WRITERS
INC
SKILLSBOOK

Editing and Proofreading Practice

a resource of student activities
to accompany
Writers INC

728-431

WRITE SOURCE

GREAT SOURCE EDUCATION GROUP
a Houghton Mifflin Company
Wilmington, Massachusetts

D1534308

A Few Words About the
Writers INC SkillsBook

Before you begin . . .

The *SkillsBook* provides you with opportunities to practice the editing and proofreading skills presented in the *Writers INC* handbook. The handbook contains guidelines, examples, and models to help you complete your work in the *SkillsBook*.

Each *SkillsBook* activity includes a brief introduction to the topic and refers you to the pages in the handbook that offer additional information and examples. The "Proofreading Activities" focus on punctuation and the mechanics of writing. The "Language Activities" highlight each of the eight parts of speech. The "Sentence Activities" provide practice in sentence combining and in correcting common sentence problems.

The Extend

Many activities include an Extend at the end of the exercise. Its purpose is to provide ideas for follow-up work that will help you apply what you have learned to your own writing.

Authors: Pat Sebranek and Dave Kemper

Project Manager: Mary Anne Hoff

Writers and Editors: Laura Bachman, Diane Barnhart, Mark Bazata, Andria Hayday, Scott Hazeu, Stuart Hoffman, Seth Johnson, Karen Park-Koenig, Lois Krenzke, Jon Leitheusser, Barb Lund, Larry Powers, Randy Rehberg, Connie Stephens, Ken Taylor, Maureen Winkler, and Claire Ziffer

Printed in the United States of America

International Standard Book Number: 0-669-47193-3 (student edition)

4 5 6 7 8 9 10 - DBH - 04 03

International Standard Book Number: 0-669-47194-1 (teacher's edition)

1 2 3 4 5 6 7 8 9 10 - DBH - 04 03 02 01 00

TABLE OF CONTENTS

Proofreading Activities

Language Activities

Sentence Activities

Sentence Basics

PROOFREADING ACTIVITIES

The activities in this section of your *SkillsBook* include sentences that need to be checked for punctuation, mechanics, or correct word choices. Most of the activities also include helpful handbook references. In addition, the Extend activities provide follow-up practice of certain skills.

Pretest: Punctuation

> **Add** the missing periods, question marks, exclamation points, commas, semicolons, apostrophes, and hyphens. **Capitalize the first word of each sentence.**

1   My grandmother was born in 1900 in a small, poor village near the

2   Italian-Swiss border. She was the first daughter to survive infancy and her

3   parents always treated her like a very special gift when she was nine

4   years old. her family immigrated to the United States. they hoped that the

5   golden shores of America would offer the opportunities and advantages so

6   lacking in their own country

7   during their arduous ocean voyage, one of my grandmothers younger

8   brothers died of dysentery. the parents were heartbroken, however, they

9   chose to view his death as a symbol of rebirth for the entire family. the

10   ship docked at Ellis Island which lies off the shores of New York City.

11   here their papers were processed and doctors examined everyone for

12   communicable diseases. did they receive a clean bill of health? indeed they

13   did. they were allowed to depart for the mainland

14   in 1910 eight long months after leaving Europe the family finally

15   arrived in San Francisco. here they set up house and began their new life

16   San Francisco was very good to them. my great grandfather immediately

17   purchased 200 acres of land in the Napa Valley. he planted grapes and

18   began the slow demanding process of developing a winery. the entire

19   family became involved in this endeavor and within five years their efforts

20   were repaid the fertile vineyards which produced some of the finest wines

21   in northern California are still in use today

> **Write _T_ before each true statement. Write _F_ if the statement is false.**

___F___ **1.** A semicolon is the punctuation mark generally used between two independent clauses that are joined by a coordinating conjunction.

_____ **2.** A comma should separate an adverb clause or a long modifying phrase from the independent clause that follows it.

_____ **3.** A comma usually precedes the opening quotation marks in a line of dialogue, setting off the speaker's words from the rest of the sentence.

_____ **4.** A comma may be used to join independent clauses that are not connected with a coordinating conjunction.

_____ **5.** Semicolons are used to separate lists or groups of words that already contain commas.

_____ **6.** A colon may be used to introduce a list.

_____ **7.** Underlining (italics) is used to punctuate titles of songs, poems, short stories, lectures, episodes of radio or television programs, chapters of books, unpublished works, and articles found in magazines, newspapers, or encyclopedias.

_____ **8.** Periods and commas should be placed inside quotation marks.

_____ **9.** The possessive form of singular nouns is usually made by adding an apostrophe and an _s._

_____ **10.** The hyphen is used correctly in these words: T-shirt, U-turn, x-axis.

_____ **11.** Common conjunctive adverbs include _besides, however, instead, meanwhile, then,_ and _therefore._

_____ **12.** A semicolon is used before a conjunctive adverb when the word connects two independent clauses in a compound sentence.

_____ **13.** Commas are used to enclose restrictive phrases and clauses.

_____ **14.** Commas are used correctly in this sentence: The banquet, which was held to honor her 60th birthday, was a surprise.

_____ **15.** Commas are used to separate coordinate adjectives that equally modify the same noun.

End Punctuation

Three different punctuation marks are used to end sentences: the period, the question mark, and the exclamation point. As you know, each indicates something different. Turn to 455.1, 467.1, and 467.5 in *Writers INC*.

> **Add** a period, a question mark, or an exclamation point at the end of each of the following sentences. Capitalize letters as needed.

1   Have you ever asked yourself, "~~w~~What is time? is time travel possible"

2   these questions have intrigued scientists and philosophers throughout the

3   ages time is still very difficult to define just check any dictionary, and

4   you'll discover that time is explained in relation to something else—an

5   event, a distance, or some other concept

6   Albert Einstein's theory of relativity ($E=mc^2$) showed that time travel

7   was possible Einstein talked about "spacetime," a four-dimensional "fabric"

8   created when time and space come together Another scientist has even

9   claimed, "I can describe how to build a time machine that adheres to the

10   laws of physics" (remember, these laws tell us what is possible, not what

11   is currently practical)

12   By now, you're probably asking, "how is time travel possible" an object

13   traveling at an exceptionally high speed ages more slowly than a

14   stationary object this means that if you could travel into outer space at a

15   velocity approaching the speed of light, you would actually travel years

16   into the earth's future could you travel into the past (think of the

17   incredible changes you could make) physicists haven't envisioned a way to

18   make this happen—not yet, anyway

Extend: Write three to five statements about something fantastic you think could happen in the future. Use each of the three end punctuation marks at least once.

Review: End Punctuation

> **Add** a period, a question mark, or an exclamation point at the end of each sentence. Capitalize letters as needed.

1   How "fast" is high-speed travel **?** you might say, "it depends on your

2   point of view"—and you're right for centuries, the stagecoach was

3   considered the ultimate transport at 10 mph in the mid-1800s, you could

4   zoom about on the early railroads—at 15 mph near the turn of the

5   century, if you owned an automobile, you could zip along at 20 mph

6   The first airplanes took off in the early 1900s, flying rather shakily

7   at 30 mph in 1939, the first jet cruised the skies at 130 mph eight years

8   later, Chuck Yeager broke the sound barrier (758 mph) when his X-1 hit

9   810 mph Yeager's X-1 was a turtle compared to the *Apollo* spacecraft—

10 which ferried astronauts to the moon at 20,000 mph

11 What does the future hold new energy sources might make speedier

12 spaceships possible Dr. W. A. Shinghton says, "an antimatter fusion ship

13 might run off energy released from matter-antimatter destruction, the most

14 powerful force in the universe an engine using this kind of energy," Dr.

15 Shinghton continues, "could send a ship into space at 225,000 mph"

16 What about "warp speed" light is the fastest thing in our universe,

17 yet it takes light from the nearest star four years to reach Earth Dr.

18 Shinghton explains, "a warp drive would compress spacetime in front of a

19 ship and expand spacetime behind it, making a starship zip through the

20 warp faster than light speed" it's possible that someday we will easily

21 explore the entire universe and go where no man—or woman—has gone

22 before

Commas Between Independent Clauses

You may join two independent clauses using a comma and a coordinating conjunction (*and, but, or, nor, for, yet,* and *so*). See 457.1 in *Writers INC.*

> **Join** each pair of sentences with a comma and a coordinating conjunction. **Choose the conjunction that you think is most suitable.**

1. Castles offer a window to medieval times , and They inspire tales of knights and valor.

2. People began building castles in the ninth century. Those early efforts bore little resemblance to King Arthur's castle in Camelot.

3. Most early castles were constructed of wood. It was not until the 1100s that builders of castles used stone.

4. Some people built castles on lakes, riverbanks, mountaintops, or steep hillsides. These settings provided natural defenses.

5. As time progressed, castles became larger. They included more advanced defensive features.

6. One example, the arrow slit, allowed an archer to shoot out of a small window. The window was so small that an attacker could not shoot in.

7. Tradespeople and peasants were not allowed to live in the nobleman's castle. They built their homes outside its walls, creating towns.

8. Some castles were almost impenetrable. A clever enemy could still find weaknesses.

9. Attackers might dig under the walls to make them collapse. They might choose a slower assault: surrounding the castle and waiting for the inhabitants to run out of food.

Extend: Turn to page 136 in *Writers INC*. Read the information pertaining to an allusion. Join the two sentences in the example using a comma and an appropriate coordinating conjunction. Write three allusions of your own using commas and coordinating conjunctions.

xq

Commas in a Series & to Separate Equal Adjectives

Use commas to separate words and phrases in a series and to separate equal adjectives. Turn to 458.3 and 457.2 in *Writers INC*.

> **Use** commas to separate items in a series and to separate equal adjectives as you combine each pair of sentences below.

1. One of the most fascinating rivalries in ancient Greece was between Sparta and Athens. It was also one of the oldest rivalries.

One of the oldest, most fascinating rivalries in ancient Greece

was between Sparta and Athens.

2. Sparta had strict discipline and great warriors. Sparta also had a strong ruling class.

_____

_____

3. Athens was known for its tremendous wealth. It was also known for its great artists and its powerful navy.

_____

_____

4. In 431 B.C.E., the Peloponnesian War broke out; the war involved Sparta and Athens. Their allies fought, too.

_____

_____

5. Ten years later, this war ended in a stalemate. This war was deadly and costly.

_____

6. In 415 B.C.E., Athens attacked again, but Sparta's army eventually won. Sparta's army was strong and well disciplined.

_____

_____

Extend: Write two sentences in which you use commas to separate words in a series and commas to separate equal adjectives.

Commas After Introductory Phrases & Clauses 1

A comma is used to separate an introductory word group from the rest of the sentence. Introductory word groups are usually clauses or phrases. Turn to 458.4 and 459.1 in *Writers INC*. Read the examples carefully. Often, you can sense when the introductory material ends and the main idea begins, but it also helps to be able to identify phrases and clauses. Turn to 520.1-521.2 for more information about phrases and clauses.

> **Add** **commas to separate introductory information from the rest of the sentence.**

1   During the Second World War‚ women played an active role in the

2   armed forces. After Pearl Harbor was attacked American factories more

3   than doubled their production of aircraft. As a matter of fact they cranked

4   out 48,000 planes in 1942 alone. Thousands of these planes had to be

5   flown from the factories to air bases. Because male pilots were fighting

6   abroad there was a shortage of pilots in the states.

7   More than 1,000 women volunteered to become pilots for the Women

8   Airforce Service Pilots (WASPs). They received the same instruction as

9   male pilots. During their 200 hours of flight school and 600 hours of

10 ground school they studied physics, navigation, flight theory, and Morse

11 code.

12   After they graduated WASPs went to air bases across the country. By

13 the summer of 1943 they were ferrying aircraft throughout the United

14 States. They flew seven days a week and had to be ready for anything.

15 One pilot left on a ferrying trip that was to take one day. After flying

16 17,000 miles in 30 days she returned to the base in the same clothes she

17 had on when she left. Although most missions involved flying in

18 noncombat zones 38 women pilots died in the line of duty.

Extend: Write two sentences; use an introductory phrase in one and introductory clause in the other.

X 10

Commas After Introductory Phrases & Clauses 2

Introductory phrases and clauses are usually set off from the rest of the sentence with a comma. By reading carefully, you will sense when the introductory material ends and the main sentence begins. Place a comma at that point. Turn to 458.4 and 459.1 in *Writers INC*. Read the examples, pausing at the commas. For information about clauses and phrases, turn to 520.1-521.2.

> **Insert** **commas wherever they are needed to separate introductory information from the rest of the sentence.**

1   After Amelia Earhart disappeared in 1937, Jackie Cochran became one

2   of America's most famous female pilots. In just 10 years Cochran set 17

3   world records in aviation. On September 23, 1938 her silver P-35 flashed

4   across the finish line in the challenging Bendix Race. Completing the

5   2,042 miles from Los Angeles to Cleveland she became the first pilot to

6   finish the race nonstop in just over eight hours.

7   Born Bessie Mae Pittman somewhere in the South Jackie Cochran was

8   raised by a foster family. In her autobiography she remembers having no

9   shoes and wearing dresses made of flour sacks. As a teenager she learned

10 how to cut hair and then headed north. On her way to New York City

11 she picked the name Jacqueline Cochran out of a phone book and decided

12 to reinvent herself. "I might have been born in a hovel," she recalled, "but

13 I was determined to travel with the wind and the stars." At the same

14 time she worked in a New York beauty salon Jackie learned to fly. "At

15 the moment I paid for my first lesson a beauty operator ceased to exist

16 and an aviator was born."

17   Meanwhile, in nearby Boston, a young woman began a career selling

18 airplanes. From a prominent Philadelphia family the young saleswoman,

19 Nancy Harkness, married Air Corps Reserve officer Robert Love.

20   As the daughter of a wealthy physician Nancy Harkness learned to

21   fly as a teenager. Though she went to the very best schools she remained

22   restless and adventurous. While she was in college she earned extra

23   money by taking students for airplane rides. When she flew too low over

24   the campus university officials were not amused and suspended her from

25   school for two weeks.

26   After their marriage the Loves formed an aviation company. Nancy

27   flew for that company and also flew for the Bureau of Air Commerce. In

28   one of the bureau's projects she tested the three-wheeled landing gear,

29   which became standard on most planes.

30   Both Nancy Harkness Love and Jackie Cochran had the same vision—

31   to form a group of women pilots that would ferry needed military aircraft

32   to air bases. In the spring of 1942 the Women's Auxiliary Ferrying

33   Squadron (WAFS) began training under Nancy Harkness Love. Shortly

34   after that Jackie Cochran's group of flying cadets also began training. Ten

35   months later the WAFS and Cochran's trainees merged into the Women

36   Airforce Service Pilots (WASPs). During the Second World War WASPs

37   flew more than 60 million miles in every type of military plane.

Explain **in your own words how you determine where you should use commas to separate introductory information from the rest of the sentence.**

_____

_____

_____

_____

_____

Review: Commas 1

Insert **commas where they are needed in the sentences below. Write the rule for each comma you insert.**

1. Although the brain comprises only 2 percent of a person's total body weight, it requires 20 percent of all oxygen used by the body.

   Rule: _Use a comma after an introductory clause._

2. My orthodontist will explain to my parents the cost of a retainer the need for it and the way I am to use it.

   Rule: _____

3. I have taken science courses all through high school and I expect to major in chemistry at the University of Wisconsin.

   Rule: _____

   _____

4. The tiny delicate hummingbird weighs less than a penny and it is the only bird—believe it or not—that can fly backwards.

   Rule: _____

   _____

   Rule: _____

   _____

5. The hummingbird has a body temperature of 111 degrees Fahrenheit beats its wings more than 60 times a second and builds a nest the size of a walnut.

   Rule: _____

6. Even though the hummingbird is hard to see it can often be spotted around red flowers or red feeders.

   Rule: _____

   _____

Commas to Set Off Contrasted Elements & Appositives

Contrasted elements usually begin with *not, but, but not, though,* or *unlike* and should be set off with commas. Turn to 457.3 in *Writers INC.* An appositive is a word or a phrase that identifies or renames the noun or pronoun that comes before it. Turn to 458.2.

> **Add** commas where they are needed in the sentences below.

1. Sir Arthur Conan Doyle created Sherlock Holmes, one of the world's best-known detectives.

2. Dr. Watson Holmes's sidekick and friend helped solve cases.

3. Sherlock Holmes always got his man not by force but through amazing use of reason and observation.

4. In 1893, Doyle wrote a story in which Holmes the great detective was killed.

5. The outcry of millions of readers all devoted fans convinced Doyle to bring Holmes back to life in another story.

6. Sir Doyle perhaps the most highly paid short-story writer of his time came to resent Holmes's fame.

7. Doyle grew agitated because Holmes his best-known character diverted attention from what Doyle considered to be his most serious literary effort historical novels.

8. Christopher Morley an English critic said about Holmes, "Perhaps no fiction character ever created has become so charmingly real to his readers."

9. Medicine not writing was Doyle's original profession; he trained as a doctor.

Extend: Write three to five sentences about one of your favorite fictional characters. Include one appositive or contrasted element in each sentence.

Commas with Nonrestrictive Phrases & Clauses 1

A nonrestrictive phrase or clause adds information that is not necessary to the basic meaning of the sentence, so it is set off with commas. If a sentence has the same meaning with or without it, the clause or phrase is nonrestrictive. Turn to 459.2 in *Writers INC*.

> **The Marshall Islands, a country in the North Pacific Ocean, consists of 29 atolls and 5 islands.** (The phrase is not necessary.)

> **The Marshall Islands consists of 29 atolls and 5 islands.**
> (The sentence has the same meaning without the nonrestrictive phrase.)

Place commas around the nonrestrictive phrases and clauses in the sentences below. Underline restrictive phrases or clauses.

1. The land area of the Marshall Islands‚which covers only about 70 square miles‚is scattered over 780,000 square miles.

2. The nationality that makes up most of the country's population is Micronesian.

3. About 30,000 people half of the country's population live on Majuro Atoll.

4. The rural areas where a traditional way of life is maintained are home to 30 percent of the people.

5. People who reside in the urban areas live with the modern conveniences of electricity, telephones, and television.

6. The islands which were controlled by Germany from 1886 until 1914 and by Japan until 1944 became a United States territory during World War II.

7. Bikini Atoll is famous for nuclear testing conducted by the U.S. military from 1946-1958 that resulted in the resettling of natives to other islands.

8. Ten years later, some people returned to the atoll which was declared safe from harmful radiation in 1968.

9. But 10 years after that, government officials finding unsafe radiation levels resettled the people again.

Commas with Nonrestrictive Phrases & Clauses 2

Commas are used to enclose nonrestrictive phrases and clauses. Nonrestrictive phrases and clauses are those that are not essential to the basic meaning of the sentence. Turn to 459.2 in *Writers INC*.

> **Place** commas around each nonrestrictive phrase or clause in the following sentences. Underline restrictive phrases or clauses.

1. If you go to New York City,which is one of the most interesting places on earth,you should visit the New York Botanical Garden.

2. My grandmother who was recently diagnosed with diabetes must watch how much sugar she eats.

3. The neighbor who lives east of us has many bowling trophies.

4. The island of Sri Lanka formerly called Ceylon is one of the most densely populated areas on Earth.

5. The invention of the videocassette recorder which some feared would bring about the demise of movie theaters has not adversely affected box-office sales in the slightest.

6. The field mouse trying to escape a swooping hawk disappeared into a hole in the barn's siding.

7. The ancient cherry tree a cherished part of the town's history became diseased and had to be cut down.

8. The ladder that has a rung missing could be dangerous to use.

9. People who wanted to buy this year's popular toy had to get to the store before it opened and wait in line.

10. Halloween when "witches" and "goblins" are out and about is offensive to some people.

Extend: Look for four examples of nonrestrictive phrases or clauses in newspapers, books, or magazines. Be prepared to share your examples with a learning partner or your class.

Other Uses of Commas 1

Use commas to set off items in a date, items in an address, dialogue, nouns of direct address, and interjections. See 460.1-460.5 in *Writers INC*.

> **Add** commas where they are needed in the sentences below. Write the rule that applies in each case.

1. Drat, Bill forgot to get my English assignment from Mr. Taylor.

Rule: _Commas set off an interjection or a weak exclamation from the rest of the sentence._

2. "I reminded you Bill to get my assignment," I spouted.

Rule: _____

_____

3. "I just forgot" Bill mumbled in apology.

Rule: _____

4. "Jeepers how could you forget something important like that?" I asked.

Rule: _____

_____

5. I told Bill that I would be visiting my mother beginning September 7 2000 and that he could e-mail the assignment or send it to me at 168 State Street Albany New York 12205.

Rule: _____

Rule: _____

6. "I'll do my best" Bill replied.

Rule: _____

7. I said "I will appreciate your help a lot."

Rule: _____

Extend: Write a sentence for each of the five comma uses covered in this exercise.

Other Uses of Commas 2

Use commas to set off interruptions, to separate numerals in large numbers, to enclose titles or initials, and to clarify or add emphasis. See 460.6-461.3 in *Writers INC*.

> **Add** commas where they are needed below. Write the rule that applies in each case.

1. The plane plunged from 38,000 feet to 16,000 feet in less than three seconds.

   Rule: *Commas separate numerals in large numbers in order to distinguish hundreds, thousands, millions, and so forth.*

2. What happened happened without warning.

   Rule: _____

3. The pilot heard the engine cough and then a terrible silence.

   Rule: _____

4. The pilot as a matter of fact would have preferred even the sound of an ailing engine to the ominous quiet.

   Rule: _____

   _____

5. "This is definitely not what John Henry Sr. had in mind when he suggested that his little boy take up flying as a hobby," thought the pilot wryly.

   Rule: _____

6. The altimeter continued to drop: 15300, 15000, 14000, . . . and an alarm began to sound.

   Rule: _____

   _____

7. The alarm grew louder by the second until finally it stopped abruptly. (I had reached over and turned off my alarm clock.)

   Rule: _____

   _____

Review: Commas 2

> **Add** commas where they are needed below. Write the rule that applies in each case.

1. Did you know, Joy, that a whale's heart beats about nine times a minute?

Rule: _Commas set off nouns of direct address._____

2. Hey please turn the music down! I'm trying to get some sleep!

Rule: _____

3. "The human body contains 206 bones" explained Mr. Brown our biology
teacher "with about 50 of them in the feet."

Rule: _____

Rule: _____

4. Although you may not believe it the body does have 60000 miles of blood
vessels.

Rule: _____

Rule: _____

5. James Rudan D.D.S. will be extracting all of my wisdom teeth.

Rule: _____

6. It is the female bee not the male that does all the work in and around the hive.

Rule: _____

7. Sari who is planning to major in psychology has already enrolled at the
University of Maryland.

Rule: _____

8. Her address will be 822 Tenth Street Apartment D Baltimore MD 00823.

Rule: _____

Semicolons

Semicolons may be used to join two or more closely related independent clauses that are *not* connected with a coordinating conjunction. They can also be used before a conjunctive adverb that connects two independent clauses. Semicolons may also be used to separate groups of words that already contain commas. See 461.4, 461.5, and 462.2 in *Writers INC* for examples.

> **Add** **semicolons where they are needed in the sentences below.**

1. Dance is the body's way of celebrating music ; it's natural to want to move to rhythm and sounds.

2. Dances can tell a story, set a mood, or express emotions offer fun, relaxation, and companionship or assist in the treatment of physical and emotional ailments.

3. Many consider Isadora Duncan the first lady of modern dance many see her as a true pioneer.

4. Modern dance can imitate the wild, often chaotic-looking movements of nature therefore, this kind of dance often uses tumbling, rolling, and other acrobatics.

5. Dance is a part of many peoples' traditions some Native American tribes perform traditional dances to bring good weather.

6. Some birds use dance as a mating ritual some people use dance as a "dating ritual."

7. Dancing is an ancient art many prehistoric paintings and sculptures have shown us that people danced 20,000 years ago.

8. Ballet had its beginnings in Italy however, it was King Louis XIV of France who made ballet a formal art.

Extend: Write three sentences illustrating the three rules you studied in this exercise. Write about dancing or about another recreational activity you enjoy.

x9

Colons

Colons have several uses. See the examples and explanations given below.

> **I know one thing: Dogs can get into a lot of trouble.**
> (The colon is used to emphasize a word, a phrase, a clause, or a sentence explaining or adding impact to the main clause. Turn to 462.5 in *Writers INC*.)

> **My dog, Zeus, gets into all sorts of trouble: chasing my baby sister, chewing on our couch, and stealing food from the kitchen.**
> (The colon introduces a list. Turn to 463.2.)

> **It was my father who said the following: "Zeus behaves, or he's a resident of the backyard."**
> (The colon formally introduces a sentence, question, or quotation. Turn to 463.1.)

> **Add** colons where they are needed in the sentences below. Then write the number of the rule in *Writers INC* that you used after each of the sentences.

1. I like a lot of different things: movies, baseball, hiking. *463.2*

2. There's one thing I like more than anything else books.

3. My mother once actually said this to me "If the world were to end, you would probably be nose-deep in a book and not even notice."

4. My shelves are lined with books of all kinds science fiction, history, humor, biographies, mysteries, and more.

5. Two years ago, I went beyond just reading books and moved to a whole new hobby collecting books.

6. There are many different ways to build a collection choosing only first editions, buying books by a particular author, or gathering books from a particular publisher.

7. I've chosen something a little different I collect books on magic.

8. Now I have more than a hundred books that explain all kinds of things card tricks; using hats, rabbits, and wands; special effects; and more.

9. Recently I added a very special title to my collection a book signed by Harry Houdini.

Review: Semicolons & Colons

Insert **colons or semicolons where they are needed in the following paragraphs.**

1   One brilliant physicist stands above all others of our time Stephen

2   Hawking. His writings have greatly advanced our understanding of the

3   universe. Dr. Hawking explains sophisticated theories in language the

4   average person can understand in other words, he has brought the outer

5   limits of space "down to earth."

6   Stephen Hawking has a disabling disease amyotrophic lateral sclerosis

7   (ALS). This disease gradually destroys the nerves and muscles needed for

8   moving. In 1962, when he was only 20 years old, doctors told Hawking

9   that he would probably die before he earned his Ph.D. however, their

10 patient, who is one of today's best-known scientists, proved them wrong.

11 Dr. Hawking is most famous for his study of black holes. These

12 phenomena—possibly formed when a star burns itself out and collapses—

13 are areas in which gravity is extremely strong anything pulled into the

14 black hole cannot get out. (Even time stops!)

15 You can learn more about this subject in Hawking's *A Brief History of*

16 *Time: From the Big Bang to Black Holes.* The book is remarkable,

17 especially when you consider this It was written by a man who cannot

18 speak or move his arms and hands.

Hyphens

Turn to the rules for hyphens at 463.4-465.2 in *Writers INC*. When using rule 465.2 to form a compound adjective, check a dictionary. You may find your word spelled without a hyphen, as in *bighearted*.

> **Add** hyphens where they are needed in the sentences below.

1. Did you end up writing a four-, five-, or six-page essay?

2. My mother doesn't like my brother's devil may care attitude.

3. Was that a velvet lined cloak that Sir Raleigh spread in the mud?

4. He is supposed to do two thirds of the chores.

5. Our town is full of one way streets, and my sister in law gets lost.

6. My great grandfather will be 99 next month.

7. He is a soft spoken person.

8. Is that an R rated movie?

9. The 65 year old woman wore a purple T shirt.

10. Do those boards come in 8, 10, and 12 foot lengths?

11. Is that really a two carat diamond?

12. In 1952, Vincent Massey became the first Canadian born governor general.

13. The flag of Canada features an eleven point red maple leaf.

14. The Civil War (1861 1865) divided Americans on a number of issues.

15. The lawyer knew that what she did would have far reaching consequences.

16. However, she mistakenly considered herself all powerful.

17. I would like to know all of my relatives, but I'll have to settle for knowing my great grandmother, my great aunt, and my two cousins.

18. I love those crescent shaped Christmas cookies.

Extend: Go back to the first five sentences above and write the number of the rule in *Writers INC* that shows why you added each hyphen.

Dashes

Dashes are used to indicate a sudden break in the flow of a sentence, to emphasize an idea, or to set off words that explain or clarify something. Turn to 466.1-466.5 in *Writers INC*.

> **Read** the following sentences by the Wyoming writer Gretel Ehrlich, who writes about the side of cowboys most people don't know. Study her use of dashes and answer the questions that follow.

1. More often than not, circumstances—like the colt he's riding or an unexpected blizzard—are overpowering him.

2. In a rancher's world, courage has less to do with facing danger than with acting spontaneously—usually on behalf of an animal or another rider.

3. What we've interpreted as toughness—weathered skin, calloused hands, a squint in the eye, and a growl in the voice—only masks the tenderness inside.

4. So many of the men who came to the West were Southerners—men looking for work and a new life after the Civil War—that chivalrousness and strict codes of honor were soon thought of as western traits.

What kinds of material do the dashes set off? _____

_____

_____

What would be the effect on these sentences if all the material between the dashes

were dropped out? _____

_____

_____

In most of these sentences, would commas work as well as dashes? Explain why or

why not. _____

_____

_____

_____

Extend: From what you have observed about dashes by reading Ehrlich's sentences and by looking at the data in your handbook, write a paragraph explaining when and how and why to use dashes. In your paragraph, make sure that at least three of your sentences use dashes—in other words, practice what you preach.

Review: Hyphens & Dashes

> Put hyphens and dashes where they are needed in the following passage.

1   If it weren't for my great-great great grandfather, I would have

2   finished my homework well, I might have finished it. Anyway, the whole

3   episode started with my sister and me playing hide and seek in the park

4   near our high rise apartment. Sometimes let's just say on those evenings

5   when my patience hasn't been used up I pretend that I don't know where

6   she is. But last night was different she didn't hide. She stood in front of

7   the Civil War Monument, pointing at it.

8   "Look," she said. I did and saw the name Patrick Flannery. "It's

9   Grandpa," she added.

10   "It can't be Grandpa," I replied. "He's eighty seven. That's too young

11   to have been in the Civil War." I pointed to a plaque that showed the

12   dates of the war: 1861 1865.

13   "Your half eaten brain is wrong!" she said. "That's Grandpa."

14   Obviously, she's a one of a kind sister. She decided to go ask Mom.

15   The elevator crawled. We watched floor numbers five, six, seven, . . .

16   My sister took advantage of the slow moving elevator and told everyone

17   inside that our grandfather was a hero a *Civil War* hero. She sounded as

18   if she had about four tenths of a brain maybe less.

19   When we got home, Mom said, "Call Grandpa."

20   Grandpa asked us to come over. When we arrived, he had spread out

21   a table full of things. It turned out that Patrick Flannery was Grandpa's

22   great grandfather. And surprise, surprise he was a Civil War hero!

Quotation Marks with Dialogue

Quotation marks are used in written dialogue, enclosing a speaker's exact words. Turn to 468.3 and 469 in *Writers INC.* Remember, a new paragraph shows a change of speaker.

> **Insert** the missing quotation marks and commas in the quotations that follow. Use the symbol ⊄ to show where a new paragraph should begin.

1. "What in the world are you doing here?" she asked, regarding her disheveled sister with well-bred surprise. ⊄ "Gathering leaves, meekly answered Jo.

—Louisa May Alcott, *Little Women*

2. It's the children said Mrs. Parsons, casting a half-apprehensive glance at the door. They haven't been out today.

—George Orwell, *1984*

3. He said Don't tell anyone our secret. I nodded my head with all the sobriety I could muster, although I wanted to scream to the world We have a secret!

—Jane Hamilton, *The Book of Ruth*

4. Suddenly Sir Kay reined in his horse in dismay. My sword! he cried. I left my sword where we lodged last night!

—retold by Emma G. Sterne and Barbara Lindsay,
King Arthur and the Knights of the Round Table

5. Stop! said the man. Good day, said Theseus. Now, listen, stranger, everyone who passes this way washes my feet. That's the toll. Any questions?

—retold by Bernard Evslin, *Theseus*

6. How long can you hold him? asks Bill. I'm not as strong as I used to be, says old Dorset, but I think I can promise you ten minutes.

—O. Henry, *The Ransom of Red Chief*

Extend: Collect three to five samples of dialogue from books, newspapers, and magazines. Study the examples with a classmate and answer these questions: (1) When do writers use dialogue? (2) Does the usage of dialogue differ between nonfiction and fiction? (3) What purposes does dialogue have?

Quotation Marks with Direct Quotations

Quotation marks enclose a direct quotation (the exact words of a speaker). See 468.3 and 469 in *Writers INC*.

> **Add** quotation marks to the direct quotations below. If a quotation is indirect, rewrite the sentence to make the quotation direct.

1. Mary says that we should test our smoke alarms to make sure they work.

Mary said, "We should test our smoke alarms to make sure they

work."

2. The state of Vermont, the travel agent said, is breathtaking in October.

_____

_____

3. If you are interested in trying out for the school play, she reminded the students, pick up a copy of the script on your way out.

_____

_____

4. The vet explained that dogs and cats raised in the same household usually get along.

_____

_____

5. I don't want to bother you, Pete whispered, but could I borrow a pencil?

_____

6. When Emily got a flat tire, she told her father she could fix it herself.

_____

_____

Extend: Write and punctuate a conversation between you and a friend, using direct and indirect quotations.

Italics (Underlining) & Quotation Marks

Some titles and special words appear in quotation marks, while others appear in italics (or are underlined). Review the rules at 468.1 and 470 in *Writers INC*.

> **Place** quotation marks around or underline (to indicate italics) the titles or special words below that require either quotation marks or italics.

1. "Where Are You Going, Where Have You Been?" (short story)

2. Introduction to French Literature (book)

3. Paris's Left Bank (magazine article)

4. Laurie Makes Mischief and Jo Makes Peace (chapter title)

5. Cat on a Hot Tin Roof (full-length play)

6. Sleep Better, Starting Tonight (magazine article)

7. Dawson's Creek (TV program)

8. Legion of Merit (video)

9. How to Choose a College (pamphlet)

10. Room at the Top of the World (song)

11. Little Miss Muffet (nursery rhyme)

12. Robert E. Lee's One Mistake (lecture)

13. Fibber McGee and Molly (radio program)

14. Enola Gay (specific name of an airplane)

15. Hartford's Free Press (newspaper)

16. Annabel Lee (poem)

17. Clueless (film)

18. lemmus (scientific classification of lemming)

19. Chicago Tribune (newspaper)

20. Pride and Prejudice (book)

21. The Hollow Men (poem)

22. Old Ironsides (ship)

23. Back on Top (CD)

24. Macbeth (full-length play)

25. McCall's (magazine)

26. The Gift (short story)

27. bien vu (foreign words)

28. Madame Butterfly (opera)

29. Spruce Goose (specific name of an airplane)

30. The Nobel Prize Winners (lecture)

Review: Quotation Marks & Italics (Underlining)

> **Add** quotation marks and italics where they are needed in the sentences below. (Use underlining to indicate italics.)

1. "You've never read <u>Moby Dick</u>!" the teacher exclaimed. "Well, to be honest," he said, "neither have I."

2. My brother told me that he went to a lecture called Physics for Poets.

3. I really hope she casts me in the role of Nora in the three-act play A Doll's House, Michelle sighed.

4. For our group presentation, you are responsible for the chapter entitled Wind and Water Energy, and I'll take the next chapter, Nuclear Energy.

5. Did you know that the Wizard of Oz is a film that is based on a book?

6. At my cousin's wedding, my uncle got up and danced when the song Blue Suede Shoes was played.

7. Sammi found this quotation to support her thesis statement: Most people who use the Internet do so because they have a desire for information, they understand how to use a computer, and they have access to the Internet.

8. Who has a favorite poem? our English teacher, Ms. Amontu, asked.

9. Raymond Healy's hand shot into the air like a missile. I love The Base Stealer, he said.

10. Really? Can you quote it? asked Ms. Amontu.

11. Sure. He began, Poised between going on and back, pulled / Both ways taut like a tightrope-walker, / Fingertips pointing the opposites, / Now bouncing tiptoe like a dropped ball.

12. Great! cried Ms. Amontu laughing. I think everyone should have a favorite poem and be able to recite it.

Apostrophes in Contractions & Plurals

An apostrophe is used to show where letters have been omitted in contractions (as in *don't*). An apostrophe is also used to form the plural of a letter, a number, a sign, or a word discussed as a word. Turn to 472.1–472.2 in *Writers INC* for examples and additional rules.

> **Insert** apostrophes where they are needed in the sentences below.

1. Theres nothing I like better than telling someone to mind their ps and qs!

2. "Youre really going to appreciate the sound quality on that new television youve got there," the salesperson assured us.

3. How many *ss* does the word *Mississippi* have?

4. I wouldnt have noticed anything was wrong if you hadnt spoken up.

5. Can you see whats holding everything up?

6. We couldnt walk around the lake because the bridge over the canal hadnt been repaired yet.

7. I didnt know you could use so many *had*s in one sentence!

8. Oh, Im great! Howve you been? Hows your brother?

9. Were going to study for the exam together so we can both get As.

10. Once a comb has lost its teeth, its no longer useful.

11. I havent been able to sleep; I keep thinking about what couldve happened to my friends and me if wed hit that truck.

12. My interviewer asked how many As and Bs I had on my last report card.

13. Are you a member of the class of 04?

14. "I'm just hangin out," Joey said. "I aint done nothin wrong."

15. Do you know the dos and donts of good writing?

Extend: Do you know the difference between *its* and *it's, who's* and *whose, your* and *you're*? Write three sentences using one of these easily confused pairs in each sentence. Exchange papers with a classmate. Correct each other's work if necessary. Turn to pages 496 and 500 in *Writers INC* for assistance.

Apostrophes to Form Possessives 1

The possessive form of a singular noun is usually created by adding an apostrophe and an *s*. Turn to 472.3 in *Writers INC*. The possessive form of a plural that ends in *s* is usually formed by adding an apostrophe at the end (*fire-eaters'*). If a plural noun does not end in *s* (*children*), the possessive is usually formed by adding an apostrophe and an *s* (*children's*). Turn to 472.4 in *Writers INC*.

> **Add** apostrophes and s's where they are needed in the sentences below.

1. You'll never figure out which poster is Mary. ʼs

2. My brother cereal bowl is still sitting on the table.

3. Where did all of the Smiths mail and packages go?

4. I hadn't even considered a lawyer involvement.

5. Monkeys tails are strong.

6. I'll never understand why Steve sister wants one of those cars.

7. Our womens basketball team is as popular as the mens team.

8. Do you know what Portugal greatest natural resource is?

9. Two months pay won't cover the bill.

10. My stepmother ex-husband still lives in upstate New York.

11. Some Greek gods temples were built on islands in the Aegean Sea.

12. Have you ever seen anything as funny-looking as Mr. and Mrs. Jones dog?

13. He is a wolf in sheeps clothing.

> **Write** sentences using both the singular and plural possessive form of these two words: *candle* and *child*.

_____

_____

_____

_____

Apostrophes to Form Possessives 2

The possessive form of a singular noun is usually created by adding an apostrophe and an *s*. Turn to 472.3 in *Writers INC*. The possessive form of a plural that ends in *s* is usually formed by adding an apostrophe at the end (*fire-eaters'*). If a plural noun does not end in *s* (*children*), the possessive is usually formed by adding an apostrophe and an *s* (*children's*). Turn to 472.4 in *Writers INC*.

> **Add** apostrophes and **s's** where they are needed in the sentences below.

1. Both dogs' toys have been gnawed into unidentifiable chunks of plastic.

2. My teacher instructions were clear and concise, but we didn't have time to finish the project.

3. Our bosses pictures hang on the wall.

4. Chaz backpack was destroyed in the same blaze that razed the public library.

5. Have you seen the triplets matching outfits?

6. Everyone in town knew that the sheriff badge had been stolen.

7. How many of the couples tickets have we collected so far?

8. Tess story was the best.

9. Please put this in the childrens room.

10. Fergus story was the most disgusting.

11. The Coen brothers movies are famous.

12. The countries flags flew over their fallen soldiers graves.

> **Write** sentences using both the singular and plural possessive form for these two words: *pizza* and *Miller* (a family's surname).

_____

_____

_____

_____

Apostrophes to Form Possessives 3

When possession is shared by more than one noun, use the possessive form for the last noun in the series (*Lonny and Sarah's house*). To form the possessive of a compound noun or of a two- or three-word indefinite pronoun, add an apostrophe and *s* to the last word (the *secretary of state's* speech, *somebody else's* truck). Turn to page 473 in *Writers INC* for more information.

> **Write** your own sentences using possessives as suggested.

1. Sarah, Laurie, and Marci own a large tent.

   Sarah, Laurie, and Marci's tent is large.

2. Show that everyone but you has sore eyes.

3. Emma and Hannah own a doghouse that has a front porch.

4. Show that nobody but you has a flashlight that works.

5. Show that there was a meeting this morning about the athletic budget.

6. Mom and Dad share possession of a car that has a sunroof.

7. Show that Opal and Jed own a new computer that operates their security system.

8. Show that Suze's mother-in-law owns a very valuable antique ring.

9. Show that someone (use "someone" as an indefinite pronoun) possesses a lawn mower that needs a muffler.

Review: Apostrophes

Write the correct form of each word that appears in italics in the blank provided. (Add apostrophes and **s**'s where they are needed.)

1. Pearl _____Buck's_____ (Buck) Nobel Prize for literature was awarded to her in 1938.

2. The _____ (boss) office had a window and an air conditioner, but _____ (Dennis) office _____ (didnt) even have a window.

3. The carpeting is being replaced in the _____ (programmers) offices.

4. Esther, Jamie, and Ed hurried into the _____ (children) room.

5. The department _____ (store) Santa Claus was tired.

6. He felt he had really earned this _____ (day) wage.

7. _____ (Somebody else) lap would have to hold the kiddies tomorrow.

8. He said, "I _____ (dont) think _____ (Ill) come to work for a week! _____ (Santa) going to rest."

9. Mrs. Sloan told us to watch our _____ (p) and _____ (q) and always be polite to our parents and our _____ (parents) friends.

10. Her _____ (great-grandmother) antiques were sold at auction today.

11. Will _____ (Black, Christer, and Tott) law firm help with that deposition?

Punctuation for Research Papers 1

This exercise is designed to help you become more familiar with the punctuation marks often needed in research papers.

> **Add** punctuation in the following sentences after checking the section in *Writers INC* that is indicated in parentheses. Answer the questions on the lines provided.

1. Edgar Allan Poe was born to David Poe, Jr., and Elizabeth Poe. (461.2)

2. To Poe, poetry was more than a job "With me, poetry has been not a purpose but a passion." (463.1)

3. One example of Poe's use of Greek references is found in his poem To Helen. Poe writes, Helen, thy beauty is to me / Like those Nicéan barks of yore. (468.1 and page 469)

4. The poem also includes consonance in some lines "The weary, way-worn wanderer bore To his own native shore." (463.1 and 471.4)

5. Poe also uses consonance in his poem The Raven. For example, consider these lines "Followed fast and followed faster till his [the raven's] songs one burden bore." (468.1 and 463.1)

   Why are brackets used? (page 474) _____

   _____

6. Poe also uses internal rhyme in his poetry when he says "Though thy crest be shorn and shaven, thou, I said, art sure no craven." (460.3)

7. He uses many techniques: "Poe's use of allusion, analogy, parallelism, rhyme, and rythm *sic* is amazing." (474.3)

8. In a magazine article, The Philosophy of Composition, published in Graham's Magazine in April 1846, Poe writes about the "tones" of beauty and sadness. (468.1 and 470.2)

9. Poe's view of tone is found in his statement "All experience has shown that this tone is one of sadness. . . . Melancholy is thus the most legitimate of all the poetical tones."

   Why is an ellipsis used? (page 456) _____

   _____

Punctuation for Research Papers 2

Research papers often include data and information from books, magazines, newspapers, computer files, and interviews. Turn to the following sections in *Writers INC* to review the punctuation marks that are often needed when you include data in a research paper: 456.1-456.2 (ellipsis), 460.3 (comma), 463.1 (colon), 474.1-474.3 (brackets), and 468.1 and page 469 (quotation marks) as well as pages 273-274 (punctuation for electronic sources).

Read the following paragraphs and focus on the punctuation that comes just before the number in parentheses. Then go to the appropriate blank at the bottom of the page and write the number of the rule that explains why each punctuation mark has been used. (*Note:* For rules on pages 273-274 and 469, just write down the page: *p. 469.*)

"The Masque of the Red Death," (1) one of Edgar Allan Poe's most famous short stories, is filled with symbolism. Both colors and numbers are symbols. According to Martha Womack, who created the Web site Precisely Poe, (2) "In this story, the plague takes the unusual form of a red death . . . (3) so that blood, the very substance of life, now becomes the mark of death." (4) Poe writes, (5) "But first let me tell of the rooms. . . . (6) There were seven." (7) Womack reminds the reader of the historical significance of seven: (8) "The history of the world was thought to consist of seven ages, just as an individual's life had seven stages. The ancient world had seven wonders; universities divided learning into seven subjects; there were seven deadly sins [pride, avarice, etc.] (9) with seven corresponding virtues [humility, generosity, etc.]."

Dr. Jorge Parkman, my instructor and a literary critic, said, "The interpretation of symbolism can show an individual's opinion and bias. Be scholarly—very scholarly—when interpreting symbols [in literature] (10)." (11)

_468.1_ **1.**	_____ **4.**	_____ **7.**	_____ **10.**
_____ **2.**	_____ **5.**	_____ **8.**	_____ **11.**
_____ **3.**	_____ **6.**	_____ **9.**	

Punctuation for Research Papers 3

The type of punctuation you use with quoted material will depend on how long or short the quotation is. Turn to pages 258 and 469 in *Writers INC*.

> **Write** answers for the following questions.

1. How many lines does a short quotation have? _*four or less*_

2. How should a short quotation be incorporated into a research paper? _____
   _____

3. What punctuation is used to set off a short quotation? _____

4. How many lines does a long quotation have? _____

5. How should a long quotation be incorporated into a research paper? _____
   _____
   _____

6. How should the second paragraph of a long quotation be included? _____
   _____

7. Are quotation marks used with long quotations? _____
   _____

8. How many lines does a short poetic quotation have? _____

9. How should a short poetic quotation be incorporated into a research paper?
   _____
   _____

10. What punctuation mark shows where a line of poetry ends? _____

11. How should poetic quotations of four lines or more be incorporated into a paper?
    _____

12. What punctuation mark shows that you have left out part of a quotation?
    _____

Using MLA Style

Turn to pages 264-274 in *Writers INC*.

> **Write** a correct MLA works-cited entry for each of the sources described below.

1. An article by Matthew Battles in *Harper's* magazine entitled "Lost in the Stacks: The Decline and Fall of the Universal Library." The article appeared in January 2000 and was printed on pages 36-39.

> *Battles, Matthew. "Lost in the Stacks: The Decline and Fall of the*
>
> *Universal Library." Harper's Jan. 2000: 36-39.*

2. A book entitled *Mexicanos: A History of Mexicans in the United States* by Manuel G. Gonzales. It was published in Bloomington, Indiana, by Indiana University Press in 1999.

3. An article entitled "Looking the Green Monster in the Eye" that appeared in *TV Barn* on the tvbarn.com Web site on November 16, 1999. The article was written by John Zipperer. It was retrieved on June 13, 2000, from the World Wide Web at this address: <http://www.tvbarn.com/111699.html>.

4. A film entitled *Mandela: Son of Africa, Father of a Nation.* It was directed by Angus Gibson and Jo Mennell and produced by Island Pictures Corp. in 1997.

5. An article entitled "Catherine the Great" in *The New Encyclopaedia Britannica* published in 1998.

Using APA Style

Turn to pages 289-295 in *Writers INC*.

> **Write** a correct APA reference entry for each of the sources described below.

1. A book called *Century of Progress: The Women's Rights Movement in the United States.* It was written by E. Flexner and published by Harvard University Press in Cambridge, Massachusetts, in 1959.

   Flexner, E. (1959). Century of progress: The women's rights movement

   in the United States. Cambridge, MA: Harvard University Press.

2. An article entitled "With the Help of God and Lucy Stone" that appeared in the journal *Kansas Historical Quarterly*. It was written by Sister Jeanne McKenna and published in 1970, volume 36, on pages 13-26.

_____

_____

3. A 1999 television documentary entitled *Not for Ourselves Alone: The Story of Elizabeth Cady Stanton and Susan B. Anthony* by Florentine Films and WETA in Washington, D.C. The film was produced by Ken Burns and Paul Barnes.

_____

_____

_____

4. An article titled "Carrie Chapman Catt" that is part of the *Votes for Women: Selections from the National American Woman Suffrage Association Collection, 1848-1921* on the Library of Congress Web site. The page is dated October 19, 1998, and it was retrieved on March 18, 2000. The Web address for the page is <http://www.lcweb2.loc.gov/ammem/naw/nawshome.html>.

_____

_____

_____

_____

Using Punctuation to Create Emphasis

Punctuation can be used to emphasize a particular word or phrase in a sentence. Dashes and colons and, of course, exclamation points often serve this purpose. Occasionally, commas are also used to emphasize a word or a phrase. Turn to 466.5 (dashes), 462.5 (colons), 467.5 (exclamation points), and 461.3 (commas) in *Writers INC*.

Study the sentences below. **Circle the punctuation marks that are used to create emphasis and underline the part of the sentence that is emphasized. Then use each sentence as a model for a sentence of your own.**

1. "He saw only dreams and memories, and heard music." (from "Home" by Langston Hughes)

   The children played with pebbles and twigs, and made fun.

2. "He's been a prisoner here longer than anyone else: thirty-three years." (from *Life Sentences* by Wilbert Rideau)

3. "He's the kind of man who picks his friends—to pieces." (Mae West)

4. "I could smell Mama, crisp and starched, plumping my pillow . . . ." (from *A Day No Pigs Would Die* by Robert Newton Peck)

5. She was on tiptoe, stretching for an orange, when they heard, "HEY YOU!"

   Note: What additional technique is used to create emphasis in this sentence?

6. "Without the hatchet he had nothing—no fire, no tools, no weapons." (from *Hatchet* by Gary Paulson)

   Note: What additional technique is used to create emphasis in this sentence?

Brackets & Parentheses

Brackets enclose words that you add to a direct quotation. Turn to 474.1-474.3 in your *Writers INC*. Parentheses (which should be used sparingly) enclose explanatory or added material. Turn to 471.1-471.2 and the first paragraph on page 258.

> **Insert** missing words and add *sic* where appropriate below, using brackets. The material is quoted directly from the 1805 journals of Lewis and Clark.

1. *Clark, July 17:* The yellow currents [sic] [are] now ripe and the fussey [sic] red chokecherries are getting ripe.

2. I climbed a spur of the mountains, which I found to be high and dificult of axcess.

3. *Lewis, July 18:* Previous to our departure saw a large herd of bighorn on the high clift opposite us.

4. *Clark, July 18:* I passed over a mountain on an Indian rode, and we camped on a small run of clear cold water. Musquitors are very troublesome.

> **Add** parentheses below to enclose explanatory material. Also add parentheses to any asides that interrupt the flow of a sentence.

1. Many of the spellings (or rather, the *mis*spellings) that Lewis and Clark used were also wrong in 1805.

2. The misspellings *fussey* for *fuzzy, clift* for *cliff, rode* for *road* confused many readers then and today.

3. Lewis's poor spelling is a surprise, considering his background. Lewis was President Thomas Jefferson's private secretary.

Extend: Write a journal entry of three sentences. Omit several words and misspell some. Exchange papers with a classmate. Use brackets to add any needed words and corrections to your partner's paper.

Pretest: Capitalization

Cross out the lowercase letter and write the capital letter above it in each word that should be capitalized in the following sentences.

1. In ~~l~~atin american history 101, one of our school's classes for juniors, we saw a movie about costa rica.

2. It's a tiny central american country, smaller than the state of west virginia.

3. costa rica is bordered by nicaragua on the north, the caribbean sea on the east, panama on the south, and the pacific ocean on the west.

4. Its capital, san jose, has approximately 300,000 people.

5. Like most central american countries, costa rica was a spanish colony until it won its independence in 1821.

6. Every year costa rica celebrates its independence from spain on september 18; the United States celebrates its independence from britain on july 4.

7. costa rica is one of the few countries in central or south america that doesn't have a standing army.

8. Just about everyone (myself included) has a hard time imagining a country without a military.

9. In 1987, president oscar arias sanchez won the nobel peace prize for his role in trying to bring peace to the region.

10. Tourists like this caribbean paradise because it has miles and miles of incredible beaches on both the east and west sides of the country.

11. *A guide to the birds of costa rica,* by f. gary stiles, tells about the toucans, parrots, and other birds that live in the rain forests in costa rica.

12. Sometimes people who visit these rain forests experience culture shock when they later visit the capital city of san jose and see neon-sign advertisements for american, european, and japanese tourists.

13. My uncle made a u-turn in his life when he moved to costa rica last spring.

14. This is what uncle charley wrote to my dad: "what I love about my home here is that there is no telephone, no computer, or no tv."

15. Sounds like my uncle (who has a ph.d. in engineering) got sick of corporate america.

16. On dad's nightstand, i saw a copy of a book called *costa rica: the last country the gods made.*

17. I hope he is not thinking of moving our family there—at least not before I graduate.

18. I think dad would have a hard time watching birds rather than the green bay packers on weekends.

Capitalize the following words that need capitalization.

1. spring, monday (M)

2. uncle zeke, my uncle

3. a japanese tea, the tearoom

4. ohio, ireland

5. the renaissance

6. the nineteenth century

7. october, middle ages

8. north of boston, turn north

9. mayor cummings, the mayor

10. fbi, a federal agency

11. *the sun also rises*

12. "the diary of a madman"

13. my english class, my math class

14. the democratic party, a political party

Capitalization 1

Turn to pages 475-477 in *Writers INC* for rules on capitalization.

> **Underline** any word below that is capitalized incorrectly (or not capitalized when it should be).

1. My <u>Mother</u> asked, "<u>when</u> are you leaving?"

2. We are driving North to Canada this Spring.

3. I love the West. The midwest is too flat for my taste.

4. During those long hours in the car (We'll drive 12 hours the first day), we can listen to Books on Tape.

5. I like listening to the british readers better than the American ones.

6. The laotian boy has learned to speak english very well.

7. The group from europe speaks a number of languages: german, spanish, and french.

8. Most italian people are catholic, but some are buddhist.

9. In the south, grits is a popular dish. (grits is a term for ground corn.)

10. In a 1955 Interview, John Mason Brown had this to say about tv: "some television programs are so much chewing gum for the eyes."

11. When auntie Anne came to visit, she read poems to us.

12. My brother hated to listen, but I liked her readings, especially the poems by robert frost.

13. Grandpa loves to shovel the garden by hand before planting his Yukon Gold Potatoes.

14. Yes, this Summer my girl scout troop will travel to nova scotia.

15. I saw signs in chicago that showed how to follow the original route 66 through the city.

Capitalization 2

Turn to pages 475-477 in *Writers INC* for capitalization rules.

> **Underline** any word below that is capitalized incorrectly (or not capitalized when it should be).

1. Pink Floyd's album *Dark side of The Moon* stayed on the charts for more than 20 years.

2. The North Cape vikings basketball uniform is black and purple.

3. Nini Purimi, ph.d, was awarded the top prize for her thesis, "The Blending of Culture In The Modern Americas."

4. John Travolta, a scientologist, became a star after he appeared in the movie *Saturday night fever.*

5. Over the thanksgiving holiday last Fall, we traveled through four States on interstate 94.

6. Laura works at the v.f.w. post, where the local Veterans hold their New Year's eve parties.

7. The Blackmailer demanded money for his silence regarding the Boston tea party.

8. The Arlington high school forensics club won the Statewide competition.

9. The latino populations in some U.S. Cities celebrate cinco de mayo, a Mexican Holiday.

10. Mayor John Jennson was surprised by a Labor day visit from Anna Lopez, the Governor.

11. Will the festival be on the last saturday in may or right before Mother's day?

12. Burlington high school has a radio station, wbsd.

Capitalization 3

Turn to pages 475-477 in *Writers INC* for capitalization rules.

> **Underline** any word below that is capitalized incorrectly (or not capitalized when it should be).

1. Nouns that refer to the <u>supreme</u> <u>being</u> are capitalized.

2. In greek mythology, Hercules was the son of Zeus, the King of the greek gods.

3. I am enrolled in a History course about the bible; it's called "History as Portrayed in The Bible."

4. When Rasheed was a Sophomore, a freshman invited him to the Sadie Hawkins dance.

5. "Ask aunt Clara if she'd like to join us," dad said. "she might have fun."

6. "Praise the lord!" my Mom exclaimed.

7. When he was President, Gerald Ford was thought to be somewhat of a Klutz.

8. Nadia is taking trigonometry 200 this semester, since she took her first Trigonometry course last year.

9. In the American southwest, native American art is very popular.

10. The owner of the Milwaukee bucks (an nba basketball team) is senator Herb Kohl, a democrat from Wisconsin.

11. Emmy, who lives in anchorage, Alaska, has her own home page on the web; she is also one of the organizers for the Dave Matthews fan club.

12. Will professor Nintri be teaching History 201 this Semester?

13. All the Juniors will be required to take either sociology or spanish.

Extend: Write five sentences that illustrate some of the capitalization rules on pages 475-477 in your handbook. Choose rules that gave you trouble in this exercise.

Review: Capitalization

> Underline any word below that is capitalized incorrectly (or not capitalized when it should be).

1. most american workers get labor day off.

2. The Mayor is going to speak every Tuesday in August.

3. Eighty-fourth Avenue is on the East side of town.

4. Isn't your Mother from the East?

5. I heard mom calling for you, Dad.

6. I've always liked History Courses.

7. Are you taking history 201 next Fall?

8. Castles were quite common in the Middle ages.

9. the battle of Bunker Hill claimed many lives.

10. an Alaskan eskimo, a Canadian pilot, and a catholic priest went fishing.

11. Have you read T. S. Eliot's "the Wasteland"?

12. Ronald Reagan, once a democrat, became a republican.

13. The State Park on highway 13 East of town was opened last summer.

14. Go north on Old Summit road.

15. My uncle Marc has worked for NASA since the Winter of '86.

16. My uncle went to the rose bowl and the super bowl.

17. Does lake michigan have car-ferry service?

18. A scenic River like the Colorado attracts many Foreign visitors.

19. let me introduce senator Bob Madsen.

20. Hawaii, the aloha state, is in the middle of the Pacific ocean.

Pretest: Plurals & Spelling

Write C above each underlined word that is spelled correctly. Write the correction above each underlined word that is misspelled.

1   Have you heard of Lilith Fair? It wasn't a county fair or a state fair; it was

2   a <u>women's</u> traveling music festival that took place during the summers of 1997,
      (C above women's)

3   1998, and 1999. It was, in fact, America's most <u>successful</u> musical tour in 1998.

4   The brainchild of singer-songwriter Sarah McLachlan, Lilith Fair <u>feachured</u>

5   well-known singers like Sheryl Crow and Queen Latifah. It also gave

6   <u>emergeing</u> artists a chance to perform. The tour <u>grossed</u> $28 million in 1999

7   and donated $2 million to women's <u>charitys</u>.

8   For years, male artists were the <u>heros</u>, the ones who sang the <u>solo's</u>. Men

9   were <u>usualy</u> the ones playing the <u>pianos</u>, strumming the <u>banjoes</u>, and beating

10   the drums.

11   But things have changed and Lilith Fair pushed that change even <u>farther</u>

12   in its three summer tours. It helped capture the attention of industry leaders

13   and record <u>studioes</u> for dozens of the performers.

14   When Lilith Fair came to our city, my <u>freinds</u> and I packed two <u>tubsful</u> of

15   fried chicken, French <u>frys</u>, some <u>loafs</u> of crusty French bread, and three

16   <u>thermoses</u> of raspberry iced tea and set off to enjoy <u>ourselfs</u>. It was <u>amazeing</u>

17   to see all those singers and musicians performing together.

18   Eventually a rain began to fall, but we were all in such a good mood that a

19   little rain <u>actualy</u> made the evening more <u>memorable</u>. Some people sang, some

20   people laughed, and some even <u>cryed</u>, but somehow everybody felt connected to

21   one another and to the music.

Write the plurals of the following nouns on the lines provided.

1. chef   *chefs* _____

2. ABC _____

3. sheep _____

4. crisis _____

5. father-in-law _____

6. 5 _____

7. spoonful _____

8. tattoo _____

9. latchkey _____

10. rash _____

11. editor in chief _____

12. party _____

13. veto _____

14. shelf _____

Fill in the blanks or circle the correct spelling. All the information you will need pertains to spelling rules.

1. Write *i* before _____ except after *c*, or when sounded like *a* as in *neighbor* and *weigh*.

2. Using the rule stated above, circle each correctly spelled word:

   receive, recieve; reign, riegn; seige, siege; belief, beleif.

3. When a one-syllable word (*mat*) ends in a consonant (*t*) preceded by one vowel (*a*), _____ the final consonant before adding a suffix that begins with a vowel (*-ing*).

4. Using the rule stated above, add the suffix *-ary* to the word *sum:*

   _____ .

5. If a word ends with a silent *e,* _____ the *e* before adding a suffix that begins with a vowel.

6. Using the rule stated above, add *ing* to the following words: make, drive, write.

   _____

Plurals 1

An *es* or *s* is added to the end of most singular nouns in order to form the plurals. But nouns ending in *y, o, f,* or *fe* present exceptions to this basic *es* or *s* rule. Turn to page 478 in *Writers INC* for more information.

> **Make** the following words plural.

1. horse _horses_

2. radio _____

3. story _____

4. holiday _____

5. potato _____

6. pass _____

7. church _____

8. wife _____

9. buzz _____

10. tomato _____

11. leaf _____

12. fly _____

13. patio _____

14. birch _____

15. monkey _____

16. push _____

> **Change** the following plurals to their singular form.

1. bowls _bowl_

2. rushes _____

3. tries _____

4. heroes _____

5. trios _____

6. ewes _____

7. jalopies _____

8. folios _____

9. fryers _____

10. satellites _____

11. roles _____

12. roofs _____

13. cries _____

14. parties _____

Extend: Create your own version of the exercise at the top of the page. Think of five new words that form plurals using the rules you've just studied. List the singular forms. Then trade papers with a classmate and complete one another's exercise.

Plurals 2

This exercise focuses on three rules: forming the plurals of words that end in *f* or *fe*; creating the plurals of foreign or irregular words; and forming the plurals of compound nouns. Turn to 478.4, 479.1, and 479.4 in *Writers INC*.

Write the plural form of each word below.

1. loaf *loaves*
2. belief _____
3. knife _____
4. calf _____
5. half _____
6. wolf _____
7. chief _____
8. cliff _____

9. thief _____
10. fife _____
11. life _____
12. sniff _____
13. staff _____
14. strife _____
15. puff _____
16. elf _____

Change each of the following irregular and compound words to its plural form.

1. die *dice (or) dies*
2. ox _____
3. mouse _____
4. goose _____
5. tooth _____
6. woman _____
7. syllabus _____

8. editor in chief _____
9. son-in-law _____
10. aide-de-camp _____
11. maid-in-waiting _____
12. secretary-general _____
13. two-wheeler _____
14. vertebra _____

Extend: Create your own version of the exercises at the top of the page. Think of five new words that form plurals using the rules you've just studied. List the singular forms. Then trade papers with a classmate and complete one another's exercise.

Spelling 1

Turn to page 484 in *Writers INC* to find spelling rules that will help you with this exercise. Learn the rules and exceptions as you work. (You may also use your dictionary.)

> Circle the word that is spelled incorrectly in each pair below. Then write the correct spelling in the blank.

1. (feild,) losing ___*field*___
2. lonly, shiniest _____
3. useful, robery _____
4. sentries, safty _____
5. peice, puppies _____
6. likly, committed _____
7. behaving, truely _____
8. nieghborhood, plier _____
9. alleys, firey _____
10. finely, ladys _____
11. biege, occurred _____
12. monkies, quitter _____
13. referred, cryed _____
14. dying, joging _____
15. luckily, refered _____
16. receipt, drugist _____
17. management, thier _____
18. nineth, freight _____
19. liesure, mileage _____
20. advertisement, pennys _____

21. mischeif, friend _____
22. living, mudied _____
23. ninteen, ponies _____
24. decieve, fiend _____
25. comeing, chief _____
26. judgment, lovly _____
27. guidance, deisel _____
28. allies, admitance _____
29. flies, arguement _____
30. lovable, hygeine _____
31. desireable, bugged _____
32. sumary, happiness _____
33. baggage, useing _____
34. likness, plugged _____
35. field, valueable _____
36. vein, niether _____
37. conceit, beautyful _____
38. canopys, approval _____
39. wierd, stately _____
40. forgetable, hurried _____

ex¹ ┼ - wkbk 10

Spelling 2

Use the spelling words listed on pages 485-489 to complete this exercise.

> **Underline** each misspelled word below and write the correct spelling above it.

really

1   The world's first roads were <u>realy</u> trails made by game animals and by the

2   hunters who undoutably followed them. After the wheel was invented (about

3   3000 B.C.E.), roads typically followed trade routs.

4   The Romans were the first great road builders, althogh other civilezations

5   had built roads previosly. The Romans laid a solid base and braught in flat

6   stones for pavement. They concieved a plan for water drainage. They made

7   sure the roads sloped adequetely from the center to both sides, and they

8   constructed ditches to carry the water away.

9   Although French enginears used gravel and stone on some roads in the

10   1700s, most roads remained little more than a clearing of mud until the 1800s.

11   It was then—during the Industral Revolution—that a road surface called

12   *macadam* (small stones packed into layers) was developped. Macadam is still

13   utillized on some roads today.

14   In the early 1900s, the demand for good roads increased. With the

15   introduction of the automobele, well-built streets were no longer a luxsury; they

16   were a necesity. Few United States highways were constructed, however, until

17   after the Great Depression of the 1930s. In 1956, the imense federel interstate

18   highway system was implemented. Nearly 40 years later, the work was

19   complete exept, of course, for that anual anoyance called "construction season."

Extend: Explain to a classmate the spelling rules (or the exceptions) you used to make four of
the corrections in the sentences above.

Spelling 3

Turn to page 484 in *Writers INC* to find spelling rules that will help you with this exercise. Also refer to the list of commonly misspelled words on pages 485-489 to find correct spellings of many of the words.

> Underline **each misspelled word below and write the correct spelling above it.**

imagine
1   When you imagin a panda, you probly picture a large, likeable, cuddly

2   bear that has a white face with a black patch around each eye. That's a

3   *giant panda,* and it's enormus—with an average heit of five to six feet

4   and an average wieght of 200 to 300 pounds.

5   But there is a diffrent species of panda, called the red panda, whose

6   appearence more closely resembles a raccoon's. A red panda has long, soft,

7   redish fur and a bushy tail with rings. It wieghs only about 11 pounds,

8   and its body measures about two feet in lenth.

9   Both species of panda live in the bamboo forests of China. The red

10   panda has three other habittats as well: the bamboo forests of northern

11   India, Myanmar, and Nepal. Each species must eat substansial quantitys

12   of bamboo. In fact, the giant panda offen consumes 85 pounds each day!

13   So, how are pandas classifyed? Should they be part of the bear family

14   or the raccoon family? Actually, zoologists disagree—not only on how

15   pandas should be classified but also on the issue of how closely the two

16   species are related. Some scientists reconize that the DNA of red pandas

17   is similer to that of raccoons, while the DNA of giant pandas paralels

18   that of bears. Perhaps these creatures—both red and giant pandas—

19   desserve a seperate family of their own.

Spelling 4

Refer to the list of commonly misspelled words on pages 485-489 in *Writers INC* for help with this exercise.

> **Underline** each misspelled word in the news story below and write the correct spelling above.

Grocery

1   The latest fire to hit Oakton this month destroyed the Streetside Grosery

2   Store. Forchunately, the store was closed, and no one was injured.

3   Oakton Fire Chief Flynn stated, "There will be an inquirey into this fire, as

4   it is of suspitious origin. The beureau will conduct a thurough investigation."

5   "The reckage caused by the fire won't be safe to remove for several days,"

6   Leutenant Wills remarked. He also noted that an aquaintance of his, musicien

7   Lamont Burrows, and several family's lost their apartments above the store in

8   the fire.

9   The chief continued, "This is the eigth fire we've been called to this month,

10   and a eunique pattern is emerging. I believe we're dealing with arson." Smoke

11   was still thick in the area, and he paused to couph. "The psycology of an

12   arsonist is such that he or she feels a need to decieve. This nesessity—some

13   might call it a dizease—might give us some clues to this criminal's

14   whereabouts. Anyone with any knowlege about how or when the fire started is

15   requested to contact me."

16   Oakton residents wishing to donate cash, food, close, or misselaneous items

17   to the former ocupants of the building can contact Marilee Singer at Oakton

18   Bank, 555-3200.

Review: Plurals & Spelling

Write the correct plural for each word that appears in parentheses.

1. The _____*people*_____ (person) went to the _____ (city) to buy _____ (grocery).

2. The _____ (wife) of the _____ (director) decided that they would try out for the _____ (solo).

3. The _____ (patio) on the _____ (house) need new _____ (brick).

4. The _____ (belief) of the _____ (woman) differed, but both said the _____ (leaf) could be used for medicinal _____ (purpose).

5. The _____ (datum) on the _____ (trout) should be given to the _____ (fishery).

6. There are three _____ (u) in the _____ (name) of my _____ (brother-in-law).

7. The _____ (family) liked the _____ (ox) and the _____ (monkey).

8. The _____ (story) of the local _____ (hero) were very interesting to the _____ (class).

9. The _____ (roof) of the abandoned _____ (factory) are in terrible shape.

10. The _____ (banjo) were stolen by _____ (thief) who tried to sell them on the Internet.

> **Study** each group of words listed below. Then, using your own words, write the spelling rule that the word group exemplifies.

1. relieve, believe, receive, sleigh, eight

(See 484.1) Write i before e except after c, or when sounded like a as in neighbor and weigh.

2. likeness, statement, ninety, nineteen

_____

_____

3. hurried, happiness, beautiful, ladies

_____

_____

_____

4. forgettable, committed, occurrence, beginning

_____

_____

_____

5. toys, plays, moneys

_____

_____

6. neither, sheik, weird

_____

_____

7. What should you remember about using a spell checker and a dictionary?

_____

_____

Numbers 1

Become familiar with some basic guidelines for using numbers so that you know when to write numbers as numerals and when to write numbers as words. Turn to page 480 in *Writers INC* for more information.

> **Write** the rule number that each statement below demonstrates. **Then give a brief explanation of each rule. (*Note:* All numbers are used correctly in the following sentences.)**

480.1   **1.** Teresa received four gifts for her birthday. _Numbers from one to nine are usually spelled out._

_____   **2.** Twelve of her gifts were from her family. _____

_____   **3.** It was a pleasant 72° F in Pittsburgh today. _____

_____   **4.** My brother gets up at 4:00 A.M. to deliver newspapers. _____

_____   **5.** I get paid $5.74 per hour. _____

_____   **6.** Sully found twenty dollars. _____

_____   **7.** I weighed 8 lbs. 3 oz. when I was born. _____

_____   **8.** About 93 percent of our class will go on to school. _____

_____   **9.** The graphic arts department made fifteen 10-foot banners. _____

Numbers 2

There are specific rules about the use of numbers in formal writing. Turn to page 480 in *Writers INC*.

> **Write** the correct form (numeral or word) above the underlined numbers below. If the form is already correct, write C above it.

1. The *five* 5 basins of the Great Lakes combine to form a single watershed with *one* 1 common outlet to the ocean.

2. Lake Superior is the largest of the Great Lakes, with an area of 31,820 square miles; Lake Ontario is the smallest, with an area of just over seventy-five hundred square miles.

3. Lake Superior is also the coldest of the 5 lakes; its average water temperature is 40° F.

4. The Great Lakes contain eighteen percent of the world's fresh surface water.

5. The total volume of the lakes is more than six quadrillion gallons.

6. Spread evenly over the continental United States, the water would submerge everything less than 9 and a half feet high.

7. The lobes of Lakes Michigan and Huron are at the same elevation and are connected by the one hundred twenty-foot-deep Mackinac Strait.

8. Mackinac Strait is not a river that separates the lakes; instead, it is a three-point-six- to five-mile narrowing of the lakes.

9. You may want to take 2 300-mile trips instead of one six-hundred-mile cruise.

10. If you left at six a.m. in a boat cruising at 40 mph, you wouldn't get to the other end of the lake until 9 o'clock at night.

Extend: Write four or five sentences about traveling. Include information about distance, time, and money, using the correct form for the numbers in your sentences.

Abbreviations

Abbreviations, acronyms, and initialisms are used to shorten a word or a phrase. Turn to pages 481-483 in *Writers INC* for more information.

Spell out the following abbreviations.

1. PTA _Parent-Teacher Association_

2. Sr. _____

3. m _____

4. lat. _____

5. inc. _____

6. JP _____

7. Que. (or) PQ _____

8. Blvd. _____

9. B.C.E. _____

10. Hon. _____

Abbreviate the following words. Refer to 481.2, 482.1, and 483.3 for the answers.

1. Connecticut _Conn. (or) CT_

2. Avenue _____

3. deceased _____

4. example _____

5. Social Security Administration _____

6. Apartment _____

7. standard time _____

8. ultra high frequency _____

9. weekly _____

10. southeast _____

List five acronyms and five initialisms that you might use in your own writing.

Acronyms	Initialisms
1. _____	1. _____
2. _____	2. _____
3. _____	3. _____
4. _____	4. _____
5. _____	5. _____

Review: Numbers & Abbreviations

Circle the correct choices. (Remember that in formal writing, most words are spelled out, with the exception of a few acceptable abbreviations.)

1. We pulled up to *(thirteen,* (13)*)* Donner *((Street,)* *St.)* at *(four,* (4:00)*)* (*p.m.,*) *post meridiem)* on Sunday afternoon.

2. *(Dr., Doctor)* Julio Mendez, *(Junior, Jr.)*, greeted us at the *(Wisconsin, WI)* *(Department, Dept.)* of Health and gave us the *(HIV, human immunodeficiency virus)* brochures to distribute.

3. The package was addressed to *(Mr., Mister)* Carter, at Mercy Hospital on Gammon *(Avenue, Ave.)*, and we needed to deliver it before *(nine, 9:00)* *(a.m., ante meridiem)* the next day.

4. The public garden was *(one hundred ten, 110)* feet wide on the *(NE, northeast)* side of the *(BBB, Better Business Bureau)* building.

5. Our teacher gave us an *(example, ex.)* of an effective *(bibliography, bibliog.)*.

6. The *(pkg., package)* *(without, w/o)* a legible address could not be delivered.

7. *(15, Fifteen)* minutes later, Luke Harrison signed and *(paid, pd.)* for the rental car and we were off.

8. We met *(7, seven)* 10-year-old Little Leaguers from Taiwan at the gas station where we filled up the car with *(8, eight)* *(gallons, gal.)* of gas.

9. *(5, Five)* students forgot to bring their permission slips.

10. Did you make the appointment for *(four p.m, 4:00 p.m.)*?

11. Dad received *(five dollars, $ five)* for his weekly allowance when he was my age.

12. Our group voted *(four to two, 4 to 2)* to go see the *(3 o'clock, three o'clock)* movie.

Pretest: Using the Right Word

Circle the correct word (or words) in each group in parentheses in the following paragraphs.

1   *(Weather,* (*Whether*)*)* or not you're a sports fan, you may have *(heard, herd)* of

2   Lance Armstrong. He's the cyclist upon *(who, whom)* the eyes of the world were

3   riveted for almost a month in 1999 as he competed in the Tour de France, the

4   bicycle race that ends on the streets of Paris, that country's *(capital, capitol).*

5   Compared to most other athletic events, the Tour de France is grueling. *(It's,*

6   *Its)* a 2,303-mile race that requires incredible endurance and stamina. That

7   Armstrong could find the *(personal, personnel)* strength to participate is

8   amazing. That he won is *(altogether, all together)* astounding.

9   Three years earlier, Lance Armstrong found out that he had cancer and

10   that it was *(already, all ready)* in an advanced stage. But Armstrong did not

11   *(accept, except)* the idea that he could not be *(healed, heeled)* and be *(good, well)*

12   again. He did not allow the doctor's grim prognosis to *(affect, effect)* his will to

13   live, which *(alot, a lot)* of people might have done under similar circumstances.

14   Instead, Armstrong *(chose, choose)* to fight his disease aggressively with every

15   tool the medical establishment could throw at it, even though the treatments

16   made him *(quiet, quit, quite)* sick for *(a, an)* entire year.

17   *(Among, Between)* cancer survivors, Armstrong is a hero. Fortunately, the

18   *(amount, number)* of people from all walks of life who are surviving and living

19   with cancer is increasing day by day. In the *(past, passed)*, people did not even

20   say the word *cancer* in polite circles. A diagnosis of cancer was considered a

21   death sentence, and the most you could expect from treatment was to

22   *(by, buy, bye)* a few extra months of life. Of *(coarse, course)*, many people with

23   the best doctors and most positive attitudes in the world still *(die, dye)* of

24   cancer, but more and more, cancer is becoming a treatable and very often a

25   curable disease.

26   Another athlete *(whom, who)* did not take her diagnosis of cancer *(laying,*

27   *lying)* down is Sweden's first gold *(medal, metal)* winner in track and field,

28   Lyudmila Engquist. She chose the day of her *(berth, birth)*, April 21, as the day

29   she had surgery. The next month she began chemotherapy treatment, and after

30   the fourth session, she felt *(good, well)* enough to compete in a track *(meet, meat)*

31   in Stockholm. Though she was still in treament, she won the 100-meter hurdle

32   with only eighteen-hundredths of a second off her best performance.

33   Of course, Armstrong and Engquist are *(different from, different than)* most

34   people in that they are both athletes in peak physical condition. Their

35   *(healthful, healthy)* regimes *(compliment, complement)* their *(good, well)* genetic

36   makeup. Good luck was a factor for both athletes, *(to, too, two)*. Nevertheless,

37   *(their, there, they're)* successes challenge all of us to look at cancer a little

38   differently. Engquist offers this wise *(council, counsel)*: "So many people

39   believe that cancer is the end, but that is not what I believe anymore."

Using the Right Word 1

Turn to pages 491-500 in *Writers INC* for help with this exercise.

> **Write** the correction above each underlined word that is misused. Write **C** above each underlined word that's used correctly.

1. It was a hot summer morning in 1939, but the people who lived in and around

tiny Orange City, Iowa, were <u>already</u> *all ready* to experience the <u>perennial</u> (happens once

each year) Fourth of July celebration.

2. In the village park, the barrel of <u>a</u> immense <u>blue</u> cannon was suspended

<u>between</u> two spoked wooden wheels.

3. <u>Besides</u> (next to) the big gun, three huge balls rested on a square wooden <u>bass</u>.

4. Two paunchy World War II veterans in uniform stood by the cannon. A large

<u>amount</u> of spectators had gathered around them.

5. The mayor was just finishing his speech: "And the reason we're <u>altogether</u> in

this safe, free, grand country of ours is not simply a result of this being our

place of <u>berth</u>."

6. "<u>A lot</u> of you older folks remember when President Wilson told us to take up

arms. We all willingly <u>excepted</u> that command."

7. "We <u>new</u> that the German guns and tanks and subs would <u>effect</u> serious

changes in our own families and in our own lives and even cause our deaths."

8. "But when the call to duty came, we also <u>new</u> that free people <u>may</u> not stand

<u>buy</u> and watch others <u>brake</u> up their democracy!"

9. "Our soldier boys <u>brought</u> their guns and bullets over to Europe so they could

<u>take</u> back a new lease on freedom for America!"

10. As the mayor's words <u>pored</u> forth, I smelled the <u>cent</u> of roasting corn.

Extend: Write your own sentences using the following words correctly: *adapt, chord, vain,* and *whom.*

Using the Right Word 2

Turn to pages 491-500 in *Writers INC.*

> Underline **each usage error in the passage below and write the correction above it.**

between
1   The late afternoon sun hovered <u>among</u> two clouds before disappearing

2   behind another. As the train chugged along, an elderly lady sat quietly

3   watching farms and villages slide buy the window. Her little nephew sat

4   besides her, unwilling to except his ant's directives: "Look at that weather

5   vain!"; "See the blew sky!"; "Aren't there alot of pigs in that pen?" The boy was

6   board by the trip—one of his aunt's perennial (twice a year) "cultural

7   experiences."

8   Even though she lived a good distance away, his aunt came twice a year

9   without fail to bring her nephew on a outing. She carefully designed each

10   "experience" as an illusion (indirect reference) to "the beauty and order this

11   world is all together full of, my dear boy!"

12   However, seeing an impressive amount of sights did not effect the nephew

13   as his ant had hoped. Traveling for five hours can be taxing. The boy was

14   interested, not in the seens outside, but in the fuzzy, stiff body of a bumblebee

15   that lay on its back in the bass of his left palm.

16   "Ah," sighed the aunt, gazing out the window. "Isn't nature alive and

17   beautiful?" And the little boy, without braking his concentrated study of the

18   bee, replied, "Yes, its pretty, Auntie, but can I bring my friend with me?" The

20   old ant looked at the boy. She saw the bee in his hand and the smile in his

21   eyes, and said, "I guess that would be alright." Then she chuckled. "After all,

22   one should accept any gift of nature . . . even if it is dead."

Using the Right Word 3

Turn to pages 491-500 in *Writers INC*.

> **Underline** each usage error in the passage below and write the correction above it.

1   Last week, the teachers in Rock River, Wisconsin, *chose* choose to picket the

2   administration building as a last coarse of action to resolve an 18-month

3   stalemate in contract talks. Radio, TV, and newspaper headlines proclaimed,

4   "Teachers Demand to Be Herd" and "Town Counsel Calls for Settlement."

5   Yesterday Shawn O'Hern, a math teacher from neighboring Raymond, went

6   to Rock River to help gain support for the teachers. It was 8:00 a.m. on a chilly

7   December morning. The streets were nearly desserted, but their was hardly

8   any room to move in the abandoned store where the picketers were meeting.

9   Shawn and other school personal whom had been sent to support the local

10   educators picked up their signs and stepped outside. "Ah," thought Shawn, "its

11   a cold morning alright, but a just protest is a capitol reason to brave the

12   elements. I haven't breathed such a brisk breeze since I immigrated from

13   Ireland in '94, but I'm not about to dye of the chill."

14   Just then, an older woman hurried to his side. "Oh dear," she panted,

15   "isn't this hole picketing business a mess?" Pale and nervous, she hugged her

16   sign as if she wanted to choke it's message. "This all makes me feel feint," she

17   said. "I can't understand how people think they can heel discord by carrying

18   these silly signs."

19   "You may be write," replied Shawn. "But isn't the fact that we do speak

20   out a complement to democracy—a system that celebrates freedom of speech?"

Extend: Write your own sentences using the following words correctly: *infer, piece, principle,* and *waist*.

Review: Using the Right Word

> Underline each usage error in the sentences below and write the correction above it.

illusions
1. Do you have any <u>allusions</u> about what Alaska will be like?

2. I do, and I think I'm already for my Alaska experience, but if I'm wrong, I'll adopt my behavior as necessary.

3. My cousin will borrow me a heavy parka and snowshoes.

4. We have an exchange program at my school, so I plan to spend next year attending school in Anchorage.

5. I expect to do a lot of hiking beside attending school, so I'm bringing my camera.

6. Alaska has all together to many trails for me to hike in just one year, but there are an amount of trails that I have chosen to hike no matter what.

7. Do I think I will get board during the long Alaskan winter? I except the fact that I may.

8. Yes, I have herd of people fainting illnesses so they could be flown out and sent back to they're homes.

9. I chose a hole bunch of books to bring; there ones I've been wanting to read.

10. My ant, who lives in Anchorage, says she watches moose wandering down desserted streets and passed empty houses.

11. Ever since my berth, it's been my dream to live in Alaska.

12. I hope I see alot of blew skies and heards of caribou, dear, and elk.

13. The scenes that I've scene in books inspire my imagination.

14. I don't no if I'll get to the capitol city of Juneau, but I hope too.

15. The year will pass much too fast, I expect, and than I'll have to let many new friends and favorite places behind.

Review: Proofreading Activities

Choose the punctuation in column B that can be used in the manner described in column A. Then write the letter in the blank.

Column A

Column B

_____ **1.** Joins prefixes like "self" to words

_____ **2.** Separates equal adjectives

_____ **3.** Set off titles of songs, short stories, and magazine articles

_____ **4.** Sets off the names of books, ships, and TV programs

_____ **5.** Used in a series if commas are already used

_____ **6.** Used to set off a word, a phrase, or a clause from the rest of the sentence (for emphasis)

_____ **7.** Used in contractions

_____ **8.** Ends an interrogative sentence

_____ **9.** Ends an exclamatory sentence

_____ **10.** Ends a declarative sentence

a. Comma

b. Apostrophe

c. Dash or colon

d. Quotation marks

e. Question mark

f. Hyphen

g. Period

h. Semicolon

i. Italics (Underlining)

j. Exclamation point

Proofread the sentences below. Correct the errors in spelling or usage.

already
1. You're <u>all ready</u> embarrasing me with these personal questions.

2. Even fourty spoonsful of sugar wouldn't make that medicine go down.

3. Throughly checking the breaks on your car is the begining of automobile saftey.

4. Relax and lay down, and I will strum soothing cords on our banjoes.

5. Whose in charge of recieving the principle guest of honor each month?

6. The visitor's unforgetable story had a chilling affect on everyone who herd it.

Proofread the essay below. Cross out any error you find in capitalization, numbers, plurals, and usage. Write the correction above it. Add or fix punctuation as necessary.

1   My friends Martha and Stewart say The small earth-friendly recycling

2   you do each each day really adds up. For example you can recycle the

3   cardboard cylinders that are found in these items gift wrap paper toweling

4   plastic wrap waxed paper and aluminum foil.

5   Martha, whose a whiz at crafts, says, Or maybe youd rather reuse

6   these tubes. Everyone can use an extra necktie or scarf rack, or a

7   custom-made window shade the cardboard tube becomes a dowel for it.

8   And why not make a cardboard napkin ring or sachet you could even

9   make a cookie cutter.

10   Cardboard tubes are not the only useful item's to recycle. Stewart

11   claims that containers such as jars, bottles, empty munchie canisters,

12   cardboard desert containers, and aluminum coffee cans can all be reused.

13   Old coffee cans can be used as safety lights just place strip's of bright

14   reflector tape on the cans then put them in the trunk of your car for an

15   emergency.

16   with these items and your creative ability, you can make lamp basses,

17   hassocks, planters, tool chests, and even canisters to hold writing supplies!

18   Martha exclaims. Speaking of VCRs, Martha and Stewart also have an

20   idea on how to reuse videotape. Once youve watched Titanic for the tenth

21   time pull the tape out of it's casing. Glue small handmade snowflakes on

22   the tape at 5 inch intervals. Voila you have garland for your holiday tree.

LANGUAGE ACTIVITIES

The activities in this section provide a review of the different parts of speech. Most of the activities also include helpful handbook references. In addition, the Extend activities encourage follow-up practice of certain skills.

Pretest: Nouns

Underline the words used as nouns in the following sentences. Label each noun twice: first, use *P* for proper and *C* for common; then, use *S* for singular and *PL* for plural.

                         C/PL

1. Are you one of those <u>people</u> who get tingles when you see a Mid-America Mall,

      Kenosha Outlet Mall, or Old Orchard Mall?

2. Or are you a person who likes to shop in the comfort of your own home?

3. If you said "yes" to the last question, you might like on-line stores.

4. To shop on-line you will need three things: a computer, a credit card, and

      access to the Internet.

Indicate the function of each of the underlined nouns in the following sentences. Use these symbols: *S* for subject, *PN* for predicate noun, *IO* for indirect object, *DO* for direct object, and *OP* for object of a preposition. Use *POS* for nouns showing ownership or possession.

      S   **1.** <u>Jupiter Communications</u>, a research company, predicts that children

                        ages 5 to 18 will spend $1.8 billion shopping on-line by 2003.

              2. Companies that sell their <u>customers</u> toys, books, clothes, and music

                        are already doing big business on the Internet.

              3. Does on-line shopping encourage an excess of <u>buying</u>, or does it

                        encourage young people to be spendthrifts?

              4. Our school choir found some great new <u>music</u> on the Internet.

              5. Our <u>family's</u> orders from shops on the Internet include books and

                        CD's, but nothing else.

              6. On-line shopping can be a real <u>convenience</u>.

Identifying Nouns 1

A proper noun names a particular person, place, thing, or idea and is always capitalized. A common noun does not name a particular person, place, thing, or idea and is *not* capitalized. Turn to 501.1-501.2 in *Writers INC.*

> Circle all the proper nouns and underline all the common nouns in the following paragraph.

1   (P. T. Barnum) was already a successful businessman when he traveled to

2   New York and purchased the American Museum in 1848. It was this

3   building—promptly renamed Barnum's American Museum—that would make

4   him a world-famous showman.

5   Barnum set out to fill his museum with both culture and curiosities. He

6   presented an enormous menagerie of animals and featured performers whose

7   talents ranged from glassblowing to snakecharming. A tiny model of Paris, a

8   dog operating a knitting machine—such wonders filled every room.

9   P. T. Barnum had an amazing talent for attracting crowds. One story says

10 that he hired a man to walk around the intersection outside the museum and

11 place a brick on every corner. Instructed by Barnum not to answer any

12 questions, the man would silently stroll around the intersection, moving each

13 brick to the next corner—and taking the last brick inside the museum.

14   Many people paid to follow the "brick man" inside, only to see him wait a

15 few minutes before he took the brick back outside to begin his circuit all over

16 again. A few people were angry, but most enjoyed the trickery by the master

17 and spent the afternoon enjoying his museum.

Extend: Quite often, both a proper and a common noun can be used to label the same person, place, or idea. For example, "showman" is a common noun referring to the proper noun "P. T. Barnum." See if you can come up with a proper noun for each of the following common nouns: *building, museum, animals,* and *performers.*

Identifying Nouns 2

The number of a noun indicates whether it's singular (one *potato,* one *person*) or plural (two *potatoes,* several *people*). A concrete noun names a thing that is tangible, while an abstract noun names an idea, a condition, or a feeling. Turn to 501.3, 501.4, and 502.1 in *Writers INC.*

> **Underline** the words used as nouns below. Write **S** above each singular noun and **P** above each plural noun.

                   S

1. My school recently underwent some unusual construction.

2. Supervisors and workmen swarmed through the building.

3. Scaffolds surrounded the six floors of the building.

4. The old doors and windows that had been damaged in a storm had to be

removed and replaced.

5. Workers hammered and ran power tools on scaffolds outside classroom windows.

6. Students and teachers found it hard not to watch the workers.

> **Underline** the nouns below. Write **A** above each abstract noun and **C** above each concrete noun.

1. The winter weather complicated and prolonged the construction work.

2. Workers carefully negotiated the slippery scaffolds and struggled to maintain

their balance in the freezing gusts of wind.

3. School staff and construction workers alike celebrated the installation of the

final window.

4. Our principal invited the workers to the cafeteria for cake and coffee.

5. The construction team was just as happy as we were that the midyear project

was over.

Extend: Write two sentences for each of these collective nouns: *crowd, faculty,* and *group.* In the first sentence, make the noun singular (it refers to the group as a unit). In the second sentence, make the noun plural (it refers to the individuals within the group).

Functions of Nouns

There are six different uses for nouns (see the chart below).   Turn to the appropriate references in *Writers INC* for information.

Writers INC	Function	Symbol	Examples
519.1	*subject*	**S**	*Children* play.
502.3, 507.3	*predicate noun*	**PN**	Bobby is only a *child*.
502.3	*possessive noun*	**POS**	A *child's* voice cried out.
508.1	*direct object*	**DO**	Someone had accidentally kicked the *child*.
508.1	*indirect object*	**IO**	We gave the *child* an adhesive bandage.
515	*object of preposition*	**OP**	The other children gathered near the *child*.

> **Using** the symbols from the chart above, label the function of the underlined nouns in the following sentences.

1. **S** Cremation is the final arrangement for the dead in Buddhist and Hindu regions of the world and is becoming more common in the United States and Canada.

2. Some cultures have other methods for taking care of their dead; in Tibet, a water burial is customary.

3. The ancient Egyptians placed their dead in tombs with food, jewels, and other things.

4. They mummified the dead, as they believed the body's spirit would return to it.

5. The tradition of burying the dead developed from a common belief in "coming back"—that the body is a seed to be planted in the earth to await rebirth.

6. Cemeteries provide people a special place to bury and memorialize the dead.

7. Arlington National Cemetery covers more than 600 acres in Arlington, Virginia.

8. It is probably the most famous cemetery in the United States.

9. The only presidents buried there are John Kennedy and William Taft.

10. Marked by an eternal flame, the grave of JFK is visited by thousands of people each year.

Nominative, Possessive, & Objective Cases of Nouns

In the *nominative case,* a noun is used as the subject or the predicate nominative. In the *possessive case,* the noun shows ownership or possession. In the *objective case,* the noun is used as the direct object, the indirect object, or the object of a preposition. Turn to 502.3.

Indicate **whether each underlined noun is in the nominative case (*N*), the possessive case (*P*), or the objective case (*O*).**

_____ *O* **1.** Scientists have dreamed of many different <u>designs</u> for tomorrow's spacecraft.

_____ **2.** Some designs resemble the spacecraft used today that burn chemical fuel for <u>propulsion</u>.

_____ **3.** Other futuristic <u>craft</u> are powered by controlled nuclear explosions. (Those <u>spaceships</u> could take people to Mars in half the time!)

_____ **4.** One <u>scientist's</u> design beams power out to spacecraft using a high-powered <u>laser</u> that orbits Earth.

_____ **5.** A few <u>concepts</u> have spacecraft sailing on the "solar wind" of tiny <u>particles</u> expelled by the sun.

_____ **6.** But <u>astronauts'</u> journeys to other solar systems will still be incredibly long, so early interstellar <u>travelers</u> may have to travel frozen in suspended animation.

Write **sentences using each of the following nouns in the indicated cases.**

1. Mars *(nominative):* _____

_____

2. Earth *(possessive):* _____

_____

3. aliens *(objective):* _____

_____

4. space station *(objective):* _____

_____

Extend: Rewrite each of your sentences using each of the listed nouns in a different case.

Using Nouns

Strong, specific nouns are essential for clear communication and lively writing. For example, you would probably be excited if you found out that you had won a car in a drawing! However, your excitement would increase if they told you that you had won a sports car—in fact, let's say it's a convertible! A specific noun makes a big difference. Turn to page 130 and 501.3-501.4 in *Writers INC*.

> **Write** a sentence containing a noun that fits each description below. Circle this noun. Be as specific and vivid as possible!

1. plural, proper, thing: _A recent ad campaign has boosted the_ _popularity of (Chihuahuas) as family pets._

2. singular, concrete, thing: _____

_____

3. collective, proper, people: _____

_____

4. singular, abstract, idea: _____

_____

5. singular, proper, place: _____

_____

6. plural, concrete, thing: _____

_____

7. singular, proper, person: _____

_____

8. plural, common, thing: _____

_____

9. singular, abstract, idea: _____

_____

Review: Nouns

> **Underline** all words used as nouns below. Identify the **first noun in each sentence:** write **PL** for plural or **S** for singular on the first blank; write **C** for concrete or **A** for abstract on the second blank.

<u>S</u> <u>A</u> **1.** <u>Snowboarding</u> has exploded onto the international sports <u>scene</u>, attracting weekend <u>skiers</u> and extreme <u>athletes</u> alike.

____ ____ **2.** The sport was originally known as "snurfing," a combination of the words "snow" and "surfing."

____ ____ **3.** Sherman Poppen invented the "snurfer" in 1965; after his daughter tried to sled standing up, he screwed two skis together.

____ ____ **4.** Many entrepreneurs tried to design a better way to surf on snow, but it wasn't until 1977—when Jake Burton Carpenter attached rubber bootstraps to a wooden board and coated it with plastic—that the modern snowboard was born.

____ ____ **5.** Jake Burton Carpenter's design led to the creation of one of the most famous snowboarding companies in existence: Burton.

____ ____ **6.** The popularity of snowboarding increased dramatically in the 1980s when snowboarding companies held international competitions.

____ ____ **7.** American snowboarders also formed the U.S. Amateur Snowboard Association (USASA) in the '80s.

____ ____ **8.** When ESPN televised the Winter X Games in the '90s, they were the first major network to televise extreme sports competitions.

____ ____ **9.** Twenty years after Burton had created his first board, in 1998, snowboarding became an official Olympic sport.

____ ____ **10.** Snowboarders from around the world gave the spectators and viewers outstanding performances as they competed for medals at the Winter Olympics in Nagano, Japan.

X Pck12
wkbk 10

Pretest: Pronouns

> Circle the correct pronoun in each pair below.

1. Many of *(us, we)* Americans have relatives or ancestors who have come to this country from other places on the globe.

2. How many American citizens do you know *(who, whom)* were born outside the United States?

3. Have you ever wondered why so many people leave *(his or her, their)* native lands to come here?

4. Between you and *(I, me),* I can't imagine permanently leaving the country where I grew up.

5. Emigrants, *(who, which)* leave their native land, often agonize over the decision.

6. In one way or another, people *(who, which)* come to America are seeking a better life for *(himself, themselves)* and for *(their, his or her)* children.

7. People for *(who, whom)* citizenship is a goal must be at least 18 years old, and they must be able to understand English if *(they are, he or she is)* under age 55.

8. My neighbor, Juan Planas, who is trying to improve his English, always has a question for my brother and *(I, me).*

9. "It is *(I, me)*, Juan," he always says proudly—and correctly—as he answers the phone.

10. Juan says that *(his, their)* naturalization test included questions on American government that many native-born Americans would not be able to answer.

11. He bought *(hisself, himself)* a United States almanac to read, supplementing the basic study materials that every prospective citizen receives.

Identifying Personal Pronouns

Pronouns are words used in place of nouns. All pronouns have antecedents (the noun that the pronoun refers to or replaces). Turn to 503.2-503.3 for further details.

> **Underline** the personal pronoun in each sentence. If the pronoun's antecedent is in the same sentence, circle it.

1. (Anne Rice) is known for <u>her</u> popular novels about vampires.

2. The author has been praised for making her supernatural characters seem believable.

3. Stephen King is another author of mystical novels, and his books are often best-sellers.

4. King's stories deal with horrifying events that he makes happen amid an everyday setting—something bound to scare us.

5. Several of King's stories take place in Maine, a state where he continues to live.

6. King was a schoolteacher before he turned to writing full-time.

7. King is one of my favorite authors.

8. Perhaps you are familiar with Edgar Allan Poe or R. L. Stine.

9. Poe and Stine are also authors of supernatural tales; their horror stories are some of the oldest and newest of the genre.

10. Manny and I read many of Stine's books—we love to be frightened!

11. Another way Manny and I scare ourselves is to go on carnival rides.

12. I do not trust the safety of some of the rides.

13. A friend broke his finger while exiting a roller coaster.

14. Once Manny did not feel well after he rode one of the rides.

15. But the designers of such rides continue to make them as scary as possible!

Extend: Write five sentences about your favorite novel, class, or amusement park ride. Include at least one personal pronoun in each sentence.

X pck 1,2
wkbk 11

Number & Person of Personal Pronouns

Personal pronouns are either singular or plural in number. A pronoun can be one of three persons: *first* (the person is speaking), *second* (is spoken to), or *third* (is spoken about). Turn to 505.1-505.2 in *Writers INC*.

> Underline and label the personal pronouns in the following sentences. Label each pronoun twice: use an **S** (singular) or a **P** (plural); also use a **1** (first person), **2** (second person), or **3** (third person).

1.   *S/2*   *S/1*
   "Lauren, you need a bath!" Mom said to my little sister.

2. We chased her and put her in the tub.

3. The minutes passed slowly as he watched the clock.

4. With a sly smile, the teacher informed us, "You are free to go."

5. Upon hearing his statement, we streamed out of the classroom.

6. "Dynice, is this your backpack?" José asked.

> Insert a personal pronoun in the blanks below so that each sentence makes sense. Label your pronouns in the same way you did in the exercise above. (Label "you" **S/P** because it can be singular or plural.)

1.   *P/1*
      We   are going on a vacation this summer.

2. Will _____ be visiting any relatives?

3. After the movie, _____ am going to get something to eat.

4. _____ is taking a typing class.

5. _____ asked _____ if _____ wanted to join _____ .

6. Dad said _____ would help _____ make dinner.

7. _____ decided to make spaghetti, but _____ forgot to watch the pot and

   _____ boiled over.

Extend: Write three to five sentences about your friends. Try to use first-, second-, and third-person pronouns in both singular and plural forms.

Functions of Pronouns

Pronouns function the same way that nouns do (see the chart below). Turn to 506.1—and to the other sections listed in the first column below—for further information.

Writers INC	Function	Symbol	Examples
519.1	*subject*	**S**	Will *you* please feed the cat?
506.1	*predicate nominative*	**PN**	The winner is *he*.
506.1	*possessive pronoun*	**POS**	He lost *his* book bag.
508.1	*direct object*	**DO**	Magda is driving *me* to school.
508.1	*indirect object*	**IO**	Julian told *her* a secret.
515	*object of preposition*	**OP**	The bus stopped right in front of *us*.

Identify the function of the underlined pronouns in the sentences below, using the symbols from the chart above.

1. I believe you've got my book, and I want it back.   POS

2. Does this bracelet belong to you or to her?

3. Come with me.

4. "The thief was she," Ronald pointed out when he viewed the lineup.

5. "It is not mine," said Mr. Grenoble.

6. Grandpa gave them a piece of his mind.

7. She was surprised to learn that he wore a toupee.

8. In addition to me, my sister and her friend participated in the neighborhood cleanup.

9. I gave him a haircut, but he didn't like it.

10. The unmarked police vehicle had its lights flashing.

11. Tara thought Russell was choosing her for his team.

12. The victory was theirs until he fumbled the ball.

Extend: Write four to six sentences about your typical day. Include pronouns in each sentence; try to use at least three of the six functions listed in the chart above.

Nominative, Possessive, & Objective Cases of Pronouns

The case of each personal pronoun tells how it is related to the other words used with it. There are three cases: *nominative, possessive,* and *objective.* Turn to 506.1 in *Writers INC.*

> **Underline** the personal pronouns below. Then identify each pronoun on the line, using **N** for nominative, **POS** for possessive, or **O** for objective.

    N   **1.** I went to Malaysia last summer.

          2. My luggage was lost on the way.

          3. How could this happen to me?

          4. We landed in the capital, Kuala Lumpur, Malaysia's largest city.

          5. Cindy went with her tour group to Mount Kinabalu, the highest mountain in Malaysia.

          6. I went with another group to see an archeological site.

          7. We learned that Malaysia's government is modeled after the British government.

          8. Our group also learned that most Malaysians speak English well.

          9. Mike toured a rubber plantation and later wrote a paper about his experience.

          10. The tour guide told us a great deal about Malaysia's economy.

          11. "Malaysia is one of the world's largest producers of tin," she said.

          12. The people who went with her had fun.

          13. This trip taught me a lot about Malaysia.

          14. Our itinerary included many historic sites.

          15. The Malaysian people are proud of their country.

          16. Tourists often marvel at its exotic beauty.

Extend: Write five to eight sentences about a place you have visited. Before you get started, figure out which personal pronouns were not used in the exercise above (they, them, etc.). Put them in your sentences. (See the personal pronouns on the chart on page 504.)

Reflexive & Intensive Pronouns

Both reflexive and intensive pronouns are formed by adding *-self* or *-selves* to a personal pronoun. Turn to 503.3 in *Writers INC* for more information.

> **Reflexive Pronoun: Cassie hurt *herself* by lifting a 50-pound dumbbell.**

> **Intensive Pronoun: The mayor *herself* gave us a tour of city hall.**

Underline each reflexive pronoun and write *R* above it. Underline each intensive pronoun and label it *I*.

1. Fabio found himself longing for a Mohawk haircut.

2. Not even Batman himself could have saved us.

3. The material was difficult, but the test itself was easy.

4. The gerbil gave itself quite a shock from the static electricity.

5. Yes, I have learned that myself.

6. The students looked at themselves as they walked by the crazy mirror.

7. We ourselves cannot imagine a brighter future for polyester.

8. You should see yourselves! You're burnt to a crisp.

9. Can you yourself honestly say it never happened?

10. Paula has not been herself since the incident.

Write five short sentences, each using a different reflexive or intensive pronoun.

1. _____

2. _____

3. _____

4. _____

5. _____

Extend: Return to the sentences you just wrote. Write an *R* above each reflexive pronoun and an *I* above each intensive pronoun.

Relative Pronouns

A relative pronoun relates an adjective clause to the noun or pronoun it modifies. Turn to 503.4 and see the chart on page 504 in *Writers INC.*

 I loved to watch the dolphins *that were following our boat.* (*Dolphins* is the noun, and *that* is the relative pronoun. The adjective clause is in italics.)

> **Circle** each relative pronoun. Then underline the noun or pronoun that each relative pronoun relates to.

1. <u>Writing</u> (that) is good requires time and attention.

2. People who fish usually do not enjoy seeing water snakes.

3. I marvel at bird behaviors—their songs, their flight patterns, their nest building, their migration—which often seem beyond explanation.

4. Mr. and Mrs. Smith, whose egos prevent them from enjoying the simple successes of others, were our neighbors.

5. The wolfhound that won the prize was raised in Ireland.

6. The thieves who robbed the train were caught when the train stopped.

7. The cleanup committee picked up all the garbage, which was later taken to the recycling center.

8. Put that book, which is a priceless copy of a first edition, on the top shelf.

9. These are the socks that have holes in the toes.

10. He was seated next to that weird man, whom he thinks is clever.

11. This is a breed of dog that loves people unconditionally.

12. Where is the birthday present that you received from your friend?

13. Were you the one who tied the yellow ribbon to the tree?

14. Make me a promise that you can keep.

Extend: Notice where commas are used above. In a brief paragraph, explain the rule for using commas with restrictive and nonrestrictive clauses. (To review the definition of restrictive and nonrestrictive clauses, see 459.2 in *Writers INC.*)

Using Relative Pronouns to Create Subordinate Clauses

Who, whom, which, whose, and *that* are relative pronouns. Writers use them to modify or subordinate (to give one idea in a sentence less importance) a noun or pronoun. Turn to 503.4 in *Writers INC.*

Combine the pairs of sentences below into one sentence. Use a relative pronoun to modify a noun in the main clause or to subordinate the less important idea.

1. An experiment does not deserve federal funding. The experiment does nothing to serve the public interest.

An experiment that does nothing to serve the public interest does

not deserve federal funding.

2. At midnight, the Duvalls were ticketed for making noise over 20 decibels. The Duvalls were celebrating Mardi Gras.

_____

_____

_____

3. I knew the comb didn't belong to the policeman. The policeman's hat had blown off, revealing a completely bald head.

_____

_____

_____

4. A small group of guests made absolute fools of themselves. The guests had been practicing their comedy routines.

_____

_____

_____

5. The accident left her paralyzed. The accident happened a year ago today.

_____

_____

Indefinite, Interrogative, & Demonstrative Pronouns

Indefinite pronouns refer to unnamed or unknown people or things and usually have an unknown antecedent. Interrogative pronouns ask questions, and demonstrative pronouns point out people, places, or things without naming them. Turn to page 504 in *Writers INC*. Also turn to page 500 for information about "*who*" and "*whom*."

Write the missing interrogative pronoun in each blank below.

1. She shopped on Second Avenue. _____ store did she visit?

2. Aaron's bike is in the garage. _____ bike is behind the house?

3. Elena invited Ted, but _____ invited Elena?

Add the missing demonstrative pronouns.

1. The hat is hideous. Do you actually wear _____ in public?

2. Those apples look wormy. I'll eat _____ instead.

3. Holding up an astrolabe, she asked, "Do you know what _____ is?"

Underline each indefinite pronoun.

1. Everyone knows that Ben Franklin was a powerful statesman.

2. Few know that he also was an inventor, a printer, a public servant, and a writer.

3. Do you know anyone who wrote his or her own epitaph?

4. The Continental Congress named several of its members to draft the Declaration of Independence.

5. Franklin, Jefferson, and Adams proposed the motto on the Great Seal, "One out of many."

6. Somebody wanted Congress to declare Franklin's birthday a national holiday.

7. Nothing would make me happier! (Okay, so maybe something would. . . .)

Review: Pronouns

1   Sometime in the seventh century—nearly 1,400 years ago—monks, <u>who</u> ^R^

2   were translating books from Latin, wrote notes in the margins. They wanted to

3   be certain everyone would know the meaning of their translations. The margin

4   notes came to be called *glosses,* from which we get the word *glossary.*

5   Around 1600, an Englishman named Robert Cawdrey published *A Table*

6   *Alphabeticall of Hard English Wordes.* What is he remembered for? As one

7   might guess, he listed the words in alphabetical order. That might not sound

8   like a big deal now, but it was in 1600 when nobody else had done so.

9   In 1721, Nathan Bailey created his own version of the dictionary. This

10   included a history of words—a distinction that helped make Bailey's book a

11   bestseller. Publishers reprinted it 30 times.

1.   *they*   *P, 3, N*   **5.** _____ _____

2. _____ _____   **6.** _____ _____

3. _____ _____   **7.** _____ _____

4. _____ _____   **8.** _____ _____

Pretest: Verbs

Underline all the main, helping, and linking verbs in the following passage.

1   The United States Customs Department <u>needs</u> good dogs. The Customs
2   Department trains dogs to sniff out illegal narcotics at airports and other ports
3   of entry. Ninety percent of the department's dogs have come from animal
4   shelters. A trained narcotics dog is a good hunter. Aggressive dogs can frighten
5   travelers and are not chosen by customs officials for narcotics work. The
6   department's beagles at O'Hare International Airport in Chicago have become
7   an attraction. The dogs are known as the "Beagle Brigade." Travelers "ahhh"
8   and "ohhh" over the cute canines. One German woman did not want to leave
9   the customs area—even though she had spent nine hours on a flight—because
10 she wanted to see the "Beagle Brigade." I understood. I saw them once, and
11 now I always hope they will be on duty when I meet friends at the
12 international terminal.

Provide the following information from the paragraph above. Always list the words for your answers in the order in which they appear in the paragraph.

1. List five of the ten present tense verbs. _needs, trains, is, can frighten,_
are chosen, are known, "ahhh," "ohhh," hope, meet

2. List two of the four past tense verbs. _____

3. List the one future tense verb. _____

4. List five of the eight helping (auxiliary) verbs. _____

_____

5. The two helping verbs _____ and _____ are used to form

perfect verb tenses.

6. The one linking verb in line 4 connects the subject _____ with the

predicate nominative _____ .

7. What is the direct object in line 1? _____

8. What verbal is used in line 2? _____

Identifying Main Verbs & Auxiliary Verbs

Verbs are words that express action (*crumble, run, think*). Auxiliary verbs, or helping verbs, help form tenses (*had* crumbled, *will* run, *did* think) as well as the passive voice (*was* crumbled) and some moods (*were* to crumble). Turn to page 507 in *Writers INC* for information and a list of common auxiliary verbs.

Underline all the verbs below. When an auxiliary verb is used, underline it twice.

1. Germany <u>ranks</u> second in population among the European countries.

2. It is growing at a rate of less than 1 percent annually.

3. In 1949, Germany was split into two different countries.

4. A communist government controlled East Germany from 1949 until the Berlin Wall was toppled in 1989.

5. On October 3, 1990, East and West Germany were officially reunited into one nation.

6. Most people agree that Germany has become one of Europe's most powerful economic leaders.

7. Germans enjoy one of the highest standards of living in Europe.

8. Germany's economy is going through many changes.

9. Germans have a rich cultural heritage that includes many famous writers, artists, composers, conductors, and philosophers.

10. Many forms of German culture and fine art are subsidized by public funds.

11. German students pursue one of three different tracks of schooling, depending upon their interests and academic skills.

12. Science education ranks at the forefront in German schools.

13. German scientists won more Nobel Prizes than scientists from any other country between 1900 and 1933.

14. Germans have decided that science will contribute most to their economic future.

Linking Verbs, Predicate Nouns, & Predicate Adjectives

A linking verb "links" a subject to a predicate noun (she *is* a carpenter) or a predicate adjective (she *looks* strong). Rather than describing an action, linking verbs describe a condition or a state of being. Turn to 507.3 in *Writers INC* for examples.

Underline the linking verb in each sentence below. Label each predicate noun **PN** and each predicate adjective **PA**.

                                                PA

1. The chocolate <u>tasted</u> so good.

2. I am allergic to chocolate.

3. My old house is drafty and homely.

4. My old house remains my castle.

5. The mustangs in the parking lot are horses, not autos.

6. Miss Catchpaw feels ill.

7. My sisters were the contest judges.

8. I'm very sleepy.

9. You look marvelous!

10. Cigarette smoke smells awful.

Compose sentences with linking verbs, following the directions below.

1. Use the linking verb *are* to connect a subject with a predicate noun.

_____

2. Use the linking verb *seems* to connect a subject with a predicate adjective.

_____

3. Use a linking verb and a predicate adjective to say something about yourself.

_____

Extend: Make a list of specific nouns and a list of colorful adjectives. Exchange papers with a classmate. Create sentences that use linking verbs to join the nouns to the adjectives.

Using Strong Nouns & Verbs

By using specific words, you can create clear and colorful word pictures for your readers. Specific nouns and vivid verbs give readers a clearer, more detailed idea of what you are saying. Turn to page 130 in *Writers INC* for information.

 George sat down on the seat.

 George collapsed on the bench. (In the second sentence, the verb *sat* and its adverb *down* have been replaced with the vivid verb *collapsed.* The noun *seat* has been replaced with the more specific noun *bench.* *Note:* Whenever possible, use a verb that is strong enough to stand alone without the help of an adverb.)

Write verbs in the "vivid verb" column below that are stronger than the verbs listed. List "specific nouns" that are stronger than the nouns listed.

Vivid Verbs	**Specific Nouns**
1. dove *plunged*	**1.** rain *cloudburst*
2. walked	**2.** room
3. said	**3.** person
4. drink	**4.** game
5. look	**5.** setting
6. show	**6.** concept
7. sing	**7.** road
8. move	**8.** darkness
9. take	**9.** jewel
10. throw	**10.** poem
11. wait	**11.** dance
12. laugh	**12.** relative
13. cry	**13.** pasta

Extend: Write five or six sentences that describe something or someone you know well. Paint a vivid picture in a reader's mind, using vivid action verbs and specific nouns. Exchange papers with a classmate. After reading one another's paper, circle the verbs and nouns that most helped you (the reader) visualize what your partner described.

X Pckt 1,2
wkbk 11

Active & Passive Verbs

Writing in the active voice places your audience closer to the action. Turn to 510.3 in *Writers INC* to see just how effective the active voice can be.

> **Identify** the voice of each sentence by underlining the verbs and writing either **A** for active or **P** for passive in the blank provided.

    A   **1.** Wayne Gretzky <u>joined</u> his first hockey team at the age of six.

    _____   **2.** Record after record was shattered by this young boy.

    _____   **3.** All over Canada the news was spread.

    _____   **4.** Fifty goals had been scored by Wayne in a nine-game tournament!

    _____   **5.** By the time he turned 17 years old, Wayne Gretzky had realized his goal of playing professional hockey.

    _____   **6.** He always wore the number 9 in honor of his hero Gordie Howe, but he changed to number 99 as a professional player.

    _____   **7.** The Hart Trophy for the most valuable player was given to Wayne after his rookie season with the Edmonton Oilers.

    _____   **8.** That same year he was also awarded the Lady Byng Trophy for sportsmanlike conduct.

    _____   **9.** After winning their fourth championship, the Oilers shocked the hockey world by trading Gretzky to the Los Angeles Kings.

    _____   **10.** Wayne Gretzky finished his career with the New York Rangers, retiring in 1999 at age 38.

    _____   **11.** During his years in the National Hockey League, Gretzky held or shared 50 NHL records.

    _____   **12.** Hockey fans have been amazed by his outstanding play for 21 years.

Extend: Locate all the sentences above that have been written in the passive voice and rewrite them in the active voice.

Present, Past, & Future Tense Verbs

Tense indicates time. The three simple tenses of a verb are present (*I think*), past (*I thought*), and future (*I will think*). Turn to 511.1 in *Writers INC*.

> **Rewrite** each sentence below, changing the verb to the tense indicated. (You may change other words as necessary to create a smooth-reading sentence.)

1. Chickadees make nests in our woodland trees.

Past: *Chickadees made nests in our woodland trees.*

Future: *Chickadees will make nests in our woodland trees.*

2. The chickadees were noisy much of the day.

Present: _____

Future: _____

3. The chickadees will feed mainly on insects.

Present: _____

Past: _____

4. Last year a chickadee nested in an old bluebird house.

Present: _____

Future: _____

5. Chickadees will line their nests with fur, feathers, moss, or other soft materials.

Past: _____

_____

Present: _____

_____

6. The female lays five to eight white eggs with brown spots.

Past: _____

Future: _____

Perfect Tense Verbs

Like simple tenses, perfect tenses deal with time. Present perfect, past perfect, and future perfect tenses use helping verbs such as *has, have, had,* and *will have* to form tenses. The past participle of verbs is also needed to form these tenses. To learn about perfect tenses, turn to 511.1 in *Writers INC.* Turn to page 509 to find past participles for irregular verbs.

Write the past participle for each of the present tense verbs listed below. Then write the verb in the perfect tense indicated in parentheses.

Present Tense	Past Participle	Perfect Tense of the Verb
1. begin	*begun*	(present perfect): **has/have begun**
2. drown		(future perfect):
3. eat		(past perfect):
4. write		(future perfect):
5. sing		(past perfect):
6. rise		(present perfect):
7. bring		(past perfect):
8. speak		(future perfect):
9. sit		(present perfect):
10. hide		(past perfect):

Select six of the perfect tenses you created above and use each in a sentence. Be certain you use all three perfect tenses.

1. _____

2. _____

3. _____

4. _____

5. _____

6. _____

All Six Verb Tenses

A writer can express an exact time by selecting one of six verb tenses. To learn more about the "times" that tenses can express, turn to 511.1 in *Writers INC*.

Write **sentences on the lines below that express the time requested.**

1. Use the present tense of *learn* to express action that is happening at the present time.

    Broderick learns quickly; I learn slowly.

2. Use the past tense of *learn* to show action completed last week or last month.

3. Use the future tense of *learn* to show action that will take place tomorrow or another future time.

4. Use the present perfect tense of *learn* to show an action that began in the past and is continuing in the present.

5. Use the past perfect tense to show an action in the past that occurs before another past action. (Choose your own verb.)

6. Use the future perfect tense to show action that will begin in the future and be completed by a specific time in the future. (Choose your own verb.)

7. Choose two tenses—either the present, past, or future and a perfect tense—to use in a sentence. (Choose your own verb.)

Extend: Select a short passage from a newspaper or magazine. Underline all the verbs and label the tenses used. Was one tense used more than the others?

Review: Verbs 1

each verb in the sentences below. State the tense and whether the verb is a main verb, a main verb with an auxiliary verb, or a linking verb.

	Tense	Class of Verb
1. I <u>experienced</u> joy.	*past*	*main verb*
2. Jane has called.		
3. They rescued it.		
4. The sun had set.		
5. It will work.		
6. She begins.		
7. They play.		
8. She was sick.		
9. We have eaten.		
10. It had begun.		
11. Snow will have fallen.		

the following sentences, changing the passive voice to the active voice. Add subjects as needed. Do not change the verb tense.

1. Mistakes were made.   *Government officials made mistakes.*

2. Fun was had by many. _____

3. They had been abducted by aliens. _____

_____

4. The decision has been made. _____

5. This show will be aired by the network in the fall. _____

_____

Transitive & Intransitive Verbs

Transitive verbs are followed by a direct object—someone or something that receives the action of the verb. (He *found* gold. He *gave* it away.)

Intransitive verbs are not followed by a direct object. (He *laughed* loudly.) Linking verbs (such as *be, seem, appear*) are always intransitive.

Depending on their meaning, many verbs can be either transitive (I *drove* his new *car*) or intransitive (He *drove* all night). Turn to 507.2 and 508.1 in *Writers INC*.

> **Label** each underlined verb in the sentences below with *T* for transitive or *I* for intransitive.

1. The earliest special effects used in movies <u>were</u> *I* incredibly simple.

2. Editors <u>created</u> lightning by scratching lines directly onto the film.

3. Special-effects crews <u>simulated</u> thunder by rattling sheets of tin, a trick invented for stage plays.

4. In the 1925 movie *The Lost World,* the filmmakers <u>created</u> dinosaurs using "stop-motion animation," shooting one frame at a time and slightly moving the dinosaur models in each frame.

5. Special-effects makeup <u>turned</u> actor Lon Chaney into a mummy, a werewolf, and Frankenstein's monster.

6. As the years passed, Hollywood's bag of tricks to create special effects steadily <u>grew</u>.

7. Snow in June, ghosts in bedrooms, trains barreling off broken bridges—these kinds of special effects <u>have become</u> increasingly realistic, and increasingly complex.

8. With the addition of powerful computers, today's special-effects technicians <u>can do</u> just about anything.

9. One thing still holds true: Only a few years need to pass before "modern" special effects <u>look</u> unrealistic to increasingly sophisticated audiences.

Direct & Indirect Objects

Direct objects and indirect objects receive the action of verbs and are usually nouns or pronouns. A sentence must have a direct object before it can have an indirect object. Turn to 508.1 in *Writers INC*.

> Circle the verbs in the sentences below. Then, underline and label the direct objects (**DO**) and the indirect objects (**IO**).

1. The cells of every living organism (contain) genes. *DO*

2. The makeup of each gene determines the organism's traits.

3. Scientists can give an organism different traits with genetic engineering.

4. As a result, genetic engineers can offer medicine, agriculture, and industry new products and procedures.

5. For example, doctors can now give patients insulin that has been manufactured in bacterial "factories."

6. Clinical trials have given doctors good results when gene therapy is used in the treatment of certain disorders.

7. Researchers have offered the pharmaceutical industry genetically engineered microorganisms that break down toxic substances.

8. In the field of agriculture, technicians have genetically engineered small plants to produce a kind of biodegradable plastic.

9. Scottish scientists handed the world an ethics debate in 1996 when they cloned a sheep.

10. Despite its benefits, genetic engineering has caused many people concern.

11. The accidental production of some uncontrollable bacteria may do people harm.

12. Scientists can now manipulate the genetic material of living creatures.

13. Genetics will give us many opportunities for discussion in years to come.

Gerunds, Infinitives, & Participles

A verbal is a word that is derived from a verb, but functions as a noun, an adjective, or an adverb. Turn to 508.2-509.2 in *Writers INC.*

Type of Verbal	Used as		
	Noun	Adjective	Adverb
Gerund (ends in *-ing*)	X		
Infinitive (introduced by *to*)	X	X	X
Participle (often ends in *-ing* or *-ed*)		X	

Underline the gerunds in the following sentences.

1. Biking through the countryside is a wonderful way to spend a spring afternoon.

2. The summer chore that Aaron likes least is cutting the grass.

3. Sounding like a foghorn, Smitty cleared his throat prior to answering the phone.

Underline the infinitives in the following sentences.

1. A great dream of mine is to write a novel before I turn 30.

2. On his way to the library, he stopped to get a hot dog and a cherry cola.

3. A good reason to drive is to see the sights along the way.

Underline the participles in the following sentences.

1. In this era of suburban sprawl, deer roaming the woods sometimes find themselves grazing in the middle of a homeowner's backyard.

2. The dog's clipped hair was scattered all over the patio.

3. Cars weaving in and out of traffic are menacing on the highway!

4. The condensed version of the speech proved very readable.

Extend: Write three sentences about a topic of your choice. Use each of the three kinds of verbals at least once.

Irregular Verbs 1

The past tense and past participle of a regular verb are usually formed by adding a -d or an -ed. Irregular verbs do not follow this pattern. (I *run*. I *ran*. I have *run*.) Turn to 509.2 in *Writers INC*.

> **Complete** the sentences using the past tense or the past participle of the verb given in parentheses.

1. Yesterday I (*am*) _____was_____ an only child; today I have a brother.

2. Jenna and Stephan (*begin*) _____ their packing last night.

3. The committee of citizens (*choose*) _____ a new slogan for our town.

4. He had (*break*) _____ his ankle and needed a ride home.

5. Those bridge builders (*am*) _____ also divers.

6. They have (*dive*) _____ many times to examine a bridge.

7. A clear, deep river (*flow*) _____ past our vacation cabin.

8. Tuckwell Forest in the spring is the most beautiful sight I've ever (*see*) _____ .

9. When we awoke, the waters had (*rise*) _____ three feet!

10. How many people have (*flee*) _____ their homes this past year?

11. We had (*swim*) _____ for more than an hour by 8:00 a.m.

12. The little kid I baby-sit has (*sing*) _____ in a commercial.

13. Mother (*lay*) _____ her purse somewhere and can't find it.

14. The bells have (*ring*) _____ in the church belfry every Easter morning for as long as I can remember.

15. The team has (*wear*) _____ these uniforms for six seasons.

16. Wow, did you see how that little kid (*catch*) _____ that ball?

17. After the international flight, they (*lie*) _____ down for a nap.

18. Mark Pajak, who is 84 years old, has (*run*) _____ four miles every day since he was 18 years old.

Irregular Verbs 2

Practice using irregular verbs. Try to memorize the forms of the most common ones. Turn to 509.2 in *Writers INC*.

> **Circle** the correct verb form in each sentence.

1. He has *(wrote, (written))* and published several short mystery stories.

2. She has *(growed, grown)* Jerusalem artichokes.

3. The choir has *(sang, sung)* every song in their repertoire.

4. We *(hide, hid)* her present, but she found it anyway.

5. The horses *(lead, led)* us to water, and we drank.

6. I *(choose, choosed)* to exercise daily because that helps me stay fit.

7. She is afraid of dogs because she has been *(bit, bitten)* several times.

> **Tell** whether the verbs below are *present tense*, *past tense*, or *past participle*.
> (Some verbs can be more than one tense.)

1. dragged *past tense/ past participle*

2. spoken _____

3. rose _____

4. dived _____

5. catch _____

6. drunk _____

7. begin _____

8. swum _____

9. write _____

10. chosen _____

11. stolen _____

12. slew _____

13. shrank _____

14. lied _____

15. come _____

16. set _____

17. given _____

18. swam _____

19. shine _____

20. lead _____

Extend: Review the chart at 509.2 in *Writers INC* and make a list of the irregular verbs that trouble you. Refer to your list whenever you proofread your writing.

Using Troublesome Verbs

It is not unusual to have trouble using certain verbs correctly (for example, *lay/lie*, *accept/except*). This exercise will offer practice in this area. Turn to pages 491-500 in *Writers INC*.

> **Circle** the correct verbs in the following sentences.

1. Roné, why don't you *(lay, lie)* the blanket on the grass?

2. I think I will *(set, sit)* on this stump for a spell.

3. Not getting enough sleep *(affects, effects)* me negatively.

4. No late assignments will be *(accepted, excepted)*.

5. The dog often *(lays, lies)* on the sun-warmed bricks of the patio.

6. Chef Renaud prepared a dessert that *(complemented, complimented)* the dinner.

7. Swimming regularly will *(affect, effect)* a noticeable change in your muscle tone.

8. At first it felt strange to *(lay, lie)* in the hammock, but he *(laid, lay)* there all afternoon.

9. Michael Caine *(accepted, excepted)* his Oscar with a gracious speech.

10. Her glasses must have been damaged when she *(laid, lay)* them on the radiator.

11. You can *(set, sit)* the dishes on the counter for now.

12. The plastic bag of garbage had *(laid, lain)* in the street for days before someone finally picked it up.

13. Please *(lay, lie)* the baby in the crib.

14. Yesterday, I *(lay, laid)* down for a nap.

15. He *(lay, laid)* the newspaper down before he spoke.

16. *(Sit, Set)* here.

17. The committee *(complemented, complimented)* Maurice for his efforts.

Extend: Write a sentence for each of the following verbs: *infer, adapt, heal, counsel, desert,* and *lead*.

Review: Verbs 2

Write a short sentence using each verb below in the form requested.

1. fly *(transitive):* __Fly the kite carefully.__

2. fly *(intransitive):* _____

3. appears *(intransitive):* _____

4. watched *(transitive):* _____

5. hope *(intransitive):* _____

Identify each of the underlined verbals as a gerund **(G)**, a participle **(P)**, or an infinitive **(I)**.

1. "An advertising agency is 85 percent confusion and 15 percent commission."

—Fred Allen

2. "Vision is the art of seeing the invisible."   —Jonathan Swift

3. "It is dangerous to be right in matters on which the established authorities are wrong."   —Voltaire

Fill in the blanks with the correct verb tenses.

Present Tense	Past Tense	Past Participle
1. swing	swung	swung
2.	laid	
3. lie (recline)		
4.		swum
5.	went	
6. lead		

Pretest: Adjectives & Adverbs

> Decide **whether the blank in each sentence requires an adjective (ADJ) or an adverb (ADV). Then write an appropriate word in the sentence.**

<u>ADV</u>   **1.** At a poetry slam, poets recite or perform their works on stage, competing
_____*aggressively*_____ to earn the most points.

_____   **2.** These public forums encourage poets to write _____ and
share their feelings with an audience.

_____   **3.** Slam poetry is as much about performing _____ as it is
about the actual words on the page.

_____   **4.** National slam poetry contests began in 1990 in Chicago and have become
_____ popular events throughout the country.

_____   **5.** The audiences at these events are not necessarily _____ ,
refined groups; they cheer wildly on occasion.

_____   **6.** Five judges, _____ selected from the audience, hold up
numerical scores after each performance.

_____   **7.** The _____ and _____ scores are thrown
out, and the sum of the middle three is the person's score.

_____   **8.** Slam poetry is a national grassroots movement that has become very
_____ .

_____   **9.** William Shakespeare may be the _____ poet of all time,
but he is very difficult for some modern readers to understand.

_____   **10.** Shakespeare probably would not think _____ of today's
poetry slams; in fact, he probably would enjoy them.

Identifying Adjectives

An adjective describes a noun or a pronoun. Articles (*a, an, the*) are a special group of adjectives. Turn to page 513 in *Writers INC*.

Underline the adjectives, including articles in the following passage.

1   So you saw a scary film and never want to go into a thick forest again.

2   But, let's say that you *are*, unfortunately, stranded in a remote wilderness area.

3   Let's say you wandered off the marked trail and find yourself lost. Here's your

4   first piece of advice: Stop where you are!

5   Second, take stock of the situation. Let's say you have a sturdy backpack

6   with an extra set of warm clothes, some dry matches, a nondigital wristwatch,

7   and a pop-up tent. But you've lost your map and compass. What do you do?

8   If you are in bright sunlight, you can follow these simple instructions to

9   make a crude compass. Push a thin stick (or even an ordinary pencil) into the

10   ground. Hold your trusty nondigital watch flat, with the face toward the sky.

11   Position the watch so that the shadow from the stick falls exactly over the hour

12   hand. Here's what your crude compass will tell you: The halfway point

13   between the 12 on the watch and the hour hand points south.

14   Try to get your bearings and remember when—and where—you became lost.

15   If you are in safe and easy terrain, you could retrace your steps. Hike in the

16   direction that you came from and look for any tracks you may have left behind.

17   If you've been lost for 10 minutes, hike back 10 minutes to find the trail. If you

18   can't find the trail (or any trail), go back to your starting point and try again.

19   Look near rivers and streams for usable paths. As you wander, mark your path

20   with small piles of rocks or sticks. If you can't find a way out easily, stay and

21   wait for rescue. Even if it's daytime, a smoky fire makes a good signal.

Using Adjectives to Compare

Adjectives have three forms: *positive* (for describing one subject), *comparative* (for comparing two people or things), and *superlative* (for comparing three or more people or things). Turn to 513.2 in *Writers INC*.

> **Write in** the adjective of your choice using the form indicated in the sentences below.

1. Even though cats and dogs come from the same ancestor, their behavior is very

   ____*different*____ *(positive)*.

2. A cat uses its _____ *(positive)* tail to balance itself when it jumps.

   A dog wags its tail to show happiness.

3. A cat chases _____ *(positive)* mice, while a dog chases cats.

4. Therefore, one would assume that the dog is the _____

   (superlative) of the three.

5. A dog will usually come when called, while a cat will usually ignore you. This

   shows that a dog is _____ *(comparative)* than a cat.

6. Cats and cat owners are often seen as being _____ *(comparative)*

   than dogs and dog owners.

7. When fetching a ball, a stick, or a disk, a dog plays until it is _____

   (positive). A cat plays only when it is in a _____ *(positive)* mood.

8. Both dogs and cats have a _____ *(comparative)* sense of smell than

   humans have.

9. A dog has 200 million smell cells in its _____ *(positive)* nose. A

   human has only 5 million.

10. Pit bulls and Doberman pinschers are _____ *(comparative)* than

    Chihuahuas and some poodles, but the Irish wolfhound is the _____

    (superlative) breed known.

Using Adjectives Like the Pros

Don't make your reader wade through a string of adjectives to find a noun buried at the end. Instead, choose adjectives carefully, and vary their positions. Professional writers often place adjectives *after* a noun. Study the following sentence from *A Day No Pigs Would Die* by Robert Newton Peck: "I could smell Mama, **crisp** and **starched,** plumping my pillow." The words used as adjectives are boldfaced.

> **Rewrite** the following sentences. Place some or all of the adjectives after the noun to strengthen the focus of the adjectives. Work thoughtfully and ask, "Which adjectives do I want to move?"

1. Then I saw his stern, cold, stony face appear at the door.

Then I saw his stern face, cold and stony, appear at the door.

2. Her sad, bottomless, and utterly vacant eyes will haunt me always.

_____

_____

3. The clear, polished, rhythmical prose resembled poetry.

_____

_____

4. The green, lush, magical fields shimmered in the sunlight.

_____

_____

5. We wept when we saw the heroic, magnificent, futile charge end in disaster.

_____

_____

6. I stopped when I heard the piercing, inhuman, high-pitched scream.

_____

_____

Extend: Write five sentences using two or three adjectives before the noun. Then rewrite the sentences, placing some of the adjectives after the noun. Read several of your before-and-after sentences to a classmate. Talk about the placement of the adjectives.

Review: Adjectives

> **Fill** in the blanks in the sentences below with adjectives. Use vivid, creative adjectives as often as possible, and don't use the same adjective twice.

1. My ___eccentric___ Uncle Matt does some really _____ things.

2. When he was a kid, he liked to swim in the _____ quarry!

3. In college, he studied _____ books about _____ subjects.

4. His first job was with an _____ company that sold _____ equipment.

5. Last summer he jumped from a _____ airplane into the ocean—to study _____ sharks.

6. His apartment is filled with _____ photographs signed by all sorts of _____ people.

7. Uncle Matt is the only person I know who has met a _____ squid.

8. These days he makes money writing articles filled with his _____ stories.

9. My mom says her brother is _____ , but I think he's just _____ .

> **Supply** the missing adjectives on the lines below.

	Positive	Comparative	Superlative
1.	funny	funnier	funniest
2.	smooth		
3.		stranger	
4.			(least) most helpful
5.	incredible		

Identifying Adverbs

An adverb modifies a verb, an adjective, or another adverb. Adverbs tell *how, when, where, why, how often,* and *how much.* Study the information on page 514 in *Writers INC* about using adverbs.

Underline the adverbs in the following sentences.

1. <u>Yesterday</u> it rained heavily, right in the middle of our annual band picnic.

2. As the first drops fell, students and teachers looked nervously at the sky.

3. The light spattering suddenly exploded into an incredible downpour.

4. Teachers stood frozen as the rain pelted down.

5. Students reacted more quickly than the teachers did and ran back to the school building.

6. The teachers hesitated briefly and then joined what had become a mad rush to escape getting totally drenched.

7. The cooks reacted the most quickly of all and instinctively threw plastic garbage bags over the food.

8. Umbrellas were hastily opened for the people grilling hot dogs.

9. Picnic food is always good, but this year it tasted even better than any other year.

10. Inside, some students raced energetically to the cafeteria, while others milled noisily in the halls.

11. Throughout the afternoon, students sat stiffly in soggy clothes while equally damp teachers squished through the day's lessons.

12. Some students wisely suggested that next year's picnic be held in the newly constructed pavilion downtown in the city park.

Extend: Write a paragraph describing an event at your school or home that turned into a near disaster such as the picnic in the exercise above. Trade paragraphs with a classmate and identify the adverbs in one another's work.

Conjunctive Adverbs

Conjunctive adverbs, with the proper punctuation, can be used to combine sentences. Turn to 461.5 in *Writers INC* for information.

Use a conjunctive adverb from the list below to combine each pair of sentences. Don't use the same conjunctive adverb twice and don't forget to punctuate correctly.

accordingly	conversely	incidentally	moreover	similarly	then
also	finally	instead	nevertheless	specifically	therefore
besides	furthermore	likewise	nonetheless	still	thus
consequently	however	meanwhile	otherwise	subsequently	

1. There have been many popular rock groups. Most groups last only a short time.

There have been many popular rock groups; still, most groups

last only a short time.

2. Many groups would like to try new styles. They follow the wishes of their fans for the same "signature sound" on each new recording.

3. Record companies are hesitant to tamper with a winning format. Groups fall into the rut of imitating their earlier successes.

4. Trends in music constantly change. New groups emerge to displace the old ones.

5. The audience for most rock groups is largely young people. The Rolling Stones attract huge crowds of older fans.

Extend: Write a paragraph describing your feelings about a particular type of music or a musician. Include at least three sentences using conjunctive adverbs.

Using Adverbs to Compare

Like adjectives, adverbs have three forms: *positive* (for describing one subject), *comparative* (for comparing two people or things), and *superlative* (for comparing three or more people or things). Turn to 514.2 in *Writers INC*.

> **Read** the sentences below. Then rewrite each adverb as directed. Some sentences will need to be slightly modified.

1. *Positive:* My dad snores loudly.

2. *Comparative:* ___My dad snores louder than my mom snores.___

3. *Superlative:* My sister snores the loudest of anyone in our family.

4. *Positive:* _____

5. *Comparative:* _____

6. *Superlative:* The third horse to compete jumped best of all.

7. *Positive:* NASCAR racers drive fast.

8. *Comparative:* _____

9. *Superlative:* _____

10. *Positive:* _____

11. *Comparative:* Tina stepped more lightly than Ed over the broken glass.

12. *Superlative:* _____

13. *Positive:* _____

14. *Comparative:* His computer processes more slowly than ours does.

15. *Superlative:* _____

Extend: Write three sentences, each with a different positive, comparative, or superlative adverb. Then trade papers with a classmate and write new sentences like those in the exercise above.

Using Adverbs vs. Alternatives

Specific adverbs can add power and meaning to vague or weak verbs. Sometimes, however, a stronger verb is a better choice altogether. Turn to pages 130-131 in *Writers INC.*

> **Replace** the underlined verb + adverb combinations in the sentences below with single, more descriptive verbs. You may refer to a thesaurus for help.

1. The massive lineman intercepted the ball and <u>ran clumsily</u> into the end zone.

lumbered   *plodded*   *lurched*

2. The quarterback <u>quickly threw</u> the ball to the tailback.

3. Susan <u>ran quickly</u> to catch the bus.

4. The soldier <u>walked heavily</u> through the ankle-deep mud.

5. The winning fighter <u>ran happily</u> around the ring.

6. The loser <u>sat tiredly</u> in his corner.

7. Angela <u>wearily carried</u> her book bag off the bus.

8. The exhausted runner <u>ran haltingly</u> toward the finish line.

9. The audience applauded as the politician <u>moved confidently</u> to the podium.

10. The sun <u>shone brightly</u> through the window.

Extend: List five specific verbs that could be used in place of "said."

Review: Adverbs

> **Underline** the adverbs in the following sentences. Write *P* for positive, *C* for comparative, or *S* for superlative above each. Circle the conjunctive adverbs.

1. The Taj Mahal is an impressive monument located in Agra, India; (furthermore,)

it is one of the world's most magnificently designed and engineered buildings.

S above "most magnificently"

2. It was originally designed by a Turkish architect and gradually constructed

between 1632 and 1648.

3. The Taj Mahal was built as a monument to eternally commemorate the love

between Shah Jahan and his second wife, Mumtaz-i-Mahal.

4. Mumtaz was his constant companion; moreover, she served better than anyone

else as his counselor and conscience.

5. She quietly inspired the shah to become more generously inclined toward his

subjects, earning Mumtaz the unquestioned loyalty of the Indian people.

6. Most amazingly, Mumtaz gave birth to 14 children.

7. Her early death resulted from the particularly difficult and painful birth of her

last child.

8. Shah Jahan immediately ordered the finest tomb to be built, but it took nearly

17 years to complete.

9. The tomb chamber is lit naturally by sunlight passing through the

most intricately carved screens.

10. "Taj Mahal" most commonly translates to "Crown of the Palace"; however, it is

more generally believed to be the abbreviated name of Mumtaz-i-Mahal.

Pretest: Prepositions, Conjunctions, & Interjections

> Circle the interjections and draw two lines under all the conjunctions in the following sentences.

1. (Okay,) either I learn a few things about chemistry, <u>or</u> I will be in big trouble.

2. Lead, mercury, gold, silver, copper, and sulfur were all discovered by early humans, and hydrogen, helium, nitrogen, and oxygen were discovered later.

3. Imagine, oxygen wasn't discovered until 1774, yet it is one of the most common elements on the planet.

4. Most people probably think oxygen is the most common element in the earth's atmosphere, but, *au contraire,* nitrogen is.

5. When common elements are joined together, they form compounds like water and salt.

> Underline the prepositional phrases in the following sentences. Write **P** above the prepositions and write **O** above the objects of the prepositions.

1. Water is a compound of hydrogen and oxygen, and salt is a compound of sodium and chlorine.

2. Both diamonds and graphite are forms of carbon.

3. Only 91 of the 112 elements occur naturally on or in the ground.

4. Though metals can be mined from the earth, it makes sense from an ecological standpoint to recycle metals whenever possible.

5. Everything that we see and use is made of elements, so you can honestly say the answer to every question ever asked in science class is, "It's elemental."

6. You may, however, need a better variety of answers than that if you want to get a passing grade in the class.

X 12

Identifying Prepositions & Interjections

A *preposition* is a word (or group of words) that shows the relationship between its object and another word in the sentence. An *interjection* is a word or an expression that communicates strong emotion or surprise. Turn to pages 515 and 516 in *Writers INC.*

Identify **each word below as either a preposition or an interjection. Then write a sentence using the word.**

1. among _____*(preposition)* *We were among the first to arrive.*_____

2. before _____

_____

3. yipes _____

_____

4. through _____

_____

5. wow _____

_____

6. away from _____

_____

7. hooray _____

_____

8. my goodness _____

_____

9. in addition to _____

_____

10. oh, no _____

_____

Coordinating Conjunctions

Coordinating conjunctions connect a word to a word, a phrase to a phrase, or a clause to a clause when these are equal or of the same type. Turn to 516.1 in *Writers INC*.

> Underline the coordinating conjunctions in the following sentences. Then write your own sentences modeling those below and using the same coordinating conjunctions.

1. Picking up a pad <u>and</u> grabbing a pencil, Andrei was ready to take a message.

Pulling on her boots and taking her walking stick, Grandma went

to get her mail.

2. He would not wear galoshes nor use an umbrella.

3. Joaquin always used brown paper bags or the comics to wrap gifts.

4. Hesitant to join the club but wanting to fit in, Leon had a decision to make.

5. She had a feeling she wasn't doing it right, for she didn't have a clue as to the proper procedure.

6. Assertive yet sensitive—that's a good combination of leadership qualities.

7. Anita never learned how to drive, so she took the bus everywhere.

Correlative & Subordinating Conjunctions

Correlative conjunctions are conjunctions used in pairs such as *either, or* and *neither, nor.* Subordinating conjunctions such as *after, before,* or *because* connect and show the relationship between two clauses that are not equally important. Turn to 516.2-516.3 in *Writers INC.*

> **Complete** sentences 2-6 below with clauses that include the conjunctions given. (Be careful not to write prepositional phrases instead; some of these conjunctions can also be prepositions.) Complete sentences 7-8 with phrases that include the conjunctions given.

1. *(before)* Samantha raised her hand ___*before she heard the question*___ .

2. *(although)* My brother is usually on time, _____

_____ .

3. *(unless)* We will all go hiking next weekend _____

_____ .

4. *(as long as)* _____

_____ , you'll be a safe driver.

5. *(after)* _____

_____ , I bought myself a new alarm clock.

6. *(while)* _____

_____ , I finished painting the clock.

7. *(both, and)* _____

_____ are dirty.

8. *(not only, but also)* _____

_____ wickedly windy.

Extend: Write sentences that include the following subordinating conjunctions: *because, if,* and *since.*

Review: Prepositions, Conjunctions, & Interjections

> Underline and label each interjection (**I**) and each conjunction (**C**) below. Circle each prepositional phrase and label the preposition (**P**) and the object (**O**).

1. "Bah humbug!" said Scrooge as he peered over his large and cluttered desk.

2. Because Elaine has chicken pox, she can attend neither the concert nor the party.

3. As she rounded the corner, the policewoman saw the suspect—just before he jumped on the bus and rode away.

4. Holy smokes! The ball not only went over the fence but also out of the park!

5. The president assured his stockholders that the company would continue to grow, provided that the scandal concerning the lawsuits did not become public.

6. We can all go to the concert, but someone has to sit on the lawn.

7. "Either take your sister skating," Mom said, "or come to the laundromat with me."

8. Dad had a dog of his own when he was young, so I want to have one, too.

> List each conjunction from the sentences above in the appropriate column below.

Coordinating	Correlative	Subordinating
		as

Review: Language Activities

Identify each underlined word or phrase in the following paragraph in the blanks on the next page. Name the part of speech or verbal each word or phrase represents; also, tell how each functions in the sentence. (*For example:* "Dad" is a noun used as a subject.)

My dad and I argue about music all the time. Dad likes classic rock, folk music, jazz, and some classical music. I stick pretty much with current rock groups, although I can put up with some Beatles material, and I sometimes tolerate the Rolling Stones. My dad is also a big fan of Kris Kristofferson, the country-and-western singer. I can put up with some of my father's music, but I draw the line at Kristofferson. Hearing Kristofferson trying to sing is painful to me. He mumbles. When I complain, Dad always tells me I should listen because Kristofferson is a better songwriter than singer. Kristofferson's singing seems so bad that anything else must be better. Wow, that doesn't say much for his singing. Dad says Kristofferson was a Rhodes scholar. That seems unusual for a country-and-western singer. Maybe I'll listen a little more closely the next hundred times Dad plays Kristofferson's songs. In the meantime, I'll stick with Phish.

1. *"Dad" is a noun used as the subject of the sentence.*

2. *"Argue"*

3. *"Music"*

4. *"Current"*

5. *"Sometimes"*

6. *"Fan"*

7. *"But"*

8. *"Hearing"*

9. *"Is"*

10. *"He"*

11. *"Mumbles"*

12. *"Always"*

13. *"Better"*

14. *"Kristofferson's"*

15. *"Wow"*

16. *"His"*

17. *"That"*

18. *"Unusual"*

19. *"Maybe"*

20. *"I'll"*

SENTENCE ACTIVITIES

The activities in this section cover three important areas: (1) the basic parts, types, and kinds of sentences as well as agreement issues; (2) methods for writing smooth-reading sentences; and (3) common sentence errors. Most activities include practice in which you review, combine, or analyze different sentences. In addition, the Extend activities provide follow-up practice with certain skills.

Pretest: Subjects & Predicates

Draw a vertical line between the complete subject and the complete predicate in the following sentences. Then underline the simple or compound subject once and the simple or compound predicate twice.

1. Ten legal <u>holidays</u> | <u>are observed</u> in the United States.

2. Columbus Day, Martin Luther King, Jr.'s, birthday, and Veterans Day are three such holidays.

3. International businesses need to keep track of all the legal holidays in all the countries of the world.

4. It is quite a nightmare!

5. Paul Spraos, a London-born entrepreneur, recognized the problem all these holidays posed for businesses.

6. He decided to create a perpetual global calendar.

7. Muslim holidays, for example, are determined by the phase of the moon and vary from one Muslim country to the next.

8. Weekends are not easy to calculate either.

9. A weekend means every Sunday and every second and fourth Saturday in Taiwan.

10. Weekends include every Sunday and the first Saturday of each month in Malaysia.

11. Lithuanians occasionally observe a one-day weekend followed by a four-day weekend.

12. Failing to pay or to collect large interest payments on holidays around the world, businesses and banks lose or gain millions of dollars.

13. Many businesses rely on Mr. Spraos' perpetual global calendar.

Subjects & Predicates

A sentence has a subject (usually a noun or a pronoun) and a predicate (verb). The subject is the part of the sentence about which something is said. The predicate is the part of the sentence that shows action or says something about the subject. Turn to pages 518 and 519 in *Writers INC*.

> **Draw** one line under the complete subject and two lines under the complete predicate in the following sentences. Circle the simple subject and simple predicate. (There is one compound sentence—it will have two subjects and two predicates. Also, two sentences have compound verbs.)

1. With the flavor of ham and biscuit still in his mouth, the boy felt good.

   —William H. Armstrong, *Sounder*

2. He kept the other key, the one to the padlock on the bear's neck.

   —Hal Borland, *When the Legends Die*

3. In a kind of furious daze, forgetting the eggs, I got a big old gray peach basket off the porch and dragged it down the path.

   —Olive Ann Burns, *Cold Sassy Tree*

4. I looked out across the ravaged fields and saw Romey, a vaporous figure in the distance, moving around in Roy Luther's garden.

   —Vera and Bill Cleaver, *Where the Lilies Bloom*

5. The wheels struck the runway and the plane pulled up by a small wooden house on the tundra, the terminal building.

   —Jean Craighead George, *Julie of the Wolves*

6. He put the big blood heart . . . into her hands.

   —Willard Price, *The Killer Shark*

7. The ride ended too quickly, in front of a large, shabby building.

   —Robert Lipsyte, *The Contender*

Extend: Write down what you know about subjects and predicates. Write to a certain audience: a young child, someone learning English, your teacher, or a friend.

Review: Subjects & Predicates

Write sentences using the words listed as your subjects and predicates.

1. Compound subject: *Sonja and Brian;* Predicate: *swim*

Sonja and Brian swim in the creek, the one that flows through the

Bartleson's meadow.

2. Subject: *name of your school;* Predicate: *displays*

_____

_____

3. Subject: *turnips;* Predicate: *are*

_____

_____

4. Subject: *elephants;* Predicate: *parade*

_____

_____

5. Compound subject: *eggs and bacon;* Compound predicate: *sizzle and crackle*

_____

_____

6. Subject: *darkness;* Predicate: *scares*

_____

_____

7. Subject: *your choice;* Predicate: *your choice*

_____

_____

Pretest: Phrases

Identify the underlined phrases using **G** for gerund, **I** for infinitive, **P** for participial, and **A** for appositive. Circle the prepositional phrases. (*Remember*: a prepositional phrase is often part of another kind of phrase.) Study the first sentence to see how to mark such constructions.

1. Morse code was one (of the greatest inventions)(of the nineteenth century.)

2. Morse code made it possible to send messages across long distances.

3. For the first time in the history of the world, people could send messages quickly.

4. Morse code, a system of dots and dashes, stands for letters of the alphabet and for numerals.

5. On May 24, 1844, Samuel Morse, the inventor of the Morse code, sent the first telegraphic message, saying "What hath God wrought!"

Underline and identify the phrases in the following sentences. Use the same symbols as above and circle the prepositional phrases.

1. *G*
Learning Morse code requires many months (of study.)

2. Sending or receiving Morse code messages at an acceptable rate of speed takes years to learn well.

3. Having learned the Morse code, people feel great pride in their skill.

4. Morse code, a remarkable system of dots and dashes, is not taught to many people nowadays.

5. For better or for worse, the Morse code is being replaced by the Internet and fax machines.

Verbal Phrases

A verbal is a word that is derived from a verb but acts as another part of speech. There are three kinds of verbals: gerunds, infinitives, and participles. See the chart below.

	Used as		
Type of Verbal	**Noun**	**Adjective**	**Adverb**
Gerund (ends in *-ing*)	X		
Infinitive (introduced by *to*)	X	X	X
Participle (often ends in *-ing* or *-ed*)		X	

A verbal phrase contains a verbal and all of its complements and modifiers. The whole phrase then functions as a noun, an adjective, or an adverb. Turn to 508.2-509.2 and 520.1 in *Writers INC*.

Identify the underlined verbal phrases in the following sentences. Write **G** for gerund, *I* for infinitive, and **P** for participial. Also label each infinitive as either **N** for noun, **ADJ** for adjective, or **ADV** for adverb.

I, ADJ   **1.** Most sports cars have low, aerodynamic bodies <u>to cut through the air easily</u>.

_____   **2.** A sports car is an automobile <u>designed for performance</u>.

_____   **3.** <u>Weighing less than other cars</u> gives a sports car improved engine performance.

_____   **4.** Low weight also makes it easier <u>to slow down and turn corners</u>.

_____   **5.** <u>To turn corners faster</u>, the cars need a firm grip on the road.

_____   **6.** Sports cars have wide tires and firm springs, <u>enabling better handling</u>.

_____   **7.** <u>Producing limited quantities</u> drives up the cost of these vehicles.

_____   **8.** <u>To own an expensive sports car</u> is a status symbol for some people.

_____   **9.** I would love <u>driving a sports car</u>.

_____   **10.** <u>Zooming around the countryside</u>, I'd fly without leaving the ground!

Extend: Write three sentences about a hobby. Each sentence should use a different type of verbal phrase.

Prepositional & Appositive Phrases

A prepositional phrase consists of a preposition, its object, and any modifiers. Turn to 515.1 and 520.1 in *Writers INC*. An appositive phrase consists of a noun and its modifiers and follows the noun or pronoun it renames. Turn to 520.1 in *Writers INC*.

> Underline the prepositional and appositive phrases below. Circle each preposition and connect it to its object with an arrow.

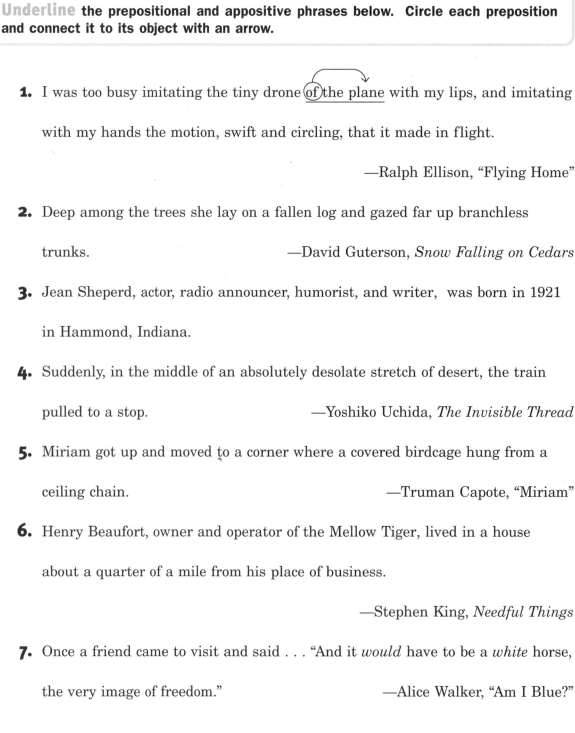

1. I was too busy imitating the tiny drone of the plane with my lips, and imitating

with my hands the motion, swift and circling, that it made in flight.

—Ralph Ellison, "Flying Home"

2. Deep among the trees she lay on a fallen log and gazed far up branchless

trunks. —David Guterson, *Snow Falling on Cedars*

3. Jean Sheperd, actor, radio announcer, humorist, and writer, was born in 1921

in Hammond, Indiana.

4. Suddenly, in the middle of an absolutely desolate stretch of desert, the train

pulled to a stop. —Yoshiko Uchida, *The Invisible Thread*

5. Miriam got up and moved to a corner where a covered birdcage hung from a

ceiling chain. —Truman Capote, "Miriam"

6. Henry Beaufort, owner and operator of the Mellow Tiger, lived in a house

about a quarter of a mile from his place of business.

—Stephen King, *Needful Things*

7. Once a friend came to visit and said . . . "And it *would* have to be a *white* horse,

the very image of freedom." —Alice Walker, "Am I Blue?"

Extend: Write three to five sentences using appositives to describe people you know. Try to include at least one prepositional phrase in each sentence.

Using Absolute Phrases

Many absolute phrases begin with a possessive pronoun: *my, his, her, its, our, their.* (Many absolute phrases also fit this pattern: If you insert *was* or *were* right after the subject in an absolute phrase, the phrase turns into a sentence.) Turn to page 521 in *Writers INC.*

> **Makem, *his eyes shining with delight,* climbed into a seat on the Ferris wheel.** (If you add *were* to the absolute phrase, it turns into a sentence: *His eyes were shining with delight.*)

Underline the absolute phrases in the following sentences.

1. Mrs. O'Tooles' cookies, <u>their insides chock-full of chocolate chips and nuts,</u> waited for us every afternoon after school.

2. Mrs. O'Tooles, her apron always full of flour and butter, baked them for us and beamed at us while we ate them.

3. Mother, who doesn't approve of sweets, convinced Mrs. O'Tooles to serve us apples and pears, their nutritious taste not equal to Mrs. O'Tooles' cookies.

Model the following sentences by professional writers to learn how to write your own absolutes. The absolute phrases have been underlined.

1. <u>Her choosing done,</u> <u>her house neat,</u> she went outside and sat on the step again.
—Hal Borland, *When the Legends Die*

Her decision made, her bags packed, Myrtle walked downstairs and waited at the curb.

2. Calvin, <u>his face screwed up with grim determination,</u> <u>his mouth scowling,</u> did not relax his hold. —Madeleine L'Engle, *A Wrinkle in Time*

3. Little Man flashed proudly past, <u>his face and hands clean</u> and <u>his black shoes shining again.</u> —Mildred D. Taylor, *Roll of Thunder, Hear My Cry*

Using Phrases Like the Pros

Using phrases well gives writing a professional quality. Turn to 520.1 in *Writers INC*.

Imitate **the following sentences written by well-known authors.   Underline your phrases.**

---

1. *(one gerund and one prepositional phrase)* My whole body would assume regular movements; my shoveling would be described by identical, even movements.
—Richard Rodriguez, "Los Pobres"

<u>My long fingers would shove the piano keys; my playing would be</u>

<u>defined by low, mournful chords.</u>

2. *(one participial, five prepositional, and two appositive phrases)* I squinted, pressing my face close to the window, and saw Baptiste, my friend from the old days at the shop, a friend from the times of long ago.
—Robert Cormier, *Take Me Where the Good Times Are*

_____

_____

_____

_____

3. *(three infinitive phrases)* Brother Coyote can't help himself; he likes man— maybe not to talk to or [to] play with, but definitely to live next door to.
—Michelle Huneven, "Living Well Is the Best Revenge— Just Ask the Urban Coyote"

_____

_____

_____

4. *(two absolute phrases)* She was not the small freckle-faced Jenny that I had known . . . but a lovely sweet sixteen . . . her nails polished and her dark hair scented.
—Christy Brown, *My Left Foot*

_____

_____

_____

_____

Review: Phrases

> Label each of the phrases enclosed in parentheses below: use **G** for gerund, **I** for infinitive, **P** for participial, **A** for appositive, and **AB** for absolute. Then underline all prepositional phrases. *Remember:* Some phrases contain another phrase (usually a prepositional phrase).

1. Cars (owned <u>by people</u> <u>in large cities</u>) [P], (like New York City, Chicago, and Paris) [A], are apt (to cause the owner stress) [I].

2. A person can drive for hours without (finding a place) (to park).

3. Drivers, (frustrated beyond reason), are always on edge.

4. (Their horns blaring loudly), dozens of yellow cabs (driven by professional drivers) muscle their way down the street.

5. It takes a genius (to decipher the parking signs).

6. Traffic police, (armed with blank citation books), patrol the streets.

7. (Getting a traffic ticket) means a hefty fine or possibly a court date.

8. Many drivers, (tired of complicated parking restrictions, daily gridlock, and other drivers' bad tempers), decide (to travel by bus or subway).

9. Many big-city car owners choose (to pay two or three hundred dollars a month for a parking space in their building's lot).

10. For many drivers, the negatives of (driving a car) far outweigh any advantages a car might provide.

11. When you don't own a car, neighborhood grocery stores—(aisles packed with people and products), (customers waiting forever in lines)—are the only places (to buy groceries).

12. (Owning a car in a big city), whether you use it or not, can be expensive and stressful.

Pretest: Clauses

Identify each underlined clause as **I** for independent or **D** for dependent. If the clause is dependent, write *adjective, adverb,* or *noun* in the blank.

adjective **1.** To some observers, 1998 <u>was the most exciting year</u> ^I <u>that baseball had in a long time.</u> ^D

_____ **2.** <u>Two baseball players, Mark McGwire and Sammy Sosa, made the year memorable.</u>

_____ **3.** Mark McGwire of the St. Louis Cardinals set a new home run record by whacking 70 balls out of the park, <u>while Sammy Sosa of the Chicago Cubs was not far behind with 66 homers.</u>

_____ **4.** We also know <u>that Sosa drove in 158 runs, a feat second only to Hank Wilson's 190 runs in 1930.</u>

_____ **5.** The two sluggers were crowd favorites all around the <u>country,</u> <u>which is a tribute to both their talent and their sportsmanship.</u>

_____ **6.** The New York Yankees set an American League baseball record <u>when they won 114 games.</u>

_____ **7.** The Yankees, <u>who beat the San Diego Padres in four straight games,</u> won the World Series.

_____ **8.** <u>Their play-off total of 125 wins set another record.</u>

_____ **9.** Cal Ripken, Jr., <u>who holds the record for the most consecutive games played at 2,632,</u> finally sat out his first game since 1982.

_____ **10.** To other observers, 1998 was a sad year <u>because Harry Caray, the Cub's legendary broadcaster, died on February 18.</u>

Independent & Dependent Clauses

An independent clause presents a complete thought and can stand alone as a sentence. A dependent clause does not present a complete thought and cannot stand alone as a sentence. The three types of dependent clauses are the adverb clause, the adjective clause, and the noun clause. Turn to 521.1-521.2 in *Writers INC*.

> **Finish** the following sentences by completing the dependent clause using the given conjunction or relative pronoun. Then identify the dependent clause by writing *adverb*, *adjective*, or *noun* in brackets.

1. Sylvia will travel to Spain next summer, unless *she is unable to save enough money. [adverb]*

2. Although _____ , he already excelled at the violin.

3. My Uncle Howard, who _____ , will retire next month.

4. I wish I could remember where _____

5. Since _____ , I decided to wear a blue dress to the dance.

6. Saturday's game, which _____ , will be held rain or shine.

7. Mother said that _____

8. The new mayor, whose _____ , wants to build three new schools.

9. As long as _____ , we will have a great time in Florida.

10. The rain that _____ ruined our picnic.

Extend: Write three complex sentences about an acquaintance. Your sentences should include one of each of the three types of dependent clauses.

Creating Adverb Clauses

An adverb clause is a type of dependent clause that modifies a verb, an adjective, or an adverb. Adverb clauses often explain *when? where? why?* or *how?* (See the categories listed below.) Adverb clauses always begin with a subordinating conjunction. Turn to 521.2 and 516.3 in *Writers INC*.

Category	Subordinating Conjunctions
To show time	before, after, when, until, since, while
To show reasons	because, since
To show purpose	that, so that, in order that
To show conditions	if, unless, although, as long as, though

Write four sentences using adverb clauses; underline the adverb clause. Use a subordinating conjunction from the chart above that matches the category listed in parentheses below.

1. (reasons) *I went straight home after school because I had said I'd*

fix supper for our family.

2. (purpose) _____

_____

_____

3. (conditions) _____

_____

_____

4. (time) _____

_____

_____

5. (reasons) _____

_____

Extend: Choose a piece of your writing. As you read it, draw one line under sentences that could be main ideas and draw two lines under sentences that could be subordinated. Finally, rewrite the selected sentences, combining them appropriately.

Creating Adjective Clauses

An adjective clause is a type of dependent clause that modifies a noun or a pronoun. Most adjective clauses begin with a relative pronoun: *who, whom, whose, which, that*. Turn to 503.4 and 521.2 in *Writers INC*. Also see the "who, which, that" entry on page 500.

> **Write** six sentences containing adjective clauses. Use a relative pronoun to create each clause.

1. Create an adjective clause that describes a person.

Tamara, who is a great singer, got the lead role in the musical.

2. Create an adjective clause that refers to a thing.

_____

_____

3. Create an adjective clause that refers to an abstract idea.

_____

_____

4. Use the relative pronoun *whose* to show possession.

_____

_____

5. Create an adjective clause that refers to a place.

_____

_____

6. Create an adjective clause that modifies a pronoun.

_____

_____

7. Use the relative pronoun *that* to indicate a specific thing.

_____

_____

Review: Clauses

> Use the word groups listed below as subjects for the sentences you will complete. Include an independent clause and the type of dependent clause indicated for each sentence. Underline your dependent clauses.

1. *(adjective clause)* The friendly police officer, _who directs traffic at Krall_ _and Oakburn, pretends he is dancing._

2. *(adjective clause)* A tired young man _____

_____

_____

3. *(adverb clause)* The soccer team _____

_____

_____

4. *(adjective clause)* Her favorite movie _____

_____

_____

5. *(adjective clause)* My hopes and dreams _____

_____

_____

6. *(noun clause)* Next Friday's exam _____

_____

_____

7. *(noun clause)* The flight attendants _____

_____

_____

Pretest: Sentences

Label each sentence below. Use **S** for simple, **CD** for compound, **CX** for complex, or **CD-CX** for compound-complex.

_CX_   **1.** Ever since the Pilgrims survived their first harsh winter in the new world, Americans have set aside a day to remember the Pilgrims and to give thanks.

_____   **2.** Do you remember dressing up as Pilgrims or as Native Americans for Thanksgiving plays in elementary school?

_____   **3.** Thanksgiving was celebrated unofficially for many years, but it took three great presidents and one editor of a women's journal to make it an official holiday.

_____   **4.** On October 3, 1789, George Washington issued the first official Thanksgiving proclamation.

_____   **5.** After Washington left office, the idea of a national day of thanksgiving was forgotten for a time; but Sarah Josepha Hale, who was editor of *Godey's Lady's Book* and the daughter of a Revolutionary War hero, revived the idea during the Civil War.

_____   **6.** Her letter to President Lincoln on September 28, 1863, arrived three months after the battle of Gettysburg, which is considered a turning point in the war, and apparently Lincoln took time to study Hale's request.

_____   **7.** That fall Lincoln proclaimed a day of "thanksgiving and praise" to a country torn apart by war.

_____   **8.** Lincoln's successors celebrated the holiday on the last Thursday of November until 1939, when President Franklin D. Roosevelt moved Thanksgiving back a week.

_____   **9.** Americans were upset; in fact, many were outraged!

_____   **10.** Roosevelt backed off, but shortly after the United States got into World War II, he signed an Act of Congress that permanently placed Thanksgiving on the fourth Thursday of November, where it has been ever since.

Kinds of Sentences

Sentences can make five basic kinds of statements: *declarative, interrogative, imperative, exclamatory*, and *conditional*. Turn to 522.1 in *Writers INC*.

> **Write** the kinds of sentences asked for using the subject and verb given. Feel free to change the form or tense of the verbs given to whatever will work best for your sentence.

1. Exclamatory: *I, love*

   I love chocolate milk shakes!

2. Imperative: *you, wash*

3. Conditional: *doctor, leave*

4. Interrogative: *dogs, run*

5. Declarative: *volcanoes, erupt*

6. Interrogative: *you, go*

7. Exclamatory: *I, swim*

8. Imperative: *you, remember*

9. Declarative: *Andy, fix*

Extend: Find an example of each kind of sentence in a textbook. If you cannot find a particular example, create one. As you search for your examples, check to see if you could add variety and impact to the writing by using different kinds of sentences.

Identifying Simple & Compound Sentences

There are four types of sentences. This exercise concentrates on simple and compound sentences. Turn to 522.2 in *Writers INC*.

> **The magician performed many tricks and illusions.**
> (Simple sentences have only one independent clause and no dependent clauses. Even so, they may contain one or more phrases, a single or a compound subject, and a single or a compound predicate.)

> **He sawed his assistant in half, and then he escaped from a straitjacket.**
> (Compound sentences are made up of two independent clauses joined by punctuation, a coordinating conjunction, or both.

Label the following sentences either *simple* or *compound.*

simple **1.** The Rolling Stones is a remarkable rock band.

_____ **2.** They began performing in the 1960s, and they are still touring today.

_____ **3.** They were one of the many bands contributing to the "British Invasion."

_____ **4.** At first they performed wearing scruffy clothes; in fact, they appeared on *The Ed Sullivan Show* wearing sweatshirts.

_____ **5.** Later, lead singer Mick Jagger would wear fancy sequined jumpsuits.

_____ **6.** Over the years, many of the members have done solo projects, but they always return to perform as a band.

_____ **7.** The members have matured, and, according to some, they may have lost their "edge."

_____ **8.** Regardless, they continue to produce enormously popular music.

_____ **9.** Songs like "Satisfaction," "Ruby Tuesday," and "Jumpin' Jack Flash" are classics.

_____ **10.** The Rolling Stones claim the title "World's Greatest Rock 'n' Roll Band," and no one disputes it.

Extend: Select four of the simple sentences above and combine them to create two compound sentences.

Identifying Complex & Compound-Complex Sentences

There are four types of sentences. This exercise concentrates on complex and compound-complex sentences. Turn to 522.2 in *Writers INC*.

> **I loved to go hiking in the woods when I was younger.**
> (Complex sentences contain one independent clause and one or more dependent clauses.)

> **The woods was always a magical place, and I marveled at the number of creatures that lived in a single acre.**
> (Compound-complex sentences contain two or more independent clauses and one or more dependent clauses.)

Label each of the following sentences. Use *CX* for complex or *CD-CX* for compound-complex.

_CD-CX_ **1.** During the last five years, my friends and I have studied and visited a number of nature preserves, so we think of ourselves as experts who have something to share.

_____ **2.** Here are some of the interesting things that we've learned over the years.

_____ **3.** Fairy rings are formed by an ever-expanding circle of mushrooms that legends say are used by fairies to dance on.

_____ **4.** Because mangroves have complex root systems, the trees only thrive in very watery conditions, such as wetlands and slow-moving rivers.

_____ **5.** Dandelions are typically hated in the United States, but they are highly desired in some parts of Europe, if you can imagine that.

_____ **6.** Venus's-flytraps capture insects in specially adapted leaves that snap shut on their prey.

_____ **7.** Cacti are tough and covered with sharp spines; they have soft, watery interiors and root systems that allow them to absorb water very efficiently.

_____ **8.** Redwoods, the tallest trees in the world, can live to be hundreds of years old; they grow well in California near the Pacific Ocean, which helps provide the moisture they need.

_____ **9.** Of course, we also learned that a few years of education about nature did not make us experts; nevertheless, we still enjoy sharing what we've learned!

Extend: Add an independent clause to two of the complex sentences above to make them compound-complex.

Pckl 1, 2
wkbk 12

Modeling a Sentence 1

Writers learn how to arrange sentences so they can achieve sentence variety and add details. One way to achieve variety is to put the main clause in different positions—at the beginning, in the middle, or at the end. Turn to 523.1 in *Writers INC*.

> Create a different arrangement for each of the sentences below, changing words as necessary.

1. Miguel pulled into the crowded parking lot and turned up the car stereo.

Pulling into the crowded parking lot, Miguel turned up the car

stereo.

2. Stepping down from the truck, I lost my balance, turning my foot under me as I crumpled to the ground.

_____

_____

3. Dancing on her hind legs and whimpering her hello, my dog welcomes me home.

_____

_____

4. Joey spent her leisure time listening to rock music on the radio in the apartment's tiny dining room that also served as her bedroom.

_____

_____

_____

5. Unable to fly due to an ear infection, Vlad rented a car and drove to his sister's wedding in Georgia.

_____

_____

_____

Extend: Select two of the sentences above and rearrange them in yet a different way.

Modeling a Sentence 2

Writers often experiment with a variety of sentence arrangements. Then they select the arrangement they think is best for the piece they are writing. Turn to 523.1 in *Writers INC*.

> **Study** the sentence below. Rewrite the sentence five times following the directions for each new arrangement.

> **"A stillness hovered in the high air, soft, quiet, peaceful."**
> —Mildred D. Taylor, *Roll of Thunder, Hear My Cry*

1. Place two of the adjectives (*soft*, *quiet*, *peaceful*) before *stillness*.

The soft, quiet stillness hovered in the high, peaceful air.

2. Add two adverbs to describe *hovered* and eliminate all the adjectives.

3. Insert an adjective clause, *that hovered in the air,* in the original sentence and add the verb *was*.

4. Insert a participial phrase, *hovering in the high air,* after *stillness* and add the verb *was*.

5. Now use the participial phrase, *hovering in the high air,* as an introductory word group.

6. Which of your four sentences do you prefer? Why? _____

Modeling a Sentence 3

Emphasis can be achieved by putting the most important idea at or near the end of a sentence. Turn to 523.1 in *Writers INC*.

> Study the following sentences written by well-known authors. Carefully note the emphasis and rhythm each author creates. Write your own sentence modeled on each example below, imitating it part by part.

1. In 1985, American unions' slow decline in membership began to turn around—mostly due to the influx of 70,000 new female members.
—Barbara Ehrenreich, "The Next Wave"

By 2005, the number of e-businesses will have exploded—owing to the entrepreneurial spirit of American workers.

2. Since advocates for the homeless claim that homelessness is entirely or primarily caused by a housing shortage, they typically deemphasize the role that disabilities like mental illness, alcoholism, and drug abuse play in the plight of the homeless.
—Thomas J. Main, "What We Know About the Homeless"

3. "Acid rain," the term for precipitation that contains a high concentration of harmful chemicals, is gradually damaging our environment.

4. I discovered—with the help of some especially sensitive teachers—that through writing one can continually bring new selves into being, each with new responsibilities and difficulties, but also with new possibilities.
—Barbara Mellix, "From Outside, In"

Review: Sentences

each sentence below. Use *S* for simple, *CD* for compound, *CX* for complex, and *CD-CX* for compound-complex.

_____*S*_____ **1.** The curfew started in London during the reign of King Alfred.

_____ **2.** Wooden houses lined the streets of London, and fire was an ever-present danger.

_____ **3.** An open fire burned in the center of every house or in its largest room.

_____ **4.** When the church bells rang in the evening, it was a signal to "cover the fire."

_____ **5.** "Cover the fire," which was slurred together in London speech, became "curfew," and the name stuck.

_____ **6.** Curfew bells were discontinued when better building practices and better fire-fighting equipment were developed.

_____ **7.** Today, curfews are used to help prevent "people" problems, not "fire" problems.

_____ **8.** When a destructive storm hits, curfews keep people who might injure themselves off the streets.

_____ **9.** Originally, "curfew" meant "cover fire"; today, it means "cool it" to potential troublemakers.

Write sentences as indicated.

1. Rewrite sentence number 1 so that it is an interrogative sentence.

_____

2. Rewrite sentence number 4 so that it is an imperative sentence.

_____

3. Rewrite sentence number 8 so that it is a conditional sentence.

_____

_____

Pretest: Subject-Verb Agreement

Underline the subject for each set of verbs in the sentences below; then circle the verb that agrees in number with the subject.

1. One <u>day</u> (*is,* *are*) plenty of time to finish this assignment.

2. The crew of the yacht *America* (*is, are*) considered the best in the world.

3. The cause of his problem (*was, were*) his bad knees.

4. The media (*was, were*) at both the Republican and Democratic conventions.

5. The counseling staff at the high school (*was, were*) honored for providing students with many new services.

6. The rescue squad, along with several police cars, (*was, were*) at the scene of the accident almost immediately.

7. One of the seven lanes (*do, does*) not have a starting block for the runner.

8. There (*was, were*) many students who favored keeping study halls.

9. (*Is, Are*) either of the girls going on the hayride tonight?

10. Here (*is, are*) the pair of gloves you left at my house yesterday.

11. (*Wasn't, Weren't*) Jen or Gabbie supposed to help clean up this mess?

12. Around the corner (*is, are*) several fresh footprints in the cement.

13. (*Has, Have*) the thunder and lightning stopped yet?

14. There in the distance (*was, were*) the remains of the ghost town.

15. In the gymnasium (*was, were*) the acrobats and their coaches.

16. Looking at the paintings in the gallery (*was, were*) 10 women.

17. Neither Janice nor Liam (*was, were*) going to the tournament.

Subject-Verb Agreement 1

Some nouns that are plural in form but singular in meaning take a singular verb. Turn to 526.4 in *Writers INC*.

> Circle the subjects (nouns) that look plural but are singular in meaning. Then underline the singular verb that accompanies each one.

1   The (news) is good for people interested in math or science. Both are now

2   hot subjects. But mathematics (my particular favorite) has been around

3   forever. Math concepts first began when primitive peoples counted by 5's and

4   10's on their hands. Later, Greek mathematicians, including Archimedes,

5   Euclid, and Pythagoras, made many advances in math. Their ideas crossed

6   into astronomy, physics, and other sciences.

7   Mathematics is the science of numbers. But mathematicians study more

8   than simple problems. Operations, relationships, and abstractions of numbers

9   are all factors in the big equation. Mathematics includes applied mathematics

10 and theoretical mathematics. Theoretical mathematicians study theories or do

11 research. Applied mathematicians apply math to practical uses. Economics is

12 a big field for applied mathematicians. Many mathematicians crunch numbers,

13 or analyze statistics, on Wall Street.

14 Physics owes its start to our Greek friend Archimedes, who invented many

15 mechanical devices such as levers and screws. Mechanics, one branch of

16 physics, covers only how objects move. Overall, physics deals with matter and

17 energy, and this science includes many branches—thermodynamics, nuclear

18 physics, geophysics, astrophysics, plasma physics, and cryogenics, among others.

19 Thermodynamics describes how heat and energy relate. Cryogenics is a cool

20 science that studies how objects react at temperatures below -238° F.

Subject-Verb Agreement 2

Compound subjects usually take a plural verb, and singular subjects take a singular verb. Turn to 526.2-526.3 in *Writers INC*.

Circle **the correct singular or plural verb in the following sentences.**

1. Past presidents, astronauts, and a United States air force general or two *(has, have)* believed in unidentified flying objects (UFO's).

2. Gerald Ford and Jimmy Carter *(was, were)* trying to get the government to tell people more about UFO's.

3. But neither Ford nor Carter *(was, were)* president when he spoke about making government UFO facts available.

4. Ronald Reagan and Jimmy Carter *(claim, claims)* to have seen UFO's.

5. From 1952 to 1969, UFO reports and alien sightings *(was, were)* collected by the U.S. Air Force in Project Blue Book.

6. Now, government reports, including the Project Blue Book file, *(is, are)* available for study through the Freedom of Information Act.

7. In 1947 near Roswell, New Mexico, either a top-secret balloon or a UFO *(was, were)* recovered.

8. Supposedly, pieces of the "flying disk" and four or five alien bodies *(was, were)* taken to Wright-Patterson Air Force Base in Ohio.

9. Neither the UFO pieces nor a single alien body *(has, have)* been seen since.

10. Alien bodies and a spaceship *(is, are)* reported to still be at Area 51, a part of the highly secured air force base near Groom Lake, Nevada.

Extend: Write three to five sentences sharing your thoughts about UFO's and aliens. Use compound subjects (include at least one subject joined by "or" or "nor"). Check to be sure your subjects agree with their verbs.

Subject-Verb Agreement 3

Do not be confused by a word or words that come between a subject and a verb. Turn to the introduction on page 526 in *Writers INC*.

> Underline the subject for each set of verbs in the sentences below and circle the verb that agrees with the subject. (Do not underline the conjunctions that join compound subjects.)

1. National <u>forests</u>, because of their size, *(offer,* offers*)* protection to many endangered species.

2. Rare and endangered species, from a tiny fern to a soaring eagle, *(find, finds)* a home in the Chequamegon-Nicolet National Forest in northern Wisconsin.

3. The goblin fern, a tiny plant that stands only one to two inches tall, *(live, lives)* in fewer than 50 places in the world.

4. The states in the western Great Lakes region *(has, have)* some of the best living conditions for the goblin fern.

5. Rare animals, including the timber wolf, *(live, lives)* in the Chequamegon forest.

6. The first timber wolf pack in Wisconsin since the 1960s, numbering about 15 wolves, *(was, were)* introduced in the 1980s.

7. The adventurous wolves of that first pack prospered and now *(number, numbers)* more than 200.

8. Wolf packs like to live in areas with few roads, and one such area deep within the forest hardwoods *(is, are)* near Bootjack Lake in the national forest.

9. The rivers and lakes of Chequamegon-Nicolet also *(offer, offers)* refuge to the bald eagle.

10. Some 689 nesting pairs of eagles, one of the largest concentrations in the United States, *(live, lives)* in Wisconsin.

Extend: Rewrite sentences 6 and 7 so that the singular subject is plural and the plural subject is singular.

Review: Subject-Verb Agreement

the subject for each set of verbs in parentheses; then circle the correct verb (singular or plural). (Do not underline the conjunctions that join compound subjects.)

1   <u>Malorie</u> and <u>Emma</u> (*are,* *is*) best friends. Each (*have, has*) known the other

2   since they attended nursery school together. Now that both of them (*are, is*)

3   older, they know that any friendship like theirs (*are, is*) dependent upon trust

4   and reliability. As trust and reliability grow, the friendship (*become, becomes*)

5   stronger. All of their friends (*wonder, wonders*) how two people who are so

6   different could remain friends for so long. Malorie says each of them

7   (*complements, complement*) the other. Emma thinks they share important basic

8   beliefs; they may look and act completely different, but their values (*is, are*) the

9   same. She also believes their friendship is not that unusual. Several of their

10   friends also (*share, shares*) long-term friendships. "Everyone," says Emma, "(*is,*

11   *are*) capable of having a long-term friendship; you just have to be yourself."

12   Neither Malorie nor Emma (*take, takes*) their friendship for granted. Friends

13   are good, and good friends (*is, are*) even better.

the subject in each sentence below; then circle the verb that agrees with the delayed subject.

1. In the library (*were,* *was*) 10 biology <u>students</u> preparing for an exam.

2. (*Is, Are*) either of the boys attending the basketball game tonight?

3. In our class (*is, are*) three students who will be studying in Spain.

4. (*Has, Have*) your mother or father given you permission to take driver's

    education this summer?

X - 11

Pretest: Pronoun-Antecedent Agreement

Underline the correct pronoun (or pronoun and verb) in each pair below. Then circle the antecedent that the pronoun refers to.

1. The two boys are sloppy; (neither) cleans *(his, their)* room.

2. The Martin twins are outdoorsmen; both spend most of *(his, their)* time in the woods.

3. Good gas mileage and reliability—*(that's, these are)* the hallmarks of a good car.

4. I'll take one of those blue shirts if *(they are, it is)* available.

5. Snakes' forked tongues have a dual purpose: *(they are, it is)* used to smell as well as to catch food.

6. Either Cindy or Nancy knows *(her, their)* way around the dance floor.

7. One of the walls looks shabby; *(it needs, they need)* repair.

8. Neither Susan nor Sheryl complains when *(she is, they are)* hungry.

9. Both planes had *(their, its)* interiors redecorated.

10. Each of the planes had *(their, its)* interior redecorated.

11. Mary and her sister took *(their, her)* brother to the concert.

12. When you find one of the sweaters I loaned you, please return *(them, it)* to me.

13. A person needs *(their, his or her)* privacy.

14. When Cory and Catherine got married, we all attended *(her, their)* wedding.

15. Each salesperson presented *(their, his or her)* new products.

16. Bring me one of those apples; make sure *(it is, they are)* fresh.

17. Neither of his cars *(were, was)* in very good condition.

Pronoun-Antecedent Agreement 1

Each pronoun has an antecedent that the pronoun refers to or replaces. Turn to page 528 in *Writers INC* for more information and examples.

Underline the correct answer in each of the following sentences. Write the antecedent above the pronoun you underline.

1. For the job hunter to get the best possible job, *(he or she needs, they need)* to
   (job) hunter
   have three or four job offers from which to choose.

2. Everyone owes it to *(himself or herself, themselves)* to become acquainted with
   all phases of the job-hunting process.

3. Both Ashley and her friend Shelli use newspaper ads to find new job leads,
   which *(she pursues, they pursue)* with a phone call and a letter.

4. The Internet now has many help-wanted sites, so *(they serve, it serves)* job
   hunters, too.

5. Job hunters make *(his or her, their)* availability known by placing information
   about themselves and *(his or her, their)* skills in newspapers or on Internet sites.

6. Most colleges have good placement services because *(they understand,*
   it understands) that finding a good job is the major reason *(their, its)* students
   come to college.

7. Some colleges offer *(its, their)* students a complete job-placement service,
   extending for years after students have graduated.

8. Other college offices, however, think *(its, their)* responsibility is completed when
   they place a student once after *(he or she has, they have)* graduated.

9. A private employment agency charges *(its, their)* customers only when *(he or*
   she gets, they get) jobs.

10. Although many people are unaware of this fact, the U.S. government offers all
    (its, their) citizens a free employment service.

Pronoun-Antecedent Agreement 2

Each personal pronoun has an antecedent that the pronoun clearly refers to or replaces. Turn to page 528 in *Writers INC* for more information and examples.

> Underline the correct personal pronouns below and write the antecedent above each.

1. Ants are incredibly diverse insects; *(it,* <ins>*they*</ins>*)* *ants* consist of 20,000 different species

   and are located throughout the world.

2. Most ant species make *(its, their)* nests underground.

3. Most species have a queen; *(she, it)* lives the longest, from about 10 to 20 years.

4. Worker ants from different communities often fight one another when *(each, they)*

   meet.

5. A fierce battle can ensue, and *(it, they)* may take many lives.

6. Army ants are such fierce fighters that other insects have come to fear *(it, them)*.

7. Some army ants live in clusters above ground; *(it, their)* queen and *(its, her)*

   brood lie amid the large cluster of bodies.

8. A harvester ant feeds on the seeds *(they collect, it collects)*.

9. Some ants collect larvae from other ant colonies; *(it brings, they bring)* *(it, them)*

   home and use them as slaves when they are full grown.

10. One species of the Amazon ant becomes so reliant on its slave ants that *(they, it)*

    can care for neither itself nor *(their, its)* young.

Extend: Write three or four sentences about ants (or some other insect). Underline each personal pronoun and write its antecedent above it.

Making Pronoun References Clear

A writer must be careful not to confuse the reader with references that are unclear or ambiguous. (*Ambiguous* means having more than one meaning.) Ambiguous pronoun reference results when it is not clear which word is being referred to by the pronoun in the sentence. Turn to 503.2 and pages 85 and 528 in *Writers INC*.

> **As he drove his car up to the service window, it made a rattling sound.** (It isn't clear what "made a rattling sound," the car or the window.)

> **As he drove up to the service window, his car made a rattling sound.** (Now the reader knows the car made the rattling sound.)

Rewrite each of the sentences below so that it is clear which word the pronoun refers to. (You will have to replace the ambiguous pronoun with the appropriate noun in several sentences.)

1. The team moved the wrestling mat off the gym floor so that it could be cleaned.

The team moved the wrestling mat off the gym floor so that the

floor could be cleaned. (or) so that the mat could be cleaned.

2. Tara entered her program into the computer, and it went completely haywire.

3. Alina asked her mother if she could carry one of the boxes for her.

4. All calendars list the holidays if they are worthwhile.

5. Check all your papers for silly writing errors so that your teacher can enjoy reading them.

Review: Pronoun-Antecedent Agreement

> Underline the correct pronoun (and verb if appropriate) in each pair below. Then circle the antecedent that the pronoun refers to.

1. When (Gary and Kurt) returned to *(his, their)* table, some of the pizza was missing.

2. Either of the boys could have found *(his, their)* bat and ball if *(he, they)* had really tried.

3. Anybody can attend the seminar as long as *(they have, she or he has)* permission.

4. Some people use scarecrows to protect *(its, their)* gardens.

5. Sinbad read the magazine from beginning to end before lending *(him, it)* to Syd.

6. Everyone should find *(his or her, their)* assigned seat.

7. Because a weeping willow can be so messy, *(they are, it is)* often shunned by homeowners.

8. Charlene was using *(her, our)* old toothbrush to clean the heating vents.

9. Some automobile dealers offer *(its, their)* customers free car-care workshops.

10. Bobbi decided she didn't want one of the items after all, so she returned *(it, them)* to the mall.

11. He said the sewing machines will be good as new as soon as *(he is, they are)* repaired.

12. Neither Robert nor his brothers ever managed to take care of *(his, their)* dog.

Pretest: Sentence Combining

Combine each of the following groups of sentences. Use the sentence-combining technique indicated in parentheses.

1. Fire is hot. Fire is wild. Fire is violent. *(Use a series.)*

Fire is hot, wild, and violent.

2. You can often put out a home fire with the right kind of fire extinguisher. This works if the fire is small when it is detected. *(Use an introductory phrase or clause.)*

3. We keep several fire extinguishers around the house to put out small fires. We keep them to provide peace of mind. *(Use correlative conjunctions.)*

4. Electrical fires and those involving flammable liquids should be put out with the spray from a carbon-dioxide extinguisher. These fires cannot be extinguished with water. *(Use a relative pronoun.)*

5. A carbon-dioxide extinguisher releases a blanket of carbon dioxide. This type of fire extinguisher keeps air from reaching the fire. *(Use a participial phrase.)*

6. Fire can be a terrifying enemy. Fire is normally one of our greatest allies. *(Use an appositive.)*

Sentence Combining 1

Sentence combining, which can be done in a variety of ways, is one of the most effective writing techniques you can practice. Turn to page 91 in *Writers INC*.

> **Combine** the following sentences using the methods indicated.

1. *(Use a semicolon and a conjunctive adverb.)* The most popular pets are dogs, cats, parakeets, and fish. Unusual pets like snakes, alligators, and monkeys are becoming more popular.

_____

_____

_____

_____

2. *(Use the correlative conjunctions "not only," "but also.")* Pets can improve a person's morale. They can also lower a person's blood pressure.

_____

_____

3. *(Repeat a key word.)* Pets are great therapy for seniors. They are especially valuable for seniors who are in care centers.

_____

_____

4. *(Use a series.)* Pets guard property. They assist blind people. They keep rodents away.

_____

_____

5. *(Use a relative pronoun.)* Children in Japan tame mice for pets. They often teach them to dance.

_____

_____

Extend: Write four brief sentences about pets. Use two different methods to combine them into two sentences.

Sentence Combining 2

Using a variety of sentence-combining methods can create sentences that work together to build a clear, interesting paragraph that reads smoothly. Turn to page 91 in *Writers INC*.

Read the following paragraphs. Combine sentences to create a paragraph that reads smoothly. (Not all sentences need combining; slight rewording is acceptable.)

1.   It was before the 1800s. Fires could destroy whole settlements. A fire would break out. All the people in the community would hurry to the scene. They arranged themselves in a line. The line started at a source of water. The line ended at the fire. The people passed buckets of water to each other to put the fire out.

_____

_____

_____

_____

_____

_____

_____

2.   Now fire departments respond to fires and other emergencies. The fire departments consist of well-trained professional firefighters and well-designed equipment. People may be trapped in cars after an accident. Firefighters rescue them. Firefighters also aid victims of tornadoes and hurricanes. They help victims of floods and earthquakes, too.

_____

_____

_____

_____

_____

_____

_____

Review: Sentence Combining

Using the list of short sentences below, follow the instructions for sentence combining.

Fire departments work hard to prevent fires.
They enforce safety laws.
Professional firefighters teach people about fire dangers.
They hope this work will help prevent fire losses.
Every year, fires kill hundreds of people.
Fires injure thousands of people, too.
Fires also destroy millions of dollars' worth of property.

1. Use a series to combine three or more similar ideas.

Every year, fires kill hundreds of people, injure thousands more,

and destroy millions of dollars' worth of property.

2. Use a relative pronoun to introduce a subordinate idea.

3. Use an introductory phrase or clause for a less important idea.

4. Use a semicolon. (Also use a conjunctive adverb if appropriate.)

5. Use correlative conjunctions to compare or contrast two ideas.

6. Use an appositive phrase to emphasize an idea.

Pretest: Sentence Problems

Identify the problems in the following sentences. Use *F* for fragment, *CS* for comma splice, *RO* for run-on sentence, *RS* for rambling sentence, *W* for wordiness, and *MM* for misplaced modifier.

_____F_____ **1.** When the calendar changed at the end of the year 999.

_____ **2.** Most people didn't know what year it was, and in Europe there were only a few educated people who knew the date, and they were concerned that going from three digits to four might destroy the symmetry of the universe, and they also worried about having enough space on documents to write four digits instead of three.

_____ **3.** Arabic numbers were being used for the first time the concept of "0" was baffling to many they wondered how a zero could stand for nothing.

_____ **4.** Things were not too civilized in Europe during that time and that period in Europe was called the Dark Ages because it was an uncivilized, lawless, barbaric time when laws were broken regularly and people cared little for others.

_____ **5.** Common people survived and never bathed with only the clothes on their backs.

_____ **6.** Sanitation was nonexistent, as was clean water, the average peasant spent most of each day trying to get enough to eat.

_____ **7.** Families slept together in one room along with the family's livestock and strangers who came in for shelter using lice-infested straw pallets for beds.

_____ **8.** *Beowulf,* an epic poem, written in Old English about 1,000 years ago.

_____ **9.** The Chinese people from Asia invented some kind of gunpowder about 1,000 years ago, which they used for fireworks and colorful blasts in the night sky instead of using it to power guns and other weapons.

_____ **10.** Huge fireworks displays marked the dawn of the year 2000 there probably was no such fanfare when the previous millennium began in 1000.

Correct each of the problem sentences above by rewriting it in a better way on the lines below.

1. *When the calendar changed at the end of the year 999, most people didn't know what year it was.*

2. _____

_____

_____

_____

_____

_____

3. _____

_____

_____

4. _____

_____

5. _____

_____

6. _____

_____

7. _____

_____

_____

8. _____

_____

9. _____

_____

10. _____

_____

_____

Revising Run-On Sentences

Run-on sentences are actually two or more sentences joined without proper punctuation—
or a connecting word. Turn to page 84 and 516.1 in *Writers INC*.

> **Correct** each run-on sentence. Insert a semicolon, add a comma with a coordinating
> conjunction, or create two sentences.

1. The Bermuda Triangle is a part of the Atlantic Ocean, it lies off the southern
   tip of Florida between Bermuda and Puerto Rico.

2. Many strange things have happened on and over this stretch of water many
   disappearances have been documented over the years.

3. Descriptions of glowing clouds, equipment failures, and extremely choppy seas
   are common elements of many Bermuda Triangle incidents many pilots also
   report losing sight of land even when flying along the coast.

4. In 1944, the Cuban ship *Rubicon* was found drifting in the Triangle without a
   trace of its crew only a dog remained on board.

5. On December 5, 1945, five Navy planes carrying 14 crew members disappeared
   they broadcast a confused message and were never heard from again.

6. Even Christopher Columbus figures into the puzzle his ship's log includes
   observations of fire in the sky and glowing white water while sailing through
   the Triangle.

7. Apollo astronauts in space reported unusual wave activity in the Bermuda
   Triangle they had no explanation for it.

8. The Triangle is still active scientists and enthusiasts continue to study the
   phenomenon.

9. How do planes disappear without wreckage how do crews vanish without a trace?

10. Perhaps one day we'll know the answer until then, it remains a mystery.

Fixing Comma Splices

A *comma splice* results when two independent clauses are connected ("spliced") with only a comma when a comma is not enough. A period, a semicolon, a comma with a coordinating conjunction (*and, but, or* . . .), or a semicolon and a conjunctive adverb (*however, moreover, besides* . . .) must be used to fix a comma splice. The more closely related the sentences are to one another, the more appropriate it is to use a semicolon. Turn to page 84 in *Writers INC*.

Identify and correct any comma splices by adding conjunctions or appropriate punctuation where necessary in the following paragraphs.

1   Jackie Robinson grew up in Pasadena, California. He was the first

2   African American to play major league baseball. His mother and four

3   older siblings worked hard to make a living, Jackie pitched in to help,

4   selling newspapers on the street corner. Jackie joined a neighborhood gang

5   called the Pepper Street Gang, taking and reselling golf balls from golf

6   courses and throwing fruit at cars got them in trouble with the police.

7   Eventually a teacher inspired him to leave the gang, telling him a strong

8   individual didn't belong in a gang.

9   Jackie lettered in football, baseball, basketball, and track in high

10   school, he impressed a lot of scouts while playing football in junior college,

11   landing him a football scholarship at UCLA. Jackie became UCLA's first

12   athlete to letter in four sports, many people were shocked and

13   disappointed when he left college early to take a job at a government

14   youth camp in order to help his mother financially.

15   Worried about being called tough on the football field but cowardly on

16   the battlefield, he refused to use an injured ankle as a military exemption

17   and was drafted. Jackie failed to qualify for Officers Candidate School, he

18   and heavyweight champ Joe Louis called for an investigation, the inquiry

19   uncovered illegal practices, and Jackie spent several years as an officer.

X 12

Identifying & Fixing Sentence Fragments

A fragment is a group of words incorrectly used as a sentence. Because it lacks a subject, a verb, or another key element, the thought is incomplete. Turn to page 83 in *Writers INC*.

Underline the fragments in the following paragraph. On the lines below, rewrite the paragraph, making the fragments into complete sentences. Add a subject or a verb or connect the fragment to a related sentence in the paragraph.

Hundreds of people have reported seeing a large animal in Loch Ness. A lake in northern Scotland. The Loch Ness monster, nicknamed "Nessie." Observers say the creature has a long, slender neck. Like a dinosaur. It also has one or two humps and flippers. Scientific expeditions have used sonar to explore the lake. Have detected large moving objects. Not sure whether the objects are one large creature or a school of fish. Underwater photographs have been taken, although many experts question their validity. Despite the doubts about Nessie's very existence. Tourists still flock to Loch Ness in the hopes of catching a glimpse.

Using Sentence Fragments

Is it ever acceptable to use fragments? Yes, when you have good reason. Single words or phrases set off as sentences can have a dramatic effect. You can also use fragments when you write dialogue, because people often use incomplete thoughts when they talk. Turn to page 83 in *Writers INC*.

> **Read** the following passages in which the writer deliberately uses fragments (shown in italics). Tell why you think the author uses each fragment.

1. "Everyone in that family, including my three cousins, could draw a horse. *Beautifully.*"
—Annie Dillard

_____

_____

_____

2. Mrs. Stokes: Weezie, come get your lunch, girl.
Weezie: *No time. Lots of homework.*

_____

_____

_____

3. *A place to rest in the middle of the lagoon. Drips from the oars.* An egret flaps its wings where it stands.

_____

_____

_____

4. *"Hurry! In the bedroom!"* Murray pleaded as he ushered the ambulance attendants in.

_____

_____

_____

Extend: Write a short passage in which you deliberately use a few fragments for special effect. With a classmate, discuss how well they work.

Revising Rambling Sentences

Rambling sentences keep going and going, which results in a muddled, monotonous message. To correct rambling sentences, remove some of the *and*'s, fix the punctuation, and reword parts when necessary. Turn to page 84 in *Writers INC*.

> **Rewrite** and clarify the rambling sentences below.

1. I returned my overdue books to the library and I paid my fine and I looked around for a while and then checked out three new books.

I returned my overdue books to the library and paid my fine.

After looking around for a while, I checked out three new books.

2. Most of the teachers and administrators attended the ceremony and so did other school personnel including the aides and custodians and even the cooks.

3. Eligia was stopped in traffic and just sat there for an hour and he listened to CD's and hoped his boss would understand the problem he was facing.

4. Karl didn't hear his alarm and woke up late and rushed like crazy but still missed his first class.

5. It was raining hard and the wind was strong and my umbrella ripped and I got totally soaked.

6. Night fell quickly and we could see the campfires dotting the hillside and hear the drums pounding in the distance and we rose to dance.

X Pdt 1,2 wkbk 12

Review: Sentence Problems 1

Edit the following paragraphs. Correct sentence fragments, comma splices, run-ons, and rambling sentences. Add or delete punctuation, capitalization, and words.

1   As a small child, he had always eaten jelly doughnuts for breakfast. Now,

2   however, at a plump and rather easily winded 29, He has switched over to

3   granola and skim milk. Along with his new eating habits, his looks are also

4   beginning to change he wears his hair a bit longer in back and thinner on top

5   and his shoes are those flip-flop kind. That are good for your posture. He

6   thinks about this. As he sits gazing out at the backyard, which the neighbor

7   kid with the nose ring mows every Saturday for a "sawbuck." He wonders if

8   the kid knows that "sawbuck" is a slang term for a ten-dollar bill.

9   Maybe his younger brother Kevin is right in his appraisal and maybe he is

10   old-fashioned and way, way out of step. He and Kevin had gone out with their

11   parents the night before, Kevin had walked into the restaurant and had

12   scanned his brother's clothes and posture, in addition, he had even seemed to

13   scan his brother's thoughts, with slow-mounting amusement, Kevin had said,

14   "You look so . . . granola." Trying to disguise his obvious embarrassment, the

15   older brother grabbed his keys and headed for his truck in the parking lot. He

16   would be glad when Kevin aged more and understood more but Kevin was the

17   kind of guy who exercised, he had been the kind of kid who played every sport

18   in high school, and he probably still played a lot of sports and, of course, Kevin

19   never did eat jelly doughnuts.

Misplaced Modifiers

You know what happens when you drag your feet along the bottom of a lake. Things become murky and obscure. That's what happens in your reader's brain when you accidentally misplace modifiers. To ensure clarity, you must be able to recognize misplaced modifiers so they can be moved or reworded accordingly. Turn to page 86 in *Writers INC*.

> **Locate** and underline the misplaced modifier in each of the following sentences. Then revise each sentence by moving the misplaced modifier to its proper location. (Make other changes to the sentence as needed.)

1. The books for the new students <u>with course-identification numbers</u> are piled in stacks.

   The books for the new students are piled in stacks with course-identification numbers.

2. Athletes must train hard to make the Olympic team for many years.

3. Quentin planted roses in his backyard garden named for Queen Elizabeth.

4. We will be visiting several four-year colleges that I am considering attending over the summer.

5. My father has gone to the library every Sunday to check out a book for years.

Extend: Experiment with misplaced modifiers in three sentences you write about school. Exchange papers with a classmate and correct one another's misplaced modifiers.

Dangling Modifiers

Dangling modifiers appear to modify the wrong word. Turn to page 86 in *Writers INC* for more information.

> Locate and underline the dangling modifier in each of the following sentences. Revise each sentence so that the modifier clearly modifies the word it was intended to. Add or change words as necessary.

1. After swimming in the lake nearly all afternoon, Bill's mother called him.

After swimming in the lake nearly all afternoon, Bill heard his mother call him.

2. While listening to my newest CD, someone came to the door.

_____

_____

3. Having never flown before, the flight attendant was especially nice to me.

_____

_____

4. Though only ten years old, my mother taught me to quilt.

_____

_____

5. After running three laps around the track, the coach signaled us to head for the showers.

_____

_____

6. Failing to see the stop sign, the car rammed into the side of an oncoming truck.

_____

_____

X 12

Wordiness & Deadwood

Wordiness and deadwood fill up lots of space but do not add anything new or important to the overall meaning of a sentence. Turn to pages 87-88 in *Writers INC.*

> Place **brackets around the unnecessary words in the paragraphs below.**

1   My mother, a native New Yorker, [who has lived in New York her

2   whole life,] recently went to Africa on an African safari. Many people

3   thought this was an odd trip for an elderly woman. I don't know when

4   or how the idea was first introduced to her, but as soon as she heard

5   about the safari trip, she began reading everything she could get her

6   hands on about Africa. The safari, which was organized last year, was

7   composed of 15 senior citizens, none of whom had ever heard of a zebu (a

8   breed of ox), and most of whom thought the Watusi (an African tribe) was

9   just a 1960s dance.

10   My mother and her fellow senior citizen explorers were very impressed

11   with the wealth of natural beauty and living animal life on the African

12   plains and in the jungles. They were also impressed with Africa's animal

13   parks and game reserves that protect and help animals to survive from

14   human hunters who are a real threat to their existence. Herd animals

15   such as zebras, wildebeest, and antelope are also protected from hunters

16   within the borders of game reserves.

17   My mother got back from her African journey and returned with

18   wonderful memories of a unique culture and wilderness that she will

19   remember for a long time.

Extend: Select something you have recently written. Exchange it for a classmate's paper and place brackets around any obvious wordiness or deadwood in your partner's work.

Unparallel Construction 1

Parallelism is the repeating of similar words, phrases, or clauses to add balance and emphasis to your writing. Inconsistent or unparallel construction occurs when the words, phrases, or clauses being used change in the middle of a sentence. Turn to pages 90, 129, and 432 in *Writers INC.*

> **We wanted to sing, to dance, and to tell stories around the campfire.**
> (repetition of infinitives)

> **Janice looked under the table, in the pantry, and behind the sofa.**
> (repetition of prepositional phrases)

> **Winning the contest, receiving the trophy, and making a thank-you speech were exciting events for Megan.** (repetition of gerund phrases)

Underline the parallel structures in the following sentences. **Explain what word groups are repeated in each sentence.**

1. Some students wanted <u>to decorate for the banquet</u>, <u>to serve appetizers</u>, and <u>to hire a comedian.</u>

   Infinitive phrases are repeated. (or) Phrases beginning with "to" are repeated.

2. Washing the dishes, feeding the cat, and taking out the garbage are my chores.

   _____

3. Vile-tasting turnips and repulsive-looking parsnips grow too well in our garden.

   _____

4. I have a grandma who listens well, who is wise, and who bakes cookies.

   _____

5. Having a bicycle to ride on campus is more useful than having a car to drive.

   _____

6. Our mother had explained, pleaded, and shouted.

   _____

7. The woods are filled with towering oaks, singing birds, and winding trails.

   _____

Unparallel Construction 2

Inconsistent or unparallel construction occurs when the kinds of words, phrases, or clauses being used change in the middle of a sentence. Turn to pages 90, 129, and 432 in *Writers INC*.

Complete the following sentences so that all the parts are parallel.

1. The police officer at the corner of 42nd Avenue and 6th Street directs traffic, chats with pedestrians, and *helps seniors cross the street.* _____

2. Waiting for the bus, standing in the rain, and _____ are not my favorite activities.

3. We strolled through Central Park to Strawberry Fields, stopped at a sidewalk cafe for coffee, and _____

_____

4. Reading the book was enjoyable; _____ the paper about it was difficult.

5. We must measure the room, order the rug, and _____

_____

6. Listen to me when I tell you to look forward to the future, when I tell you to plan to work hard, and _____

7. Yes, of course, there are times when I am lonely, and there are times when I am bothered by the quiet, but there are also times _____

_____

8. Turn the stove down to low, let the applesauce simmer, and _____

_____

9. Tired and sore, the bicyclist sat under a tree; _____

_____ , the other biker drank from her water bottle.

10. I love the smell of grass after it's mowed; I love the sound _____

_____ ; and I love the sight _____

Unparallel Construction 3

There's a good chance your writing will improve if you use repetition of similar words, phrases, and clauses. Parallel construction adds rhythm, emphasis, unity, and impact to your writing. Professional writers use this kind of repetition to give their passages impact. Public speakers use it to give their messages rhythm and emphasis. Turn to pages 90, 129, and 432 in *Writers INC*.

> **Study** the parts of each sentence below. Imitate the models as well as you can.

1. Goldilocks sat in Papa Bear's chair, but it was too hard. She sat in Mama Bear's chair, but it was too soft. She sat in Baby Bear's chair, and it was just right.

—as retold by mothers and fathers everywhere

_____

_____

_____

_____

2. "If you can laugh at it, you can live with it."

—Erma Bombeck

_____

_____

3. "The test of our progress is not whether we add more to the abundance of those who have much; it is whether we provide enough for those who have too little."

—Franklin D. Roosevelt

_____

_____

4. "Once there was a lot of sound in my mother's house, a lot of coming and going, feasting and talking."

—N. Scott Momaday, "My Kiowa Grandmother"

_____

_____

_____

Extend: If you like parallel structures, look for examples as you read. Record the best examples in a notebook for future reference.

Review: Sentence Problems 2

Rewrite the following sentences to eliminate misplaced or dangling modifiers.

1. Working hard to pass the exam, John's mother agreed to help him.

Working hard to pass the exam, John persuaded his mother to

help him.

2. The woodpecker is causing damage to our wooden boat we keep trying to get rid of.

3. Hernando tripped over his skateboard running down the street.

4. Before leaving Montana for vacation, the horses needed grooming.

Put brackets around any words that are unnecessary in the following sentences. When necessary, rewrite sentence parts adding your changes above the line.

1. Regardless of any opposing opinions, I am going to do what I think is right, and I don't care what anyone else thinks.

2. With winter fast approaching, it's a good idea to prepare our cars for the cold months ahead.

3. Due to the fact that the storm knocked out our electricity and the electrical power to our area, it seems that we should be in the process of trying to find some dry ice for the purpose of keeping our milk and other perishables that might spoil chilled.

Make all the words parallel to the first word in each set. Then use your words in a sentence.

1. running, ~~jumped~~, ~~throw~~ *jumping throwing*   *Running, jumping, and throwing are skills*

   many athletes need.

2. rakes, listening, took _____

   _____

3. played cards, watching a video, eat junk food _____

   _____

Create sentences that are parallel in structure. Follow the directions for each sentence.

1. Use infinitive phrases: _____

   _____

   _____

2. Use participial phrases: _____

   _____

   _____

3. Use prepositional phrases: _____

   _____

   _____

4. Use gerund phrases: _____

   _____

   _____

Pretest: Shifts in Construction

Shifts in construction can be shifts in *number* (singular to plural, plural to singular), in *person* (using a combination of 1st, 2nd, and 3rd persons), in *tense* (using an inappropriate combination of tenses), or in *voice* (active to passive, passive to active).

> Correct the first underlined part in each sentence below by writing the correction above it. (The two underlined parts in each sentence represent an incorrect shift in construction.) On the blank, identify the kind of shift: number, person, tense, or voice.

number **1.** *students work*
When a student works hard in a class, it is a shame if they have trouble taking exams.

_____ **2.** One must not bring a cart loaded with groceries to the express lane, or you might be asked to go to another checkout.

_____ **3.** While the librarian waits for her computer to download the information, she cataloged the new reference books.

_____ **4.** The fans were shouting and waved their hands at the camera during the seventh-inning stretch.

_____ **5.** We would shop at the mall with the designer outlets if they were not so far from our home.

_____ **6.** If you are told by your teacher to finish your paper by Friday, but you forget it, he or she can lower your grade.

_____ **7.** A person may not truly learn a lesson until something very painful happens to them.

_____ **8.** We skated on the frozen pond; then we were drinking hot chocolate in the lodge.

_____ **9.** The seeds were eaten by the birds, and they build nests nearby.

_____ **10.** We wanted to sing, but she didn't know any French songs.

Shifts in Verb Tense 1

Consistent verb tenses clearly establish time in your writing. When verb tenses change without warning or for no reason, readers can become confused. Turn to page 90 and 511.1 in *Writers INC* for more information about past, present, and future verb tenses.

> Underline the verb in the first sentence of each pair. Change the verb tense in the second sentence to be consistent with the first. Finally, identify the tense that is used.

present **1.** The Channel Tunnel <u>is</u> a railway tunnel beneath the English
Channel. The tunnel ~~linked~~ *links* England and France.

_____ **2.** The "Chunnel" opened in 1994. How many passengers will ride the
tunnel trains that year?

_____ **3.** The tunnel has three types of trains. One kind, the shuttle train,
carried automobiles, trucks, buses, and their passengers.

_____ **4.** The other two types of trains were designed for high-speed passenger
traffic. The trip through the tunnel takes about one-half hour.

_____ **5.** To take the train, you will enter the tunnel in Folkestone, England.
On the French side, you go into the tunnel at Coquelles, near Calais.

_____ **6.** The tunnel measures nearly 31 miles from entrance to entrance.
Nearly 24 of those miles lay underwater.

_____ **7.** The structure consists of three parallel tubes. Two tubes will
accommodate the railroads.

_____ **8.** A third tube lies between the other two. It supplied fresh air and
maintenance access to the rail tubes.

_____ **9.** The third tube will provide for emergency evacuation. The design of
this structure contributes to the safety of the riders.

_____ **10.** The three tubes generally lie about 130 feet beneath the seabed.
Rings of concrete or iron formed a continuous lining in the tubes.

Shifts in Verb Tense 2

Tense shifts, also called tense sequences, are sometimes necessary to help a writer show more than one time in a sentence. Just make sure your tense shifts are correct. Turn to page 90 and 511.1 in *Writers INC*.

 He was certain that he had left me a message.
(The first verb *was* shows past action. The second verb *had left* shows an action that occurred before the past action. This verb sequence past/past perfect is often used.)

Place a verb in the blank space in each sentence below. Choose a verb tense that differs from the first verb in the sentence and makes clear that the two actions described in the sentence occur at different times.

1. Although the dynamite had exploded, the building _____*remained*_____ intact.

2. The snow will soon accumulate, so the plows _____ out.

3. It rained here yesterday, but the sun _____ most of the time.

4. We lost this week's game, but we _____ when we play next week.

5. Because it rained all week long, the playing field _____ into a quagmire.

6. John failed his driver's test last week, but he _____ to take it again next week.

7. Since Yolanda had sprained her ankle two days before, she _____ yesterday's track meet.

8. If Terrell wins the election, it _____ the third time in a row he has been elected.

9. Based on the winning margin in the past two elections, I think he _____ this time as well.

10. Because a thunderstorm had darkened the sky, the maintenance crew _____ the stadium lights on early.

Shifts in Verb Tense 3

Tense shifts made for no reason can add confusion to your writing. Changes in tense to describe time changes in your writing are, however, necessary. For more on tenses, turn to 511.1 in *Writers INC*.

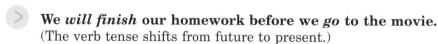

> We *will finish* our homework before we *go* to the movie.
> (The verb tense shifts from future to present.)

> My mom *had declined* the invitation before I even *read* it.
> (The verb tense shifts from past perfect to past.)

Underline and label the two verb tenses used in the following sentences.

1. The train <u>future</u> <u>will be</u> late tomorrow because the railbed <u>is</u> <u>present</u> under water.

2. I hope Dad will buy a new car soon.

3. Mom is certain she added the eggs to the cake.

4. Grandma remembers that she came to the United States in 1919.

5. Will you please fix the faucet before you go to work?

6. Claire claimed she had written all her thank-you letters.

7. Mr. Dickens has remembered that his mother will have a birthday tomorrow.

8. The state of Alaska has offered invitations to all distance runners; Alaska wants these athletes to run in the Solstice Marathon.

9. After the gate had been opened, the horses ran out.

10. We will wear earplugs when we mow the lawn next time.

11. Before the exam begins, we will want to go over our notes again.

12. The stew tasted strong because so many root vegetables had been added.

13. The stapler is out of staples, so someone will have to fill it.

14. If she hangs the sheets on the line, they will smell like fresh air and sunshine.

15. He said, "Give me a break."

16. If he takes that long to pack again, the train will have left without him.

Pronoun Shifts 1

In a well-written sentence, pronouns should not shift in number, person, or gender. Turn to page 90, 505.1-505.2, 506.2, and 527-528 in *Writers INC*.

Replace the underlined pronouns with ones that match the number, person, and gender of the other pronoun in the following sentences. (The first five antecedents are in italics.) Also change any verbs as necessary. If an underlined pronoun is correct, write **C** above it.

1. *You* may be able to tune a guitar, but can <u>one</u> tune a car engine?

   you

2. When *a person* plays guitar for a while, <u>they</u> should know how to tune a guitar.

3. *Anybody* can tune <u>their</u> guitar in a few simple steps, except electrics with Floyd Rose whammy bars.

4. An in-tune guitar means that all *strings* are at *their* proper tension so that <u>they</u> produce the correct pitches, or sounds.

5. Every *guitarist* starts the tuning process with the sixth string (the thickest one) on <u>your</u> guitar.

6. And because you are probably an ace guitarist in a rockin' band, <u>one</u> should do an absolute, or concert, tuning.

7. When concert tuning, one uses a tuning fork (A or E) to determine the correct tone for that string, no matter what guitar <u>they</u> play.

8. When tuning her guitar, Julie strikes the E fork on <u>his</u> knee and places the tuning fork's base on the guitar near the strings.

9. Julie then plays the guitar string that matches the fork's pitch, and <u>you</u> try to match the tone by tightening or loosening the string.

10. Peter brings in his guitar. He sits next to Julie, and both match the tone of the fifth string. Then <u>they</u> tune the other strings, one after the other.

Pronoun Shifts 2

Using indefinite pronouns is tricky because they can easily shift in number or person as you write. Turn to pages 90, 505, and 528 in *Writers INC.* Also see 527.2 for information on which indefinite pronouns are singular, plural, or either singular or plural.

> **Circle** the correct pronoun in each sentence below.

1. When anybody buys a used car, *(he or she,* they) should inspect it thoroughly.

2. You might begin by looking for rust on the car. If someone painted the car recently, it could mean that *(he or she, they)* may have been covering up damage.

3. Someone should slam the car's doors, open its windows, and pop its trunk. If one sees something not fitting properly, *(he or she, they)* may need to ask more questions about the car's history.

4. For example, if one of the car's doors fits badly, it may indicate that *(it was, they were)* damaged.

5. Everyone should check tailpipes for black, gooey soot, and *(they, he or she)* should also check the car's oil level.

6. However, be careful not to wear *(your, his or her, their)* light-colored clothes when doing this kind of check.

7. When checking headlights, taillights, brake lights, backup lights, and directional signals, several friends might work together so that *(he or she, they)* can complete the checks quickly and accurately.

8. Just remember, none of the tasks mentioned above are really that aggravating if *(it helps, they help)* you avoid a buyer's biggest nightmare—buying a lemon.

Extend: Write three to five sentences on how you would go about inspecting an item that you are interested in buying. Think about how you would use the item. Add your own special inspection points. Check for pronoun shifts in your writing.

Pronoun Shifts 3

Within a sentence, a pronoun must agree in number, person, and gender with the word it refers to—its antecedent. Turn to pages 90 and 528 in *Writers INC*. Also see 527.1 for information on collective nouns and how to determine if they are singular or plural.

Circle the correct pronoun in each sentence below.

1. The team was awarded a trophy for *(its, their)* winning record.

2. The coach awarded each player *(his or her, their)* letter.

3. Both the players and coach expressed *(their, his)* pride in the team.

4. All team members had something good to say about *(its, their)* coach.

5. The team promised to do *(its, their)* best the following season.

6. The coach gave the team the privilege of keeping *(its, their)* uniform jerseys.

7. Both Nassir and Joel rode down the freeway in silence until *(he, they)* reached the O-Kee-Doke Diner.

8. Neither Nassir nor the other patrons knew that *(he was, they were)* in for a big surprise.

9. Along with the entree, all the diners could have *(your, their)* choice of garlic mashed potatoes or roasted peppers.

10. Uncle Raymond drove *(her, his)* truck through the cornfield while the kids and Auntie Fay screamed *(her, their)* usual—"Whoopie!"

11. A ballet dancer is one of those athletes who must stay in excellent condition and keep on *(their, his or her)* toes.

12. Tonight either the Blue Soxs or the Mustangs will receive *(its, your)* official notification to move to Muddville.

13. John lost his keys because his pair of pants had holes in *(its, their)* pockets.

14. Neither Sharmin nor Joy remembered to do *(their, her)* homework.

Review: Shifts in Construction

Underline the incorrect pronoun and verb shifts in the following sentences. Look for shifts in person, number, voice, and tense. Correct each shift by writing the correct word or words above the underlined portion.

1. Some people fly kites, while other people *ride* <u>rode</u> bicycles.

2. If you love to write, draw, paint, and act, one should probably not go into accounting.

3. Juliana hopes to go to college and planned on applying to several schools.

4. I planted zinnias and petunias in the red containers, but cosmos and sweet peas have been planted in the blue containers.

5. The students finished the essay test before he or she went to the auditorium.

6. Jack and his buddy finished his homework early and went skateboarding.

7. I walked into Grandma's kitchen and spied the pie of your dreams.

8. There is a cricket, maybe two, who are singing in my basement.

9. The members of the class were hungry; it wanted more pizza.

10. Astronomy 406 is very difficult, and I wished I had not taken the course.

11. Does my lawn mower need a new engine, or can they be repaired?

12. When the alarm rang early on the morning of the trip, she turns it off.

13. Several of the students met to discuss his or her ACT scores.

14. Nobody really wanted to reveal how they had done on the test.

15. All Mondays are the same: long and boring; most Tuesdays will not be great either.

16. Jan will finish her homework, and she used the rest of her time to do the laundry.

17. Neither my uncle nor his children wanted to take down his Christmas tree.

Review: Sentence Activities

Underline the simple or compound subject once and the simple or compound predicate twice in the following sentences. Then, on the line, identify the sentence as **S** for simple, **CD** for compound, **CX** for complex, or **CD-CX** for compound-complex.

_____ **1.** Although broadcasting is the most popular use of radio, it has many other uses as well.

_____ **2.** Pilots, police, and other professionals use it to communicate quickly.

_____ **3.** Scientists learn about weather by sending radio waves into the sky, and radio enthusiasts operate amateur stations all over the country.

_____ **4.** RADAR, which is a special form of radio, not only aids in the safe operation of airplanes and ships, but it also helps police departments to apprehend speeders.

Identify the underlined phrases in the following sentences as **A** for appositive, **G** for gerund, **I** for infinitive, **P** for participial, or **PREP** for prepositional.

1. Believe it or not, cooking food is something that radio waves can do well—

in a microwave oven.

2. Spies use bugs, hidden radio devices, to secretly listen to conversations.

3. Doctors can use a miniature radio transmitter enclosed in a capsule

to help them diagnose stomach ailments.

Identify the underlined clauses as adverb, adjective, or noun.

_____ **1.** Before the development of radio revolutionized communication, people had only two other means of quick, long-distance communication: the telegraph and the telephone.

_____ **2.** The drawback of both of these methods was that communication was possible only between places connected with wires, since they were required to send the signals.

_____ **3.** Radio signals, <u>which pass through the air</u>, enable people to quickly communicate between any two points on land, sea, air—even outer space.

_____ **4.** Radio's first practical use was for ship-to-ship and ship-to-shore communication; operators found <u>that it aided greatly in sea rescues</u>.

Circle the correct verb in parentheses in the sentences below.

1. The cheerleading squad *(are, is)* taking the bus to the next game.

2. Either the cats or the dog *(was, were)* responsible for this mess.

3. The six o'clock news *(are, is)* coming on next.

4. Everyone in the group *(was, were)* heading for the exit at the same time.

5. There *(was, were)* an abundance of lilacs on the bushes this year.

6. Rasheed and I *(is, are)* the distance runners on our team.

7. All of the children *(are, is)* required to have their immunizations.

8. The result of the race *(are, is)* not one, but two winners.

Circle the misplaced modifier in the following sentences, and draw an arrow to the word it modifies.

1. Coffee is what most diners like with milk.

2. People need to protect their computers from viruses who use the Internet.

3. Adrian really wants a car to take to a summer concert with great speakers.

4. We tried scuba diving at a vacation resort in the lake.

5. Ricardo got a video game that enables the user to act as a pilot for his children.

EDITED BY KRISTEN IVERSEN
WITH
E. WARREN PERRY AND SHANNON PERRY

DOOM
WITH A
VIEW

HISTORICAL AND CULTURAL
CONTEXTS OF THE ROCKY FLATS
NUCLEAR WEAPONS PLANT

FULCRUM

D1534290

Library of Congress Cataloging-in-Publication Data

Names: Iversen, Kristen, editor. | Perry, E. Warren, Jr., editor. | Perry, Shannon, editor.
Title: Doom with a view : historical and cultural contexts of the Rocky Flats nuclear weapons
    plant / edited by Kristen Iversen with E. Warren Perry and Shannon Perry.
Description: Golden, CO : Fulcrum, [2020] | Includes bibliographical references.
    | Summary: "Tucked up against the Rocky Mountains, just west of Denver, sits the remnants of one of the most notorious nuclear weapons sites in North America: Rocky Flats. With a history of environmental catastrophes, political neglect, and community-wide health crises, this site represents both one of the darkest and most controversial chapters in our nation's history, and also a conundrum on repurposing lands once considered lost. As the crush of encroaching residential areas close in on this site and the generation of Rocky Flats workers passes on, the memory of Rocky Flats is receding from the public mind; yet the need to responsibly manage the site, and understand the consequences of forty years of plutonium production and contamination, must be a part of every decision for the land's future"-- Provided by publisher.
Identifiers: LCCN 2020008211 | ISBN 9781682752548 (paperback)
Subjects: LCSH: Rocky Flats Plant (U.S.) | Rocky Flats Environmental Technology Site (U.S.) | Nuclear weapons plants--Environmental aspects--Colorado. | Nuclear weapons plants--Health aspects--Colorado. | Radioactive pollution--Colorado.
Classification: LCC TD195.N85 D66 2020 | DDC 363.17/990978884--dc23
LC record available at https://lccn.loc.gov/2020008211

10 9 8 7 6 5 4 3 2 1

Fulcrum Publishing
3970 Youngfield Street
Wheat Ridge, CO 80033
800-992-2908 • 303-277-1623
https://fulcrum.bookstore.ipgbook.com/

DOOM WITH A VIEW

HISTORICAL AND CULTURAL CONTEXTS OF THE ROCKY FLATS NUCLEAR WEAPONS PLANT

EDITED BY KRISTEN IVERSEN
WITH
E. WARREN PERRY AND SHANNON PERRY

CONTENTS

FOREWORD

Christopher Hormel

*"Every man, woman and child lives under a nuclear
sword of Damocles, hanging by the slenderest of threads,
capable of being cut at any moment by accident
or miscalculations or by madness. The weapons of war
must be abolished before they abolish us."*

– President John F. Kennedy,
September 25, 1961, UN General Assembly

The nuclear sword is still hanging over us, by a thread tragically close to
being cut. At worst a nuclear war would result in the end of civilization
and death to most life on the planet. A limited nuclear exchange would
immediately kill millions in a radioactive firestorm, and the debris that
collects in the atmosphere would cause a nuclear winter, changing the climate around the globe, disrupting food production, causing many more
deaths from starvation and war among the survivors.

We have somehow avoided nuclear Armageddon, but the damage to
the health of the planet and all life upon it from the development of nuclear weapons and nuclear energy has already manifest. We have contam-

inated our world with atmospheric nuclear testing, uranium mining and milling, accidental and illegal dumping of waste, radioactive fires, and core meltdowns. The nuclear weapons industry has been negligent in the extreme, leaving enormous levels of contaminated materials everywhere they have operated. Nuclear power plants release radiation daily, and all have large amounts of spent fuel stored on site. Three Mile Island, Chernobyl, and Fukushima remind us of the danger. There is no safe dose of radiation, yet governments around the world have allowed safety limits to be more relaxed, instead of making them more protective. Given the ignorance and negligence with which we have handled nuclear materials, the lives of many of our descendants will be degraded by more cancers, birth defects, mutations, and other health issues. Our "nuclear age" will have a negative impact on living beings for millions of years.

We may be able to improve the prospects for future generations, but it will take all of us to speak out and force our leaders to listen to reason. There is a treaty banning nuclear weapons that came out of the United Nations in 2017. In the United States we don't hear much about it, but there are many countries in the rest of the world who are challenging us to examine the morality of threatening the world with annihilation. Will we listen? Will we as Americans examine our past behavior and admit our responsibility for the extreme danger to life we have created?

Reading this book is a good place to start. *Doom with a View* provides an honest appraisal of the consequences of nuclear weapons manufacturing by telling the story of Rocky Flats. This story is not subject to the greenwashing of corporate and government agency spin doctors. There is no nefarious political agenda driving the writers of these essays. These good people are neither scaremongers nor agents of foreign powers. Every one of the contributors to this book has borne witness to the suffering of the victims of the blind ambition to achieve a superior nuclear arsenal that was the driving force behind the Rocky Flats Nuclear Weapons Plant.

I am grateful to Kristen Iversen and E. Warren Perry, Jr. for assembling this collection of essays about Rocky Flats, the mess that was made, how it was closed, the resulting so-called cleanup, and the toxic legacy that remains. It takes courage to tell this story because many in the area around Rocky Flats don't want to hear it. The truth of the story is bad for business. Radioactive contamination deters tourists, home buyers, and employers. So the storytellers must take a deep breath and persevere. They must endure being dismissed by politicians and business leaders. They must tolerate having their patriotism questioned.

Support these brave people by reading what they have written about downwinders and workers who became ill from exposure to radioactive and toxic contamination, and how many have died without receiving compensation; how the federal government and their contractors kept massive releases of radioactive materials secret from the people in surrounding communities; how a grand jury investigation of Rocky Flats was "ambushed" and justice not served; how the Colorado Department of Public Health and Environment consistently looked the other way while the federal Department of Energy rushed the manufacture of plutonium pits for nuclear bombs while worker and community health and safety were taking a back seat; how the Fish and Wildlife Service relies on biased testing methodologies to proclaim to the public that the Rocky Flats National Wildlife Refuge is safe for public recreation; and how the City of Arvada allows homes to be built on land that was once part of the Superfund site at Rocky Flats.

Let us thank these writers who speak truth to power about Rocky Flats in these pages. We need such courage as an example for the rest of us to find a way forward that acknowledges the harm done, and perhaps more importantly, that breaks through the delusion that war is the way to resolve our differences.

The courage to tell the truth is our only hope. We can create a culture of Nuclear Guardianship rather than sweeping the problem under the rug. Instead of a wildlife refuge that doesn't acknowledge the radioactive contamination on the land, we can use the mistakes of the past to create an intergenerational investigation to learn about how radioactive materials behave in soil, water, and air; how they move in the environment; and how people can protect themselves from the danger. If we tell the truth we have an opportunity to learn from our mistakes and thereby help future beings understand what they are up against.

There are no signs around Rocky Flats that tell visitors about the danger of nuclear contamination. There is but a lonely *Cold War Horse* in a red hazmat suit and a respirator standing by to hint at the truth. I feel the eyes of our descendants upon us. Let us begin the work of helping them understand and keep safe from the nuclear legacy we are leaving behind.

PREFACE

Kristen Iversen and E. Warren Perry, Jr.

This book represents the research and analysis of scientists, medical researchers, philosophers, artists, writers, and activists who have been impacted by one of the most notorious nuclear weapons sites in the United States: Rocky Flats. The history and catastrophes of the Rocky Flats Nuclear Weapons Plant just outside Denver, Colorado, had environmental, political, and health effects that extended beyond just the Front Range of Colorado. At the heart of the Cold War effort in the United States, Rocky Flats produced more than 70,000 plutonium pits for nuclear weapons. Plutonium pits, the radioactive cores or "triggers" of nuclear weapons, essentially provide the heart of a nuclear bomb. The production of plutonium pits resulted not only in extensive toxic and radioactive contamination in the environment but also negative public health effects, deeply divisive social and cultural attitudes among workers and local residents, and ongoing political ramifications. Beyond Colorado, the consequences of the forty-year nuclear weapons buildup that took place in Oak Ridge, Tennessee; Hanford, Washington; and Pantex, Texas, as well as numerous other sites across the country, are still being felt on environmental, political, and cultural levels. In many ways, the plutonium pits that were manufactured at Rocky Flats – and that served as the nexus of the nuclear weapons constructed to fight the Cold War – are symbolic of the larger network of Cold War nuclear production.

Twenty-five years after the closing of the Rocky Flats Nuclear Facility and more than ten years after the Department of Energy's (DOE's) modified cleanup of the area, the question of radioactivity in suburban areas close to the site remains contested and acrimonious. The "first generation" of Rocky Flats protesters included cultural luminaries such as Daniel Ellsberg, Allen Ginsberg, and Anne Waldman, as well as hosts of local, ordinary people who spoke out against the Cold War nuclear arms race. These were people who testified with their voices and bodies to the dangerous work of manufacturing parts for the U.S. nuclear weapons industry. Now, a "second generation" of artists, activists, concerned scientists, and academics continues to warn a public – some knowing, some unwitting – about the potentially negative health and environmental consequences that resulted from forty years of nuclear production at the Rocky Flats site.

The past, present, and future of Rocky Flats remains controversial. The historical disagreement over the plant breaks out according to the two competing master narratives of the Cold War. The first narrative strain celebrates American labor and the technological prowess that went into developing and manufacturing a powerful nuclear arsenal; it was this arsenal that prevented the Soviet Union from firing the first shot. The second narrative strain laments the sheer number of nuclear weapons produced, the long-term environmental degradation, and the apparent and invisible public health consequences that resulted from the large-scale production of nuclear weapons.

Since the cleanup of the plant ending in 2005, we have been faced with the ongoing question of what to do with Rocky Flats, which lies 16 miles west of downtown Denver, one of the fastest growing cities and metropolitan areas in the United States. Because the area is so close to a major metropolitan area, and because it sits atop a scenic high plateau that overlooks the Denver valley, there is a great deal of pressure to develop the area for housing, business, and transportation, including a major highway. The future of Rocky Flats remains controversial.

These controversies are intensified by a variety of citizen, business, and governmental interests that compete against each other to tell the Rocky Flats story and to determine the future use of the land. For instance, the DOE's Rocky Flats Legacy Management Project, as well as DOE-funded groups such as the Rocky Flats Stewardship Council, aim to convince the public that the site has been satisfactorily remediated and that residential areas cropping up around the perimeter of the old Rocky Flats boundaries pose no risks to inhabitants. Indeed, the DOE and the US Fish and Wildlife Agency opened wide swaths of the former nuclear facility for day hikers, mountain bikers, and school field trips. On the flip side, citizen action groups also vie for the public's attention and strive to make accurate and complete information about Rocky Flats more accessible. The Rocky Mountain Peace and Justice Center and other groups, including Candelas Glows, Rocky Flats Downwinders, and Rocky Flats Right to Know, work to alert homeowners and residents in the Rocky Flats area of potential health dangers. Further, in response to ongoing anecdotal evidence of health effects in residents, local universities, including Metropolitan State University of Denver, the University of Colorado, Boulder, and Regis University have joined efforts to launch a scientifically valid health study of people who live or have lived around Rocky Flats. And despite the challenges of adequate funding, these efforts continue.

Because of former secrecy and the sensitivity and controversy surrounding Rocky Flats, places of public memory have not been supported by local and federal officials. For instance, a fledgling Rocky Flats Museum has been searching for a home for more than a decade. Officials in the neighboring town of Arvada are decidedly uninterested in funding a space of public memory that reminds citizens of the nuclear production that took place there over the course of two generations. The same is true for objects of art, such as Jeff Gipe's *Cold War Horse*. Installed on private property adjacent to the old Rocky Flats site over Labor Day weekend in 2015, the sculpture was promptly pulled down and damaged by unknown vandals. (The statue was immediately reconstructed, and now stands surrounded by a security fence and camera.) In addition, a public commemoration of the twenty-fifth anniversary of the FBI raid of the Rocky Flats site, hosted by the Arvada Center for the Arts in June 2014, was characterized by acrimonious debate among former government officials, Rocky Flats workers, and citizens of the Front Range.

But, as time passes, as the DOE gradually erases traces of the old plant, and as the generation of former Rocky Flats workers passes on, the memory of the site is receding from the public mind. The DOE, for instance, quietly took down signage that signaled the old entrance to the plant, and the historical records are scattered, highly contested, and often prevented by public officials from scrutiny and analysis by the public and other interested parties. The Rocky Flats Reading Rooms, which provided some information to the public, have all been closed, and documents that researchers or the public might want to examine have been taken to the Federal Center in Littleton, where entry is difficult.

Just as there have been attempts to gloss over the legacy of Rocky Flats, a growing body of imaginative work has begun to explore the personal and national history of the site and how, as individuals and as a culture, we think about and understand it from both a historical perspective and with eyes to the future. This is particularly important as we face decisions regarding how to responsibly manage the land – as well as surrounding areas – that was the Rocky Flats Plant.

Rocky Flats is a social and political problem that cannot be solved or understood through the lens of any single academic discipline. A full understanding of the history and the consequences of forty years of plutonium production demands an inter- and cross-disciplinary set of perspectives that includes academic, activist, and nonacademic voices, opinions, and ideas. This collection of essays, then, invites a wide range of writers and thinkers to examine the local problem of Rocky Flats and, by default, the larger problem of the nuclear legacy in the United States.

THE ACCIDENTAL ACTIVIST

Kristen Iversen

Every Sunday after church, my parents forced us four kids to endure long, winding drives through the Colorado mountains. Later, of course, I learned to love the mountains – but at that time in my life, as a child, I didn't care. My siblings and I punched and tickled each other in the back seat and thought we would die of boredom. But some things out the window were worth noticing. As we headed west on our way toward the hills, we'd pass lines of protesters standing with signs at the gate of the Rocky Flats plant. "Hippies and housewives," my father would grumble, and my mother nodded silently. "Students, too," he'd add. "Wait 'til they get out into the real world."

 We were made to understand that in the real world, you accepted what the government did. You accepted what the government said. You were grateful to be an American, and you didn't ask questions.

 Years later – after I became a Rocky Flats employee – I learned that the plant was making nuclear weapons. Radioactive and toxic contamination, including plutonium, was ubiquitous both on-site and off-site. Our neighborhood was contaminated. The protesters were right. My family and our neighbors were being lied to.

But when I was a kid during the era of Cold War secrecy, we had no idea what was going on at Rocky Flats. The parents of many of my friends worked at the plant, but no one was allowed to talk about it. You could get fired for saying anything about your job or what was going on. So people kept their mouths shut, pocketed their paychecks, and felt grateful for the job.

In the early years, when Dow Chemical operated the plant, word on the street was they were making household cleaning supplies. Even the newspapers repeated the lies and half-truths put out by the Department of Energy (DOE), Dow, and Rockwell. In fact, Rockwell earned tax-payer-funded bonuses for coercing local media to publish stories that cast Rocky Flats in a positive and shrouded light. For years my mother thought Rocky Flats made Scrubbing Bubbles. The government, and the corporations that operated the plant, repeatedly denied that anything dangerous was going on. *It's safe*, they said. *Don't worry.*

"Surely," my mother used to say, "the government would tell us if there was anything we needed to worry about."

For the first ten years of my life we lived in a modest three-bedroom house in what's now known as Old Arvada. Back then it was new, and our little neighborhood of identical red brick tract homes was about 7 miles downwind from Rocky Flats. Long fields and farms spread in every direction, and even then the soil held traces of plutonium from the first big, uncontrollable fire at the plant back in 1957. With a half-life of 24,000 years, that contamination was still there.

After the birth of my little brother, we moved to a bigger house in one of the new housing tracts. This house was even closer to Rocky Flats, just 3 miles away, and I could see the plant's water tower from our back porch. My sisters and I rode our horses in the fields around the plant and galloped up and down Indiana Street, where the boys in the neighborhood raced their dirt bikes and motorcycles. Home builders advertised with slogans like "Country Living with City Amenities!" and it did seem that we had our own outdoor paradise, at least for a time – until the housing development took over. My siblings and I spent every possible minute outside with our dogs and horses.

Some of my best childhood memories are of swimming with my horse in Standley Lake, just downstream from Rocky Flats. Sassy was a tall sorrel mare with a golden mane and tail that I wove into long braids. I liked to ride bareback with nothing to curb Sassy's enthusiasm but a noseband and braided leather reins, and I was proud of my record of never falling off. Sassy loved to swim. We'd tiptoe gingerly along the sandy bank, looking for just the right spot to go in, and then Sassy would slowly wade into the lake until the water reached just above her knees. Then we'd hit the end of the rock shelf and she'd plunge into the deeper water, head held high, legs pumping forward like pistons, and I had to twist my fists into her mane to keep from sliding off her slick back. The water was dark and icy cold and all around us was blue sky, the fantastic Colorado deep turquoise sky, with a few puffy white clouds floating flat-bottomed above us. We'd swim until she began to tire, nostrils flaring in short blasts of fiery breath, and then we'd emerge, dripping wet, ecstatic. I'd slide from her back as she shook herself thoroughly like a dog coming in from the rain, and then I'd scramble back on and we'd gallop home in time for supper.

I loved my horse, I loved the lake, I loved my life.

Years later, following an FBI raid on Rocky Flats, we learned there was plutonium in the sediment of Standley Lake. It was in the soil. It was in the air.

Maybe there was a reason why there was so much cancer in my neighborhood.

Where I grew up, "activist" was a bad word. It wasn't a label I would have chosen for myself. But I was well on my way to wearing the label with pride.

"Whistleblowers will be dealt with severely and completely." When Rocky Flats worker Jacque Brever heard the words of manager Bill Weston, just one week after the FBI raid on Rocky Flats, her heart sank. Was she a whistleblower for telling the truth?

Seven years earlier, in 1982 when Jacque first took a job at Rocky Flats, she was a high-school dropout and single mother desperate for a good-paying job. Like many workers, she started out in the plant cafeteria and didn't really know what went on at Rocky Flats. She'd been taking art classes part-time at the community college, and when she started at the plant she learned she could move up from the cafeteria if she added a few chemistry and physics classes and became a chemical operator.

That meant she'd be making real money. To her surprise it turned out she was good at chemistry and physics. She applied for a national-security government clearance, and by the time Jacque became a crew leader, her salary had jumped to $30,000 a year – a small fortune in her eyes. She was immediately assigned to Building 771, one of the "hot" areas of the plant.

Jacque didn't know much about Rocky Flats, and she knew almost nothing about nuclear weapons. But she worked hard to learn her job and do it right. What she really cared about was a daughter she was raising on her own and the good salary.

But the job was harder than she expected. As a "chem op," Jacque worked on the glovebox line where workers wore lead-lined gloves to handle plutonium. Even in minuscule amounts, plutonium was deadly. A single leak, slip, or mishap could have devastating consequences. Workers also had to deal with uranium, beryllium, americium, and other highly toxic metals and chemicals, including carbon tetrachloride. Jacque was especially worried about the company's "production first, safety second" attitude. She began to keep a journal, not only to keep track of the new procedures she was learning but also to make note of her concerns about safety violations and accidents and what she felt was a lack of response from management.

There were other hazards as well. Most women at Rocky Flats worked as secretaries or servers in the cafeteria, and few women worked in plutonium processing. Tall and blond, Jacque made friends at work but she was also the target of sexual comments, pranks, and jokes by male co-workers. So she learned to be tough and roll with the punches. Some men felt women didn't belong in the production areas, but from others she earned a begrudging respect.

Fortunately, Jacque found a kindred spirit in Karen Pitts, another female chem op. Karen was muscular and athletic – she played tournament racquetball – and both women were proud of the fact that they were contributing to the country's national defense. They intended to work at Rocky Flats until they retired. As one company official had said to Karen, "You can stay here till you die."

Then things changed. Early on the morning of June 6, 1989, a line of thirty vehicles filled with seventy-five armed agents of the FBI and Environmental Protection Agency (EPA) raided the plant for suspected environmental crimes. For eighteen days agents carried out more than 200 boxes of materials, and the raid led to a grand jury investigation.

One of the primary alleged violations was the illegal operation of a long-standing incinerator in Building 771, the building where Jacque and Karen worked. This incinerator burned plutonium-contaminated waste, which was then carried by winds over unsuspecting residents in nearby Arvada and the entire metro Denver area. A successful lawsuit by the Sierra Club had temporarily halted the incineration – yet flyover evidence from an FBI plane indicated that Rockwell was likely continuing to use the incinerator illegally for midnight incineration. The charge listed very specific dates in 1988 and 1989.

When Jacque saw the allegation, she was immediately alarmed. "Oh my gosh," she thought. "That was one of my overtime days in Building 771. I think we did that." Worried that she and her crew might end up in jail, she spoke to her manager and asked to see the documents they had signed for that day's work to confirm they had done nothing illegal.

Instead, on June 13, Rocky Flats management called a staff meeting to discuss the FBI investigation. Workers were given little information but instructed to remain quiet. William Weston, Rockwell's Manager of Plutonium Operations, threatened that "whistleblowers will be dealt with severely and completely. Everyone knows the incinerator did not run between October 7, 1988, and February 25, 1989." Jacque was stunned. Jacque and Karen, as well as other workers, were specifically told not to cooperate with FBI investigators. "If the FBI comes to me," Karen said, "I'm not going to lie to protect anyone."

The following day, managers refused to allow Karen Pitts and Jacque Brever access to documentation that would confirm the dates and nature of their duties with respect to the Building 771 incinerator. When they were subpoenaed by the grand jury, they agreed to testify.

Reaction at the plant was swift. Everyone – management and co-workers – knew the women planned to testify to the grand jury regarding safety violations at the plant. Angry coworkers confronted them and talked about how their actions were going to shut down the plant and make them lose their jobs. Jacque and Karen received threatening phone calls and their cars and homes were vandalized. "If you make me lose my job," a male coworker told Jacque, "I'll hunt you down and kill you." Jacque feared for her safety and she was worried about sending her young daughter to school. Karen's husband, who also worked at the plant, was ostracized. But neither woman backed down.

Shortly before the court date, on September 14, 1989, Jacque was getting ready to work in a glovebox in Building 771. She pulled on her lead-lined gloves. The moment she extended her arms into the box, she felt a puff of ash on her face. Simultaneously the SAAM alarm (Selective Alpha Air Monitor) went off. Karen, who was working in the same room, was at her side immediately. They headed for the door. "I had a strange metallic taste in my mouth," Jacque later recalled, "as if I were sucking on a penny." Another alarm went off and a radiation monitor appeared. He instructed Jacque to put on paper coveralls for transportation to the decontamination room. As she stood waiting for the van, two men from the previous shift came down the hall. "That's what you get for making waves," one remarked. Both men laughed.

Someone had poked a hole in her glove. Tests confirmed that Jacque had been contaminated with plutonium and americium.

Jacque Brever testified before the grand jury on October 23 and 24 in 1989. Karen Pitts testified on October 25. They were subject to so much hostility at the plant that for their own safety, the FBI and the Department of Justice ordered the women to be transferred to the "cold" part of the facility. As they were cleaning out their lockers, the women were heckled and jeered. "Bitches!" one worker yelled. "Why don't you just quit?" said another.

But they didn't quit. They wanted to stand their ground as the grand jury continued its work – and further, both women knew that not only had their careers been destroyed, but they were also contaminated. Who would hire a contaminated worker from Rocky Flats? No company would take that health risk. They had to stick it out. In her journal, Jacque wrote,

> What about [our] futures? We can never do our jobs again. Our reputations are ruined.... We can never make this wage on the outside and we now have the reputation of being whistleblowers, therefore there aren't any companies we can think of who will hire us. We are unable to get outside insur-

ance because we are now health risks.... How long will it be before this all comes to an end?

For twenty-one months the grand jury investigation continued. Eventually Rockwell pleaded guilty to criminal violations of the Federal Hazardous Waste Law and the Clean Water Act, and the company was convicted of five felonies and five misdemeanors. Although the grand jury wanted to indict nine DOE and Rockwell employees, that didn't happen. Rockwell paid an $18.5 million fine (although ironically that amount was equivalent to the DOE bonus they received that year). Even today the case remains highly controversial.

For Jacque and Karen, the harassment never stopped. In 1991 they filed a civil suit against Rockwell and EG&G, the new operator of the plant. The suit alleged they had been labeled "whistleblowers" for cooperating with the FBI, and they were "harassed, intimidated, threatened, subjected to unsafe working conditions, deterred from testifying before a grand jury, and retaliated against after testifying." They also listed thirty-nine specific individuals as defendants, their former friends and co-workers at the plant.

Despite extensive evidence and testimony, the lawsuit was dismissed for lack of adequate detail. The court also noted that the individual defendants were "acting for their own personal purposes and not blindly executing corporate policy."

The working conditions became unbearable. Fearing for both herself and the safety of her family, on April 17, 1991, Karen Pitts resigned her position as chemical operator at Rocky Flats. One week later Jacque Brever resigned as well. Jacque left the state and went into hiding with her daughter.

Karen Pitts dropped from public view. After a decade in hiding, Jacque returned to Colorado to pursue a master's degree in environmental policy and management despite the fact that she had been diagnosed with thyroid cancer and reactive airway disease. "I'm really ashamed that we're leaving this mess for people like my daughter and her generation," she said in an interview. "The best thing I can do is what my conscience tells me to do while I'm here. I'm not afraid of dying, but at least I can do something to clean up the mess we made."

In one of her final interviews, Karen Pitts was asked, "Would you do it again? "I was brought up to tell the truth," she said. "When your government asks you questions, you're supposed to answer them honestly. I couldn't live with myself if I didn't do that."

In 2004 Jacque returned to Colorado to join former grand jury foreman Wes McKinley and FBI agent Jon Lipsky for a press conference in Denver. The rally was to protest plans to open the Rocky Flats National Wildlife Refuge to the public despite the fact that contamination remained on-site and off-site, and there were continuing reports of residents who were ill.

After years of fighting thyroid cancer and other illnesses, Jacque Brever died in 2015 at the age of 58.

Nearly every house in our neighborhood had cancer.

Back in the spring of 1968, just after we moved into our new house, there was a fire in Building 771. Denver came very close to a Chernobyl-like total disaster, and a radioactive plume traveled over my neighborhood and over the entire metro area. There was no warning, no evacuation, no information available to the public. My family was sitting outdoors having Mother's Day brunch on the day the radioactive cloud floated over our heads. Most people never knew about this fire, or any of the other accidents and spills at Rocky Flats. Even when the Cold War ended, the plant was shrouded in secrecy.

By this time there had been many fires – more than 200 – at Rocky Flats. The worst was on September 11, 1957, when a fire occurred in one of the gloveboxes and set the entire line of gloveboxes ablaze. At the time, it was the largest industrial fire in the history of the United States – and the primary contaminant was plutonium. The fire was so extreme it burned out the filters and measuring equipment, so it will never be known exactly how much radioactive and toxic contamination spread over the Denver area, but two years later there was an increase in childhood leukemia. There has never been an epidemiological study of public health in the area around Rocky Flats, so even now it's difficult to determine precisely how the metro Denver community has been affected by the plant's activities.

The first well-known incident of cancer in my neighborhood was Kristin Haag, the daughter of the home builder who designed our house, Rex Haag. Kristin was diagnosed with bone cancer when she was eleven. Her leg was amputated, but the treatment was unsuccessful, and she died a few months later. Aware of the fires and off-site contamination and concerned about how much time his daughter had spent playing outdoors in their backyard, Rex Haag tried to sue Rocky Flats. But the suit never got very far. People in the neighborhood whispered about how it was "God's will" that the child had died. Mr. Haag was just looking for a scapegoat, they said.

My fifth-grade crush was a brown-eyed boy with sandy hair who lived just up the street from our house. He had a red dirt bike and was almost as shy as I was. We stood at the bus stop together each school morning and silently blushed. When he was diagnosed with testicular cancer, his family packed up and moved away.

The stories grew. Another school friend and neighbor who lived up the street had a thyroid tumor removed at age seventeen. Later, in his early thirties, he had prostate cancer. The Smith family lived just around the edge of Standley Lake, not far from our house and directly downwind from Rocky Flats. They liked to live off the land and raise their own vegetables. Tamara Smith was in her early twenties when she was diagnosed with brain cancer, and she's now lived for more than a decade with recurring brain tumors, cancer, and brain surgeries. Her doctors in Colorado and New York feel certain her illness is tied to Rocky Flats

But people around Rocky Flats don't like to talk about cancer and illness. They take it personally. Coloradans are supposed to be tough – especially if you worked at the plant and consider yourself a "Cold War Warrior." If you get sick, it's your own damn fault. It's probably because you smoked, or got too much sun, or inherited a bad gene somewhere. It's bad form, a kind of personal failing, to look for blame. And besides, even if contamination from Rocky Flats does cause cancer, there's no way to prove it. Or so people say.

Jacque Brever and Karen Pitts were blamed by many of their coworkers for leaking information to the FBI that led to the raid, but that action belongs to other workers – workers like Jim Stone.

Following a family tragedy, Jim Stone and his sister were raised in an orphanage. Educated by nuns, he went on to serve in the army and then earned a graduate degree in engineering.

Hired in 1952 to help design Rocky Flats before it even opened, Jim Stone was ultimately fired for doing exactly what he was hired to do. A trained and experienced engineer, Jim Stone was employed to work on power and ventilation systems for the plutonium-processing buildings and to be a troubleshooter. His job was to prepare weekly reports that identified key problems and then recommend how they should be fixed.

He found plenty of trouble.

Stone's first warning was about the location of the plant itself. Rocky Flats had a unique problem. Other nuclear weapons sites, such as Los Alamos in New Mexico, were relatively distant from high population areas and kept their workers on-site. At Rocky Flats, the presence of a nuclear weapons factory would pose a significant danger to the local population – the plant could contaminate residential areas, and it was number one on the Soviet hit list – but the plant also needed local workers. Lots of workers. Stone warned against the location of Rocky Flats "because Denver is downwind a few miles away."

The Department of Energy ignored his warning.

Stone then pointed out that the original site plans were based on faulty information regarding wind patterns. The DOE had used wind maps from Stapleton Airport, which was far on the other side of Denver. Those patterns had little to do with the fast-moving chinook winds that roared down the canyons and would carry any contamination from the site directly over the metro Denver area.

The Department of Energy ignored his warning.

Over the years, Jim Stone took issue with a number of things. There was too much radioactive waste stored at the plant – 13.2 metric tons, to be exact – and Rockwell had a hard time figuring out what to do with it. This included not only plutonium in drums and containers but also liquid from contaminated pond water that was being sprayed through an irrigation pump onto fields of grass. This water then traveled into local streams, lakes, and residential areas. Monitoring of water wells was inadequate.

Stone further noted that plutonium was clogged in the ductwork of the plutonium-processing buildings, with most of the piping underground. And the company continued to burn plutonium-contaminated waste in an incinerator that wasn't properly licensed or filtered, and those contaminants were floating up into the Colorado sky.

But the problem that worried Stone the most was "pondcrete," a desperate effort by the plant to deal with overflowing radioactive waste. Beginning in the 1950s, Rocky Flats stored liquid hazardous waste in five shallow human-made ponds, similar to small swimming pools. This liquid, low-level radioactive waste was then poured into large ponds, where it was heated by the sun to evaporate moisture and reduce its overall weight. The DOE wanted the ponds phased out. Rockwell intended to mix the toxic sludge from the ponds with concrete in order to immobilize it and then pour the toxic pudding into plastic lined cardboard boxes the size of small refrigerators.

In October 1982 Stone sent a memo to Rockwell's management. Pondcrete was not going to work, he wrote. The cement will not harden and the plutonium will not stabilize. He was warned by his coworkers. "Don't rock the boat!" they said. But Stone was adamant. His job was to tell Rockwell what they needed to know, whether they liked it or not.

Rockwell ignored his warning.

Despite Stone's strongly worded memos, Rockwell decided to go ahead and manufacture pondcrete. But, just as Stone had warned, the plutonium pudding never gelled. Like huge soggy Lego blocks, 12,000 one-ton ton blocks of pondcrete stood out in the open air, unprotected from sun, wind, and snow. In a few months they started falling apart, and toxic liquid containing nitrates, cadmium, and low-level radioactive waste leaked and leeched into the ground, where it ran downhill to Walnut Creek, Woman Creek, and local neighborhoods. Stone was told by Rockwell not to tell the Department of Energy.

Nevertheless he continued his work. Then one morning during a meeting, there was a knock on the office door. A Rockwell manager and a security guard stood on the other side. "You have one hour to leave," he was told. Jim Stone was stunned. Under the watch of an armed guard, he gathered a few things from his office and was forced to turn in his security badge. He would never work again in the nuclear weapons industry.

Eventually, 16,500 one-ton pondcrete blocks were stacked on the asphalt pad, exposed to the elements, just upwind of Arvada, Broomfield, and the city of Denver.

When the FBI and EPA began preparing for the raid on Rocky Flats, they called Jim Stone. He'd been waiting for a call like this. A calm, polite, slightly stout man wearing a fedora, Jim Stone didn't look much like an activist or a troublemaker. But he described in detail everything he knew, dating all the way back to the early days of Rocky Flats. "They blackballed me," he added. "The industry is spooky about whistleblowers. But I don't see myself as a whistleblower. I see myself as a good engineer."

Jim Stone took the stand during the grand jury investigation and talked about pondcrete, the incinerator, and the spray fields. He discussed the plutonium in the air duct pipes and how there was enough lost radioactive material in those pipes and ducts to make several bombs. He was one of the driving forces behind the raid and subsequent grand jury investigation.

Stone's courage and truthfulness on the stand contributed significantly to Rockwell's guilty plea and the eventual closing of the plant. But his career was ruined. He filed a whistleblower lawsuit under the False Claims Act, designed to help recover billions of dollars stolen by government contractors. This act includes a provision that allows citizens who know of fraud to sue contractors on behalf of the government. In 1999 Stone won a $4.2 million judgment against Rockwell. He had sued along with the federal government to recover environmental cleanup costs and bonuses paid to Rockwell. As part of the lawsuit, he produced his 1982 order in which he explained how mixing toxins in cement to create solid blocks "would result in an unstable mixture that would later deteriorate and cause unwanted release of toxic wastes to the environment." This was exactly what happened.

But after eighteen years of legal wrangling with Rockwell in several different courts, the Supreme Court decided 6–2 against Stone based on the court's strict definition of who is an "original source," a prerequisite to filing a federal whistleblower lawsuit. The citizen, who must have "original knowledge" of fraud, can share in any funds recovered. But Rockwell defended itself by claiming Stone was not the only source of knowledge, and thus technically he was not due any compensation.

Many in the legal community felt this decision was not only an affront to the legacy of an engineer whose career was ruined by his decision to step forward, but that it would also discourage others from calling attention to government waste and fraud. "Fewer whistleblowers are going to come forward to take action," predicted James Moorman, president of Taxpayers Against Fraud, a nonprofit that guides whistleblowers and lawyers.

When Jim Stone died in 2007 of Alzheimer's at the age of eighty-two, most of the world had forgotten who he was.

The world has also nearly forgotten the work of Dr. Carl Johnson – perhaps the most important character in the sad saga of Rocky Flats. Carl Johnson was hired as the health director of Jefferson County, which included Rocky Flats and its surrounding neighborhoods, in 1976. This was a tumultuous time, particularly at Rocky Flats – the first big national protest at the plant had attracted tens of thousands of people from all over the country. From his first day on the job, Johnson was faced with serious public health and public relations problems.

Like Jim Stone, Carl Johnson had a rough start in life. Born in Indiana in 1929, at age twelve he was diagnosed with tuberculosis. But he was determined to live a normal life. He began working out and lifting weights and focused on eating a healthy diet. His health improved and he went on to serve in the army and then attend Michigan State University, Ohio State University College of Medicine, and the University of California–Berkeley, where he received a master's degree in public health.

As soon as Johnson took office, home builders who wanted to build near the Rocky Flats plant approached him. The land, once relatively remote, was ideally located between Denver and Boulder, and it afforded prime real estate for developers. Jefferson County was one of the fastest growing areas in the country.

Based on citizen complaints of cancers and health issues, Johnson refused to provide permits and declared that soil testing for plutonium had to be done before any home development moved forward. With support from the National Institute of Health, the testing found forty-four times more plutonium in the soil than the DOE admitted to. Based on further testing, in 1977 Johnson found higher-than-average rates of leukemia and cancer in local residents. He continued to oppose development. In 1980 he began to focus on the workers at Rocky Flats as well, and he found that they had had eight times more brain tumors than should be expected. He insisted that more studies were needed.

Asked to testify in a lawsuit filed by unhappy landowners who believed their health and their properties had been negatively impacted by Rocky Flats, Johnson stated on the witness stand that he felt there was a serious cover-up going on at the plant. Testing had discovered the presence of plutonium and cesium in local neighborhoods, and he and other specialists testified that this was likely the result of a single criticality incident – a nuclear chain reaction – at the plant, a charge the DOE had long denied. Johnson recommended additional testing of soil samples and analysis of forage, vegetables, and other fresh produce in the area, as well as evaluation of livestock and milk and testing of air, groundwater, and water in reservoirs. He also felt there should be a full and adequate public Emergency Response Plan in place if there was an accident at Rocky Flats or if the plant was subject to a nuclear strike from another country. Johnson stood his ground in interviews with the press.

That was not what home developers wanted to hear, however. The chairman of the Jefferson County Board of Health favored home development in the county, and stated that Johnson should not have released his findings to the public but rather only to specific agencies that had been approved by the board. Johnson disagreed and said there had been no such restriction. He felt that the public needed to know about past and ongoing radioactive contamination at Rocky Flats, particularly those people who lived within 10 miles of the plant or were thinking of buying new homes. "A radioactive plume," he said, "is similar to a dust storm, and plutonium is likely to lodge in windowsills, breaks, and cracks in wood. It's not just a matter of a sort of gaseous cloud passing overhead that will dissipate. We're talking about particles that drop to the ground and remain dangerously radioactive. Even getting in the car and rolling up the windows may be safer than staying indoors." Johnson also believed the government's levels for acceptable plutonium exposures were far too high and would result in the rise of radiation-related cancers.

The Jefferson County Board of Health and home developers had by now had enough. The chair appointed a new member to the board for the express purpose of firing Johnson, which was done in 1981. Due to the harassment he and his family endured, Johnson decided to accept a job as health director in another state. But he didn't give up. He continued his studies and became an internationally renowned expert on the effects of radiation. Carl Johnson's work included a significant study of people in Utah, the "downwinders" – those who were subject to the fallout from nuclear bomb testing in the 1950s and 1960s. This study, and his studies on Rocky Flats, were published in respectable scientific journals.

Further, Carl Johnson filed a whistleblower lawsuit against Jefferson County, Colorado – and won. The Colorado State Supreme Court commissioners settled with Johnson for $150,000. The money was not important, but the moral victory was huge. Still, few people in Colorado knew that Johnson had won his battle. The victory attracted very little press coverage.

The stress on Johnson had taken its toll, but he kept fighting. On December 18, 1988, he published an article in the *New York Times* entitled "Rocky Flats: Death Inc." His words were damning. "The actual number of people who have been injured or died because of the operations of Rocky Flats can never be fully known," he wrote. He continued,

> Thus, communities near nuclear weapons and nuclear power facilities must insist on detailed investigations of all activities and emissions. I was a whistleblower... I was forced out of office. If the nation is to be properly protected, all studies of nuclear contamination and associate health packs should be conducted primarily by independent scientists who are insulated from cynical retaliation from a nuclear establishment as well as advocates of urban development.

Eleven days later, the man who had overcome tuberculosis as a child died of complications from heart surgery at age of fifty-nine. He was buried with military honors at Fort Logan National Cemetery in Denver.

Rocky Flats was a death sentence for many, regardless of politics or status. Thousands of Coloradans worked at Rocky Flats and many became ill. More than 4,000 workers and their families applied for government compensation for deaths and illnesses, but the process has been difficult and convoluted. After years of trying to get numerous presidents and cabinet secretaries to address the workers' concerns, in 2014 the Obama administration took steps to ensure that many Rocky Flats workers were able to more easily secure the care they needed under the Energy Employees Occupational Illness and Compensation Program Act. Illnesses that were covered included leukemia, lymphomas, and multiple myeloma; cancers of the lung, brain, bones, breast, ovary, esophagus, stomach, colon, small intestine, urinary, bladder, renal system, bile ducts, gall bladder, salivary gland, pharynx, thyroid, pancreas and liver; and chronic beryllium disease and chronic silicosis.

Even many of the managers at Rocky Flats, some of whom even refused to go into the "hot" areas, became ill. Dominic Sanchini worked for Rockwell for decades as a rocket scientist before taking a position as DOE manager at Rocky Flats for two years, including during the raid. A year and a half after the raid, he died at age sixty-three after a brief struggle with cancer. Mark Silverman, a West Point–trained engineer, became DOE manager at Rocky Flats in 1993. He understood more than anyone how much radioactive waste was unsafely stored at Rocky Flats. "We may have done too good of a job convincing the public that we're doing things safely at the site," he said in an interview with the press. "As a result, people aren't so concerned about the site. If the people don't care, the elected officials don't care, and if the elected officials don't care, we can't get the funding to do the job out here." Silverman stepped down from his position in April 1996 when he was fifty-seven because he felt the job was taking too big a toll on his personal life. Four years later Silverman was diagnosed with an inoperable brain tumor and died not long after.

But there has never been any compensation or public health monitoring for people who live around Rocky Flats. There is no hotline, no clinic, nowhere for people to turn for help and information.

Later, like many of the people in my neighborhood, I went to work at Rocky Flats myself. I was a single parent of two young boys, putting myself through graduate school at the University of Denver. The job had what I needed: a good hourly wage, flexible hours, and benefits. And I knew scores of people who had worked there. It seemed to be a good opportunity, at least until I finished school.

As a writer, my job was to meet with managers and project managers and prepare reports that were sent on to Albuquerque, New Mexico; Washington D.C.; and other Department of Energy offices. I began to understand what was really going on at Rocky Flats. I made friends with people who worked in the hot areas of the plant, and others who worked in administration or management. I heard lots of stories, including stories of local residents – farmers, ranchers, new homeowners in the newly developing suburbs – who were ill.

My own health took a turn for the worse. I began to experience fevers, swelling, enlarged lymph nodes, and extreme fatigue. I went from doctor to doctor and received various diagnoses: chronic fatigue syndrome, fibromyalgia, allergies. "It's mostly in your head," one doctor said. But I'd always been healthy and athletic. It didn't make sense. My symptoms worsened. Finally, a physician at National Jewish Hospital said it was likely lymphoma or Hodgkin's disease. I would need biopsies and surgery, and he asked me to think about who might be able to raise my children if things went badly.

I had the surgery just days before my PhD dissertation defense. I showed up in front of my examination committee freshly bandaged and with a heavy brace around my neck. I was determined to graduate.

I quit my job at Rocky Flats. The day I quit was the day I knew I would write a book – a book that would eventually involve more than ten years of research, including extensive archival research, and hundreds of interviews. It was a book that many people at Rocky Flats said could never be published. "Let sleeping dogs lie," they said. "Don't rock the boat."

Today, that book has been read by people all over the world. It's a standard text in many university classrooms. I moved away to take a new teaching job, and my health slowly – but never fully – improved.

I've taught at universities all over the country, yet my heart will always be in Colorado.

The fight over Rocky Flats continues. The Department of Energy and US Fish and Wildlife Service have now opened the "Rocky Flats National Wildlife Refuge" for public hiking, biking, and – unbelievably – field trips for local school groups. Yet toxic and radioactive contamination remains, and 1,300 acres of the 5,000-acre site, now a Superfund site, is so profoundly contaminated with plutonium that it can never open to the public and the rest of the site is controversial. Attorneys representing environmental groups argue the U.S. Fish and Wildlife Service neglected federal environmental regulations when planning to open the site. Numerous grassroots organizations, including the Rocky Mountain Peace and Justice Center, Rocky Flats Right to Know, Rocky Flats Downwinders, Candelas Glows, and others actively oppose opening the Rocky Flats site to the public as well as home development near the site. Based on recent, potentially dangerous contamination measurements, several neighboring counties have barred school groups from visiting the site.

I grew up riding my horse across those fields, swimming in Standley Lake, climbing in the foothills and deep blue mountains that form the backdrop for this beautiful prairie land. This is my land, this is your land, this is our land. We have poisoned it and it breaks my heart. But plutonium has a half-life of 24,000 years and we must face this heavy legacy. The best we can do is to prevent our children and grandchildren from paying for our mistakes with their health and with their lives.

I am an activist. And no longer an accidental one.

Works Cited

Sources for this essay include extensive interviews with Jacqueline Brever, Jim Stone, Jon Lipsky, and other Rocky Flats workers and activists archived at the Maria Rogers Oral History Program of the Carnegie Library, Boulder Public Library, Boulder, Colorado.

"A Sad Final Note for Flats Whistleblower: An Engineer Who Helped Expose Problems at the Former Nuclear Plant Deserves Thanks," *Denver Post*, March 28, 2007.

Ackland, Len. "A Dump Called Rocky Flats." *The Bulletin of the Atomic Scientists* 11, no. 2 (Nov./Dec. 1994): 12–13.

Brever, Jacqueline. "Nuclear Whistleblower," *The Progressive*, 1993.

———. "Inside Rocky Flats: A Whistleblower's Journal," *Harper's Magazine*, Feb. 1992.

Frank, Laura, and Ann Imse. "Rocky Flats Whistleblower Dies at 82," *Rocky Mountain News*, Apr. 12, 2007.

Gallo, Nick. "Bitter Truth: They Risked Their Jobs, Their Happiness, Even Their Lives." *Family Circle*, Apr. 21, 1992.

Johnson, Carl J. "Rocky Flats: Death, Inc." *The New York Times*, Dec. 18, 1988.

Lemonick, Michael D. "Rocky Horror Show: Why Can't Rocky Flats' Plutonium Be Cleaned Up?" *Time*, Nov. 27, 1995.

———. "Sometimes It Takes a Cowboy," *Time*, Jan. 25, 1993.

Lippman, Thomas W. "Two Women at Rocky Flats Plant Tell of Intimidation, Safety Violations," *Denver Post*, Dec. 28, 1991.

"Rocky Flats Whistleblower Wins Suit Against Rockwell, *Denver Post*, Apr. 12, 2007.

"The Rocky Flats Cover-Up: Continued," *Harper's Magazine*, Dec. 1992.

Rothstein, Linda. "Yes, Haste Made Waste: The FBI's Raid on Rocky Flats Uncovered a Toxic Disaster – and a Management That Didn't Need to Care." *The Bulletin of Atomic Scientists* 51, no. 3 (May/June 1995): 14–15.

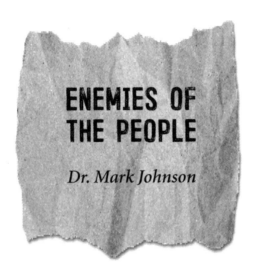

ENEMIES OF THE PEOPLE

Dr. Mark Johnson

"You killed my husband!"

"You and Jefferson County killed my husband!" The woman on the telephone was almost screaming now. The emotional anger and mental agony were palpable as she spat the words at me. "I will never talk to you or anyone from Jefferson County," she shouted as she slammed her telephone receiver down.

It was the summer of 1990. I had recently been appointed as the executive director of the Jefferson County Health Department. Jefferson County, metropolitan Denver's gateway to the Rocky Mountains, contained the Rocky Flats Plant, the US Department of Energy's (DOE) industrial site that made plutonium triggers for nuclear bombs. It had been a year since Operation Desert Glow, the raid on the Rocky Flats Plant by the FBI and the US Environmental Protection Agency (EPA). As the government official statutorily responsible for protecting the health of Jefferson County's residents, I was trying to learn all I could about the nuclear weapons fabrication site and its potential impact on the health of the community.

I knew little about Rocky Flats when I took the job. I had dated a girl from Boulder in the late 1960s who had pointed it out to me one day as we drove by on US Highway 93. "That's where they make atomic bombs," she said. I couldn't see anything of interest going on there. I had also heard about the antinuclear protesters who had picketed Rocky Flats. I thought it was ironic that they had not been able to surround the plant when they attempted to hold hands and form a human chain around it. That was about all I knew about Rocky Flats until I applied for the job in Jefferson County.

I subsequently learned that Rocky Flats was a very controversial place. In fact, Rocky Flats should never have been built. Its proximity upwind from a large population center, with prevailing winds moving in that direction, as well as its history of not-infrequent hurricane-force winds should have disqualified the site before it was ever chosen. Allegedly, those assigned to find a site for an atomic bomb trigger facility used wind maps from Stapleton Airport, on the east side of Denver, instead of wind maps from Rocky Flats. Fires at the plant, as well as leakage from drums stored on-site that were full of radioactive and hazardous waste, were known to have contaminated the site and the surrounding environs. The controversy was around how much contamination had taken place and how dangerous it might be. It still is.

I had read about some of the demonstrations that occurred in the 1970s, and I had seen pictures of some of the protestors sitting on the railroad tracks to stop the trains going in and out of the site. I also learned a bit about the FBI and EPA raid on Rocky Flats, one based on insiders' claims that environmental crimes were being committed, but I knew nothing about the work that had been done there or the scope of the criminal activity being alleged. I knew there were growing concerns in the country about nuclear and hazardous waste contamination and disposal, but I was not aware how these might be affecting the health of the residents of Jefferson County – and the greater Denver area.

When I accepted the position in Jefferson County, my new administrative assistant asked me two questions before I officially began my duties: Would I be willing to review the county's new policies on dealing with employees with AIDS, and would I like to have my name submitted to be on the Governor's Health Advisory Panel, the task force being formed to look into the potential health impact of the situation at Rocky Flats? I said yes to both questions.

The next time we spoke, my assistant told me she had been informed by the Colorado Department of Health that membership of the Health Advisory Panel had already been determined, but I was welcome to attend their meetings as an observer. She then said something that I didn't understand at the time. "They probably think you're related to Carl Johnson."

I had never heard of Carl Johnson.

From 1973 until 1981 Dr. Carl J. Johnson (no relation) was the director of the Jefferson County Health Department, where he had had a very rocky tenure. In 1974 the chair of the County Commissioners asked his opinion about a proposal to rezone several square miles of ranchland near Rocky Flats for residential development. The request had already been approved by federal agencies and the Colorado Department of Health. After conferring with Dr. Edward Martell at the National Center for Atmospheric Research in Boulder, Colorado, Johnson recommended against the proposal. According to Dr. Martell, the soil in the area had been found to have plutonium contamination that was seven times higher than what was permitted by the state health department's guidelines for construction workers' exposure. Based in large part on Dr. Johnson's recommendation, the commissioners did not approve the zoning permit request.

Carl Johnson went on to extensively study the contamination around Rocky Flats and its effects on the health of those living near it. Using cancer diagnosis data from the National Cancer Institute and plutonium exposures based on analysis of a group of soil samples collected in neighborhoods and ranches around Rocky Flats, he concluded that plutonium contamination of the soil around the plant was indeed very high and that numerous cancer types for persons living in exposed areas were much higher than expected when compared with control subjects living farther away. His studies also implicated the Rocky Flats Plant as the source of increased rates of malformations in the animals living near it.

In my first few months as the executive director of the Health Department, I read as many of Carl Johnson's studies as I could find and learned much about his own tenure as the director. In 1981 he resigned in lieu of being fired by the Board of Health but subsequently sued them to be reinstated in his position. He was not reinstated but had finally been convinced to take what his attorney considered a generous monetary offer from the Board of Health to drop his claims. His lawsuits against the Jefferson County Board of Health and County Commissioners established several technical legal precedents for public health law in Colorado that are still widely referenced in the Colorado statutes. I would love to have talked to him about his experiences, but, unfortunately, he died in 1988, at the relatively young age of fifty-nine, from surgical complications for coronary heart disease.

I learned rather quickly that Rocky Flats was a major topic of conversation in Jefferson County. The recent raid on the plant and the subsequent media and legal interests had raised many questions about what it all meant for the county's residents. In fact, during the first few months in my new job I was asked to give several public presentations on Rocky Flats and its impact on the health of the community, so I needed to do a great deal of research to try to catch up with events. Almost everything I could find in the scientific literature supported the US federal agencies' claims that very little contamination had occurred off the Rocky Flats site, and that there was no discernable increase in diseases related to exposure to Rocky Flats, other than some unique conditions among some of the plant's workers. Carl Johnson's work was severely criticized as having been produced by an amateur investigator with a political agenda, and statements were made asserting that recent, more sound research had invalidated his key findings. Hoping to get more information regarding his work and his history with the department, it seemed like a good idea to contact his wife.

It was not a good idea.

The woman with whom I had spoken on the telephone was Carl Johnson's justifiably enraged widow. She clearly felt that her husband's early demise was directly related to the stress he had suffered in his battles with the boards of Jefferson County. Her chilling and indignant response accentuated the tragedy through which she had lived. She well knew that her husband's activities had enraged powerful political and commercial forces in Colorado, and that the state and federal governmental agencies had done what they could to portray him as a prototypical "enemy of the people." She grieved that the reputation of her husband, whom she knew was a good man, had been so badly tarnished.

The term "enemy of the people" has a long and storied past. It apparently originated in Roman times as *hostis publicus*, or "public enemy." Shakespeare used it in the play *Coriolanus* as one common citizen's description of a wealthy senator. The citizen claimed that if the mob would just kill the senator, who was an enemy of the people, they could have corn at their own price. The term has been used more recently by the

Nazis in Germany, the leaders of the Soviet Union, and China, and as an epithet against the media by President Donald Trump.

Perhaps the most applicable use of the term for this chapter is found in Henrik Ibsen's 1882 play entitled *An Enemy of the People*. The story plot may sound familiar. A public health physician discovers a source of contamination that he believes is of great danger to the health of the community. The source, however, provides the community with numerous well-paying jobs, an improving local economy, and an illustrious civic reputation. While many in the community initially side with the physician in his quest to contain the pollution, over time, as more and more individuals realize what this will mean to their own personal prosperity, the community turns on him. For his honesty he is eventually persecuted, ridiculed, and declared an "enemy of the people" by the townspeople, including some of those who had originally been his closest allies. To those with whom I spoke in Jefferson County government, Carl Johnson had indeed been viewed as another enemy of the people.

In my quest to educate myself about Rocky Flats and the country's nuclear program, I was soon reminded of some of the difficulties I had had in my college physics classes understanding the world of quantum mechanics. Comprehending descriptions of nature at the smallest scale and the levels of energy held in atoms and subatomic particles had not come easily to me. Complicating things even further, not only is the way radioactive substances interact with objects and the human body complex, it seemed to me that the physicists who worked in this field had gone out of their way to make things as obscure as possible to the average person. I could begin to understand the differences between alpha-, beta-, gamma-, and x-rays and how they each have different effects on the human body, but the nomenclature used to describe their nature and activities was bewildering.

There are two major scientific classifications of measurements, English, or imperial, units and the International System of Units, or the *Système International D'unités* (SI). Measuring radiation in these two systems includes terms such as roentgens (R), coulombs/kilogram (C/kg), curies (Ci), becquerels (Bq), rads, grays (Gy), rems, sieverts (Sv), and disintegrations per minute. Because there is a move in the scientific community to replace one system with another, these terms are deliberately duplicative, but each conversion between systems has a different formula or conversion factor. Each system also has its own way of describing the special ways radioactivity moves, exposes things, and is absorbed by objects and beings. Unfortunately, some authors move back and forth between the systems in their writings, making things even more confusing. The mathematics involved in quantum physics is also incredibly challenging, traveling from the smallest of extremes in size to gigantic measures of energy.

In an attempt to make sense of it all, someone came up with the acronym "R-E-A-D." The "R" stands for radioactivity, which is the ionized radiation released by a material, and is measured in curies (Ci) or becquerels (Bq). The "E" represents the exposure, which is the radiation traveling through the air, measured in roentgens (R) or coulombs/kilogram (C/kg). "A" is the absorbed dose, the radiation that is absorbed by an object or a person, measured in rads or grays (Gy). The "D" corresponds to the dose equivalent, the combined amount of radiation absorbed and the medical effects of that type of radiation. It is measured in rems and sieverts (Sv).

Explaining to most people what this means to them personally is almost impossible. Comparisons to the radiation exposure encountered during a medical procedure, such as a chest x-ray or a CT scan of the body, are often used. If you are exposed to 155 mrem (millirem), it's like having a whole-body CT scan. If you are exposed to 155 sieverts, it is like getting 1,550,000 chest x-rays. More significantly, you'd be instantly vaporized. (This claim is widely debated by physicists on the internet, but for this purpose I think the term works). This is the dose of radiation that hit the ground directly underneath the atomic blast at Hiroshima.

The reason we have systems of nomenclature is to simplify and stabilize the naming of objects to improve human communication. As a physician, however, I know this is not always the case. The language of medicine does, indeed, improve communication between medical clinicians, but it is also purposefully used at times to obscure things from patients, families, insurance companies, and the uninitiated. In my search to make sense out of radiation physics and quantum mechanics I became convinced that the same thing was being done by nuclear scientists to keep the rest of us in the dark.

One thing I have learned in my life is that I am not good at ascertaining other people's motives. In studying the history of the discovery and subsequent use of radioactive materials, I have concluded that, for the most part, mistakes and miscalculations were made from ignorance more often than malevolence. Although there was often an unwarranted level of arrogance and hubris exhibited by the scientists, politicians, and military advisers involved in this effort, I believe that most of the disastrous errors that occurred were caused by general unfamiliarity with the substances with which they were working. This was clearly true of a number of deaths that occurred early in the era of radiation. Even with the United States' use of nuclear weapons in Japan to end World War II, physicians and scientists were unaware of the extent of physical and pathological signs, symptoms, and diseases that would occur in the exposed populations.

The clandestine nature of the work at Rocky Flats could be justified – to a point. The Russians' detonation of an atomic bomb in 1949 and a hydrogen bomb in 1955, along with their technological advances, as evidenced by the launching of the Sputnik satellite in 1957, sent shock waves through the US military establishment. The Cold War, with its race for a stockpile of atomic weapons, was on. Workers at Rocky Flats had every right to be proud of the historic labor in which they were involved. Initially, the drive to produce as many bomb triggers as possible as fast as possible had some degree of justification. Over time, however, as the contractors at Rocky Flats learned more and more about the dangers of contamination and the difficulty of hazardous and nuclear waste disposal, it seems to me that greed and fear of discovery overtook patriotism as the incentive for secrecy.

Over the years, I learned an increasing amount about the secrecy surrounding the nation's nuclear program – including the mining, milling, testing, refining, and fabrication of the components for atomic weapons – and the obfuscation enveloping the storage and disposal of the nuclear and hazardous waste that accumulate in these processes. As a result I came to believe that the government and its commercial contractors intentionally used both an unhealthy mix of patriotic zeal and the complexity of describing the work being done as a smokescreen to keep the uninitiated citizenry from knowing what was going on at Rocky Flats.

When I moved to Jefferson County I felt I was open-minded regarding Rocky Flats and the nation's nuclear weapons program. What I didn't recognize at the time was that I brought and formed several significant biases and attitudes that influenced my approach to this issue.

I was pronuclear.

Welcome sign for visitors to Grand Junction in the 1950s.
©Museums of Western Colorado.

I grew up in Grand Junction, Colorado, a city that used an atomic isotope symbol for a logo and was the commercial heart of the nuclear-industrial complex of the Colorado Plateau. Grand Junction had been a central part of the Manhattan Project's secret effort to mine and refine domestic uranium. It was the home of the only domestic procurement program for uranium, and the site of a large uranium processing mill. While the parents of some of my classmates labored for the Union Mines Development Corporation, a front for Union Carbide's classified work with uranium, and experimented on uranium milling and processing techniques for the United States Atomic Energy Commission, their children and I sat in classrooms, played on playgrounds, and golfed on golf courses built on radioactive uranium sand and soil – the "tailings" from the "yellowcake towns"[1] that surrounded us.

We were proud of the role our town was playing in the Cold War against communism. It was only years later, when these friends and classmates began being diagnosed with cancer, and I found that I myself had a brain tumor, that I began to question the overall cost of growing up in "The City That Glows."

I also grew up listening to my father's stories of World War II. He was one of the soldiers scheduled to be among the first wave in the occupation of Japan in the summer of 1945. His unit had been told by their commanding officers that it was anticipated that a million American soldiers would die in the battles of the occupation. Numerous times during my childhood my father told me, "If it wasn't for the atomic bomb, you never would have been born." I was definitely pronuclear.

I was also progovernment.

That may not be the best way to describe this sentiment. It's kind of a mixture of proscience, progovernment, and anticonspiracy theory. I had done my postgraduate medical studies in Baltimore, Maryland. Many of our lectures had been given by federal government scientists, and many field trips were taken to government facilities. Most of the research papers and studies we reviewed and dissected were written by scientists from the Centers for Disease Control and Prevention and the National Institutes of Health, and several of my classmates went on to work for these federal institutions. I had also worked for the state health department in Wyoming and done elective rotations with the Colorado Department of Health. It had been my experience that both the federal and state health employees with whom I interacted were intelligent, serious scientists with great integrity, who believed in the scientific method and who were simply searching for fact-based evidence in their work.

I was skeptical of conspiracy theories, and my default position was to believe the government. I believed Oswald assassinated Kennedy and that the Warren Report was not a cover-up. I believed we had sent men to the moon. I did not believe the government was hiding UFOs and extraterrestrials at Area 51 in Nevada. I believed AIDS was caused by a natural virus, and that the CIA had had nothing to do with its manufacture or spread. I also believed that the USSR was a nuclear threat, that our stockpile of nuclear weapons was helping to deter World War III, and that our government would take good care of those who were working in these industries to protect us.

I soon became anti–Dr. Carl Johnson – at least for a while.

I am embarrassed to say this, but it is true. I had never met the man, but from my limited knowledge of his work in Jefferson County, I found myself siding with his critics. Many of those who had denounced his scientific work and methods were themselves, for the most part, credible physicists and nuclear scientists. Also, as I reviewed his work in Jefferson County, I tended to agree with those who felt he had focused too much attention on Rocky Flats and not enough time on the leading causes of death, disease, and disability in the county. It appeared to me that he had become consumed with Rocky Flats to the detriment of other important health issues such as tobacco-related diseases and the health impacts of other personal behaviors and lifestyle choices. It seemed he had neglected dealing with and preventing the negative consequences of important social determinants of health such as poverty, access to health care, education, health equity, and nonnuclear environmental factors.

I also have to admit that it hurt my professional pride to be constantly and negatively compared to Dr. Carl Johnson by his numerous devotees. Most of his detractors had moved on to other things, so almost all of the public appraisals contrasting him with me were from those who strongly admired him. Most of the comparisons cast me in a negative light. He had heroically battled the political and commercial powers that be. I was supporting a corrupt government-industry enterprise that was poisoning the environment. He was devoted to protecting the health of the residents of Jefferson County. I was only interested in protecting my job. He had invented an innovative new way of sampling dust for radioactivity. I had done… nothing. I got tired of hearing about Dr. Carl Johnson. I also determined that the legacy of my work in Jefferson County would not be related to Rocky Flats.

I found many of the antinuclear community advocates off-putting.

Probably due in large part to my knowledge limitations and the aforementioned biases, I found attendance at most public Rocky Flats meetings very unpleasant. I had been sheltered most of my life from the raw, aggressive, in-your-face approaches that many of the community advocates took in these deliberations. The open distrust of the Colorado Department of Health, the Department of Energy, and its Rocky Flats' contractors was palpable and pervasive. The contentious, and often rude, accusations and allegations made me uncomfortable. The hostile and cynical view they displayed toward the scientific evidence was offensive to me as an epidemiologist. The lack of respect for authority seemed impertinent. Their behavior initially solidified my support for the government's position.

Not all of my attitudes and biases, however, predisposed me toward supporting the work at Rocky Flats. I had an inherent suspicion of business and was wary of politicians.

Growing up in western Colorado I had seen the ecological devastation that had been caused by a century of exploitation of our rich natural resources, mostly by eastern commercial interests. Although as children we loved exploring the old "ghost towns" that had been left behind by the nineteenth-century mining interests and collecting the rusty railroad spikes and whatever pieces of machinery we could carry away, it was obvious even to a child that great damage had been done to our environment. Later, as a history major in college, I learned that this was the dominant underlying theme of history in the American West – eastern commercial interests had always used their money and influence with the federal government to exploit and despoil western lands, peoples, and resources.

Public health as a discipline is also rather agnostic about business in general. While it recognizes the beneficial consequences of a robust economy on the health of populations, from its inception as a distinct field of endeavor it has been fighting with powerful but toxic trades. Beginning with battles against medical quacks and moving up to today's campaigns against the tobacco industry, Big Pharma, and Big Alcohol, public health has had, and made, many powerful commercial adversaries. Conversely, because of its regulatory powers, it is also viewed with disdain and suspicion by many in business. Three popular movies around the turn of the century, *A Civil Action* (1998), *The Insider* (1999), and *Erin Brockovich* (2000), highlighted the mutual levels of distrust between public health and industry.

In addition, public health focuses on prevention, and prevention and politics are natural enemies. While prevention gets a great deal of public lip service, intervention and treatment get the funds. Politicians know instinctively that they need to be seen by their constituents as providing, or at least supporting, immediate, visible solutions. Such actions usually cannot wait for evidence-based data. Further, the impacts of prevention may take decades to be appreciated, while politicians are usually focused on the next election cycle. Politics also depends on public approval polls, whereas public health is often called upon to take unpopular positions.

The more time I spent conversing with politicians and contract managers from Rocky Flats, and the more I learned about the nuclear and hazardous waste pollution occurring around the plant, the more I came

to question the underlying narrative that this was fundamentally a patriotic enterprise protecting America from its enemies. Gradually I came
to view it as an industry that was greatly benefiting from the veil of secrecy and the apparently total level of liability indemnity that was being
supplied to it by the US Department of Energy. Because of this screen
of secrecy and an ultimate lack of accountability, it appeared to me that
the Rocky Flats contractors had contaminated Jefferson County and its
residents indiscriminately with no fear of consequences.

I attended as many of the various Rocky Flats committees and councils as I could work into my schedule, but I soon recognized an interesting pattern. I was welcome to attend, and at times even encouraged to
participate in the deliberations, but decisions on the social and political
issues about Rocky Flats were always passed on to the Board of County
Commissioners and health matters were always assigned to the Colorado
Department of Health. It was made clear, both explicitly and implicitly,
that the Jefferson County Health Department had no role in the oversight of Rocky Flats. The legacy of Carl Johnson cast a long shadow.

To be fair, I can understand some of the reasoning behind this. The
local health department in Jefferson County had no engineering or nuclear physics expertise and no funding with which to obtain any. The
wisdom and the power clearly resided at the federal level. Even the state
health department had limited resources in this area, and the more I
watched the various community groups debate the situation at Rocky
Flats, the more I became convinced that the US Department of Energy
was making the ultimate decisions. Our department continued to monitor the activities, and often we had representatives at the community
meetings, but we rather quickly began to focus our attention on other
areas of public health in Jefferson County where it seemed that we could
have more impact.

Analyzing any public health issue calls for viewing it under the lenses
of what are called the core public health functions: assessment, assurance,
and policy development. The assessment function calls for monitoring
the environment to diagnose and investigate health problems and hazards
in the community. Rocky Flats was clearly a potential health hazard to the
community, but my own review and analysis of the various studies that
had examined the health and disease rates of the surrounding population
did not seem to support elevating it to the level of a major priority for
departmental action. The crass way this is sometimes described is to ask,

"Where are the bodies?" Although I subsequently came to doubt the veracity of much of the data we received regarding Rocky Flats, I trusted the information in the state's cancer registry, and it did not seem to support the presence of a cancer cluster in those living near Rocky Flats, particularly those cancers most closely associated with exposure to plutonium.

Additionally, under the assurance function of public health, if another appropriate entity, such as the state health department, was actively addressing the potential hazard, our department could focus on other health issues in the community. Finally, it was made crystal clear to us by both the state and federal agencies involved that we were not going to play a role in the policy development surrounding the concerns identified at Rocky Flats. So, for many years of my tenure as the executive director, our department focused on preventing the environmental issues related to food service and clean air and water, and the leading causes of death, disability, and disease in Jefferson County, such as those associated with heart disease, stroke, tobacco-related diseases, obesity, and reproductive health.

Although our focus was elsewhere, Rocky Flats continued to weave its way into our work and consciousness. In 1996 we were funded by the DOE to conduct a community health assessment in Arvada with the University of Colorado's School of Nursing. We were invited to have our Environmental Health team inspect their on-site canteen. We were also asked to review and share advice on the plans for a proposed water retention pond that was never completed. But for the most part, our department was minimally involved with the plans and cleanup activities going on at Rocky Flats.

Then in 2009 I received a telephone call from Colorado representative Wes McKinley. Representative McKinley was a cowboy and rancher from Baca County, Colorado, the county in the farthest southeast corner of the state. Although we had never met, I had practiced medicine in Baca County for three years, and Wes and I knew each other by reputation. He had been the foreman on the Rocky Flats grand jury and was still very concerned about the community's exposure to the plant, especially now that it was scheduled to be opened to the public as a national wildlife refuge. He was sponsoring a bill that required posting signs at the entrance to the refuge and wondered if I would be willing to testify in support of it. The signs needed to disclose to the public "information about the presence of, and risks posed by, plutonium and other toxic substances that were used in the production of nuclear weapons" at the site, which would be open for recreation. This seemed prudent, so I told him I would testify.

Before I testified, however, I wanted to know more about Wes McKinley's experience on the grand jury. This led me to search for a copy of the book he had written with attorney Caron Balkany, *The Ambushed Grand Jury: How the Justice Department Covered Up Government Nuclear Crimes and How We Caught Them Red Handed.* I ended up having to order a copy of the book, but while searching for it in a used bookstore in Boulder, I ran across a copy of *Making a Real Killing: Rocky Flats and the Nuclear West,* by Len Ackland. It was the reading of these two books that did the most to change my attitude toward Rocky Flats. They did not move me all the way into the antinuclear activist camp, but they made me reevaluate my stance and become much more skeptical of the official government position. Having now worked with and watched the DOE for several years, I was much more open to claims that they and the US Department of Justice had "conspired" to deceive us.

Representative McKinley's bill was killed in committee, but as I recall, this was where I first met Jon Lipsky, the head agent in the FBI raid on Rocky Flats in 1989. I was struck by the fact that the two men who knew the most about the history of contamination on and around the Rocky Flats plant site were both zealous opponents of opening the refuge to public visitors. It gave me pause and made me wonder what they knew that the rest of us were prohibited by court order from learning.

On October 13, 2005, the site contractor at Rocky Flats declared cleanup of the site complete. Substantial on- and off-site contamination consisting of plutonium, beryllium, and other hazardous substances, along with unknown quantities and chemical configurations of plutonium remaining in the site's piping and tanks, had made this one of the most significant and challenging nuclear weapons plant cleanups to date. A project that had originally been estimated by the DOE to take up to sixty-five years at a cost of $37 billion had been completed in fewer than ten years at a cost of $7 billion. Interestingly, this was the exact amount that Congress had appropriated for the cleanup. The Central Operating Unit, where most of the industrial buildings and work had been done, was the only site on which remediation took place. It was still determined to be too contaminated for public access. The DOE Office of Legacy Management is responsible for the maintenance and long-term surveillance of this portion of the site.

Congress had approved the Rocky Flats National Wildlife Refuge Act in 2001, allowing for the establishment of a wildlife refuge in the security buffer zone, or Peripheral Operating Unit, the approximately 8.2 square miles that surround the Central Operating Unit. In this area, as well as in the off-site areas around Rocky Flats, no cleanup activities took place. Plans were being made for designated refuge trails to be built here for year-round public hiking, biking, cross-country skiing, snowshoeing, and horseback riding.

After completion of the cleanup, the main concerns regarding the Rocky Flats history of contamination were twofold. The first had to do with opening the refuge to public travel. The second was the Jefferson County Parkway, a proposed highway to be built along the east side of the buffer zone to complete a transportation beltway around the Denver region.

In 2017 I was interviewed by a local television station about a bill in the legislature dealing with registration of naturopathic doctors. At the end of the interview, as the cameraman was tearing down and putting away his camera, the reporter asked if there were any big public health stories going on in Jefferson County about which he should be reporting. I mentioned that there was a lot of discussion about the school, residential, and commercial areas that were being built adjacent to the Rocky Flats refuge, particularly in light of the 2012 publication of *Full Body Burden: Growing Up in the Nuclear Shadow of Rocky Flats*, written by Kristen Iversen, which had reported on "the government's sustained attempt to conceal the effects of the toxic and radioactive waste released by Rocky Flats." The reporter immediately told the cameraman to set up again, and we proceeded to do an interview about Rocky Flats and the encroaching neighborhoods.

During that interview the reporter asked me a question that has considerably changed my professional life. "Would you buy a house or send your children to a school so close to Rocky Flats?" he asked. "I probably would not at this time, no," I answered, making it clear that I was speaking for myself, not for our department or for the Jefferson County government.

Knowing that the interview would be on the evening news that night, I felt I should alert the Jefferson County Boards of Commissioners and Health that this would be broadcast and attempt to clarify for them my position regarding Rocky Flats and the growth of residential neighborhoods in the vicinity. My central position was that I had spoken in a personal capacity and not as a departmental or county representative; that from past experience and reputation I did not have a great deal of trust in the DOE or its contractors; I did not have the expertise, nor did I feel I had credible evidence on which to make a reliable determination as to how safe it was to live or work in that area; and I felt that all available data needed to be reviewed by independent experts.

To me, it was neither a bold nor a courageous statement, but it apparently fit into an important public narrative and gave solace to a great many people. I received numerous phone calls, e-mails and letters thanking me for being so forthright and daring. I also learned, however, that many people were now concerned about living in the area. I thought I had been rather circumspect and cautious. Whatever the case, I quickly learned that I now had many new friends and a great many new critics. To those critics, I, too, was now an enemy of the people.

One particularly harsh critique came from an opinion columnist in the *Denver Post*, the major daily newspaper in Colorado. I was labeled an alarmist and was accused of "undermining the credibility and professionalism of every scientist, technician, statistician, and epidemiologist, both federal and state, who worked on the cleanup at Rocky Flats." I was labeled the "general of the scare brigade." I was called "reckless" and "irresponsible," in part for questioning the veracity of the Department of Energy, an agency that is responsible for 107 Superfund and cleanup sites around the country, including Rocky Flats, which was ranked as the most dangerous nuclear site in the country and which had two of the ten most contaminated buildings in America on its property. This is also the federal agency that hid its known off-site nuclear contamination from the public for more than a decade until it was forced by community testing to admit their pollution. To undermine credibility there must be a semblance of credibility already present.

It is uncontested by all involved that there has been a detectable level of nuclear contamination in both the refuge buffer zone and on the private property outside of the Rocky Flats reserve. What is still contested is how much contamination took place, how far the contamination spread, and what risk there is to the public from the contamination, both on- and off-site. The government agencies, including the Department of Energy, the Environmental Protection Agency, the US Fish and Wildlife Service, and the Colorado Department of Public Health and Environment present reams of data supporting their claim that the risk is low. Their studies state that there is a less than a one in a million chance of getting cancer from exposure to the Rocky Flats refuge. Community groups and antinuclear activists have also revealed credible science that supports their claim that the risk is not trivial. At least eleven studies have found plutonium contamination just east of the plant at levels hundreds of times greater than background radiation, and at least three epidemiological studies have found significantly increased rates of cancer near and downwind from the plant.

In the HBO miniseries on the Chernobyl nuclear disaster, Valery Legasov, the first deputy director of the Kurchatov Institute of Atomic Energy, compares the uranium-235 atom to a bullet traveling nearly at the speed of light, "penetrating everything its path. Wood, metal, concrete, flesh." He states that each bullet is capable of damaging our genetic code and of bringing sickness, cancer, and death. "Most of them will not stop firing for a hundred years. Some of them will not stop for fifty thousand years." Plutonium-239 atoms, which make up most of the nuclear contamination at and around Rocky Flats, are different in many ways from uranium atoms. Their most likely route of entry into the human body is through inhalation. But if inhaled, or ingested, they, too, are like bullets, capable of damaging our genetic code; bringing sickness, cancer, and death; and they, too, will not stop firing for thousands of years.

Some of those plutonium "bullets" will hit their mark. There will be cancer cases caused by Rocky Flats plutonium. I do not know how many cases there will be. If the government data is correct, there will be very few; if the community studies' data are correct, there will be more than expected. With today's current technology, we will never be able to prove how many cases there are. That may change. Already studies are under way to determine the source of radioactive materials in solid tumors.

I have called for an independent review of all the collected Rocky Flats data to determine where the risk lies. I have also called for the unsealing of the Rocky Flats grand jury report. I believe the public has the right to know what occurred at Rocky Flats, and what the risk may still be of recreating on or living near the refuge. As I wrote in my response to the *Denver Post*'s opinion piece, "Two of the men who have seen the most evidence concerning the level of contamination at Rocky Flats, the lead agent for the FBI raid and the foreman of the grand jury, continue to advocate for the prohibition of public access to the site. This gives me great pause."

Enemies of the people may actually have the best interests of the community at heart.

Endnotes

1. "Yellowcake towns" refers to the processing centers that converted uranium ore into uranium oxide, which is known as "yellowcake" from its color. This is what was then sent to special processing centers for conversion into fissionable material.

DEADLY DEVELOPMENT AND THE RADIOACTIVE REFUGE:
BUILDING AND RECREATING ON PLUTONIUM–CONTAMINATED LAND

Randy Stafford

Executive Summary

The author, a third-generation Jefferson County resident whose relatives worked at Rocky Flats, was in his fifties when he read Kristen Iversen's *Full Body Burden*. Subsequently, he became active in civic engagement regarding public recreation and road development at the Rocky Flats site, stemming from his belief that the government has a moral obligation to protect public health from plutonium. Based on an extensive review and analysis of the history of the site, this chapter chronicles the establishment of the Rocky Flats National Wildlife Refuge and the rapid growth of home development in contaminated areas. It summarizes a dozen off-site soil studies from multiple sources spanning half a century, all demonstrating plutonium contamination at levels that are hundreds of times higher than background radiation. A survey of the extant epidemiological studies of cancer incidence in the downwind population, as well as the expert opinions of pioneering scientists in the fields of health physics and nuclear chemistry, provide evidence of public health impact. Further, the threat of respirable plutonium-laden dust raised by road and home construction is demonstrated. The chapter concludes with an evaluation of the government's fulfillment of its moral obligation to protect public health from Rocky Flats plutonium.

Rabbit Holes, Research, and Activism

Rocky Flats is a rabbit hole. My fall down it began with reading Kristen Iversen's *Full Body Burden* in 2012 and hasn't stopped since. I became obsessed with the issue, reading every book, watching every documentary, and listening to every interview about it. I delved into deeper research, reviewing special collections and archives at the University of Colorado, Boulder (CU) library from the first scientists to raise alarms about Rocky Flats, making Freedom of Information Act requests to the Department of Energy (DOE), and visiting the Federal Records Center and US district court clerk's office, all to obtain rare reports and court case exhibits related to off-site Rocky Flats contamination and its consequences.

As a fifty-something, third-generation Jefferson County resident, I'd always been vaguely aware of the place in the background. I knew my aunt worked there. I remember the "hippies" (as I regarded them during my high school and college years) protesting it. Later, my biking routes would take me up Indiana Street, bordering the site on the east, but I was as ignorant of the contamination as I'd been of those people's heroic activism. I saw metal sheds and equipment in the fields and accurately suspected they were for air and water monitoring, without grasping the implications. Only after going down the rabbit hole did I begin to understand the complexity, and the horror, of Rocky Flats.

Amusingly, I became what I'd dismissed before: an activist, although I prefer research and direct persuasion of decision makers to public protest. Two government plans moved me to oppose actions I regard so dangerous to public health that I'm dumbfounded by our officials' lack of moral responsibility. The first was to open the Rocky Flats National Wildlife Refuge (RFNWR) to the public on September 15, 2018. The other is to build the Jefferson Parkway along the site's eastern border. The latter is but one example, although the most ominous one, of the mind-boggling amount of development on contaminated land immediately downwind of one of the world's worst nuclear sites.[1]

Those plans are dangerous because that land is contaminated with plutonium from the Rocky Flats Nuclear Weapons Plant. Plutonium is carcinogenic if it enters the human body; it bombards surrounding cells with alpha particle emissions and, over a latency period of decades, can cause cancers where it settles in the body (Agency for Toxic Substances and Disease Registry [ATSDR] 2010, D-9). The exposure pathway of greatest concern is inhalation of micron-sized (0.000039 inch) particles of plutonium oxide dust (Johnson 1981, 177).

Soil studies on that land have consistently found plutonium levels representing hundreds of times background radiation.[2] In downwind neighborhoods there is an increased incidence of cancer. This impact is evident in the few studies that exist of the surrounding population, and more poignantly in the stories of area residents whose relatives and friends have suffered and died from such diseases associated with radioactivity. Meeting those people is a life-changing experience, and the consequences of Rocky Flats on their health are what motivate me.

In this chapter I examine the refuge and the new development downwind of Rocky Flats, including the Jefferson Parkway. I explain the soil studies showing plutonium contamination in the area. I lay out the evidence of public health impact and discuss the dangers of disturbing respirable plutonium-laden dust. I conclude with my beliefs about government's moral obligations with respect to refuge access by the public and development in the area.

The Rocky Flats National Wildlife Refuge

After the Federal Bureau of Investigation (FBI) raided Rocky Flats in 1989 and a subsequent three-year grand jury investigation, coinciding with the end of the Cold War between the United States and the Soviet Union, debate ensued over what to do with Rocky Flats (Ackland 1999, 215–246). The plant's mission changed from producing plutonium cores of US nuclear weapons to cleanup and closure of the site. In 2001 the US Congress passed the Rocky Flats National Wildlife Refuge Act, and management responsibility for the federally owned land transferred from the

DOE to the Department of the Interior, for administration by the US Fish and Wildlife Service (USFWS) when cleanup and closure was completed (US Congress 2001).

The act was sponsored to "preserve the value of the site for open space and wildlife habitat" and "promote the preservation and enhancement of those resources for present and future generations." The act contains several important provisions. First, it provides that the Superfund area (roughly, the former industrial area) is retained by the DOE; only the former "buffer zone" around the industrial area was transferred to

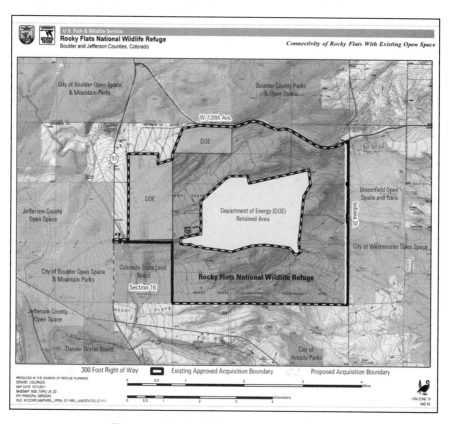

Figure 1. Rocky Flats, showing the DOE-retained Superfund area surrounded by the refuge, with the transportation right-of-way along the eastern border. All land contained within the "proposed acquisition boundary" was acquired by USFWS for the refuge after this map was produced. Source: US Fish and Wildlife Service.

USFWS to become the refuge. Second, it provides a 300-foot transportation right-of-way "along the eastern boundary of Rocky Flats for the sole purpose of transportation improvements along Indiana Street," which would be used for the Jefferson Parkway. Third, it provides that "wildlife-dependent recreation and environmental education and interpretation are the priority public uses of the refuge." Figure 1 maps the results of these provisions.

As mentioned, the area that became the refuge is roughly the former "buffer zone" around the industrial area of the plant. Prior to 1975, the boundary of the plant was much smaller than it is today, as depicted in Figure 2. In 1971 a committee of employees of plant operator Dow Chemical found plutonium contamination in the soil outside the original plant boundary and recommended purchase of that land to expand

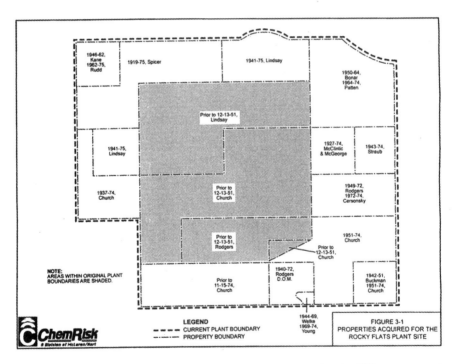

Figure 2. Properties acquired by the US government for the plant. The 1951–1975 plant boundary is shaded in gray (Fig. 3.1 from Flack et al. 1994, prepared for Colorado Department of Public Health and Environment). Source: US Department of Energy (see Flack et al., 1994, Fig. 3.1).

the plant's "buffer zone" (Seed et al. 1971, 50). The US government implemented that recommendation by 1975, and the additionally acquired plutonium-contaminated land, not remediated at all in the Rocky Flats cleanup, is now part of the refuge.

Unremediated contamination notwithstanding, the USFWS opened the refuge to the public on September 15, 2018, and is proceeding with plans to construct a visitor's center and trail system on the refuge, both of which will disturb contaminated soil. The land is open to hiking, mountain biking, and horseback riding, likely to raise plutonium-contaminated dust for trail users to breathe. It's also likely refuge visitors will track contamination off-site into other spaces (Kaltofen 2018).[3]

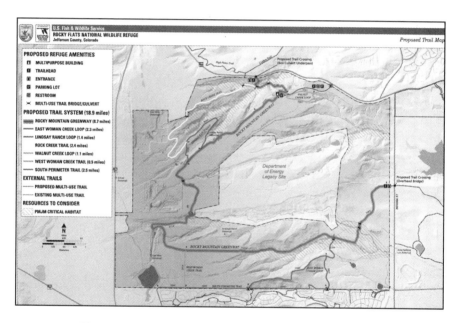

Figure 3. Proposed trail system on the Rocky Flats Wildlife Refuge. Source: US Fish and Wildlife Service.

Figure 3 shows the proposed trail system. The Rocky Mountain Greenway Trail passes through the wind-blown area east of the 903 Pad, the worst source of plutonium soil contamination at the site (Krey 1970, 1–4). Contamination there reaches levels as high as 20 picocuries[4] per gram of soil, which represents 1,023x background radiation, according to government data (Colorado Department of Public Health and Environment [CDPHE] 2018b). Because experts in health physics have testified that there is no safe level of plutonium exposure (as quoted later in this chapter), it is morally irresponsible for the government to claim that recreating there would pose no health risk to trail users.

New Development in the Indiana Street Corridor

When the US Atomic Energy Commission (AEC) selected Rocky Flats in 1951 as a new nuclear weapons plant site, the area was a hinterland 16 miles northwest of Denver, at the foothills of the Colorado Front Range between Golden to the south, Boulder to the north, and Arvada and Broomfield to the southeast and northeast, respectively. There wasn't much but a handful of ranches, Standley Lake, and pasture for grazing livestock. In fact, the AEC acquired some of the Church family's ranchland for the plant site (Ackland 1999, 64–66).[5] Not until the 1960s was the east gate to the plant added from Indiana Street, a country road; prior to that the only entrance was off Highway 93, on the west side.

But suburban expansion was creeping northwest, and that trend continues to this day. For land developers and local governments alike, big money can be made from ever more development. Government officials are motivated by the additional tax revenue with which to fund services, and real estate developers, including the Church family, are motivated by profits from development (Young 2019).[6]

For perspective, the Google Earth Engine time-lapse view shows how the area has changed from 1984 (the inception of Google's imagery) through 2018. Figure 4 shows the 1984 and 2018 satellite images of the area. The industrial area of the plant is clearly visible in the upper-left quadrant of each image. All the areas showing new development between 1984 and 2018 are contaminated with Rocky Flats plutonium in varying concentrations, according to multiple corroborating studies by independent, government, and industry scientists.

The Candelas neighborhood, south of the plant, is the outcome of the Churches' desire to develop some of their ranchland for profit (Maher 2009a). In 1975, the Church family sued the US government and its Rocky Flats contractors for contaminating their remaining landholdings surrounding the plant, thereby devaluing that land for development. The

Figure 4. Google Earth Engine time-lapse images of the Rocky Flats area in 1984 (top) and 2018 (bottom), showing suburbia sprawling from the southeast. Source: Google Maps/Google Earth.

DOE contractors settled the suit before trial with an agreement awarding the plaintiffs $8,750,000 (*Perry S. McKay v. United States of America* 1984). The agreement further stipulated that:

1. Plaintiffs refer to DOE contractors any inquiries from prospective land buyers about contamination;

2. DOE contractors disclose facts necessary to inform prospective buyers of contamination "including that the risks associated with those amounts of such materials are sufficiently small that they can be disregarded in any consideration relating to use of the lands";

3. Colorado and Jefferson County agree the Church family's lands were suitable for development, and any rezoning requests for those lands would not be denied; and

4. The lands would be certified to have plutonium contamination less than the state's standard (set in 1973 at 2.0 disintegrations per minute per gram of soil, which is 46 times background radiation, to match the existing level of contamination).

Thus in the settlement of this lawsuit the Church family's lands, including those on which Candelas was developed, were essentially declared suitable for any use and in compliance with arbitrarily set Colorado contamination standards.

But larger forces than residential neighborhood development are at work. A new grocery store strip mall was developed on the northwest corner of Indiana Street and Candelas Parkway and opened in spring 2018. Indiana Street was widened to four lanes at that intersection and new drainage systems installed on the shoulders. A new medical facility will be built just east of Welton Reservoir. Like residential development, all these commercial and infrastructure developments disturb soil contaminated with plutonium.

One of the largest developments planned for the Rocky Flats area is the Jefferson Parkway. This project by three local governments – Jefferson County, the City of Arvada, and the City of Broomfield via the Jefferson Parkway Public Highway Authority (JPPHA) – will build a four-lane toll highway between Highway 93 near Golden and Highway 128 between Indiana Street and Wadsworth Boulevard. It's part of a decades-old vision to complete a beltway around the Denver metropolitan area (Maher 2009b). The southwestern, southeastern, and northeastern portions of the beltway are already completed as C-470, southeastern E-470, and northeastern E-470, respectively, and half of the northwestern portion is completed as the Northwest Parkway. The Jefferson Parkway along with two more future projects, named West Connect and Northwest Parkway Extension, would complete the remaining half of the northwestern portion.

JPPHA chose a public-private partnership to build the Jefferson Parkway instead of approaching the Federal Highway Authority for funding because that would have required intensive environmental analysis (Jefferson Parkway Public Highway Authority [JPPHA] 2018a, 5). JPPHA also took the position that the alignment of the Jefferson Parkway was nonnegotiable, and preselected from seventy-three potential alignments studied during previous attempts at the northwest portion of the beltway (JPPHA 2018b, 2). The chosen alignment, depicted in Figure 5, goes along Indiana Street, using the right-of-way created by the RFNWR act. The Indiana Street corridor is one of the most contaminated places outside the former industrial area of the plant, with plutonium levels of hundreds of times background radiation. The construction concepts for the Jefferson Parkway call for "cut and fill" of the undulating terrain along Indiana Street, which would disturb contaminated soil (JPPHA 2018b, 6). Construction of the Jefferson Parkway would raise plutonium-contaminated dust, and it could blow downwind into populated areas.

Plutonium Contamination in the Indiana Street Corridor

Eleven studies from a variety of sources spanning forty-three years have all found plutonium contamination in the soil along the Indiana Street corridor at levels representing hundreds of times background radiation. This soil was not remediated in the Rocky Flats cleanup, limited to roughly just the former industrial area of the plant. Because plutonium-239 has a half-life of 24,100 years, that contamination remains except to the extent the plutonium is moved by weather elements or the activities of animals and humans. Figure 6 shows the locations of soil samples from these studies and the multiples of background radiation found in the samples.

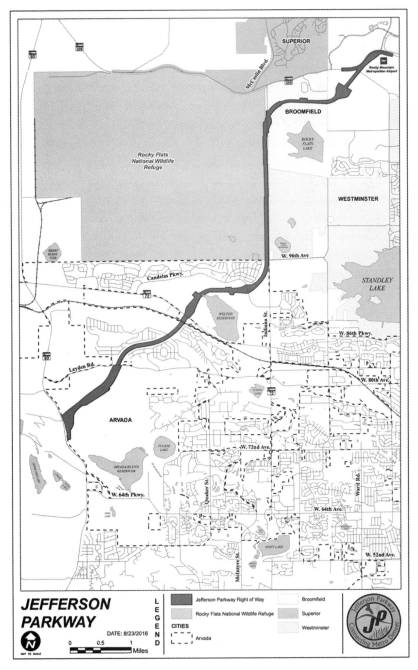

Figure 5. The JPPHA's chosen alignment of the Jefferson Parkway.
Source: Jefferson Parkway Public Highway Authority.

The first study of off-site soil contamination was conducted by radiochemist Dr. Edward Martell after the Mother's Day 1969 fire at the plant. A West Point graduate who'd studied radiation effects on humans from nuclear weapons tests in the Pacific, Martell was working in Boulder at the time and became concerned about possible contamination releases. He collected off-site soil samples in August 1969 and first published his findings in a January 1970 letter to the chair of the AEC (Martell 1970). He found 311x background radiation at Indiana Street and Woman Creek. Martell also measured background radiation at 0.0434 disintegrations per minute per gram (dpm/g) of soil at Boyd Lake, Colorado.

In response to Martell's findings, the AEC sent two scientists from its Health and Safety Laboratory, P. W. Krey and E. P. Hardy, to conduct their own study. They confirmed Martell's findings and produced the widely circulated Krey-Hardy map, showing off-site plutonium isopleths, or contour lines indicating amounts of radioactivity (Krey and Hardy 1970). Figure 7 shows an enhanced version of the Krey-Hardy map.

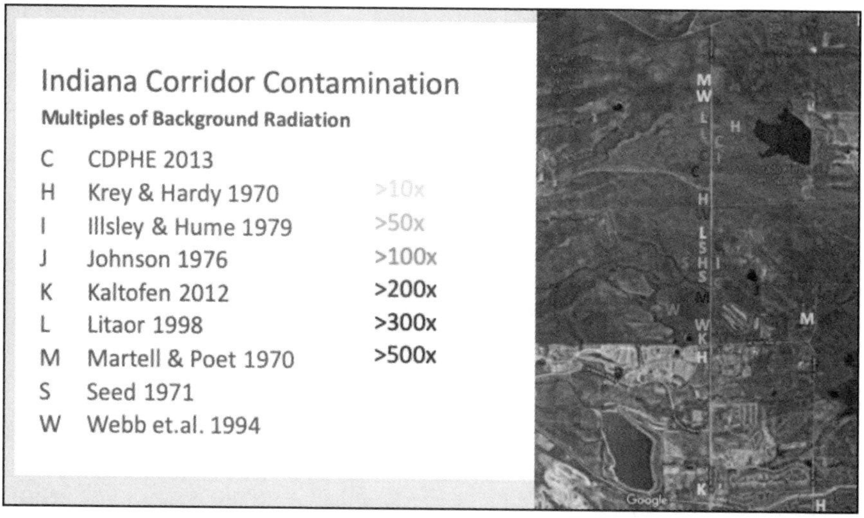

Indiana Corridor Contamination
Multiples of Background Radiation

C	CDPHE 2013	
H	Krey & Hardy 1970	>10x
I	Illsley & Hume 1979	>50x
J	Johnson 1976	>100x
K	Kaltofen 2012	>200x
L	Litaor 1998	>300x
M	Martell & Poet 1970	>500x
S	Seed 1971	
W	Webb et.al. 1994	

Figure 6. Locations of samples containing high multiples of background radiation from studies of off-site soil contamination. The letter identifies the study containing the sample, and the color indicates the multiple of background radiation found in the sample, using 0.0434 dpm/g (disintegrations per minute per gram) as background.
Source: Courtesy of Randy Stafford.

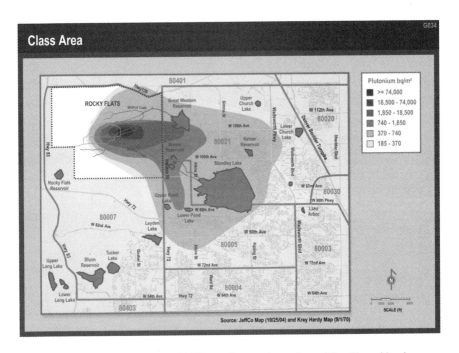

Figure 7. The enhanced version of the Krey-Hardy map, with colored plutonium isopleths in Bq/m2. Note that 1,850 Bq/m2 represents 171x background radiation, using 0.0434 dpm/g as background (P. W. Krey and E. P Hardy 1970). Source: Jefferson County/US Department of Energy (see Krey and Hardy 1970).

Plant operator Dow Chemical then appointed a committee of its employees, chaired by Robert Seed, to assess the accuracy of those scientists' findings. The Seed Report corroborated Martell's and Krey and Hardy's findings and produced a new isopleth map the committee deemed more accurate than the Krey-Hardy map (Seed et al. 1971, 18–20). The Seed map is reproduced as Figure 8. The 100–50 pCi/g (picocuries per gram) band crossing Indiana Street represents 341–171x background radiation.

After the initial spate of studies triggered by the 1969 fire, the next significant off-site soil contamination study was conducted by Jefferson County Public Health Department director Dr. Carl Johnson and published in *Science* magazine (Johnson et al. 1976). Johnson held an MD degree from the Ohio State University and an MPH (master of public health) from the University of California at Berkeley and specialized in

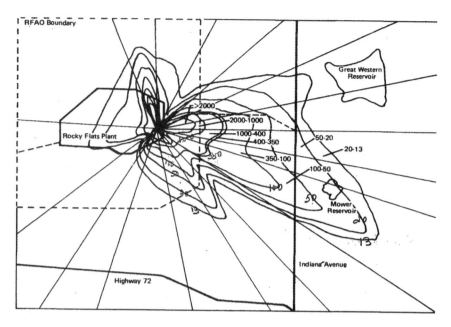

Figure 8. The plutonium isopleth map from the Seed Report, in picocuries per gram (pCi/g) of soil. Source: Jefferson County/US Department of Energy (see Seed et al. 1971, Fig. 7.2).

radiation and epidemiology. His study was requested by the Jefferson County Board of Commissioners upon a rezoning application for new residential development east of Rocky Flats (Johnson 1985, 1). Johnson analyzed soil in sections of land between Indiana and Alkire Streets and 88th to 112th Avenues. Some of his findings are shown in Table 1.

Location	Concentration	x Background
Section 7 (Indiana to Alkire, 104th to 112th)	14.1 dpm/g	325x
Section 18 (Indiana to Alkire, 96th to 104th)	2.96 dpm/g	68x
Section 19 (Indiana to Alkire, 88th to 96th)	0.23 dpm/g	5x
Section 8 (Alkire to Simms, 104th to 112th)	0.72 dpm/g	17x

Table 1. Johnson's findings of plutonium concentrations in off-site soils east of Rocky Flats (Johnson 1981).

In 1975, as previously mentioned, Marcus Church had sued the US government for contaminating his ranchland and thereby lowering its value for development. As part of the defense in that lawsuit, C. T. Illsley and M. W. Hume of Rockwell International Corporation, which had succeeded Dow Chemical as plant operator, sampled soil at seventy-one locations outside the plant boundary (Illsley and Hume 1979). They found hotspots as high as 174x background radiation just east of Indiana Street, as circled in Figure 9.

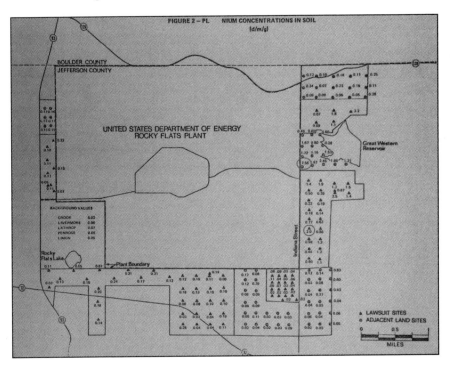

Figure 9. Hotspots found by Illsley and Hume (1979) in dpm/g. Note 7.56 dpm/g is 174x background radiation. Source: Rockwell International Energy Systems Group (see Illsley and Hume 1979, Fig. 3).

Former Rocky Flats engineer and whistleblower Jim Stone teamed with Colorado State University professor Dr. Ward Whicker in 1994 to conduct another study, "The Spatial Distribution of Plutonium in Soil Near the Rocky Flats Plant." Their soil sampling locations are shown in Figure 10. At location AX6, on the southwest corner of Indiana Street and East Gate Road, they found a hotspot of 211x background radiation. Farther south at location CX6, they found a 100x background radiation hotspot and at location CX7 a 40x background radiation hotspot 12–15 inches deep in the soil (Webb et al. 1994, 24).

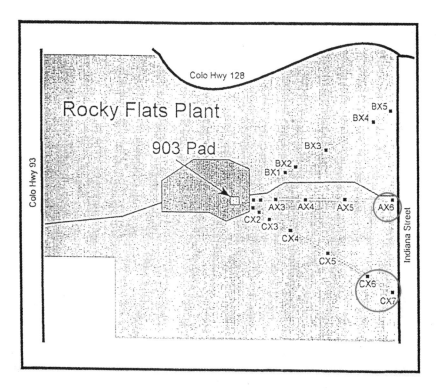

Figure 10. Sampling locations in the Stone, Webb, and Whicker 1994 study. Source: Courtesy of F. Ward Whicker and James M. Stone (see Webb et al. 1994, Fig. 8b)

Dr. Iggy Litaor had worked at Rocky Flats since 1990 for successive operators EG&G and Kaiser Hill. His PhD and postdoctoral research were in soil geochemistry. Litaor not only found plutonium hotspots of 111x and 71x background radiation just east of Indiana Street but also analyzed the ratio of plutonium isotopes in the soil samples to confirm Rocky Flats as the origin of the found plutonium (Litaor 1999).[7] Ratios of 0.06 are Rocky Flats plutonium. Ratios of 0.16 are global fallout plutonium. Ratios in between are a weighted blend. Figure 11 shows the isotope ratios and off-site isopleths Litaor found.

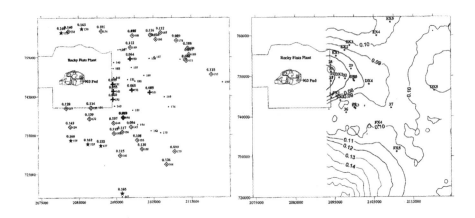

Figure 11. Plutonium isotope ratios (at left) found by Litaor. At right, sampling location 30 yielded 111x background radiation, and location 28 yielded 73x. Source: Litaor 1999, Fig. 5).

The Agency for Toxic Substances and Disease Registry (ATSDR) maintains toxicological profile documents for a vast number of environmental contaminants, including plutonium. With respect to Rocky Flats off-site soil contamination, the ATSDR toxicological profile for plutonium states: "The highest offsite concentration of ^{239,240}Pu observed during a remedial investigation was 6,500 pCi/kg (240 Bq/kg). A separate sampling study conducted in the 1990s at 42 locations adjacent to RFETS measured ^{239,240}Pu concentrations in soil ranging from 0.22 to 14.80 Bq/kg (5.9–400 pCi/kg)" (Litaor 1999) (ATSDR 2010, 177). Note that 6,500 pCi/kg represents 332x background radiation, and 400 pCi/kg represents 20x background radiation.

A more recent report of off-site soil contamination is from Marco Kaltofen of Boston Chemical Data Corporation, under contract to Dr. LeRoy Moore of the Rocky Flats Nuclear Guardianship organization. Kaltofen's study collected fifty soil samples in 2010 and 2011 at locations in the Indiana Street corridor and elsewhere (Kaltofen 2012, 4). Kaltofen detected 81x background radiation just west of Indiana Street at 96th Avenue. He summarized: "Plutonium exceeded reported background levels by two orders of magnitude at locations that match those noted in the Krey-Hardy report. (P. W. Krey and E. P. Hardy, 1970, "Plutonium in Soil Around the Rocky Flats Plant").... There was no statistically significant

Figure 12. Locations and concentrations of plutonium detections in Kaltofen's 2012 study Source: Courtesy of Rocky Mountain Peace and Justice Center (see Kaltofen 2012, Fig. 3a).

difference between this data set and the 1970 data set. Plutonium losses appear to be approximately equal in magnitude to plutonium inputs in the Indiana St. area" (Kaltofen 2012, 14). The plutonium inputs to which Kaltofen alludes are most likely from contaminated soil areas upwind. Figure 12 shows the locations of plutonium detections in his study.

Most recently the Colorado Department of Public Health and Environment (CDPHE) presented data to the Rocky Flats Stewardship Council (RFSC) in 2013. Carl Spreng of the CDPHE gave a presentation, "Operable Unit 3 Offsite Areas," to the RFSC explaining the decision of "no action" in those off-site areas (Spreng 2013). That presentation contained a CDPHE/DOE plutonium isopleth map in picocuries per gram of soil; see Figure 13 (Spreng 2013, 7). Just west of Indiana Street at East Gate Road, there is a 10 pCi/g isopleth line. That concentration of plutonium, 10 pCi/g, represents 512x background radiation. There is also a 5 pCi/g isopleth, representing 256x background radiation, crossing Indiana Street to the east side.

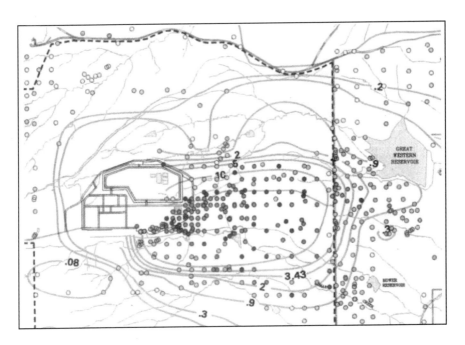

Figure 13. Plutonium isopleths in pCi/g from Carl Spreng's 2013 presentation to the RFSC. Source: Colorado Department of Public Health and Environment (see Spreng 2013).

Evidence of Increased Rates of Disease in the Downwind Population

Compared with the number of off-site soil contamination studies, there have been few studies of potential health effects of that Rocky Flats contamination on the downwind population. During the course of Rocky Flats' history, six studies of cancer incidence have been performed in towns surrounding the site. Another study analyzed plutonium content in tissues collected at autopsy from downwind residents compared with those of a control population. There never has been a comprehensive health-monitoring program for nearby residents, and no studies have been performed on potential health effects aside from those on the incidence of cancer. However, there have been anecdotes about public health impacts for decades in surrounding neighborhoods and cities.

Johnson was first to study cancer incidence in the population downwind of Rocky Flats in comparison to cancer rates farther from the site. He is the only investigator ever to have published such an epidemiological study in a peer-reviewed medical journal. Johnson reported the following findings based on comparing cancer incidence in geographical areas around the Denver metropolitan area at varying distances from Rocky Flats (Johnson 1981, 179–182). The data were obtained from the National Cancer Institute's Third National Cancer Survey 1969–1971 (i.e., new diagnoses for those years by census tract).

1. Cancer incidence in males was 24 percent higher and in females 10 percent higher in the most contaminated suburban area nearest the plant, compared with the unexposed area.

2. The excess cases of cancer consisted of mostly leukemia, lymphoma, and myeloma, along with cancer of the lungs, thyroid, breasts, esophagus, stomach, and colon. This is a pattern similar to that observed in the survivors of Hiroshima and Nagasaki.

3. In males, cancer of the gonads (especially of the testes) and liver and in females cancer of the pancreas and brain contributed to the higher incidence of all cancer in areas nearest the plant.

4. The increase in incidence of all cancer and for certain classes of cancer in the exposed population supports the hypothesis that exposure of general populations to small concentrations of plutonium and other radionuclides can have an effect on cancer incidence.

5. A preliminary study of congenital malformations coded at birth found a rate of 14.5 per 1,000 births for a large suburban city near the plant, compared with a rate of 10.4 for the remainder of the county and 10.1 for the state of Colorado.

6. An unusually high incidence of cancer of the testes (40 cases observed/18 expected) was discovered throughout the exposed population. The incidence of cancer of the ovary was also higher (24 percent). The higher incidence of cancer of the testes in the three exposed areas merits special attention. One possible explanation is the demonstrated propensity of plutonium to concentrate in gonads. The higher incidence of cancer of the ovary is also consistent with this hypothesis.

Plaintiffs' counsel in *Church v. United States* hired CU physicist Stephen Chinn to perform additional analysis on the same data set Johnson had studied. With advice from renowned radiation epidemiologist Dr. Alice Stewart and others, Chinn performed multiple regression analysis on the data set to identify which of some fifty factors were most strongly correlated with the increased cancer incidence in populations near the plant. Chinn found:

1. Residence downwind of the Rocky Flats facility or in the area with plutonium contamination were the most significant risk correlates [in the higher cancer incidence nearer the plant].

2. Control for the other factors [socioeconomic status, air pollution, urban/rural factors, population mobility, and possible sources of carcinogens], singly or in combination, failed to account for the excess risk.

3. The excess was primarily of organs considered to be radio-sensitive by the ICRP [International Commission on Radiological Protection] and was more pronounced in men than in women. (Chinn 1981, i)

Chinn's report was part of the plaintiffs' pretrial statement in *Church v. United States*. Figure 14, excerpted from Chinn's report, shows the average wind direction and speed from Rocky Flats for the years 1953–1970. The prevailing winds at Rocky Flats are from the west, sometimes with a northerly or southerly component, with an average velocity of 12 miles per hour (mph).

In response to the studies by Johnson and Chinn, a DOE-funded cancer incidence study was led by Kenny S. Crump for the Inhalation Toxicology Research Institute, a longtime AEC contractor. Crump's report, "Statistical Analyses of Cancer Incidence Patterns in the Denver Metropolitan Area in Relation to the Rocky Flats Plant," states:

In Section II of this report, cancer incidence data for 1969 to 1971 are analyzed in a manner similar to that reported by Johnson.... Johnson's results were closely reproduced using data collected for this study. Statistically significant differences occurred between Area I and Area IV in total cancer and in the cancer categories of lung and bronchi, lymphoma and myeloma, colon and rectum, and testes for males, and in total cancer and colon and rectum cancer for females. (Crump et al. 1984, 1)

However, Crump then applied an urbanization adjustment to his and Johnson's and Chinn's findings that negated Johnson's and Chinn's conclusions of greater cancer incidence with closer proximity to Rocky Flats.

In the landmark case *Cook v. Rockwell*, the court found in favor of the plaintiff class, homeowners east of Rocky Flats whose property was contaminated by the plant, and awarded the plaintiff class $375,000,000 in settlement (PR Newswire 2017). Plaintiffs' counsel presented Dr. Richard Clapp, an epidemiologist and a former director of the Massachusetts Cancer Registry, as an expert witness in the case and admitted into evidence a study he conducted on cancer incidence downwind of the site. Clapp

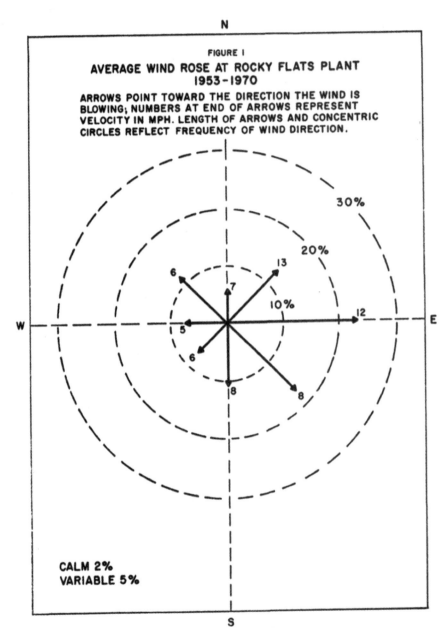

Figure 14. Average wind direction and speed from Rocky Flats plant, 1953–1970. Source: Chinn 1981.

reviewed all previous studies of cancer incidence in the downwind population, criticized the Crump study as "highly unorthodox" and stated that Johnson's and Chinn's findings "provide justification for purposeful and ongoing medical surveillance of exposed populations" (Clapp 1996, 5). He analyzed lung and bone cancer incidence for the years 1979–1992 as a function of proximity to Rocky Flats, and the following from his report was admitted into evidence:

> The most relevant finding is that for the time period 1989–1992, the risk of lung cancer was elevated in all the exposure scenarios comparing the two contours closest to the Rocky Flats plant to other contours farther away. The odds ratios range from 1.09 to 1.29 depending on the exposure scenario and the sex of the cases.... These years correspond to an approximate latency of 20–35 years from the time of maximum plutonium emissions from the plant and may therefore be more representative of a health effect in the exposed population.
>
> In addition, bone cancer incidence was examined in the same time periods and with respect to plutonium levels in soil (Krey and Hardy, 1970).... In this analysis, there is evidence that the incidence of bone cancer in the Zip Codes in the inner two contours (the areas associated with the highest plutonium levels) was greater than in areas associated with lower plutonium levels farther away. This is especially true in the period 1984–1988 when the adjusted odds ratio was 1.9. (Clapp 1996, 7)

The "odds ratio" of 1.29 for lung cancer means that according to the cancer incidence data, people closer to Rocky Flats had 29 percent more lung cancer cases than did people farther away. The odds ratio of 1.9 for bone cancer means that people closer to Rocky Flats had 90 percent more bone cancer cases than did people farther away. The relevance of the twenty-to-thirty-five-year latency period is that for cancers caused by internal bodily exposure to low-level ionizing radiation, there can be a latency period of decades for adults between exposure and disease onset (ATSDR 2010, D-9).

The CDPHE conducted cancer studies in 1998 and 2016. Although the CDPHE's website states that the 1998 study was independent, its acknowledgments page states, "This project was supported in part by the U.S. Department of Energy State Health Agreement Program through grant #DE-FG01-94EH89530" (CDPHE 1998). The studies analyzed incidence of ten selected types of cancer in ten regional statistical areas (RSA) "selected primarily for their proximity to Rocky Flats." The 1998 study's findings were that "for the entire 10-RSA region and the 10 individual RSAs, the incidence of all [10 studied] cancers combined for persons of all ages and for children from 1980 through 1989 was not higher than expected compared to the remainder of the Denver Metro area. Also for the entire 10-RSA region, none of the ten selected cancers for persons of all ages was found to be higher than expected" (CDPHE 1998). However, the CDPHE studies have a number of design flaws limiting their ability to detect increased cancer incidence in the downwind population. Those flaws are:

1. The ten RSAs selected "for their proximity to Rocky Flats" include mostly areas that were not downwind and were not contaminated; for example, north of US 36 and Highway 128, east of I-25, west of I-70, and so on. See Figure 15 for a map of the RSAs studied. Because these areas were not as contaminated, it is expected that cancer incidence there would be lower. That lower incidence dilutes the incidence found across the entire 10-RSA region. In Figure 15, only RSAs 202 and 203 should have been compared with "the remainder of the Denver Metro area."

2. Even the RSA granularity is too large to isolate cancer incidence increases as a function of distance and direction from the site. For example RSA 202, containing Standley Lake, stretches all the way from Highway 93 to east of US 36, whereas Johnson worked at census tract granularity, and Dr. Clapp worked at zip code granularity, allowing their studies to focus on finer geographical units in relation to distance and direction from the site.

3. The list of cancer types studied had important omissions from the perspective of radiosensitive cancers; for example,

cancers of the gonads and thyroid. Therefore the studies weren't designed to find all of the data necessary to answer the question of whether there is increased incidence of radiosensitive cancers downwind of Rocky Flats.

4. The studies used estimates of population; therefore, the accuracy of their findings is sensitive to the quality of their population estimation approach.

5. The 2017 supplement covering thyroid and "rare" cancers only analyzed 1990 to 2014 data, not including the 1980 to 1989 data as in the 1998 study. Thus the 2017 supplement is incomplete.

Radioecologist Bernd Franke, upon reviewing the 1998 CDPHE study, stated, "It appears the study design was chosen for public relations purposes, to calm people down, rather than for any real scientific reason" (McKinley and Balkany 2004, 200). Dr. LeRoy Moore has also criticized the CDPHE study (Moore 2017, 1–2).

In making assessments and representations about the safety of the Rocky Flats area, CDPHE relies upon mathematical models based on assumed safe standards of radioactivity in soil and assumed permissible doses of radioactivity in humans. Through different exposure scenarios for different groups of people, the models relate contaminant concentrations in soil to committed doses of radiation in people, and then relate those committed doses to excess cancer risk. But a model is not reality. A model is an abstraction of how its creators think and hope a system works. What is actually observed from the system is almost always different (Rechtin 1991, 58–59).

Johnson's, Chinn's, and Clapp's epidemiological studies more accurately reflect reality. Metropolitan State University's (MSU) Rocky Flats Downwinders Health Survey, although not an epidemiological study, suggests the need for new, comprehensive epidemiological studies. The survey's preliminary findings revealed that 414 (49 percent) of 848 reported cancer cases were designated rare cancers – twice the national rate of rare cancers (Jensen 2016, 1–2). The survey produced geo-plots, shown in Figure 16, of the addresses of respondents reporting cancer, overlaid with the path of the 1957 fire smoke plume and with the Krey-Hardy

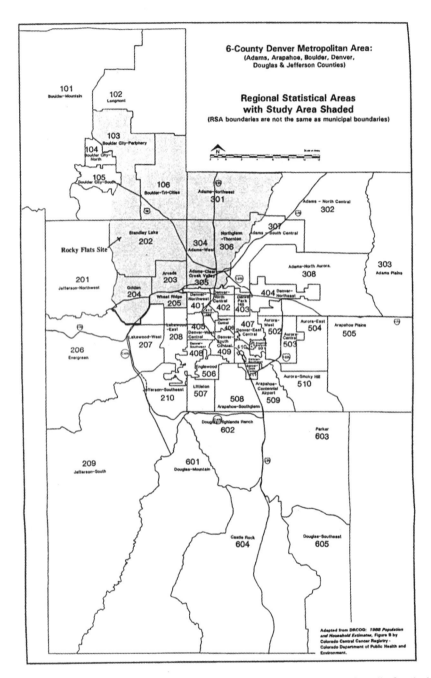

Figure 15. Regional statistical areas (RSAs) "selected primarily for their proximity to Rocky Flats" in the CDPHE 1998 and 2016 cancer incidence studies. Source: Colorado Department of Public Health and Environment.

map. Those geo-plots are striking visual evidence of the potential correlation between Rocky Flats contamination releases and downwind disease incidence.

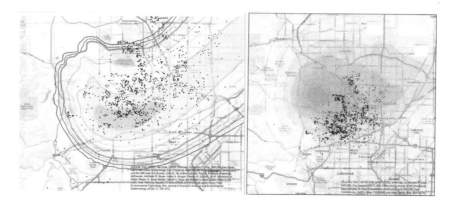

Figure 16. MSU health survey geo-plots (black dots) of cancer sufferers' addresses overlaid at left with the path of the 1957 fire smoke plume and at right with the Krey-Hardy map isopleths. Source: Jensen 2016.

The disease incidence in Five Parks, a relatively new neighborhood 3 miles downwind of the 903 area, also reflects reality. Only ten years after Five Parks was developed, residents had two cases of the extremely rare heart cancer, cardiac angiosarcoma; multiple cases of other radiosensitive cancers; and multiple cases of neurological disease.[8] Like the story of cardiac angiosarcoma victim Brian McNeely, anecdotes abound among Arvada residents, with multiple family members, neighbors, friends, and classmates dying of cancer or having neurological diseases or thyroid conditions (McNeely 2018).[9]

A study by Dr. John Cobb, former professor and chair of the Department of Preventative Medicine at the CU School of Medicine, shows the real impact of Rocky Flats. Cobb conducted a long-running, EPA-funded study of plutonium content in deceased downwinders' lung and liver tissue, compared with plutonium content in the lungs and livers of a control population of deceased persons from Pueblo, Colorado (Cobb et al. 1983). The researchers collected tissues at autopsy, with permission, from a total of 519 people. Although the amount of plutonium in the downwinders' tissues was only slightly higher than the amount in the Puebloans' tissues, the important finding from Dr. Cobb's study was that plutonium in the downwinders' tissue was definitely from Rocky Flats, based on analysis of ^{240}Pu:^{239}Pu isotope ratio (Cobb 1983).[10]

Establishing a causal connection between Rocky Flats contamination and cancer by analyzing tumor tissue or decedents' remains for Rocky Flats–specific plutonium is reality, as opposed to the CDPHE's claims of a not higher than expected cancer incidence. Precedent for establishing such a causal connection exists in the cases of Lloyd Mixon and Kristen Haag, for example. Mixon, a rancher who lived downwind of Rocky Flats, developed cancer (and observed a number of deformities in his ranch animals). In the movie *Dark Circle*, Mixon describes having his excised malignant tumors analyzed for plutonium, with positive findings (*Dark Circle* 1982). Kristen Haag was a downwind teenager who died of cancer after having a leg amputated because of that cancer. She was cremated and her ashes were analyzed for Rocky Flats plutonium, with positive findings. In *Dark Circle*, Kristen's father, Rex Haag, tells her story, and her case is also described in *Full Body Burden* (Iversen 2012, 46–47). Work is under way to develop new capabilities to analyze human tissue samples, such as excised primary tumors, for radionuclide content (Ketterer 2019). Positive findings of Rocky Flats–specific plutonium by isotope ratio in excised primary tumor tissue would constitute smoking-gun evidence of causality.

In light of those realities, the assumptions about safe standards of plutonium in soil and permissible doses of plutonium in humans on which CDPHE relies, might be invalid. In January 1973, then-director of the Colorado Department of Health (CDH), which later became CDPHE, established for the first time a plutonium soil standard of 0.2 dpm/g for Colorado, stating that that level of contamination "presents a sufficient radiation hazard to the public health to render the land unfit for residential use, subdivision development, or commercial and industrial uses" (Colorado Department of Health [CDH] 1973a). But the standard was changed to 2.0 dpm/g just a few months later, perhaps because the existing contamination already exceeded the earlier threshold by an order of magnitude as far away as east of US 36 and south of 64th Avenue (CDH 1973b).

Regarding permissible doses of plutonium, pioneers in the fields of health physics, nuclear chemistry, and radiation epidemiology have stated under oath that there is no safe level of plutonium exposure for humans (*Decision at Rocky Flats* 1979). Dr. Karl Morgan testified that "there is no dose, no exposure, to ionizing radiation so low that the risk is zero," that "the cancer risk is much, much greater than it was thought to be when these earlier standards were established," and that those earlier standards create a false sense of security.[11] Dr. John Gofman testified, "I don't find any permissible dose to be permissible, because to me a standard or a permissible dose is simply a legalized permit to commit murder. So I don't think of things as a permissible; I think of things only in how many deaths there will be per unit dose, which is the only scientifically meaningful thing."[12] A UK government committee also found that cancer risk from plutonium might be an order of magnitude greater than previously thought (Edwards 2004).

CDPHE's mission is "to protect and improve the health of Colorado's people and the quality of its environment" (CDPHE 2017). Yet the department has never conducted a health-monitoring program for the population downwind of Rocky Flats, instead choosing to rely on modeling and assumptions, to publish studies with major methodological flaws, and to attack or ignore the large body of dissenting work from credible sources. Measurement of actual public health impact would far outweigh modeling of hypothetical health risk and would better align with CDPHE's stated mission.

Respirable Plutonium-Laden Dust

For the population downwind of plutonium-contaminated soil, the exposure pathway of greatest concern is inhalation of plutonium-laden dust. ATSDR's toxicological profile for plutonium warns:

> **Plutonium can enter your body when it is inhaled or swallowed:** When you breathe air that contains plutonium, some of it will get trapped in your lungs. Some of the trapped plutonium will move to other parts of your body, mainly your bones and liver. The amount of plutonium that stays in your lungs depends on the solubility of the plutonium that is in the air you breathe. (4)

Plutonium in your body will remain there for many years:
Plutonium leaves your body very slowly in the urine and fe-
ces. If plutonium were to enter your lungs today, much of the
plutonium would still be in your body 30–50 years later. (4)

Cancer is the major latent harmful effect produced by ionizing radiation and the one that most people exposed to radiation are concerned about. The ability of alpha, beta, and
gamma radiation to produce cancer in virtually every tissue
and organ in laboratory animals has been well demonstrated. The development of cancer is not an immediate effect.
Radiation-induced leukemia has the shortest latent period
at 2 years, while other radiation-induced cancers have latent periods >20 years. The mechanism by which cancer is
induced in living cells is complex and is a topic of intense
study. Exposure to ionizing radiation can produce cancer at
any site within the body; however, some sites appear to be
more common than others, such as the breast, lung, stomach, and thyroid. (D-9)

Johnson's study of cancer incidence in the downwind population
specifically emphasized the inhalation risk:

The major route of exposure is the inhalation of airborne
particles of Pu and other radionuclides by people living in
the path of exhaust plumes from the plant, and (for those
living near the plant), the inhalation of Pu in resuspended
surface dust.

Resuspension of Pu-contaminated soil increases with wind
speed to the 2.1 power, and the ratio of Pu 238 to Pu 239 increases from about 2 percent (surface soil) to 20–40 percent
in airborne soil (31). As much as 50 pCi/g of Pu in airborne
soil has been reported in the area. A study of Pu particle size
in the soil suggested that single Pu atoms and Pu particles
with diameters less than the minimum detectable equivalent diameter (0.09 pm) accounted for the majority of Pu
239 and Pu 240 activity in the soil (32). (Johnson 1981, 177)

Thus, all it might take to get carcinogenic Rocky Flats plutonium into a person's lungs is one unlucky breath on a breezy day – for example, if one were on the refuge in conditions such as depicted in Figure 17. In that picture, dust devils and clouds were raised on the refuge by winds of less than 25 mph on July 3, 2018 – and winds at Rocky Flats are frequently much stronger.

Figure 17. Dust resuspended into the air on the refuge on July 3, 2018. Source: Courtesy of Drake Panzer.

Construction of the Jefferson Parkway will certainly raise dust into the air from plutonium-contaminated soil in the Indiana Street corridor. Figure 18 depicts construction activity on C-470 between Broadway and Santa Fe Drive at 12:53 p.m. on April 12, 2018, when the wind at nearby Chatfield Reservoir was blowing 27 mph and gusting to 44 mph. The dust from a dump truck's tires, and from a bulldozer ahead of it, is plainly evident in the photograph, to the extent that it was creating a driving hazard on westbound C-470. There is no reason to believe the same degree of dust resuspension will not occur during Jefferson Parkway construction, given the scope of the project and amount of cut-and-fill work contemplated.

Figure 18. Dust resuspended by construction on C-470 on a breezy day, April 12, 2018. Source: Courtesy of Randy Stafford.

Government's Moral Obligation

I believe government has a moral obligation to protect public health from risks associated with Rocky Flats contamination. The available evidence indicates that off-site soil is contaminated with Rocky Flats plutonium and that disease incidence in area residents correlates with proximity to Rocky Flats, influenced by direction from it. But currently, government at all levels overlooks or downplays the public health risk. No government entity or official wants to own up to, or own, the problem of Rocky Flats contamination and consequences. Most government entities and officials want to depend on plausible deniability, in the name of avoiding accountability or defending development or accomplishing ill-advised missions.

In reference to DOE's responsibility for Rocky Flats, former US representative Pat Schroeder (D-CO) once quipped, "I've yet to see an agency study itself and turn itself in" (Brown 1979). The DOE has negative incentive to accept accountability for the contamination and consequences it ultimately caused – to admit it is responsible for the suffering and death of innocent citizens unwittingly participating in an unintentional experiment.

The current CDPHE is also complicit in denial of these health risks in its official publications (CDPHE 2018a). CDPHE merely regulates to existing standards for contamination (JPPHA 2018d, 168) – not to more conservative standards that could be informed by health monitoring of the downwind population or by attention to reputable epidemiological studies' findings.

Earlier in Rocky Flats history, the CDH took responsible and conservative positions with respect to Rocky Flats; for example, when CDH director Dr. Frank Traylor advised that "industrial development would be more appropriate than residential zoning around the plant because of part-time occupancy, no children present, and the ease of communication for possible evacuation from industrial property. Agricultural use, because of its low density, and 'open space,' of course, would also be appropriate" (CDH 1979).

But under the Rocky Flats Legacy Management Agreement, entered into in 1996, CDPHE became a support agency to DOE per the provisions of the 1980 Superfund legislation. Under that agreement, CDPHE's Rocky Flats oversight activities are also funded by DOE (CDPHE 2018a, 11). Sometime between the 1970s, when CDH took responsible and conservative positions with respect to Rocky Flats contamination, and the present day, in which CDPHE downplays contamination levels and public health risks, their position on Rocky Flats matters changed markedly. It would seem a conflict of interest for CDPHE to carry out its stated organizational mission with respect to Rocky Flats while simultaneously accepting funding from the federal agency that caused the public health consequences in the first place.

Another example of government flouting its moral obligation was the Jefferson County Board of Commissioners' dismissal of Johnson. After his cancer incidence study was published, the board appointed new members to the Jefferson County Board of Health, and the new majority on the latter board asked Johnson to resign. It was later discovered that the new appointees to that board of health had real estate and business interests in the vicinity of Rocky Flats, and their appointment reflects duplicity on the part of the county commissioners (Johnson 1985).

Jefferson Parkway development follows a different course. The JP-PHA appointed a citizen's Jefferson Parkway Advisory Committee (JPAC, on which I served). The public health risk of disturbing the soil along Indiana Street for parkway construction was voted the committee's top-priority agenda item (JPPHA 2018a, 8). In November 2018 the committee concluded a year of work by formally making recommendations to the JPPHA Board of Directors, consisting of elected officials from Jefferson County, the City of Arvada, and the City of Broomfield. Those recommendations included a spectrum of risk characterization and mitigation efforts, such as obtaining an independent review of all past contamination and health studies by a qualified national institution, commissioning new soil-contamination studies, developing techniques to use during parkway construction for mitigating plutonium resuspension and migration, and realigning the parkway to go up Highway 93 instead of Indiana Street (JPPHA 2018c). However, JPPHA's executive director subsequently responded to the JPAC's recommendations in a dismissive way (JPPHA 2018e).

The USFWS's only motivation for opening the refuge to public access is to implement a law passed in 2001. There is no other compelling reason to open it, and a quite compelling moral obligation not to open it – namely, protecting the public from exposure to plutonium contamination.

When foreman Wes McKinley of Colorado Special Grand Jury 89-2, empaneled to weigh evidence of environmental crimes at Rocky Flats, heard about plans to turn the plant into a wildlife refuge for the public, he ran for and became a Colorado state representative specifically to sponsor legislation requiring strongly worded informed-consent signage at the refuge to advise people of the risk they would take in visiting it (Colorado General Assembly, 2009). In another example of government officials failing to protect the public health from the impact of Rocky Flats, the bill did not pass, partly because Carl Spreng of CDPHE spoke in opposition to the proposed signage.

However, encouraging examples have emerged recently of government entities honoring this moral obligation. In the previous two years, seven local school districts have banned field trips to the refuge out of concern for the safety of students and staff. These responsible decisions by school district boards and superintendents will eliminate exposure of district students to Rocky Flats contamination through school activities, especially important because children are most vulnerable to the health impacts of ionizing radiation.

In addition, a coalition of local citizens' groups, along with the Town of Superior, filed suit in 2018 to prevent the refuge from opening, on grounds that the necessary environmental reviews required by law had not been performed properly (*Rocky Mountain Peace and Justice Center v. United States Fish and Wildlife Service* 2018; *Town of Superior v. United States Fish and Wildlife Service* 2018). In filing its suit, the Town of Superior set an example for other governments in the region of honoring its moral obligation to protect public health.

In my view, it is irresponsible and unethical for government at any level to evade its moral obligation to protect public health from Rocky Flats contamination. It's simply not justifiable via any excuse or rationalization. Citizens' lives and well-being are in the balance. Experience to date suggests that at present, only the school boards and the courts are listening. Other officials need to listen, too: city mayors and council members, county commissioners, governors, state representatives and senators, and even US representatives and senators. The more political support these concerns have, the more likely change will be effected in the future course of Rocky Flats–related matters.

This means we need more citizens to become concerned and lobby their elected officials, to go down the rabbit hole, research the issues, and become active. It's up to us to protect our fellow citizens from the failings of our governments.

Endnotes

1. See Pearce (2018) for a global catalog of the worst nuclear sites in world history, in which Rocky Flats warrants its own chapter.

2. Background radiation from plutonium is the result of fallout from aboveground nuclear weapons testing in the 1950s and 1960s, which sent radioactive materials into the atmosphere, where they circled the world and settled out. See US Environmental Protection Agency, www3.epa.gov/radtown/fallout-nuclear-weapons-testing.html.

3. Also see Vartabedian (2018) for news reporting on Kaltofen's studies.

4. A picocurie is one trillionth of a Curie, a unit of radioactivity equaling 37,000,000,000 decays per second.

5. Henry Church settled in the Rocky Flats area in the 1860s. Brothers Charlie and Perry McKay are the current heirs of the Church family; they are the nephews of Marcus Church, whose grandfather was Henry Church.

6. Doug Young was district policy director for US Representative Mark Udall (D-CO) and authored the Rocky Flats National Wildlife Refuge Act of 2001.

7. Rocky Flats plutonium has a different isotope ratio than does background fallout plutonium.

8. See also KDVR (2018) for a news story highlighting the disease incidence in Five Parks.

9. The Facebook groups Arvada Neighbors and Let's Talk, Arvada, are gold mines of such anecdotes.

10. Rocky Flats plutonium has a different ratio of those isotopes than does atmospheric fallout plutonium.

11. Dr. Morgan was known as the "father of health physics" and, while at Oak Ridge National Laboratory, set standards for human exposure to plutonium. See "Karl Z. Morgan" (2018).

12. Dr. Gofman was the first person to isolate milligram quantities of plutonium. See "John Gofman" (2018).

Works Cited

Ackland, Len. *Making a Real Killing: Rocky Flats and the Nuclear West.* Albuquerque: University of New Mexico Press, 1999.

Agency for Toxic Substances and Disease Registry (ATSDR), US Department of Health and Human Services. Toxicological Profile for Plutonium, 2010. www.atsdr.cdc.gov/toxprofiles/tp143.pdf, accessed Feb. 17, 2019.

Brown, Jerry. "Rocky Flats Study Should Be Given to Outside Experts, Schroeder Says," *Rocky Mountain News*, Aug. 18, 1979.

Chinn, Stephen. "The Relation of the Rocky Flats Plant and Other Factors to 1969–1971 Cancer Incidence in the Denver Area." Denver, CO: Fairfield and Woods, P.C. 1981.

Clapp, Richard. "Report of Dr. Richard W. Clapp." Philadelphia: Berger & Montague, P.C. Nov. 13, 1996.

Cobb, John. "Affidavit of John Chandler Cobb." University of Colorado, Boulder, Special Collections and Archives, Nov. 17, 1983.

Cobb, John, B., Charles Eversole, Philip G. Archer, Roxanna Taggart, and Deward W. Eford. "Plutonium Burdens in People Living Near the Rocky Flats Plant." US Environmental Protection Agency, Las Vegas, NM: EPA-600/S4-82-069, 1983. https://cfpub.epa.gov/ols/catalog/advanced_bibliography.cfm?&FIELD1=SUBJECT&INPUT1=nuclear&TYPE1=EXACT&LOGIC1=AND&COLL=&SORT_TYPE=MTIC&start_row=926.

Colorado Department of Health. "Public Notice of Plutonium Contamination in the Area of Dow Chemical Rocky Flats Plant," Denver, CO: Jan. 24, 1973a.

———. "Notice of Publication of Amendment to Rules and Regulations Pertaining to Radiation Control," Denver, CO: Apr. 19, 1973b.

———. "Development Around the Rocky Flats Plant," Denver: Apr. 12, 1979.

Colorado Department of Public Health and Environment (CDPHE). 2016–2019 Strategic Plan, 2017. www.colorado.gov/pacific/sites/default/files/OPP-StrategicPlan2016-19-July2017.pdf, accessed Feb. 17, 2019.

———. "Rocky Flats Cancer Study," 1998. www.colorado.gov/pacific/cdphe/cdphe-rocky-flats-cancer-study, accessed Feb. 17, 2019.

———. "Rocky Flats: Myths and Misunderstandings," 2018a. rockyflatssc.org/public_comment/Myths%20and%20Misunderstand-

ings%20CDPHE%20presentation%20at%20RFSC%20with%20
notes%20%282018-2-5%29%20.pdf, accessed Feb. 17, 2019.

————. "What Are the Risks to a Rocky Flats National Wildlife Refuge
Visitor?" 2018b. www.colorado.gov/pacific/cdphe/rocky-flats-risks-
to-refuge-visitor, accessed Feb. 17, 2019.

Colorado General Assembly, House, House Bill 09-1060, 2009.

Crump, Kenny S., Tie-Hua Ng, and Richard G. Chuddihy. "Statistical
Analysis of Cancer Incidence Patterns in the Denver Metropolitan
Area in Relation to the Rocky Flats Plant." Inhalation Toxicology Re-
search Institute, 1984.

Dark Circle. Directed by Judy Irving. New York: New Yorker Films, 1982.

Decision at Rocky Flats. Pamela Roberts, filmmaker. Rocky Flats Truth
Force, 1979. vimeo.com/groups/161968/videos/45547905, accessed
Feb. 17, 2019.

Edwards, Rob. "Plutonium Cancer Risk May Be Higher Than Thought."
New Scientist (July 18, 2004). www.newscientist.com/article/dn6152-
plutonium-cancer-risk-may-be-higher-than-thought, accessed Feb.
17, 2019.

Flack, Susan et al. "Project Task 7 Report: Demography & Land Use Reconstruction of the Area Surrounding the Rocky Flats Plant." Ala-
meda, CA: ChemRisk (a division of Dow Chemical Company), April
1994, Fig. 3.1.

Illsley, C. T., and M. W. Hume. "Plutonium Concentrations in Soil on
Lands Adjacent to the Rocky Flats Plant." Rocky Flats Plant, Golden,
CO: Rockwell International Energy Systems Group, 1979.

Iversen, Kristen. *Full Body Burden: Growing Up in the Nuclear Shadow of
Rocky Flats.* New York: Crown, 2012.

Jefferson Parkway Public Highway Authority (JPPHA). "Jefferson Parkway Advisory Committee Meeting Summary," Feb. 20, 2018a. www.
jppha.org/citizen-engagement, accessed Feb. 17, 2019.

————. "Jefferson Parkway Advisory Committee Meeting Summary,"
Jan. 18, 2018b. www.jppha.org/citizen-engagement, accessed Feb. 17,
2019.

————. "Jefferson Parkway Advisory Committee PowerPoint Presented to JPPHA Board." Nov. 15, 2018c. www.jppha.org/citizen-engagement, accessed Feb. 17, 2019.

————. "Jefferson Parkway Advisory Committee (JPAC) Final Report," 2018d. www.jppha.org/citizen-engagement, accessed Feb. 17, 2019.

————. "Executive Director's Recommendations on JPAC Final Report," 2018e. www.jppha.org/citizen-engagement, accessed Feb. 17, 2019.

Jensen, Carol. "Rocky Flats Downwinders Health Survey, Metropolitan State University of Denver." Rocky Flats Downwinders, 2016. rockyflatsdownwinders.com/wp-content/uploads/2016/05/RFD-Health-Survey-Executive-Summary-Final.pdf, accessed Feb. 17, 2019.

"John Gofman." Wikipedia. en.wikipedia.org/wiki/John_Gofman, 2018, accessed Feb. 17, 2019.

Johnson, Carl. "Cancer Incidence in an Area Contaminated with Radionuclides Near a Nuclear Installation." *Ambio* 10, no. 4 (1981): 176–182.

————. Letter to Kitty Kinsman, Sept. 30, 1985. rockyflatsambushedgrandjury.com/wp-content/uploads/19850930-Carl-Johnson-letter-to-Kitty-Kinsman.pdf, accessed Feb. 17, 2019.

Johnson, Carl J., Ronald R. Tidball, and Ronald C. Severson. "Plutonium Hazard in Respirable Dust on the Surface of Soil." *Science* 193 (Aug. 6, 1976): 488–490.

Kaltofen, Marco. "Field Investigation and Laboratory Report for LeRoy Moore, PhD." Boston: Boston Chemical Data Corporation, 2012.

————. "Microanalysis of Particle-Based Uranium, Thorium, and Plutonium in Nuclear Workers' House Dust." *Environmental Engineering Science* 36, no. 2 (2019): 219–226.

"Karl Z. Morgan." Wikipedia, en.wikipedia.org/wiki/Karl_Z._Morgan, 2018, accessed Feb. 17, 2019.

KDVR. "Safety Concerns Continue at Rocky Flats Months Ahead of New Trails Opening Up." Fox 31 Denver KDVR-TV, Apr. 2, 2018. kdvr.com/2018/04/02/safety-concerns-continue-at-rocky-flats-months-ahead-of-new-trails-opening-up, accessed Feb. 17, 2019.

Ketterer, Michael. "Cadenas de Evidencia: Tracing Pu from Nucleosynthesis to the Environment, and the Human Body." Presentation to Rocky Flats Right to Know, Jan. 23, 2019. Trinity Presbyterian Church, Arvada, Colorado.

Krey, P. W., and E. P. Hardy. "Plutonium in Soil Around the Rocky Flats Plant." New York: US Atomic Energy Commission, Health and Safety Laboratory. HASL-235, 1970.

Litaor, Iggy. "Plutonium Contamination in Soils in Open Space and Residential Areas Near Rocky Flats, Colorado." *Health Physics* 76, no. 2 (1999): 171–199.

Maher, Jared. "The Rocky Road to Developing Around Rocky Flats," *Westword*, Jan. 15, 2009a. www.westword.com/news/the-rocky-road-to-developing-around-rocky-flats-5102336, accessed Feb. 17, 2019.

———. "Will the Proposed Jefferson Parkway Toll Road Take Colorado Commuters for a Ride?" *Westword*, Jan. 15, 2009b. www.westword.com/news/will-the-proposed-jefferson-parkway-toll-road-take-colorado-commuters-for-a-ride-5102326, accessed Feb. 17, 2019.

Marcus F. Church v. United States of America. US District Court for the District of Colorado,1975.

Martell, Ed. 1970. Letter to Dr. Glenn T. Seaborg, chair, US Atomic Energy Commission, Jan. 13, 1978. Special Collections and Archives Unit, University of Colorado, Boulder, Norlin Library.

McKinley, Wes, and Caron Balkany. *The Ambushed Grand Jury.* Lanham, MD: Apex, 2004.

McNeely, Elaine. Public comment, Rocky Flats Stewardship Council, Apr. 2. Rocky Mountain Metropolitan Airport, Broomfield, Colorado, 2018. www.youtube.com/watch?v=9XTtu2DRb3k at 59:10, accessed Feb. 17, 2019.

Moore, LeRoy. "Rocky Flats Nuclear Guardianship, Series 4: Rocky Flats Legacy – Nuclear Workers' Stories," 2017, 2011. leroymoore.wordpress.com/2011/02/21/rocky-flats-legacy-nuclear-workers-stories, accessed Feb. 17, 2019.

———. "Health Risk of Living Downwind of Rocky Flats." Rocky Flats Nuclear Guardianship, 2017. www.rockyflatsnuclearguardianship.

org/single-post/2017/01/16/Health-Risk-of-Living-Downwind-of-Rocky-Flats-By-LeRoy-Moore-PhD-January-2017, accessed Feb. 17, 2019.

Mulvaney, Kevin. "A Brief History of Amchitka and the Bomb." Greenpeace, 2007. www.greenpeace.org/usa/a-brief-history-of-amchitka-and-the-bomb, accessed Feb. 17, 2019.

Pearce, Fred. *Fallout: Disasters, Lies, and the Legacy of the Nuclear Age.* Boston: Beacon Press, 2018.

Perry S. McKay v. United States of America. US District Court for the District of Colorado, 1984. rockyflatsambushedgrandjury.com/wp-content/uploads/19841214-McKay-v-Ackard-75-M-1162-EIN.pdf. Accessed Feb. 17, 2019.

PR Newswire. "Court Grants Final Approval of $375 Million Settlement in Cook v. Rockwell International Corporation." PR Newswire, May 1, 2017. www.prnewswire.com/news-releases/court-grants-final-approval-of-375-million-settlement-in-cook-v-rockwell-international-corporation-300448960.html, accessed Feb. 10, 2019.

Rechtin, Eberhardt. *Systems Architecting.* Boston: Prentice Hall, 1991.

Rocky Mountain Peace and Justice Center v. United States Fish and Wildlife Service. US District Court for the District of Colorado, 2018.

Seed, Robert R, K. W. Calkins, C. T. Illsley, F. J. Minor, and J. B. Owen. "Committee Evaluation of Plutonium Levels in Soil Within and Surrounding AEC Installation at Rocky Flats, Colorado." Dow Chemical Company, Rocky Flats Division, RFP-INV-10, Golden, Colorado, 1971.

Spreng, Carl. "Operable Unit 3 Offsite Areas." Presentation to the Rocky Flats Stewardship Council (RFSC), Feb. 4, 2013. www.rockyflatssc.org/OU3-RFSC-4Feb13.pdf, accessed Feb. 17, 2019.

Stone, James M., Scott B. Webb, and F. Ward Whicker. 1994. "Soil Sampling Site Characterization Near the Rocky Flats Plant." https://www-static.bouldercolorado.gov/docs/370_Stone_James_Soil-1-201307161155.pdf?_ga=2.45715428.1727737747.1579734718-79796889.1528124342.

Town of Superior v. United States Fish and Wildlife Service. US District Court for the District of Colorado, 2018.

US Congress. House of Representatives. H.B. 812 – Rocky Flats National Wildlife Refuge Act, 2001. www.congress.gov/bill/107th-congress/house-bill/812, accessed Feb. 17, 2019.

US Environmental Protection Agency (EPA). "Radioactive Fallout from Nuclear Weapons Testing," 2019. www3.epa.gov/radtown/fallout-nuclear-weapons-testing.html, accessed Feb. 17, 2019.

Vartabedian, Ralph. "Hidden Danger: Radioactive Dust Is Found in Communities Around Nuclear Weapons Sites." *Los Angeles Times*, Sept. 28, 2018. www.latimes.com/local/california/la-na-radiation-hazards-2018-story.html, accessed Feb. 17, 2019.

Webb, Scott B., James M. Stone, Shawki A. Ibrahim, and F. Ward Whicker. "The Spatial Distribution of Plutonium in Soil Near the Rocky Flats Plant." Colorado State University Department of Radiological Health Sciences, Fort Collins, 1994.

Young, Doug. Interview with author, Feb. 5. Littleton, Colorado, 2019.

ART AND PLUTONIUM AT ROCKY FLATS

Jeff Gipe

At a 2014 event honoring the twenty-fifth anniversary of the FBI raid at Rocky Flats, the master of ceremonies, Philip Sneed, introduced a panel of artists with the provocative question, "What is the role of artists in helping to effect change; does their work make any difference at all?" (Sneed et al. 2014).

While it is difficult to measure the effect of art on social and political change, Rocky Flats artwork has offered "alternative" systems of truth that help counteract the avoidance of actual truth, which has plagued Rocky Flats' contentious past. I've included several artists in the following chapter who bring clarity to issues surrounding Rocky Flats. In their effort to effect change, these artists have brought national and international attention to Rocky Flats and helped shape the broader dialogue surrounding nuclear weapons. Chronologically ordered, the following artworks – a small sample of Rocky Flats' rich creative history – provide a historical context that challenges our understanding of Rocky Flats and the legacy it has left us.

The critical issues that these works examine have also been an influence on my own artwork, and impelled me to create a memorial for the Rocky Flats plant. Beyond the selection of artworks that I cite as viable and important responses to the legacy of the Rocky Flats plant, I also narrate my personal struggle to memorialize the former nuclear weapons facility.

ROBERT ADAMS
Our Lives and Our Children: Photographs Taken Near the Rocky Flats Nuclear Weapons Plant

At age fourteen, Robert Adams and his family moved to Wheat Ridge, Colorado, just northwest of Denver (Adams 1994, 178). There was a plateau within sight of his home that rises between the plains and the Rocky Mountains. Recalling the first time his family visited the plateau, Adams wrote, "The view was like nothing we had ever known – windswept, sun-bleached, vast" (1994, 178).

Adams (1994, 180) was especially drawn to the plateau after taking up photography. He remarked about his keen desire to capture this beautiful and rapidly changing landscape: "The plateau has been the focus of my work for twenty years both because it was near my home and because the location was and is characteristic of the American West in general, and even the world. Though not many landscapes are at once as beautiful and as damaged as this one, most are, as we have invaded them, similarly discordant."

Native Americans previously inhabited the landscape to which Adams refers. Now, non-indigenous civilization's imprint on the land is so present that it is increasingly difficult to imagine the area's natural topography. In his acclaimed photographic book, *The New West*, Adams documents billboards, strip malls, freeways, and neighborhoods of tract housing engulfing the beautiful landscape of the Rocky Mountain Front Range (Adams and Szarkowski 2008). If the visible damage weren't telling enough, Adams notes, "worse, in relative secrecy there was constructed at the center of this geography an atomic-weapons factory. The Rocky

Flats Nuclear Weapons Plant is a collection of low buildings, uncompromising to the eye, inside of which the United States shaped plutonium for nuclear detonators. In the process, it exposed those living in Denver to plutonium suspended as smoke" (Adams 1994, 180).

Robert Adams and his wife actually witnessed smoke rising above the Rocky Flats Nuclear Weapons Plant in the early 1970s. "For an hour they watched the plume grow and experienced a sense of helplessness before what appeared to be a nuclear accident in progress" (Adams and Szarkowski 1983). They would eventually learn that the smoke they saw didn't originate at Rocky Flats. However, Adams and his wife certainly had reason for concern. Just a few years prior, on Mother's Day in 1969,

West Edge of Denver, ca. 1980. Photograph by Robert Adams.
© Robert Adams, courtesy Fraenkel Gallery, San Francisco.

Rocky Flats experienced a major plutonium fire that sent a plume of smoke toward Denver and out to the plains.

Influenced by these events, Adams (1983) turned his camera to what "of absolute worth" stood to be lost in the event of a nuclear catastrophe. The greatest threat, Adams felt, came to families living near the nuclear weapons plant. For the first time, Adams set out to depict the inhabitants of the damaged landscape he often photographed. The occupants of this altered land became victims themselves, paradoxically threatened by their own creation, intended for defense.

At first glance, the photographs can appear unremarkable, even banal, and like much of Adams's work, the poetic underpinnings take time to coalesce. The photographs of ordinary people doing ordinary things could be any of us, or our friends and family. There's a subtle feeling of unease, though, as if you can sense the helplessness that Adams and his wife experienced when they witnessed smoke rising over Rocky Flats. The implied peril faced by these individuals becomes a metaphor of the greater threat we all face from the production, and possible use, of nuclear weapons.

In a short essay that accompanies the photo series, Adams summarizes (1984, 93): "The plutonium triggers built at risk to Denver became part of a worldwide system so open to error and malfunction that it is reasonable to believe many of us will, at a scarcely imaginable but exact time, die from them". While Adams's photographs can leave the viewer with a sense of despair, he finds beauty within all of his subjects – and in that beauty Adams offers a glimpse of hope. "I think if I had one goal, it's to convince people to care and to look. I don't think that the game is over. It looks bleak, but I think we're obliged to keep trying, and that's why I think art is important" (Blevins 2012, 316).

BARBARA DONACHY
Amber Waves of Grain

As Cold War tensions were escalating in the early 1980s, the United States and the Soviet Union maintained thousands of nuclear weapons aimed at each other. Many people feared that nuclear war was imminent (Schloss-

Barbara Donachy's installation *Amber Waves of Grain* at the Museum of Science, Boston, in 1986. This photograph titled *All The Warheads in the United States Arsenal* was taken by nuclear photographer Robert del Tredici.

er 2014, 446). During the height of the standoff, Barbara Donachy was standing in downtown Denver, watching giant planes flying low overhead and bombs starting to drop (Moore et al. 1999). "It was the end; it was all-out nuclear war, and it was the end of everything that had happened. And then I woke up" (Moore et al. 1999).

For Donachy, the threat of nuclear war felt more present than ever after the nightmare. She soon took action and began volunteering with the American Friends Service Committee in Denver and working on the national nuclear FREEZE campaign (Moore et al. 1999). The nuclear FREEZE campaign was unveiled at Rocky Flats in 1980 with the goal of halting the nuclear arms race (Wilson 1999). The grassroots campaign grew quickly and sparked an international resistance to the ongoing nuclear buildup. While working on the campaign, Donachy started to question how many nuclear warheads the United States had built and stockpiled (Moore et al. 1999). The contents of the US stockpile were not publicly known because of the secrecy surrounding nuclear weaponry (Friedman et al. 2010).

Donachy concluded, after months of research, that in 1982 the US stockpile contained "12,000 strategic nuclear warheads, 15–20,000 tactical warheads, 1,000 inter-continental ballistic missiles, 640 submarine launch missiles, and some 3,500 cruise missiles." She also found that the nuclear core, or "trigger," for each of the warheads deployed and ready to be used were all manufactured at Rocky Flats (Sneed et al. 2014). Unable to grasp the magnitude, Donachy came up with an idea that she hoped would make tangible the vast numbers she had compiled.

Donachy and her husband soon turned the second story of their Denver home into a full-time production studio and began enlisting friends, family, neighbors, and other volunteers to help produce the massive project (Moore et al. 1999). After more than six months of work, and using 6 tons of clay slip, Barbara and nearly seventy volunteers successfully cast and fired 35,000 miniature cone-shaped warheads. They also created 33 miniature submarines and 400 B-52 miniature bombers, which represented the actual vehicles designed and built to deliver the warheads.

The repetition of the thousands of clay warheads resembles a field of wheat, and the name *Amber Waves of Grain*, referring to the song "America the Beautiful," was adopted as the title. The installation was first displayed in TriBeCa, New York, at an event hosted by the Performers and Artists for Nuclear Disarmament (Moore et al. 1999). Once the show was up, a reporter from the *Wall Street Journal* published a short article on the exhibit and sparked an outpouring of press coverage (Moore et al. 1999).

In the subsequent nine years, Donachy, with the help of many volunteers, set the show up in eighteen locations in the United States and Europe. Hundreds of thousands of viewers saw the exhibition, and for the first time the public was able to visualize the United States' massive nuclear weapons stockpile.

Amber Waves of Grain was produced and displayed at the height of the nuclear arms race, helping to focus international attention on the issue of nuclear proliferation (Morreale 2014, 197; Salzman 2003). At the Arvada Center's *Rocky Flats Then and Now: 25 Years After the Raid* event in 2014, Donachy concluded her presentation by saying, "It was tedious, difficult, obsessive, and probably the most rewarding thing I've done in my life" (Sneed et al. 2014).

JOHN CRAIG FREEMAN
Operation Greenrun II

John Craig Freeman was shocked to witness the public's apathy toward Rocky Flats when he moved to Boulder, Colorado, in 1987. "I became increasingly amazed that a community would allow such a beautiful place to be tainted with plutonium (Cameron 1992, 39)."

As a fine arts student at the University of Colorado, Boulder, Freeman began contemplating ways to raise awareness through art (Cameron 1992, 38). His first response was a public installation at Boulder's Civic Park, in 1988. It consisted of four sequential 4-foot-by-6-foot images depicting a nuclear worker in a HAZMAT suit (Freeman, *Sculpture in the Park*). With each successive image, the focus narrows, until the final image reveals only the worker's face mask. Freeman utilized an emerging

Operation Greenrun II. Eleven 10-foot-by-40-foot mosaic laser prints on billboards. Highway 93, Rocky Flats, Colorado. November 1990 through April 1991. Photo by John Craig Freeman.

computing technology that allowed him to enlarge an image up to thousands of times its original size and print it, piece by piece, using an early model LaserWriter printer.[1]

The extraordinary FBI and EPA raid at Rocky Flats occurred the following year, on June 6, 1989, and plutonium production was halted. However, the Department of Energy and its contractors were determined to restart plutonium work at the site. While government officials lobbied for funding to restart plutonium operations (Day 1990) Freeman was eyeing a row of unused billboard structures that lined the west side of Rocky Flats on Highway 93. He envisioned taking his innovative printing technique to a massive scale in an "attempt to bring about tangible political change" (Freeman, personal communication, July 10, 2016).

Freeman negotiated with the owner of the billboards and the company eventually agreed to loan the structures for six months (Cameron 1992, 38). During the negotiations, the activist organization Greenpeace offered to collaborate on the project and donated funds toward production costs (Cameron 1992, 38). Once realized, *Operation Greenrun II* encompassed eleven 10-foot-by-40-foot billboards, each consisting of more than 2,000 individual 8.5-inch-by-11 inch prints (Cameron 1992, 38).

A firestorm erupted when the project was revealed. The project's size, scope, and political nature made it newsworthy in itself, but the controversy escalated when a lawyer representing a group called Citizens Against Billboards on Highway 93 interrupted a news conference (Engel 1990).

Freeman's project garnered national and international attention (*Harper's; Time; Der Spiegel*). One side of the billboards depicted nuclear workers, and sequentially read, "Today," "We Made," "A 250,000 Year," "Commitment." The statement references the amount of time plutonium will remain harmful to humans. From the opposite direction, the billboards depicted a nuclear explosion, reading, "Building," "More Bombs," "Is A," "Nuclear," "Waste." A separate billboard urged citizens to call then-Colorado governor Roy Romer and demand he put an end to Rocky Flats (Lipard). While *Operation Greenrun II* was on display, and in the midst of the media frenzy, the decision was made to shut down Rocky Flats for good (Freeman, personal communication, July 8, 2016).

ZOE STRAUSS
Rocky Flats

Zoe Strauss grew up amid the climate of nuclear fear during the Reagan administration and became particularly interested in the Cold War (Strauss, communication, Aug. 3, 2016). She fixated on the American West as a mythic land where nuclear weapons are manufactured and detonated (Scott and Swenson 2015, 82).

Strauss pursued her Cold War obsession in 2008, traveling to the Trinity bomb site in White Sands, New Mexico, and to the Rocky Flats Nuclear Weapons Plant (Strauss, communication, Aug. 3, 2016). Rocky Flats was always of tremendous interest to Strauss. For her, the facility represents the "mistake, horror, and power of nuclear munitions." When Strauss arrived at Rocky Flats in 2008, the site was not what she had envisioned: "I was not prepared for the reality of what had happened after the plant had closed." Strauss toured the Rocky Flats site and photographed the open prairie that once housed the massive bomb factory. She also met with former Rocky Flats workers and their families and with great compassion photographed intimate moments and learned of their ongoing struggles.

An image titled *Nila Holding Shirt* depicts the widow of Rocky Flats worker, Danny Adkins, holding a long-john shirt he was given to wear

Nila Holding Shirt, 2008. Photo by Zoe Strauss.

home after being exposed to high levels of radiation at work. The clothes he dressed himself in that day became so radioactively "hot" they had to be confiscated and destroyed (Strauss, Billboard Project, n.d.). Danny passed away in 2003 at age forty-seven (Draper 2014).

Strauss also met with Judy Padilla, who worked at Rocky Flats for twenty-two years. In her fifteenth year on the job, Judy developed breast cancer and had to undergo a radical double mastectomy. Padilla took six months off to fight the illness, and then returned to work at Rocky Flats (Trumbule 2010). In Strauss's series, Judy wears an American flag T-shirt that carries the slogan "Remember the Rocky Flats Cold War Vets." In one of Strauss's photos, Judy holds up paperwork from the government denying that her illness is related to her work at Rocky Flats.[2]

Charlie Wolf is the subject of another series of photographs by Strauss. Charlie, a chemical engineer, was assigned as a project manager for the decontamination and deconstruction of Building 771 ("As Likely as Not" 2009). Building 771 was legendary for its horrific past and became known as "the most dangerous building in America" ("The Most Dangerous Building in America" 2007). In one of Strauss's photos, Charlie prepares to give himself his daily chemo injection; in another, he brushes his fingers over a scar that runs the length of his skull (Strauss 2008). Charlie passed away in 2009 after a seven-year battle with brain cancer (Strauss 2009).

In the book *Critical Landscapes*, Julian Bryan-Wilson writes that Strauss utilizes "bodies to register the invisible toxicity of the nuclear landscape and to make palpable the discursive dynamics of nuclear culture" (Scott and Swenson 2015, 78). Many Americans think of the Cold War as a war without death. However, there is indeed a human and environmental price that is paid in the name of national defense, and Strauss's photographs draw attention to this cost ("A Little-Known Casualty of the Cold War?" 2015).

SARAH KANOUSE and SHILOH KRUPAR
National TLC Service

As a response to the fading memory of Cold War legacies, artists and scholars Sarah Kanouse and Shiloh Krupar joined forces in 2011 to cre-

National Toxic Land/Labor Conservation Service logo.
Courtesy of National Toxic Land/Labor Conservation.

ate the "satiric and sincere" hypothetical government agency known as the National Toxic Land/Labor Conservation Service (National TLC Service). The National TLC Service takes a multidisciplinary approach and calls on the participation of artists, environmentalists, activists, nuclear workers, Native communities, scholars of the bomb, and more. The duo travels the country conducting lectures, organizing design charrettes ("a collaborative workshop in which a group of people and designers draft solutions to a problem or issue"), and setting up interactive gallery exhibitions (Krupar and Kanouse 2016).

The National TLC Service parodies the US Fish and Wildlife Service (USFWS), which is overseen by the Department of the Interior. The USFWS is tasked with the repurposing and ongoing management of hundreds of former military sites across the country (Department of Defense [DOD] 2017), including the Rocky Flats National Wildlife Refuge which the USFWS received in 2007 and opened to the public amid controversy in 2018 (US Fish and Wildlife Service 2018). Mark Udall, a former Colorado representative who helped introduce the Rocky Flats Wildlife Refuge Act, said about Rocky Flats' conversion from a nuclear weapons factory to a national wildlife refuge, "We are in essence converting bombs into birds, weapons into wildlife, armaments into open space" (Blatt 2003).

Federal regulators boast about hundreds of species of wildlife and plants at Rocky Flats, including rare and endangered species (US Fish and Wildlife 2018), but they are more reluctant to talk about what was left behind – the buried buildings, the remaining contamination in the water and soil and the legacy of sick nuclear workers, of ill residents. This is where the National TLC Service comes in. They aim to fight the amnesia of the Cold War and to acknowledge past and ongoing injustices across the nuclear weapons complex. The TLC service states that they work to "develop justice-oriented forms of public memory and a future orientation to the permanent conditions of the Cold War" (Krupar, communication, Nov. 14, 2016).

> A video introducing the *National TLC Service* explains,
> As a wishful federal agency working for you, the National TLC Service addresses the continuing ecological, cultural, and human effects of the Cold War and the ongoing military state.... We will work in Rocky Flats, Colorado where the demolition of a former bomb trigger plant did more to erase the memory of the facility's troubled history than reduce the hazards of buried wastes. You will find us in Chicago, where missiles once pointed skyward along the beaches of Lake Michigan, and in the countless communities where workers mined, milled and lived in the shadow of the el-

ements that fueled the arms race.... We will honor per-spectives too often omitted for the dominant triumphant narratives of the Cold War: the voices of activists, of sick workers, of our so-called enemies, of downwind and down-stream communities, of test subjects, and of native nations (Kanouse and Krupar 2012).

Due to the invisible nature of contamination and ongoing secrecy and misinformation, many Cold War legacies, such as Rocky Flats, are difficult to ascertain. The National TLC Service seeks to fill the gap left by federal agencies. "Our Mission is to do for you what the Department of Energy and Department of Defense have been unwilling or unable to do – to recognize that the Cold War isn't past" (Kanouse and Krupar 2012).

DAVID WESTMAN
Nuclia Waste

Nuclia Waste (David Westman), is a Denver performance artist, comedi-enne, and drag queen. Nuclia utilizes Cold War kitsch and camp humor in her performances and digital artwork as the living embodiment of Rocky Flats nuclear waste. "I'm my own canvas; my art is me!" said West-man, who created Nuclia (Vickstrom).

Westman has no direct intent to address political commentary sur-rounding Rocky Flats; however, Shiloh Krupar (National TLC Service) points out in her 2013 book, *Hot Spotter's Report: Military Fables of Toxic Waste*, that Nuclia's antics form a new way of questioning how humans think of, and live with, the remains of US bomb production: "Her perfor-mance practices offer some tangible responses to the purifying discourse surrounding Rocky Flats, such as visibilizing the porosity of body and environment and the ways humans and nonhumans have been irrevoca-bly altered by nuclear projects" (*Hot Spotter's Report 2013*, 234). Through Nuclia's alternative artistic approach to addressing nuclear waste, Krupar suggests, "She opens the possibility for different social practices in relation to Rocky Flats that acknowledge mutation rather than recover the site or bodies as normal/natural" (234).

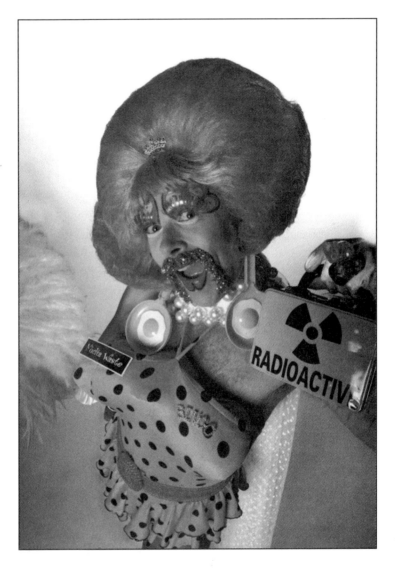

Nuclia Waste. Photo by David Westman.

On Nuclia's former website, the "Plutonium Princess" laid out her origin story:

> As the daughter of two Rocky Flats workers who were regularly exposed to radiation, Nuclia was born with a full head of green hair. The town of Rocky Flats was shocked and

amazed, but accepted her just as they had accepted that all the fish in Rocky Flats Lake have three eyes. Special lead diapers had to be designed for Nuclia, since her radiation destroys natural fibers, and cotton bursts into flames. Nuclia's intense radiation caused the local insect population to mutate into bioluminescent butterflies, which helped to "make Rocky Flats the tourist mecca it is today."

On Nuclia's last website you could, among other activities, visit strange roadside attractions, dress up a Nuclia doll, and take the toxic tour of Rocky Flats. Rocky Flats has been transformed into Nuclia's Plutonium Palace and comes complete with a nuclear reactor core, where "Nuclia gets her special powers," and a missile tower, because "no radioactive goddess would be caught dead without a few nuclear warheads lying about the place. They're ready to launch at a moment's notice to spread radioactive joy wherever needed in the world" (Westman).

JEFF GIPE
Cold War Horse

The buildings at Rocky Flats have been razed and buried, the signs have been removed, and the east entrance and guard station where my father entered work for two decades is no longer recognizable. Scott Surovchak, a former Rocky Flats worker and current Department of Energy Rocky Flats Legacy manager, remarked in 2014, "There's times when I'll stand there and try to remember what building used to be here and what did this look like and I just can't do it anymore. It's now just a grassland" (Dondero 2014). The Rocky Flats site, which was so familiar to me having grown up in the area, and especially to my father, has become arcane.

As a response to the erasure of Rocky Flats, in 2011 I designed a model for a monument to Rocky Flats and attempted to gain funding to build the large-scale project. My efforts ultimately proved futile, and a year later the land around Rocky Flats, which stood largely barren because of known widespread contamination, began to be developed for housing (Fleming 1995).

A city-sized development project on the southern border of Rocky Flats, named Candelas, has been pitched as an earth-conscious "leader in green-living, and there are plans for thousands of homes and millions of feet of commercial real estate." The development's Community Brochure states, "Candelas site has rich, historic roots to match the breathtaking, picture perfect scenery encompassing it." The brochure and the development's website fail to mention the historic former nuclear weapons facility. The brochure goes on to assert, "Candelas is a natural wonderland" and the "landscape boasts nature's untamed beauty." The denial goes even deeper, with the insistence that the encompassing land is in "mint condition" (Candelas).

During Candelas' grand opening event in 2013, I joined several concerned citizens at the entrance of the development in an action to raise awareness about the former nuclear weapons plant. Many visitors and prospective homebuyers were surprised to learn about the former nuclear bomb factory. One woman, who had recently purchased a house, said that she would not have bought there if she had known the history of the site.

That experience made clear to me that someone, or some symbol, needed to be present at all times. After increasing dismay, I came back to the idea of creating a memorial, and I began designing a new sculpture that I could produce without having to find or depend on funding. My original intention to acknowledge the site and its workers remained, but the sculpture evolved into a more radicalized visual to counter the silent denial. I worked for several months to produce a sculpture that has become known as the *Cold War Horse*—a slightly larger-than-life-sized horse wearing a bright red HAZMAT suit, fitted with goggles and a respirator.

I originally planned to perform a renegade installation of the memorial along the edge of the Rocky Flats site, but I was dissuaded after it became clear that tensions were high enough that the threat of swift destruction was likely. Six months after I finished the sculpture, on June 12, 2014, a local Denver paper reported, "Where the site ends to the south, the building begins; the Candelas development is going up quickly." The article concludes, "There are no signs that tell you the history of the 6,500 acres just up the hill" (Calhoun 2014). I was still unable to find a way to display the memorial.

Having exhausted all other options, I began going door to door and talking with local residents and business owners. Most people were un-

The *Rocky Flats Cold War Horse* monument stands in front of the Denver skyline. Pictured October, 2016. Photo by Jeff Gipe.

receptive to the idea because of the memorial's controversial nature. My efforts seemed hopeless until I eventually knocked on the door of Janice and Bruce Roberts. Bruce had worked at Rocky Flats for a short time, and both Janice and Bruce felt that people should understand the history of the area, and they agreed to display the memorial.

With Bruce's help, the sculpture was installed within a week – over a year and a half after it was built – and there was an immediate response from the public. Seen clearly from the highway, many people driving by honked and waved or stopped by share their personal stories about Rocky Flats.

Not everyone welcomed a Rocky Flats reminder, however. Less than two weeks after the piece was installed, the sculpture was hooked to a vehicle and ripped from its concrete foundation, then subsequently beaten with a sledgehammer. The day of the attack, a Denver news station headline read, "The Vandalism of a Controversial Piece of Artwork on Hwy 72 Was Not a Random Act." (Oh.) The malicious sabotage led many people to believe that local developers might be the culprits.

Despite the agenda of whoever wanted to destroy the memorial, the attempt to suppress awareness of the nuclear plant only accomplished the opposite. The vandalism provoked outrage in the community and led to an outpouring of support and media coverage. The monument was rebuilt, resurrected, and fortified with security features. A little more than a month after the vandalism, and on the week of the ten-year anniversary of the "cleanup" at Rocky Flats, a dedication ceremony was held on October 18, 2015.

> A stone sign was also erected and reads, in part:
> This memorial was created to acknowledge the history of Rocky Flats, its workers, and the surrounding community... safety concerns still exist due to remaining contamination and questions of risk. Nonetheless, the history of this important national and international site, and the workers who sacrificed so much, have yet to be acknowledged by federal, state or local governments. This memorial stands as a reminder of a history that we must not forget.

CONCLUSION

Rocky Flats stopped producing nuclear weapons more than a decade ago, and today there is no visible trace of what happened there. Radioactive plutonium will remain in the environment for thousands of generations – long after the *Cold War Horse* has deteriorated and the refuge designation fails. Who will carry this information into the future when the topic is no longer newsworthy? When generations have passed, who, or what, will make the public aware of Rocky Flats' buried past? Hannah Nordhaus, who worked for several years to collect oral histories of former workers, activists, and others involved with Rocky Flats, wrote in a 2009 article, "Plutonium has a half-life of 24,000 years. The half-life of memory, by contrast, is a much briefer thing. The contamination at Rocky Flats will long outlive our efforts to control or even remember it... like the waste trenches and the rumors and the memories, Rocky Flats' contested history is now invisible to the naked eye" (Nordhaus 2009).

The events being played out at Rocky Flats and across the nuclear weapons complex demonstrate that it is up to us as citizens to remember what happened. Without knowledge there are no safeguards. If the Rocky Flats Nuclear Weapons Plant and its legacy of contamination is to be remembered generations from now, it will be credited to ongoing creative acts that compel others to pay attention. The story of art and plutonium at Rocky Flats is not over; it's only just beginning.

Endnotes

1. Although this sounds dated, the technology for large-scale printing was not available until several years later (Cameron 1992, 38).

2. "We were acutely aware of how important our jobs were for the country and we felt that the country would protect us in return" (Strauss 2008).

Works Cited

"A Little-Known Casualty of the Cold War? U.S. Nuclear Workers," PBS, aired Dec. 12, 2015. www.pbs.org/newshour/show/a-little-known-casualty-of-the-cold-war-u-s-nuclear-workers.

"As Likely As Not." Exposé America's Investigative Reporter, PBS, aired Apr. 1. 2009.

Adams, Robert, "Why People Photograph: Selected Essays and Reviews," *Aperture*, 1994.

Adams, Robert, and John Szarkowski. "The New West," *Aperture*, 2008.

———. "Our Lives and Our Children: Photographs Taken Near the Rocky Flats Nuclear Weapons Plant 1979–1983," *Aperture*, 1983.

Blatt, Jeanna. *Countdown to Closure: Making the Impossible Possible.* Rocky Flats closure video produced for Kaiser Hill and Department of Energy, est. 2003.

Blevins, Tim. *Film and Photography on the Front Range.* Pikes Peak Library District, Colorado Springs, Colorado, 2012.

Calhoun, Patricia. "The Secrets of Rocky Flats Won't Stay Buried Forever," *Westword*, June 12, 2014.

Cameron, Andy. "Digital Dialogues, Street Digital." *TEN•8*, vol. 2, no. 2: 32-39, (Oct. 1992), Birmingham, England.

Candelas. "Life Wide Open: The Story of Candelas," Candelas Community Brochure. Arvada Colorado, www.candelaslife.com/Community-Brochure/Candelas-Community-Brochure.html, accessed May 12, 2018.

Day, Janet. "Flats Start-Up Set for June Plutonium in Air Ducts Still Poses Problem For Plant Officials," *Rocky Mountain News*, May 18, 1990.

Der Spiegel. "Personalien," 49/1990, 281.

DoD Natural Resources, and Alison Dalsimer. "Threatened and Endangered Species on . DoD Lands." *DoD Natural Resources*, 2017.

Dondero, Michael. "Interview with Scott Surovchak." *Colorado's Cold War* transcripts. Rocky Mountain PBS, Aug. 6, 2014.

Draper, Electa. "They Just Want Us to Die and Go Away," *Denver Post*, Feb. 23, 2014.

Engel, Marnie. "Environmentalists Clash with Anti-Flats Activists," *Daily Camera*, Nov. 16, 1990.

Fleming, Richard. "Hot Property," *Westword*, June 4, 1995.

Freeman, John Craig. "Sculpture in the Park," n.d. johncraigfreeman. wordpress.com/sculpture-in-the-park/, accessed June 7, 2014.

Friedman, Emily, Kirit Radia, and Luis Martinez. "Clinton, Pentagon Reveal State Secret: Size of U.S. Nuclear Arsenal," aired May 3, 2010, ABC News. abcnews.go.com/Politics/International/hillary-clinton-reveal-size-us-nuclear-arsenal/story?id=10539450, accessed Dec. 12, 2018.

Harper's. March 1991.

"In Miniature, The U.S. Nuclear Arsenal," *New York Times*, Jan. 1, 1986.

Kanouse, Sarah, and Shiloh Krupar. *Introducing the National Toxic Land/ Labor Conservation Service*. National Toxic Land/Labor Conservation Service introduction video, Aug. 27. nationaltlcservice.us/, accessed Dec. 12, 2018.

Krupar, Shiloh, and Sarah Kanouse. *National Cold War Monuments and Cold War Heritage Trail Workbook.* Produced by National TLC Service for an event in Colorado Springs, Colorado, March 19, 2016.

Krupar, Shiloh R. *Hot Spotter's Report: Military Fables of Toxic Waste.* Minneapolis: University of Minnesota Press, 2013.

Lipard, Lucy L. "Snipers Nest," *Z Magazine,* Oct. 1991.

Moore, LeRoy et al. "Barbara Donachy Oral History." *Maria Rogers Oral History Collection,* https://localhistory.boulderlibrary.org/islandora/object/islandora%3A31728?solr_nav%5Bid%5D=103e597db-b8228220c09&solr_nav%5Bpage%5D=0&solr_nav%5Boffset%5D=0 vol. OH1500, Sept. 3, 1999.

Morreale, Don. *Cowboys, Yogis and One Legged Ski Bums.* Bloomington, IN: XLibris, 2014.

"The Most Dangerous Building in America." *Nightline,* aired Dec. 20, 1994, ABC News. DVD release date May 17, 2007.

Nordhaus, Hannah. "The Half-Life of Memory," *High Country News,* Feb. 17, 2009.

Oh, Jessica, and KUSA. "Cold War Horse Vandalism Was Not Random, Jeffco Says," KUSA newscast, Sept. 8, 2015. www.9news.com/news/local/cold-war-horse-vandalism-was-not-random-jeffco-says_20160412015535742/128836498, accessed Dec. 12, 2018.

Salzman, Jason. *Making the News: A Guide for Nonprofits and Activists.* Boulder, CO: Westview Press, 2003.

Schlosser, Eric. *Command and Control.* London: Penguin Books Ltd: 2014.

Scott, Emily Eliza, and Kirsten Swenson. *Critical Landscapes: Art, Space, Politics.* Berkeley: University of California Press, 2015.

Sneed, Philip et al. "Imagining the Real: Art and Rocky Flats." *Rocky Flats Then and Now: 25 Years After the Raid.* Arvada Center for the Arts and Humanities, Arvada, Colorado, June 7, 2014.

Strauss, Zoe. Billboard Project. Official webpage for Zoe Strauss's *Billboard Project.* zoestraussbillboardproject.com/billboards/billboard-5/.

————. *Charlie's Daily Self Injection.* Official webpage of Zoe Strauss, Posted March 29, 2008. zoestrauss.blogspot.com/2008/03/charlies-daily-chemo-self-injection.html.

————. *Rest in Peace, Charlie Wolf.* Official webpage of Zoe Strauss, posted Jan. 31, 2009. zoestrauss.blogspot.com/2009/01/rest-in-peace-charlie-wolf.html.

————. *We Were Acutely Aware of How Important.* Official webpage of Zoe Strauss, posted March 29, 2008. zoestrauss.blogspot.com/2008/03/we-were-acutely-aware-of-how-important.html.

Time. "Nuclear Confrontation," November 26, 1990.

Trumbule, Gerald. *"Rocky Flats Worker Judy Padilla Part 3."* Denver Direct, posted to YouTube March 17, 2010, www.youtube.com/watch?v=rLdXY7TWC80.

US Fish and Wildlife Service. "Home – Rocky Flats – U.S. Fish and Wildlife Service." www.fws.gov/refuge/rocky_flats/, accessed Sept. 17, 2018.

Vickstrom, Anne Hopper. *Have You Met? David Westman aka Nuclia Waste,* Blacktie Colorado. www.blacktie-colorado.com/have-you-met/david-westman-aka-nuclia-waste/.

Westman, David. Nuclia Waste, An Experiment Gone Bad. Web archive of Nuclia Waste's official webpage. web.archive.org/web/20130226025543/http://www.nucliawaste.com/whonuc.html, accessed Feb. 26, 2013.

Wilson, David, Return to the Nuclear Crossroads: Resistance at Rocky Flats (Part 1), David Barsamian/Alternative Radio, recorded in Boulder, CO, 1999.

COOK v. ROCKWELL LAWSUIT

Louise Roselle

In July 2016, after twenty-six years of litigation, the defendants agreed to pay $375 million to settle the class action lawsuit of *Merilyn Cook, et al. v. Rockwell International Corp. and Dow Chemical Company*, Case Number 90-cv-00181, in the United States District Court for the District of Colorado. During that twenty-six-year period, there had been more than 2,400 pleadings filed in the United States District Court, fifteen published decisions of the District Court,[1] a four-month jury trial, seventeen days of jury deliberation, two published decisions by the Tenth Circuit Court of Appeals, and two petitions for writ of certiorari filed in the United States Supreme Court. Attorneys for the plaintiffs spent in excess of 160,000 hours (the equivalent of eighty person-years of work) working on the case and more than $7 million in out-of-pocket expenses. In 2008, the plaintiffs had a judgment against defendants for $926 million inclusive of compensatory damages, punitive damages, and prejudgment interest. That judgment was reversed by the court of appeals in 2010, leaving the plaintiffs with nothing. In 2015, in the second court of appeals decision, the court reinstated the case and remanded it to the trial court for further proceedings. Finally, the case settled. While these statistics are daunting, they don't convey the bitterness of the fight, the intensity of the emotions, or the innumerable controversies that this litigation embodied.

The Lawsuit Commences

On June 6, 1989, the FBI raided Rocky Flats. The raid was the result of an investigation concerning environmental crimes at the plant. Two of the immediate effects of the raid were that the neighbors of the plant became concerned about their safety, and the real estate market plummeted. The neighbors sought legal counsel and, after an investigation, a class action lawsuit was filed on January 30, 1990, by and on behalf of the residents who lived near the plant, alleging Colorado nuisance and trespass claims as well as claims under the federal Price-Anderson Act (PAA), arising from the defendants' alleged releases of plutonium and other hazardous materials into the surrounding environment, contaminating private property and jeopardizing human health. The two defendants were Dow Chemical Company, which managed the plant from 1951 to 1975, and Rockwell International,[2] which managed the plant from 1975 to 1989. The US Department of Energy (DOE) and its predecessors hired these companies to operate the plant. The plaintiffs alleged that their property had lost value and that they needed medical monitoring.

The two main causes of action were trespass and nuisance. A nuisance is an unreasonable interference with the use and enjoyment of land. A trespass is a physical invasion of another's land. Plaintiffs sought to prove that the management at Rocky Flats had operated the plant in violation of state and federal environmental laws, and that defendants released radioactive and other hazardous materials into the class area and caused the plaintiffs' property to be diminished in value. The defendants' position was that Rocky Flats had not affected the property values and that any releases of radioactive and hazardous materials were so minor as not to pose any health threat. Some facts were undisputed. Both parties agreed that there had been two major fires at the plant, that plutonium and other hazardous materials were released into the environment, and that environmental laws had been violated. By the time of the trial in

2006,[3] the plant had been torn down, and the government took the position that remediation of the site had been completed. New homes were being constructed near the site.

The Lawyers Representing the Parties

The lawyers in the case were experienced litigators who had worked cases involving nuclear sites and class actions. For the plaintiffs, there were three main law firms:[4] Berger & Montague, a law firm in Philadelphia that had been involved in the Three Mile Island litigation surrounding the release of radioactive material in 1979; Silver & DeBoskey, a Denver law firm that had been involved in issues relating to Rocky Flats for many years; and Waite, Schneider, Bayless & Chesley,[5] a Cincinnati law firm that had litigated the Fernald atomic weapons plant off-site residents' lawsuit between 1985 and 1989. Peter Nordberg, an attorney with Berger & Montague, devoted endless hours to this case and was primarily responsible for all motions and other writings until his untimely death in 2010.

Defendant Dow Chemical Company was represented by Kirkland & Ellis, a law firm headquartered in Chicago; and Sherman & Howard, a Denver law firm. Rockwell International was represented by Shea & Gardner, also a Denver law firm. All were nationally known litigation firms. Kirkland & Ellis took the lead for the defense. David Bernick, who has since left Kirkland & Ellis, was the key advocate for the defendants. The defense law firms were paid by DOE and therefore had no incentive to either resolve the lawsuit or streamline it. As a result, the work involved in this case was of the epic proportions described above.

The Class Representatives

One of the plaintiffs who filed the lawsuit was Merilyn Cook. Merilyn grew up in Golden, Colorado. She has loved horses and worked with them all of her life. She has had national, regional, and world champions and at one point was known in the Colorado area as one of the top breeders of show horses.

On the day of the FBI raid in 1989, Merilyn had a horse farm situated directly south of the Rocky Flats plant, where she boarded and trained horses and gave riding lessons. She had purchased two thirty-six-acre tracts at the corner of Ninety-Sixth and Indiana Streets in 1983, paying $306,000 for the property. She previously owned property close by and had sold it at a profit in 1983, so she did not question the purchase of more property in the vicinity of the Rocky Flats plant. Merilyn hoped to build an equestrian center as the focal point of a residential development designed around use of the horse facility. The equestrian center would have barns, an arena, housing for horse-loving families, and a use area for horses.

But when Merilyn went to the County for multifamily construction and zoning permits, she was told that it was not possible; the property was within a circle where that type of development was not allowed because of Rocky Flats. Merilyn then decided that she would subdivide the 72 acres into six 12-acre tracts and then improve and sell the properties as horse operation locations for people with horses. She proceeded to subdivide the properties. Merilyn built a house on one of the properties. It was a brick home of approximately 2,000 square feet with a fireplace, three bedrooms, and two baths. The house was used by trainers whom she employed or by families that rented it. Merilyn also built a 14,000-square-foot arena and stable complex. She also added a modular home to the property as well as utilities. On one of the other parcels, Merilyn built another 14,000-square-foot barn. Between the two improved parcels, she spent $700,000 for the improvements. To make these improvements, Merilyn borrowed $500,000 from the Colorado National Bank. The improvements were completed by 1985, but by that time, she had fewer customers than expected. Media attention to Rocky Flats was increasing, and Merilyn's customers expressed concerns about coming to her facility because it was so close to the plant. By the end of 1985, she was in financial trouble. Merilyn sold one of the 12-acre parcels to her friends Lorren and Gertrude ("Trudy") Babb, who were also plaintiffs in the lawsuit. The Babbs paid $128,000 for the lot. Merilyn used the Babbs' money to pay on the bank loans. In 1986, business was worse. Fewer customers were willing to do business with Merilyn at the location close to Rocky Flats. They were concerned about their children drinking the water and breathing the dust. People were unwilling to board their horses there. In 1987, she sold a parcel to Helen Phillips for $100,000. This money was used to pay debts and banks. Throughout 1987 and 1988, Merilyn's business continued to decline, and she was unable to sell any additional properties.

Before the FBI raid, Merilyn contacted the operator at Rocky Flats on at least two occasions because she needed help. She expressed her concerns that her business was deteriorating and that she was unable to sell her land due to the presence of Rocky Flats. Neither DOE nor Rockwell provided her with any assistance. By the time of the FBI raid, Merilyn had sold two parcels (to the Babbs and Helen Phillips). She was unable to sell the remaining four, and they went back to the holders of the notes. After the FBI raid, and having lost her business and her property, Merilyn moved to Springfield, Missouri, where she stayed for eight years. But she missed her family and her home and eventually decided to return to Colorado to the property on Indiana Avenue and the house she had built but never lived in.

Merilyn believed that Rocky Flats destroyed the value of her property, which would have been worth $2.2 million based on comparable sales in the neighborhood and like properties with like uses. She testified in the case that defendants polluted her property and caused a lack of confidence in the real estate marketplace, a lack of confidence in the horses that she was raising because of potential contamination, and a steady decline in her business. Merilyn testified that she agreed to be a class representative in this case "because I know that there [are] a lot of people, thousands of people in that area that suffered in various ways. I want to make that known, and I want to be part of seeing that that does not happen again."[6]

Sally and Richard Bartlett also are plaintiffs and class representatives in the case. Dick Bartlett was a successful banker in Arvada, Colorado, a mayor of Arvada, and a member of the Jefferson County Parks and Recreation Board. Sally is a registered nurse and had a long career in nursing; she also worked as a Realtor for several years. The couple has three children. The Bartletts agreed to be class representatives because they felt they had been harmed by the operations at Rocky Flats and were concerned and alarmed about the contamination. They also sought the truth about the work at the plant and the release of hazardous and radioactive chemicals. Like Merilyn Cook, the Bartletts were lifelong residents of the Denver area. In 1978, they bought vacant land on Alkire Street near Rocky Flats for $55,000. Before purchasing the land, the Bartletts had soil and water sampling done, and the results were within normal limits. The property was beautiful land with a gorgeous view of the Flatirons.[7] The family lived across from Standley Lake, and their property was exactly the size that they wanted – 10 acres. They built a 3,000-square-foot house on the property, a 1,200-square-foot multipurpose building that could be used as a barn, and a 20,000-square-foot equestrian building. There was also a modular home (1,800-square feet) and a trailer. The Bartletts' daughter and son-in-law, Karen and Mark Bannister, used the equestrian center for training horses, which had cost $300,000 to build.

In 1988, the Bartletts decided to downsize and put the property up for sale, listing it for $675,000. After ten years, they finally sold the property for $700,000. The Bartletts believe the property would have sold for twice as much if not for its proximity to Rocky Flats.

William and Delores Schierkolk[8] were two additional class representatives. Bill grew up in Nebraska and Kansas. He served in the US Navy, then worked for International Harvester Company in Denver for thirty-seven years as a mechanic. Delores worked for Miller Supermarkets for thirty years. The Schierkolks have four children. They purchased the property near Rocky Flats because they could look out their window at the Front Range of the Rocky Mountains. The property consists of 3.2 acres, with a four-bedroom house and a barn. They paid $92,000 for the property in 1978 and spent $34,000 on improvements. Bill still lives in the house on the property.

Within two years of moving to the property, Mrs. Schierkolk raised her concerns about Rocky Flats to the county health department and was told that it might not be safe to have a garden on the property. So the Schierkolks ceased gardening.

After the FBI raid, Bill and Delores did not consider selling their property as it would not have any value; furthermore there would not have been any buyers. The information that Bill and Delores learned about Rocky Flats caused a lot of stress in their family. In 1993, the Schierkolks filed an appeal related to the valuation of their property for real estate taxes. As a result of the appeal, the valuation was lowered from $167,700 to $150,940. Bill became a class representative because he was concerned about his safety, and what happened at the plant is reflected in his property's value. He thinks that it is questionable whether it can be sold.

Lorren and Gertrude ("Trudy") Babb[9] also were class representatives. At one time Lorren Babb was the mayor of Golden, Colorado, and he worked for Meyers Hardware and Coors Company and also sold real estate in Golden. Trudy Babb had a number of jobs, including work for the Jefferson County Schools and the Jefferson County treasurer. She came to Denver in the 1940s, and the Babbs were living in Golden when the plant opened in the early 1950s. They never lived in the class area, but they owned a 12-acre parcel of land purchased from Merilyn Cook. The Babbs put a barn on the property that could hold ten horses; they also dug a well. The couple spent at least $70,000 on the improvements. By the time they were finished, the they had almost $200,000 invested in the property. The Babbs' daughter and son-in-law used the property for their horse business, but after they divorced, Lorren and Trudy had to take care of the horses on the property. The Babbs could not handle the business and decided to sell the property in 1989 or 1990. Initially, they listed the property for $200,000 but eventually sold it for $137,000.

In addition to the class representatives, many other members of the class testified either by deposition or at trial. Most of their stories were similar – they believed that Rocky Flats had interfered with their use and enjoyment of their property and caused their property to diminish in value.

The Motions

After the complaint was filed in January 1990, defendants' first move was to file a motion to dismiss. Dow also filed a motion for summary judgment, arguing that the lawsuit was filed too late.[10] They claimed that the "publicity and events predating the FBI raid (including previous litigation by a few local landowners, state governmental enforcement actions, antinuclear protests outside the plant, and federal government studies of environmental problems at Rocky Flats) precluded recovery under each of plaintiffs' claims."[11] In February 1991, the Court issued its decision denying the motion to dismiss based on the failure to timely file the lawsuit but granted certain other motions. Plaintiffs filed an amended complaint and there followed another wave of motions.

In 1993, the case was assigned to Judge John L. Kane[12] who has retained the case since then.[13] Judge Kane certified a property class[14] defined as "all persons and entities owning an interest (including mortgagee and other security interests) in real property situated within the

Property Class Area, exclusive of governmental entities, defendants, and defendants' affiliates, parents and subsidiaries" as of June 7, 1989,[15] the day after the FBI raid of Rocky Flats. The Property Class Area is the area where, according to a DOE study, there was plutonium off-site. It is an irregularly shaped ellipse, and 12,000 people live in the class area.

Fact Discovery

As part of the litigation process, each party is entitled to discover facts that are relevant or may be relevant to the issues of the litigation. This discovery can be initiated by requesting documents, taking depositions, asking written questions (known as interrogatories), and asking the opposing party to admit that certain statements are true. The discovery process is often the longest portion of a lawsuit. In this case, the discovery process began shortly after the lawsuit was filed and continued right through trial. By the time discovery concluded, the plaintiffs had served on the defendants' 120 requests for production of documents.

In this case, many of the documents were under the DOE's control, since the plant is owned by the federal government. The DOE asserted that the documents could not be released because they contained information that was classified for national security reasons. A four-day hearing was held in 1995 concerning the documents that the DOE was withholding. Judge Kane concluded that the department's conduct was wrong and awarded plaintiffs their fees and costs of $500,000 for withholding documents.

Magistrate Judge Donald E. Abram[16] was assigned to handle discovery disputes. Many of his rulings were against the plaintiffs. For example, in 1992, Magistrate Judge Abram adopted an approach under which the plaintiffs were required to state the factual basis of their claims in precise detail even though they had not yet conducted discovery. The plaintiffs complied to the best of their ability, but the defendants argued that the plaintiffs' filing did not comply with the court's order and asked the court for sanctions against the plaintiffs, including dismissal of the class claims. On December 30, 1992, Magistrate Judge Abram found that the plaintiffs' statement was insufficient and ordered the plaintiffs to provide in even more detail the factual basis of their claims supported by expert reports. The plaintiffs appealed this order to Judge Kane, who modified the order to allow further discovery. As Merrill Davidoff, the plaintiffs' lead counsel, has explained:

> In a nutshell, although the Magistrate Judge (as urged by the Defendants) had ordered Plaintiffs to provide a statement of the factual basis of their claims, including a listing of the hazardous substances and doses to which each Plaintiff had been exposed, Defendants continually threw up roadblocks to impede Plaintiffs' access to the evidence in Defendants' hands (and in the possession of DOE) that was needed to comply with the Magistrate Judge's order.[17]

After Judge Kane's ruling, the defendants and DOE began producing discovery materials.

Over the next several years, approximately 800 boxes of paper documents were produced and ninety-nine fact witnesses were deposed, resulting in 22,500 pages of testimony. In order to review the 800 boxes of documents, plaintiffs hired contract employees to review the documents and identify those that should be copied and indexed for further use. A database of documents was made that allowed plaintiffs to search for documents they needed. For example, if a deposition was being taken of an employee, the database could be searched for documents the employee authored or received. Then those documents could be used in the deposition to question the witness. The plaintiffs also served sixty-six document subpoenas on other organizations not parties to the litigation, such as the DOE, the Environmental Protection Agency, and the Colorado Department of Health. These subpoenas contained a total of 638 requests for categories of documents and information.

The defendants also conducted discovery, serving 35 sets of interrogatories, requests to produce documents, and requests for admissions. These consisted of: 730 individual interrogatories; 88 separate requests to admit, and 729 individual requests for production of documents.

Expert Discovery

The parties are required in most cases to have experts testify. These experts give opinion testimony that supports the parties' allegations. In this case, because of the highly technical and specialized evidence, the plaintiffs engaged nineteen experts to opine on matters, including "what the appropriate standard of care was for the operation of a nuclear weapons facility generally, and for the safe handling of plutonium specifically; the health risks of plutonium exposure; the pathways by which Class members were exposed or were at risk of being exposed to plutonium, and how the effect of the contamination and health risks from Rocky Flats had affected property values in the Class area."[18]

The defendants engaged twenty-seven experts of their own, who expressed opinions that opposed those of the plaintiffs' experts.

Summary Judgment and Motions to Exclude Expert Testimony

In September 1996, after the experts gave their depositions and the fact discovery was completed, the defendants filed additional motions for summary judgment, which, if granted, would dismiss the case. In addition, the defendants asked the court to strike all of the plaintiffs' experts. Two years later, in July 1998, the court issued its opinion. It decertified the medical monitoring class but reaffirmed certification of the property class and denied summary judgment on the trespass and nuisance claims, finding that the plaintiffs had sufficient evidence that the properties in the class area had diminished in value as a "result of actual invasion by plutonium or interference with class members' use and enjoyment of their property."[19] The defendants filed a petition for appeal in the Tenth Circuit Court of Appeals, but that court denied the petition on October 8, 1998.

Judge Kane held a two-day hearing on whether the plaintiffs' experts should be excluded, after which he indicated that issues relating to the experts would be decided "once the parties presented a trial plan defining the issues and witnesses to be presented at trial."[20]

With regard to damages for nuisance and trespass, Judge Kane ruled that the plaintiffs could seek recovery of prospective damages for the continuing invasion of their land with plutonium. The measure of such damages would be the decrease in the value of their land caused by the prospect of the continuance of the invasion calculated as of the time when the injurious situation "became complete and comparatively enduring."[21] The case then proceeded to trial.

Trial and Verdict

The jury was selected on October 6, 2005, and the trial began on October 11. It lasted through January 20, 2006, and the verdict was rendered on February 14, 2006. The jury heard testimony from forty-one witnesses, and the trial transcript is more than 10,000 pages. "A total of 385 exhibits,[22] 200 demonstrative exhibits, and 21 videos were admitted into evidence."[23] The plaintiffs' core trial team consisted of nine attorneys, two paralegals, and a graphics team.[24] While it is unknown exactly how large the defendants' trial team was, it was most likely at least twice the size of the plaintiffs' team.

Since the trial teams were primarily attorneys from out of state, each party set up offices in Denver and rented living facilities. The plaintiffs were housed in apartments near the courthouse. They also had a two-bedroom apartment that they used as an office. With the use of the internet, the plaintiffs were able to do all their trial preparation from the apartments. This included filing motions with the court, legal research, internet research concerning witnesses, serving correspondence, and other matters attendant to a jury trial. The team worked around the clock. Each trial day, the attorneys who were arguing motions, preparing witnesses for their testimony, or accompanying witnesses went to court. The balance of the trial team remained in the apartments preparing for the next few days of trial. At the end of each day, the team met to allocate the work for the next day. The court allowed each party to file motions concerning upcoming testimony the day before the testimony. Thus, attorneys were working throughout the night to respond to the motions before they were argued the next morning. This process was grueling on all concerned, but perhaps most difficult for Judge Kane and his staff as the judge was required to decide all of the motions and preside over the trial.

Defendants rented an entire floor of an office building for their trial work area.

During the four months of trial, the jury heard testimony on corporate wrongdoing, corporate responsibility, corporate accountability, secrecy at the plant, conduct at the plant, health effects of radiation, and damages. Among the fact witnesses who testified were local governmental officials who talked about the effects of Rocky Flats on real estate and business and the former FBI agent who spearheaded the June 1989 raid, Mr. Jon Lipsky. Michael Norton, the federal prosecutor in charge of the secret grand jury investigation of Rocky Flats that was convened to investigate the environmental crimes, testified about the decision to settle the criminal case rather than proceed with litigation. Also, former plant employees testified about the releases of hazardous and radioactive materials from the plant. In addition, there was testimony concerning 2,600 pounds of plutonium that has not been accounted for, known as "MUF," which stands for "material unaccounted for."

The expert testimony covered many disciplines. In addition to the fact witnesses, the plaintiffs proved property value loss through three experts: Dr. John Radke, Mr. Wayne Hunsperger, and Dr. Paul Slovic. Dr. Radke, a geographer and professor at the University of California, Berkeley, presented "a highly complex regression analysis that measured the effect of proximity to Rocky Flats on property values in the Class Area, while controlling for a wide range of other factors that can affect property values such as demographics and local amenities and disamenities."[25] Dr. Radke determined that property values definitely had decreased as a result of Rocky Flats. Mr. Hunsperger, a certified real estate appraiser, did a multifaceted analysis of the impact of Rocky Flats on the properties in the class area. He used five different methods to estimate the "diminution in property value: (1) real estate market research, (2) analogous case studies, (3) comparison of market sales data, (4) multiple regression analysis, and (5) the public opinion surveys conducted by Flynn and Slovic and surveys or reports by others."[26] The public opinion survey determined that attitudes about Rocky Flats had stigmatized property in the class area. Dr. Slovic, a professor of psychology, testified about "how people perceive different types of risk and why radiation risk tends to elicit an especially negative reaction."[27] The plaintiffs' experts' concluded that, as a result of Rocky Flats, the average residential property lost 10 percent of its value, while vacant land lost 30 percent. So, according to the plaintiffs' evidence, a house that should have sold for $150,000 would only sell for $135,000 because of the plant.

The plaintiffs also presented several health experts, including Dr. Richard Clapp and Dr. Steven Wing, both epidemiologists who discussed the health impact of the releases, and Dr. Rob Goble, a health physicist, who testified about the health risks of plutonium and the classwide exposures. Dr. Wing testified that all scientific bodies agreed that any exposure to radiation increases the risk of cancer. Dr. Clapp testified that he conducted a study of the area around Rocky Flats and that, for the period of 1989 to 1992, there were 23 percent more lung cancers among men and 29 percent more among women living near the plant as compared to a control area. Dr. Clapp also testified that in his opinion, to a reasonable degree of scientific certainty, the elevated lung cancer rates were associated with exposures to hazardous substances from Rocky Flats.

The defendants also presented evidence through fact and expert testimony. Like the plaintiffs, they had experts in many disciplines. Their real estate expert, Dr. Kenneth Wise, performed a study in which he found that the FBI raid had no impact on property values. The defendants' experts also took the same model that Dr. Radke had used but changed a few variables and reweighed some factors and determined that the property values in the class area had not been diminished. The defendants' health experts testified that there was no impact from Rocky Flats' releases on human health.

Even though the defendants' experts were able to present evidence to challenge the testimony of the plaintiffs' experts, there were some facts they had no way to dispute. These facts included that there were environmental and waste storage problems at Rocky Flats, that the plant was not designed as a waste storage facility, that radioactive and hazardous waste had traveled off-site, that people did not want to live near Rocky Flats, and that it is possible people could not sell their property because of Rocky Flats.

Closing Arguments

Both sides gave closing arguments to the jury after the testimony was completed. Closing arguments are summaries by the attorneys of evidence that the attorneys think is the most persuasive and that they want the jury to consider. Closing arguments are not evidence. During the plaintiffs' closing argument, counsel spoke about the evidence of wrongdoing at the plant and argued that

this is a case about wrongdoing that has increased the future risk of cancer and the diagnosed cases of cancer; that
has caused contamination of two major water supplies, the
Great Western Reservoir and Standley Lake; that has left a
legacy of plutonium and hazardous waste contamination of
the water and soils both on and off site and has caused permanent damage to the environment.[28]

The defendants' closing argument was designed to cast doubt on the
plaintiffs' claims and the opinions of the plaintiffs' experts. For example,
Mr. Bernick argued that Dr. Clapp's study was "junk science. It's not revealed truth."[29] He also emphasized that the jury instructions required
intentional conduct and that the defendants did not intend to cause off-
site contamination or violation of environmental laws. They argued that
the plea agreement related to environmental permit violations, and that
none of the items in the plea agreement showed any intent to engage in an
activity that led to contamination.[30] The defendants also emphasized the
requirement that the plaintiffs prove damages throughout the class area.
The defendants argued that there is no proof that plutonium was there.
The defendants trivialized the health risks associated with the off-site
contamination – comparing the risk to the radiation you get from flying
back and forth from Denver to California or having one chest X-ray. The
defendants argued that there is no real health concern, just a theoretical
risk. The defendants then discussed the evidence that supported their
position that property values had not gone down because of Rocky Flats.
They mentioned the new real estate developments right next door to the
former plant, the downturns in the economy, and the problems with the
plaintiffs' experts' studies. Finally, Mr. Bernick told the jury that

the story needs a last chapter, of course, and you write the last
chapter. It's kind of trite, but it's true. You are given the obligation and the prerogative to say, well, how does this end?
And we have urged the following. Look at the evidence, then
the emotion. How will you do justice? What's justice? What's
the paths of justice? It's following the rules of the court and
doing a good job with the evidence. That's what justice is in
the United States. It's not little guy versus big guy. In some
cases that's true, and in some cases it's not true.[31]

Before the jury began deliberations, Judge Kane gave jury instructions to the jury. These are instructions concerning the law that applies to the facts of the case and the procedures that the jury should follow in deciding the case. Each party submitted proposed jury instructions to the judge for his consideration, and eventually the judge determined what he believed the jury instructions should be. In this case, the jury instruction process, like every other step in the litigation, was contentious and time-consuming. One year before the trial commenced, the parties exchanged their proposed jury instructions. Oral arguments concerning the instructions took place on three separate days in 2004. After that, the parties were submitting proposed changes to the instructions right up until October 11, 2005, when the court gave initial instructions to the jury. But, the changes to the instructions continued even while the trial was ongoing. Judge Kane issued the final jury instructions on January 18, 2005, after the evidence was complete and the parties were about to give closing arguments.

After the court instructed the jury, the jury began deliberations which lasted for seventeen days. Shortly after deliberations began, one juror was excused because she was too emotionally distressed to continue serving.

The Verdict

On February 14, 2006, the jury returned their verdict in a tumultuous court proceeding. The jury found both Dow and Rockwell liable on nuisance and trespass and awarded $176.8 million in compensatory damages and $200 million in punitive damages. The verdict totaled $376.8 million. The court added prejudgment interest to the verdict, which increased the judgment to $926 million. The day the verdict was announced, the parties became emotional. The plaintiffs were thrilled that the jury had awarded everything they had asked for. The defendants seemed shocked that they lost. Mr. Bernick asked the court to poll each individual juror to see if all joined in the verdict. All did.

First Tenth Circuit Decision in September 2010

Despite Mr. Bernick's closing argument, during which he told the jury that they would write the last chapter of the story. That did not happen. The case continued for another decade before settlement was achieved. The defendants appealed the judgment to the Tenth Circuit Court of Appeals, raising several alleged errors in the trial. On March 10, 2010, the Tenth Circuit heard oral arguments. One new argument raised by the defendants on appeal was that the "PAA contained an additional element (above and beyond state law requirements) requiring proof of a 'nuclear incident,' which the PAA defines as an occurrence causing 'loss of or damage to property, or loss of use of property.'"[32] Following the oral argument, the appellate court ordered supplemental briefing on this issue.

On September 3, 2010, the court of appeals[33] vacated the judgment and the class certification, and sent the case back to Judge Kane. Even though the defendants had never raised the argument that the PAA required proof of loss of or damage to property, or loss of use of property before the trial court during the almost two decades the case was pending in the lower court, the court of appeals found that the PAA required such proof. The Tenth Circuit held that the jury had been properly instructed on Colorado nuisance law. The Court also ruled that any punitive conduct had to predate the 1988 PAA amendments. The plaintiffs filed a petition for certiorari with the United States Supreme Court, which was denied. On August 7, 2012, the case went back to Judge Kane for him to proceed pursuant to the direction given by the Tenth Circuit.

Proceedings in the District Court

Twenty-two years after filing the complaint, the plaintiffs were back in the district court without a judgment and without a class. The plaintiffs proposed that the parties brief the issue of reinstating the judgment under Colorado nuisance law and other issues. After briefing the issue, on January 28, 2014, Judge Kane found that the PAA preempted the plaintiffs' state law claims and refused to enter a new judgment based on the original nuisance verdict.

Second Tenth Circuit Decision in June 2015

The plaintiffs kept fighting. They appealed the District Court's 2014 decision to the Tenth Circuit Court of Appeals. After briefing, oral argument was held on November 20, 2014. On June 23, 2015, the Tenth Circuit reversed Judge Kane's 2014 decision and sent the case back to him again. The court of appeals agreed with the plaintiffs that the jury had been properly instructed on Colorado nuisance law and, based on the jury's express finding of a nuisance under that law, directed that the district court "proceed to judgment on the existing nuisance verdict promptly, consistent with resolving the outstanding class action question, wary of arguments that have already been rejected or forfeited."[34]

The Tenth Circuit wrote:[35]

> We can well understand why the plaintiffs on remand renounced a new trial and sought entry of a judgment based on the existing nuisance verdict. Indeed, without some specific mandate or identified error requiring so much we can imagine only injustice flowing from any effort to gin up the machinery of trial for a second pass over terrain it took fifteen years for the first trial to mow through. Injustice not only in the needless financial expense and the waste of judicial resources, but injustice in the human costs associated with trying to piece together faded memories and long since filed away evidence, the emotional ordeal parties and witnesses must endure in any retrial, the waste of work already performed by a diligent and properly instructed jury, and the waiting – the waiting everyone would have to endure for a final result in a case where everyone's already waited too long, longer even than the lives of today's college graduates. When the district court receives this case it should proceed to judgment on the existing nuisance verdict promptly, consistent with resolving the outstanding class action question, wary of arguments that have already been rejected or forfeited. This long lingering litigation deserves to find resolution soon.[36]

The defendants filed another petition for writ of certiorari in the United States Supreme Court. At the same time, the case was remanded to Judge Kane because the Tenth Circuit refused to stay the action while the petition for writ of certiorari was filed. The day before the Supreme Court would have decided whether to accept the case, the case settled.

Hearing Approving Settlement

On April 28, 2017, Judge Kane held the settlement hearing where he approved the settlement of $375 million dollars, attorney fees, expenses, and service awards to the class representatives.[37] At that hearing, Judge Kane made the following observation:

> While there are two corporate defendants named in this case, and both of them litigated vigorously, indeed, relentlessly, in defending the claims both as to liability and damages and at every stage of the proceedings, the United States Department of Energy was the shadow defendant. The reasons for the length of this litigation and the heightened degree of contention cannot be accurately portrayed without reference to the influence and control of the defense exerted by the Department of Energy. Irrespective of its motion or characteristics of conduct, I believe, based on my years presiding over this case, that had the Department of Energy conducted itself with greater candor and less belligerence, a fairer settlement could have been achieved much, much earlier.[38]

Judge Kane also noted some statistics and impressions about the case:

> Class counsel took 99 depositions of fact witnesses, resulting in 22,539 pages of testimony, and defended or attended 52 other depositions. The parties also conducted 46 expert witness depositions. I have never in the years that I have been both a lawyer and judge encountered the degree of technicality and complexity and sophistication of expert witnesses

as took place in this case.... The trial lasted four months, from 2005 into 2006, and had over 300 substantive motions filed during it. A total of 385 exhibits, 200 demonstrative or graphic exhibits, and 21 videos were admitted into evidence.[39]

Judge Kane addressed the quality of the jury in this case:

I want to recognize the truly extraordinary civic service rendered by the members of the jury in this case. They served with considerable personal sacrifice and distinguished themselves by their dedication. I was privileged to work with them and to know them. For anyone who asks about the future of trial by jury in this country and whether it should be defended at all costs, my response is this: Look to the jury in *Cook v. Rockwell* and be proud and be grateful.[40]

Conclusion

By the time settlement money is finally distributed to the class members, more than three decades will have passed since the FBI raid on June 6, 1989. The immediate need that the plaintiffs had for relief from their property and business losses is long past. The class members had to suffer through their losses without timely compensation. In the case of Merilyn Cook, that meant losing her property and her business and moving to Missouri for eight years. In the case of the Bartletts, that meant selling their property at a loss and moving away. In the case of the Babbs, they died before receiving any compensation. And in the case of the Schierkolks, who chose not to move away, that meant staying on the property and worrying about their health and future. Delores Schierkolk died before receiving any compensation. Within the first year after the FBI raid, two-thirds of the class members had moved away from the neighborhood.

The attorneys have spent thousands of hours on this case. Their expenses were millions of dollars. The case has been pending in the federal courts for 30 years. Was it worth it? Did the long delay before settlement constitute a system failure? Did the settlement fail to accomplish its mission of helping the people affected by the plant because it was so long overdue?

Why did it take so long to settle? Perhaps the answer to the last question is that the federal government and the lawyers representing the contractors had no incentive to settle. In a normal lawsuit, both parties watch the costs and when the costs become too high, they often choose to negotiate a settlement. In this case, that normal financial incentive for settlement was missing. Another reason may be that the case was so complex that neither side could realistically assess the risks it posed for them. Perhaps the defendants and the federal government were so entrenched in their thinking about how the nation's nuclear weapons plants were operated that they could not believe a jury would hold them liable to off-site residents for the contamination and economic damage the operations at Rocky Flats have caused.

Were there other goals associated with the litigation that were accomplished? Class members wanted to uncover the truth about the operations at Rocky Flats and make that information public.[41] To a large extent, the plaintiffs did uncover and publicly present evidence that described what happened at Rocky Flats. However, a large quantity of information remains confidential for national security reasons.

Another goal was to show that what happened at Rocky Flats was wrong. The jury award of $200 million in punitive damages demonstrated that this jury did, in fact, conclude that the conduct at the plant was wrong.

Finally, the plaintiffs wanted medical monitoring for the early detection of cancer and other illnesses. This part of the case was lost because of the legislatively imposed limitations of the PAA.

Endnotes

1. These decisions resolved pending motions. As part of a lawsuit, a party may file a motion asking that the court take certain action, such as dismissing a case, requiring production of records, precluding witnesses, and numerous other actions.

2. Rockwell International Corp. sold its defense and aerospace business to Boeing Integrated Defense Systems in 1996.

3. In 2005, the federal government released a draft memorandum of understanding concerning the transfer of administrative jurisdiction for certain lands within the Rocky Flats site from the Department of Energy to the Department of Interior, and the transition of Rocky Flats from a defense nuclear facility into the Rocky Flats National Wildlife Refuge.

4. Additional law firms were involved during the twenty-six-year litigation, but these three law firms represented the parties throughout the trial and for the majority of the period of the litigation.

5. Waite, Schneider lawyer Louise Roselle left the firm in 2012 and now practices with Biller & Kimble, LLC also in Cincinnati, Ohio.

6. Trial transcript, 2049.

7. The Flatirons are rock formations in the western United States, near Boulder, consisting of steeply sloping triangular landforms.

8. Delores Schierkolk did not participate in the trial and she passed away prior to the settlement.

9. Both Lorren and Trudy Babb were deceased at the time the case settled.

10. The statute of limitations governs how long a plaintiff has to file a lawsuit after he or she knew or should have known that he or she has been injured by the wrongful conduct of another.

11. Declaration of Merrill G. Davidoff, attorney with Berger & Montague filed in support of Class Counsel's Motion for an Award of Attorneys' Fees, Reimbursement of Expenses, and Incentive Awards to Class Representatives [Doc. 2435-2], para. 7.

12. Judge John L. Kane, Jr. is an Article III federal judge who joined the court in 1977 (43 years ago) after being nominated by President Jimmy Carter. He graduated from the University of Colorado with a bachelor's degree in 1958 and from the University of Denver College of Law with his Juris Doctorate degree in 1960.In 1967-68, he was the Deputy Director for the Peace Corps, Eastern Region of India, Calcutta, India and in 1968-1969 he was the Peace Corps country

representative to Turkey. Before joining the bench, Judge Kane's legal career in Colorado included work as a law school professor, a deputy district attorney, and an attorney in private practice.

13. The case was assigned to Judge Richard Matsch from April 1, 1999, until August 2, 2000, when it was reassigned to Judge Kane.

14. A medical monitoring class was also certified, but it was later decertified.

15. *Cook v. Rockwell Int'l Corp.*, 151 F.R.D. 378 (D. Colo. 1993).

16. Magistrate Judge Donald E. Abram served as a federal magistrate judge from 1981 to 2000. He began as a trial attorney in 1963, and in 1975, he was appointed to serve as a state court judge in the Tenth Judicial District (Pueblo).

17. Declaration of Merrill G. Davidoff, *Supra.*, para. 19.

18. Id., para. 59.

19. Id., para. 83.

20. Id., para. 102.

21. Id., para. 121

22. Exhibits included, for example, documents describing how the plant functioned and real property records.

23. Davidoff declaration., *Supra*, para. 162.

24. Two trial technology and graphic presentation consultants were present throughout "to craft demonstrative exhibits for key concepts and for use with expert witnesses." Id., para. 150.

25. Id., para. 152.

26. Id., para. 161.

27. Id., para. 156.

28. Trial transcript, 12036. Argument of Louise Roselle.

29. Id., 10486.

30. Id., 10509.

31. Id., 10550.

32. Davidoff declaration, *Supra.*, 185.

33. The Tenth Circuit judges were Michael Murphy, Stephen Anderson, and Jerome Holmes. Judge Murphy wrote the opinion.

34. *Cook v. Rockwell,* 790 F.3d 1088 at 1105.

35. The Tenth Circuit judges were Neil Gorsuch, Gregory Phillips and Nancy Moritz. Judge Gorsuch wrote the opinion.

36. *Cook v. Rockwell,* 790 F.3d at 1105

37. Transcript of the April 28, 2017, hearing.

38. *Id.*

39. *Id.*

40. *Id.*

41. The grand jury spent three years investigating Rocky Flats, but their investigation is not publicly available.

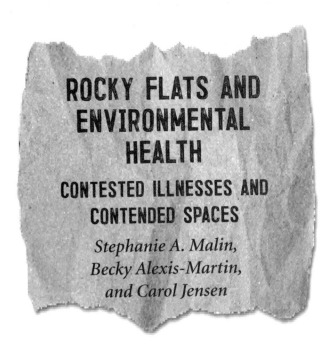

ROCKY FLATS AND ENVIRONMENTAL HEALTH

CONTESTED ILLNESSES AND CONTENDED SPACES

Stephanie A. Malin,
Becky Alexis-Martin,
and Carol Jensen

The Rocky Flats Nuclear Weapons Plant near Arvada, Colorado, represents an important space when considering the contested illnesses that fringe many US nuclear Superfund sites. For communities surrounding Rocky Flats, this fragment of the military industrial complex contains many secrets – some of which could potentially provide vital insights into people's health experiences. Difficult interactions between Rocky Flats site managers, local communities and advocacy groups, the medical community, and the state have meant that vital information about health risks and environmental contamination has not been presented in a way that is useful to the lay public. In addition, previous studies of health and environment have been subject to contestation, as have the contemporary health experiences of people living downwind and down-gradient from the former plant. Long-standing politicization of local people's illness experiences – and a deep-seated culture of secrecy – have undermined the public's ability to understand, engage with, and utilize information about the environmental public health implications of Rocky Flats. Ultimately, this continues to undermine protection and preservation of public and environmental health in surrounding communities, as illnesses are contested and as members of the public lose trust in officials.

Contested illnesses refer to medical conditions that either have not been formally recognized as diseases (for instance, Gulf War Syndrome) or that *are* formally recognized but have not yet been "officially" causally linked to exposure to environmental toxicants (such as breast cancer's potential link to pesticides like atrazine) (Brown 2007; Brown et al. 2011). When the diagnostic process does not provide adequate explanation for the patient's experiences, this may encourage them to challenge their diagnosis and to seek alternative explanations. Some commonalities occur across contested diagnosis experiences, including chronic illness experiences, biomental components, fuzzy diagnostic boundaries, and legal difficulties in recognition of illness – all of which create a need to challenge the boundaries and categories of diagnosis (Trundle et al. 2014; Barker 2011).

Environmentally induced illnesses fall beyond the dominant epidemiological paradigm, which focuses on health at the individual level (lifestyle, genetics, diet, etc.) and can therefore become contested illnesses with contested diagnoses (Brown 2007; Brown et al. 2011). This can be caused by a lack of understanding within the medical community of symptoms of chronic toxic exposure, or due to outright denials of exposure and/or its environmental links by the medical community or state (McCormick 2009). This challenge is exacerbated by the dearth of toxicological data on synergistic effects of toxicants both in the environment and in bodies, the compound nature of contamination, and the potentially long latency periods between exposure and onset of symptoms (Malin 2015; Brown et al. 2011; Malin and Petrzelka 2010). Rarely is just one contaminant released to the surrounding environment during a potential exposure, leading to complexities regarding human and environmental exposure (Oughton and Howard 2012). This creates difficulties for communities to justify or "prove" their exposure to environmental harms and to establish causal links between exposure and health outcomes. Any attempts to contest or challenge the way that medicine and science define their experiences may be dismissed due to lack of orthodox evidence (Brown et al. 2011; McCormick 2009).

Contamination has no respect for human sociopolitical boundaries. Toxicants cannot be constrained by fences or property lines near contaminated places such as Rocky Flats. Historically, when contamination was discovered and recognized beyond the frontiers of the industrial complex, land was purchased, boundaries were extended, exposure thresholds were increased, and space was adapted to suit the needs of production rather than the population. Additionally, spatiotemporal problems arise in accurately estimating the time between any original occasion(s) of contamination, and the later detection and remediation of pollution across the surrounding hinterland (Cohen and Ottinger 2011). These jumbled latency periods between exposure, contamination detection, and emergent symptoms of illness add elements of uncertainty to the timescales of exposure, and the thoroughness of remediation and health assessments for affected communities (Brown 2007; Brown et al. 2011; Malin 2015).

Colorado residents who lived near the Rocky Flats Plant as it operated and during its remediation, and contemporary residents concerned about residual contamination, live each day with a pernicious uncertainty regarding their health, their risk of toxic and radioactive exposure, their support from the medical community and the state, and eventual outcomes for their families. While we cannot know precisely what risks lie beneath the grassy prairies that surround Rocky Flats, we can share preliminary data and context from our community-driven Rocky Flats Exploratory Health Study. In particular, we analyze the environmental health and contested illness experiences of community members through historical and archival review, preliminary participatory survey results, and oral history studies. As we show, politicization of illness experiences linked to Rocky Flats have had negative public and environmental health outcomes. The culture of secrecy surrounding Rocky Flats has served to fortify and institutionalize patterns of contested illness in surrounding communities, creating significant procedural inequity for members of the public.

Contextualizing Rocky Flats

Originally, Rocky Flats was pastoral farmland. However, its underlying geological stability, proximity to uranium sources, and nearness to other atomic industrial installations made it ideal for nuclear weapons manufacturing, so the US Atomic Energy Commission purchased it. Facilities were rapidly constructed, and the Rocky Flats Plant was opened in 1952 to produce plutonium pits, or triggers, for nuclear weapons. At the time, the plant provided stability and well-paying, if risky, jobs for local people, precipitating socioeconomic growth embedded in Cold War opposition to Communism.

Rocky Flats is a place of concealment and contestation (Iversen 2012). Today, it is difficult to believe that it was once a site of industry. Even during its operation, few nearby residents knew what was produced at the plant. Rocky Flats forms a small component of a much larger nuclear defense industry of extraction, processing, and manufacturing. Other spaces shaped by nuclear warfare include some of the most polluted sites in the United States, such as the Hanford Site (known by many names, including the Hanford Engineer Works and Hanford Nuclear Reservation), Oak Ridge National Laboratory, Denver Radium Site, the Cotter Uranium Mill and adjacent Lincoln Park Superfund site, the Uravan Uranium Project (Union Carbide Group), and less-visible sites such as the Monticello Mill in southern Utah and the Fernald Feed Materials Production Center in Ohio (Malin 2015).

Dangerous levels of contamination were recognized at these locations, and legislation was developed to address the inherent risks.[1] In 1980, the US Congress passed CERCLA (Comprehensive Environmental Response, Compensation, and Accountability Act) legislation to create a national mechanism for determining which contaminated places required a long-term, extensive, and expensive remediation to become "clean." Many radioactive sites were placed on a National Priorities List and became Superfund sites, including Rocky Flats – signaling that these sites were too contaminated for human habitation and required immediate remediation. Despite the name, funding has been consistently reduced to the Superfund. Since the early 2000s, there has been decreased reliance on the polluter-pays principle as taxes on industry expired (Larson 2005); instead, taxpayers and uneven appropriations have been responsible for the bulk of financing during remediation efforts. Even with other mechanisms for remediating nuclear contamination – including the US Department of Defense's Environmental Restoration Program (DERP), the DOE and US Army Corp of Engineers Formerly Utilized Sites Remedial Action Program (FUSRAP), and the various Department of Energy programs for remediating uranium contamination – few sites are cleaned each year and approaches to remediation are often economically lean (Pearce 2018).

The Hanford Site, for example, has an extensive legacy of pollution that dates back to 1943. It initially housed the first plutonium production reactor that produced materials for the Trinity bomb, and later expanded to include nine more nuclear reactors and five plutonium-processing complexes (Schwartz 2011). Much of this plutonium was transported to Rocky Flats for processing into triggers for nuclear weapons. Plutonium production ceased at the end of the Cold War (for now), and the Hanford Site subsequently became an informal repository for high-level radioactive waste (Gerber 2007; Lichtenstein 2004). In 2007, Hanford contained two-thirds of the United States' high-level radioactive waste by volume (Chilvers and Burgess 2008). It continues to release radionuclides to the environment, and tritium, technetium-99, and iodine-129 have been identified in local ground and surface waters, alongside a non-radionuclide suite of contaminants, including chromium, arsenic, and sulfate compounds (Adeniji 2004). This contamination is being remediated, but the process has been slowed by infrastructure complications (Gutman 2017) and impacts to the health and safety of workers charged with decontamination efforts (K. Brown 2013; Brown et al. 2011). Hanford demonstrates the challenges associated with understanding the public and environmental health risks of nuclear installations for nearby communities (Pearce 2018), particularly when secrecy surrounding nuclear sites wields immense cultural power. It is notable that low mortality rates have been reported among plutonium workers at the Hanford facility, potentially due to increased screening and monitoring (Wing et al. 2004). Additionally, combined studies of Hanford, Oak Ridge, and Rocky Flats workers provided no evidence for correlation between radiation exposure and mortality from eleven different types of cancer, with only myeloma exhibiting a statistically significant correlation with radiation exposure (Gilbert et al. 1989).

Nuclear installations have immensely powerful cultures of secrecy that lead to situations of contested illness, where people's claims of illnesses related to nuclear exposures are dismissed by the state and medical practitioners (Brown et al. 2011; Cable et al. 2008). For instance, Oak Ridge, Tennessee, hosted an extensive hidden complex for uranium enrichment and weapons production activities. Today, former nuclear workers assert that their health problems were caused by various exposures at the Oak Ridge facility, but their illness claims have been consistently contested by the Department of Energy (Cable et al. 2008; Mix et al. 2009). Monticello Mill in southeastern Utah processed uranium for twenty years, and although cancer clusters have emerged in the surrounding community since that time, their connection to environmental exposures have been rejected by the federal government (Malin 2015; Malin and Petrzelka 2010, 2012). Only rarely have nuclear workers been able to substantiate their claims and have their illnesses formally recognized and compensated, as with the workers of Fernald Feed Materials Production Center (Cianciolo 2015).

Importantly, few studies explore incidences of poor physical and mental health among communities and members of the public surrounding nuclear places such as Hanford or Rocky Flats. Several studies showing positive correlations between exposure and adverse health effects for these communities have been dismissed as invalid or inaccurate, despite qualitative and historical evidence that social, cultural, and medical challenges are present (see the following history). In this way, scientific knowledge relating to community and environmental public health impacts of the nuclear military industrial complex has been controlled by state and industry (Quigley et al. 2017). This has important underexplored consequences for public and environmental health.

A History of Rocky Flats Health and Safety Culture

Since the advent of nuclear technology, our cultural understanding of environmental risks has grown, and our attitudes toward health and safety have changed. We expect access to transparent information about occupational risks, and we expect compensation for harm for which an employer may be liable. While this cultural shift in expectation has occurred, there are still challenges associated with how responsible parties and institutions respond to historical outcomes from the Cold War.

The 1950s were a boom time in the States, with high wages and powerful manufacturing sectors making everything from automobiles to atomic bombs. Manufacturing was also often dangerous (Wildavsky 1988) – especially in nuclear facilities such as Rocky Flats. Cloaked in secrecy, the US nuclear industry enjoyed protection from regulation and oversight, impacting the lives of workers (K. Brown 2013), as social conditions in the country became more restrictive during the 1950s. Social policy was being dismantled, as the States transitioned from welfare state to warfare state in response to Cold War anxieties. A safety culture had yet to evolve, while the American Dream instigated an attitude of conformity and compliance, with everyman aspirations of white picket fences and new suburban conveniences. By creating a classless recharacterization amid inequality that continues to widen, voices of labor groups and unions – traditionally the ombudsmen of the working classes – were suppressed by the 1980s (Harvey 2005).

At Rocky Flats, the toxic legacy stealthily snowballed. The earliest accidents were classified, and swaths of land were purchased to remove the potential for public exposure – and public scrutiny. By the mid-1960s, some residents and antinuclear protesters became concerned about environmental and health impacts. Activist mobilization escalated throughout the 1970s and 1980s, as several thousand people showed up to organized protests and sit-ins. A large-scale protest referred to as the Encirclement occurred in October 1983, attracting enough participants to hold hands and encircle the site's perimeter (Iversen 2012).

This sustained public outcry was ignored by the nuclear sector. However, it was not possible to stifle whistleblowing by Rocky Flats workers to the Environmental Protection Agency. A case was developed through FBI agent Jon Lipsky's extensive work with informants. Operation Desert Glow was implemented by the US Department of Justice, and the Rocky Flats plant was raided on June 6, 1989 (Krupar 2011; Iversen 2012) – uncovering multiple violations of antipollution regulations. The plant was shut down, and the reputation of Rocky Flats was downgraded from place of industry to place of pollution.

Meanwhile, the Cold War was ending. The perception of risks to national security could no longer be used as an impermeable excuse for concealing the mistakes of the military industrial complex. The United States moved to increase transparency and accountability surrounding environmental challenges resulting from military industrial activity. This meant revealing hitherto hidden nuclear places and spaces. While transparency had increased, people felt they could no longer trust nuclear operators or the state (Lodwick 1993; Lowrie and Greenberg 1999). By 2007, after completing what was the largest remediation operation in American history at Rocky Flats (between 1996 and 2005), more than 4,000 acres of Rocky Flats buffer zone became the charge of the US Fish and Wildlife Service (USFWS) (Coates 2014). More than ten years later, it is still mired in a highly contested process of becoming a National Wildlife Refuge.

There has been focus upon environmental upheaval and the physical renewal of Rocky Flats, but people who have illnesses they relate to radiation and chemical exposure from the site want a community-based health study led by state institutions. These requests have not been entertained; instead, the deep culture of secrecy surrounding Rocky Flats makes health-related inquiries controversial and divisive, and uncertainty continues to dominate people's daily lives. Even in the simplest context, making causal links between environmental exposures and resultant illnesses is difficult. This is due to latency periods, incomplete toxicological data on chemicals and their synergistic reactions, and the hegemonic influence of the biomedical model – as opposed to environmental public health perspectives – in individualized medical approaches dominant in societies such as the United States (McCormick 2009; Brown et al. 2011). Of course, environmental pollution can be sensed with monitoring equipment that provides measurements of contamination, made visible by the readings of spectroscopy and Sievert meters. However, it is far harder to form linkages between the landscape of the body and environmental pollution. Our bodies are incredibly resilient, absorbing and processing contaminants, detoxifying us, protecting us from outside harm, and temporarily obscuring traces of environmental trauma. This is further confounded by the selectivity of the data available, as institutions remain focused on the health experiences of heavily monitored and managed Rocky Flats employees, rather than local members of the public (Dreyer et al. 1982; Daugherty et al. 2001; Falk et al. 2006).

Early research exploring contamination from the Rocky Flats Plant and its relationships to the health of surrounding communities and members of the public was often dismissed or demonized – along with the researchers publishing the work (Volchok 1972; Putzier 1982; Rood et al. 1999, 2001, 2002). Public health experts were publicly derided, their findings rejected, and some even lost their livelihoods. Within this culture of secrecy, public health and public access to crucial, useful information had been seriously and repeatedly compromised.

The experiences of Dr. Carl Johnson, a public health physician who directed the Jefferson County Health Department from 1973 to 1981, illustrate how data in this case have been so historically politicized that public health can be negatively affected – in part by impacting and limiting people's access to reliable information. In the early 1970s, Johnson was asked to review permit applications from developers proposing to build residential subdivisions near the site, on land potentially contaminated from Rocky Flats. Instead of issuing the permits outright, Johnson conducted community health analyses to carefully, rigorously capture any potential public health risks for community residents. He found excess incidences of multiple cancers in all age groups. He mapped specific areas or zones where certain cancers such as lung, ovarian, testicular, and bronchial cancers had spiked, even 13 miles from the site. He found that rates of leukemia and other types of cancer were elevated in local populations. He discovered that levels of plutonium in soils surrounding the Rocky Flats Plant were more than forty times greater than reported. He found multiple clusters of cancers in various areas or zones surrounding the site. And he even discovered elevated rates of brain tumors and triple the normal rates of malignant melanoma in plant employees (Johnson 1987; Iversen 2012).

This evidence of contamination-linked health issues led Johnson to campaign for a green belt of undeveloped land to be maintained across a 10-mile radius surrounding the site to protect public health. Johnson's alarming findings and his subsequent recommendations were not well-received by federal and state institutions, nor were they welcome news for real estate agents and developers looking to build and sell new homes near the site. Johnson's data elicited such strong responses precisely because his findings contradicted reports from the federal government and Colorado Department of Health. Johnson's research was dismissed, and he was fired from his role as director at the Jefferson County Health Department in 1981. While he was forced to resign, development continued apace.

Since then, other studies have explored the links between nuclear contamination and health outcomes – but for workers, not members of the public living in nearby communities. One study updated analyses of mortality data on workers at Hanford, Oak Ridge, and Rocky Flats – identifying health risks that may have originated from low-dose exposure to ionizing radiation (Gilbert, Cragle, and Wiggs 1993). The study's P values (statistical values showing relationships are not happening by chance or due to spurious variables) were statistically significant for cancers of the esophagus, larynx, and Hodgkin's lymphoma (cancer of the lymphatic system). Evidence of an increase in the excess relative risk with increasing age at risk was found, with significant correlations for all twenty-four cancers associated with ionizing radiation exposure among the cohort members who were seventy-five years or older. While, from a biomedical model perspective, there are legacies of confounding social and health factors associated with this age of cohort (including increased tobacco and alcohol consumption and poorer diet), the prevalence of rare cancers suggests that there have been health effects beyond the influence of poor lifestyle.

The Rocky Flats Beryllium Health Surveillance Program (BHSP) began in June 1991 (Stange, Furman, and Hillmas 1996; Barnard et al. 1996). This study explored the likelihood of worker exposure to beryllium – an important component of the plutonium pit manufacturing process at Rocky Flats (Aronchick 1992; McGavran 1999) – and found an above-average prevalence of specific degenerative effects associated with exposure to ionizing radiation. Another study examined lung cancer mortality of workers by matching pairs of workers over decades with individually matched controls, finding that lung cancer risk was elevated among workers with cumulative internal lung doses of more than 400 mSv (millisievert, the scientific unit for one year of background radiation exposure, excluding radon exposure, in the United States) in several different analytical models. Yet, no associations were found between lung cancer mortality and cumulative external penetrating radiation dose or cumulative exposures to asbestos, beryllium, hexavalent chromium, or nickel (Grogan 1999; Brown et al. 2004), known carcinogens or toxicants.

Today, challenges remain in defining risks related to these contaminated sites. Current tools for assessment of radiation exposure impacts are reliant on the detectability of radiation exposure to humans, and these interpret risks presented by radiation in a fairly uniform way for all people. For instance, the US standard linear no-threshold (LNT) model of exposure correlates radiation exposure and risk estimation, but this model cannot take into account the individual's personal sensitivity to ionizing radiation exposure, which is inherently variable from person to person (Breckow 2006). It also requires knowledge of exposure thresholds, which cannot be constructed within this particular cohort.

Chronic exposure to ionizing radiation above background levels (or average levels of environmental exposure to radiation from the sun or "cosmic rays," from radon exposure, and from other natural, ambient exposure) is associated with a number of different conditions and cancers, which are statistically rare within the average population (Cardis et al.

1995; Cardis et al. 2005). In this way, the incidence of unusual cancers, and especially related cancer clusters at increased frequency when compared to a normal baseline population, can be used to discern if health effects are present. Within the context of nuclear sites, significant conditions associated with exposure to ionizing radiation include multiple myeloma, retinoblastoma, nevoid basal cell carcinoma and other leukemia-type cancers due to bone marrow radiosensitivity; squamous and basal cell carcinomas of the skin; thyroid cancers; cancers of the prostate, nasal and sinus cavity, pharyngeal and laryngeal cancers; and pancreatic cancer (not all rare, of course) (Richardson et al. 2015). However, this does not necessarily mean that any clusters are attributable to a specific nuclear installation or military industrial complex, due to complications such as people moving to and from affected areas. For instance, the incidence of leukemia clusters around Sellafield (a large multipurpose nuclear facility on the coast of Cumbria, England) that were originally believed to be due to ionizing radiation exposure have instead been attributed to population mixing (McNally et al. 2017). The Rocky Flats Plant is unique in the sheer amount of plutonium on-site and released via ambient contamination, because of illegally incinerating plutonium until the FBI raid, as well as through other pathways for radioactive and chemical contamination that were officially noted during the Superfund remediation (Iversen 2012).

Today, health-aware activism related to the site, interactions with the state, and struggles over contested illnesses and diagnoses continue. The process of conversion from military industrial complex to nature reserve and bourgeois, eco-friendly subdivision is almost complete, and Rocky Flats National Wildlife Refuge surrounds the invisible, decommissioned, and remediated Rocky Flats plutonium pit manufacturing facility. However, the psychosocial, public health, environmental health, and cultural traces of this contaminated Superfund site remain.

The Rocky Flats Exploratory Health Study: Community-Driven Science

While attention has been paid to the workers of Rocky Flats, there is a significant gap in studies that explore the health experiences of members of the public in the aftermath of substantial radioactive environmental contamination. The Rocky Flats Downwinders, the Rocky Flats Right to Know, Candelas Glows, and other groups have mobilized to fight for community-based health studies and transparency for people moving to the area – especially subdivisions now being constructed on the perimeter of the Rocky Flats Plant site buffer zone. Yet, the public has met significant structural barriers, systemic forms of denial regarding their illness claims, and continued secrecy throughout this process. It was as if the site did not exist. We were contacted by these groups and codeveloped this study with input from several community partners, including the groups named above.

Below, we share the preliminary results of the community-driven Rocky Flats Exploratory Health Study. The study was a multi-university effort between Colorado State University in Fort Collins, Metropolitan State University in Denver, and University of Denver. Multiple researchers designed and implemented this study, with expertise spanning cancer care and nursing, sociology of nuclear sites and contested illness, nuclear geography, epidemiology, biostatistics, and soil science. Identifying an appropriate survey instrument was the first step, and researchers contacted Utah Department of Health epidemiologists who had conducted a similar community-driven study in Monticello, Utah. The exploratory study went live in May 2016. In total, 1,744 participants took part in the pilot study through an open online survey.

At the same time, we developed our oral history interview guide to examine the psychosocial experiences of being diagnosed with rare cancers and/or of contested illness experiences personally or in one's immediate family. This guide drew from questions already asked of respondents for the Maria Rogers Oral History archive at the University of Colorado, Boulder, so that these data could enhance those earlier oral history databases. This approach provides more holistic insights into communities such as those surrounding Rocky Flats, whereby the incidence of unusual and contested illnesses, alongside social trauma, indicate that there are challenges that need to be resolved. Importantly, this data is not statistically representative and does not claim to be, but as scientists continue to uncover pockets of potential plutonium contamination around the former plant site (Associated Press 2019), members of the public have reason to demand transparent information and accountability from state agencies.

Exploratory Health Study: Preliminary Survey Data

Participants, who lived in the Arvada, Westminster, and Denver areas, self-reported 848 cases of cancer, of which 414 (48.8 percent of reported cancers) could be considered rare. In the United States and Colorado, the most common cancers in order of prevalence are breast, prostate, lung, and colon, with thyroid cancer ranking ninth. Figure 1 provides greater insight into the types of cancer that have been reported by people living near the Rocky Flats site as a percentage of the study cohort. In the pilot study, the most common cancers in order of prevalence are breast, thyroid, prostate, and colon. However, there are also important incidences of rare cancers, including cancer of the gall bladder, pancreas, and heart – along with multiple myeloma. Some of the cancers could be associated with toxic exposures to radionuclides or other carcinogens, but unfortunately it is not possible to trace exposure timelines through this exploratory and nonrandomized data. The pilot phase of the survey relied on

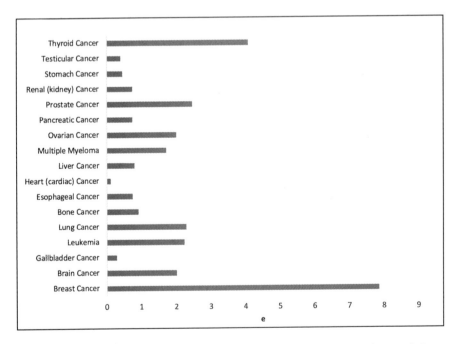

Figure 1. Percentage of the Rocky Flats cohort reporting each type of cancer (n = 1744). Created by Becky Alexis-Martin, using data from the exploratory Rocky Flats Exploratory Health Study.

self-reported data about illnesses, which complicates its validity as a piece of quantitative research. However, our exploratory survey has highlighted the sheer number of rare cancers and other unusual ailments reported in the region. While further statistical study is still needed, the research provides a contemporary snapshot of the Rocky Flats Plant and contested illnesses. Indeed, these findings support the need for a more rigorous, comprehensive, and community-based health study led by state agencies.

In addition to a significant incidence of a variety of cancers, a greater incidence of autoimmune conditions has also been reported by this study, as shown by Figure 2. Significantly, these findings echo the greater incidence of autoimmune conditions also reported by the British nuclear test veteran community (Brent 2010). To provide more context, Hashimoto's thyroiditis has a comorbidity with thyroid carcinoma, but is only expected to affect 2 percent of the population at a given time (Kipolla et al. 2005). Strikingly different, our preliminary findings from the Rocky Flats Health Study reveal an incidence of 6.1 percent for Hashimoto's thyroiditis among the respondents to the Rocky Flats Health Study, which is notably higher.

The Exploratory Health Study has also uncovered evidence of increased incidence of other types of autoimmune disorders, though again we are working with self-reported data that should be confirmed through a comprehensive community-based health study. For instance, Type 1 diabetes could be anticipated to affect 0.3 percent of the population, but is reported by 1.4 percent of respondents of this survey; 0.3 percent of the population suffer from Multiple Sclerosis globally, with slightly greater incidence in the Northern Hemisphere, yet 2.9 percent have reported experiencing this health challenge in this study. Our findings show that Lupus is also reported in greater numbers than expected. Lupus is a rare autoimmune disease, normally affecting just 0.024 percent of the population (Danchenko et al. 2006). However, 1.8 percent of Rocky Flats survey respondents have reported this condition.

While this diverse range of rare autoimmune conditions are not usually associated with exposure to ionizing radiation, it is evident that there are health challenges in Rocky Flats that should not be ignored. Environmental contaminants of industrial origin, including mercury, trichloroethylene, silica, and solvents, are associated with the development of autoimmune diseases (D'Cruz 2000; Cooper et al. 2009; Zahir et al. 2005; Miller et al. 2012). It may be necessary to review not just the radioac-

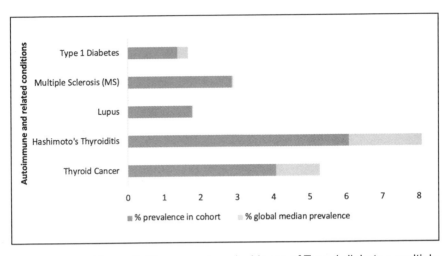

Figure 2. The percentage incidence of Type 1 diabetes, multiple sclerosis, lupus, Hashimoto's thyroiditis, and thyroid cancer in our study, compared to global median prevalence for these conditions (Maahs et al. 2010; You and Henneberg 2016; Ron et al. 1987; Brent 2010). Created by Becky Alexis-Martin, using data from the exploratory Rocky Flats Exploratory Health Study.

tive burden to the surrounding environment of Rocky Flats, but other plausible contaminant loads from nuclear industrial production that are associated with these conditions.

In January 2017, in a partial nod to community requests, the Colorado Department of Public Health and Environment (CDPHE) released the results of a replicated 1998 study, which examined rates of ten specific cancers in ten communities near Rocky Flats using secondary data from sources such as the state Cancer Registry. Their analysis included three of the four most common cancers in the United States and Colorado and five rare cancers (there are dozens), but did not include thyroid cancer – despite residents' requests for its inclusion. They concluded that any increased rates of cancer that they found were explained by tobacco and alcohol use, or early treatment due to screening. The CDPHE has rejected public requests to conduct their own community-based health study – and so contested illnesses have become a central feature of Rocky Flats' legacy.

Health Study: Findings from Oral Histories

Oral histories, collected via in-depth interviews, have provided rich insights into people's experiences of living with the uncertainty of environmental contamination and contested illness. Our team of researchers is compiling a growing database of detailed oral histories of rare cancer survivors who lived near the plant site, which offers unique perspectives on the experiences of living with contested illnesses intimately linked to the military industrial complex.[2]

Preliminary assessments of our interview data highlight two important findings. First, interviewees report that their diagnoses with rare cancers or illnesses are intertwined with experiences of contested illness and contested diagnosis when they share their observations with medical practitioners that their illnesses are linked to environmental exposures from Rocky Flats. Second, our participants report experiencing an acute lack of transparency and feel they lack access to useful information about risks related to the site. For our respondents, secrecy and lack of useful, translated information about public health risks permeate their illness experiences, their knowledge of Rocky Flats, and their ability to rectify their experiences of contested illness and diagnosis.

Rare and Contested Illness Experiences

Our interviewees have all been diagnosed with rare cancers or other highly unusual health problems, and/or their immediate family members have experienced these diagnoses. Each study participant described experiencing deep fear, uncertainty, and isolation accompanying their initial diagnoses. As they describe it, medical practitioners have been consistently unable to diagnose their unique health outcomes; often, practitioners end up piecing together diagnoses and treatments. While these experiences permeated the recollections of our respondents throughout each interview, we offer a few examples here to illustrate the disruptive, isolating, and stressful circumstance of being diagnosed with a rare disorder, connecting that disorder to environmental contamination, and then having those observations contested or denied by medical providers and/or the state.

Lizette participated in our study after seeing her now-deceased husband and a young neighbor both diagnosed with the same rare "heart cancer," formally diagnosed as cardiac angiosarcoma. She and her family had lived for several years in a neighborhood that sat downwind from the former Rocky Flats site. As she explains it:

> He [her husband] started having all this pain in his left side.... So our doctor sent us to Boulder in the ER to do a cat scan.... And they came out and said, "You have a mass in your heart, and it looks like your ribs have been eaten through." We were like, "oh no... nah." They said, "We've never seen anything like this. It's so very rare, very... very weird...." We went to Rocky Mountain Cancer Center in Boulder, and they did a PET scan. And the doctors there said, "I don't know what it is. We haven't seen anything like that, but it's in about nine places in your bones." They did test after test. They had to do... all kind of scans and biopsies. They took one of his ribs. They couldn't tell what it was, it was so rare.... We [got] a second opinion and went to Dana Farber in Boston.... He said, "I don't ever see this. I mean it's very, very rare." They told him he would have seven weeks to live if he didn't have chemo, that it's so aggressive. And it's just a horrible cancer that can't be cured.... I went to a church lady's group and they said, "What's wrong with your husband?" I said "I don't know, it's kind of like heart cancer." And they said, "Well, we know someone else who has heart cancer." We're like, "Nah, can't be." Anyway, they told me the name of the boy.... Eleven years old. And he's in our neighborhood.... I went and knocked on their door, and I said, "I'm so and so. I heard your son has whatever." And she just started crying and said, "No way. We're not really telling anyone what it is. But that's the name that they gave us." He [their son] had just been to Children's [Hospital], and he couldn't breathe, he fainted, and there was no oxygen getting through to his body. And they said, "You have a mass in your heart, and we have to operate right now." So he had... emergency open heart surgery, and they took as much of the mass as they could out of his heart. They told him he had cardiac angiosarcoma and, of course, he's a young boy. Eleven years old at that time.

Potential environmental links were contested; medical practitioners did little to examine the possibility, raised by Lizette and her husband, that these rare cancer cases resulted from exposure to radioactive, toxic contamination from Rocky Flats. Lizette explains, "Our doctor said 'I don't know, I don't know if there's a correlation or not.' And we told him about the boy at Children's that lived next door.... And he just said, 'That's really weird....' He just doesn't want to make waves."

Another study participant, Veronica, discussed her own diagnoses with a suite of maladies, some rare, that she has suffered for nearly three decades after growing up in Broomfield and the Arvada area. Several months ago, struck be the sheer number of diagnoses, she says "I finally had to sit down and actually say 'Well, if I am going to die, I need this record and my family needs this record.' So I had to make myself sit down and actually document stuff and... I gave it to my daughter and my son." These maladies included, in chronological order from the early 1990s to the present: partial hysterectomy/endometriosis; positive miscarriage (miscarriage of one twin); sarcoma with large margin removal; gall bladder removal; fibromyalgia; thyroidectomy; chronic bladder infections; kidney stones; little bumps all over her body; tumor near spine; "non-diagnosable mini tumors" throughout her lungs, which grew and led to removal of her middle right lung; paralyzed vocal cord after lung surgery; and psychosocial stress as these diagnoses accumulated. Further, Veronica sees multigenerational impacts, as her son was just treated for colon cancer.

When she was first diagnosed with sarcoma, a rare cancer, Veronica began to wonder if her health outcomes resulted from living near Rocky Flats throughout her childhood, particularly from their community's source of drinking water. She explains: "At some point, we heard tritium had leaked out of the plant into the creek water.... There was a creek that went into the reservoir, the Great Western Reservoir, and that was our drinking water and so we had been, you know, drinking that for years." Over time, Veronica became more convinced that environmental contamination from Rocky Flats had affected her health. When her still–best friend and childhood neighbor was subsequently diagnosed with the same rare cancer – on her face instead of her ankle – Veronica persisted in making these links and requesting her medical practitioners and state officials do the same. Yet, her doctors were not persuaded, nor were Cancer Registry officials to whom she reported her sarcoma. As Veronica recollects:

At the time, they [her doctors] said, "We really don't know what this is, and we don't know that much about it. We don't feel like you need chemo or radiation, we think we got it all".... Nobody had any answers. But since they said it was rare, I called the cancer line, the Registry. And what I was told at that time was, "Well, where are you living?" I said, "Evergreen, but I grew up in Broomfield." "Well, we don't care where you grew up. You're in Evergreen, so that's where we put down where you got your cancer." And I said, "Well, I haven't lived here that long." And I said, "I was by Rocky Flats." "Well, sorry...." So I was really disheartened by that and I still am because, what does that do? How does that help anybody? Well, I found out at the same time, one of my best friends who lived not even a block from me – she got the same rare cancer, with the same name, on her face by her eye.

More frustrating for Veronica were medical practitioners' inabilities to diagnose or treat many of her ailments – especially the rare "mini tumors" in her lungs and her particular sarcoma – even as they continued to reject her observations that her maladies were related to Rocky Flats. This created stress, uncertainty, and depression – in addition to her other health problems. Veronica explains:

With the two rare cancers, I had to say to myself, "Ok, this isn't normal. Right?"... A lot of doctors did not recognize it, they would not talk to you about it, and they would not treat you. They thought it was all in my head, or I could do something different or whatever. So I kind of tuned out Rocky Flats for quite a few years because I really couldn't handle knowing.... [It leaves you] kind of hopeless in a way, you know, kind of depressed. I had two kids and I was working full time and trying to have a regular, normal life like everyone else. But I'm having these weird things, symptoms. And they can't tell me what or why or really help.

Even now, her doctors contest her concerns about her illnesses' links to Rocky Flats – which has important implications for access to medical specialists. Veronica explains:

> It's not a coincidence to me.... But as I was going to different doctors, if I ever mentioned Rocky Flats, that was it. They didn't want to talk about it because they didn't know what to do about it. They didn't want to hear it, and they didn't want to be involved. So they basically say, "Well, why are you here today? How can I help you today with the symptoms?" Not to say, "Oh my gosh, let's look at this whole picture and see why you might have this or what else we can do," you know? I kept thinking, "Well, if I could get to an internist or someone who would really investigate." But I never did because you go to your doctor and they have to refer you and you have to have insurance and all of that, so I never got there.

Experiences of contested illness and diagnoses were strong patterned findings throughout this project's interview data. For instance, another study participant, Henry, experienced devastating loss as a result of a rare cancer called osteosarcoma. Now in his mid-fifties, Henry was diagnosed at nineteen, when his knee buckled under him at a track meet. He recalls:

> That was a horrific year. I mean, straight up horrific.... [My knee] just buckled under me. I told [my coach] I couldn't stop it... the way I understand, osteosarcoma usually hits boys and girls when they're adolescents. I was pretty much grown when it hit me. It's really rare to hit a nineteen-year-old kid. Really rare. I was nineteen years old and at Sloan-Kettering in New York. They couldn't figure out why someone my age was getting osteosarcoma.

Soon after, he had to have his leg amputated above the knee because of the osteosarcoma's extensive and aggressive spread. Henry recollects eventually connecting his situation to Rocky Flats, largely because he was in a position to see more collective illness experiences in the region:

I was a counselor for seven years after cancer and did a lot of volunteer work at Children's Hospital and met lots of kids from the Jefferson County area that had one form of cancer or another.... You kept hearing Jefferson County, but you don't hear Douglas County or Denver or Park County. A lot of Jefferson County and, more specifically, a lot of Arvada, Jefferson County.

In a departure from most other study participants' experiences, Henry's doctors consistently affirmed causal links between his osteosarcoma and Rocky Flats contamination. However, contested illness narratives remain strong in some local media coverage, despite opportunities to report on people's illness experiences. Says Henry:

They [the media] don't think the community really cares at this point. They think it's past history. These are comments that have been passively made to me. I've called them, said, "What about the people that have had cancer? What about all of the people that have been irreparably ill, probably due to Rocky Flats?" "Well," they ask, "is there a certain correlation? Do you know something that we don't know?" Well, no, I don't. I have common sense.

Study participants observed division within the local medical community, some supporting people's claims and others contesting their illness experiences. Warren, one of three in his immediate family suffering from a rare syndrome related to exposure to ionized radiation that affects hemoglobin and platelet production in blood, explained it like this:

We talk to the nurses up there [at the blood transfusion center]. They're broken into two divisions, a group of RNs who understand the problem and are horrified by that and don't understand how anybody could even think of living out there. And then there's a few of them that are buying homes out there, are living out there and totally denying it.... The house is cheap, what a deal. Unfortunately, what they don't realize is that they've just mortgaged their kid's life.

Study participants like these, without cancer diagnoses but with other rare ailments they connect to environmental exposures from the Rocky Flats Plant, report experiencing stress and uncertainty when medical and public health practitioners or institutions reject their illness experiences or obscure possible risks. Their trust in these experts and institutions falters. For instance, Rachel, who has been afflicted with thyroid, ovarian, and lymph tumors, and now a rare thyroid disorder – but never with cancer – observes:

> People were sick all around me. My best friend in third grade had a brain tumor, my brother had bouts of mono, people in the neighborhood got sick, but it's random stuff. When you're a kid you're like, "Oh my goodness, that's crazy. How could my best friend have a brain cancer?"...Your brain doesn't want you to believe because we are taught that we live in a kind of safe world where the government protects us and we're not going to be contaminated.... I would never have thought I had to question information that is out there from those agencies, you know, until I started to see that there were some inconsistencies... but you can't even trust those sources.

Although study participants such as those highlighted above illuminate the important presence of rare cancers and other ailments around the former Rocky Flats Plant, their illness experiences continue to be contested. The role of useful, translated public health information in this struggle has been a central point of tension, and we turn now to exploring this second finding.

Information Inaccessibility Facilitating Contested Illness

In our interviews, participants have observed that a lack of transparent, translated, and useful information about environmental public health risks related to the Rocky Flats Plant creates significant procedural and structural barriers to understanding the nature and potential environmental causes of their illnesses. They can access very little useful information about levels of contamination, quality of the Superfund remediation, and many other pertinent details about the Rocky Flats site. Instead, the nontranslated information available online or presented at public meetings requires high levels of expertise in topics such as toxicology, chemistry, or epidemiology – an unrealistic, perhaps risky expectation for the lay public (Alexis-Martin and Malin 2017). The lack of useful, accessibly translated information has affected our interviewees' abilities to process and cope with their diagnoses or counter professionals or institutions that contest their illness experiences.

These experiences have had deep psychosocial impacts on our interviewees, who often had hyperindividualized and alienating experiences when they were initially diagnosed. With little useful information to rely on, people often made significant time commitments to understand information related to the site, and our respondents described how costly, lonely, and stressful this could be. Rachel, whom we met above, took time away from work and other daily activities after her thyroid tumor diagnosis so she could learn about potential causal links and risks of growing up near Rocky Flats. Rachel explains:

> It was crazy. I was at the downtown library and I was freaking out… It was like, my whole life I felt like something had happened to me… I felt strongly something has gone on… And then I found this out, and I was like holy shit…. They didn't know if I had cancer about that time, but everyone I was talking to did. So my everything fell apart.

Like many of our study participants to date, Lizette, whose husband suffered from the rare heart cancer angiosarcoma, observed that the lack of useful information about the site's risks was stressful and allowed her family to move into the middle of an invisible risk, one which was then contested as they dealt with life-changing health impacts. Lizette observes:

> When we bought the house we didn't ask, nobody told us, we didn't have any idea… A few people said something about Rocky Flats, but they said, "Oh it's all cleaned up." We had a friend and her husband helped do the cleanup and she said, "Oh yeah, they cleaned it up"…. It's so covered up. It just irritates me because they need some truth, they need to have truth of what really happened. People aren't crazy…. They

told us it was safe, so we believed them. I guess we were just oblivious like everyone else.

Although the Rocky Flats Plant belonged to the US government, it was frequently managed and operated by private corporations that oversaw day-to-day operations and hiring, as well as on-site safety issues. The collusion between state and corporate entities, and their abilities to obscure or conceal environmental risks and information about them, affected trust in those institutions for many of our participants. For instance, Henry asserts:

> It makes you really angry. I worked in Cedar Rapids for seven years after grad school... home of Rockwell [the last corporation to run the plant]. I know a lot of people worked for that company, and they are all good people. It just makes you wonder about the efforts to cover up, you know, spills or seepage. Those are the things that make you really concerned because people in the area just don't know what's coming at them. And you'd almost have to be criminally negligent to know that that's going on and not do something to stop it. And I mean like, treasonous. I couldn't do it, could you?

Our study participants have continually highlighted that historical access to reliable and valid information about Rocky Flats and related contamination could have helped them alleviate much uncertainty in their daily lives now. Further, even with hundreds of pages of technical information now provided by the CDPHE's website, the information requires such expertise that it is not readily accessible or useful to the lay public. This effectively prevents another generation of residents from fully understanding the nature of potential contemporary risks, as homes are constructed near the buffer zone and public access to the Wildlife Refuge is debated. Like many of our participants, Veronica – who suffered from multiple maladies and two rare cancers – observed that useless, highly specialized information diminished her capacity to make an informed decision about how to approach public health risks:

> It's been wonderful when I do see stuff on the news because... all of these years, they didn't say anything. And I

know there's information out there, and I think... there needs to be more education that it [the site] is out there. I do feel so, so bad for people moving into that area [who] don't know about it... I've gone through so many different things, and there still isn't anger about it because it's still very hard for me to think that anybody that would know that people could get hurt or it could affect their lives would do that, would not let you know and would not let you choose. If we knew better, then we could have gone somewhere else. I just feel like I trusted them, and they let me down. They let my family down. They let this whole community down.

Conclusions

The Rocky Flats Exploratory Health Study has been successful in identifying a number of initial findings and challenges to be tackled during the next phase of research. From our interview data, we have two important findings. First, contested illnesses and diagnoses have defined the experiences of people we interviewed who had rare cancers or maladies that they connect with environmental exposure from Rocky Flats. Second, a lack of useful, translated information about potential environmental public health risks related to the site has created significant barriers for the public in assessing the nature and extent of potential contemporary public health risks.

Contested illness saturates this story. Some former Rocky Flats employees have expressed concerns about making claims like this, concerned that their pensions or retirements may be affected. There have also been some challenging interactions with the CDPHE as they have publicly challenged the study and our findings, as is often the case with new academic studies of contested illness. Health Department representatives have even come to our community meetings, where we translate our findings for community members and answer their questions, and have announced to audience members that these cancer cases and rates are completely normal, while denigrating this study. Yet, continued requests from affected community members show that the public strongly desires a community-driven health study conducted by a state agency.

Alas, this Exploratory Health Study continues even as this book goes into print. Future goals include a continuation of oral history collection, institutional analyses of contested illness and environmental justice and health issues, and a more robust survey distribution and sampling design to add representative data to our exploratory data from the survey's first round.

Akin to other once-contested illnesses such as chronic fatigue and Gulf War Syndrome, it is challenging to irrefutably link the environmental toxicants that were historically detected – and are still present – around Rocky Flats with the chronic morbidity and self-reported but seemingly elevated incidences of rare conditions in surrounding communities. While public health monitoring has been unable to provide concrete records of exposure, and the baseline values for chemical toxicity are subject to individual variability that is difficult to gauge, people living near Rocky Flats over the last sixty years wait for honest, transparent answers.

Acknowledgments

We would like to thank the American Sociological Association's support for this research, funded through their Spivack Community Action Research Initiative Grant program.

Works Cited

Adeiji, Adebowale. "Bioremediation of Arsenic, Chromium, Lead, and Mercury." Washington, DC: National Network of Environmental Management Studies Fellow for US Environmental Protection Agency Office of Solid Waste and Emergency Response Technology Innovation Office, Washington, DC, 2004.

Alexis-Martin, Becky and Stephanie Malin. "An Unnatural History of Rocky Flats National Wildlife Refuge." *Arcadia* (2017).

Aronchick, Judith M. "Chronic Beryllium Disease." *Radiologic Clinics of North America* 30, no. 6 (1992): 1209–1217.

Associated Press (AP). "Tests Show Conflicting Levels of Plutonium at Rocky Flats." Colorado Public Radio, Aug. 21, 2019.

Barker, Kristin K. "Listening to Lyrica: Contested Illnesses and Pharmaceutical Determinism." *Social Science & Medicine* 73, no. 6 (2011): 833–842.

Barnard, Anthony E., Janet Torma-Krajewski, and Susan M. Viet. "Retrospective Beryllium Exposure Assessment at the Rocky Flats Environmental Technology Site." *American Industrial Hygiene Association Journal* 57, no. 9 (1996): 804–808.

Breckow, Joachim. "Linear-No-Threshold Is a Radiation-Protection Standard Rather Than a Mechanistic Effect Model." *Radiation and Environmental Biophysics* 44, no. 4 (2006): 257–260.

Brent, Gregory A. "Environmental Exposures and Autoimmune Thyroid Disease." *Thyroid* 20, no. 7 (2010): 755–761.

Brown, Kathryn L. *Plutopia: Nuclear Families, Atomic Cities, and the Great Soviet and American Plutonium Disasters.* New York: Oxford University Press, 2013.

Brown, Phil. *Toxic Exposures: Contested Illnesses and the Environmental Health Movement.* New York: Columbia University Press, 2007.

Brown, Phil, Rachel Morello-Frosch, and Stephen Zavestoski. *Contested Illnesses: Citizens, Science, and Health Social Movements.* Berkeley, CA: University of California Press, 2011.

Brown, Shannon C., Margaret F. Schonbeck, David McClure, Anna E. Barón, William C. Navidi, Tim Byers, and A. James Ruttenber. "Lung Cancer and Internal Lung Doses among Plutonium Workers at the Rocky Flats Plant: A Case-Control Study." *American Journal of Epidemiology* 160, no. 2 (2004): 163–172.

Cable, Sherry, Thomas E. Shriver, and Tamara L. Mix. "Risk Society and Contested Illness: The Case of Nuclear Weapons workers." *American Sociological Review* 73, no. 3 (2008): 380–401.

Cardis, E., E. S. Gilbert, L. Carpenter, G. Howe, I. Kato, B. K. Armstrong, V. Beral, G. Cowper, A. Douglas, and J. Fix. "Effects of Low Doses and Low Dose Rates of External Ionizing Radiation: Cancer Mortality among Nuclear Industry Workers in Three Countries." *Radiation Research* 142, no. 2 (1995): 117–132.

Cardis, Elisabeth, M. Vrijheid, M. Blettner, E. Gilbert, M. Hakama, C. Hill, G. Howe, J. Kaldor, C. R. Muirhead, and M. Schubauer-Berigan. "Risk of Cancer after Low Doses of Ionising Radiation: Retrospective Cohort Study in 15 Countries." *BMJ* 331, no. 7508 (2005): 77.

Chilvers, Jason, and Jacquelin Burgess. "Power Relations: The Politics of Risk and Procedure in Nuclear Waste Governance." *Environment and Planning A* 40, no. 8 (2008): 1881–1900.

Cianciolo, Patricia K. "Compensating Nuclear Weapons Workers and Their Survivors: The Case of Fernald." *Michigan Family Review* 19, no. 1 (2015): 51–72.

Coates, Peter. "From Hazard to Habitat (or Hazardous Habitat): The Lively and Lethal Afterlife of Rocky Flats, Colorado." *Progress in Physical Geography* 38, no. 3 (2014): 286–300.

Cohen, Benjamin R., and Gwen Ottinger. *Technoscience and Environmental Justice: Expert Cultures in a Grassroots Movement.* Cambridge, MA: MIT Press, 2011.

Cooper, Glinda S., Susan L. Makris, Paul J. Nietert, and Jennifer Jinot. "Evidence of Autoimmune-Related Effects of Trichloroethylene Exposure from Studies in Mice and Humans." *Environmental Health Perspectives* 117, no. 5 (2009): 696–702.

D'Cruz, David. "Autoimmune Diseases Associated with Drugs, Chemicals and Environmental Factors." *Toxicology Letters* 112 (2000): 421–432.

Danchenko, N., J. A. Satia, and M. S. Anthony. "Epidemiology of Systemic Lupus Erythematosus: A Comparison of Worldwide Disease Burden." *Lupus* 15, no. 5 (2006): 308–318.

Daugherty, N. M., R. B. Falk, F. J. Furman, J. M. Aldrich, and D. E. Hilmas. "Former Radiation Worker Medical Surveillance Program at Rocky Flats." *Health Physics* 80, no. 6 (2001): 544–551.

Dreyer, N. A., J. E. Loughlin, F. H. Fahey, and N. H. Harley. "The Feasibility of Epidemiologic Studies of Cancer in Residents Near the Rocky Flats Plant." *Health Physics* 42, no. 1 (1982): 65–68.

Falk, Roger B., Nancy M. Daugherty, Joe M. Aldrich, F. Joseph Furman, and Duane E. Hilmas. "Application of Multi-Compartment Wound Models to Plutonium-Contaminated Wounds Incurred by Former Workers at Rocky Flats." *Health Physics* 91, no. 2 (2006): 128–143.

Gerber, Michele Stenehjem. *On the Home Front: The Cold War Legacy of the Hanford Nuclear Site*. Lincoln: University of Nebraska Press, 2007.

Gilbert, Ethel S., Donna L. Cragle, and Laurie D. Wiggs. "Updated Analyses of Combined Mortality Data for Workers at the Hanford Site, Oak Ridge National Laboratory, and Rocky Flats Weapons Plant." *Radiation Research* 136, no. 3 (1993): 408–421.

Gilbert, Ethel S., Shirley A. Fry, Laurie D. Wiggs, George L. Voelz, Donna L. Cragle, and Gerald R. Petersen. "Analyses of Combined Mortality Data on Workers at the Hanford Site, Oak Ridge National Laboratory, and Rocky Flats Nuclear Weapons Plant." *Radiation Research* 120, no. 1 (1989): 19–35.

Grogan, H. A., P. A. McGavran, K. R. Meyer, H. R. Meyer, J. Mohler, A. S. Rood, W. K. Sinclair, P. G. Voilleque, and J. M. Weber. *Technical Summary Report of the Historical Public Exposures Studies for Rocky Flats Phase II.* (Health Studies on Rocky Flats: Phase II: Historical Public Exposures.) Denver, CO: Colorado Department of Public Health and Environment. RAC Report No. 14-CDPHE-RFP-1999-Final, 1999.

Gutman, David. "Thousands of Hanford Workers Take Cover after Cave-in of Tunnel with Radioactive Waste." The Seattle Times. May 9, 2017. https://www.seattletimes.com/seattle-news/environment/hanford-declares-alert-emergency-evacuates-workers-because-of-problems-with-contaminated-tunnels/.

Harvey, David. *A Brief History of Neoliberalism*. Oxford, UK: Oxford University Press, 2005.

Iversen, Kristen. *Full Body Burden: Growing up in the Nuclear Shadow of Rocky Flats*. NY: Broadway Books, 2012.

Johnson, Carl J. "Re: 'Cancer Incidence Patterns in the Denver Metropolitan Area in Relation to the Rocky Flats Plant.'" *American Journal of Epidemiology* 126, no. 1 (1987): 153–155.

Kate Brown. "A People's Truth." *Aeon*, Dec. 3, 2012. https://aeon.co/essays/downwinders-the-noxious-legacy-of-the-hanford-nuclear-site.

Krupar, Shiloh R. "Alien Still Life: Distilling the Toxic Logics of the Rocky Flats National Wildlife Refuge." *Environment and Planning D: Society and Space* 29, no. 2 (2011): 268–290.

Larson, Eric Thomas. "Why Environmental Liability Regimes in the United States, the European Community, and Japan Have Grown Synonymous with the Polluter Pays Principle." *Vanderbilt Journal of Transnational Law* 38 (2005): 541

Lichtenstein, Noah D. "The Hanford Nuclear Waste Site: A Legacy of Risk, Cost, and Inefficiency." *Natural Resources Journal* 44, no. 3 (2004): 809–839.

Lodwick, Dora G. "Rocky Flats and the Evolution of Distrust". *Research in Social Problems and Public Policy* 5 (1993): 149–170.

Lowrie, Karen, and Michael Greenberg. "Cleaning It Up and Closing It Down: Land Use Issues at Rocky Flats." *Federal Facilities Environmental Journal* 10, no. 1 (1999): 69–79.

Maahs, David M., Nancy A. West, Jean M. Lawrence, and Elizabeth J. Mayer-Davis. "Epidemiology of Type 1 Diabetes." *Endocrinology and Metabolism Clinics* 39, no. 3 (2010): 481–497.

Malin, Stephanie A. The Price of Nuclear Power: Uranium Communities and Environmental Justice. New Brunswick, NJ: Rutgers University Press. 2015.

Malin, Stephanie A., and Peggy Petrzelka. "Left in the Dust: Uranium's Legacy and Victims of Mill Tailings Exposure in Monticello, Utah." *Society and Natural Resources* 23, no. 12 (2010): 1187–1200.

Malin, Stephanie A., and Peggy Petrzelka. "Community Development Among Toxic Tailings: An Interactional Case Study of Extralocal Institutions and Environmental Health." *Community Development* 43, no. 3 (2012): 379–392.

McCormick, Sabrina. *Mobilizing Science.* Philadelphia, PA: Temple University Press, 2009.

McGavran, Patricia D., Arthur S. Rood, and John E. Till. "Chronic Beryllium Disease and Cancer Risk Estimates with Uncertainty for Beryllium Released to the Air from the Rocky Flats Plant." *Environmental Health Perspectives* 107, no. 9 (1999): 731.

McNally, Richard JQ, Peter W. James, Karen Blakey, Nermine O. Basta, Paul D. Norman, and Mark S. Pearce. "Can Changes in Population Mixing and Socio-Economic Deprivation in Cumbria, England Explain Changes in Cancer Incidence around Sellafield?" *Spatial and Spatio-Temporal Epidemiology* 21 (2017): 25–36.

Miller, Frederick W., Lars Alfredsson, Karen H. Costenbader, Diane L. Kamen, Lorene M. Nelson, Jill M. Norris, and Anneclaire J. De Roos. "Epidemiology of Environmental Exposures and Human Autoimmune Diseases: Findings from a National Institute of Environmental Health Sciences Expert Panel Workshop." *Journal of Autoimmunity* 39, no. 4 (2012): 259–271.

Mix, Tamara L., Sherry Cable, and Thomas E. Shriver. "Social Control and Contested Environmental Illness: The Repression of III Nuclear Weapons Workers." *Human Ecology Review* (2009): 172–183.

Oughton, Deborah H., and Brenda J. Howard. "The Social and Ethical Challenges of Radiation Risk Management." *Ethics, Policy & Environment* 15, no. 1 (2012): 71–76.

Pearce, Fred. "After 60 Years of Nuclear Power, What About the Cleanup?" *The Atlantic*, May 28, 2018. https://www.theatlantic.com/science/archive/2018/05/the-60-year-downfall-of-nuclear-power-in-the-us-has-left-a-huge-mess/560945/.

Putzier, E. A. "The Past 30 Years at Rocky Flats: A Summary of Experiences and Observations at Rocky Flats Plant Over the Past 30 Years with Emphasis on Health and Safety." *Health Sciences Division. Repository Document HS-371*, 1982.

Quigley, Dianne, Amy Lowman, and Steve Wing. *Tortured Science: Health Studies, Ethics and Nuclear Weapons in the United States.* NY: Routledge, 2017.

Richardson, David B., Elisabeth Cardis, Robert D. Daniels, Michael Gillies, Jacqueline A. O'Hagan, Ghassan B. Hamra, Richard Haylock, Dominique Laurier, Klervi Leuraud, and Monika Moissonnier. "Risk of Cancer from Occupational Exposure to Ionising Radiation: Retrospective Cohort Study of Workers in France, the United Kingdom, and the United States (INWORKS)." *BMJ* 351 (2015): h5359.

Ron, Elaine, Ruth A. Kleinerman, John D. Boice Jr., Virginia A. LiVolsi, John T. Flannery, and Joseph F. Fraumeni Jr. "A Population-Based Case – Control Study of Thyroid Cancer." *Journal of the National Cancer Institute* 79, no. 1 (1987): 1–12.

Rood, Arthur S., Helen A. Grogan, and John E. Till. "A Model for a Comprehensive Assessment of Exposure and Lifetime Cancer Incidence Risk from Plutonium Released from the Rocky Flats Plant, 1953–1989." *Health Physics* 82, no. 2 (2002): 182–212.

Rood, Arthur S., George G. Killough, and John E. Till. "Evaluation of Atmospheric Transport Models for Use in Phase II of the Historical Public Exposures Studies at the Rocky Flats Plant." *Risk Analysis* 19, no. 4 (1999): 559–576.

Rood, Arthur S., Patricia D. McGavran, Jill W. Aanenson, and John E. Till. "Stochastic Estimates of Exposure and Cancer Risk from Carbon Tetrachloride Released to the Air from the Rocky Flats Plant." *Risk Analysis* 21, no. 4 (2001): 675–696.

Schwartz, Stephen I. *Atomic Audit: The Costs and Consequences of US Nuclear Weapons since 1940.* Washington, DC: Brookings Institution Press, 2011.

Stange, Arthur W., F. Joseph Furman, and Duane E. Hilmas. "Rocky Flats Beryllium Health Surveillance." *Environmental Health Perspectives* 104, Suppl. no. 5 (1996): 981.

Trundle, Catherine, Ilina Singh, and Christain Bröer. "Fighting to Be Heard: Contested Diagnoses." In *Social Issues in Diagnosis: An Introduction for Students and Clinicians* (pp. 165–182). Baltimore: Johns Hopkins University Press, 2014.

Tubiana, M., A. Arengo, D. Averbeck, R. Masse, M. Tubiana, A. Aurengo, D. Averbeck, A. Bonnin, B. Le Guen, and R. Masse. "Linear-No-Threshold Is a Radiation-Protection Standard Rather than a Mechanistic Effect Model." *Radiation Research* 167 no. 6 (2007): 742–744.

Volchok, H. L., R. H. Knuth, and M. T. Kleinman. "The Respirable Fraction of Plutonium at Rocky Flats." *Health Physics* 23, no. 3 (1972): 395–396.

Wildavsky, Aaron B. *Searching for Safety.* Vol. 10. NY: Routledge Press. 1988. (Transaction Publishers, reprint 2017.)

Wing, Steve, David Richardson, Susanne Wolf, and Gary Mihlan. "Plutonium-Related Work and Cause-Specific Mortality at the United

States Department of Energy Hanford Site." *American Journal of Industrial Medicine* 45, no. 2 (2004): 153–164.

You, Wenpeng, and Maciej Henneberg. "Cancer Incidence Increasing Globally: The Role of Relaxed Natural Selection." *Evolutionary Applications* 11, no. 2 (2018): 140–152.

Zahir, Farhana, Shamim J. Rizwi, Soghra K. Haq, and Rizwan H. Khan. "Low Dose Mercury Toxicity and Human Health." *Environmental Toxicology and Pharmacology* 20, no. 2 (2005): 351–360.

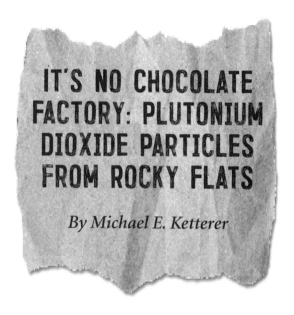

IT'S NO CHOCOLATE FACTORY: PLUTONIUM DIOXIDE PARTICLES FROM ROCKY FLATS

By Michael E. Ketterer

Executive Summary

On a map of North America depicting plutonium activities in North American soils, the zone near the former Rocky Flats nuclear weapons plant in the steppes northwest of Denver stands out, prominently and alarmingly. Surface soils in the future location of the Jefferson Parkway along Indiana Street, in the proximity of the plant's former East Gate, contain plutonium at activities tens or hundreds of times those found from weapons-testing fallout at control locations elsewhere in Colorado's Front Range. The Rocky Flats Plant grounds and central operating unit were later remediated to contain fewer than 50 picocuries per gram of the two major isotopes ^{239}Pu and ^{240}Pu (i.e., $^{239+240}$Pu); however, the surrounding Rocky Flats National Wildlife Refuge, and the proposed Jefferson Parkway corridor consist of nonremediated soils of < 50 pCi/g in areas that were deemed suited for unrestricted uses.

In August 2019, renewed public attention was focused on the Indiana Street corridor east of Rocky Flats, as the Jefferson Parkway Public

Highway Authority (JPPHA) hired contractors to sample and analyze soils from the corridor to collect contemporary results. The JPPHA was fully expecting to demonstrate that the $^{239+240}$Pu activities were well under the 50 pCi/g $^{239+240}$Pu standard, and that was found to be the case, with the exception of one 264 pCi/g result. Both JPPHA and the Colorado Department of Public Health and Environment (CDPHE) characterized this finding as an anomaly, although JPPHA's contractors correctly ascribed the result to the presence of a single 8.8 micrometer diameter "hot particle" of plutonium dioxide in that specific sample portion. The presence of any PuO_2 grains is concerning, as respiring a single particle of PuO_2 can lead to long-term internal exposure of one's lung tissue to a very high dose of radiation within the ~ 50 micrometer penetration range of an alpha particle.

Synthesized under conditions where Pu metal reacts spontaneously with oxygen, plutonium dioxide particles were released from multiple fires at the former weapons plant, with well-documented events in 1957 and 1969. Besides these discrete grains of essentially pure plutonium, Rocky Flats proximity soils also contain other physical/chemical forms of Pu from the facility that are distributed more uniformly in the soil. Maps and reports published by the US Government and collaborators report a prevailing pattern of elevated $^{239+240}$Pu in locations east of the former weapons plant; however, there has been little focus on discrete PuO_2 particles in soils. US Environmental Protection Agency's determination of suitability was based solely on the simplistic comparison of the soil $^{239+240}$Pu activity to an arbitrary standard of 50 pCi/g.

In July 2019, the author and collaborators obtained soils from Jefferson County right-of-way property in the Indiana Street corridor, and found $^{239+240}$Pu activities that largely agreed with JPPHA's 2019 findings. However, these recent independent studies have also pursued measurements of the "hot particles." Multiple replicate preparations of a specific soil sample allow these to be detected by the increase in activity observed above the baseline of homogeneously distributed Pu activity. In these experiments, the author found PuO_2 grains in six out of twelve soil subsamples from a soil collected near the former East Gate of the facility; interpretation of the results reveals that PuO_2 particles ranging from 0.8 to 2.6 microns are present.

Both the JPPHA's and the author's findings of hot particles in soils near the Rocky Flats facility underscore the urgent need to further characterize the prevalence, size distribution, and geographic range of the plutonium dioxide particles. The precautionary principle mandates a new risk assessment for refuge visitors, parkway construction workers, and nearby residents who may be exposed to air-entrained respirable PuO_2 particles.

Northwest of Denver, Colorado, along the roller-coaster corridor of Indiana Street, lies a section of the proposed Jefferson Parkway, a missing segment that will almost complete the intended 360-degree bypass route circumnavigating the heart of the metropolitan area.[1] The parkway design traverses the zone of contaminated soils directly east of the former Rocky Flats plutonium pit production facility, now the site of the newly opened Rocky Flats National Wildlife Refuge. On a contour map of soil plutonium inventory for all of North America, the Rocky Flats-impacted zone would stand out, prominently and alarmingly. Activities of the two major isotopes, expressed in picocuries per gram as their sum $^{239+240}Pu$, are tens and hundreds of times more than the ubiquitous global background in surface soils that stems from Cold War–era aboveground nuclear weapons tests. There is little dispute regarding its source: the soils contain weapons-grade plutonium from Rocky Flats. Routine stack emissions, episodic fires, and negligent open-air storage of rusting drums containing contaminated oils are collectively responsible for this aberration.

Plutonium is present in soils worldwide as a result of atmospheric nuclear weapons tests, conducted mainly by the United States and former Soviet Union, during the Cold–War era.[2,3] In aquatic sediment records, one can identify the first global appearance of plutonium in the early 1950s, with its peak deposition corresponding to the year 1963.[4] In my own backyard or yours, if the surface has been stationary since the middle of the last century, one could anticipate finding about one picogram (10^{-12} g, pg) of ^{239}Pu per gram of soil. The element's major isotope, ^{239}Pu, would be accompanied by 0.2 picograms of ^{240}Pu, and much smaller masses of the additional isotopes ^{238}Pu, ^{241}Pu, ^{242}Pu, and ^{244}Pu. A picogram of any form of matter is completely invisible to the naked eye; nonetheless, one picogram of ^{239}Pu still represents a population of 2.5 billion atoms. The US environmental standards for radioactive isotopes are given in units of curies (Ci), named in honor of two-time Nobel Laureate

Madame Marie Curie, the discoverer of the elements radium and polonium. The quantity of radioactivity in one curie, corresponding to one gram of ^{226}Ra, is enormous; a Curie of a radioisotope corresponds to 3.7 x 10^{10} disintegrations per second (i.e., 3.7 x 10^{10} becquerels, Bq) of that nuclide. The US government sought to remediate the Rocky Flats site to achieve activities of fewer than 50 picocuries (pCi) $^{239+240}$Pu per gram of surface soil.[5]

Translated into mass, the 50 pCi/g remediation standard corresponds to 670 pg ^{239}Pu together with an additional 37 pg ^{240}Pu per gram dry mass of soil. It seems inconsequential; one might make light of these very low concentrations as analogous to a couple of heartbeats out of a long human lifetime. Nevertheless, in the first decade of the 2000s, the US government expended billions of dollars to remediate contaminated soils on the former plant site, to achieve post-cleanup levels of less than 50 pCi/g. Surface soils containing only a few nanograms (10^{-9} g) Pu per gram soil were assayed, and removed from the Central Operating Unit, the former location of the weapons plant itself. The surrounding buffer zone, the site of the then-future Rocky Flats National Wildlife Refuge, was extensively characterized; risk assessment modelers concluded that soils containing up to 50 pCi/g $^{239+240}$Pu represented acceptable, inconsequential risk to human health and the environment. Following the directive of the US Congress, the refuge was created, and opened to public access in 2018, having been deemed safe for unlimited recreational uses. As all portions of the refuge apparently exhibited less than the 50 pCi/g threshold, no soil remediation was conducted on its present site.

In the summer of 2019, the Colorado-based environmental consulting firm Engineering Analytics conducted sampling and analysis of soils from the Indiana Street corridor, under contract with the Jefferson Parkway Public Highway Authority. The transuranic or "beyond uranium" elements, having atomic numbers exceeding 92, were atop the laboratory menu; the Parkway Authority sought to confirm decades of previous studies supporting an expectation that the maximum activities encountered would be well below 50 pCi/g $^{239+240}$Pu. The US government released its first study admitting to soil contamination in the Rocky Flats proximity on August 1, 1970[6]; these investigators from the US Atomic Energy Commission's Health and Safety Laboratory collected and analyzed a series of samples from near Rocky Flats and elsewhere along the Front Range. Referred to as the Krey-Hardy map (Figure 1), a relatively

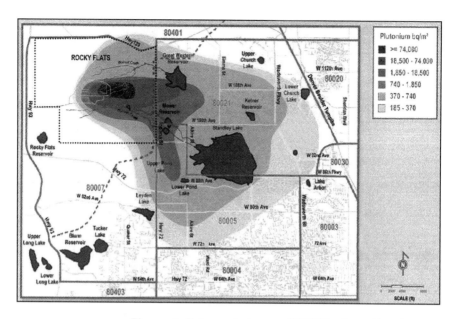

Figure 1. Color-coded map of $^{239+240}$Pu deposition, in units of becquerels per square meter, constructed based upon the Krey-Hardy HASL-235 report of August 1, 1970. The dashed line coincides with the proposed route of the Jefferson Parkway. In comparison, North American mid-latitude inventories of $^{239+240}$Pu are on the order of 50–100 Bq/m2 (see note 3).

simple contour map of the deposition of Pu near Rocky Flats pointed to the elevated soil Pu content near Rocky Flats. Krey and Hardy measured the inventory of $^{239+240}$Pu (i.e., depth-integrated deposited per unit area, expressed in becquerels per square meter, Bq/m^2, or millicuries per square km, mCi/km^2; the Krey-Hardy study developed inventory contours drawn from a relatively few data points. Decades of subsequent, more detailed work (e.g. as summarized in note 5), has generally validated and added much detail to the original Krey-Hardy map.

At a June 18, 2019, meeting of the Broomfield City Council, Engineering Analytics staff reported preliminary results, confidently expressing that the highest activity soils contained only 1 to 2 picocuries $^{239+240}$Pu per gram soil. As one of the local government partners in the JPPHA, Broomfield had a stake in the parkway construction process. A functionary of the Colorado Department of Public Health and Environment

(CDPHE) presented a legal opinion that a Colorado state standard of two decompositions per minute [239+240]Pu per gram of soil (0.9 pCi/g) was inapplicable, and would not be enforced.[7] *You've got the green light to build the parkway,* was the imputed message from CDPHE to the polarized audience gathered in the city council auditorium.

On August 16, 2019, I received a call from *Denver Post* reporter John Aguilar, with whom I'd previously spoken several times regarding Rocky Flats. John related that the JPPHA had just disclosed a perplexing result from one particular soil sample Engineering Analytics had collected along the highway's intended path. It seemed that the lab reported a much higher result for one of a pair of 1-gram subsamples from the same jar of soil. *Well,* I told John, *this can only mean that they found a specific result above the cleanup threshold of 50 picocuries per gram.* Why else would JPPHA go to the trouble of making a proactive public announcement about a single data point? *How can this inconsistency happen,* John asked. We had talked previously about what I referred to as the hot particle phenomenon in a previous conversation, and I continued, *John; here's a hot particle for you, and it must be a big one, of several microns in diameter.* Further announcements from JPPHA's technical consultants described the result as stemming from the presence of a single 8.8 micron (8.8×10^{-6} meter) diameter plutonium dioxide particle in this one specific 1-gram soil portion. Adding this mammoth PuO_2 particle to 1 gram of soil had resulted in an increase in the measured [239+240]Pu activity, from a baseline of 1.5 to an observed value of 264 pCi/g.

Gold prospectors have long referred to the same phenomenon as the nugget effect,[8] and mining companies that wanted to stay in business for very long heeded the nugget effect when conducting its sampling and assaying of gold ores. Starting from the veins underground and the glistening flakes in streambeds, to the balance pan and all through each intervening step, the careful analyst and mining engineer collaborated to acknowledge the nuggets' presence and to generate a credible result for the value in an ore body. The mining companies find it imperative to address this so-called nugget effect, considering how stock prices and everyone's future employment depend upon accurate assays of railroad cars full of low-grade ore with interspersed nuggets.

It is not a surprise, John, I continued. *They've just mined a PuO_2 nugget,* one might say. One should expect to find these nuggets occasionally, and Engineering Analytics' radiochemistry lab, ALS Laboratories had been fortunate, or perhaps unfortunate, enough to obtain a sizable nugget at the analytical balance. A PuO_2 nugget of 8.8 microns is a giant, and the result of 264 pCi/g for that single spatula full of soil had kicked the anthill on what to do about a soil that exceeded the 50 pCi/g soil abatement standard adopted by the US Department of Energy. Smaller particles are more numerous, and yet still can produce obvious, detectable deviations in replicate analyses. One major deviation, totally outside normal statistical control, had just showed up.

John, let's see what the JPPHA, CDPHE, and DOE will have to say about this finding, but I'm certain how I interpret it. John continued by bringing up questions about the health effects and risks to humans. I related that plutonium was an alpha emitter, and its capacity for harm stems from internal, as opposed to, external radiation exposure. In other words, *Don't inhale these guys. How likely is that?* John countered. I replied that I wouldn't be too concerned about it most of the time, but it could conceivably happen, if the soil was disturbed during road construction or on one of those windy days that scoured and denuded surface soils on the native shortgrass prairie. Under the gun to produce nuclear weapons during the early Cold War, the US government had built the plant in a veritable wind tunnel, directly in the path where the Chinook winds roared down from the Continental Divide and pushed warm air in an easterly direction. The downwind areas were much less densely developed in the 1950s than today, but the wind patterns have remained the same. Even so, inhaling a particle this large would still not be a high-probability event – rather like winning the Powerball jackpot. Yes, it could happen, and if you get that guy in your lungs, that one particle will be generating a dozen decays per second in a pinpoint volume of tissue. *No, it's not a surprise,* as I refreshed my memory on a 2-micron particle I'd similarly encountered in one of my own samples I had collected in 2002 from property to the east of Indiana Street.

I'd been thinking about plutonium-laden particles since a September afternoon in 1980, when I first gazed upon the Rocky Flats Plant, visible in the brown cloud after I'd reached the pinnacle of Bear Mountain on a day hike. I pointed to the facility, and asked one of my fellow hikers relaxing on the summit, *WTF is that place over there?* A ripple of mirth came from my colleagues. *Oh, that's Rocky Flats, and it's no chocolate factory; what they do is make nuclear bomb parts out of plutonium metal. Haven't you heard of the big fire in 1969 and the protests? You must be a newcomer to Boulder.* Indeed I was. Yet, as a newly enrolled graduate student in analytical chemistry at the University of Colorado, I digested the relevant chemical properties: plutonium metal is pyrophoric, a term indicating that the substance reacts rapidly and violently with oxygen gas. For these reasons, the plant had been constructed to handle the Pu metal in large inert gas dry glove boxes; nevertheless, it is impossible to believe that even the most careful practices would preclude occasional metal fires and releases of plutonium oxide aerosols into the ambient environment. When plutonium metal burns, it releases heat and generates temperatures well in excess of $1000°$ centigrade (C), in what is referred to as an exothermic process. The temperatures created are high enough to occasionally excite individual Pu atoms into elevated energy states; as these excited states return to their normal, ground-state configuration, photons of light are emitted. Plutonium metal fires are characterized by a visible glow, analogous to the emission of white light from a magnesium sparkler. Plumes of smoke containing the reaction product, plutonium dioxide, escape into the atmosphere. An ignited sparkler or metal-cutting oxyacetylene torch produces similar plumes of aerosol.

Stay away from the heat and smoke from that sparkler, Michael, my mother warned my nine-year-old self on a Fourth of July evening as I watched its atomic emissions and billowing clouds of magnesium oxide fumes with giddy fascination. Had my family been living in Colorado in that same year of 1969, and had Mom happened to know what they actually did at Rocky Flats, she'd have warned me away from the smoke from the plutonium that burned and glowed on that Mother's Day of 1969. The radioactive smoke escaped the plant, and the hot particles spread with the winds, landing wherever chance wind patterns and Stokes's Law dictated. The Mother's Day particles of 1969 blended with the particles from fires in 1957 and other years, the particles that managed to escape the main stack filters on a daily basis, and the Pu-contaminated oil-soaked soil that blew to the east from the 903 Pad with the Chinook winds.

Before leaving the summit of Bear Mountain, I thought briefly on the subject of entropy: order does not forever persist, and the universe tends to become disordered. Having had some experience working in chemistry labs, and now as a first-year graduate teaching assistant supervisor of two General Chemistry sections, I realized that humans were not perfect in handling dangerous materials. Entropy is the root cause of environmental pollution; I'd grown up in New York near the site of the Love Canal, and quickly imagined the mess wrought at Rocky Flats. At neither place could omelets have possibly been prepared without cracking and scattering egg-shells. I left my fellow hikers with their lunches on the summit, pondering to myself, *The whole surroundings must have been dusted with PuO$_2$ particles; yes, you guys are right – the place is no chocolate factory.*

In the summer of 2018, I'd testified in a US District Court hearing, brought by the Rocky Mountain Peace and Justice Center, requesting an injunction to keep the Rocky Flats National Wildlife Refuge closed to public use. I'd been working for nearly two decades in studies of pluto-nium in the environment, and early on, I was drawn to Rocky Flats as a natural laboratory to study different aspects of this element's behavior in the ambient environment. During my 2000 and 2002 Christmas breaks, I'd traveled to visit family and friends in Colorado, while also collecting soil cores from areas near the refuge. One of the top 5-cm surface inter-vals of an off-site soil core had exhibited the same disparity as the 2019 JPPHA soil, which I had interpreted as arising from the presence of a 2-micron diameter PuO$_2$ particle. I'd strategized with the plaintiff's at-torney, Randall Weiner, to discuss this particle during my direct examina-tion. The eager young Department of Justice attorney defending the gov-ernment's opening of the refuge was anxious to cross-examine me. *Dr. Ketterer, would you say that your findings agree with previous Rocky Flats environmental studies conducted by the government?* Surviving periodic cross-examinations in my career had taught me to be wary of the Trojan horse syndrome. Indeed, I considered, there is a Trojan horse here, but it works in my favor, unlike whatever opposing counsel might be conclud-ing. *Yes*, I answered, as I imagined classified reports and KGB dossiers I'd never read, yes, I do agree with the government. The one-word answer on cross-examination is best, when possible. I let out a very slight smirk with that answer. The defense attorney had gotten the smirk she'd hoped for, and returned mine. I'd gotten the truth into the record: yes, counsel-or. Had I chosen to expand on my answer, I'd state and affirm that the Central Operating Unit, the Rocky Flats National Wildlife Refuge, and unknown points beyond, have all been dusted with hot particles of PuO$_2$. Yes, these particles are out there, but their concentrations, particle sizes, and geospatial distributions, not to mention their health implications, have yet to be disclosed by the government and discussed with the com-munity. Yes, defense counselor, I do agree with the government. The De-partment of Energy and their predecessor agencies have definitely sampled and characterized these particles in soils outside the former Rocky Flats plant, as surely as did spies of the United States' Soviet adversaries during the Cold War.

David Abelson, executive director of the Rocky Flats Stewardship Council, commented in the *Denver Post* on the significance of the JPPHA 8.8 micron hot particle: *There were not readings historically this high in the buffer zone…. It is something that demands a much more in-depth look, a much more in-depth conversation as to what it means.*[9] I had encountered Mr. Abelson previously at a Stewardship Council meeting; I read David's words, and a lack of any mention of the hot particle phenomenon, and imagined the next line of reasoning: *this is an outlier, so let's throw it out.* Go ahead, throw it out; you'll be throwing out the single relevant data point that reveals precisely the scientific truth.

Grains of concentrated radioisotopes represent an altogether different situation from having the same activity dispersed uniformly on the surface of all the billions and trillions of mineral grains in a macroscopic sample. In most soils, Pu is present from aboveground nuclear weapons testing deposition from the Cold War era, and this "fallout" Pu is relatively uniformly distributed on the surfaces of an enormous number and variety of soil particles. A gram of soil containing a billion Pu atoms might contain a Pu atom here and there on some of the grains; perhaps a large particle surface might even contain a half dozen Pu atoms. There is fallout Pu at Rocky Flats a second variety of similarly dispersed Pu stemmed from the dispersion of soil contaminated with cutting oils from the 903 Pad. The Pu emissions from fires did not yield individual atoms that subsequently became adsorbed to the soil particles; instead, these processes synthesized chemically inert ceramic beads of nanometers to micrometers (microns) in diameter, and they were now demonstrating their presence as individual PuO_2 particles. Since ^{239}Pu has a half-life of 24,110 years, a single ^{239}Pu atom on the surface of a soil particle is unlikely to disintegrate even over the course of a century. However, a macroscopic collection of PuO_2 atoms in a PuO_2 grain will yield a steady stream of alpha particles. Even a tiny, 1-micron diameter PuO_2 particle, with a mass of 60 picograms, contains about thirteen billion (1.3×10^{10}) plutonium atoms. A micron-sized PuO_2 particle will emit, on average, about 1,000 alpha particles on a daily basis, over a future period of tens of thousands of years. Soil with homogeneously distributed Pu is akin to a large bag of Skittles, with coatings and occasional Pu atoms on the surfaces of an enormous collection of particles; add PuO_2 particles to that collection, and it would be analogous to adding some jalapeño-flavored jellybeans to the bag. Most of the spicy flavor in the entire bag would stem from the jellybeans. Imagine trying to sample that bag of Skittles, in order to determine how spicy the whole bag was: occasionally one would grab a jellybean in a specific handful, but most mouthfuls would not bite the tongue.

After the 1986 Chernobyl accident in Ukraine, radioecologists conducted extensive characterization studies of regionally distributed hot particles of nuclear fuel and their more volatile concomitants from the failed reactor. Their deposition in eastern Europe, and their accompanying risks are now well understood. The reader can go to scholar.google.com, type in the terms "Chernobyl" and "hot particles," and investigate. I'll summarize hundreds of peer-reviewed papers in four words: *don't inhale these guys.*

Yet, a similar Google Scholar search for Rocky Flats reveals a paucity of analogous hot particle studies. The most direct mention of Rocky Flats hot particles in US government publications is from the National Institute of Standards and Technology (NIST). Radiochemistry labs throughout the world buy "Rocky Flats Soil" as a standard reference material from NIST, and the fine print on the certification sheet makes mention of PuO_2 particles. This caveat emptor to the laboratory radiochemist advises that one may see inconsistencies in the activity results, stemming from hot particle effects.[10] Scoop a spatula full of pulverized soil that contains a sizable PuO_2 particle, and one will measure a higher activity than the other scoops that lack a nugget. The activity increase, measured by alpha spectrometry or mass spectrometry, reveals the presence of a hot particle. The plutonium activity equates directly to mass of the element, the mass of its oxide, the volume of the PuO_2 particle, and hence its diameter. I had applied that rationale in characterizing the PuO_2 particle from my own 2002 soil core, as had Engineering Analytics in interpreting their finding of an 8.8-micron particle in the construction zone where workers and earthmoving equipment would soon be kicking up dust.

The anthill had indeed been kicked by JPPHA's August 16, 2019, disclosure of the 8.8-micron particle, and different perspectives emerged. Jennifer Opila, director of CDPHE's Hazardous Materials and Waste Management Division stated, "We do believe that further sampling and analysis is needed to assess what this elevated sample may mean for long-term risks, and whether it is an isolated instance or a sign of a wider area of relatively high contamination." Nevertheless, the CDPHE's official position was that they "do not believe there is an immediate health threat." Retired FBI special agent Jon Lipsky, who had directed the 1989 criminal search warrant of the then-operating Rockwell facility, was rather matter of fact: "Rocky Flats refuge visitors should beware" (see note 9). David Wood, retired professor of Physics at Colorado School of Mines, took a stance quite opposed to Lipsky's, in penning an information sheet entitled "The Great Jefferson Parkway Hot Sample Kerfuffle," with an elaborate opinion that the nonuniform dose from hot particles was somehow less dangerous than an equivalent dose of radiation uniformly delivered, and that one would need to inhale thousands of 3-micron diameter PuO_2 particles to even raise one's risk of cancer by 1 percent. On September 6, 2019, the US Fish and Wildlife Service, custodians of the Rocky Flats National Wildlife Refuge, announced the completion of a new dataset of forty-eight soil samples collected along the intended route of the Rocky Mountain Greenway, cutting across the refuge property; $^{239+240}$Pu activities ranged from 0.013 to 3.51 picocuries per gram soil. According to the Fish and Wildlife Service, "The new soil sampling results are consistent with previous conclusions and recommendations by state and federal public health experts, indicating that the area is safe for public use."[11] David Abelson added that the new study "confirms what we've always known," namely, that there is no evidence that human health is at risk in the refuge (see note 11).

Who exactly is David referring to by "we" in the "we've always known," I pondered as I boarded a flight from Denver to Flagstaff, Arizona, where I intended to search for additional answers about hot particles in the vial of soil I carried in my backpack in a sealed custody package. I had collected this soil in July 2019 on Jefferson County right-of-way to the west of Indiana Street, and had obtained six composite samples, each consisting of a blend of thirty to fifty individual shovels of surface soil from a ~ 15 meter-x-15 meter square area. I had retained 1-kilogram splits of the six soil samples, and completed the preliminary steps of oven drying. Using a ten-mesh sieve with 2 mm openings, I obtained what is operationally regarded as "soil," removing twigs, roots, pebbles, and few unfortunate desiccated invertebrates. On August 2, 2019, I had completed a report on plutonium in the six soils for Tiffany Hansen, a local researcher and director of the Rocky Flats Downwinders. The results revealed $^{239+240}$Pu activities of between 0.9 and 2.7 picocuries per gram in the soil, which appeared to fit the story of what JPPHA and the US Fish and Wildlife Service had found.

In this trip to Northern Arizona University (NAU), I intended to delve further into one of the composite samples, to specifically look for discrepancies in measured plutonium activities of a series of small-mass portions of a specific individual soil. To prepare the key sample for analysis, I used a 200-mesh sieve to sift the soil, obtaining a working quantity of particles of fewer than 75 microns in diameter. It is within this finer particle size fraction that I anticipated finding the hot particles, if they were present.

As an emeritus faculty member at NAU, I had access to the laboratories in the Department of Chemistry and Biochemistry, where I had previously taught and researched for fifteen years. The department is equipped with an instrument known as an inductively coupled plasma mass spectrometer (ICPMS); an ICPMS employs a high temperature, atmospheric pressure argon gas plasma, similar to a metal-cutting or welding discharge, to vaporize samples into individual gas-phase atoms.[12] I'd first become fascinated with ICPMS in 1988 while working as an analytical chemist for the US Environmental Protection Agency with one of the first installed instruments in the United States. In the high temperatures of the plasma, many of the free atoms lose an electron to form a charged ion, which one might represent as M^+ (g). At temperatures of about 7000° C achieved in the plasma, all introduced Pu atoms are converted to gasphase Pu^+ and Pu-bearing polyatomic ion species. I had purchased two new ICPMS's and installed two secondhand instruments during my time at NAU, and one of the systems I had purchased in 2009 was still operational. The 2009 Thermo X2 instrument, located in the lab of a colleague, Professor Jani Ingram, served the needs of researchers with radionuclide measurements. In addition to many other tasks involving stable element measurements, and the Ingram group's extensive studies of legacy uranium mining contamination in the Navajo Nation, the X2 had completed more than 10,000 Pu determinations during its operational history. NAU maintains a radionuclide license with the state of Arizona for use/handling of solutions of ^{242}Pu, which serves as a calibration material in measurements of ^{239}Pu and ^{240}Pu by ICPMS methods. I would spend the next two days on three urgent analytical projects, including the hot particle analysis of my own Rocky Flats Soil Composite No. 3.

It is common practice in ICPMS to introduce samples that have been converted into an aqueous liquid, using an aerosol of dried water droplets that are sprayed into the plasma with an argon gas stream by a nebulizer, a device similar to an airbrush used for spray painting. The ionized gas atoms are extracted from the plasma into a vacuum chamber, focused and steered, and thereafter, the beam is directed into a mass-selective filter known as a quadupole. The quadrupole, a 20-cm long bundle of four machined nickel rods with appropriate DC and high-frequency AC voltages applied in a precisely controlled and programmed fashion, is systematically tuned and switched to transmit ions of a specified mass-to-charge ratio. Since the charges of most of the ions are +1, in essence the ICP mass spectrometer filters and then counts individual atoms as a direct function of mass. The filtering performed by the quadrupole is not a perfect process; nevertheless, it is a realistic way to measure atoms that differ by one atomic mass unit; for example, ^{239}Pu vs. ^{240}Pu can be distinguished, whereas ^{238}Pu and ^{238}U cannot. However, the quadrupole conditions can be rapidly and repeatedly switched to obtain count rate information as a function of mass. Referred to as the mass spectrum, the data output contains information about multiple isotopes that is measured in a matter of minutes (Figure 2). When the liquid and gas flow rates, the spray chamber evaporation and condensation chamber parameters, and many additional variables associated with the plasma and mass spectrometer were reasonably tuned, one could record signals to record the atom counts of each Pu isotope. One seeks to integrate the mass spectrometric peaks of ^{238}U$^+$, ^{239}Pu$^+$, ^{240}Pu$^+$, and ^{242}Pu$^+$ in multiple "runs" over a three-to-five minute period of time. The quadrupole filter conditions are adjusted to transmit ionized atoms of each mass in a "peak jump" sequence with dwell times of ten milliseconds. Over the several minutes before the sample liquid is expended, reasonable ion count data can be generated with ~ 10 femtograms (1 fg = 10^{-15} g) or more of a specific Pu isotope. I anticipated Rocky Flats nectars would contain considerably more than 10 fg Pu, and accordingly, it would be relatively straightforward to collect good results for the Pu extracted from 200-milligram soil subsamples. It is not possible to directly introduce the soil into the plasma in order to measure the Pu; instead, a sequence of chemical steps must first be undertaken to dissolve the sample, and thereafter, to extract and purify the Pu. From soil samples of milligrams up to 200 grams, I had experimented with many different procedures for converting the Pu

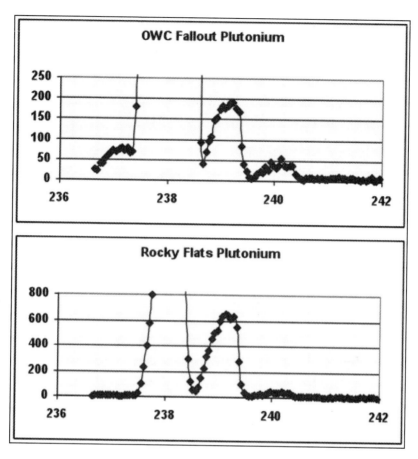

Figure 2. Inductively coupled plasma mass spectra of plutonium solutions obtained with a VG PQII ICPMS instrument, during early experiments at NAU in 2001. A liquid containing the Pu was extracted from a sediment sample containing "global fallout" Pu (top), and a soil sample containing Pu of Rocky Flats origin (bottom). The large off-scale peak in both spectra corresponds to 238U, and the smaller peaks at mass 239 and 240 represent 239Pu and 240Pu, respectively. The vertical scale represents the average number of ionized atoms counted per second during the spectral acquisition; the horizontal scale represents mass-to-charge ratio. Note that the relative peak heights of 240Pu vs. 239Pu spectra are routinely measured, allowing one to distinguish between different sources of Pu. A small 237Np peak is evident in the top spectrum; this isotope is also present in nuclear weapons testing fallout. Courtesy of Michael Ketterer.

from the solid sample into a 1-to-2 milliliter volume of nectar to present to the mass spectrometer.

Chemistry is like cooking, my physicist colleague from Krakow, Jerzy Mietelski once related, and it was indeed true; I would expend the majority of my lab time performing chemical processes to produce the Pu nectars, and a minor fraction of the time was expended actually measuring the nectars with the ICPMS. When things were running well, the ICPMS could measure ten to fifteen Pu nectars per hour. To start the cooking, I weighed a dozen 200-milligram portions of the soil into small vials along with 2.0 grams of solid potassium hydroxide, and a 100 microliter volume of a "spike" solution that contained 105 picograms of ^{242}Pu. I commenced a thirty-minute furnace heating of the mixtures at 600° C, which melts the potassium hydroxide, dissolving the sample in the process. The ^{242}Pu isotope is not indigenous in the Rocky Flats samples at significant levels, hence it functions as a suitable internal reference for measuring the amounts of ^{239}Pu and ^{240}Pu in the sample. Moreover, once the ^{242}Pu from the spike and the Pu atoms from the sample are brought into a common chemical form, as is achieved in the molten potassium hydroxide, the sample and spike atoms are "equilibrated"; the ratios of ^{239}Pu and ^{240}Pu from the sample vs. ^{242}Pu from the spike would remain constant even after performing a series of chemical steps to separate the Pu into a nectar. The upshot is, one can get the correct answer for the quantities of ^{239}Pu and ^{240}Pu by measuring their ratios to ^{242}Pu, even if some of the Pu was lost – I could be a sloppy cook, and spill or lose most of the atoms. If the proportional losses of ^{239}Pu, ^{240}Pu, and ^{242}Pu were the same after sample-spike equilibration, the chef would nevertheless be successful for measuring the quantities of ^{239}Pu and ^{240}Pu.

After taking the potassium hydroxide melts out of the furnace, I added water to remove the solid gelatinous precipitate and a clear liquid phase. The Pu partitions into the solid phase, centrifugation removed the solids, which I dissolved in dilute nitric acid. A series of reactants were added to convert all the Pu into its +4 oxidation state; the Illinois firm EIChrom manufactures polymeric "TEVA resin" beads that retain Pu in the +4 oxidation state from nitric acid solutions.[13] A total of 100 milligrams of the resin beads, added to 10 milliliters of solution, would remove the majority of the Pu from the solution. Another beneficial property of TEVA is that it has a low affinity for binding uranium; in most soils, the naturally occurring U atom concentrations are millions of times higher than those of Pu. Getting rid of at least 99.99 percent of the U from the dissolved sample uranium was imperative for measuring Pu, as ^{238}U and ^{239}Pu are neighbors in the mass spectrum. An enormous ^{238}U$^+$ peak would produce a "peak tail" that would interfere with accurate measurements of ^{239}Pu$^+$; furthermore, U forms a ^{238}U^{1}H$^+$ "hydride" species in the plasma, which the quadrupole cannot resolve from ^{239}Pu$^+$. Uranium is, indeed, the enemy in this recipe for measuring plutonium by mass spectrometry. Fortunately, the TEVA resin chemistry worked well. Invented at Argonne National Labs, TEVA resin mimicked the solvent extraction chemistry used during the Manhattan Project and Cold War era to recover ^{239}Pu from neutron-irradiated ^{238}U. One simply had to collect the resin beads from the solution suspension after a thirty-minute agitation step; I used inexpensive, disposable 8-milliliter transfer pipets equipped with glass wool plugs to collect the TEVA resin beads into a columnar geometry. A nitric acid rinse was used to elute, or strip off, nearly all of the residual U, to achieve Pu nectars within specifications for successful measurement. After several rinse steps, I collected 1.5 milliliters of eluted solution using water and aqueous ammonium oxalate solution. The majority of the Pu from each of the 200 milligrams of the soils had finally been obtained in small centrifuge tubes, and the mass spectrometry could commence.

It's great to sit in front of you once again, my old X2 friend, I thought, while starting the machine. When tuning adjustments had been completed, I programmed a block of three 46-second measurements for each of the nectars. In between samples, I'd rinse the nebulizer and aerosol heating/condensation system with dilute ammonium oxalate to remove remnants of the previous sample. While the instrument was collecting peak integrations, the computer monitor would display, in real time, a horizontal strip with a series of momentarily illuminated dots, each indicating that one or more ions had been detected within a ten millisecond measurement dwell time of the quadrupole at each mass. It was relaxing and reassuring to sit in front of the instrument, while the dots flickered as the nebulizer drew in and consumed the cook's creations. I stared at the flickering dots as the detector recorded Pu atoms, and repeatedly checked the reported ion count data as each sample's integrations concluded.

Within two hours, the results were complete: all twelve of the 200-milligram subsamples contained elevated levels of plutonium. It was also apparent that all of the subsamples exhibited Pu originating from Rocky Flats; as Pu is of synthetic origin, its isotope composition varies among different specific sources. The mass spectrometer also measured the ^{240}Pu/^{239}Pu atom ratio, to distinguish between the global baseline of nuclear weapons testing fallout (0.18) vs. the weapons-grade Pu that had been used at Rocky Flats (0.05 – 0.06). A simple division of the atom counts recorded at ^{240}Pu and ^{239}Pu, respectively, revealed this ratio. All twelve of the samples exhibited weapons-grade ^{240}Pu/^{239}Pu signatures; while undoubtedly, they also contained some weapons testing fallout, the measured ratio reflected a weighted average of the two sources, and these ratios indicated essentially 100 percent Rocky Flats origin. Isotope ratios are akin to truth serums, in establishing provenance of elements and compounds in the environment; I'd employed Pu isotope ratios on many different studies. Here at Rocky Flats, few would dispute that the Pu near the former facility had originated from historic plant operations, although I'd heard claims that the uranium at the site could have originated from the Schwartzwalder Mine. *Let the isotope ratios do the talking,* was my philosophy, whenever someone offered conjecture testable with a truth serum.

My heart skipped beats as I started to digest the other significant revelations of the ion count data. Each of the potassium hydroxide melts had been prepared from nominal 200-milligram aliquot; for homogeneous samples, the results would be in close agreement, with a relative standard deviation of only a few percent. Nevertheless, it was apparent that the ^{239}Pu/^{242}Pu atom ratios being measured by the mass spectrometer varied by nearly a factor of 10, revealing that the individual samples contained quite different masses of ^{239}Pu. Six of the samples reported concentrations of 67 ± 3 picograms $^{239+240}$Pu per gram of soil, but the remaining half dozen samples exhibited disparate values, ranging from contents of 80 to 585 picograms $^{239+240}$Pu per gram of soil.

The interpretation followed the same rationale as had been stated by Engineering Analytics: the disparate results arose from the presence of individual PuO$_2$ particles. Some straightforward calculations implied that the highest-concentration sample contained a particle of 96 picograms of Pu, chemically equivalent to 109 picograms of PuO$_2$. A 109-picogram particle of Pu occupies a volume of 9.5 x 10^{-12} cubic centimeters, corresponding to a sphere of radius 1.3 microns and a diameter of 2.6 microns. Following the same logic, the remaining 5 particle-containing sample data points translated into particles from 0.8 to 1.7 microns in diameter – in other words, precisely in the ideal size range to be inhaled and persist in the inner recesses of the lungs. *Don't inhale these guys.*

Sleep escaped me for a long time that same night, as I pondered the implications of the results. What I had first envisioned on that afternoon in 1980 was indeed manifested in the day's data: the refuge and its proximity had been dusted with PuO_2 particles. Herein, I had used a very short experiment to indirectly show the particles' presence, and to calculate their sizes, but my thoughts led to many confirmatory experiments; the essence of a scientific truth lies in its repeatability. At a minimum, this same experiment would need to be repeated on a much larger scale, using soils obtained from different locations near the site, as well as more distant, control locations. One expects the presence of PuO_2 particles to be sporadic, and it would be necessary to perform many preparations with several different masses of soil in order to get a reasonable handle on this size distribution in a single soil sample.

A series of thoughts that night focused on how one could directly isolate and characterize these PuO_2 particles. The PuO_2 particles are small and dense; sifting with fine mesh sieves could discard a lot of the larger, extraneous fraction of the soil. Starting with a sieved fraction of particles of 20 microns and smaller, one might next proceed using density-based heavy liquid separations. This idea was certainly not original; igneous petrologists have long used liquids such as methylene iodide (CH_2I_2) or aqueous sodium polytungstate to recover heavy minerals such as zircon.[14] In a vessel filled with methylene iodide, most of the soil particles, having densities of less than 3 grams/centimters^3, would float in a column of higher density fluid, while PuO_2 grains (11.5 g/cm^3) would sink, along with the zircons and other indigenous heavy minerals. One could gather and dissolve the heavy mineral fraction, which might only comprise a milligram or 2 from 1 gram of soil. Alternatively, a scanning electron microscope could be used to acquire images of the particles. With an X-ray emission spectrometer attachment, the Pu-containing grains could be identified readily, using the characteristic X-rays emitted by atoms excited by the imaging electron beam. A specialized type of mass spectrometer, referred to as a secondary ionization mass spectrometer (SIMS), could even perform imaging of individual particles and measure their isotope compositions.[15] The investigations of particles with SEM or SIMS methods were not my expertise, although I had collaborated with colleagues who were versed in collecting this type of data.

If indeed Rocky Flats soils contained PuO_2 particles from the fires, their geographic distribution would need to be investigated, and hence, this type of experiment would need to be repeated with soils from the refuge, the Indiana Street corridor, and locations throughout the northwest section of greater Denver. Where had the plumes from the 1957 and 1969 fires traveled to, and what additional fires had deposited PuO_2 particles in the proximity? There is no reason to assume that the geospatial distribution of PuO_2 particles coincides precisely with the government's Pu activity contour maps that had been published; we still know very little with regards to where PuO_2 particles from the fires are found today. We lack insights into realistic scenarios about PuO_2 inhalation by refuge visitors or residents of downwind communities. It is easy for the Colorado Department of Public Health and Environment to state that the refuge is safe when that conclusion rests on a simplistic comparison of soil activity to a 50 pCi per gram threshold; understanding the probability of inhaling a radioactive particle, and the subsequent processes when said particle irradiates lung tissue, was an altogether different question. The CDPHE, it would seem, has its work cut out, if it seeks to fulfill the agency's mission to protect human health and the environment.

Perhaps, however, David Wood is correct: one can inhale thousands of PuO_2 particles and only minimally raise one's risk of carcinoma. Who among us is willing to try that experiment?

Notes

1. Jefferson Parkway. https://www.jppha.org/about-the-jefferson-parkway/, accessed Sept. 16, 2019.

2. J. H. Harley. "Plutonium in the Environment – A Review," *Journal of Radiation Research* 21 (1980): 83–104.

3. J. M. Kelley, L. A. Bond, and T. M. Beasley. "Global Distribution of Pu Isotopes and [237]Np," *The Science of the Total Environment* 237/238 (1999): 483–500.

4. Ketterer, M. E., and S. C. Szechenyi. "Review: Determination of Plutonium and Other Transuranic Elements by Inductively Coupled Plasma Mass Spectrometry: A Historical Perspective and New Fron-

tiers in the Environmental Sciences." *Spectrochimica Acta* B 63 (2008): 719–737.

5. D. L. Clark, D. R. Janecky, and L. J. Lane. "Science-Based Cleanup of Rocky Flats," *Physics Today* 59, no. 9 (2006): 34–40.

6. P. W. Krey, and E. P. Hardy. "Plutonium in Soil around the Rocky Flats Plant," US Atomic Energy Commission 1970, Health and Safety Laboratory, HASL-235. https://www.osti.gov/servlets/purl/4071339, accessed Sept. 16, 2019.

7. Letter from Jennifer T. Opila, Hazardous Materials and Waste Management division director, Colorado Department of Public Health and Environment, to Bill Ray, executive director, Jefferson Parkway Public Highway Authority, June 14, 2019. Copy available from author.

8. C. O. Ingamells. "Evaluation of Skewed Exploration Data – The Nugget Effect." *Geochimica et Consmochimica Acta* 45 (1981) 1209–1216.

9. Aguilar, J. "Potential Plutonium Hot Spot Found on the Eastern Edge of Rocky Flats," *Denver Post*, Aug. 16, 2019. https://www.denverpost.com/2019/08/16/rocky-flats-plutonium-hot-spot-jefferson-parkway/, accessed Sept. 16, 2019.

10. National Institute of Standards and Technology, Certificate for Standard Reference Material 4353A, Rocky Flats Soil Number 2. https://www-s.nist.gov/srmors/certificates/4353A.pdf, accessed Sept. 16, 2019.

11. J. Aguilar. "New Soil Samples from Inside Rocky Flats Refuge Show Low Plutonium Levels," *Denver Post*, Sept. 6, 2019. https://www.denverpost.com/2019/09/06/rocky-flats-plutonium-samples-soil/, accessed Sept. 16, 2019.

12. R. S. Houk. "Elemental and Isotopic Analysis by Inductively Coupled Plasma Mass Spectrometry," *Accounts of Chemical Research* 27 (1994): 333–339.

13. E. P. Horwitz, M. L. Dietz, R. Chiarizia, H. Diamond, S. L. Maxwell, and M. R. Nelson. "Separation and Preconcentration of Actinides by Extraction Chromatography Using a Supported Liquid Anion Exchanger: Application to High-Level Nuclear Waste Solutions," *Analytica Chimica Acta* 310 (1995): 63–78.

14. H. W. Fairbairn. "Concentration of Heavy Accessories from Large Rock Samples." *American Mineralogist: Journal of Earth and Planetary Materials* 40 (1955): 458–468.

15. R. Pöllänen, M. E. Ketterer, S. Lehto, M. Hokkanen, T. K. Ikäheimonen, T. Siiskonen, M. Morin, A. Martín Sánchez, and M. P. Rubio Montero. "A Non-Destructive and Destructive Multi-Technique Characterization of a Nuclear Bomb Particle from the Palomares Accident," *Journal of Environmental Radioactivity* 90 (2006): 15–28.

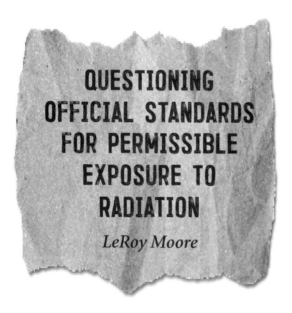

QUESTIONING OFFICIAL STANDARDS FOR PERMISSIBLE EXPOSURE TO RADIATION

LeRoy Moore

Executive Summary

The purpose of this chapter is to examine official standards for permissible exposure to radiation. Such standards are intended to protect the health of workers in the nuclear industry and of people who could be exposed to radiation because they live or work near nuclear facilities. Do these standards actually protect those likely to be exposed? My concern is to answer this question with respect to Rocky Flats, the now-closed nuclear weapons production facility near Denver, Colorado.

Background: My Introduction to Rocky Flats

In 1974 I arrived in Colorado to teach at the University of Denver. Since 1969 I'd been trying to convince students that we humans face three fundamental threats to our continued existence on this planet: nuclear holocaust, environmental disaster, and authoritarian or non-democratic governance. Since all these threats are produced by humans, if we vanish from the planet, it will be our doing. Likewise, only we humans can solve our problem.

When I arrived in Colorado, I had never heard of the Rocky Flats Nuclear Weapons Plant located 16 miles northwest of downtown Denver. I was in Denver for several years before I learned about the plant in 1978 when a small group of nonviolent activists occupied the railroad tracks leading into the facility. I soon joined those on the tracks in my first act of civil disobedience. My primary reason for opposing the plant was to eliminate the possibility of a nuclear war that could end human life on this planet.

Someone handed me a slim activist-produced booklet about Rocky Flats entitled *Local Hazard, Global Threat.* Looking at the booklet, I realized immediately that Rocky Flats combined in a concentrated way all three of the threats to which I had been alerting students. It made bombs for a nuclear holocaust. It contaminated the environment with highly toxic radioactive material. And it was carrying out decisions made behind a veil of secrecy that violated the principles of democracy.

I was already familiar with what the booklet called the "global threat." But I knew nothing about the "local hazard," especially related to Rocky Flats. Looking inside the booklet, I found this:

- "Plutonium-239 (Pu-239), the key ingredient in nuclear bombs, is one of the most lethal substances known."

- "Nearly invisible plutonium oxide smoke particles… can be carried for miles by the wind, later resuspended and carried further."

- "When beagle dogs inhaled one-thousandth of an ounce of Pu-239… as tiny smoke particles, their lungs were damaged by the alpha radiation, and they died in a matter of days to weeks. As little as one millionth of an ounce caused cancers over a period of years."

- "Inhaled plutonium dust would probably produce similar effects in humans…. Even tiny doses can cause cancer in the lungs, bones, and liver, and may cause premature aging and heart attacks."

- "Inhaled plutonium oxide particles produce intense alpha radiation to the lung."

- "If plutonium from RFP is being redistributed as some soil tests indicate, the lung cancer rate for Denver could increase as much as 10%."

- The rate that a radioactive material decays or loses its radioactivity is indicated by its "half-life." After one half-life, a given material will be half as radioactive as at the beginning of the period; this continues until the material has totally decayed. "With a radioactive half-life of 24,000 years, an ounce of plutonium would still be lethal after decaying for 250,000 years."[1]

The booklet said much more, but the above makes clear that plutonium is dangerous in very small amounts and for a very long time – far longer than humans have existed on this planet. With tiny wind-blown particles of plutonium widely distributed in the environment, the Denver area is indeed a "local hazard" – not a temporary hazard but a permanent one. I realized, looking at the booklet, that I had much to learn.

Learning about Radiation from a Physician

Dr. Jock Cobb, MD, professor at the University of Colorado medical school, was convening a seminar on radiation. I decided to attend. He was just what I needed – a genial medical doctor who opposed nuclear weapons and was thoroughly familiar with the science of radiation.

At the outset, Dr. Cobb said he would talk only about "ionizing radiation"; that is, substances that emit energy in the form of electromagnetic waves or particles that modify or "ionize" the atoms of material contacted. Ordinary atoms are stable, but ionizing energy upsets an atom's balance. Ionized atoms are very unstable and themselves are able to ionize or upset the balance of other atoms. Non-ionizing radiation may induce heat, light, or electricity, but ionizing radiation modifies atoms.

Dr. Cobb emphasized the following:

- There are three main types of radiation – alpha, beta, and gamma. A fourth, x-ray, is similar to gamma radiation, although x-rays are emitted by a machine while gamma rays are emitted naturally from a radioactive substance, such as uranium.

- Among the many radioactive elements, the most important ones at Rocky Flats are uranium, plutonium, and americium.

- Each radioactive material will have many forms, called isotopes. A specific isotope is indicated by a number, such as plutonium-239, uranium-235, or americium-241.

- The principal radioactive isotopes at Rocky Flats are uranium-235 and plutronium-239. Only a very small percentage of natural uranium is uranium-235; the uranium-235 at Rocky Flats had been isolated and enriched to increase the quantity of uranium-235. Plutonium-239, very rare in nature, is primarily produced in reactors; it came to Rocky Flats from either the Hanford Site in Washington state or the Savannah River Site in South Carolina.

- The plutonium at Rocky Flats contains a very small amount of the isotope plutonium-241, which has a short half-life, meaning it decays or gives off its radiation rapidly. As it decays, its "daughter product" is americium-241. So the americium at Rocky Flats is actually produced there as the plutonium-241 decays. Americium-241 also has a brief half-life. Its importance at Rocky Flats is that it emits alpha radiation quickly, creating a public health danger.

This was just the beginning. I asked myself: What have you gotten yourself into? This is incredibly complex. But anything that can be learned can be learned. So I stayed with it.

Jock Cobb was a wonderful teacher, always clear, always patient. He explained the origin of Rocky Flats by pointing out that the two atom bombs dropped on Japan were not identical. The one dropped on Hiroshima was a uranium bomb; the one dropped on Nagasaki was a plutonium bomb. Both uranium-235 and plutonium-239 can undergo fission – in which atoms split and release enough energy to destroy a city. US scientists soon realized that plutonium bombs produce a bigger blast with less material and thus less weight. They decided that the fissile core (or "pit") of all US nuclear weapons would be made with plutonium. The Rocky Flats plant came into existence to produce plutonium pits for warheads.

Although plutonium was the principal material used at Rocky Flats, uranium continued to be used as well. Dr. Cobb spoke of the distinctly different types of radiation – alpha and gamma – emitted by these two materials. He said almost nothing about beta radiation, since it is rare at Rocky Flats. I thus will concentrate on gamma and alpha.

Uranium emits gamma radiation, while plutonium emits alpha. Gamma radiation is strongly penetrating, readily passing through a human body. A large hit of gamma radiation can kill enough cells in the body to be harmful or fatal. But because it passes through the body and is gone, at lower levels of exposure gamma radiation may do little or no harm; any cells it kills directly will be discarded. The body can be shielded to prevent exposure. As Figure 1 shows, lead or concrete can block it.

The alpha radiation emitted by plutonium is quite another story. As Figure 1 shows, alpha radiation is blocked by skin. This suggests that alpha radiation is not harmful. But in fact it can be enormously harmful if a tiny particle of an alpha emitter, especially plutonium, is inhaled or otherwise taken into the body. If it enters the body through an open wound, blood carries it elsewhere, perhaps to the liver, the gonads, the brain, or the surface or marrow of a bone. Plutonium that is ingested – taken in with food or drink – will usually be excreted as waste rather quickly. Otherwise, internalized plutonium will lodge in the body, and wherever it lodges it will constantly irradiate a very small area of nearby cells, typically for the rest of one's life. These cells will not be killed, but they will be harmed. Replication of these injured cells becomes cancer. This is the source of the greatest harm from plutonium exposure.

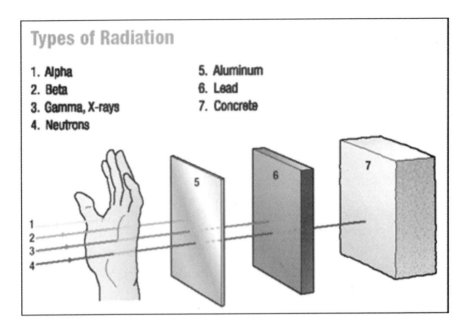

Figure 1. Types of radiation and what blocks each type. Gamma radiation, emitted by uranium, passes through the body but can be blocked by lead or concrete. Alpha radiation, emitted by plutonium, cannot penetrate human skin. Image courtesy of Robert Del Tredici.

The Beginning of Radiation Exposure Standards

From what has just been said, it is clear that exposure to radiation can be harmful. Herman Muller realized this as early as the 1920s. In 1946 he received the Nobel Prize for his discovery two decades earlier of genetic mutations in fruit flies exposed to radiation – harming future generations. That radiation exposure could be harmful thus was known well before the Manhattan Project to build the first atomic bombs. When the bomb project began, one of the first acts of the government was to hire Karl Z. Morgan to determine how much radiation nuclear weapons workers could be exposed to without endangering their health. His evolving views on this subject are very important. I will discuss him more fully later.

No legally binding standards for exposure to radiation were created for the Manhattan Project. A technical group, predecessor to today's National Committee on Radiation Protection and Measurements (NCRP), proposed the first US standards in 1934, but these standards were arbitrary and not legally binding. According to Catherine Caufield's book on this topic, these early standards "rested on scientifically shaky grounds – on studies too short to detect long-term effects; on inadequate samples; on ill defined and inconsistent units of measurement; on untested assumptions" – problems that, she says, have continued to characterize most efforts to set exposure limits.[2] Standards did not become legally binding until 1957 when the Atomic Energy Commission (AEC), which was responsible for both US nuclear weapons and nuclear power programs, "wanted standards to be legally binding, so that they could not be altered at the NCRP's whim."[3]

There was a difference between the views of the AEC and the NCRP. The AEC held that there was a threshold below which radiation exposure would not be harmful. By contrast, the NCRP's "guiding principle of radiation protection then, as now, was explained in 1956 by Lauristan Taylor.... 'Any radiation exposure received by man must be accepted as harmful. Therefore, the objective must be to keep man's exposure as low as possible and yet at the same time, not discontinue the use of radiation altogether.' Thus, the NCRP exposure limits could not and did not promise absolute safety."[4]

Today the NCRP continues to study radiation health effects and to make recommendations for exposure standards. The International Commission on Radiological Protection (ICRP) does similar work at the international level, as does the United Nations Scientific Committee on the Effects of Atomic Radiation.

A variety of US agencies currently establish and enforce radiation standards. For the nuclear weapons industry, two sets of standards apply, one for employees in the plants and another for the general public. Standards for the latter are enforced by the Environmental Protection Agency (EPA) and state agencies, such as the Colorado Department of Public Health and Environment. The Department of Energy (DOE) enforces standards for nuclear weapons workers; the Nuclear Regulatory Commission enforces standards for nuclear power workers. All these agencies rely on recommendations from NCRP, ICRP and other bodies, such as the National Academy of Sciences, especially its periodic BEIR (Biological Effects of Ionizing Radiation) studies.

My Own Experience and Activities

Thanks to Jock Cobb, I devoted thirty-five years to the "local hazard" of exposure to plutonium in the environment, released from Rocky Flats. Because of my academic background, I brought to this work the skills of research and writing. Here are a few highlights from my experience:

- Wrote the *Citizen's Guide to Rocky Flats* (1992), an eighty-page work that builds on and much enlarges the twenty-page *Local Hazard, Global Threat.*

- Studied and wrote about Edward Martell, PhD, of the National Center for Atmospheric Research, and Carl J. Johnson, MD, director of the Jefferson County Department of Health, independent scientists who revealed the public health danger of Rocky Flats.[5]

- Participated in a half dozen advisory and oversight bodies related to public health issues at Rocky Flats.

- Attended nine years (1991–1999) of meetings for the Historical Public Exposures Studies on Rocky Flats (the dose reconstruction study).

- Participated in two courses on adverse health effects from exposure to radiation, one in Seattle, the other in Washington, DC.

- From 1999 to 2004 served on two committees of the National Council on Registration and Measurements, an organization that studies radiation health effects and recommends exposure standards.

- Published two articles in the *Bulletin of the Atomic Scientists*, one countering efforts to make radiation exposure standards less protective,[6] the other a critique of the Superfund cleanup at Rocky Flats.[7]

- On the twenty-fifth anniversary of FBI raid on Rocky Flats, published a history of activism at Rocky Flats.[8]

Lessons from Others about
Plutonium in the Environment

The important activity of biologist Harvey Nichols, PhD, specialist on sampling airborne particles, influenced me. In 1975, at the height of production, he was commissioned by the Energy Research and Development Administration (predecessor to the Department of Energy) to sample airborne particles at Rocky Flats. He found, first, that the monitoring equipment in place along the site's downwind boundary could not measure the airborne plutonium particles being released and thus provided essentially worthless data. Second, from his own sampling he concluded that billions of tiny plutonium particles released in routine operations at the plant had been deposited and were then being deposited throughout the site and beyond.[9]

The second influence came from meteorologist W. Gale Biggs, PhD. Not long after the 1989 FBI raid of Rocky Flats to collect evidence of alleged environmental crime at the site, then-governor Roy Romer gave Biggs the job of finding out the size of plutonium particles released from Rocky Flats, the quantity released, and where it went. Biggs found that the average size of plutonium particles released from the plant was 0.045 microns, far smaller than the average size of a human hair of about 50 microns. As for the other two questions, neither the airborne monitors at the edge of the site nor the monitors within the ventilation system could measure the particles. So there was no way to know how much plutonium was being emitted or how much was being carried by wind across the plant boundaries.[10]

Both Biggs and Nichols found the sampling for airborne particles done by DOE and other agencies worthless. They concluded that the periodic official reports asserting that very little plutonium was leaving the site were public relations moves to provide false assurance to a worried public. We don't know how much plutonium has been deposited in the environment or when it will be picked up by the wind and carried to another location. We do know that both the EPA and the DOE say the worst way to be exposed to plutonium is to inhale tiny particles. According to Nichols and Biggs, there is reason to believe that multitudes of particles lie in wait in the environment.

Why Radiation Exposure Standards Are Faulty

Based on my studies over thirty years, I concluded that, although radiation exposure standards provide some protection by setting limits that make high-dose exposures less likely, they otherwise provide insufficient protection, especially from the low-dose exposure emitted by tiny plutonium particles taken into the body. The National Academy of Sciences (NAS) BEIR studies mentioned earlier affirm that any exposure to ionizing radiation is potentially harmful. There is no such thing as a safe exposure.[11] Although this view is accepted by the NAS and the NCRP, the agencies that recommend and set radiation exposure standards allow some exposure. They create a legal framework that allows some people to be harmed and some to die. As Lauriston Taylor of the NCRP said back in 1956, the standards need to be as low as possible, but not so low that they "discontinue the use of radiation altogether."[12]

In the words of Ulrich Bech, "Whoever *limits* pollution has also *concurred* in it." Exposure standards "may indeed prevent the very worst from happening, but they are at the same time 'blank checks' to poison nature and humankind *a bit*."[13] Despite the fact that their standards allow some exposures, government officials often call contaminated sites "safe." This happened repeatedly at Rocky Flats and continues to happen today. The only thing that has changed is that different people now say that meeting standards means the site is safe. In what follows, I explain some of the problems with official standards.

1. Failure to Protect the Most Vulnerable

The whole edifice of standards for permissible exposure to radiation rests on the dubious foundation of cancer incidence among survivors of the Hiroshima and Nagasaki bombings. In the bombings, the most vulnerable people died. Those who ended up being studied were thus the stronger survivors. Basing exposure standards on what happens to survivors protects the strong more than the weak.[14] The resultant standards, based on Hiroshima and Nagasaki survivors, are biased in favor of a population of healthier survivors.

2. Conclusions from These Studies Are Not Reliable

First, the data used in the study consisted of interviews of survivors done not immediately after the bombing but rather five years later. How accurate were people's memories after so long? Second, estimates of exposure are uncertain because they do not rely on direct medical observation or measurement; much guesswork went into estimating the doses people had received. Third, the investigators were US personnel from the militarily victorious occupiers, not Japanese medical personnel or advocates who had observed what happened to the people of their country. Although more recent work on the data has combined Japanese and US specialists – a positive development – there have been ongoing changes in the way the study is done that, according to the late John W. Gofman, create "a real threat to the scientific credibility of the whole study."[15]

3. Affected Populations Excluded from the Standard-Setting Process

Nuclear workers and people who live or work in the vicinity of a nuclear facility are excluded from the task of setting standards for radiation exposure likely to affect them. All such standards are developed by a self-selected scientific elite without any direct input from affected populations, much less their consent. The standards are called "standards for permissible exposure," but permission to expose is not given by the exposed. When I was serving on an NCRP committee, two colleagues and I made a presentation before the NCRP at their 2004 annual meeting in Washington, DC. We urged them to include affected parties in the task of studying radiation health effects and setting standards. Our appeal was later published in *Health Physics*.[16] They rejected us. The NCRP functions like a self-appointed medieval priesthood that decides the earthly fate of people exposed to radiation.[17]

4. Exposure Standards: Radiation That Passes through the Body versus Radiation Lodged in the Body

The studies done on the Japanese survivors were of radiation exposure from a one- time bomb blast that emitted penetrating gamma radiation to the whole body. The studies locked in a precedent still followed by organizations responsible for exposure standards. Penetrating radiation exposure may be severe, but it passes through the body and thus is temporary. This is very different from the chronic exposure to alpha radiation emitted by plutonium particles lodged in the body. Columbia University scientists have shown that a single plutonium particle taken into the body can be harmful.[18] As discussed earlier, once inside the body, the plutonium stays in a specific location – a lung, a bone, the liver, the brain, the gonads, or elsewhere. Thereafter, typically for the rest of one's life, the plutonium repeatedly bombards nearby cells with radioactive alpha particles. Alpha radiation is not like gamma radiation, which passes through the body and generally proves harmful only in doses large enough to kill many cells. Plutonium, by contrast, is harmful not because it kills cells but because it damages them, and it is the replication of these injured cells that produces a cancer. Plutonium may also compromise one's immune system or cause genetic harm that gets passed on to offspring and future generations. One plutonium particle may prove harmful, not instantly but slowly. A cancer may take thirty years before it manifests. Harm from plutonium exposure is best addressed not at the bodily level but instead at the cellular level. The only sure form of protection from exposure to alpha radiation is to allow no exposure. But as noted previously, exposure standards allow some exposure.

5. Insufficient Protection for Internalized Radiation

Internal alpha emitters, like plutonium-239 and americium-241, are much more harmful than the equivalent dose from penetrating gamma radiation, because, as noted above, alpha particles lodge at a specific location in the body and continually irradiate nearby cells, while penetrating radiation passes through the body and is gone. To account for the difference, the ICRP refers to the "relative biological effectiveness" (RBE) of alpha emitters. Looking at the potential harm to different organs and for different disease end points, ICRP concludes that the average RBE for alpha emitters is twenty. This means that, on average, internalized plutonium is twenty times more harmful than penetrating radiation of the same dose. But because twenty is an average, for some body organs and certain cancers as well as for particular individuals the actual RBE can be higher, sometimes much higher. For example, the RBE for bone cancer ranges as high as 320, which is sixteen times twenty.[19] But agencies that set standards (such as those for the Superfund cleanup at Rocky Flats) use in their calculations the RBE of twenty. Such standards again fail to protect the most vulnerable.

6. Bias: Protecting "Reference Man"

Almost all radiation exposure standards have been calculated to protect "Reference Man," a Caucasian male twenty to thirty years of age, 5 feet and 7 inches tall, weighing 154 pounds, and living in a mild climate, such as in western Europe or North America.[20] Again, the standards by design do not protect those who are more vulnerable – females, infants, the elderly, the infirm, and the non-Caucasian. In 2013 Mary Olson publicized the fact that National Academy of Sciences' BEIR VII study of 2006, *Health Risks from Exposure to Low Levels of Ionizing Radiation*, showed conclusively that "a woman is at significantly greater risk of suffering and dying from radiation-induced cancer than a man who gets the same dose of ionizing radiation." She said, "This is news," because it had been "under-reported." She noted that, although it is often said that children are at higher risk from exposure to radiation than adults, "it is rarely pointed out that the regulation of radiation and nuclear activity (worldwide) ignores the disproportionately greater harm to both women and children."[21]

7. Karl Morgan's Challenge to the Standards for Low-Dose Exposure

Earlier I mentioned that in the mid-1940s Karl Morgan pioneered radiation standards to protect nuclear workers in the Manhattan Project. He said that at the time, "We all had… a serious misconception, in that we adhered universally… to the so-called 'threshold hypothesis,' meaning that if a dose were low enough, cell repair would take place… and there would be no resultant damage. In other words, we believed there was a safe level of radiation." By 1949, however, "The majority of us realized that there really wasn't a so-called safe level of exposure." Convinced that risk increased in exact proportion to dose, those responsible for radiation safety rejected the threshold model in favor of the "linear no-threshold" or "LNT" hypothesis – that harm increases as exposure increases. Both the NCRP and the ICRP, the leading organizations for recommending exposure standards, adopted the LNT approach, making it the orthodoxy of the nuclear establishment.[22]

Morgan eventually rejected the LNT in favor of the more stringent "supralinear" approach, because he had become convinced that it "fits the data more appropriately." He explained:

> Down at the very low doses you actually get more cancers per person-rem [rem is a unit of radiation] than you do at the high doses. Now, I'm not saying that you get more cancers at these low doses than at high doses. I'm saying that damage per unit dose is greater at these levels. And that's true in part because the high levels will more often kill cells outright, whereas low levels of exposure tend to injure cells rather than kill them, and it is the surviving, injured cells that are the cause for concern."

Over time, a damaged cell may become cancerous: "It divides, it divides again and again, and, on the average, if it's leading to a solid tumor, after 30 years it will be large enough that it will be recognized as a malignancy."[23]

Before saying more about these two approaches to radiation exposure, the LNT orthodoxy of the nuclear establishment and the supralinear approach favored by Morgan, I will briefly mention two other approaches the reader may encounter. The first is the "threshold" approach indicated by the T in LNT – Linear No Threshold. I earlier quoted Morgan's words that he had once adhered to the idea that there is a threshold below which radiation exposure is not harmful. A little radiation won't hurt you. He later rejected the threshold approach for the LNT idea, as did both the NCRP and the ICRP. The second approach to mention here is what is called "hormesis," which is a modification of the threshold approach. Advocates of hormesis believe that radiation exposure below the threshold is not only harmless, it's beneficial. A little radiation not only won't hurt you, but it will actually do you good.[24] This minority viewpoint pops up every once in a while; it was expressed in early 2016 by a person from the Nuclear Regulatory Commission (which deals solely with nuclear power), who reminded the agency that all its work would be cheaper if for setting standards it adopted hormesis.

While there are advocates of all four of these positions (see Figure 2), the real conflict is between the LNT orthodoxy of the nuclear establishment and the supralinear approach of Morgan and others.[25] Between

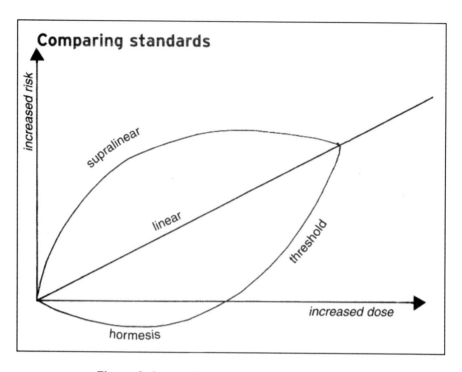

Figure 2. Approaches to setting standards for exposure to radiation. For the linear approach, risk increases as dose increases. The supralinear approach says harm at low doses increases more rapidly than the dose itself. Both the threshold and hormesis approaches say no harm occurs below a threshold; according to hormesis, exposure below the threshold is actually beneficial. Image from LeRoy Moore, "Lowering the Bar," *Bulletin of the Atomic Scientists*, May 2002.

these two, the key question is: What is best for the public health, including offspring and future generations? The answer is simple: That is best which is most protective. Obviously, this is the supralinear approach, with its recognition that any exposure can be harmful and its concern to protect people from harmful effects of low-dose exposure. If people are protected at this level, they are protected at all levels. Unfortunately, those who recommend and establish radiation exposure standards violate even the LNT approach by setting standards that allow some exposure. They say they accept the idea that any exposure is potentially harmful, yet establish standards that allow harm. They believe the harm they allow is small because the exposure is small, which is where advocates of the supralinear approach disagree.

8. Hereditary Damage of Radiation Exposure

As noted previously, Herman Muller received the 1946 Nobel Prize in medicine for his discovery of genetic mutations in fruit flies exposed to radiation. Toward the end of his life he published an article on the genetic effect in humans of radiation exposure. Although radiation exposure may cause birth defects, far more serious is the cumulative effect of exposure "over a virtually unlimited period." The damaged gene will "be passed along in inheritance… before it happens to turn the scales against the individual carrying it. When it does so, it will cause the extinction of its own line of descent," because a person in the chain of the harmed gene will suddenly lose the ability to reproduce, resulting in "genetic death…. The losses are spread out over centuries, even millennia, with only a few thousand genetic deaths resulting from them in any one generation." The damage to posterity will be massive. "Therefore the hereditary damage should be the chief touchstone in the setting of 'permissible' or 'acceptable' dose limits…. We must learn, through experience, to tackle our problems of today that affect tomorrow in a truly responsible way – one that our successors will thank us for."[26]

Reminiscent of Muller, genetic specialist Diethard Tautz says that effects of radiation exposure on a given species of wildlife may not be readily apparent in the individuals of that species until the passage of several generations. He calls this a "genetic uncertainty problem."[27] His work suggests that wildlife at Rocky Flats could in the long term be hurt by conditions at the site. Such harm would not be confined to the site. Some observers have taken a very sanguine approach to reports that plutonium has been found in the bodies of deer killed near Rocky Flats. Ecologist K. Shawn Smallwood, who in 1996 studied wildlife at Rocky Flats, "found it remarkable that no genetic studies" of wildlife had been done there or at "other nuclear sites."[28]

9. Distinct Character of Standards for Nuclear Workers

Nuclear workers are noteworthy in that, unlike the rest of us, while on the job they wear dosimeters to collect real-time data on the level of their exposures. Also, official radiation exposure standards for them are much higher than those for the general public. In 1990 ICRP recommended that standards for US nuclear workers be reduced 150 percent. This recommendation was not followed. Standards for US nuclear workers remain at the level established in 1956.[29]

10. Excess Cancers among Rocky Flats Workers with Low Exposures

In 1987, Gregg S. Wilkinson of DOE's Los Alamos Lab published results of a study of Rocky Flats workers, comparing those exposed to plutonium to those not exposed. He found excess cancers among the exposed workers, but the most disturbing finding was that some workers with health problems had been exposed to internal plutonium deposits as low as 5 percent of DOE's standard for permissible lifetime exposure.[30] That is, according to DOE's standards it would have been safe for these workers to be exposed to 95 percent more plutonium than in fact they were. The study thus showed that DOE's standards for workers were far from protective. Wilkinson was ordered by his supervisor to alter the results to "please the customer" – that is, the DOE – but he refused and published his study without change.[31] A physician at Los Alamos told him that if his study was correct, it would shut down the nuclear industry.[32] He was soon forced out of his job at Los Alamos. I have yet to meet a Rocky Flats worker who was told about this study.

11. Follow-Up Study: Inadequacy of Worker Exposure Standards

James Rutttenber of the University of Colorado Health Sciences Center spent a decade studying records of 16,000 Rocky Flats workers at the plant between 1952 and 1989. He built on Wilkinson's study, but examined records of far more workers. His conclusions, published in 2003, were similar to Wilkinson's, although Ruttenber found more lung and brain cancers. He said his results call into question whether current standards for permissible radiation exposure are sufficiently protective.[33] However, Doug Benevento, then head of the Colorado Department of Public Health and Environment, called the results "reassuring," since they don't conclusively prove that cancer increases came from workplace exposures.

Thus the man who at the time was the State of Colorado's leading public health administrator dismissed a central conclusion from years of research that his agency had supported.[34]

12. Fate of Exposed Workers

Things changed for nuclear weapons workers in 1999 when then Energy Secretary Bill Richardson publicly admitted for the first time that the health of many workers at DOE nuclear weapons plants had been harmed due to workplace exposures to toxic materials. The Energy Employees Occupational Illness Compensation Program Act was enacted in October 2000 to compensate exposed workers or their survivors. The law was originally intended to shift the burden of proof of harm from workers to their employers at DOE plants, but it hasn't worked out this way. Administrators of the program often insist that a worker provide proof of exposure, while the record the worker has, if there is a record, was kept by companies that operated the plants. Numerous workers have found themselves unable to get compensation to which they believe they are entitled because they have no record or do not think the record they have received is credible. Some ailing workers unable to get compensation were exposed, according to the record, at levels well below that permitted by the standards. Others who were exposed have no record showing it. Workers exposed while producing nuclear weapons for a government that allowed their exposure must deal with the complexities of radiation exposure standards. In response, workers and former workers created what is now called the Alliance of Nuclear Workers Advocacy Groups, a national program that provides help to DOE nuclear weapons workers in need. It is administered by Terrie Barrie, whose husband formerly worked at Rocky Flats.

13. Off-Site People Exposed

The health of some people who lived or worked downwind of Rocky Flats has been compromised. Unlike workers at the plant, they didn't wear dosimeters and were never monitored to see if they had been exposed. Jock Cobb analyzed plutonium content of tissues collected from cadavers of people who died in hospitals either near Rocky Flats or near Pueblo, more than 100 miles away, well outside the orbit of Rocky Flats. Although fallout plutonium from atmospheric tests of bombs was present in all the bodies he examined, Rocky Flats plutonium, sometimes in quantity, was present in the bodies of those from near Rocky Flats.[35] But nothing has ever been done to provide people near Rocky Flats with medical care or compensation.

An example of what is needed but has never been available for people near Rocky Flats is the Fernald Medical Monitoring Program established at DOE's Fernald uranium processing facility near Cincinnati, Ohio. Created as the result of a class action lawsuit, this program, which ended in 2007, provided comprehensive health monitoring for about 9,500 individuals over a period of eighteen years. The monitoring relieved some individuals of worry while for others it provided an early warning of problems in need of attention. A program of this sort should have been set up by the federal government for all DOE nuclear weapons facilities.

Conclusion

Standards for permissible exposure to radiation rest on a questionable foundation. They are misleading and inadequate. They do not protect the most vulnerable. They overlook the effects of radiation emitted internally. And they are established with no participation of those most likely to be exposed. We have been told time and again that the standards exist to protect us, and government officials never tire of telling us we are safe, but the protection these standards provide is only partial. Although it has been recognized for decades that low levels of exposure to ionizing radiation can be harmful, we are repeatedly told that official radiation exposure standards protect us. These standards are not simply misleading and inadequate. They provide false assurance that makes it possible for a harmful industry to operate. They are in fact a sham.

Radiation Standards: A Prediction

(For Jock Cobb, Herman Muller, and Karl Morgan)

Standards for permissible exposure
  to radiation
  fail to protect sufficiently
They are a dam that holds back
  a flood of illness and death
  but lets pass
  an "insignificant" trickle
  of the diseased and damned.
These standards are a damn dam
  that lets a harmful enterprise thrive.
Today's trickle is a warning:
  In time, the dam will break
in a flood of illness and death.

1. *Local Hazard, Global Threat: Rocky Flats Nuclear Weapons Plant* (Denver: Rocky Flats Action Group, 1977), pp. 2–3.

2. Catherine Caufield, *Multiple Exposures: Chronicles of the Radiation Age* (Chicago: University of Chicago Press, 1989), p. 21.

3. Ibid., p. 73.

4. Ibid., p. 120.

5. LeRoyMoore, "Democracy and Public Health at Rocky Flats: The Examples of Edward A. Martell and Carl J. Johnson," in *Tortured Science: Health Studies, Ethics, and Nuclear Weapons in the United States,* comp. Dianne Quigley, Amy Lowman, and Steve Wing (Amityville, NY: Baywood, 2012), pp. 69–97. Online at http://media.wix.com/ugd/cff93e_5d3b6b6a12204505a3bc0fd2e2f504eb.pdf

6. LeRoy Moore, "Lowering the Bar," *Bulletin of the Atomic Scientists* (May–June 2002): 28–37. Online at http://media.wix.com/ugd/cff93e_0d1d35fb8d8140698e530f1095352eb3.pdf

7. LeRoy Moore, "Rocky Flats: The bait-and-switch cleanup," *Bulletin of the Atomic Scientists,* January-February 2005, pp. 50-57. On line at http://media.wix.com/ugd/cff93e_7711d2b2a9d84f28ab1986706f1c-da75.pdf

8. LeRoy Moore, "Local Hazard, Global Threat," in *A Year of Disobedience and a Criticality of Conscience,* comp. Joseph Daniel (Boulder, CO: Story Arts Media, 2013), pp. 106–135.

9. ForNichols,seehttp://media.wix.com/ugd/cff93e_409f499ec9f9479d916db728e2952cbc.pdf.

10. For Biggs, see http://www.rockyflatsnuclearguardianship.org/#!Page%2001/zoom/c1s3u/i2149z.

11. *Health Risks from Exposure to Low Levels of Ionizing Radiation, BEIR VII* (Washington, DC: National Academies Press, 2006).

12. Caufield, *Multiple Exposures,* p. 120.

13. Ulrich Bech, *Risk Society,* trans. Mark Ritter (London: Sage Publications, 1992), p. 64.

14. David Richardson, "Lessons from Hiroshima and Nagasaki: The Most Exposed and Most Vulnerable," *Bulletin of the Atomic Scientists,*

vol. 68, no. 3 (May-June 2012): 29–35. http://bos.sagepub.com/content/68/3/10.full.pdf+html.

15. John W. Gofman, *Radiation-Induced Cancer from Low-Dose Exposure* (San Francisco: Committee for Nuclear Responsibility, 1990), pp, 5–8.

16. Lisa Ledwidge, LeRoy Moore, and Lisa Crawford, "Stakeholder Perspectives on Radiation Protection," *Health Physics*, vol. 87, no. 3 (Sept. 2004): 293–299.

17. See Rosalie Bertell, "Critique of ICRP Structure and Membership" (1993), http://www.ratical.org/radiation/inetSeries/wwc2_10.txt.

18. Tom K. Hei et al., "Mutagenic Effects of a Single and Exact Number of Particles in Mammalian Cells," *Proceedings of the National Academy of Sciences*, vol. 94 (April 1997): 3765–3770.

19. Helen A. Grogan et al., *Assessing Risk of Exposure to Plutonium* (Neeses, SC: Risk Assessment Corporation, Feb. 2000), pp. 6.27–6.39. Prepared for the Rocky Flats Historical Public Exposures, Colorado Department of Public Health and Environment.

20. Arjun Makhijani et al., "Healthy from the Start," *Science for Democratic Action*, vol. 14, no.4 (Feb. 2007). See http://www.nuclearfreeplanet.org/ieer-healthy-from-the-start.html and http://www.nuclearfreeplanet.org/ieer-healthy-from-the-start.html.

21. Mary Olson, "Atomic Radiation Is More Harmful to Women" (Takoma Park, MD: Nuclear Information and Resource Service, 2013). Online at http://www.nirs.org/radiation/radhealth/radiationwomen.pdf.

22. *Health Risks from Exposure to Low Levels of Ionizing Radiation*, BEIR VII (Washington CDC: National Academies Press, 2006).

23. Morgan, quoted in Robert Del Tredici, *At Work in the Fields of the Bomb* (NY: Harper & Row, 1987), pp. 133–134.

24. Gofman, *Radiation-Induced Cancer from Low-Dose Exposure*, chapter 35.

25. Ibid., throughout; and Ralph Graeub, The Petkau Effect: *The Devastating Effect of Nuclear Radiation on Human Health and the Environment* (NY: Four Walls Eight Windows, 1994).

26. Herman J. Muller, "Radiation and Heredity," *American Journal of Public Health and the Nation's Health*, vol. 54, January 1964. http://www.ncbi.nlm.nih.gov/pmc/articles/PMC1254569/?page=9.

27. Diethard Tautz, "Genetic Uncertainty Problem," *Trends in Genetics*, vol. 16 (Nov. 2000): 475–477.

28. K. Shawn Smallwood et al., "Animal Burrowing Attributes Affecting Hazardous Waste Management," *Environmental Management*, vol. 22, no. 6 (1998): 834.

29. Caufield, *Multiple Exposures*, p. 21; US Department of Energy, *Closing the Circle on the Splitting of the Atom: The Environmental Legacy of Nuclear Weapons Production in the United States* (Washington, DC: DOE, 1995), p. 38.

30. Gregg S. Wilkinson et al., "Mortality among Plutonium and Other Radiation Workers at a Plutonium Weapons Facility," *American Journal of Epidemiology*, vol. 125, no. 2 (1987): 231–250.

31. Keith Schneider, "Panel Questions Credibility of Nuclear Health Checks," *New York Times*, Feb. 28, 1990.

32. Gregg S. Wilkinson, "Seven Years in Search of Alpha: The Best of Times, the Worst of Times," *Epidemiology*, vol. 10 (1999): 340–344.

33. For the text of the study, see http://www.cdphe.state.co.us/rf/rfp-workerstudy/RockyFlatsFinalNIOSHReport_text.pdf.

34. Katy Human, "Flats Workers May Be at Risk," *Boulder Daily Camera*, Apr. 18, 2003.

35. See interview with Jock Cobb in Rocky Flats Oral History Collection, OH1180 http://oralhistory.boulderlibrary.org/interview/oh1180/.

ROCKY FLATS: POISONED CHALICE?

Harvey Nichols, Ph.D.

Executive Summary

This personal narrative of my forty-six-year study of the contamination history of the Rocky Flats Nuclear Weapons Plant arose from chance, and changed my opinions of how federal bureaucracies behave. The lessons I draw are that independent-minded research into complex environmental problems, contrasting with official explanations, in alliance with multi-disciplinary colleagues, can uncover public health hazards that are astonishing. If young people reading this can be persistent in standing up to criticize officials in public and can deal with that potential discomfort and embarrassment, that can be a real key to success.

During the Cold War, Rocky Flats produced 70,000 semicircular "pits" of plutonium that were to be atomic bomb "triggers" for the H-bomb (hydrogen bomb), amidst much understandable secrecy. The machining and finishing of those parts inevitably produced plutonium residues and other hazardous wastes that severely contaminated the Rocky Flats' central industrial site, comprising about 2 square miles; and the surrounding "buffer zone" of about 8 square miles was contaminated too. Against community protest, that latter area was converted into a national wildlife refuge, opened for recreation in 2018.

My invited DOE (Department of Energy) 1975–1976 research contract showed that the official air samplers around that industrial zone were seriously inefficient in detecting airborne particles, meaning dangerous emissions would not be properly detected and the public would not be warned. I also found puzzling numbers of radionuclide particles in snowfall in the buffer zone/Refuge. Plant officials deceptively explained that away, but after thinking for years about those data I extracted an admission from officials that nuclear production had released plutonium dust into the surrounding areas throughout four decades of plant operation. And I found enormous numbers of such particles in snowfall that had "scavenged" plutonium dust from the contaminated air the plant had released, depositing radioactive dust all over the Refuge. If inhaled, a microscopic particle of plutonium can cause cancer, as is clearly implied by Professor Tom Hei's research (letter to H. Nichols 6/25/2018, cf. Hei 2011). As Rocky Flats is an especially windy site, Refuge visitors could be endangered. The plutonium is still there in topmost soil and almost certainly in the vegetation of the Refuge, although the Refuge managers refuse to allow analysis of those plants. So my colleagues and I later testified to the Air Quality Control Commission to effectively stop large-scale federal burning of contaminated Refuge vegetation.

It's hard to believe this account if you think that surely the EPA (Environmental Protection Agency) and the CDPHE (Colorado Department of Public Health and Environment), along with our political representatives, would not allow such dangers to affect Refuge visitors or neighboring communities. But several accounts I give in the following chapter show the inadequate thinking of officials and their resistance to independent criticism by qualified citizens. We should not be afraid of critical thinking that contradicts officialdom, and the energy and bravery of educated young people in such situations is enormously effective. I saw this in my senior biology class when the undergraduates questioned a visiting EPA scientist from Rocky Flats and revealed his disturbing inadequacies.

Early Days

I had no particular interest in nuclear weapons when I moved to Boulder in 1969 to take up a professorial position at University of Colorado, after postdocs at Yale (biology) and University of Wisconsin–Madison (meteorology). I was solely focused on my "ivory tower" paleo-ecology and paleo-climate research and on teaching. I'm originally English, and here is my personal account of how my esoteric research opened my eyes to a potential public health scandal here in my new home, Colorado.

In 1974 I was working on samples of Boreal Forest pollen windblown into the Canadian Arctic, when Dr. William Osburn of the US Energy Research and Development Administration (ERDA, later the Department of Energy) entered the room. Bill had noticed my arctic aerobiological work, and would I like to study airborne particles at Rocky Flats nuclear weapons plant? I said, "No, I'm too busy and I have no interest in Rocky Flats." Dr. Osburn persisted and took me to Rocky Flats for a "site visit" which surprised me.

There I noticed perimeter air samplers, supposed to warn of dangerous emissions, but their inlets did not rotate to face the wind nor did their suction adjust to draw air inside to match wind speed, thus they were not isokinetic (Gregory 1973). The samplers had roofs, preventing particles from entering via gravity, rain, or snowfall. The bad design intrigued me so I accepted the contract.

My ERDA/DOE research was funded from 1975 to 1976, so I obtained used filters from the samplers to check my suspicions. By setting up comparative pollen sampling slides I found the official samplers were not efficiently collecting very lightweight pine pollen that have particularly slow depositional rates (Gregory 1973, 377). Finding almost no pine pollen on sampler filters while my nearby sticky slides captured large numbers confirmed my doubts about the official equipment (cf. Biggs 2015, 11).

Sampling Equipment:
"Good enough for government work"?

My DOE report stated, "Sampling airborne pollen throughout the Rocky Flats area demonstrated the Rocky Flats air samplers were deficient in their abilities to properly collect large lightweight pollen grains [such as pine]. [This has] implications of sampling inefficiency in some particulate size ranges…" (Nichols 1977a, 24). Consultant micro-meteorologist Gale Biggs, Ph.D., later enlarged my criticism of the air samplers. Biggs when chairman of Governor Romer's Rocky Flats Air Committee accessed the inner industrial zone and found the high-volume air sampling equipment there missed plutonium particle sizes most hazardous to health (Biggs 2011). The effluent stack radionuclide samplers were in the *most unlikely* places to properly record the plutonium particles emitted and had not been calibrated since 1952. Dr. Biggs concluded it was not known how much plutonium was released from the stacks or from "the site's soil surfaces since the ambient air monitors did not represent the airborne plutonium concentrations at Rocky Flats" (Biggs 2015, 11).

My early doubts about the samplers' effectiveness were further confirmed when in 2016 a retired Rocky Flats senior security official, Tom Sanford, told me his technical officer said the air samplers "missed nearly all the plutonium dust that was going past them." I responded, "So they were in effect 'pacifiers' for public consumption?" and Tom agreed.

The "Hot Snow" Puzzle

While sampling Buffer Zone (later Refuge) soils, plant operatives told me about extensive oil-barrel leakage of plutonium at the "Hot Spot" (now the 903 Pad). Light snowfall in early winter 1975 revealed the level landscape of the Buffer Zone had slight hollows where snow gathered, contrasted with some slightly higher spots bare of snow. Might there be erosion of elevated spots and accumulation of radionuclides in hollows? The official soil sampling was on a regular grid pattern, but maybe that missed fissionable accumulations? My speculations led to unexpected discoveries.

During the winter of 1975 1976 my assistant and I promptly sampled every substantial snowfall in the Buffer Zone. The melted snow was pumped through a 0.5-micron Nuclepore filter and a 0.05 micron Nuclepore filter. Resulting particles were sandwiched with plastic microscope slides and polycarbonate film; then, with the assistance of my nuclear physicist wife, irradiated at the Denver US Geological Service (USGS) reactor (Nichols 1977, 24). The polycarbonate film was treated with re-agents to microscopically reveal alpha radiation tracks from radionuclide particles. The microscopic fissile particles were visible on the film as "star bursts" made by radionuclide particles >0.5 microns, while 0.5- to 0.05-micron particles appeared as "fission tracks." The results were surprising. We counted very large numbers of starbursts and fission tracks from all of my eight sites around the Rocky Flats Buffer Zone. The freshly fallen snow was "hot," but why? This puzzle remained a conjecture with me for years while I episodically turned it over in my mind.

The numbers of radionuclide particles we counted were so large that I later extrapolated from each snowfall to the decades of routine emis-sions, estimating billions of plutonium particles cumulatively deposited per acre of the Refuge. In 2016 Dr. Michael Ketterer, professor of chemis-try specializing in environmental plutonium, explained the microscopic starbursts we'd recorded were from "hot particles" of plutonium metal emitted from plant operations (Ketterer and Szechenyi 2008).

Incurious Operatives?

But in the 1970s the plant operatives explained my findings as being from the "nearby Schwartzwalder uranium mine." In 1976 I asked them to per-form radiochemical analyses to determine if they were uranium or pluto-nium particles, but they replied, "It would cost too much." Perhaps they knew the origin of the radionuclide dust and did not want to admit it. I lat-er visited a UK AEA atomic energy establishment, and they said they could have done the analyses at only one-tenth of the suggested federal costs.

The Schwartzwalder uranium mine proved to be five miles away in a valley, where an official gamma radiation aerial survey showed uranium dust was very localized. On 3/22/2003 I asked meteorologist Dr. Biggs if that dust could reach Rocky Flats; he replied, "Not likely." Here we see part of a pattern of behavior at Rocky Flats where the operatives were either incurious or deceptive about their work. The source of the radio-nuclide dust was much closer, as we will see.

The Key Question

By the late 1980s I had thought through the "hot snow" puzzle and took an opportunity to ask the Rockwell site contractors the question. Colorado senator Dorothy Rupert convened a House committee to examine Rocky Flats health matters on September 30, 1987. Colorado Department of Health (CDH, later CDPHE) and Rocky Flats contractors Rockwell International were questioned by Chairwoman Dorothy Rupert, her committee, and invited citizens, including myself. When Rockwell stated that "there are no health implications from the operations at Rocky Flats," I had my question ready:

"Do you emit plutonium in tiny volumes of very small particles on a routine daily basis?"

Rockwell: "Yes."

Nichols: "Do you consider plutonium to be dangerous?"

Rockwell: "Yes."

I said quietly to enator Rupert: "What do you think of that?" and she replied to me, "They're schizophrenic!" Senator Rupert noted privately to me that of the three parties present (CDH, Rockwell, and citizens), "our state health people were the weakest," and she was concerned about CDH.

This Rockwell admission solved the puzzle of the hot snow: the falling snowflakes had physically scavenged the effluent stack plutonium particles from the air, and since snowflakes have electrical charge, they attracted the airborne metal dust emitted from the stacks nearby, resulting from machining operations. The public was never warned.

Confirmation of chronic release of plutonium dust came in a dose reconstruction study by Voilleque (1999) and Rood, Grogan and Till (2002) funded by Dow Chemical (first Atomic Energy Commission [AEC] contractor at Rocky Flats) and authorized by the Colorado Department of Public Health and Environment. They made clear that as a minimum the official records showed >600 million nanocuries (billionths of a curie) of plutonium were emitted, excluding uncounted releases from major fires (1957, 1969) and rusted lathe-oil drums. A substantial Colorado State University contract study by Webb, Ibrahim, and Whicker (1997), found plutonium soil exceedances in the eastern Refuge and off-site Indiana Street, as did Marguilies et al. (2004).

Public Health Implications

What does it mean in potential health terms that the site had been dusted with plutonium particles on this scale, and then to open it for recreation? DOE admits that a millionth of a gram (a microgram) of plutonium-239 can be fatal if inhaled, and it admits that for the general public inhalation is the most dangerous route of plutonium exposure when it can irradiate internal tissues. A microgram of Pu-239 would release about 60 nano-curies of alpha radiation (=2,300 decays per second "which is astronom-ical," according to chemistry professor Michael Ketterer (cf. Ketterer and Szechnyi 2008). This means DOE is being parsimonious with the truth in saying that a microgram can be fatal when in fact it's more it far exceeds a fatal dose!

In 1974 a *Science* study by Bair and Thompson (1974) of beagle dogs deliberately exposed to plutonium dust showed the toxicity of plutonium inhalation. Subsequent studies of plutonium inhalation in animal sub-jects showed that exposure to nanocurie levels and even below a billionth of a curie of Pu had serious health effects.

Keeping in mind the >600 million nanocuries of plutonium report-ed by Voilleque (1999) and Rood et al. 2002 Till (1999) released from Rocky Flats, I recall the EPA scientist at Rocky Flats, Tim Rehder, saying to me emphatically, "A nanocurie is a massive dose." So, based on the above, it appears that more than 600 million potentially fatal doses of plutonium dust were released from Rocky Flats stacks during four de-cades of operation.

The larger plutonium particles I studied could eventually form lung cancers if inhaled, while the smaller particles could penetrate the lung alveoli and enter the bloodstream, circulating there, later to form tumors, especially in the gonads, brain, and bones. Such plutonium particles were deposited in astronomical numbers at Rocky Flats according to my snow-fall measurements (Nichols 1977a, 11–19).

I presented my findings (Nichols, 1977b) at a public meeting in Boulder organized by Rocky Flats officials and Rockwell International on March 4, 1977. There was no rebuttal from the Rocky Flats audience or the meeting chairman, Douglas C. Hunt, who merely said after my presentation, "There seems to be plutonium everywhere!"

At another public meeting in Boulder on May 1, 2001, when Dr. John Till (Voilleque 1999; Rood et al. 2002; Till 1999) presented his data on Rocky Flats plutonium releases and health implications, I rose to ask him to criticize my study, which found orders of magnitude more plutonium particles than his DOE contract study. Dr. Till replied, "Harvey, I've seen your study and I believe your data" (witnessed by Dr. LeRoy Moore and the audience).

The Rockwell Incinerator Plan

After I dispatched my final report to DOE in 1977 and sending it to the Colorado governor's office, I was impelled to act on another related matter. Rather than maintaining my "green card" immigrant status and British passport, I applied for US citizenship because I wanted to speak to my representatives *as a citizen* about the implications of radionuclide contamination of the site. That was a positive outcome of my research at Rocky Flats.

However, Rocky Flats' management episodically creates citizen concerns by proposing schemes so ill advised they alarm the public. Thus by the mid-1980s DOE contractor Rockwell announced they would incinerate unpermitted excess low-level radioactive waste. A newspaper letter by Jan Pilcher (American Friends' Service Committee) asked for volunteers to look into the matter. Six Boulder-area scientists responded: meteorologist Gale Biggs, combustion engineer Joe Goldfield, radiochemist Ed Martell, chemistry professor Niels Schonbeck, hydrogeologist David Snow, and me, as aerobiologist. We concluded this Rockwell incinerator would spread radioactive particles into our communities (see McKinley and Balkany 2004).

We raised enough questions that our congressman, David Skaggs, secured money from local municipalities to bring national specialists to examine our claims of incinerator dangers. Our presentations satisfied the panel except for our combustion engineer colleague, Joe Goldfield. He noted since Rockwell was new to building incinerators this scheme would be risky, and he urged the trial-run not use radioactive waste as Rockwell planned. I recall being embarrassed for Joe as the expert from MIT said,

"If Mr. Goldfield is correct, we could expect every domestic heater in the nation to be at risk for explosion!" Rockwell did use innocuous materials for their incinerator trial, and the official account read: "As ignition proceeded, the stainless steel of the incinerator began to glow orange, then the thermal glass viewing port broke and flaming debris burst into the room." Joe Goldfield was fully vindicated!

In June 1987 Al Hazle, head of radiation at Colorado Department of Health, released a newspaper report that a lifetime spent at Rocky Flats would mean no more than "1 in 64 quadrillion chance of any health risk" from the incinerator emissions. So I phoned him (July 1, 1987) and said, "Al, where did you get that statistic?" Answer: "I got it from Rockwell." "Did you or your staff analyze the assumptions?" "No." This was one of my earliest experiences of the weakness of the Colorado Department of Health concerning Rocky Flats. This agency withholds personnel CVs, but a medical colleague reported Al had a bachelor's degree in agricultural science, with formal radiological education of less than two weeks.

The Boulder scientists found no CDH allowance for age factors (children are more active, respire more, and their cellular development means they are more prone to cancer) health status, or sex. We agreed the "1 in 64 quadrillion" report was bogus.

We needed media attention on this misreporting. One of my students attended a play featuring TV actor Ed Asner. Afterward, he 'went backstage to ask if Mr. Asner would help advertise our health worries. Ed agreed, so I called TV stations to film him at a press conference outside CDH where a colleague and I explained our Rocky Flats concerns. The TV recording shows Ed was extraordinarily gracious, and after introducing our cause he said on camera, "But these are the important people, so I'll turn it over to them." Note to young activists: contact TV and movie stars to see if they will help.

January 21, 1989: "A Public Forum on Rocky Flats" and a Warning from DC

By 1988 public concern about Rocky Flats was growing, and the Sierra Club hinted they would fund a conference. Unbeknownst to me, there was a tsunami gathering at the FBI that on June 6, 1989, would break open the Rocky Flats scandal. But on January 21, 1989, I had organized a public meeting at the University of Colorado, Boulder, entitled "A Public Forum on Rocky Flats." Among the luminaries I invited were Governor Roy Romer and US representative (later senator) Hank Brown (R-CO); the latter called for closing the plant and a cleanup. At lunchtime I was invited to eat privately with Robert (Bob) Alvarez and Tara O'Toole from Washington. Bob was radiation advisor to Ohio US senator John Glenn and took me to lunch for a purpose: "Harvey, now that you are so deeply into this Rocky Flats business, I have to tell you that your telephone will be listened into for the rest of your life. Not just a recording, but a live person will listen to everything you say from now on."

So a citizen who criticizes government errors may lose lifetime privacy? I recall Congresswoman Pat Schroeder's forceful remark on a Colorado Channel 7 KMGH-TV program entitled *Rocky Flats; Critical Mass*, which aired June 19, 1989: "If you dare criticize DOE about Rocky Flats they even question your patriotism!"

Death of a Medical "Activist"

In January 1989 former US secretary of the interior Stewart Udall was to speak at the University of Colorado Boulder Law School. Previously he'd criticized AEC/DOE mistreatment of US military atomic veterans, and while thinking about the upcoming talk I speculated how secrecy at Rocky Flats had created quasi-Soviet behavior by exclusion of oversight by the Occupational Safety and Health Administration (OSHA), EPA, and the US Congress, a train of thought that disturbed me. Stewart Udall began by eulogizing my prematurely deceased colleague, Carl Johnson, MD MPH, Jefferson County health director, who was driven from office for reporting plutonium and excess cancers in Rocky Flats neighborhoods (Johnson 1976, 1981), (Iversen 2012). During his eulogy Secretary Udall described operatives at Rocky Flats as (quasi-Soviet) "apparatchiks." When afterward I told him my speculations about Rocky Flats, he said, "We're on the same page"). At Dr. Johnson's funeral the minister described the scandalous way Johnson was treated for defending his constituents' health: "We pay the DOE very well to lie to us."

Is Rocky Flats National Wildlife Refuge Seriously Contaminated?

Dr. Iggy Litaor was a Rocky Flats professional soil scientist (Litaor 1995) and publicly supported the DOE view that plutonium, when incorporated in soil, became immobilized. However, in spring 1995 Colorado's Front Range experienced prolonged heavy rains; on May 17, 1995, Dr. Litaor's instruments recorded 10 millicuries of plutonium (potentially 10 million fatal doses) released from Refuge soils by sheet-flooding). Dr. Litaor wanted to publish these data despite his previous (official) belief. He admitted to me that "Mother Nature taught me a lesson!" But DOE's contractor dismissed him "to save money" (Litaor p.c.) and sequestered his data so he could not publish those results. Iggy is still angry about this official burial of his evidence, another example of DOE antagonism to independent science that contradicts their official belief system.

Dr. Litaor wrote a letter to the Boulder *Daily Camera* on March 23, 2004, warning against opening the Refuge for recreation. His unpublished letter described digging soil pits in the Refuge: "During my extensive soil sampling in the (Refuge) buffer zone and beyond I commonly found that my personal protection equipment (PPE) was 'hot' by day's end and was discarded into the 'hot' contaminated bin. On this basis I strongly recommend that the buffer zone/wildlife refuge be highly limited for public use.... I sent this recommendation to US Fish and Wildlife Service March 10 [2004]" (Prof. M. Iggy Litaor, Tel-Hai Academic College, Israel).

Public Health Protected by State and National Agencies?

Rocky Flats illustrates government failure of due diligence. Citizens assume their health is protected by our representative government, the EPA, etc. Personal observation of the Colorado Department of Health (CDH) and its successor, Colorado Department of Public Health and Environment (CDPHE), illustrates historic weaknesses regarding Rocky Flats' radiation and health effects, some already referred to in this chapter. We need targeted epidemiological studies of the older community populations around Rocky Flats related to site history, especially as healthy homeowners migrate into this area without knowing the industrial record. Dr. Carol Jensen, retired professor of nursing at Metropolitan State University of Denver, surveyed residents from nearby Rocky Flats for unusual incidences of rare cancers, possibly related to Rocky Flats operations (Jensen 2017). Chemistry professor Michael Ketterer is starting to research whether isotopic "fingerprinting" of any plutonium found to cause Colorado cancers could be linked to Rocky Flats. If there is no association of plutonium with cancer we could all "breathe easier" around Rocky Flats.

The Question of Radiation Standards

The official justification for Rocky Flats being "safe enough" in public comments by DOE manager Scott Surovchak and CDPHE director Dr. Larry Wolk is that Refuge radionuclide soil levels are within allowable exposure limits. There seems no official recognition that "safe" radiation standards have progressively reduced over time as experience accumulates, and this process may continue. There's no mention that Dr. Karl Morgan (founder of US health physics) and radiochemist Dr. Ed Martell stated in a 1993 *Frontline* PBS TV program (*Secrets of a Bomb Factory*) that US radiation exposure standards might be 500 times (K. M.) to 1,000 times (E.M.) too high. One would think that officials would be cautious in a debatable public health issue, but at Rocky Flats the opposite occurs. Dr. Larry Wolk, director of CDPHE wrote September 8, 2016, to Jon Lipsky: "The protectiveness level of the (Rocky Flats Refuge) Site is consistent with the CERCLA risk range of 10x-4 to 10x-6 (1 in 10,000 to 1 in 1,000,000) excess cancer risk and therefore meets accepted human health protectiveness standards." This relies on DOE in-house data unverified by independent scientists and cannot safely justify choice of a recreational pathway across an unremediated nuclear weapons site. US Fish and Wildlife Service (FWS) admitted the Refuge plutonium contamination in a formal reply on October 21, 2003, to Congressman Bob Beauprez (R-CO), based on my question to FWS (letter held by author).

How Do Rocky Flats Officials Behave Toward Citizens Concerned about the Radioactive Refuge Being Ignited to Clear Weeds?

The approximately eight square miles of the Refuge surrounding the Superfund core has native tallgrass prairie ecosystems invaded by alien weeds, normally controlled elsewhere by burning. Critics oppose this at Rocky Flats, as a prairie fire would raise a radioactive smoke cloud over the neighborhoods.

An obvious precaution is to test the vegetation for plutonium, but senior DOE ecologist at Rocky Flats, John Rampe, stated publicly at a 2000 Rocky Flats Stewardship Council meeting, "There is no uptake of plutonium in vegetation." I asked my students to research this, and they promptly located eight published reports; e.g.. "Plutonium-239 and Americium-241 Uptake by Plants from Soil," by Kenneth W. Brown, EPA Ecological Research Series, March 1979, and Lee et al. 2002.

However, at that 2000 meeting of the Rocky Flats Stewardship Council, when I questioned the safety of burning the Refuge prairie, Mr. Rampe was unpersuaded. Council Member Lisa Morzel followed my lead and asked Rampe to test Refuge vegetation before burning, but he refused: "It would cost too much." Dr. Morzel responded that as a USGS scientist, she would test the vegetation at no charge. Morzel tried again to get Rampe to agree, but he replied, "The answer is no, we have a basic philosophical disagreement on the issue and that is the end of it."

A reflection of this belief by USFWS that there is no or "very little" uptake of plutonium from soil by plants is found in page 2, paragraph 5 of a July 30, 2003, letter from FWS' regional director to Congressman Bob Beauprez, arising from my correspondence with FWS via the congressman.

On April 6, 2000, there was an FWS test burn of 50 acres (about 20 hectares) of prairie at Rocky Flats. My students and I watched it from the fourth story of the building in which I held my undergraduate class that day. The smoke cloud was surprisingly large, so I telephoned the NOAA (National Oceanic and Atmospheric Administration) Aeronomy Lab in Boulder to ask if NOAA had been tasked to detect the smoke. A meteorologist said no, and I mentioned it would be weeks before officials reported the smoke analyses. She replied, "That would give them enough time to massage the data!" So at least one professional federal meteorologist on that day implied her disbelief in the accuracy of particulate reports from Rocky Flats prairie burnings. Perhaps the reader will anticipate that the subsequent in-house federal reports found nothing dangerous in the smoke cloud. It is vital to require that FWS involve the independent professional environmental scientists of Colorado in planning any large-scale burn at Rocky Flats.

In January 2015 the State of Colorado Air Quality Control Commission (AQCC) received an FWS request to ignite 701 acres (1.10 square miles or 2.8 sq. km.) of the Refuge to control invasive weeds. This was to be a repeated biennial procedure proceeding in a circular manner around the Superfund core of Rocky Flats.

Retired FBI agent Jon Lipsky of the Rocky Flats Technical Group had noted this hearing, and he and Mary Harlow (water quality specialist formerly representing City of Westminster, Colorado, at Rocky Flats) attended AQCC to protest. I sent the commission a 3,200-word evidentiary letter (Nichols 2015) before the hearing, and Dr. Gale Biggs sent a subsequent letter. Some of the AQCC were scientists.

A year later (January 11, 2016), Mr. Gordon Pierce, program manager of the Technical Services Program for AQCC, wrote to Jon Lipsky to declare that the FWS burn permit for the Refuge was denied from that date forward, and if another FWS application for the same purpose was received it would not be considered until a full public hearing evaluated the case. It was noteworthy that Mr. Pierce's official ruling named three individuals: Jon Lipsky, Mary Harlow, and Dr. Harvey Nichols (specifically, his letter) as having influenced the AQCC decision. Later in 2016 FWS Refuge manager David Lucas said that he still hopes to burn weeds at the Refuge (Freedman 2016).

What a program of repeated large-scale burning of officially admitted, plutonium-contaminated prairie would logically achieve would be, in addition to weed control, the fiery export in massive smoke clouds of much of the plutonium dust in the surface soil and vegetation throughout the Denver Metro area. This arguably would eventually "cleanse" the Refuge of plutonium and other contaminants at the cost of neighborhood health.

Alternatives to weed control by burning the radioactive prairie certainly exist, such as browsing by goats (they love weeds!) and also predation by insects, and these would be far safer than igniting *untested* Refuge vegetation on a large scale. My undergraduates (e.g., Katie Chell, now an MD) researched this issue, contacted the Lamming family of goat-herders (www.goatapelli.com) and found these methods were well-established and cheaper than burning. FWS managers objected they were "not staffed to deal with such a weed control method" although the Lammings were interested in running a trial program. An alternative was published by Dr. Jody K. Nelson who described insect control of weeds at Rocky Flats during the 2013 Weed Management Conference in Phoenix, Arizona: "Integrated Weed Control for Land Stewardship at Legacy Management's Rocky Flats Site in Colorado – 13086," thus these alternatives have been made known to FWS, and appear safer and cheaper than controlled burning.

After the 2000 Refuge test burn, I gave Congressman Mark Udall (D-CO) documentation of my work and talked at length with him; at that time he recognized the danger from large-scale burning at Rocky Flats, and said, "I'm on board" and he wrote a cautionary congressional letter concerning any further burns at the Refuge.

But despite my providing evidence to him of Refuge plutonium contamination, Representative Udall, following federal advice, later stated publicly to me and my surprised students at a University of Colorado, Boulder political forum that the Refuge was "pristine," and the Refuge vegetation "does not contain plutonium" (KGNU radio February 21, 2001). He, with Senator Wayne Allard (R-CO), created the Rocky Flats National Wildlife Refuge, and their legislation changed much of the former Buffer Zone" into the present Refuge, thus prophylactically preventing it from being developed for housing or industry. Representative Udall said his legislation relied on the site being remediated to a safe standard (Udall 2005); this does not appear to be the case, thus the "Poisoned Chalice" in the title.

During my forty-six years of involvement in this topic I've noticed wariness by politicians when faced with unpalatable truths about Rocky Flats; I suspected there might be some powerful force steering legislators away from tackling the health threat. When I met the then majority leader of the Colorado Senate, Brandon Shaffer, at a fund-raising event in Longmont, Colorado, in 2012, I found that my suspicion was not mine alone. On hearing my hypothesis, senator Shaffer agreed that he'd noticed something similar about Rocky Flats, and his wife, Jessica, said they called the effect "the Rocky Flats dark cloud."

Or is this a recognition by politicians that this is how the federal bureaucracy works, brushing aside citizen concerns when the governmental juggernaut gets under way?

Here's another example of federal attitude toward citizen concerns about Refuge safety: Congress required FWS to explain publicly their plans for the Refuge, so Dean Rundle of US Fish and Wildlife Service appeared to do that in 2001 in local communities. At East Boulder Recreational Center he stated FWS envisaged four plans, ranging from no public access to open Refuge recreation: "…Plans A, B, C and D. **We favor Plan B**, *but we will listen to you*" (boldface and italics added). I knew immediately which plan they would choose, and indeed it was "Plan B," full public access. The meetings were very tightly controlled; no questions were allowed about safety. FWS' Rundle said Rocky Flats Refuge was clean enough, so there was nothing to discuss on that issue. Written public comments were allowed but did not change FWS' decision. Dr. LeRoy Moore accessed the numerous written comments to FWS and more than 80 percent favored very limited or no public access, Plans A and C. When I politely raised a scientific point with FWS at a later public meeting, I was faced with raised fists, witnessed by my colleague the inorganic chemist Anne Fenerty who reprimanded the FWS officer.

EPA Faces a Classroom

A last example of officialdom's behavior regarding Rocky Flats involves an unexpected phone call to me in March 2000 from Tim Rehder, senior EPA scientist at Rocky Flats, who demanded that he address my class to correct the impression he said I'd given my students (how did he know?) that burning the Refuge prairie was dangerous. Plans for the April 2000 50 acre (20 ha) test burn at the Refuge had been announced. My final-year undergraduate biology students had all written term papers on Rocky Flats for my class called Critical Thinking on Environmental Problems. They gave Mr. Rehder a polite re-education.

Twenty-four out of twenty-five students from the class's morning section asked him a question, and EPA's Rehder ended up with his arms clasped self-protectively around him. Mr. Rehder's intellectual inadequacy shocked my class; he appeared to be quite uncritical of the DOE. He argued that since we in Colorado were already at increased cancer risk from high elevation solar exposure and the radon effects from uranium in Colorado soil, "a little bit more [from Rocky Flats] won't matter." When I pointed out the obvious flaw, that it was all the more important to avoid further public exposure, I could see from his expression that his mind was slowly opening, and he said, "That's what [NCAR radio-chemist] Dr. Martell says, too."

CDPHE depends for assurance by EPA and DOE that prairie burning is safe at Rocky Flats but critical thinking by officials here is in calamitously short supply. However, they provided my classes with extraordinary educational insights into government realities and may have guided some career plans. For example, Colorado state representative Wes McKinley proposed legislation of a "signage bill" to warn potential visitors to the Refuge's history and that contamination remained. Wes had been foreman of the Rocky Flats grand jury following the FBI raid on Rocky Flats. Forbidden to reveal the findings on pain of jail, he ran for office to try to warn the public. Wes invited me and my class to testify to the Colorado House of Representatives health committee to support his bill, and this gave the students insights. The students testified first, and a class member named Adam was immediately "attacked" by a Republican representative from Colorado Springs: "Who put you up to this? Was it that professor?" Adam calmly replied, "Sir, I wrote a fifteen-page term paper on this, with twenty-six references from the medical literature. Would you like a copy?" The representative gave an angry "No!" and bustled out of the room "to make trouble for the university" as he told the University of Colorado, Boulder lobbyist in the capitol. Adam is now an MD. Another student who testified had previously intended to join his family business, but seeing how medical evidence affected legislation (the health committee approved the bill), he changed his career plans to pursue a master of public health.

After a positive vote by the health committee, Representative McKinley's bill was approved by the Colorado House of Representatives. Approval by the state Senate was expected, but the legislative term eventually ended without further action on the bill from the senate. Representative McKinley investigated and reported to me that a senior member of the Colorado Congressional delegation told senate majority leader Joan Fitz-Gerald, "I don't want that bill to go anywhere," and so the bill died. Doesn't this raise questions about our democracy?

Conclusions

There are serious environmental problems at the Rocky Flats National Wildlife Refuge left unaddressed by the rapid, cheap "cleanup" of only the industrial site's core; the Refuge was not remediated. Original DOE estimates for site remediation were $40 billion (1990s dollars) over seventy years (Iversen, 2012). Instead Congress allowed $7 billion, with only $473 million (7 percent of that total) for industrial zone soil and water treatment, with "mission accomplished" declared in 2007. For comparison, the Sellafield nuclear site in England will take a century to decommission and remediate to British government standards, costing more than a billion dollars each year (BBC News Radio 4, 2015, and Wikipedia 2020).

Multigenerational health impacts are possible (omitted here due to space limitations; see chapter 8 by Dr. LeRoy Moore), and there could be economic impacts. If local rare cancer rates rise and are linked to Rocky Flats exposure via isotopic analysis of tumor causality, then Colorado's reputation for a clean entrepreneurial environment could be at risk. Politicians without scientific training confess themselves unable to judge the conflicting evidence while federal officials act as propagandists for management plans, undercutting citizen efforts to educate those politicians. Could this be a future Flint, Michigan, scandal?

Recent Accomplishments

In 2016 I met Laurie Albright, president of the Boulder Valley School Board (BVSB), and persuaded her of the dangers of school trips to the Rocky Flats Refuge. Then in 2017 my Rocky Flats Technical Group (RFTG) and I testified to the BVSB, and we got a unanimous vote to ban all school field trips to the Refuge. Jon Lipsky and the RFTG got the same result from the St. Vrain School Board. Rocky Mountain Peace and Justice Center along with other community groups followed our lead and persuaded Thornton, Westminster, and Denver school boards similarly, while my RFTG persuaded Jefferson County's superintendent Dr. Jason Glass to agree "in an abundance of caution." The total stands at seven Denver metro school boards that have adopted this policy and the *Denver Post* headline on April 29, 2018, announced: "Nearly 300,000 Colorado public school students now barred from making field trips to Rocky Flats." The *Guardian*'s Daliah Singer reported on the issue August 22, 2018: "Amid Plutonium Fears, Schools Ban Visits to New Colorado Wildlife Refuge."

Works Cited

Bair, W. J., and R. C. Thompson. Plutonium: Biomedical Research. *Science* 183 (1974): 715–722.

BBC News Radio 4 broadcast, 2015 (heard in UK by author).

Biggs, W. G. Emissions Monitoring and Health Effects of Plutonium from Rocky Flats in Relation to the Proposed Burn at Rocky Flats. Unpublished, pp.1–11, 2015, and many letters to EPA regarding Rocky Flats plutonium emissions.

Brown, K. W. 1979. Plutonium-239 and Americium-241 Uptake by Plants from Soil.

US EPA-600/3-79-026, p. 16.

Freedman, E. "Repurposing Rocky Flats National Wildlife Refuge." *Earth Island Journal, Truthout* (March 20, 2016).

Gregory, P. H. *Microbiology of the Atmosphere*, 2nd ed. New York: Halsted Press, 1973.

Hei, T. K. letter to H. Nichols, June 25, 2018.

Hei, T. K., H. Zhou, Y. Chai, B. Ponnaiya, and V. N Ivanov. "Radiation Induced Non-Targeted Response: Mechanism and Potential Clinical Implications." *Current Molecular Pharmacology* 4 (2011): 96–105.

Iversen. K. Full Body Burden: Growing Up in the Nuclear Shadow of Rocky Flats. New York: Crown, Random House, 2012.

Jensen, C. 2017, Rocky Flats Downwinders' Health Survey, unpublished, Metropolitan State University of Denver.

Johnson, C. J. "Cancer Incidence in an Area Contaminated with Tadionuclides Near a Nuclear Installation. *Ambio* 10 (1981): 176–182

Johnson, C. J., R. R. Tidball, and R. C. Severson. "Plutonium Hazard in Respirable Dust on the Surface Soil." *Science* 193 (1976): 488–490.

Ketterer M. E., and S. C. Szechenyi. "Determination of Plutonium and Other Transuranic Elements by Inductively Coupled Plasma Mass Spectrometry: A Historical Perspective and New Frontiers in the Environmental Sciences." *Spectrochimica B* 63 (2008): 719–737.

KGNU Radio Boulder, Colorado, broadcast by Cong. Mark Udall on Rocky Flats, recorded by Dan Fernandez, Feb. 21, 2001.

Lee, J. H., L. R. Hossner, M. Attrep Jr., and K. S. Kung. "Comparative Uptake of Plutonium from Soils by *Brassica juncea* and *Helianthus annuus*." *Environmental Pollution* 120 (2002): 173–182.

Litaor, M. I. "Comprehensive Appraisal of 239+ 240Pu in Soils around Rocky Flats, Colorado." *Health Physics* 69 (1995): 923–935.

Margulies, T. D., N. D. Schonbeck, N. C., Morin-Voilleque, K. A. James, and J. M. LaVelle. "A Comparative Study of 239,240Pu in Soil Near the Former Rocky Flats Nuclear Weapons Facility, Golden, CO." *Journal of Environmental Radioactivity* 75 (2004): 143–157.

McKinley, W., and C. Balkany. *The Ambushed Grand Jury*. New York: Apex Press, 2004.

Moore, L. 1992. *A Citizen's Guide to Rocky Flats*. Boulder, CO: Rocky Mountain Peace and Justice Center, 1992.

———. *Plutonium and People Don't Mix: Rocky Flats*. Boulder, CO: Rocky Mountain Peace and Justice Center, 2019.

Nelson, Jody K. Integrated Weed Control for Land Stewardship at Legacy Management's Rocky Flats Site in Colorado – 13086. Weed Management Conference Phoenix, Arizona, Feb. 2013:

Nichols, H. 1977a *Some Aspects of Organic and Inorganic Particulate Transport at Rocky Flats*. Final Report on (ERDA) Contract EY-76-S-02-2736, 1977.

———1977b Some Aspects of Organic and Inorganic Particulate Transport at Rocky Flats. Transactions of Rocky Flats Buffer Zone Ecological and Environmental Research Meeting, Rockwell International, 1978, 63–66.

————, convenor. A Public Forum on Rocky Flats: An Educational Program on Current Environmental and Economic Issues at the Rocky Flats Nuclear Weapons Plant. University of Colorado, Boulder, Jan. 21, 1989.

————. "To the Air Quality Control Commission, Colorado Department of Public Health and Environment." Jan. 25, 2015.

PBS. "Secrets of a Bomb Factory." PBS TV *Frontline*, aired Oct. 23, 1993.

Rood, A. S., H. A. Grogan, and J. E. Till. "A Model for a Comprehensive Assessment of Exposure and Lifetime Cancer Incidence Risk from Plutonium Released from the Rocky Flats Plant 1953–1998. *Health Physics* 82, 2 (2002): 182–212.

Rundle, Dean. Public appearance as US Fish and Wildlife Service representative at East Boulder Recreation Center, Boulder, Colorado to explain FWS plan for the Rocky Flats National Wildlife Refuge, 2001.

Udall, Mark. "Udall Urges Care in State Law Efforts on Rocky Flats Cleanup." News release, Congressman Mark Udall's congressional office. Jan., 4, 2005.

US Fish and Wildlife Service letter to Congressman Bob Beauprez, signed by FWS regional director Ralph O. Morgenweck, Oct. 21, 2003.

Voilleque, Paul G. 1999, *Review of Routine Releases of Plutonium in Airborne Effluents at Rocky Flats*. RAC report no. 6-CDPHE-RFP-1998 FINAL. Neeses, SC: Radiological Assessments Corporation, 1999.

Webb, S. B., S. A. Ibrahim, and F. W. Whicker. "A Study of Plutonium in Soil and Vegetation at the Rocky Flats Plant." In Environmental Health Physics, ed. R. L Kathren, D. H. Denham, and K. Salmon.. Richland, WA: Research Enterprises Publishing Segment, 1993, pp. 611–623

Wikipedia. "Sellafield," 2020.

THE GRIEVING LANDSCAPE: WOMBS AND WALLS DO NOT PROTECT

By Heidi Hutner

In legends lives a woman. Turned monster from loneliness. Turned monster from agony and suns exploding in her chest. She gives birth to a child that is not so much a child but too much a jellyfish. The child is struggling for breath. Struggling in pain. She wants to bring the child peace. Bring her home. Her first home. Inside her body.

– Kathy Jetñil-Kijiner, "Monster,"
from *Iep Jaltok: Poems from a Marshallese Daughter*

At thirty-five, I was diagnosed with Hodgkin's disease. One year before my diagnosis, my mother died from complications after heart surgery. At the time of her death, my mother had cancer – lymphoma. Five years prior to Mom's death, my father passed away from a brain tumor, a metastasis from the cancer melanoma. Two years after I had completed my chemotherapy treatment for cancer, I gave birth to Olivia. My miracle.

At first, I was ecstatic about the pregnancy. I had always wanted children, and with the cancer I feared this would never happen. The doctors said I was lucky to give birth to a biological child at my age (late thirties) *and* after chemo (my treatment left me with a 50 percent chance of remaining fertile afterward). But now, a mother-to-be, I was also afraid. How could I protect my baby from our family cancer blight? From the pollution all around me? I wondered: Were our family cancers genetically induced or environmentally so? Or both? "Cancer rates are way up," said Dr. Wisch, my oncologist, an Alan Alda look-alike, when I asked him his opinion. "Yes, I think our polluted environment has a lot to do with the rising numbers."[1]

My desire to protect my baby daughter from a future cancer diagnosis drove me into a rabbit hole of reading and learning about carcinogenic contamination. My journey began with reading Rachel Carson's classic *Silent Spring*; Sandra Steingraber's *Living Downstream: An Ecologists Personal Investigation of Cancer*, and *Having Faith: An Ecologist's Journey to Motherhood*; Theo Colburn and Dianne Dumanoski's *Our Stolen Future*; Jonathan Harr's *A Civil Action*; and many more.

Women Strike for Peace march, July 15, 1962,
Mercury, Nevada. Photo by Harvey Richards.

Everything I learned confirmed my worst fears: Our world swirls with carcinogens, these carcinogens are in our bodies, they penetrate mothers' wombs and breasts. Synthetic chemicals and ionizing radiation change our makeup, harm our genes. Our babies are born poisoned, their umbilical cords have hundreds of synthetic chemicals in them at birth.[2] Mother's milk is a toxic cocktail.[3]

Rachel Carson's worst predictions back in the early 1960s had come true: 80,000 plus unregulated carcinogens now fill our world. An uncontrolled experiment. We are the guinea pigs.

Fast forward about eleven years: one summer day, in 2009, on the Upper West Side of Manhattan, at lunch with a close friend (and cousin) of my deceased mother, Phyllis Resnick, I stumbled upon a story about my mom that I had never heard before. The tale Phyllis told would radically change my life. My then preteen, Olivia, who was by my side, listened rapt with me as we learned of our maternal nuclear legacy.

Phyllis described how my mother and she, along with their good friend Thalia Stern Broudy, had been a members Women Strike for Peace (WSP), an antinuclear group led by Dagmar Wilson and Bella Abzug in the 1950s and 1960s. In the 1950s, during the Cold War period in which a hundred aboveground nuclear test bombs had been detonated in the Nevada desert, a team of physicians and scientists initiated a survey to determine the effects of nuclear fallout through the examination of baby teeth for the presence of cancer-causing, radioactive material – strontium-90. With a chemical makeup similar to calcium, strontium-90 is easily absorbed in teeth and bones in humans and animals. Thousands of baby teeth were collected between 1958 and 1971 by the Greater St. Louis Citizen's Committee for Nuclear Information to be used in the St. Louis Baby Tooth Survey. In 1961, preliminary results of the survey showed high levels of strontium-90 in baby teeth of children born after 1945. This terrifying information drove the mothers of Women Strike for Peace to band together and protest atmospheric bomb testing. In the early 1960s, my mother, along with 50,000 women from WSP, wrote letters, gathered petitions, lobbied congressional representatives, initiated lawsuits, and protested through marches and street demonstrations, tactics rarely seen before the Vietnam War and the height of the civil rights movement. In 1963, the United States, England, and the Soviet Union signed the Partial Nuclear Test Ban Treaty, an agreement to halt atmospheric, underwater, and outer space bomb testing. The signing of the treaty in the United States has been attributed, in large part, to the efforts of Women Strike for Peace.[4]

After discovering the story of my mother's involvement with WSP, I became obsessed with feminist nuclear history. On March 11, 2011, in the midst of my deep dive into the material, a massive earthquake and Tsunami hit the Tohoku region of Japan. Three out of five nuclear plants at Fukushima Daiichi Nuclear Power Plant exploded and fully melted. I followed this story in the news and attended many Fukushima disaster events in New York City near to where I live.

A few years after the Fukushima disaster, I met with visiting Hibaku-sha women, survivors of the Hiroshima and Nagasaki bombs, at several Hibakusha Stories events in New York City. Hibakusha Stories[5] brings Hiroshima and Nagasaki survivors to schools to speak about their experiences in 1945, when their cities were attacked with atom bombs. At these talks, I met Kristen Iversen, the author of *Full Body Burden*, an investigative memoir about growing up next-door to Rocky Flats, the former nuclear weapons facility in Arvada, Colorado.[6] In the Hibakusha Stories presentation, Kristen and the other speakers explored the connective link that binds all nuclear disasters. After Kristen spoke, we chatted about our nuclear histories, and she invited me to visit her in Arvada to uncover more about Rocky Flats.

In the summer of 2016, I traveled to Colorado to meet with Kristen – as well as with scientists, mothers, and fathers – to learn more about the Rocky Flats former nuclear weapons facility. It was my daughter Olivia's last month at home before she went off to college, and as the history of women and nuclear disasters is part of our maternal family legacy, I asked her to join me.

I drove the Prius rental from the Denver airport to Boulder and arrived at the Colorado Chautauqua National Historic Landmark in the afternoon. The sight of the tall, flat, conglomeratic sandstone unsettled me as we entered the park property. The immense rocks looked unreal, like something biblical or darkly fantastical – a mountain in a science fiction film that contains, within it, a dangerous and secret realm. The sharp upward angle of the earth leading to the tall rocks threw me off balance. Beyond those foreboding crags sits the closed Rocky Flats Nuclear Facility, now a Superfund site and wildlife refuge, a grieving land at the base of the snowcapped Rocky Mountains. The terrain is laced with plutonium, uranium, beryllium, cesium 137, many other forms of ionizing radiation, and a long list of toxicants.

As I pulled into the main road on the Chautauqua property, I turned and saw a large grassy area with groups of picnicking families at the base of the large lodge. A perfect summer day. Blankets covered with baskets of food and toys. Parents and children eating, frolicking, talking, throwing Frisbees, and playing catch. Dogs romped about. Colorado families on a sprawling green lawn at the base of the Flatirons.

Olivia asked me to stop the car for a moment so she could get out and take pictures of the mountainscape. She walked toward the trailhead, also filled with pretty young families walking and running upward on the wide sloped path, leading toward the crags.

She snapped photos of the sky and rocks and wildflowers.

Olivia returned to the car and we headed to the big lodge to register and collect keys for a periwinkle-blue, wood-shingled cottage.

The sign over its door said, "Morning Glory." Our temporary home. The next morning, I rose early while Olivia still slept, and hiked in the hills just beneath the crags, through fields of wild grasses and flowers –

Aerial photo of Rocky Flats Nuclear Weapons Plant
before being leveled. Photographer unknown.

asters, blazing stars, western wallflowers, stonecrops – and into the cool of the evergreen trees. It was hard to make sense of these two very different but overlapping realities: a stunning Colorado landscape and nuclear horror. As I hiked, I tried to quiet my mind and push away the frightening scientific facts and stories that I had read about Rocky Flats. Mothers, children, and former workers all sick with cancers. Dead-too-soon loved ones. A contaminated land.

As I circled back and descended to the small streets toward our light-blue cottage, I passed people walking their dogs, children playing, and families chatting inside screened-in porches. This was all "normal" Americana – summer vacation in the Colorado Rockies. But the normalcy shook me. Did these people have any idea about the nuclear disaster on the other side of the mountain?

Wombs and walls cannot protect.

After an early breakfast, Olivia and I met Kristen Iversen[7] in the Chautauqua parking lot. She would be our tour guide through Arvada. Tall and blonde, Kristen wore a long, flowing, colorful skirt and blouse with a wide leather belt and silver buckle cinched at the waist. In her arms, she held her small dog, Emma, a papillon. Kristen looked the part of a Colorado gal who had grown up riding horses. This was her territory. She had seen so much cancer in her friends and neighbors in the community. She also worked at the plant as a young adult and raised her two sons here during their early years.

I drove, Kristen sat in the passenger seat next to me, and Olivia crouched down in the back seat with the windows firmly sealed shut. Olivia wore an oversized sweatshirt and red baseball hat with the embroidered words, "Make America Kind Again." I glanced back and wondered, *Should I have brought my daughter here? Is it safe?* All it would take is the smallest bit of plutonium to enter her lungs and her health could be compromised, or the health of her children, and their children's children.

We traveled down Indiana Street, past fields of brown grass, dry scrub bushes, gently rolling hills, and the unmarked property of the former plant. Bicyclists flew by. I wondered if they knew about Rocky Flats and the dangerous air they were breathing.

Photo of cows next to Rocky Flats and
Candelas advertising sign, 2016. Photo by Michael Kodas.

Olivia asked Kristen questions: "Those cows, are they contaminated? What are those people doing playing miniature golf? Aren't they concerned?"

"Studies have shown that local cows do have plutonium in their bodies," Kristen replied. "And, yes, it's amazing that people just go on as if everything is fine."

Kristen pointed to a group of houses. "Over there, that's where Bini Abbott had a horse farm. Many of her horses had birth defects, organs outside their bodies, and some were sterile. Some of the women in the neighborhood were sterile, too. I told you about the rancher, Lloyd Mixon, who had a deformed pig, Scooter? He would take Scooter with him to city council meetings and try to get the government to tell him what was going on." We drove a little further down the road. "This was where the Jackson Turkey Farm used to be," she said. "The family who owned it said DOE officials would come by unexpectedly to test the turkeys, and sometimes take them away. No one ever found out what they did with the turkeys or what they discovered."

We drove to Kristen's childhood home, which looked like a 1960s Disney movie set: barn, bridge, creek. "That barn and field over there held my horses," she said. "But the water in the creek, the whole area, has been affected by off-site plutonium contamination. New people live here now." We gazed at the bubbling water that ran under a small wooden bridge – a tempting area for children to play in – potentially polluted with plutonium. There were no "stay out" signs or warnings.

"I don't get it," Olivia said.

"Yes, it's very sad," Kristen sighed.

Further on, we approached Standley Lake. The water was wide and still, bounded by a landscape covered with the same dry grasses and scrub bushes, and a few thin, sickly looking trees. A well-worn dirt path led to the shoreline. Kristen told us the lake was a drinking water source for the cities of Westminster, Northglenn, and Thornton, even though plutonium is in the sediment. There were signs for boat rentals – paddleboard, canoes, and kayaks.

"People aren't supposed to swim here," Kristen noted. "It's dangerous to kick up the sediment. But they waterski and fish."

Olivia asked, "Do they eat the fish?"

"Yes, sadly, many do." Kristen replied.

We drove on and parked on the side of the road, with a view of the lake, near a white clapboard home. An older man exited the front door and carried a box to the rear of the house. He did not look our way. Kristen said that the man was the father of her childhood friend, Tamara. Kristen told us how Tamara grew up in this lakeside house, how her parents were deeply committed to their Mormon faith. She was eventually diagnosed with brain cancer, but her parents didn't believe the plutonium had anything do with it. I watched Tamara's father walk into his house while listening to Kristen speak. I wondered about the safety of the soil and the dust on the soles of his shoes.

Two years ago, Michelle Gabrieloff-Parish,[8] who lives nearby in Superior, took her video camera and filmed the lake during a rainstorm. She watched the contaminated water from Rocky Flats rushing beyond its containment areas and flooding Standley Lake. She filmed the bubbling runoff at the top of the body of water at the edge of the shoreline. The residents whose water comes from the lake were never warned by authorities to avoid drinking from or bathing or recreating in the water.

The final stop on our tour was the new housing development, Candelas. Candelas looks like new suburbia in Anywhere, USA, but as we entered the development, Kristen pointed out that many of her scientist colleagues believe the community isn't safe for residence. Plutonium has been detected in the soil, although real estate brokers are not required to inform prospective buyers about the contamination or about the history of Rocky Flats. Plutonium has also been detected in a nearby drinking water source. As I parked the car in front of the model houses, I realized just how close we were to the Refuge. *Too close.*

"I wouldn't live here in a million years," Olivia blurted out incredulously.

I turned back and saw fear in my daughter's sky-blue eyes. I debated getting out of the car but decided to go for it – I would not be giving birth to more children, so I convinced myself it would be okay. My damaged genes would not impact another generation.

Olivia stayed in the car as Kristen and I stepped out to ask the real estate agent a few questions. It was only a few feet from the car to the office, but with each step on the ground, I thought of invisible plutonium and the soles of my shoes. No turning back. I was exposed. I noted there was no wind today. But, then, there was my daughter. I worried (again) that perhaps I should not have brought Olivia with me on this trip. Yet, all around us were playgrounds and recreation areas and homes and schools – all within range of the strong Chinook winds and the former plumes from the weapons plant. The families in Arvada, Westminster, and Broomfield live with plutonium contamination from birth to death. New people move in every day. They come here to Arvada and to these new developments like Candelas, where it's much cheaper to buy a house than in Boulder. They have no idea. It's Colorado. The good life. Land of hikers, skiers, bikers. Land of the wealthy, healthy, and athletic.

We entered the small real estate office. The cheery agent greeted us with brochures and asked us our names. She played up the benefits of raising kids here in Candelas. She boasted about the excellent new schools, a new swimming pool and rec center, the hiking trails running from the development through the "natural habitat" of the refuge of Rocky Flats with its "elk, deer, owl." Then she told us about Standley Lake, "A great place to boat and fish, right nearby." I felt my cancer cells divide as she spoke. My hand flew to my neck – automatically checking my lymph nodes – where my scar remained from having tissue removed when I had Hodgkin's disease. My cancer tied me to Rocky Flats, even though I was not from there, but so many residents have the same cut on their neck, the proverbial downwinders' scar.

How the hell do they allow people to live here? My mind raced. Not one word was said by the agent about plutonium from the former plant site. Or the risks of raising kids here. Or the rare cancers in the community. She smiled her Teflon smile, handed us paperwork with price points, and we took a tour of one model house. It had the standard stainless-steel kitchen, large walk-in closets, large picture windows, and high ceilings. Through the window glass, I could see snowcapped Rocky Mountains in the distance. If the mountains could speak, I'm sure they'd be screaming.

This is the American Dream.

Imagine a time when American soldiers came home from war, went to school for free on the GI Bill, and were offered economic incentives to move out of the cities and into suburbia. Freeways and highways were etched into the earth, making way for more cars and swift travel out of cities and into the brave new world of the suburbs. Gender roles had shifted during World War II – women took over jobs traditionally held by men as many men went to war, and it was expected that such roles would revert as soldiers returned home. And as World War II ended, with the bombing of Hiroshima and Nagasaki, the "ideal" middle-class white American woman tended to the house and children, while her husband worked outside the home. Little houses on the hillside would be built, "all made of ticky-tacky," as the song goes, and people from the working classes would move up the social scale and live well in these new domestic boxes. Machinists and carpenters and plumbers and electricians would make more money than they ever imagined, and each house would come equipped with new appliances for every task that had previously been done by hand. TV was born. Fast food was born. Mass consumption was born. Every family had a car, and then two or three. Suburban communities seemingly offered upward mobility, safety, and comfort.

As it turns out, the spread of suburbia was as much about "white flight"[9] as it was about the fear of atomic weapons hitting urban areas and the need for population dispersal in case of nuclear attack.[10]

While the suburban home expanded to include more gadgets, more bedrooms, more privacy, more ease, across the nation and around the world nuclear bombs were being built and tested to support the Cold War. The new suburbia seemed safe, but toxic dangers lurked. Many of these new communities were built next to bomb factories and nuclear facilities such as in Hanford, Washington;[11] Oak Ridge, Tennessee; Brookhaven, New York;[12] Los Alamos, New Mexico; and the suburbs of Denver, Colorado. Nuclear families provided workers for nuclear factories. Historian Kate Brown suggests developers of the bomb industry understood that happy families living in upscale suburban settings made for happy nuclear workers.[13] Nuclear homes and nuclear families normalized atomic war, a war that in many ways was being secretly waged on its own citizens. According to Carole Gallagher,[14] "This nation's dirty little secret is that for [more than] 50 years the only nation on which we have declared a nuclear war is the United States." As the saying goes, "We are all downwinders."[15]

So, picture living in a community that appears clean, safe, middle class, where the children play outside all day, ride their horses and dirt bikes, swim, fish, and waterski. The windy Colorado plateau offers spectacular views of the Rocky Mountains. Horse and cattle graze in local fields. According to Barbara Hoskinson,[16] a mother who raised her children in the suburb of Arvada in the 1960s and 1970s, life was "ideal – apple pie, church, and picnics. It was good."

Right next door to this *Father Knows Best* and *Leave It to Beaver* suburb, there was the very busy and quickly expanding Rocky Flats Nuclear Weapons Facility, at which they were secretly constructing plutonium triggers for nuclear bombs – triggers that are, in and of themselves, nuclear bombs. These plutonium triggers would set off the very test bombs my own mother fought to shut down. For most of the plant's operational years, local Arvada mothers like Hoskinson had no idea what was being made at Rocky Flats. They were not informed of the fires or leaks. Years later, Hoskinson and her daughter developed thyroid cancers, and other family members developed cancers as well – rectal, kidney, lung, and thyroid. When Hoskinson learned the history of Rocky Flats, she became angered and saddened about the losses her family suffered and the destruction of such a beautiful landscape. She felt betrayed by her government. This is a common story. Kristen told me, "We lived a very good life in many ways. Arvada was a great place to grow up." That is until her teenage boyfriend developed testicular cancer, her friend Tamara developed multiple brain cancers, and she eventually learned the true story of Rocky Flats.

Operating from 1952 to 1992, the Rocky Flats nuclear weapons facility was located approximately 15 miles northwest of Denver, a city built by an influx of miners during the gold rush in the nineteenth century. During the years of its operation, the plant constructed more than 70,000 triggers for nuclear bombs. Rocky Flats would be the site of two major secret plutonium fires, blowing radioactive poison into sections of Arvada and Denver in 1957 and 1969. Hundreds of smaller fires also took place, as well as regular leaks, spills, and atmospheric plutonium releases. Plutonium clouds blew over houses, swimming pools, schools, churches, farms, fields, and streams. Rocky Flats is known for powerful Chinook winds – winds that would blow plutonium dust into local neighborhoods. Liz Martin,[17] a Rocky Flats neighbor for five years, developed cervical cancer; she now has leukemia. She lost one pregnancy when living there. Martin recalls the frightening sound of the intense winds blowing through her house, "violently shaking the windows and walls." Martin is convinced the plutonium dust made its way into her home, and that is why she's sick now. She regrets having ever lived there and would never move back. She worries for her living children and hopes they don't get sick. Today, the Chinook winds from Rocky Flats continue to pose a problem, according to meteorologist W. Gale Biggs.[18] Buried contamination is brought to the surface by animal and plant life and then blown downwind. Just downwind, of course, there are large populations of families living in neighboring communities.

Locals did not know that Rocky Flats was a weapons factory for most of its years of operation. Workers employed there were forbidden to speak of their work and often didn't comprehend the full extent of the factory's activities. Many workers would become sick with cancer and die far too young.[19] The families living in the neighborhoods surrounding Rocky Flats did, and they continue to suffer from cancers and strange illnesses. In addition, many of their pets were born with deformities or developed cancers. A preliminary report from a recent health survey shows a high rate of cancers in humans in the area, and of those reported, 48.8 percent are rare cancers.[20] Dr. Carl Johnson's 1981 health research shows high rates of cancer in the neighboring communities as well, and newer studies show a high percentage of rare cancers.[21] "I grew up on a farm [next to the plant property] and my horses died of brain tumors," Nikki Willems[22] says. "When I was a teenager, we'd go fishing out at Standley Lake; the guys would pull up fish with two heads and three eyes. We didn't think anything of it. We were just kids. You know, there's plutonium there. Kids swam in it when I was growing up." Today, Willems has Hashimoto's disease, and many of her friends from high school have had cancer or have died from cancer.

By 1989, The FBI and EPA suspected criminal negligence at Rocky Flats, which led to a raid focused on investigating broken safety regulations. A federal grand jury began an investigation, a settlement was negotiated, the court documents were sealed, and the plant closed. The story of this federal grand jury is fraught and complex, and cover-ups are suspected in the sealing of the documents and lack of full prosecution.[23] The Rocky Flats cleanup was officially completed in 2004;[24] however, numerous scientists, nuclear experts, local citizens, and antinuclear activists argue the cleanup is far from finished. Unknown but large amounts of plutonium and other contaminants remain on the land in what has been turned into a Superfund site, a designation made under the Comprehensive Environmental Response, Compensation, and Liability Act of 1980. The primary industrial site (the Superfund area – 485 acres) was never completely remediated. There is a buffer zone, also heavily contaminated, although the EPA claims this area is fully remediated. The surrounding area, now called a National Wildlife Refuge, was not remediated;[25] contamination has been detected there by scientists Edward Martell and Harvey Nichols.[26] Research shows "there are more than 20 million potentially fatal doses of plutonium per square mile at the refuge."[27] Groundwater tested by the Rocky Flats Stewardship Council found elevated levels of plutonium and americium in groundwater testing stations in the side of the refuge on the southeast corner and closest to the new Candelas housing development in 2015.[28] A host of other toxic and radioactive contaminants have also been found at Rocky Flats, including americium, uranium, cadmium, PCBs, and beryllium.[29]

Homes, children, and radiation disaster obviously don't belong together; however, they intersect in ecosociological contexts such as Rocky Flats. There are grave implications here: science shows that females and children are most harmed by radiation, and babies and fetuses most of all,[30] and families, women, and children garner the least attention in health studies of radiation exposures at Rocky Flats.[31] Regulatory radiation safety standards are based on a white male adult body, the standard "Reference Man." The reference man model fails to account for differences of age, race, and gender in radiation exposures. According to Mary Olson's[32] and Arjun Makhijani's[33] analyses of radiation and cancer risk in the Beir VII report, when we hear a level of radiation is safe, we need to adjust the dial and redo the math; an adult woman is twice as likely to get cancer from the same exposure to radiation as a white adult man. These numbers go way up with children – girls are at least seven times as likely to get cancer from the same exposure to radiation as an adult white male, boys are at least five times as likely as an adult male, and babies and fetuses are the most vulnerable of all. Adult females are almost twice as likely to die from exposures as adult males, and so on.[34] Safety standards make no adjustment for those who are most at risk: fetuses, babies, children, and women – neighbors of nuclear facilities such as Rocky Flats.[35]

"Go ask the mothers," said Dr. Alice Stewart, an epidemiologist, as she attempted to locate the reason behind an epidemic of childhood cancer in 1950s England.[36] Stewart discovered that a single X-ray to the womb nearly doubled a fetus's chance of developing cancer in childhood. Going door to door, Stewart asked mothers what they had done differently during their pregnancies to possibly bring on cancer in their children. Her approach was radical. She threatened the nuclear industry, calling attention to the health hazards of radiation, and was therefore denounced. Stewart's gender did not help matters. In the 1970s, Stewart's research on the dangers of X-rays to the fetus would be proven accurate by male researchers. What about pregnant women living nearby to Rocky Flats? What about developing young women of reproductive age who are exposed to radiation? What about their ova? What about the sperm of the men? Grave mutagenic harm may be done even before conception.[37]

Like a mother's womb, we like to think of the home as a safe space. Radiation pollution undoes all that. Ingested and internalized radiation travels through the mother's bloodstream and crosses the placenta. External radiation, such as X-rays and gamma rays, penetrate the womb. Wombs and homes, as permeable spaces, put the unborn and children at risk.[38]

Rocky Flats is "a national sacrifice zone," says Robert Alvarez,[39] associate fellow at the Institute for Policy Studies and former senior policy advisor to the secretary at the US Department of Energy. "That's what it is, although no one will say so officially. How much remains buried there? A tremendous amount – plutonium doesn't go away. No one has done this yet – it's costly and complex – but someone needs to go into those houses nearby in Arvada and take samples. We don't know how much plutonium is in them."[40]

Houses and families do not belong next to radioactive sacrifice zones. Home sweet home. Home is where the heart is. Home, home on the range. Home is where it starts. Dream home. Don't sit at home. Love starts at home. Home, home is where I want to be / pick me up and bring me down. This space in which we grow occupies so many cliché, trite, and nostalgic phrases and song lyrics, yet we know home may be a place of horror, where violence remains hidden. We long for the perfect American Dream home, but we know secret dangers lurk there. Post-World War II, those dangers include toxic and radioactive contamination.

Today, when driving by Rocky Flats, there are no signs, no warnings, no walls, only thin wire fencing. The only symbol of the past is Jeff Gipe's eerie sculpture of the *Cold War Horse*. The landscape looks inviting and beautiful. Cattle graze. Wind turbines line one section of the refuge property, part of a new green power project. Dig a little, knock on a few doors, and tragic family stories of cancer spill out of the mouths of residents as my interviews and other oral histories show. The refuge opened to families and visitors for recreation purposes on September 15, 2018. Environmentalists and community activists continue to oppose the opening. Harvey Nichols, a biologist who has examined plutonium in the soil at Rocky Flats, argues that children should not be allowed "out there," as the potential for their developing cancer is too great. W. Gale Biggs also offers scientific evidence for why people should be concerned about using the site for recreation and living nearby.[41]

Shaunessy Keely,[42] MPH (master of public health), grew up in Arvada, only a few miles from Rocky Flats, and she recently lost her father, Brian, to an extremely rare form of cardiac cancer. He lived in the Village of Five Parks, a development in Arvada under 2 miles from Rocky Flats. In a wistful tone, she explains, "Some people don't want to face what's going on. There's a lot of denial. In every fourth house in my parents' neighborhood, someone is very sick. The family next door – the woman has

Cold War Horse, sculpture by Jeff Gipe.
Photo courtesy of Heidi Hutner.

MS, but her husband, my dad's close friend, refuses to talk about Rocky Flats. My good friend who just lost her husband says she won't move; she says her house is her best investment." A child, Nathan, living only a few blocks from Keely's father, developed the same rare heart cancer. They were diagnosed in the same year. Nathan is battling that cancer now. He underwent a surgery to remove the large primary cancer tumor from his heart and received chemotherapy treatments for a number of years. His future is uncertain. Nathan's mother, Elizabeth Panzer,[43] speaks of the heartbreak of her situation: "When we moved here from Chicago, nobody warned us that this housing and land might be polluted with plutonium. We didn't know much about Rocky Flats. We believed that it was all cleaned up." Panzer notes: "So many people in Arvada don't want to think about the dangers here. The government says it safe and they want to believe it. I wanted to believe it, too." Panzer pauses and then says, "But my son could die any day and I think there may be a cancer cluster here. People *need* to know." Panzer and her family chose to stay in their house so Nathan could continue to live a normal life during his illness. Now she questions that decision. "What about the health of my other children? And if I sell my house and move away, what about the next family? What about those kids?"[44]

In the 1950s, suburban housing began cropping up all around the Rocky Flats landscape in and around Arvada. The new development, Candelas, which I visited with my daughter and Kristen Iversen, will include 1,450 homes on 1,500 acres of plutonium-contaminated land right next door (approximately 1 mile) to the Rocky Flats Wildlife Refuge. Candelas is labeled "green" because of the buildings' LEED certification, Energy Star ratings, solar rooftops, and solar streetlamps.[45] Real estate agents and local home sellers in the area are under no legal obligation to alert homebuyers about the history of Rocky Flats and the risks of buying downwind. At the Candelas website, there is reassuring information about the cleanup at Rocky Flats; two official letters posted their report on the limited soil testing in sections of the Candelas property in 2013 and 2011.[46] The device used to test for radiation on-site was the Ludlum 19 Micro-Meter; and, based on soil testing done with this device, the radiation levels are declared as "background" and safe for housing. However, this information is misleading, as the Ludlum 19 does not pick up plutonium; it detects gamma rays, and plutonium emits alpha rays.[47] There is also no mention of radioactive materials found in the groundwater and soil tests nearby. The words on the Candelas housing site do not account for the intense local winds blowing contaminated materials from the nearby refuge and Superfund site; these winds and the natural movement of biological materials pose an ongoing hazard to Candelas residents and the local community.

Today, community activists try to warn others of the ongoing dangers of living near the refuge and former plant, and many of these spokespeople are mothers. Michelle Ramon Gabrieloff-Parish[48] founded the activist watchdog group Candelas Glows to raise awareness about the area's dangers to homebuyers. In addition to Candelas Glows,[49] she led a protest in front of the development and wrote an article for *Elephant Journal* about the health risks of living there. Gabrieloff-Parish is concerned that "there are no plans in place for disasters such as floods and extreme weather, no protections in place for future radical ecological events" at and around the Rocky Flats site. She recently monitored the flow of water from the former plant during a major flood and observed that the overflow, which is supposed to be diverted away from drinking and bathing water sources, ended up in the local water supply.

Tiffany Hansen, another mother activist, founded the community support group, Rocky Flats Downwinders.[50] Hansen grew up 3.75 miles from the plant. She now lives in Denver. "I had a pillow seat in my bedroom window growing up," Hansen explains.[51] "I spent many nights looking out at the plant's lights, but I had no idea what was really going on." Now, she is outraged at the dangers she and her peers were exposed to without their knowledge or consent. It wasn't until a few years ago, after developing an ovarian tumor and experiencing other "debilitating health" symptoms (including Graves' disease), that she Googled and discovered the Rocky Flats' contamination story. Hansen then read Kristen Iversen's memoir and became deeply upset with the news that she had grown up next to a bomb factory: "We played outside all day in that stuff, exposed, unaware. I was hysterical when I found out. I called many of my old friends and discovered too many stories of cancer."

"We thought we were living the dream," Hansen[52] continues. Her father owned an electrical contracting company that did work at the Rocky Flats site. He was well compensated. They had a nice house with a pool, she had fancy toys like "four wheelers," and her mother drove a Corvette. In addition to her ovarian tumor, Hansen has had one miscarriage (common to women who live nearby), and she had a benign lymph tumor on her neck as a child. In her youth, Hansen was often hospitalized for mysterious debilitating symptoms. She bears the downwinder's scar on her neck: "Just like Kristen Iversen describes in her book about her own scar." Her brother, who worked at the plant, has heart and thyroid problems. Hansen's childhood best friend had a brain tumor in the third grade. Another friend had ovarian cancer and passed away at forty-three. Hansen's high school boyfriend, Curtis, had stage four thyroid cancer and he survived, as did his mom; Curtis's dad passed away from thyroid cancer.

"As a mother, I feel a sense of responsibility about Rocky Flats," Hansen says. "I get so many calls from sick people, and I feel so bad for those who remain unaware of the dangers at the plant. I see families moving into this area, to all those beautiful houses, where it looks safe. But, a few years from now, they may develop cancer. Kids are running around there. Knowing what I know, I feel so sad for them." In response to these many health and safety concerns, Hansen sought out Carole Jensen, RN, and asked her to help create the Rocky Flats Health Survey. This survey is the first since Dr. Carl Johnson[53] looked at the health impacts of ionizing radiation on the local community surrounding Rock Flats. She recently initiated another citizen-led health survey and a soil study with Dr. Micheal Ketterer.

Another mother, Denise Leonard, newly discovered the history of Rocky Flats' contamination and health risks. She raised her family next to the facility and now lives in California. Her two sons, both born in Arvada, had brain birth defects – hydrocephalus – a condition that may be caused by ionizing radiation exposure in utero. After discovering the true history of Rocky Flats, Leonard joined the board of Rocky Flats Downwinders and became an active member. Alice Paetzel,[54] a two-time cancer survivor and another mother from the community, lost her adult daughter Dawn to ovarian cancer. Alice's surviving daughter Heidi had childhood epilepsy and now has growths on her ovaries, and Alice's husband just passed away from prostate cancer. Paetzel says, "We sent our kids to the small private Arvada Christian School, right near Standley Lake. So many of those children and teachers have died. We thought we were protecting our kids by sending them there, but we marched those little angels to their deaths."

This legacy of the fraught toxic maternal and familial spaces (wombs and homes) goes back to World War II. Female scientists and health experts such as Rachel Carson, Rosalie Bertell, Helen Caldicott, and Alice Stewart, among others, warned us about our future if we continued poisoning ourselves with toxic and radioactive contamination. My own mother participated in combatting the dangers of ionizing radiation in her work with Women Strike for Peace and later during Nuclear Freeze in the 1980s. A legacy of mothers and women fighting this battle continues today across the United States and the globe – including the predominantly female ICAN (International Campaign to Abolish Nuclear Weapons) 2017 Nobel Peace Prize winners who work to support the 2017 UN Treaty to Ban Nuclear Weapons.

Like so many activist mothers and women at nuclear disaster sites around the world who rise up, demand information, and fight for their children's safety, Arvada mother Elizabeth Panzer says: "I cannot stay silent anymore," and let "such suffering happen to more children. The denial must end."

Again and again, I hear my daughter's words, "I wouldn't live here in a million years."

Endnotes

1. See, for example, Song Wu, Scott Powers, Wei Zhu, and Yusuf A. Hannun, "Substantial Contribution of Extrinsic Risk Factors to Cancer Development," *Nature* (2015) https://doi.org/10.1038/nature16166. There is much additional literature on the links between cancer rates and environmental pollution.

2. See, for example, Environmental Working Group, *Body Burden: The Pollution in Newborns*, July 14, 2005, https://www.ewg.org/research/body-burden-pollution-newborns. Paul Terry, Craig V. Towers, Liang-Ying Liu, Angela A. Peverly, Jiangang Chen, Amina Salamova, "Polybrominated diphenyl ethers (flame retardants) in mother-infant pairs in the Southeastern U.S." *International Journal of Environmental Health Research* (2017), https://DOI.org/ 10.1080/09603123.2017.1332344.

3. Jenny Pronczuk, James Akre, Gerald Moy, and Constanza Vallenas, "Global Perspectives in Breast Milk Contamination: Infectious and Toxic Hazards," *Environmental Health Perspectives* 110, no. 6 (2002): 349–351, https://doi.org/10.1289/ehp.021100349. Philip J. Landrigan, Babasaheb Sonawane, Donald Mattison, Michael McCally, and Anjali Garg, "Chemical Contaminants in Breast Milk and Their Impacts on Children's Health: An Overview," *Environmental Health Perspectives* 110, no. 6 (2002): 313–315, https://doi.org/10.1289/ehp.021100313.

4. Amy Swerdlow, *Women Strike for Peace: Traditional Motherhood and Radical Politics in the 1960s* (Chicago: University of Chicago Press, 1993).

5. Hibakusha Stories, [Homepage 20], http://hibakushastories.org/.

6. Kristen Iversen, *Full Body Burden: Growing Up in the Shadow of Rocky Flats* (New York: Broadway Books, 2013).

7. Kristen Iversen, personal interview, Aug. 4, 2016.

8. Michelle Ramon Gabrieloff-Parish, personal interview, Nov. 11, 2016.

9. On white flight, see Jan Blakee, "On 'White Flight' to the Suburbs: A Demographic Approach," *Focus: Institute for Research on Poverty Newsletter* 3, no. 2 (1978–1979).

10. See Kathleen A. Tobin, "The Reduction of Urban Vulnerability: Revisiting 1950s American Suburbanization as Civil Defense," *Cold War History* 2, no. 2 (2001): 1–32.

11. On the building of the nuclear suburb at Hanford in Washington State, see Kate Brown, *Plutopia: Families, Atomic Cities, and the Great Plutonium Disasters* (Oxford, UK: Oxford University Press, 2015). Brown also offers an in-depth report on plutonium disasters at Hanford and the Mayak plant in the former Soviet Union.

12. On growing up next to Brookhaven National Laboratory, see Kelly McMasters, *Welcome to Shirley: Growing Up in an Atomic Town* (New York: Farrar, Straus and Giroux, 2008).

13. Brown, *Plutopia*, 39.

14. Carole Gallagher, *American Ground Zero: The Secret Nuclear War* (Cambridge, MA: MIT Press, 1993).

15. Carole Gallagher, "In Nuclear Tests, We All Live Downwind," *New York Times*, May 30, 1993, http://www.nytimes.com/1993/05/30/opinion/l-in-nuclear-tests-we-all-live-downwind-558593.html. The phrase "we are all downwinders" was first used by a lieutenant testing the spread of fallout in the Nevada desert after he realized the radiation from the Nevada test site could not be contained.

16. Barbara Hoskinson, personal interview, July 29, 2016.

17. Liz Martin, personal interview, Aug. 3, 2016.

18. W. Gale Biggs, personal interview, Aug. 2, 2016. See also W. Gale Biggs, "Airborne Plutonium Contamination and Rocky Flats," YouTube video, posted by Highland City Club, August 25, 2015, https://www.youtube.com/watch?v=rs-BZZJolYs&feature=youtu.be.

19. Ted Zeigler, Larry Hankins, Harvey Nichols, and W. Gale Biggs, personal interviews, Aug. 2, 2016.

20. Carol Jensen, *Rocky Flats Downwinders Health Survey*, Metropolitan State University of Denver, May 2016, http://rockyflatsdownwinders.com/wp-content/uploads/2016/05/RFD-Health-Survey-Executive-Summary-Final.pdf. See also Malin et al.'s chapter in this volume.

21. For example, see Carl J. Johnson, "Cancer Incidence in an Area Contaminated with Radionuclides Near a Nuclear Installation," *Ambio* 10, no. 4 (1981): 176–182; and Carl J. Johnson, "Cancer Incidence Patterns in the Denver Metropolitan Area in Incidence Patterns in the Denver Metropolitan Area in Relation to the Rocky Flats Plant," *American Journal of Epidemiology* 126, no. 1 (1987): 153–155. For more on health studies, see Iversen, *Full Body Burden*, where there is an exhaustive list on Rocky Flats health impacts.

22. Nikki Willems, personal interview, Nov. 30, 2016.

23. For more on the legal story, see Wes McKinley and Caron Balkany, *The Ambushed Grand Jury: How the Justice Department Covered Up a Nuclear Crime and How We Caught Them Red Handed* (New York: Apex, 2004).

24. Environmental Protection Agency, Search Superfund Site Information, 2017, https://cumulis.epa.gov/supercpad/cursites/.

25. Ibid.

26. Harvey Nichols, personal interview, Aug. 2, 2016.

27. S. E. Poet and Edward Martell, "Plutonium-239 and Americium-241 Contamination in the Denver Area," *Health Physics*, 23 (1972): 537–548, https://doi.org/10.1097/00004032-197210000-00012.

28. See contamination reports through 2015. Rocky Flats Stewardship Council, Monthly Updates, January 2019, http://www.rockyflatssc.org/updates.html.

29. Stephanie Malin and Becky Alexis-Martin, "Flatlining: Exploring Hidden Toxic Landscapes and the Embodiment of Contamination at Rocky Flats National Wildlife Refuge, USA," *Toxic News*, Feb. 8, 2017, https://toxicnews.org/2017/02/08/flatlining-exploring-hidden-toxic-landscapes-and-the-embodiment-of-contamination-at-rocky-flats-national-wildlife-refuge-usa/.

30. See Arjun Makhijani, *The Standard Reference Man in Radiation Protection Standards and Guidance with Recommendations for Change*, rev. ed., Apr. 2009, http://citeseerx.ist.psu.edu/viewdoc/download?doi=10.1.1.394.358&rep=rep1&type=pdf; and Mary Olson, *Radiation Is More Harmful to Women*, Nuclear Information and Resource Service, Oct. 2011, https://www.nirs.org/wp-content/uploads/radiation/radhealth/radiationwomen.pdf. The updated gender/age-sensitive safety models have now been incorporated in the language of the 2017 UN

Treaty to Ban the Bomb, thanks, in large part, to the work of Mary Olson; see Nuclear Information and Resource Service and the Institute for Energy and Environmental Research, "Radiation and Gender: One Basis for New Nuclear Weapons Treaty," Pressenza International Press Agency, May 25, 2017, https://www.pressenza.com/2017/05/radiation-gender-one-basis-new-nuclear-weapons-treaty. See also, Heidi Hutner, "Invisible Victims," *Ms. Magazine*, Summer 2015.

31. Malin and Alexis-Martin, "Flatlining."

32. Olson, *Radiation.*

33. Makhijani, *Standard.*

34. Olson, *Radiation*; Makhijani, *Standard.*

35. Notably, studies on animals in Chernobyl and Fukushima also reveal that radiation most negatively impacts females (butterflies, birds, and bats); see P. Lehmann, Z. Boratynski, T. Mappes, T. A. Mousseau, and A. P. Møller, "Fitness Costs of Increased Cataract Frequency and Cumulative Radiation Dose in Natural Mammalian Populations From Chernobyl," *Scientific Reports* 6 (2016): 19974, https://doi.org/10.1038/srep19974; A. P. Møller, T. A. Mousseau, G. Milinevsky, A. Peklo, E. Pysanets, and T. Szép, "Condition, Reproduction and Survival of Barn Swallows From Chernobyl," *Journal of Animal Ecology* 74 (2005): 1102–1111; A. P. Møller, A. Bonisoli-Alquati, G. Rudolfsen, and T. A. Mousseau, "Chernobyl Birds Have Smaller Brains," PLoS One 6, no. 2 (2011): e16862, https://doi.org/10.1371/journal.pone.0016862; A. P. Møller, A. Bonisoli-Alquati, G. Rudolfsen, and T. A. Mousseau, "Elevated Mortality among Birds in Chernobyl as Judged from Biased Sex and Age Ratios," *PLoS One* 7, no. 4 (2012): e35223. The research team is currently studying these effects in Japan post-Fukushima March 2011 and has determined similar findings regarding gender and radiation. Tim Mousseau, personal correspondence, June 28, 2015 and April 2, 2017.

36. On Alice Stewart, see Gayle Greene, *The Woman Who Knew Too Much: Alice Stewart and the Secrets of Radiation* (Ann Arbor: University of Michigan Press, 1999).

37. "The potential effects of radiation on a conceptus [embryo or fetus] include prenatal death, intrauterine growth restriction, small head size, severe mental retardation, reduced intelligence quotient, organ malformation, and childhood cancer" write Cynthia H McCollough, Beth A. Schueler, Thomas D. Atwell, Natalie N. Braun, Dawn M. Regner, Doug-

las L. Brown, and Andrew J. LeRoy, in "Radiation Exposure and Pregnancy: When Should We Be Concerned?" *Radiographics* 27, no. 4 (2007): 909–917, https://doi.org/10.1148/rg.274065149. On reduced fertility in women exposed to radiation see Jennifer Y. Wo and Akila N. Viswanathan, "The Impact of Radiotherapy on Fertility, Pregnancy, and Neonatal Outcomes of Female Cancer Patients," *International Journal of Radiation Oncology, Biology, Physics* 73, no. 5 (2009): 1304–1312.

38. Alice Stewart's work on X-rays and children with cancer first illustrated this; on toxics (not radiation) and the permeability of the womb and the impact on the developing fetus; see Sandra Steingraber, *Having Faith: An Ecologist's Journey Into Motherhood* (Cambridge, MA: Perseus, 2001).

39. Robert Alvarez, personal interview, Nov. 30, 2016.

40. Some work on this has begun, such as Marco Kaltofen's 2019 study, which includes an examination of plutonium dust taken from one house approximately 1 mile from the former nuclear weapons plant facility. See LeRoy Moore, "Rocky Flats Nuclear Guardianship #6: Marco Kaltofen, Plutonium in Respirable Dust with Harvey Nichols and Gale Biggs," *LeRoy Moore's Blog*, March 17, 2011, https://leroymoore. wordpress.com/2011/04/01/rocky-flats-nuclear-guardianship-6-marco-kaltofen-plutonium-in-respirable-dust-with-harvey-nichols-gale-biggs-3-17-11/; and Marco Kaltofen, "Microanalysis of Particle-Based Uranium, Thorium, and Plutonium in Nuclear Workers' House Dust," *Environmental Engineering Science* 36, no. 2 (2009), https://doi. org/10.1089/ees.2018.0036. Also, Dr. Michael Ketterer has analyzed soil near housing on Indiana Street; see Michael Ketterer, *Activities of 239+240Pu and Pu Atom Ratios In Hemp Study Soils* (Report for Hansen Roddenberry Catalyst Grant Award), available from Tiffany Hansen, tiffany@rockyflatsdownwinders.com.

41. Jeff Todd, "Scientists Debate Rocky Flats Safety," 4 CBS Denver, July 27, 2017, http://denver.cbslocal.com/2017/07/27/rocky-flats-plutonium; W. Gale Biggs, *Airborne Plutonium Contamination and Rocky Flats*, YouTube video, posted by Highland City Club, August 25, 2015, https://www.youtube.com/watch?v=rs-BZZJolYs&feature=youtube, W. Gale Biggs, personal interview, Aug. 2, 2016; Harvey Nichols, personal interview, Aug. 2, 2016.

42. Shaunessy Keely, personal interview, Jan. 6, 2017.

43. Elizabeth Panzer, personal interview, Aug. 6, 2017.

44. This same question comes up in the documentary film *Dark Circle* (1982), about Rocky Flats activism in the 1980s, when a mother activist in the community wants to move away to protect her children, but doesn't want to sell her home to another young family. She doesn't want to endanger more children.

45. Candelas, "Candelas Awarded Prestigious LEED® Gold Certification," n.d., https://www.candelaslife.com/news-candelas-awared-leed-gold-certification.

46. Candelas, [Homepage], 2017, http://www.candelaslife.com.

47. John Saxton, *Request for Additional Information on Submittal Regarding License Condition 12.8, Ross ISR Project, Crook County, WY, Source Material License SUA-1601, DOCKET NO. 040-09091, TAC J00735*, Oct. 15, 2015, https://www.nrc.gov/docs/ML1527/ML15278A115.pdfLetters at Candelas website, CTL Thompson, 2013, and 2011, http://www.candelaslife.com/faqs.

48. Michelle Ramon Gabrieloff-Parish, personal interview, Nov. 11, 2016.

49. Candelas Glows, [Homepage], 2019, https://candelasglows.com.

50. Rocky Flats Downwinders' mission is to "Bring about awareness of Rocky Flats in order to educate the community, to sensitize medical professionals regarding potential adverse health effects suffered by Downwinders, and to obtain medical monitoring for Rocky Flats Downwinders, as well as inclusion under the Radiation and Exposure and Compensation Act (RECA)." Rocky Flats Downwinders, http://rockyflatsdownwinders.com/about-us/goals-for-rocky-flats-downwinders/.

51. Tiffany Hansen, personal interview, Nov. 6, 2016.

52. Ibid.

53. Johnson, "Cancer Incidence."

54. Alice Paetzel, personal interview, July 29, 2016.

Works Cited

Biggs, W. Gale. "Airborne Plutonium Contamination and Rocky Flats." YouTube video, posted by Highland City Club, August 25, 2015. https://www.youtube.com/watch?v=rs-BZZJolYs&feature=youtube.

Blakee, Jan. "On 'White Flight' to the Suburbs: A Demographic Approach." *Focus: Institute for Research on Poverty Newsletter* 3, no. 2, 1978–1979.

Brown, Kate. *Plutopia: Families, Atomic Cities, and the Great Plutonium Disasters.* Oxford, UK: Oxford University Press, 2015.

Candelas. "Candelas Awarded Prestigious LEED® Gold Certification," n.d. https://www.candelaslife.com/news-candelas-awared-leed-gold-certification.

Candelas Glows. [Homepage]. 2017. https://candelasglows.com.

Colburn, Theo, and Dianne Dumanoski. *Our Stolen Future: Are We Threatening Our Fertility, Intelligence, and Survival? – A Scientific Detective Story.* New York: Plume, 1997.

Dark Circle. Directed and produced by Judy Irving, Christopher Beaver, and Ruth Landy.

Environmental Protection Agency, Rocky Flats Plant (DOE) Golden, CO.. n.d. https://cumulis.epa.gov/supercpad/SiteProfiles/index.cfm?fuseaction=second.Cleanup&id=0800360#bkground.

Environmental Protection Agency. Search Superfund Site Information. 2017. https://cumulis.epa.gov/supercpad/cursites/.

Environmental Working Group. "Body Burden: The Pollution in Newborns," Environmental Working Group, July 14, 2005.

Gabrieloff-Parish, Michelle. "Green Housing on Plutonium," *Elephant Journal,* May 30, 2013. https://www.elephantjournal.com/2013/05/angelina-jolie-cuts-off-both-breasts-to-prevent-cancer-while-we-prepare-to-build-housing-on-plutonium-michelle-gabrieloff-parish/.

Gallagher, Carole. *American Ground Zero: The Secret Nuclear War.* Cambridge, MA: MIT Press, 1993.

———. "In Nuclear Tests, We All Live Downwind," *New York Times,* May 30, 1993. http://www.nytimes.com/1993/05/30/opinion/l-in-nuclear-tests-we-all-live-downwind-558593.html.

Greene, Gayle. *The Woman Who Knew Too Much: Alice Stewart and the Secrets of Radiation.* Ann Arbor: University of Michigan Press, 1999.

Hibakusha Stories. [Homepage]. 2017. http://hibakushastories.org/.

Hutner, Heidi. "Invisible Victims," *Ms. Magazine,* Summer 2015.

Iversen, Kristen. *Full Body Burden: Growing Up in the Shadow of Rocky Flats*. New York: Broadway Books, 2013.

Jensen, Carol. *Rocky Flats Downwinders Healthy Survey*. Metropolitan State University of Denver. May 17, 2016. http://rockyflatsdownwinders.com/wp-content/uploads/2016/05/RFD-Health-Survey-Executive-Summary-Final.pdf.

Jetñil-Kijiner, Kathy. "Monster." *Iep Jaltok: Poems From a Marshallese Daughter*. Tucson: University of Arizona Press, 2017.

Johnson, Carl J. "Cancer Incidence in an Area Contaminated with Radionuclides Near a Nuclear Installation." *Ambio* 10, no. 4 (1981): 176–182.

———. "Cancer Incidence Patterns in the Denver Metropolitan Area in Incidence Patterns in the Denver Metropolitan Area in Relation to the Rocky Flats Plant." *American Journal of Epidemiology* 126, no. 1 (1987): 153–155.

Kaltofen, Marco. "Microanalysis of Particle-Based Uranium, Thorium, and Plutonium in Nuclear Workers' House Dust." *Environmental Engineering Science* 36, no. 2(2009). https://doi.org/10.1089/ees.2018.0036

Ketterer, Michael. *Activities of 239+240Pu and Pu Atom Ratios In Hemp Study Soils* (Report for Hansen Roddenberry Catalyst Grant Award). Available from Tiffany Hansen, tiffany@rockyflatsdownwinders.com.

Landrigan, Philip J., Babasaheb Sonawane, Donald Mattison, Michael McCally, and Anjali Garg. "Chemical Contaminants in Breast Milk and Their Impacts on Children's Health: An Overview." *Environmental Health Perspectives* 110, no. 6 (2002): 313–315. https://doi.org/10.1289/ehp.021100313.

Lehmann, P., Z. Boratynski, T. Mappes, T. A. Mousseau, and A. P. Møller. "Fitness Costs of Increased Cataract Frequency and Cumulative Radiation Dose in Natural Mammalian Populations from Chernobyl." *Scientific Reports* 6 (2016): 19974. https://doi.org/10.1038/srep19974.

Makhijani, Arjun. *The Standard Reference Man in Radiation Protection Standards and Guidance with Recommendations for Change*, rev. ed., Apr. 2009. http://citeseerx.ist.psu.edu/viewdoc/download?doi=10.1.1.394.358&rep=rep1&type=pdf.

Malin, Stephanie, and Becky Alexis-Martin. "Flatlining: Exploring Hidden Toxic Landscapes and the Embodiment of Contamination at Rocky

Flats National Wildlife Refuge, USA," *Toxic News*, Feb. 8, 2017. https://toxicnews.org/2017/02/08/flatlining-exploring-hidden-toxic-landscapes-and-the-embodiment-of-contamination-at-rocky-flats-national-wildlife-refuge-usa/.

McCollough, Cynthia H., Beth A. Schueler, Thomas D. Atwell, Natalie N. Braun, Dawn M. Regner, Douglas L. Brown, Andrew J. LeRoy. "Radiation Exposure and Pregnancy: When Should We Be Concerned?" *Radiographics* 27, no. 4 (2007): 909–917. https://doi.org/10.1148/rg.274065149.

McKinley, Wes, and Caron Balkany. *The Ambushed Grand Jury: How the Justice Department Covered Up a Nuclear Crime and How We Caught Them Red Handed.* New York: Apex, 2004.

McMasters, Kelly. *Welcome to Shirley: A Memoir from an atomic town.* New York: Farrar, Straus and Giroux, 2008.

Møller, A. P., T. A. Mousseau, G. Milinevsky, A. Peklo, E. Pysanets, and T. Szép. "Condition, Reproduction and Survival of Barn Swallows from Chernobyl." *Journal of Animal Ecology* 74 (2005): 1102–1111.

Møller, A. P., A. Bonisoli-Alquati, G. Rudolfsen, and T. A. Mousseau. "Chernobyl Birds Have Smaller Brains." *PLoS One* 6, no. 2 (2011): e16862. https://doi.org/10.1371/journal.pone.0016862.

Møller, A. P., A. Bonisoli-Alquati, G. Rudolfsen, and T. A. Mousseau. "Elevated Mortality among Birds in Chernobyl as Judged from Biased Sex and Age Ratios." *PLoS One* 7, no. 4 (2012): e35223.

Moore, LeRoy. "Rocky Flats Nuclear Guardianship #6: Marco Kaltofen, Plutonium in Respirable Dust with Harvey Nichols and Gale Biggs." *LeRoy Moore's Blog.* March 17, 2011. https://leroymoore.wordpress.com/2011/04/01/rocky-flats-nuclear-guardianship-6-marco-kaltofen-plutonium-in-respirable-dust-with-harvey-nichols-gale-biggs-3-17-11/.

Nuclear Information and Resource Service and the Institute for Energy and Environmental Research. "Radiation and Gender: One Basis for New Nuclear Weapons Treaty." Pressenza International Press Agency, May 25, 2017. https://www.pressenza.com/2017/05/radiation-gender-one-basis-new-nuclear-weapons-treaty.

Olson, Mary. *Radiation Is More Harmful to Women.* Nuclear Information and Resource Service, Oct. 2011. https://www.nirs.org/wp-content/uploads/radiation/radhealth/radiationwomen.pdf.

Poet, S. E., and Edward Martell. "Plutonium-239 and Americium-241 Contamination in the Denver Area." *Health Physics* 23 (1972): 537–548. https://doi.org/10.1097/00004032-197210000-00012.

Pronczuk, Jenny, James Akre, Gerald Moy, and Constanza Vallenas. "Global Perspectives in Breast Milk Contamination: Infectious and Toxic Hazards." *Environmental Health Perspectives* 110(6) (2002): 349–351. https://doi.org/10.1289/ehp.021100349.

Rocky Flats Downwinders. "Mission." 2016. http://rockyflatsdownwinders.com/about-us/goals-for-rocky-flats-downwinders/.

Saxton, John. *Request for Additional Information on Submittal Regarding License Condition 12.8, Ross ISR Project, Crook County, WY, Source Material License SUA-1601, DOCKET NO. 040-09091, TAC J00735,* Oct. 15, 2015. https://www.nrc.gov/docs/ML1527/ML15278A115.pdf.

Steingraber, Sandra. *Having Faith: An Ecologist's Journey into Motherhood.* Cambridge. MA: Perseus, 2001.

———. *Living Downstream: An Ecologist's Personal Investigation into Cancer and the Environment.* Cambridge, MA: Da Capo, 2010.

Swerdlow, Amy. *Women Strike for Peace: Traditional Motherhood and Radical Politics In the 1960s.* Chicago: University of Chicago Press, 1993.

Terry, Paul, Craig V. Towers, Liang-Ying Liu, Angela A. Peverly, Jiangang Chen, and Amina Salamova. "**Polybrominated Diphenyl Ethers (Flame Retardants) in Mother-Infant Pairs in the Southeastern U.S.** *International Journal of Environmental Health Research* (2017). https://DOI.org / 10.1080/09603123.2017.1332344.

Tobin, Kathleen A. "The Reduction of Urban Vulnerability: Revisiting 1950s American Suburbanization as Civil Defense." *Cold War History* 2, no. 2 (2001): 1–32.

Todd, Jeff. "Scientists Debate Rocky Flats Safety." 4 CBS Denver, July 27, 2017. http://denver.cbslocal.com/2017/07/27/rocky-flats-plutonium.

Wo, Jennifer Y., and Akila N. Viswanathan. "The Impact of Radiotherapy on Fertility, Pregnancy, and Neonatal Outcomes of Female Cancer Patients." *International Journal of Radiation Oncology, Biology, Physics* 73, no. 5 (2009): 1304–1312.

Wu, Song, Scott Powers, Wei Zhu, and Yusuf A. Hannun. "Substantial Contribution of Extrinsic Risk Factors to Cancer Development." *Nature* (2015). https://doi.org/10.1038/nature16166.

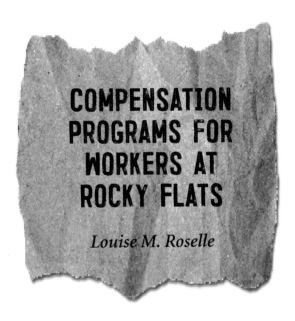

COMPENSATION PROGRAMS FOR WORKERS AT ROCKY FLATS

Louise M. Roselle

Introduction

Judy Padilla worked at Rocky Flats for twenty-two years beginning in November 1983. For the first six years she worked in the foundry, melting weapons-grade plutonium. She was diagnosed with breast cancer, a cancer which is known to be radiogenic,[1] fifteen years after she began working at Rocky Flats. After treatment and recovery, she returned to Rocky Flats where she worked for another seven years.

Charles Padilla, Judy's deceased husband, began working at Rocky Flats in 1986 as a chemical operator. He was diagnosed with bladder, kidney, and liver cancer.

Charles Saunders,[2] who was known as Cotton, worked at Rocky Flats for sixteen years from 1978 through 1993. He developed asbestosis, beryllium disease, and thyroid cancer.

These are but a few of the stories of Rocky Flats' workers. These individuals, each of whom worked at a plant located 1,500 miles from Washington, DC, had their lives profoundly impacted by decisions made by the Atomic Energy Commission (AEC),[3] the US Congress, and by various presidents.

Beginning on the day the plant opened in 1952, Rocky Flats workers were exposed to radioactive and other hazardous chemicals. Radiation is not detectable by human senses – it cannot be tasted, smelled, seen, or felt. Rocky Flats operations "routinely involve[d] handling radioactive, hazardous and/or toxic material."[4] Even though the plant was owned by the federal government, Colorado's workers' compensation program was supposed to provide remuneration to injured Rocky Flats workers. However, when workers at the facility became ill, as many of them did, they were unable to collect workers' compensation[5] or other benefits needed to support themselves and their families. While this unquestionably was a failure of the Colorado workers' compensation system, the federal government played a significant part in the denial of coverage by submitting "evidence" that the workers' exposures were too low to have caused the illness. For decades workers complained about the federal government ignoring them and their health concerns.

In 1990, the Rocky Flats workers sought relief in federal court, but their claims were dismissed for the ironic reason that their claims were compensable not through the court system but rather through the Colorado workers' compensation system. Finally, fifty years after Rocky Flats opened, workers began receiving benefits[6] from the Energy Employees Occupational Illness Compensation Program Act (EEIOCPA),[7] which Congress enacted in 2000 to compensate the workers and their families. As of December 31, 2019, this federal program[8] has paid more than $669 million dollars in benefits to Rocky Flats workers,[9] but many of the claims have been denied. Many of the workers died before they received benefits, and through no fault of their own, many workers have been unable to prove that exposures at Rocky Flats caused or contributed to their illnesses. This has been the outcome, despite the fact that these workers suffered illnesses and shortened lives due to the exposures they received at Rocky Flats.

Workplace Exposures

"The primary mission of Rocky Flats was the processing and machining of plutonium and other materials into detonators, also called 'triggers' for nuclear weapons."[10] Production activities at the facility involved fabrication of parts from plutonium, uranium, and other materials. In addition to plutonium, Rocky Flats used "more than 8,000 chemicals during the production… and cleanup from the contamination took more than a decade."[11]

Sixteen thousand people worked at Rocky Flats between 1952 when production began at the plant and 1989 when it ended.[12] From the beginning, the AEC somewhat half-heartedly attempted to address worker safety while keeping its primary attention focused on production. The monitoring of workers had two purposes: (1) to protect the workers from illness and (2) to protect management from claims that the workers were ill due to workplace exposures. The AEC promulgated regulations on allowable limits of exposure to radiation and monitoring of workers, including urinalysis[13] and dosimeter badges.[14] Rocky Flats had a safety and health division that included a medical department where workers received annual physical examinations and treatment for workplace injuries. The plant also had industrial hygienists who monitored the air in the plants. The workers relied on the employer to monitor their exposures and to keep them safe.

The monitoring data could be used to see if a worker was exposed to more radiation than the regulatory limits. If a worker was overexposed, he/she could move to a different job to avoid further exposure. The records also could be used to calculate a lifetime dose[15] for a worker. Further, these records were used by management in defense of workers' compensation claims – when a claim was filed, management could submit a record showing that the worker's exposures were too low to have caused his/her illness. For many reasons, several of which are discussed below, these standards and programs were woefully inadequate and did not protect the workers from illness. They were misused to shield the government from having to pay compensation.

Health and Safety Problems at Rocky Flats

There were many reasons for the inadequacies in the health and safety program at Rocky Flats, one of which was that the AEC was responsible for both production and safety. In 1981, the Government Accounting Office (GAO)[16] noted,

In lieu of OSHA[17] oversight of non-radiological and radiological workplace conditions, DOE must ensure that safe and healthful working conditions exist and are maintained at DOE's contractor-operated nuclear facilities. This role places DOE in the awkward position of both operating and regulating its facilities.[18]

Another reason for worker exposures was that the AEC did not promulgate or enforce strict standards for minimizing any exposure to radiation. During the 1950s, the AEC took the position that workers could be exposed to a certain amount of radiation – that a de minimis dose of radiation would produce effects that were "so small that they wouldn't affect mortality and morbidity statistics for the industry as a whole."[19] In the early 1960s, the AEC "stopped relying on a threshold theory and went to a no-threshold theory."[20] The AEC recognized that "almost all of the cancers that are seen in humans will occur more frequently in an irradiated population."[21] However, the AEC continued to have regulations that provided that a worker could be exposed to 5 rem per year of radiation. The AEC's nod to the no-threshold theory was to adopt the As Low As Reasonably Achievable (ALARA) principle, which provided that the plant should try to keep exposures as low as reasonably achievable. In 1988, more than two decades later, GAO noted that Technical Safety Appraisals conducted by the Department of Energy (DOE), successor to the AEC, found that there was "a lack of understanding by plant personnel regarding DOE's 'As Low As Reasonably Achievable' (ALARA) program."[22]

According to a September 9, 1988, internal appraisal, plant personnel, including those who monitor radiation, have a limited understanding of how to apply an ALARA program in their particular building. Few people could describe the radiation exposure goals set for their buildings; radiation areas were not posted consistently (some not at all); and floor supervisors were not familiar with radiation levels encountered during specific tasks.[23]

Another problem resulting in radiation exposure was that situations causing contamination were not immediately corrected. At Rocky Flats there were glove boxes, which are sealed boxes in which workers, using gloves attached to and passing through openings in the box, could handle radioactive materials from the outside. However, these glove boxes could leak and the work area would become contaminated with radioactivity in excess of allowable standards. GAO noted one instance in which an employee reported that a filter was improperly installed on a glovebox and that the condition "existed for 3 days... because the supervisor did not want to disrupt production to correct the problem."[24] In another instance GAO found that "workers performing certain glove box operations were routinely exposed to air contaminated with radioactivity in excess of allowable standards."[25]

Another issue was that neither management nor workers gave adequate attention to safety issues. DOE reports "suggest a lack of management attention toward safety issues."[26] Issues raised by DOE were not resolved for years.[27] Workers did not always give adequate attention to radiological protection, either. For example, DOE noted that "workers have been observed handling contaminated items without surgical gloves, not surveying themselves for contamination and improperly wearing dosimeters (badges used to measure exposure to radiation)."[28]

On October 7, 1988, DOE took the unusual action of ordering the shutdown of activities in one building (Building 771) because of concerns over health and safety:

> Among the staff's concerns were the frequent need for respirators in the work areas, a general lack of cleanliness and good housekeeping practices, inadequate air sampling to monitor the radiation levels, and a weak health physics program for the building.[29]

The contractors and the DOE for decades not only denied any health and safety problems at Rocky Flats, they actually boasted of their fine safety record. This contributed to complacency about contamination among both management and workers. For example, in 1956, Dow Chemical was honored by the National Safety Council for completing more than 3 million hours of work without a disabling injury.[30] In 1974, Rocky Flats employees received cash rewards equivalent to 6.5 percent of their 1973 base pay "in recognition of superior performance in safety, environmental control, production and energy use reduction."[31] In 1981,

"DOE release[d] its health study that demonstrate[d] lower cancer rates in male Rocky Flats employees than in a national control group."[32] In 1985, "Employees celebrate[d] as they surpass[ed] a 22-year record for continuous safe work hours under the SENTRY[33] Safety Program when they rake[d] in 25.000.000 continuous safe hours."[34] During the 1950s there were even dinner-dance events to recognize safe performance at the plant.[35]

One of the methods DOE used to compensate its contractors was an award fee. If the performance of the contract was good, the contractor could receive an award. Between 1986 and 1988, despite many GAO and DOE reports condemning the health and safety program at Rocky Flats, DOE gave the Rocky Flats contractor, Rockwell, an extra $26.8 million in award fees.[36] This was yet another indication that DOE was satisfied with Rockwell's performance at the plant.

The federal government was aware of the health and safety problems at Rocky Flats, as well as other plants. GAO did numerous investigations of the weapons plants' health and safety issues. In 1994, after production at Rocky Flats ceased, GAO[37] testified:

> Workers within DOE's industrial complex face hazards from being exposed to radiation and toxic chemicals, cleaning up the complex, and repairing and maintaining aging facilities. Historically, the overemphasis on weapons production, along with complacency about workers' safety, has meant that DOE management has given limited attention to the potentially adverse health effects of working at DOE sites. Beginning in the early 1980s, we have repeatedly reported on problems with DOE's oversight of health and safety issues within the complex. In addition, DOE's own technical safety appraisals, implemented in 1985, have identified the extent of the Department's health and safety problems....
>
> Inadequate radiological protection programs and procedures were a major deficiency throughout DOE.... For example, a 1988 appraisal at the Rocky Flats plant in Colorado found inadequate capabilities for monitoring and sampling air to detect radiation releases.

For every worker at the plant, there should have been sufficient records from which the dose of radiation that the worker received from his/her employment could be determined. Sadly, this is not the case, whether at Rocky Flats or elsewhere in the government's nuclear weapons complex.

Workers' Compensation Program

At Rocky Flats, the two contractors during the production years, Dow and Rockwell, had insurance policies that required coverage for workers' compensation claims. These policies complied with Colorado workers' compensation requirements.[38] If a worker was injured on the job, such as a broken leg, then he/she received Colorado workers' compensation. However, if a worker became ill due to repeated exposure to radiation or other hazardous chemicals during his/her employment (occupational illness), generally workers' compensation would not allow the claim. President Bill Clinton recognized that

> because of the long latency periods, the uniqueness of the hazards to which they were exposed, and inadequate exposure data, many of these individuals have been unable to obtain State workers' compensation benefits. This problem has been exacerbated by the past policy of the Department of Energy (DOE) and its predecessors of encouraging and assisting DOE contractors in opposing the claims of workers who sought those benefits.[39]

Congress recognized that

> the policy of the [DOE] [w]as… to litigate occupation illness claims, which has deterred workers from filing workers' compensation claims and has imposed major financial burdens on such employees who have sought compensation. Contractors of the [DOE] have been held harmless and the employees have been denied workers' compensation coverage for occupational disease.[40]

There were a few exceptions where the worker or his/her family found a lawyer who was willing and able to litigate the claim; for example, the family of a worker who died of brain cancer at the age of thirty-one after working at Rocky Flats for ten years was awarded workers' compensation.[41]

Federal Litigation

In 1990, the Building & Construction Trades Department at Rocky Flats and others filed a lawsuit in federal court alleging that Rockwell and Dow, the operators at the plant, exposed workers to both radioactive and non-radioactive hazardous substances and concealed or misrepresented the risk to the workers. The plaintiffs sought a medical monitoring program and a surveillance fund and other damages arising out of defendants' alleged negligence, absolute or strict liability, misrepresentation and concealment, and outrageous conduct. The District Court dismissed the lawsuit holding that the claims are barred by the exclusivity provisions of the Colorado Workers' Compensation Act (Colo. Rev. Stat. §§8-42-102), and the Tenth Circuit Court of Appeals affirmed the dismissal.

Federal Legislation

For many years, workers, unions, lawyers, and other advocates fought to obtain compensation for the workers who developed cancer and other diseases while working at nuclear weapons facilities. The workers became known as the Cold War Patriots, "A community of former nuclear and uranium workers who helped keep America free during the Manhattan Project through the Cold War to present day by building the nation's nuclear stockpile."[42] Finally, on October 30, 2000, Congress enacted EEIOC-PA, stating that "it is the sense of Congress that (1) a program should be established to provide compensation to covered employees; (2) a fund for payment of such compensation should be established on the books of the Treasury; (3) payments from the fund should be made only" after proper procedures were followed.[43] Congress found that nuclear weapons production and testing have involved unique dangers... and recurring exposures to radioactive substances and beryllium... even in small amounts, can cause medical harm. Since the inception of the nuclear weapons program and for several decades afterwards, a large number of nuclear weapons workers at sites of the [DOE]... were put at risk without their knowledge and consent for reasons that, documents reveal, were driven by fears of adverse publicity, liability, and employee demands for hazardous duty pay. Many previously secret records have documented unmonitored exposures to radiation and beryllium and continuing problems at these sites..., at which the [DOE] and its predecessor agencies have been, since World War II, self-regulating with respect to nuclear safety and occupational safety and health. No other hazardous Federal activity has been permitted to be carried out under such sweeping powers of self-regulation."[44]

Congress further found that

over the past 20 years, more than two dozen scientific findings have emerged that indicate that certain of [the] employees are experiencing increased risks of dying from cancer and non-malignant diseases. Several of these studies have also established a correlation between excess diseases and exposure to radiation and beryllium. While linking exposure to occupational hazards with the development of occupational disease is sometimes difficult, scientific evidence supports the conclusion that occupational exposure to dust particles or vapor of beryllium can cause beryllium sensitivity and chronic beryllium disease. Furthermore, studies indicate tha[t] 98% of radiation-induced cancers within the nuclear weapons complex have occurred at dose levels below existing maximum safe thresholds.[45]

On December 7, 2000, President Clinton recognized the contributions that these workers made to the nation at the expense of their health when he signed Executive Order 13179:

> Since World War II, hundreds of thousands of men and women have served their Nation in building its nuclear defense. In the course of their work, they overcame previously unimagined scientific and technical challenges. Thousands of these courageous Americans, however, paid a high price for their service, developing disabling or fatal illnesses as a result of exposure to beryllium, ionizing radiation, and other hazards unique to nuclear weapons production and testing. Too often, these workers were neither adequately protected from, nor informed of, the occupational hazards to which they were exposed."[46]

EEIOCPA consists of two distinct compensation programs: (1) Part B provides compensation of $150,000 and payment of medical expenses from the date a claim is filed for a worker[47] who develops a radiogenic cancer or chronic beryllium disease; and (2) Part E provides compensation for a worker[48] up to $250,000 for wage loss and impairment for an illness caused by exposure to toxic substances including radiation, chemical solvents, acids and metals.[49] In addition, under Part E the worker can recover medical expenses from the date a claim is filed. A worker can recover under both Parts B and E.

Rocky Flats Workers' Fight for EEIOCPA Benefits

The passage of the legislation was just the beginning of yet another fight for the workers before they would get benefits. When the legislation was passed, workers believed that the government was finally recognizing its commitment to keeping the nation safe during the Cold War and that they would be compensated. Unfortunately, for the majority of the workers, the legislation had not provided any compensation. The primary reason for this is that the burden of proof was on the worker to show that his/her workplace exposure was as likely as not to have caused the disease. This placed an enormous burden on the worker who had little or no ability to calculate his/her dose or prove that the illness was caused by workplace exposure.

Congress could have chosen different methodologies for compensation. For example, it could have provided that the government, not the worker, had the burden of proving that the workplace exposure was as likely as not to have caused the disease. Alternatively, the legislation could have provided compensation based on disease without requiring any proof of dose.

The legislation provided that the National Institute for Occupational Safety and Health (NIOSH) had the responsibility to re-create doses for every worker who made a claim. This process has been both time consuming and expensive. When NIOSH tried to re-create doses, there were many problems with the available data. As an example, in 2000, NIOSH reported on the information needed for the evaluation of health effects due to occupational exposures for DOE site remediation workers.[50,51] NIOSH found

> the current environment of decentralized management and increased subcontracting at DOE sites has led to fragmented and inconsistent data collection and maintenance. In this environment, rosters of remediation workers are rarely maintained and are difficult to compile from other site data. In addition, the availability of exposure data varies across disciplines. Radiation monitoring practices are standardized throughout the complex, leading to reasonably comprehensive exposure data. In contrast, industrial hygiene monitoring and data collection requirements are not codified or standardized, so non-radiologic exposure data tend to be incomplete.

Another problem with Rocky Flats' monitoring data is related to neutron dose calculations originally performed by the plant in the 1950s and 1960s. A *Report of Epidemiologic Analyses Performed for Rocky Flats Production Workers* by the Department of Preventive Medicine and Biometrics, University of Colorado Health Sciences Center and the Colorado Department of Public Health and Environment found that data for doses from external exposures to neutrons were incorrectly estimated for some years."[52]

Congress had recognized that there could be limited situations where doses could not be accurately calculated, and the legislation provided for the designation of Special Exposure Cohorts (SEC).[53] This unique category of employees would be compensated without having to go through the dose reconstruction process. The president of the United States, who delegated the responsibility to the secretary of health and human services, is authorized to add classes of employees to the cohort if the dose reconstruction cannot be completed because there is insufficient data to determine doses with sufficient accuracy. Once a designation is made, the worker would receive benefits if he/she could establish that he/she had worked in the facility for at least 250 days, and he/she had at least one of twenty-two specified cancers[54] without having to show that his cancer was as likely caused by workplace exposure as not.

In 2007, an SEC was approved for Rocky Flats workers who were monitored or should have been monitored for neutron exposures from April 1, 1952, through December 31, 1966.[55] This was a limited SEC that did not help most workers. The Rocky Flats workers submitted another SEC petition, and in 2014, an SEC was approved for

> all employees of the DOE, its predecessor agencies, and their contractors and subcontractors who worked at the Rocky Flats Plant in Golden, Colorado from April 1, 1952, through December 31, 1983, for a number of work days aggregating at least 250 work days, occurring either solely under the employment or in combination with work days within the parameters established for one or more other classes of employees included in the Special Exposure Cohort.[56]

The SEC extension was based on the inability to estimate dose with sufficient accuracy for exposures to thorium, uranium-233, and neptunium.[57] Without the SEC, workers were being denied awards because proving that the dose was high enough to cause cancer is almost impossible.

Current Status of Compensation Pursuant
to Federal Legislation

The claims for workers who had been denied benefits before the SEC was approved and then qualified for compensation under the 2014 SEC were reopened and many of those claims have now been paid. In order for workers to be compensated for cancer under Part B, it is very important that the worker be included in the SEC.

Take, for instance, Charles Saunders. He worked at Rocky Flats from 1978 through 1993 as a machinist, mechanic, and maintenance worker. He was approved for Part E benefits for asbestosis shortly after Part E was enacted. However, with regard to Part B benefits for thyroid cancer, for which he first applied in July 2001, he did not receive anything until the special exposure cohort was approved in 2014. He was receiving benefits under both Part B and Part E, but before he died he elected a lump sum settlement.[58]

Judy Padilla had a different experience. She applied for Part B benefits for her breast cancer in 2001. She was denied benefits twice because NIOSH determined that her dose was too low. When the SEC was approved, she still did not receive benefits because she began working at Rocky Flats in November 2003, so she did not have the requisite 250 days of employment during the SEC period. As of today, Judy has not received any compensation for her cancer.[59]

Charles Padilla was not in the SEC because he did not begin his employment at Rocky Flats until 1986. He was denied Part B benefits because the dose reconstruction calculation found that he did not have a 50 percent probability of causation. However, he did receive Part E benefits because he was exposed to carcinogenic chemicals. He was awarded benefits one week before he died.[60]

Claims for workers who are part of the SEC (who worked at the plant before 1984) and workers who are not part of the SEC are still being denied. There are many reasons why Rocky Flats workers are still being denied benefits even after the SEC was approved in 2014.

A major problem for workers who were at the plant before 1984 is that the SEC only covers twenty-two cancers. If the worker has a cancer or other health problem that is not specifically enumerated, such as prostate cancer, then he must prove that it is as likely as not that his cancer was due to employment at Rocky Flats. Prostate cancer can be caused by radiation, but it requires a large dose. So, a Rocky Flats worker with prostate cancer must prove a very high dose to be awarded compensation and, through no fault of his own, he is unlikely to be able to marshal such evidence. Throughout the country, 4,975 male genitalia claims were made through September 23, 2015 of which 165 were approved.[61] For the balance of 4,810 claims, the dose reconstruction determined that the 50 percent probability of causation was not met. Similarly, with breast cancer, there were 1,120 claims made and only 17 were approved.[62]

The problem of proving causation for cancer also applies to the post-1983 workers. Post-1983 workers must prove that every cancer was caused by Rocky Flats' exposure, even if the cancer is on the list of twenty-two cancers. The plant continued operating until 1994 and then remediation workers were inside the plant for another decade. Thus, there is a time span of twenty years for which there is no SEC, which means that a worker during that period still has to prove that it is as likely as not that his/her cancer was caused by workplace exposure.

It is very difficult for an individual worker who has no access to his/her monitoring data to meet that burden. When a dose reconstruction is necessary the case is referred to NIOSH. As of January 26, 2020, 52,640 claims for all facilities, including Rocky Flats, have been referred to NIOSH for dose reconstruction; 23 percent of these claims have been approved for compensation.[63]

There are also other problems that apply to both pre- and post-1983 workers. In some instances it is difficult to prove where the worker worked at Rocky Flats. Rocky Flats was a large facility with hundreds of buildings. For example, welders and pipefitters were all over the plant – in and out of every building.

Sometimes, the worker has trouble proving that he/she worked at the plant for at least 250 days. EEIOCPA provides benefits for the workers (and their families) who worked at the plant from the time the plant opened in the early 1950s, and some of these workers died decades ago. It is the workers' heirs who are trying to prove their entitlement to benefits, and that is often very difficult because there is no one to ask about their parent's or grandparent's work at Rocky Flats. Further, there was a cloak of secrecy at the nuclear weapons facilities, including Rocky Flats, which meant that workers were not permitted to talk about their work to anyone, and families knew nothing about the work that was done at Rocky Flats.

This compensation program should be reconfigured to help workers get compensated. Instead, the program is burdened with paperwork and procedures that are daunting. The dose reconstructions are "extremely difficult, slow and arduous for the worker and the agency. The process drags out while workers... suffer and wait for compensation they need – in some cases, to help them pay for cancer treatments or care for other deadly illnesses."[64] In addition to the dose reconstruction, medical and employment records must be collected, if they are available. If records, such as pathology reports that diagnosed cancer, are no longer available, then affidavits can be completed.

In 2009, Colorado Senator Mark Udall (for himself and Senator Michael Bennet) introduced a bill to amend EEIOCPA "to expand the category of individuals eligible for compensation, to improve the procedures for providing compensation, and to improve transparency, and for other purposes."[65] The bill was referred to the Committee on Health, Education, Labor and Pensions and no further action occurred.

Conclusion

Men and women were exposed to radioactive and hazardous materials at Rocky Flats while they produced nuclear weapons that the federal government deemed necessary for the nation's security. For more than fifty years these workers were not compensated when they developed cancers and other workplace illnesses. Their families had the burden of paying medical expenses and other bills when the workers were unable to work. In instances too numerous to count, these workers sacrificed their lives for their country. Many workers died before any compensation was paid. Even now, twenty years after EEIOCPA became law, fewer than half of the claims submitted have been approved. More than 317,000 claims have been made by workers or their families for all the eligible facilities in the country, and only 123,671 claims had been paid as of January 26, 2020.[66] It is time that the program be simplified and that the workers whose claims have been denied be compensated. Judy Padilla worked at Rocky Flats for twenty-two years and developed breast cancer, a known radiogenic cancer. The fact that she has received no compensation is evidence that the EEIOCPA is flawed and needs to be retailored.

Endnotes

1. *Radiogenic* means it is produced by radiation.

2. Mr. Saunders died in July 2019.

3. From 1953 until 1975, the Atomic Energy Commission was the government agency responsible for production at Rocky Flats. The operations were conducted by Dow Chemical Company pursuant to written contract. Rockwell International replaced Dow Chemical Company as the plant operator in 1975. The same year the Energy Research and Development Administration (ERDA) became the government organization responsible for production. In 1977 ERDA was replaced by the Department of Energy (DOE).

4. GAO Report, *Nuclear Health and Safety Summary of Major Problems at DOE's Rocky Flats Plant*, GAO/RCED-89-53BR, 9.

5. Workers' compensation is a no-fault insurance program that provides compensation to a worker who is injured on the job regardless of what caused the injury. However, in many states workers' compensation is the sole compensation that a worker can recover from his/her employer.

6. The first Rocky Flats worker received compensation on October 18, 2001. Cumulative EEIOCPA Compensation Paid – Rocky Flats Plant dated March 31, 2016, from EEIOCPA website.

7. The Energy Employees Occupational Illness Compensation Program Act of 2000, 42 U.S.C. §7384 et. seq. (EEIOCPA) was enacted in October 2000.

8. Statistical data from the Department of Labor website is updated weekly on Mondays. DOL.gov.owcp.DEEOIC.

9. Cumulative EEIOICPA Compensation and Medical Paid-Rocky Flats Plant data as of Dec. 3, 2019, from DOL.gov.owcp.DEEOIC.

10. *Rocky Flats History*, Patricia Buffer, July 2003, 3. www.doe.gov Rocky Flats Site History Office of Legacy Management–Department of Energy.

11. Letter to The Honorable Thomas Perez, Secretary, US Department of Labor, dated January 16, 2014, signed by US Representative Ed Perlmutter, US Senator Mark Udall, US Senator Michael Bennet, and US Representative Jared Polis.

12. Leroy Moore, Rocky Flats Nuclear Guardianship, Series 4: Rocky Flats Legacy: Nuclear Workers' Stories. Leroymoore.wordpress.com.

13. Even though urinalyses were done, internal doses were not calculated until 1989.

14. Each worker wore a badge while at Rocky Flats that was designed to measure the ionizing radiation that the worker received.

15. *Dose* is the quantity of radiation the worker received.

16. The Government Accounting Office (GAO) is the investigative arm of Congress charged with examining matters relating to receipt and payment of public funds.

17. OSHA is the Occupational Safety and Health Administration, which was established in 1970 to protect workers.

18. GAO Report, *Better Oversight Needed for Safety and Health Activities at DOE's Nuclear Facilities*, EMD-81-108 (Aug. 4, 1981), 12.

19. Oral History of Merril Eisenbud. DOE Openness.Human Radiation Experiments: Roadmap to the Project DOE/EH-0456. Oral history of Merril Eisenbud conducted Jan. 26, 1995. US DOE Office of Human Radiation Experiments, May 1995.

20. Id.

21. Id.

22. GAO Report, *Nuclear Health and Safety Summary of Major Problems at DOE's Rocky Flats Plant*, GAO/RCED-89-53BR, 2.

23. Id., 13.

24. GAO Report, *Better Oversight Needed for Safety and Health Activities at DOE's Nuclear Facilities*, EMD-81-108 (Aug. 4, 1981), 7.

25. Id., 7–8.

26. GAO Report, *Nuclear Health and Safety Summary of Major Problems at DOE's Rocky Flats Plant*, GAO/RCED-89-53BR, p. 11.

27. Id., 11.

28. Id., 11.

29. Id., 5.

30. *Rocky Flats History* by Patricia Buffer, July 2003.

31. Id., 13.

32. Id., 14.

33. Altec SENTRY programs are computer-aided safety programs.

34. *Rocky Flats History* by Patricia Buffer, July 2003.

35. Id., 9.

36. GAO Report, *Nuclear Health and Safety Increased Rating Results in Award Fee to Rocky Flats Contractor*, GAO/RCED-92-162, 3.

37. GAO testimony before the Subcommittee on Oversight and Investigations, Committee on Energy and Commerce, House of Representatives, *Protecting Department of Energy Workers' Health and Safety*, GAO/T-RCED-94-143, 2.

38. Building & Construction Trades Dep't v. Rockwell Int'l Corp., 756 F. Supp. 492, 496 (U.S.D.C. Colo., 1990).

39. Executive Order 13179, signed by President Bill Clinton on Dec. 7, 2000, Section 1.

40. 42 U.S.C. §7384 – Findings; Sense of Congress.

41. Dow Chemical Co. v. Gabel, 746 P.2d 1357 (Colo. App. 1987).

42. Cold War Patriots website, Aug. 2, 2016. Coldwarpatriots.org.

43. 42 U.S.C. §7384 Findings; Sense of Congress.

44. Id.

45. Id.

46. Executive Order 13179, signed by President Bill Clinton on Dec. 7, 2000, Section 1.

47. If a worker is deceased, then his/her spouse, children, parents, and grandparents are eligible for the payment under Part B.

48. If a worker is deceased, then his/her spouse and, in limited circumstances, his children may be eligible for Part E benefits.

49. Part E was enacted in 2005 and replaced Part D. Part D allowed DOE to help its contractor employees file state workers' compensation claims for illnesses determined by a panel of physicians to be caused by exposure to toxic substances in the course of employment at an energy facility.

50. Remediation workers are workers involved in the cleanup of the facilities. These are but one group of workers at the weapons' facilities.

51. NIOSH Evaluation of Data for DOE Site Remediation Workers, Sharon Silver et. al., Dec. 2000, Abstract, iv. CDC-NIOSH Occupational Energy Research Program-Rocky Flats…cdc.gov.

52. *Report of Epidemiologic Analyses Performed for Rocky Flats Production Workers Employed Between 1952-1989*, March 3, 2003 by Ruttenber, et al. HM_sf-rocky flats-NIOSH rpt.pdf

53. 42 C.F.R. Part 83.

54. The twenty-two cancers are bone, renal, leukemia (other than chronic lymphocytic leukemia), lung, multiple myeloma, lymphoma (other than Hodgkins' disease), bile duct, brain, breast (male), breast (female), colon, esophagus, gall bladder, liver (except if cirrhosis or hepatitis B is indicated), ovary, pancreas, pharynx, salivary gland, small intestine, stomach, thyroid, and urinary bladder. For many cancers there are minimum latency periods after first exposure.

55. NIOSH home webpage for NIOSH Radiation Dose Reconstruction Program for Rocky Flats Plant. Petition 30 .DOL.gov.owcp.DEEOIC. special exposure cohort employees.

56. Id. Petition 192.

57. Rocky Flats Plant SEC Petition 192, David Kotelchuck, PhD, MPH, RF Working Group, chairperson, Nov. 19, 2015.

58. Telephone interview by Louise Roselle on Aug. 8, 2016, with Charles Saunders. Telephone interview with Mrs. Saunders on January 31, 2020.

59. Telephone interview by Louise Roselle on Aug. 11, 2016, with Judy Padilla.

60. Telephone interview by Louise Roselle on Aug. 11, 2016, with Judy Padilla.

61. Centers for Disease Control Chart Compensation Results by NIOSH-IREP Cancer Model Based on Claims with Dr. Approved and Submitted to DOL through September 23, 2015 (37,155 claims). This chart does not include claims submitted through the SEC process.

62. Id.

63. DOL.gov.owcp.DEEOIC.

64. March 31, 2009, Congressional Record – Senate S4082 statement by Senator Mark Udall.

65. Id., S4081.

66. DOL.gov.owcp.DEEOIC.

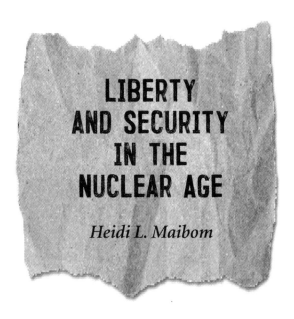

LIBERTY AND SECURITY IN THE NUCLEAR AGE

Heidi L. Maibom

The conjunction of an immense military establishment and a large arms industry is new in the American experience. The total influence – economic, political, even spiritual – is felt in every city, every state house, every office of the federal government. We recognize the imperative need for this development. Yet we must not fail to comprehend its grave implications. Our toil, resources and livelihood are all involved; so is the very structure of our society.

In the councils of government, we must guard against the acquisition of unwarranted influence, whether sought or unsought, by the military-industrial complex. The potential for the disastrous rise of misplaced power exists and will persist.

We must never let the weight of this combination endanger our liberties or democratic processes. We should take nothing for granted. Only an alert and knowledgeable citizenry can compel the proper meshing of the huge industrial and military machinery of defense with our peaceful methods and goals, so that security and liberty may prosper together.

– Dwight Eisenhower, January 17, 1961

The unleashed power of the atom has changed everything save our modes of thinking, and we thus drift toward unparalleled catastrophes.

– Albert Einstein (as quoted in Lapp 1964)

Eisenhower warned that the military-industrial complex poses a threat to liberty and democracy under the guise of security. This was nowhere more evident than in the nuclear arms race during the Cold War. During this time, plutonium and uranium were mined, refined, transported, made into nuclear triggers, and stored in silos at sites all over the United States. As a result, hundreds of thousands of tons of nuclear waste were produced. Nuclear materials are among the most toxic on earth, and are known to cause a range of life-threatening diseases. Despite this fact, workers and people living close to nuclear weapons production sites have been systematically misinformed and deceived about the risk of contamination to which they have been exposed. Tens of thousands of workers suffer, or have died, from radiation-related illnesses. A major health study is now under way in the hopes of establishing a connection between cancers in the larger Metro Denver area and radiation exposure from the former Rocky Flats Nuclear Weapons Plant.

This chapter argues that the government deception surrounding the nuclear weapons program in the United States is an unjustified violation of liberty. The evidence points to the fact that the US government deceived its citizens with regards to the location of plants, and the risks both to workers involved in nuclear weapons and to people living in areas adjacent to such production. I first discuss the concept of liberty and its centrality to the US Constitution. I then address the demands of national security, specifically on the issue of weapons production. Last, I consider the clash of the values of liberty and security in the case of Rocky Flats.

Liberty

The Declaration of Independence states:

> We hold these truths to be self-evident, that all men are
> created equal, that they are endowed by their Creator with

certain unalienable Rights, that among these are Life, Liberty and the pursuit of Happiness. – That to secure these rights, Governments are instituted among Men, deriving their just powers from the consent of the governed,–That whenever any form of Government becomes destructive of these ends, it is the Right of the People to alter or to abolish it, and to institute new Government, laying its foundation on such principles and organizing its powers in such form, as to them shall seem most likely to effect their Safety and Happiness.[1]

In these passages are contained the ideals of self-governance, liberalism, and individual freedom. A basic tenet of liberal democracies is that the government will not sanction one particular way of life as the good life. Instead, it safeguards its citizens' freedom to choose their own good and to live according to it, as long as they do not harm others. In this way, life, liberty, and the pursuit of happiness operate together. I shall focus on liberty, but with the proviso that this idea is closely associated with the other two. John Stuart Mill said: "The only freedom which deserves the name, is that of pursuing our own good in our own way" (Mill 1859/1963, vol. 18, 226). We may be denied this freedom by brute force or unjust laws. Freedom of religion was a particular concern for the Founding Fathers. But liberty covers many things, including liberty to pursue relationships with consenting partners, freedom of thought, freedom of speech, and so on. The most obvious way in which someone can exercise her liberty is by exploring different ideas about living. In "On Liberty," Mill says so-called experiments in living are only possible if there is free exchange of ideas. In other words, we cannot truly pursue our freedom to live as we please – to seek our own good in our own way – without awareness of what the options are. Liberty, therefore, is endangered by restricting or controlling the information people have available. Totalitarian regimes keep tight control over the media, in part to restrict the flow of ideas, some of which are invariably at odds with the governing ethos.

One of the longest sections of "On Liberty" discusses the importance of free speech, which makes clear the intimate connection between freedom to live as one chooses and the free exchange of ideas. True liberty requires access to information. I must know what living in a certain way implies, and once I know it, I must know how I go about living the way I want. Suppose I decide to work as a coal miner like my father before me. I am aware that some people die of black lung disease, but I am told by the company that they comply with the Mine Safety and Health Administration's safety standards. I am, however, not aware of the widespread fraud in sampling. What sense does it make to say that I am free to choose my profession when I am deceived about the health risks involved? What could be more important to my decision than knowing the risk of my occupation to my health and longevity?[2]

It may be that nobody is responsible for furnishing us with information about how to achieve what we value. However, governments typically publicize guidelines for healthy eating and drinking, which are meant to help us pursue universal goals, such as health and longevity, and they finance large-scale community studies on the health effects of pollution and other dangers. In the United States, how much the government should be involved in such activities is a contested issue. What is less debated is whether it is permissible for someone, or some organization, to deceive us about how to pursue our good. This is particularly true when it comes to our health and safety. If someone misleads us as to the safety of an activity we engage in, how can we choose to do so freely? In many cases, we would not have done as we did, had we known the truth. Take the Ford Pinto scandal in the 1970s. Ford knew that if rear-ended, the car's fuel filler might separate and puncture the fuel tank, spraying fuel into the passenger compartment and igniting. This happened in most safety tests before full production began. A memo revealed that the company decided it was cheaper to pay the estimated resulting lawsuit than it was to make the car safe. Between 500 and 900 people died as a result, with many more being victims of severe burns (Dowie 1977). Who would have bought a Ford Pinto over one of its competitors, had they known of the danger? Some might. After all, most of us choose to consume drugs, such as aspirin or naproxen, even after reading the dizzying list of sometimes life-threatening potential side effects. We determine that the benefits outweigh the risks, or that the risk is too remote or too small to be concerned about. The point is that we choose whether or not to take the risk. In the case of drugs, we know about the risk of taking them because of government regulation. Safety standards and published lists of risk factors are ways in which government agencies both keep citizens safe and enhance their ability to make informed choices. Conversely, deceiving people about the risk they incur when purchasing a certain product denies people the ability to choose freely. Hence it is often punishable by law.

If we turn from businesses to the government, the protection of people's liberty becomes even more central. Whether or not you believe the government should ensure people's positive liberty, you will most likely agree that the government has a duty to protect free thought, speech, and action on the part of its citizenry. If the government discredits information that it knows to be true, it is complicit in a de facto restriction of the liberty of its citizens. Discrediting information is simply a different way of restricting it. The thought is not that the government is failing by not producing the conditions under which true freedom can be exercised – often called positive liberty – but that it is suppressing, denying, or discrediting information that either it or other individuals or institutions already possess. By doing so, it prevents the spread of information that may be essential to people's ability to make decisions about how to lead their lives. If liberty is an inalienable right, and freedom to choose requires knowledge of what we are a choosing, it is impermissible for a government, particularly one in place precisely for the purpose of securing our liberty, to prevent us from attaining that knowledge. In short, government deception is a threat to liberty.

However, liberty is not the only consideration in politics, nor is it in life generally. Most people marry, although that restricts their freedom significantly. There are many other values against which liberty must be balanced. At the end of his famous essay, "Two Concepts of Liberty," Isaiah Berlin wrote: "The extent of a man's, or a people's, liberty to choose to live as he or they desire must be weighed against the claims of many other values, of which equality, or justice, or happiness, or security, or public order are perhaps the most obvious examples" (Berlin 1969, 30). And so it is not unusual for agencies to not inform the public of risks if the fear is that it would cause panic, which would lead to worse consequences. For the government, as for people generally, values must be balanced against one another. Some argue that in order to safeguard true liberty, people must have available to them certain resources, such as money needed to subsist, access to health care and pension, access to legal aid, and so on. Others would regard such measures as restricting their liberty. Most, however, agree on the paramount importance of national security or defense. If deception is perpetrated in the interests of national defense, it is often thought to be justified. Let us examine this type of justification.

Security

The two World Wars saw large-scale production of weapons. This typically involved substantial risks to workers and people living in the vicinity of the production sites. Apart from the atomic bomb, the most hazardous was the production of explosives and chemical weapons. Handling TNT (Trinitrotoluene), the most common explosive agent used during the World Wars, turns skin yellow, and prolonged exposure causes anemia and abnormal liver function. Moreover, it is probably a carcinogen. Workers handling TNT were typically not informed about the risks involved in doing so. In addition, there were rarely acceptable safety standards in place. At least 400 people died from TNT poisoning in Britain during World War I, mainly women (Braybon and Summerfield 1987). More serious were the effects on chemical weapons workers. Both World Wars saw massive production of toxic gases, including chlorine, phosgene, cyanogen chloride, and, most famously, mustard gas. Although German factories were the safest, as many as one-third of the workers were absent due to poisoning at any one time (Norris 1919). Mustard gas is the most toxic of the weaponized gases; it causes respiratory cancers, skin cancer, leukemia, chronic respiratory diseases, eye diseases, skin abnormalities, sexual dysfunction, and a range of psychological disorders (Pechura and Rall 1993). Because of long-term exposure, workers suffered from chronic poisoning just like exposed soldiers did. Many found it difficult to work after the war due to frequent illnesses and difficulties breathing (Norris 1919; Haber 1986). In the United States, around 60,000 servicemen were used as human subjects to test the effectiveness of such gases without any real knowledge of what was happening to them (during World War II).[3]

The demands of national security are supposed to justify these infractions of people's liberty. But why deception was required is actually not obvious. There are a couple of possibilities. First, we might suppose that the suspicion was that if people knew the true risk involved in their occupation, they would refuse to work. This cannot justify much of the deception. In Britain, women were drafted to support the war effort, and their work included weapons production. Even though they knew the risks, they were not at liberty to refuse. Drafting is always available to any government. Second, one might suppose that secrecy was required for the enemy to remain ignorant of the sources and sites of production. But this justification is also not plausible. It is clear that the location of sites of weapons production should be kept secret as far as possible, but the people who worked in these facilities were obviously aware of where they were. When it came to the nature of what was produced, this could hardly be a secret either. The enemy was surely smart enough to know what went into building weapons of a certain kind. In other words, it is hard to see what the justification for deception of weapons workers would be.

When we look at compensation of workers or soldiers taken ill from chemical weapons in the United States, we see a disconcerting pattern. After the end of the war, when secrecy due to national security was no longer an issue, many were kept in the dark as to what they were exposed to, and how it might have impacted their health.[4] Even after committees were formed and resolutions agreed on for compensation, information was not well disseminated, and claims were regularly denied for spurious reasons. But arguably, people producing weapons are essential to warfare and should receive the same benefits as soldiers do. Compensation is a particular concern in the United States where there is no socialized health care and relatively meager social support of those too sick to work. It is hard not to conclude that ongoing deception about the ill effects of weapons production – when no longer at war – is an attempt to save money, and is not justified by considerations of national security. People have a right to know why they are ill and to seek compensation.

Before moving on, let me touch on the concern about security threatening democracy. Government deception and propaganda may be thought to be justifiable because it is simply a different form of coercion. If we accept that the state can coerce citizens to engage in armed battle against enemies against their will, why not also accept that the state is justified in providing false or misleading information about a foreign government or a certain group of people, if this is in the interest of national security? The problem, however, is that if the true reasons for war are unknown, the government cannot be held accountable by its citizens. Any form of deception on the part of a government undermines the democratic process, since it prevents voters from knowing what they are voting for. It is paramount that voters can hold politicians and government institutions accountable. If the true costs of war are kept secret, citizens are not in a position to make informed choices in elections that follow.

Rocky Flats

Nuclear weapons production is an extremely hazardous activity, as weapons-grade uranium and plutonium are some of the most poisonous materials on earth. In order to produce such weapons, uranium and plutonium must be mined, refined, and transported before they arrive at facilities that produce nuclear triggers. Contamination is likely during any part of this process. Moreover, during the production of nuclear weapons triggers, a great deal of very hazardous waste is produced, which must be stored safely in order to avoid widespread environmental contamination. Because of the longevity of radioactive materials – the half-life of plutonium is 24,100 years – this problem is not going away any time soon. The Rocky Flats Nuclear Weapons facility produced a staggering number of plutonium triggers, and remains the most contaminated site in the country. The story is similar to other types of weapons production we have considered. It is dangerous work, and workers are often not informed of the risks, or are misled about them. People involved in many parts of the process, and therefore all at risk of exposure to radiation, have often been unaware of the true nature of their work. For example, people working in the offices at Rocky Flats did not know they were working next to tons of plutonium waste, much of it unsafely stored (Iversen 2012). Finally, not only were people living in the vicinity of Rocky Flats not informed about what was produced at the plant, they were repeatedly misled by government agencies as to this fact.

Before we move on to consider the justification behind such deception, it is important to remind ourselves of the dangers of nuclear contamination. As LeRoy Moore makes clear in Chapter 8 of this volume, problems were apparent from the beginning. The Atomic Energy Commission sought safety standards that kept workers as safe as possible compatible with the production of nuclear weapons. Having safety standards that are not safe, as such, but only as safe as is compatible with nuclear production, is misleading to say the least. Indeed, workers developed cancers while their exposure to radioactive materials was within the "life-time body burden" limit (Wilkinson 1987, 1999). Already by 1969, people who worked on the Manhattan Project recommended the federal safety limits on low-level exposure to radiation be reduced by 90 percent (Gofman 1990). Despite the federal levels being high for some, we now know that workers were routinely exposed to above-safe levels, mostly without their knowledge. And although records of workers' dose levels were supposed to be kept, such records have been found to be incomplete, missing, or wrong when workers have sought compensation.

In 2000, almost fifty years after work at Rocky Flats commenced, President Bill Clinton created the Energy Employees Occupational Illness Compensation Program Act. This program recognizes that at least twenty-two types of cancer are caused by radiation exposure, including cancer of bone, kidneys, lungs, bile duct, brain, breast (male and female), colon, esophagus, gall bladder, ovary, pancreas, pharynx, salivary glands, small intestine, stomach, thyroid, urinary/bladder, and leukemia. It is far from clear that this list is exhaustive. At the time of writing this chapter, 48,751 people had received compensation for medical complications due to working in the nuclear weapons production industry, and 44,718 have had their claims denied. There is mounting evidence that claims are regularly denied without justification.[5] Moreover, many people have found the process of applying for compensation impossibly cumbersome, or have been unable to retrieve the relevant documents from their employers (to determine dose exposure).

The danger to civilians posed by nuclear weapons production does not merely affect workers. Atmospheric nuclear testing, both global and national, exposed civilians worldwide to radioactive materials. Caesium-137 can be found deposited in the red bone marrow of US citizens in significant doses, and iodine-131 has been found in increased amounts in thyroid glands, and is believed to cause cancer. One group has estimated that the increased risk of thyroid cancer due to global fallout following atmospheric nuclear testing is 10 percent (Simon, Bouville, and Land 2006). Worst affected are people living downwind from nuclear test sites. Senate Resolution 330 acknowledges that people "who, during the Cold War, worked and lived downwind from nuclear testing sites (referred to in this preamble as "downwinders") were adversely affected by the radiation exposure generated by the above ground nuclear weapons testing, and some of the downwinders sickened as a result of the radiation exposure."

Compared to the progress made on compensating nuclear weapons workers, little progress has been made when it comes to people living in the vicinity of current or former nuclear weapons plants. There were two major fires at Rocky Flats, which released masses of radioactive materials into the atmosphere. These materials were carried by the wind over the Denver metro area. As documented by Iversen (2012), there were also frequent releases of contaminated materials along with slow leaks from inadequately stored radioactive waste. Although government agencies have repeatedly denied that there is a problem with contamination from Rocky Flats, it is important to recall that in 1984, Charles Church McKay won a billion dollar lawsuit because of plutonium contamination of his land (*McKay vs. United States*, No. 75-M-1162 [D.Colo.]). Part of the evidence was the high level of plutonium in the bones of his cows in 1974. That land was later sold off to private developers, without having been cleaned up. Several housing estates, such as Candelas, have sprung up on this land. In 2016, *Cook et al. vs. Rockwell* was settled. Rockwell who, together with Dow Chemical, was operating the Rocky Flats plant for the US government, accepted responsibility for contaminating surrounding property with plutonium, and agreed to a $375 million dollar settlement. In the end, the US government, which is to say taxpayers, will pay. The case took twenty-six years to settle, during which time many of the original plaintiffs died.

Long term, the most pressing concern for Americans is the storage of nuclear waste. The money spent on such storage is not sufficient to keep the soil and groundwater safe from contamination. This is clear not only at Rocky Flats, but also at Hanford Nuclear Reservation in Washington, where two-thirds of the country's radioactive waste is stored. The Department of Energy acknowledges that several dozen aging storage tanks are leaking at Hanford, and that around 1 million gallons of radioactive waste have been deposited in the soil (DOE, RPP-14193, p. 7). This is particularly serious, as the Hanford site sits atop the Columbia River watershed, which is crucial for agriculture and provides drinking water for three medium-sized cities. Washington State Department of Ecology claims that there is no immediate danger, but acknowledges that the contamination will "eventually" reach the groundwater if it is not retrieved and treated.[6]

If we sum up what we have found so far, the production of nuclear weapons poses grave risks to workers and people living in the areas of such production. Government agencies have consistently denied or downplayed the danger. Can such deception be justified in terms of the demands of national security?

The counterpoint to the tremendous dangers and ill effects of nuclear weapons production is easy to state. Once nuclear weapons proliferated sufficiently, it is naive to think that one can remain secure without possessing some such weapons. Nor would it now be wise to push for abolishment of nuclear weapons, at least if done unilaterally. It is hard to know with any certainty whether the strategy of developing ever more nuclear weapons prevented a World War III in the twentieth century, or whether other factors were at play. However, the common wisdom is that it was the threat of mutual assured destruction that kept the United States and USSR from engaging in direct warfare. This is not the place to debate whether or not the United States should have engaged in the arms race. Let us assume that it would have been impossible to keep the nation safe without producing such weapons. However, this does not, by itself, answer the question of whether deceiving the people affected by such production was justified.

As we saw above, it is hard to justify deceiving weapons workers about the risk they are undertaking in terms of national security. The people working directly with radioactive materials knew that this was what they were doing. Might they have been deterred from doing so had they known the risk? Perhaps. It is unlikely, though, that everyone would have refused to work producing nuclear weapons if the compensation had been good enough. Indeed, Iversen (2012) repeatedly points out that many people worked at the plant despite misgivings, because the pay and the benefits were so good. Moreover, it is hard to see what justification would be proffered for deceiving workers about the increased doses they were exposed to. Or rather, it is obvious that there were financial incentives to withhold or deny such facts, but national security was hardly the issue.

Because of its highly toxic effects, nuclear production at Rocky Flats posed other problems to citizens not directly involved in the actual production. People living around such production sites were put at risk, without their having any knowledge of the danger they were in. It might be argued that the choice to deceive these people was a matter of national security, so as to keep the location of these sites secret. Not only would the destruction of such sites be catastrophic for national defense, but it would also endanger people living in the area more than the risk of contamination. This might have served as a decent justification at the beginning of the arms race. However, it quickly became clear that a nuclear war would be swift and devastating. Primary targets were not production plants but rather missile silos and big cities. In other words, there was no reason to think that places involved in producing parts of nuclear weapons were at particular risk, or certainly no more so than New York, Chicago, or Los Angeles. This again raises the questions of secrecy, deception, and lies. What justification could government agencies have for deceiving residents in areas of nuclear weapons production sites, if it was not to keep these residents safe?

In the absence of further information, it is hard not to suspect that the reason for secrecy was ultimately monetary. There was little will to cover the true cost of nuclear production: decreased land value; medical care for, and compensation to, sick workers and their families and perhaps even to people affected by off-site contamination; proper monitoring of water and air; and so on. Instead, the deception has ensured that the cost of nuclear weapons production is disproportionately borne by only certain segments of the population. That costs enter into this calculation was made rather clear when the Environmental Protection Agency, Department of Energy, and Colorado Department of Public Health changed the safe limit for soil contamination for the Rocky Flats cleanup. The final decision to clean only the first 3 feet of soil, so that it contains no more than 50 picocuries per gram of soil, leaves the site the most contaminated in the country. This so-called cleaned up site is more contaminated than former test sites and nuclear waste storage sites, such as Hanford. The economic incentive is glaring. Instead of paying $36 billion dollars for the cleanup, the price was lowered to a mere $7 billion. This might seem like a lot, but it pales when compared to the cost of nuclear weapons production proper, which was estimated at $5.48 trillion in 1993 (Wald 1998).

There is no reason to go into further detail. Even if you agree that liberty can – even must – be sacrificed for national security, you might find it harder to accept that it can or ought to be sacrificed for financial expediency. People have a right to choose whether they will work in, or live nearby, heavily contaminated sites, and they cannot do so if the government deceives them about such facts.

What if no one would choose to work producing nuclear weapons if they knew the true risks of doing so? Then other ways must be explored. Conscription is a pretty standard way of coercing citizens to engage in warfare. Advances in artificial intelligence also hold the promise of obviating the need for workers at the most contaminated sites. Realistically, however, good wages, benefits, and pensions are usually sufficient for persuading many people to take the risks that such work imposes. Whichever way we look at it, it is hard to deny that the deception surrounding the operation of nuclear weapons production centers cannot be justified in terms of national security.

Conclusion

Eisenhower was concerned about how people can "compel the proper meshing of the huge industrial and military machinery of defense with our peaceful methods and goals, so that security and liberty may prosper together." They can do so only through democratic means, which require transparency at the level of government. The nuclear weapons program in the United States was carried out in such a way that people most at risk from such production were either kept in the dark or simply deceived about the dangers they were facing. As we have seen, such deception cannot be justified in terms of national security. The more likely cause of the deception was monetary. This raises the larger issue of the communal responsibility to shoulder the burden of national security. Arguably, if there is to be nuclear weapons production, then the cost of it must be borne by the country as a whole. Just as soldiers who risk their lives for their country must be provided with medical care and compensatory payments for inability to work due to injury, so must people exposed to radiation due to nuclear weapons production. If nuclear weapons are deemed to be too expensive, taking into consideration their true costs (including contaminated land and medical costs), then an intelligent discussion must be had of how to proceed. It is simply not justifiable for government agencies to deceive people about matters crucial to their health and well-being in order to save money.

People might choose to live close to, or on, contaminated land because in their minds the benefits outweigh the risks. But they cannot choose to do so freely if relevant information about the level and danger of contamination is discredited by government agencies, agencies that are supposed to be in place to inform and protect. Similarly, individuals may choose to work in nuclear weapons production out of concern for the safety of their country and their fellow citizens. They cannot do so freely, however, if they are misinformed about the true risks of undertaking such labor.

Endnotes

1. See also preamble to the Constitution: "We the People of the United States, in Order to form a more perfect Union, establish Justice, insure domestic Tranquility, provide for the common defence, promote the general Welfare, and secure the Blessings of Liberty to ourselves and our Posterity, do ordain and establish this Constitution for the United States of America."

2. The incidence of black lung has risen explosively in the last five years, including among young workers. NPR, Dec. 15, 2016, on *All Things Considered*, "Advanced Black Lung Cases Surge In Appalachia." Louisville's Courier-Journal led a one-year investigation in which they found widespread cheating in measurement, but unfortunately also that the federal government had known about the cheating for at least thirty years (as reported in the Seattle Times, Apr. 22, 1998, "The Dust They Breathe – Black Lung Killing Nation's Coal Miners," by Gardiner Harris).

3. Secret World War II Chemical Experiments Tested Troops by Race." *Morning Edition*, NPR. June 22, 2015, https://www.npr.org/2015/06/22/415194765/u-s-troops-tested-by-race-in-secret-world-war-ii-chemical-experiments.

4. "The VA's Broken Promise to Thousands of Vets Exposed to Mustard Gas." *Morning Edition*, NPR. June 23, 2015. https://www.npr.org/2015/06/23/416408655/the-vas-broken-promise-to-thousands-of-vets-exposed-to-mustard-gas.

5. The information used to determine whether there is a causal relation between a disease and radiation exposure was created by just one doctor and never peer reviewed. Instead of being evaluated by a qualified doctor, Department of Labor employees review the first stage of the claims. Astounding errors are made. Take the instance of Melissa Web, who developed Parkinson's disease at age thirty-three

after working at the Mound nuclear facility near Dayton, Ohio. In her compensation claim, she listed exposure to carbon disulfide as a possible cause. Her claim was denied because, as the letter stated, although she had been exposed to this chemical, there is no evidence that such exposure causes Parkinson's. However, a bulletin from the Department of Labor's Occupational Safety and Health Administration has carbon disulfide at the top of their list of toxic links to Parkinson's (Frank 2009). In other words, the same governmental department that has drawn a causal connection between Parkinson's and exposure to carbon disulfide denies to claimants that such a connection exists! The problem goes deeper than mere incompetence. A doctor formerly employed by the Department of Labor says he was forced out of his job after he testified to the problems regarding the compensation system. The same doctor provided evidence that the Department of Labor sent letters to doctors examining prospective claimants giving false information meant to reduce the number of successful claims (Frank 2009). Parts of this letter is available at http://s3.amazonaws.com/propublica/assets/docs/dol_radiation_instructions.pdf?_ga=1.80532370.445997195.1472407897.

6. See https://ecology.wa.gov/Waste-Toxics/Nuclear-waste/Hanford-cleanup/Tank-waste-management.

Works Cited

Berlin, I. "Two Concepts of Liberty." In *Essays on Liberty*. Oxford, UK: Oxford University Press, 1969.

Braybon, Gail, and Penny Summerfield. *Out of the Cage: Women's Experiences in Two World Wars*. London: Pandora Press, 1987.

Department of Ecology, Washington State. *Hanford Site Cleanup: Progress and Challenges*

Department of Energy (DoE) RPP-14193. Title 42, Chapter 84, Subchapter XVI: Energy Employees Occupational Illness Compensation Program.

Dowie, M. 1977. "Pinto Madness," *Mother Jones*, Sept./Oct., 1977. http://www.motherjones.com/politics/1977/09/pinto-madness.

Eisenhower, D. 1961. Farewell Address. The Eisenhower Archives. https://www.eisenhower.archives.gov/research/online_documents/farewell_address/Reading_Copy.pdf.

Fitzgerald, G. J. "Chemical Warfare and Medical Response during World War I." *American Journal of Public Health* 98 (2008): 611–625.

Frank, L. "Plan to Pay Nuclear Workers Unfairly Rejects Many, Says Doctor. *Pro Publica*, July 31, 2009.

Gofman, J. W. *Radiation-Induced Cancer from Low-Dose Exposure: An Independent Analysis*. San Francisco: Committee for Nuclear Responsibility, Book Division, 1990.

Haber, L. F. *The Poisonous Cloud: Chemical Warfare in the First World War*. Oxford, UK: Clarendon Press, 1986.

Harris ,G. "The Dust They Breathe – Black Lung Killing Nation's Coal Miners," *Seattle Times*, Apr. 22, 1998.

Iversen, K. *Full Body Burden: Growing Up in the Nuclear Shadow of Rocky Flats*. New York: Broadway Paperbacks, 2012

Lapp, R. E. 1964. "The Einstein Letter That Started It All; A Message to President Roosevelt 25 Years Ago Launched the Atomic Bomb and the Atomic Age," *New York Times Magazine*, Aug. 2, 1964.

Mill, J. S. "On Liberty." In *Collected Works of John Stuart Mill*, ed. J. M. Robson. Toronto: University of Toronto Press.

National Public Radio (NPR). "The VA's Broken Promise to Thousands of Vets Exposed to Mustard Gas." *Morning Edition*, June 23, 2015. https://www.npr.org/2015/06/23/416408655/the-vas-broken-promise-to-thousands-of-vets-exposed-to-mustard-gas.

———. "Secret World War II Chemical Experiments Tested Troops by Race." *Morning Edition*, June 22, 2015, https://www.npr.org/2015/06/22/415194765/u-s-troops-tested-by-race-in-secret-world-war-ii-chemical-experiments.

Norris, J. F. "The Manufacture of War Gasses in Germany." *The Journal of Industrial and Engineering Chemistry* 11 (1919): 817–829.

Pechura, C. M., and D. P. Rall. *Veterans at Risk: The Health Effects of Mustard Gas and Lewisite.* Washington, DC: The National Academic Press, 1993.

Simon, S. A. Bouville, and C. Land. "Fallout from Nuclear Weapons Test and Cancer Risks." *American Scientist* 94 (2006): 48–53. DOI: 10.1511/2006.1.48.

DOE Office of River Protection. "The Accelerated Retrieval, Treatment, and Disposal of Tank Waste and Closure of Tanks at the Hanford Site Environmental Impact Statement: A Guide to Understanding the Issues." DOE Office of River Protection, Washington State, RPP-14193, Jan. 2003, 7.

Wald, M. L. "U.S. Nuclear Arms' Cost Put at $5.48 Trillion, *New York Times,* July 1, 1998.

Wilkinson, G. "Study of Mortality among Plutonium and Other Radiation Workers at a Plutonium Weapons Facility." *American Journal of Epidemiology* 125 (1987): 231–250.

———. "Seven Years in Search of Alpha." *Epidemiology* 10 (1999): 340–344.

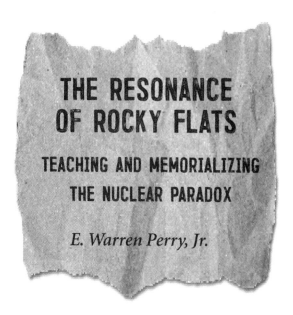

THE RESONANCE OF ROCKY FLATS

TEACHING AND MEMORIALIZING THE NUCLEAR PARADOX

E. Warren Perry, Jr.

In 1990, literary critic and cultural philosopher Stephen Greenblatt published the seminal essay, "Resonance and Wonder." Greenblatt's short discourse quickly became required reading in the burgeoning discipline of museology, or museum studies. Although not restricted to cultural exhibition or museum settings, "Resonance and Wonder" established two distinct and efficacious paradigms whereby audiences are impacted. Greenblatt writes:

> By resonance I mean the power of the object displayed to reach out beyond its formal boundaries to a larger world, to evoke in the viewer the complex, dynamic cultural forces from which it has emerged.... By wonder I mean the power of the object displayed to stop the viewer in his tracks, to convey an arresting sense of uniqueness, to evoke an exalted attention. (Greenblatt 1990)

In discussing possible scenarios for a museum at Rocky Flats, Colorado, Greenblatt's notion of objects and lessons that "reach out beyond... formal boundaries" and that "convey an arresting sense of uniqueness" should be considered. What singles out Rocky Flats? Why should Rocky Flats have a Cold War museum when other museums – even regionally – provide scientific, historical, and political overviews of the atomic age? Would a Cold War museum at Rocky Flats be redundant, or does the Rocky Flats experience offer something unique that would serve both community and tourism?

This chapter will have three parts, the first of which will contend that a Rocky Flats Cold War museum would serve a regional and national interest not served by other institutions. The creation of the Rocky Flats Nuclear Weapons Plant was a direct result of escalating tensions between the United States and the Soviet Union. While museums at Oak Ridge, Tennessee; Los Alamos, New Mexico; and Albuquerque, New Mexico; among others, all participate in scientific and historical discourse surrounding the invention of the bomb, a thorough treatment of the Cold War's impact on the average American community is lacking.

Part two of this chapter will discuss object-oriented curatorial choices that could shape a Rocky Flats museum. The material culture of the assembly plant would provide a wealth of scientific wonder. Equally significant is the resonance of images of American antinuclear activists, including Daniel Ellsberg, Allen Ginsberg, Anne Waldman, Bonnie Raitt, and Jackson Browne, protesting or supporting protesters at Rocky Flats. The history of protest and the cries for transparency are models for the practice of the First Amendment.

The final part of this chapter will contend that the history of the compromised assembly plant at Rocky Flats provides the opportunity to educate and enlighten patrons on the potential horrors of unaccounted-for nuclear materials, and that such educational platforming is not mutually exclusive of historical, Cold War programming. The human and environmental lessons to be taught in a Rocky Flats Cold War museum are as critical as the geopolitical lessons. A museum with the mission of representing both sides of this experience stands a chance of approaching the very complex truth that is Rocky Flats – such a museum stands a chance of getting it right.

Part I: The Case of the American Museum of Science and Energy at Oak Ridge, the National Museum of Nuclear Science and History at Albuquerque, and the Bradbury Museum at Los Alamos

Oak Ridge, Tennessee, is about 30 miles from downtown Knoxville, both cities being locked solidly inside the beautiful mountains of east Tennessee; they are also, by virtue of their geography, a pair of Appalachian sequins studding the mighty American Bible Belt. Knoxville – perhaps accidentally, perhaps intentionally, but certainly symbolically – contains within its downtown perimeter the intersection of Church and State Streets. Oak Ridge is a different story. However deep spirituality ran in the nearby bucolic district that became Oak Ridge, the US government's interest in securing a victorious ending to World War II ran deeper.

When the federal government bought the land and fenced off the space for the Manhattan Project, the effort displaced families, mowed over farms, and put a couple of churches out of the salvation business, among them the New Bethel Baptist Church. There might be an intersection of Church and State in Knoxville, but Oak Ridge would be all state, specifically, the US Department of War.

The major war effort at this facility was the production of uranium-235, which was done at the Y-12 plant. The U-235 that this plant yielded would be the nuclear material used in the bomb known as Little Boy; that is, the atomic weapon dropped on Hiroshima, Japan, on August 6, 1945. Oak Ridge, known as the "Secret City" because of its surreptitious origins, cloaked inside a national security apparatus, would open its gates three and a half years after World War II's conclusion. Several hundred buildings never seen by the public would suddenly appear as a municipality, its citizens the workforce behind the atomic bomb. With the new city came a museum.

Beginning in 1942, Oak Ridge evolved rapidly over less than a decade, thanks to a building program overseen by Manhattan Project director General Leslie Groves. Oak Ridge, formerly a series of small farming communities, was, by the early 1950s, one of the world's foremost centers of study of the atomic sciences. In its early years, the Museum of Atomic Energy in Oak Ridge branded itself as an homage to the new American nuclear culture. Later, the museum rebranded itself as the American Museum of Science and Energy (AMSE); it is under this name that the museum still operates. Of late, however, the Department of Energy (DOE) has threatened to pull the plug on its own invention. Desirous of leaving the museum business, the DOE has opted to turn the museum over to the US General Services Administration for disposal.

In January 2017, the DOE surrendered the property and building which housed the American Museum of Science and Energy. The City of Oak Ridge accepted the land and structure with the intention of moving AMSE to a smaller facility within a large retail complex across the street from the existing structure. While the museum's future is bleakly perceived by the staff and the community, AMSE has a proud past. Averaging 60,000 visitors a year, it is a servant to the generations, exhibiting and interpreting the sciences and the history of atomic energy since 1949.

The AMSE collection is a keen one. Not only does it contain those anomalies of atomic history such as 1940s-era signage stating "Reactor On" and Manhattan Project lab equipment, tools, and uniforms, but also therein lie some true wonders of the nuclear and early postnuclear moments. A collection of letters from young G. I. Carl V. Bretz forms part of the research collection; these letters begin with his experiences after basic training and wind through Bretz's visit into Nagasaki in the early autumn of 1945, when he was one of the first Americans to enter after the August 9 bombing of that year.

Also in the collection are documents signed by then vice president Richard Nixon; Tennessee senator Albert Gore, Sr.; General Leslie Groves; and objects handled by key figures in the history of atomic science. Although the mission of the museum is dedicated to education in science, technology, engineering, and math, the collection representing the Manhattan Project period is one of the finest historical collections of its kind in the world. Many objects came not through the lab's donations or through the DOE, but rather through the community – and not just the Oak Ridge community. The American atomic community of workers, scientists, and scholars contributed much of the material, ephemeral, and intellectual content of AMSE.

AMSE is the only museum solely dedicated to science in the east Tennessee region. Also, since AMSE is within the metropolitan confines of Oak Ridge, it is a launching point for historical tours of the Manhattan Project efforts in that government-built city. AMSE assistant director Ken Mayes has long been an advocate of a living history presence in Oak Ridge. "This town is perfect for such interpretation," Mayes notes, adding, "It would be easy to line the streets with Manhattan Project period automobiles and buses, and many of the original homes and building from that era are still in place" (Ken Mayes, personal interview, June 2017). It is easy to imagine such a Dick Tracy-esque retro presence in Oak Ridge, and Mayes further cites the success of living history programs at Williamsburg and many Civil War battlefields as evidence that such endeavors both educate and attract tourism dollars (Ken Mayes, personal interview, June 2017).

However, the DOE and the City of Oak Ridge are not entertaining this sort of creative increase in the museum's presence. The DOE is rapidly washing its hands of the museum, and as of February 2017, orders were being created to store AMSE's collection in a DOE storage facility, and the City of Oak Ridge seemed to be primed to bulldoze the museum. In a time when arts funding is thin, it is no surprise that a museum might close. However, a museum whose purpose is educate in the science, technology, engineering, and math (STEM) disciplines would seem to have a solid footing in this technology-driven world. That is not the case.

From April 2016 until early 2017, I served as a contract curator for the DOE, and although my initial job was largely to conduct an inventory of the museum collection, it rapidly became apparent that I was performing the museum equivalent of an autopsy. My job was to locate and record all of the objects, with the aftermath being the burial of the museum.

As of this writing, the future of AMSE remains uncertain. With a weakened, powerless board and a series of interim directors who have been given no authority to advocate for the museum, AMSE struggles with leadership and funding. Although the staff is committed to the success of the institution, and a large, dedicated volunteer corps has been in place since the museum's inception, the DOE's decision to pull funding and surrender the museum to the City of Oak Ridge seems to be a move fraught with the damnation of a previously hardy institution. At $1.5 million dollars a year operational funding, one would believe that the good of influencing generations of young people through STEM education might outweigh the (relatively speaking) meager costs of keeping the museum operating at a minimal level.

But far from being an advocate for the museum, as of late 2016 the City of Oak Ridge and Mayor Warren Gooch were planning to surrender the museum and the land upon which it sits to a retail developer (Habegger 2019). The museum and its collection were to be relegated to another location – a bay in a strip mall across from the museum's current, spacious environment – and AMSE's facility at Tulane Avenue was scheduled to close in December 2017. In 2018, the museum relocated to the smaller strip mall facility. As of 2019, the museum is still governed by the DOE through a management and operating contractor, Alutiiq, and is supported by a nonprofit foundation, but its future is uncertain (American Museum of Science and Energy 2019).

While these problems may only seem important to AMSE and Oak Ridge, this experience suddenly becomes germane to the entire Rocky Flats mission when one considers both the collection and educational components of such an enterprise. If a museum that has been open and sponsored by a government agency since 1949 suddenly has its funding jerked from beneath it, forcing that museum either into a smaller space (best-case scenario), into a hiatus (middle but acceptable scenario), or into closure (worst-case scenario), what are the implications for a proposed museum wrought out of a controversial nuclear weapons manufacturing site/center of US Cold War efforts?

Under a somewhat patriotic banner in conservative east Tennessee, the American Museum of Science and Energy openly shares the history of World War II, the fight to defeat the Japanese, the harnessing of the atom, and the development of nuclear energy. Since 1945, Oak Ridge has participated strongly in the national discourse on energy. Scientists in that community have played significant roles in major discoveries up to and including the December 2016 "unveiling" of element 117 on the periodic table, Tennessine. Oak Ridge remains a key player in the world scientific community, but it is unable to sustain a museum sailing under the flag of science.

Other museums serving the atomic theme have also had to face challenges resulting from close affiliation with or reliance on government agencies. After the September 11, 2001, attacks, the National Museum of Nuclear Science and History (NMNSH) in Albuquerque had to move out of the newly secured area at Kirtland Air Force Base. At that time, immediate measures were taken to secure government facilities from further attacks, and steps were taken to assure public and institutional safety in federally operated buildings all over the world. Institutions such as the Smithsonian in Washington, DC, installed metal detectors at public entrances and enhanced security by increasing guards, installing protective architectural features (the notoriously ugly Jersey barriers that eventually gave way to less homely networks of steel reinforced bollards and landscaped walls), and inculcating safety awareness with operations staff such as retail personnel, educators, and docents.

Although the NMNSH had obstacles to overcome, they did so with a diligence many institutions lack. Director Jim Walther notes:

> Our non-profit was already in the process of considering a move out of Kirtland Air Force base by 9/11 because we had been intermittently closed after the African Embassy bombings in 1998. So, we knew we needed to get out of KAFB, and our facility (provided by DOE and the Air Force) was truly sub-standard; (that was my assessment as the new director in 1996). After 9/11 and our total lockout at KAFB as the base closed, we went into high-gear with our $10M capital campaign to prepare to construct our own facility. The intent was that the non-profit would do it independently, not the lab, DOE or the government. We wanted to no longer be held up by these organizations. Raising that much money took about eight years and a LOT of work. Back since I got here, I was building the financial base of the non-profit which had 1 [part-time] staff when I arrived, and Sandia Lab (which then ran the museum for DOE) had nine [full-time] staff. By 2005 that had shifted to 6 non-profit and six Sandia staff. In 2005, all Lab staff went back to jobs at Sandia and the non-profit took over all jobs. We opened the new facility in 2009 and now have 16 [full-time] staff, all non-profit. The museum building is owned by the non-profit and has no mortgage or debt. (Jim Walther, personal email communication, June 20, 2017)

The NMNSH is a military and twentieth-century historian's dream. The collection contains everything from comic books to B-17s. The new facility, opened in April 2009, is vast. One of the biggest challenges museums face in the new millennium is establishing leadership and financial security. Museums, like universities, operate under the auspices of education and enlightenment, but make no mistake about it: *museums are big business.* The NMNSH seems to have overcome this with some aplomb. Walther also notes:

> The Board is the owner/operator of the museum now. They approve the annual budget that I present to them (now $2.2M) and the strategic plan. They set the "values" of the organization. I do not ask DOE or Sandia for "permission" to mount exhibitions or hold events. I have a great relationship with our Board based on many years of mutual trust in our work together to bring the museum to its present operational level. And the future is bright, still holds a new warehouse (now funded at $200K), a replica Trinity Tower (funded at $100K) and 2 expansion wings yet to be fundraised for in future years.

Another important museum in the nuclear franchise is the Bradbury Science Museum. Located in Los Alamos, New Mexico, one of the three locations of the most intense research and activity during the Manhattan Project (along with Hanford, Washington, and Oak Ridge), the Bradbury grew from a small archive of classified historical weapons-research materials that were moved into an old ice house in 1954, meant for official visitors only, to an additional small exhibition area of unclassified material meant for the general public in 1963 (Bradbury Science Museum n.d.). The public museum moved to a larger facility in 1965 and in 1970 was named for Norris Bradbury, the first Los Alamos Laboratory director (from 1945 to 1970). In 1987 the museum's success spurred a move to downtown Los Alamos, where a new facility could better accommodate the museum's eighty-thousand-visitor annual attendance. The Bradford is a small, focused institution that keeps its mission close to that of AMSE. It is driven by science, but it also gives the visitor some gallery space in which to explore the history of nuclear physics, the political circumstances that led to World War II, and the deployment of the atomic bomb. It is very much the public face of the lab. Its position as a museum run by the DOE, similar to AMSE, means that it can also be seen as having a dual mission: to advocate the DOE/Los Alamos National Laboratory's interests and justify continued nuclear weapons research, and to commemorate US nuclear and Cold War history.

Bradbury director Linda Deck is very positive about the role of her museum inside the Los Alamos community. "We are unique as a museum," she notes, and continues, "We are actually part of Los Alamos National Laboratory, so we are a function of the communication and public affairs division of the laboratory.... We derive our funding for keeping our doors open, and the exhibits that we do, and our staffing, and our rent, and our operations cost, from the laboratory" (Linda Deck, personal interview, Aug. 25, 2017).

In short, to the Bradbury's advantage, its financial security is tied to the lab's pocketbook. The Bradbury is a science museum with a strong focus on the scientific achievements and the works of the Los Alamos National Laboratory. Linda Deck affirms:

> The laboratory uses the Bradbury as a public venue all the time. Hardly a week goes by or even a few days, where we don't have some official function of the laboratory taking place here in the museum. Just yesterday I welcomed a group that was part of an official conference to the laboratory, and they spent two hours in the museum to learn the background of the lab and more about the across-the-board work that the laboratory does. And they wouldn't be able to do that any other way here at the lab. And for a lot of the visitors that come, they just cannot access many, many parts of our laboratory. We are still an ongoing NNSA [National Nuclear Security Administration] laboratory, and it is off-limits to the general public and especially foreign nationals. So we are able to host them here; we are a general access area. Anybody who is in the United States legally can come in our doors and enjoy the exhibits we have here, and the information, and the films and everything else. Take photos – all of our information is unclassified, for sure, we check that out. So it is the preeminent public venue for Los Alamos National Laboratory. (Linda Deck, personal interview, Aug. 25, 2017)

This note of Director Deck's, "*all of our information is unclassified*," is not an insignificant one. As part of the National Park Service's Manhattan Project National Historical Park chain, with Oak Ridge and Hanford, Washington, Los Alamos is a repository for classified information, although much of it is archaic and no longer sensitive. Like so many other institutions in the United States, and like a proposed museum at Rocky Flats, the issue of security looms largely, and not just because of the collection. Deck further notes:

> This museum, the Bradbury, is in the downtown of the Los Alamos area, and we are not within the laboratory footprint. So after 9/11, that really did not change our access at all. [However] we are part of the laboratory, and you know, there were heightened – there was certainly heightened awareness… after 9/11. Across the country – if you see something, say something, those kinds of things. And of course we all are very aware of that here, but we basically just follow those really good general safety and security guidelines. We are an official lab facility, but like I said we are not behind the fence, so we've got all of our activity security plans. We do exactly what we need to do as a lab facility, but it's a general access area, so, not a problem. (Linda Deck, personal interview, Aug. 25, 2017)

When one considers the cost of building a new facility, protecting collections, maintaining the facility, and then *protecting* the facility – and, more importantly, the general public who attend the museum – money becomes the issue through which all other issues flow.

As with every other sector of the tourism industry, the costs of operating a museum have skyrocketed. Coupled with the perception of political incorrectness and the general unpopularity of all atomic culture, the efficacy of remaining in business has been questionable for the Manhattan Project museums. However, that same historical moment, the aftermath of 9/11, inspired a rise in patriotic culture, resulting in the creation of September 11 memorials, military memorials, and military museums. In Washington, D.C., the period from 2002 to 2016 brought in the dedication of many new and costly memorials. A large US Air Force monument representing jet contrails opened at the Naval Annex in 2006, while a September 11 memorial was unveiled at the Pentagon a few hundred yards away in 2008. The much-awaited World War II Memorial opened on the National

Mall in 2004, and a large US Marine Corps museum in the symbolic configuration of the flag raisers at Iwo Jima opened at Quantico 25 miles south of the beltway in 2006. In 2009, the US Army opened a 190,000-square-foot museum at Fort Benning, Georgia, the infantry training grounds, and September 11 memorials flew up all over the nation.

Part II: Shaping a Rocky Flats Museum

There are more than 35,000 active museums in the United States, with a large number of those museums being 501(c)3 institutions, which means many things, but chiefly that as nonprofit institutions, they pay no taxes and are eligible to receive grants from municipal, state, and federal agencies (Institute of Museum and Library Services 2014). The United States has museums that collect the material culture of world history, science, the arts, athletics, and most forms of human endeavor.

From a museum approach, Rocky Flats is an ideal case study in planning possibilities. First, there already exist collections such as the original Rocky Flats collection of material culture curated by Murph Widdowfield and the collection of Rocky Flats portraits created by artist Jeff Gipe. While the administration and directorship of a large, categorical Rocky Flats museum could be facilitated by an extracommunal scholar or museum professional, the curatorships representing the Cold War stakes, the environmental stakes, and the memorial efforts could easily be filled by citizen-scholars and Rocky Flats stakeholders such as Widdowfield, Gipe, and many other qualified locals whose voices are those of direct experience.

However, a distinction must be made between what such a museum potentially *has* versus what such a museum potentially *needs*. Local voices are important, certainly, but in order for a museum to fulfill its educational mission, objects and narratives must be considered by parties with objectivity. Local passions run high on all sides of the Rocky Flats narrative, and the creation of any museum that is worth its salt must be grounded in a journalistic-style objectivity. This discussion begins, per Smithsonian scholar Steven Lubar, when we define the roles of history and history museums:

> One difference between historians and the general public
> is the extent of critical distance we put between ourselves

and our subjects. We share an interest in history, but the approach we take is different. Our sources are different also; historians want to use archives and objects, the public more often turns to memory, personal connections, and family stories. We use those sources in different ways; historians are careful to assess the bias of their sources, to question the evidence. And we consider different contexts; historians must cast a broader net. These factors help to determine our critical distance. Our stories of the past can be commemoration, remembrance, reminiscence, explanation, interpretation, or analysis. Objects move from keepsake to memento to souvenir to reminder to evidence. Our presentations move from celebration to memorial to exhibition. (Lubar 1997, 16)

Although this looks like a reasonable daisy chain – taking an object that has personal resonance and emotional connections to an individual's attachment to a moment and then placing that object and that moment at a critical distance in order to see the object and moment through intellectual, theoretical, and historical lenses – it is not an easy set of links to accomplish. Every human consideration, from personality to patriotism, can stop a moment from receiving objective treatment and placing upon historians what Lubar refers to as "the bias of their sources." Complicating this, of course, is the fact that every theory and methodology carries its own set of biases. But that does not mean that the goal should be less lofty.

History museums have a… difficult task. The goal of a history exhibit is to move people from the ideas and information that they bring with them to the exhibit to a more complex, problematized, and nuanced view of the past. Exhibits should not be limited to reminiscence or commemoration; they should add perspective by aspiring to a greater critical distance and by putting the artifacts in context (Lubar 1997, 16).

Like Oak Ridge, this community was chosen because of its access to labor and resources, and because of its geographically secure location. And although there were victims in the process, they did not see themselves as victims so much as soldiers in the supply side of the Cold War. Building a museum with a dual purpose at Rocky Flats – paying homage to Cold War patriots while raising awareness of the health threats brought about by the plant's long-term occupancy (and subsequent poor remediation) would seem to be an ideal solution for bringing the nuclear culture of the community together.

Establishing a large-scale, comprehensive museum at Rocky Flats will be no small achievement, but it would certainly not be outside the scope of other similar ventures. Partners in a national network for the exchange of objects and expertise could be sought in museums such as those in the National Park Service Manhattan Project institutions and the various Cold War museums, presidential archives, and twentieth-century history museums scattered across the United States.

Fortunately for a potential Rocky Flats museum, a network is being put into place by none other than Francis Gary Powers, Jr., son of the famous pilot whose name is synonymous with Cold War espionage. In 1996, Powers established a Cold War Museum, which is now headquartered near Warrenton, Virginia. Like most recent non-profit museum start-ups, the Cold War Museum is seeking funding. Their mission statement is compact: "The Cold War Museum is a 501(c)(3) charitable organization dedicated to education, preservation, and research on the global, ideological, and political confrontations between East and West from the end of World War II to the dissolution of the Soviet Union" (Cold War Museum 2019).

They list their goals as follows:

- Develop permanent Cold War Museums to preserve local and regional Cold War history with the headquarters and National Museum facility located in the Washington, DC metropolitan area.

- Erect Cold War Memorials with the National Cold War Memorial located near Arlington National Cemetery to honor the men and women who were killed as part of Cold War events and activities.

- Establish a reference library and research center to help maintain the historical accuracy of the Cold War. (Cold War Museum 2019)

In a July 2017 interview, Powers described his motivation for wanting to establish such a museum:

> I started giving lectures to high school students in about 1992 to 1995, so a few years after the end of the Cold War. I was shocked, sometimes, when I would go into classrooms, including AP classrooms, and I would give a talk about the U2 incident. I would get blank stares from the kids. They thought I was there to talk about the U2 rock band. That was one of the reasons why I founded the Cold War Museum. I wanted to make sure that we educate future generations about this time period and teach them about what we struggled to endure and eventually win, in that forty-six-year period between 1945 and 1991. The mission [was] to educate the kids and the students about the Cold War time period – I thought it was important to honor our Cold War veterans. Korea, for many years, was the forgotten war. I now call the Cold War the forgotten war. It was not a declared war, per se, so that added some more complications of how to commemorate it and advocate for it, and get support for it. It was just this forty-six-year period of time that was a Cold War, but not an official declaration of war at any time during that time period between the Soviets and the Americans. So we just wanted to make sure that we could honor the veterans, preserve the history, and educate the kids about this time period. That was the reasoning behind the founding of the Cold War Museum. (Francis Gary Powers, Jr., personal interview, July 2017)

However, just because it is a good idea does not necessarily mean that it will be easy to execute. Funding such an institution is a difficult task, and this is exactly what is in front of any potential venture to memorialize Rocky Flats in *any* context. In our interview, Powers told his story of what might seem to be a "slam-dunk" idea taking years to put into the physical world.

> When I first did my business plan in 1996, I thought it would take three years, fund-raise three million dollars – it

shouldn't be difficult to do. What I found out was it took fifteen years to get brick and mortar. And in that fifteen-year time period, between ninety-two and two thousand seven-ish, we started to collect Cold War artifacts from various locations around the country and internationally. We got donations in from veterans, from veteran groups, from officials from the former Soviet Union and East Germany, from various locations around the country, and internationally we started collecting these artifacts. Very easy to find in the early nineties – very difficult to find nowadays. And so over the fifteen-year time period we were collecting, we were always reaching out to other museums, we created mobile displays that would go around the country to showcase our efforts and what we were doing. We would lecture internationally, talk to media – everywhere we could to gain support for the mission. In 2011, we finally opened our doors at Vint Hill. Vint Hill is a former army communication base located forty-five miles from Washington, DC. So it is an authentic Cold War historic site. We are now open in a two-thousand-square-foot facility, full of Cold War artifacts. There is an additional two-thousand-square-foot facility next door that is full of storage, so we are looking to grow our site at that location at Vint Hill. We are looking to partner with other museums around the country and internationally to preserve Cold War history for future generations. (Francis Gary Powers, Jr., personal interview, 2017)

Given that such an institution has been established with a similar mission by an individual whose family name evokes the Cold War experience at its most tense, it is reasonable that a stabilized Rocky Flats museum could find a worthwhile partner in trade. But the story of the creation of the Cold War Museum at Vint Hill should be a warning to any who might wish to tackle such a project: *do not enter the terrain believing that the mission will be an easy one.* Powers added an encouraging codicil to his tale of memorializing the Cold War:

I do believe that there is plenty of room in America and in the international arena for other Cold War–type museums to develop and prosper. But it all comes down to money. And oftentimes, some museums will go after the same pool of funding through foundations or grants. So I would like to work with other museums through an initiative – the Cold War Museums Association – and [for] any museum that would participate in Cold War activities and displays, we would try to help with resources and outreach to assist with their efforts. It would be a group effort and not just an individual effort. (Francis Gary Powers, Jr., personal interview, July 2017)

The problem of the creation of a Rocky Flats museum herein is an odd one, with a bit of a twist. *There is already a Rocky Flats museum.* Established in 2001, it has gone through large and small iterations, and currently its board is trying to find a permanent location. Such a complex endeavor has a very tight but important mission statement: "To document the historical, social, environmental, and scientific aspects of Rocky Flats, and to educate the public about Rocky Flats, the Cold War, and their legacies" (Rocky Flats Cold War Museum). The museum is a bit of a collection of objects without a home, and it has suffered some fairly abject setbacks in its history. In December 2015, Patricia Calhoun of the Denver weekly *Westword* reported that the Rocky Flats Cold War Museum, a collecting institution which was first bounced from its home in an Arvada post office, had been forced to leave its rental space in a building in Olde Town Arvada.

In November 2016, I spoke with Murph Widdowfield, the president of the Rocky Flats Cold War Museum. The museum has since found a small place for exhibition and interpretation inside the larger Arvada museum. Widdowfield was succinct and interested in pursuing an institution representative of the entire history of the plant. Mostly, as a resident and former worker at the plant, he was interested in a stable environment for the floating collection and a situation of permanence. In response to several questions about building an institution on top of his museum's current and previous efforts, he noted:

There are over ten thousand items in our collection with which to create a solid museum. I believe this museum would be very important to Colorado and to everyone interested in the Cold War and the nuclear aspects of the deterrent. Our primary mission would be to tell the story of Rocky Flats, including the Cold War in Colorado, the workers story, the protest story and the unknowns, as they are all parts of the history.

We have objects large and small, such as glove boxes, storage tanks, and others that depict how the plant was used and others that are smaller to fill in the knowledge of how it was done. We have a few hundred objects that are part of the activist movement to show what the feeling was of those who were against the development of nuclear weapons and also what the feelings were toward the plant site and its proximity to the surrounding area and population. We also have displays to show radiation and its effects and the sources of radiation.

The history must be told in its entirety. The story is what was Rocky Flats, how did it come about…, and what it did to our communities, county, and the state. The activist story is a part of this history and must be included for it to be complete. We contracted for the design of the museum layout, which was completed about five years ago, and it includes an area called "Pride and Protest" which tells the workers story and the activists story…. The entire story needs to be told so that everyone understands what Rocky Flats was all about. We have had many good conversations with all comers regarding this museum and would always be willing to discuss it further, especially if there were a chance to build it. Our Board of Directors over the past years has involved members who have ties to every part of this history (Murph Widdowfield, personal email communication, Dec. 6, 2016).

By 2017, the Rocky Flats Cold War Museum had still been unable to secure funding for a public space, and the collection remains in storage, the cost supported by individual donors (Miller 2017).

Part III: How Rocky Flats Has the Chance to
Tell a Complex Truth and Get It Right

It would be easy to say that a museum for the entire Rocky Flats experience – from the Cold War patriotism component to the victims of the corporate chemical and nuclear disasters – was possible, but it would be difficult to build it. Rocky Flats is symptomatic of the entire American political climate. Like America, the population of the Rocky Flats experience is divided and many are unwilling to compromise.

The Rocky Flats Cold War patriots are committed to preserving the legacy of Rocky Flats during the Cold War, while those who have lost loved ones or suffer currently because of careless chemical and nuclear policies are determined to preserve the memories of those who have died or seek justice for those affected. Also, there are those who seek to educate the public on the environmental dangers of the plant site. The clearest path to success in the creation of a Rocky Flats Museum lies in the direction of total community commitment.

Is there any crossover inside the groups?

Perhaps. However, many of the possible opportunities to create exposure are cloaked in distrust. Many retired professionals from the plant view the health and environmental protests as counter to the achievements of the plant, if not downright subversive. Also, many of those with health and environmental concerns view the first group with suspicion.

All sides have moral ground, but from a memorializing and educational point of view, it is quite possible that all parties involved are missing a seminal opportunity to capitalize on the Rocky Flats experience. All narratives within this history are compelling, and the history of this community's involvement in the American Cold War effort is quite complex. If James Michener's epic *Centennial* is the fictitious saga of Colorado from the dawn of time to the American industrial age, then Rocky Flats is the multifaceted, tragi-heroic, real-life tale of the atomic age and its pyrrhic outcomes.

Although there are multiple narratives, there need not be multiple institutions. To tell the story of the Rocky Flats experience, one museum with many galleries situated on one ground with many memorials would likely be a greater whole than the sum of so many individual stakeholders trying to create many spaces in many places; the total narrative would quickly become confused and lost over geography, ticketing mechanisms, multiple missions, and lack of funding.

The advantages of a unified community effort here are numerous. Large American cities such as Denver host hundreds of nonprofit organizations, and many of them are clamoring for the same grant money, patronage, and support. Currently there are at least 965 institutional members of the Colorado nonprofit association in the Denver metro area (Colorado Nonprofit Association). Two to three organizations trying to sustain themselves under multiple umbrellas stand much less of a chance for survival than a focused and united organization willing to share narrative space and funding. In a time when hospitals, religious organizations, museums, symphonies, libraries, ballets, amateur athletics, parks, and zoos all seek the charity dollar, the fiscal efficacy of joining hands is apparent.

Also, the creation and administration of such an institution is not so difficult as it might seem, but it can be a challenge to the stakeholders to move their interpretive lenses out from the nucleus of their lives and toward an objective, peripheral point of view. After all, passions run high in communities when history and legacy are being recorded for posterity. No one wants to be written down as the bad guy in history.

Works Cited

American Museum of Science and Energy. "Governance" and "History." amse.org/about-amse/governance/; amse.org/about-amse/history/, accessed Feb 22, 2019.

Bradbury Science Museum. "About the Museum." www.lanl.gov/museum/visit/about-museum.php, accessed Feb. 2019.

Calhoun, Patricia. "Rocky Flats Cold War Museum Is Out in the Cold," *Westword*, Dec. 21, 2015.

Cold War Museum. Mission Statement. 2019. www.coldwar.org/museum/index, accessed Feb. 22, 2019.

Colorado Nonprofit Association. Nonprofit Member Directory. www. coloradononprofits.org/membership/nonprofit-member-directory, accessed Feb. 22, 2019.

Greenblatt, Stephen. "Resonance and Wonder." *Bulletin of the American Academy of Arts and Sciences* 43, no. 4 (1990): 11–34. JSTOR, www. jstor.org/stable/3824277.

Habegger, Becca. "DOE, Oak Ridge Seal AMSE Land Transfer Deal." WBIR 10News, Dec. 30, 2016. www.wbir.com/news/local/doe-oak-ridge-seal-amse-land-transfer-deal/380730207 accessed Feb. 2019.

Institute of Museum and Library Services. "Government Doubles Official Estimate: There Are 35,000 Active Museums in the U.S," May 19, 2014. www.imls.gov/news-events/news-releases/government-doubles-official-estimate-there-are-35000-active-museums-us.

Lubar, Steven. "Exhibiting Memories." In *Exhibiting Dilemmas:Issues of Representation at the Smithsonian*, edited by Amy Henderson and Adrienne L. Kaeppler. Washington DC: Smithsonian Press, 1997

Miller, Amanda. "Fighting to Tell Its Atomic Tale, a Wandering Cold War Museum Finds a New Spark." Military Times Rebootcamp. Jan. 12, 2017. https://rebootcamp.militarytimes.com/education-transition/education/2017/01/12/fighting-to-tell-its-atomic-tale-a-wandering-cold-war-museum-finds-a-new-spark/.

Rocky Flats Cold War Museum. www.rockyflatsmuseum.org/, accessed Feb. 22, 2019.

THE NUCLEAR POWER–NUCLEAR WEAPONS CONNECTION

Linda Pentz Gunter

In the opening sequence of Errol Morris's documentary, *A Brief History of Time* (based on the book by physicist Stephen Hawking), we see a shot of a star-scattered night sky while a comical chicken bobs in and out of the frame. Then we hear Hawking's electronically generated voice ask that perpetually confounding question: "Which came first, the chicken or the egg?"

In Hawking's case, the question applied to the universe. Did it have a beginning? And if so, what happened before that, and how did it get here?

It is a question that baffles us deeply as we try to grasp the concept of infinity. It boggles the human brain and seems to dwell in a realm beyond conceptual thinking. Is there a right answer, or even *any* answer? We may never know.

When we apply the chicken-and-egg question to nuclear power and nuclear weapons, we are faced with the possibility that the answer might not be one or the other, but is in fact "both at the same time."

There is no uncertainty about the evolution of either one. New Zealand–born British scientist Ernest Rutherford, working in Manchester, UK, at the time, first split the atom in 1917. This event released not only energy but a new realization about the power of the atom. Rutherford's "split" involved a nuclear reaction between nitrogen and alpha particles. During this experiment he also discovered and named the proton.

Rutherford had already discovered alpha and beta particles, which he also named, as well as the concept of radioactive half-life – the time required for one-half of the atoms of a given amount of radioactive substance to lose half their radioactivity.

But it was not until 1942, when Italian-born physicist Enrico Fermi engineered the first controlled, self-sustaining nuclear chain reaction in Chicago, that the nuclear reactor saw life. The project was conducted with a team that included Hungarian-born physicist Leo Szilard, who had first conceived of the nuclear chain reaction in 1933.

Despite helping to unleash this awesome power, Szilard quickly had misgivings, foreseeing that its application would lead to a deadly arms race with the Soviets. He tried to warn President Franklin D. Roosevelt, and then-President Harry S. Truman about these dangers, but without success. In July 1945 Szilard sent a petition to President Truman, which was signed by sixty members of the Manhattan Project, arguing on moral grounds against the use of the atomic bomb on Japan. Distressed and disappointed that this fell on deaf ears, he went on in 1962 to found the Council for a Livable World to promote policies to reduce and eventually eliminate nuclear weapons.

Fermi's chain reaction, at what was known as the Chicago Pile, and which occurred at 3:25 p.m. on December 2, 1942, is generally heralded – if such a celebratory word should, in hindsight, be applied here – as the official dawn of the Atomic Age. But what exactly was it ushering in?

The Chicago Pile experiment was part of the Manhattan Project and therefore provided a key step in the development of the atomic bomb. Arguably then, in the US case, nuclear weapons development came first. The Chicago chain reaction was the crucial initial step in what became a massive atomic arms buildup. It put Navajo Native Americans to work in uranium mines under deadly conditions without proper health protection. And it put workers and surrounding communities into harm's way at Rocky Flats, producing the plutonium pits – the key trigger components of a nuclear weapon – for tens of thousands of nuclear weapons.

Today, the United States still possesses an estimated 6,450 warheads – 2,800 retired and waiting to be dismantled, 4,018 stockpiled, and most frighteningly,1,750 still deployed, meaning they could be launched within minutes. (Russia still has a total of 6,850, similarly broken down).

The activities that were launched at the Chicago Pile fell under the purview of the Department of Defense, but "Offense" would be the more appropriate moniker; nothing humankind has ever invented is more offensive or destructive than the massive power unleashed by even a single atomic bomb. This was to manifest most horrifically, although it did not end with, the atomic bombings of the Japanese cities of Hiroshima and Nagasaki in August 1945.

The horrors of those two devastating bombings are generally thought to have spurred President Dwight D. Eisenhower's creation of the so-called Atoms for Peace program. It was the title of a speech he gave on December 8, 1953, but it was also believed to be an effort at damage control, or possibly fear management. As concerns about the atomic arms buildup grew, the Eisenhower administration sought ways to assuage public anxieties by promoting a "peaceful use" of the atom. (The more cynical view is that it was political maneuvering to bring Europe in line with the US nuclear weapons program.)

Whatever the public posturing, behind the scenes, any so-called peaceful use of the atom was then – and remains today – inextricably linked to nuclear weapons. While Eisenhower established a seemingly civilian nuclear energy pathway with his Atoms for Peace speech, seven months earlier, the Atomic Energy Commission (AEC) had produced a report entitled *Nuclear Power Reactor Technology.*

The report, dated May 1953, detailed industry proposals for "dual-use" reactors; that is, reactors that would generate electricity but, at the same time, produce plutonium for nuclear weapons. In preparing its report, the AEC had invited the US industrial complex to take a seat at the table to participate in US military security interests. This sits in ironic contrast to Eisenhower's outgoing speech in 1961 when he warned that "we must guard against the acquisition of unwarranted influence, whether sought or unsought, by the military-industrial complex."

One of the contributors to the AEC report was Dow Chemical – already by then installed as the first contractor managing the Rocky Flats bomb production facility. Significantly, along with Dow, the other companies involved – Monsanto, Union Electric, Commonwealth Edison, Public Service Company of Northern Illinois, Detroit Edison, Pacific Gas and Electric Company, and Bechtel Corporation – expressed interest in the dual-use endeavor, but only if the profit assigned to plutonium production was the chief driver.

The AEC study concluded that commercial nuclear reactors would not be economically feasible if they were used solely to produce electricity. Nuclear power, the AEC said, would not survive without nuclear weapons. The inextricable link was cemented firmly in place.

However, while the dual-use concept was eventually largely abandoned for solely "commercial" nuclear power reactors; one such remains, operated by the Tennessee Valley Authority (TVA) at its Watts Bar Nuclear Plant in Spring City, Tennessee. Watts Bar Unit 1 was modified to operate as a dual-purpose reactor in the fall of 2003. TVA uses Watts Bar 1 to irradiate tritium-producing rods for the commercial production of electric power as well as the military production of tritium as a key ingredient to maximize the explosive yield of hydrogen bombs. Because tritium has a relatively rapid radioactive decay rate, it is perishable and must periodically be replenished in nuclear warheads. Just a few grams of tritium added to a nuclear weapon substantially increases the explosive yield with the same amount of plutonium or enriched uranium. This strategically translates into smaller, lighter, and more deliverable warheads.

The launch of a dual-use reactor as late as 2003 is indicative of how far down the nuclear power–nuclear weapons path we have traveled, despite decades of concerns raised about crossing the line between the two sectors. Things might have been altogether very different if Eisenhower had foregone Atoms for Peace and had instead adopted a recommendation made under the preceding Truman administration. Concerned about the exhaustibility of raw materials and the likely impact on national defense as well as the economy, Truman had in 1951 established a President's Materials Policy Commission (also called the Paley Commission), to explore the matter.

Truman appointed William S. Paley, after whom the Commission was named, to lead the investigation. Writing to Paley on January 19, 1951, Truman expressed his chief concern: "We cannot allow shortages of materials to jeopardize our national security nor to become a bottleneck to our economic expansion." A five-volume report was duly published in June 1952 called *Resources for Freedom.*

The report saw limited utility for nuclear power. It its Summary and Conclusions, it noted: "Nuclear fuels, for various technical reasons, are unlikely ever to bear more than about one-fifth of the load." Instead, the Commission strongly advocated solar energy development. "Efforts made to date to harness solar energy economically are infinitesimal," it concluded. "It is time for aggressive research in the whole field of solar energy – an effort in which the United States could make an immense contribution to the welfare of the world."

These words have a bitter ring today. This was clearly not only an economic opportunity lost but could well have changed the energy trajectory of the entire world. Had Eisenhower adopted, rather than tossed away, the recommendations of the Paley Commission, there might be no climate change today.

The Paley Commission report did not miss the fact that intentions for nuclear energy at the time centered almost entirely on dual-use nuclear reactors, and that while the AEC was indeed looking into "how electricity can be produced economically with nuclear reactors," the "method under consideration is, in effect, to generate electricity as a byproduct of plutonium production."

If electricity was the byproduct of the nuclear weapons program, it also became the byproduct of the commercial nuclear energy program. While nuclear energy has contributed at best around 20 percent of the nation's electricity, its major byproduct has been the mounting and unsolved radioactive waste problem. This is one of the many problematic legacies of the fateful decision to take the atomic rather than the solar path.

The solar road not taken, then, set us on the path to mutually assured destruction, and not just because the nuclear choice ballooned into a devastating nuclear arms race that could still destroy the planet in the blink of an eye. It also ensured that nuclear energy, with its extractive and wasteful use of resources, deadly potential for accident or terrorist attack, and mountains of radioactive waste, would block the path for renewable energy development, thus contributing to the climate change crisis we face today, a crisis that could also finish life on Earth as we know it.

The inextricable link between nuclear weapons and nuclear power begins at the very start of what is known as the nuclear fuel chain, although it should more properly be called the uranium fuel chain. Indeed, it is arguable that had uranium energy not been sanitized by the adoption of the word "nuclear" – which is also associated with beneficial medical practices that treat cancers and other maladies – there might have been greater understanding of, and resistance to, its power and origin. Calling it "uranium energy" would bring nuclear power in line with the names for all our other electricity sources identified by their fuel – coal, gas, oil – even the good ones like solar and wind.

Uranium, of course, is the raw material that fuels both nuclear power and atomic bombs. And that raw material must be mined. Early on, the methods for mining were the traditional "hard rock" or underground mining as well as open pit mining. (The in-situ leach mining method, which injects vast quantities of chemical-laced water – usually sulfuric acid or ammonium carbonate – to extract uranium ore, began in 1974 but ultimately became the most widely used method in the United States.)

Most uranium miners in the States came from Native American communities. While they were told they were making a patriotic contribution by extracting the raw materials for the US nuclear weapons program, they were not told about the health risks of the mining process itself. Consequently, without protective gear or any fundamental health education, miners early on were exposed to radioactive gases and dust. Even their wives suffered. Miners returned home in their work clothes, which their wives washed. Radioactive dust was tracked into homes.

Even today, Navajo and other uranium miners are still fighting for compensation for the resulting and often deadly health consequences they suffered. These illnesses, which resulted from radiation exposures caused by uranium mining and its legacy of contamination, included lung cancer from inhalation of radioactive particles as well as bone cancer and impaired kidney function from exposure to radionuclides in drinking water. Native Americans and others continued mining for decades, mainly in Arizona, Colorado, New Mexico, Utah, and Wyoming, and were soon producing uranium for the burgeoning nuclear energy program as well as the atomic arsenal.

Today, there are an estimated 15,000 uranium mine locations in fourteen western states; most are closed and abandoned. On Navajo sovereign land alone, nearly 30 million tons of uranium ore were extracted between 1944 and 1986. The Navajo Nation has now banned uranium mining on their land but still must deal with the cleanup and environmental consequences of 500 abandoned mines.

Exposure initially came from the mining process itself, but it lingers on today due to the contamination present in the radioactive rocks and detritus left behind after the milling process, known as "tailings." Indeed, around 85 percent of the initial radioactivity of the ore is left behind as sludge, including between 5 and 10 percent of the uranium initially present in the ore. Piles of tailings leach into water supplies, while radioactive dust is carried on the winds.

Accidents can also occur. One particularly deadly case – which has been underreported but was arguably even more serious than the 1979 Three Mile Island reactor accident – occurred at Church Rock, New Mexico, a poor Native American farming community.

On July 16, 1979, just fourteen weeks after the Three Mile Island reactor accident, and thirty-four years to the day after the Trinity atomic test, 90 million gallons of liquid radioactive waste, and 1,100 tons of solid mill wastes, burst through a broken dam wall at a tailings pond at the Church Rock uranium mill facility. The breach created a flood of deadly effluents that permanently contaminated the Puerco River. The giant spill washed into gullies, contaminated fields and the animals that grazed there, and poisoned drinking water relied on by the largely Navajo population. Today, the Church Rock disaster is acknowledged as likely the largest single accidental release of radioactive contamination ever to take place in US history (outside of the very deliberate atomic bomb tests).

Compensation for the health consequences of uranium mining has been hard-won. The Radiation Exposure Compensation Act (RECA) has so far obliged the US Justice Department to award more than $2 billion in compassionate compensation to eligible claimants. In January 2017, a bipartisan coalition of western US senators introduced legislation to extend RECA to cover Americans exposed to airborne radiation during nuclear weapons tests in the 1950s and 1960s.

Typically, the companies who owned the uranium mines walked away from the sites when they closed, indemnified from any cleanup responsibilities. Multiple lawsuits have sought – mainly successfully – to force those responsible, whether corporations or the federal government, to shoulder the financial responsibility of uranium mine site remediation. But these victories have come only recently. Meanwhile, generations of Native Americans and others have lived on and farmed land, and have drunk water, contaminated with radioactive elements.

Heavy metals are also released through uranium mining, some of which are even more harmful to human health than some radioactive elements. These, too, have contributed to the poor health of mining communities, and are as much a part of the uranium fuel chain legacy as uranium itself.

Early in 2017, even before Donald Trump took office, the Environmental Protection Agency withdrew a proposed requirement for companies to clean up groundwater at uranium mines across the United States and to monitor their former mines potentially for decades. These kinds of walk backs have plagued efforts to get land and water adequately cleaned up around disused and abandoned uranium mines.

Few people think about this phase of the industry when turning on their lights or talking about Hiroshima and Nagasaki. Atomic weapons were the invention of brilliant (if misguided) scientists. Nuclear power is invisible and misrepresented as "clean" energy. Consequently, the question of who worked to unearth the uranium that armed atomic bombs or powered the nuclear reactors turning on our lights, rarely comes up. The human face of the nuclear legacy has remained largely invisible.

Today, most uranium used in US nuclear power plants is imported, with only about 8 percent still produced from domestic mines, predominantly in Wyoming, but also in Nebraska and Texas. Uranium mined overseas is extracted by peoples far away, out of the sight and mind of most Americans.

Uranium mining around the world is largely conducted by Indigenous people on their own and often sacred lands, including Aborigines in Australia, Touareg in Niger, and First Nations in Canada. It is a consistent story of environmental injustice and abuse, a facet of the nuclear power–nuclear weapons connection that is usually only given prominence at the end of the chain – when the atomic bomb was used on people of color, or when the radioactive waste is dumped back into underprivileged communities.

For example, studies conducted in Niger, Africa, by the French independent research laboratory Commission for Independent Research and Information about Radiation, found that people were using household goods contaminated with radioactive materials left behind from uranium mining. Such is the level of poverty and deprivation in Niger, often ranked as one of, if not the poorest country in the world, that residents around the uranium mines collect leftover scrap metals to fashion into household utensils. They were even used to build the houses – or more properly, shacks – in which they dwell.

Most of us are more familiar with the victims at the other end of the nuclear weapons chain – in Hiroshima and Nagasaki – where the two devastating US atomic bombs were dropped. The Nagasaki bomb, nicknamed "Fat Man," was a plutonium bomb. The Rocky Flats facility went on to produce such plutonium pits for the American nuclear weapons stockpile and, contrary to popular belief, these bombs were used again. And again.

Just as uranium mining targeted mainly Indigenous communities around the world, so too did atomic "testing." Between 1946 and 1958, the United States detonated sixty-seven atomic bombs over the Marshall Islands in the Pacific. The legacy of this endless exposure – equivalent to dropping 1.6 Hiroshima bombs every day for twelve years – has been passed down the generations through birth defects, yet the faces of these victims remain relatively invisible.

The United States also exposed its own people through multiple detonations in the Nevada desert. The French briefly used Algeria – then a French colony – as their "testing" arena, before political pressure forced a shift to the South Pacific. The British detonated theirs on Aboriginal land in Australia. Russia tested at Semipalatinsk in Kazakhstan, claiming no one lived there but in fact using the rural population as human guinea pigs. In all these communities, the health impacts continue down the generations.

While uranium is mined and milled both for the nuclear power and nuclear weapons sector, it is at the next phase – uranium enrichment – that the nuclear power and nuclear weapons pathways, in principle, diverge. But not necessarily.

There are two commercial uranium enrichment processes: gaseous diffusion and gas centrifugation. Most commercial nuclear reactors require uranium-235 enriched to no more than 5 percent. Uranium is considered "highly enriched" at 20 percent or higher. Uranium-235 enriched to above 85 percent is generally considered "weapons grade."

But there is also a gray area in the middle – between 20 percent and 85 percent – where highly enriched uranium is considered "weapons usable." It would not be easy to make a nuclear weapon with weapons usable enriched uranium, but it is not impossible.

This is precisely the debate at play over Iran and its allegedly civilian nuclear program. It is why the Joint Comprehensive Plan of Action (JCPOA), known informally as the Iran nuclear deal, became necessary and why the Obama administration fought so hard to put the deal in place. Iran insisted it was enriching uranium entirely for civilian purposes and for use in electricity generation. But the Obama White House estimated that, without the JCPOA, Iran could transition to a nuclear weapons program within two to three months given what it already has in place. The US, under the Trump administration, announced its intention to withdraw from the JCPOA in May 2018. Since doing so, the Americans have further exacerbated tensions between the two countries with a political assassination and increased economic sanctions. This has prompted Iran to threaten to withdraw from the nuclear Non-Proliferation Treaty (NPT). Doing so would free the country to manufacture nuclear weapons without penalty.

Iran uses the centrifuge method to enrich its uranium and already has a large enough enriched-uranium stockpile to make at least eight atomic bombs. To do so, Iran would also need tens of thousands of centrifuges, a goal well within reach given that the country is already operating around 20,000 centrifuges.

The Iran nuclear deal obligated the country to reduce its stockpile of uranium by 98 percent and maintain its level of uranium enrichment at 3.67 percent – significantly below the enrichment level needed to create a bomb. It would also have to reduce its centrifuge inventory to 6,104 for the next ten years.

Plutonium is also a concern in Iran. The country's Arak reactor is of the heavy-water design, which means it could produce plutonium. The Iran nuclear deal cut off this pathway to the bomb by mandating that the Arak reactor be redesigned so it cannot produce any weapons-grade plutonium.

Inevitably, the deal also required monitoring, inspection, and verification. A secret nuclear weapons program would still be possible otherwise, given the "civilian" nuclear power programs and materials Iran already has in place. Iran, therefore, is emblematic of the secrecy under which a country could transition from nuclear power to nuclear weapons development and the blurry line between them.

Iran should not be the only cause for concern. There are twenty-two countries around the world still generating electricity from nuclear power plants, outside of the nine also in the Nuclear Club (see p. 325). As stability wanes in certain regions, these countries may become a concern. There are also countries eager to develop nuclear power programs, the most recent and alarming example being Saudi Arabia.

Saudi Arabia's justification for nuclear power is that it will replace the energy now generated by domestic oil, thus allowing the kingdom to export more oil for profit, while reducing its carbon emissions. In 2019, the US government signaled its intent to sell nuclear technology to Saudi Arabia, but without the uranium enrichment and verification restraints imposed on Iran through the original Iran deal.

Clearly Saudi Arabia, a sun-soaked desert country, is perfectly suited to the development of solar and wind power. Consequently, the only logical explanation for its choice of nuclear power over renewable energy is clearly a nuclear weapons agenda. This was made explicit by Saudi crown prince Mohammed bin Salman, who said in 2018 that the kingdom would develop nuclear weapons if Iran did.

Among countries already using nuclear power generation, Japan has at least nine tons of surplus plutonium stored in the country and another twenty-one tons stranded in the UK as a result of the failed UK Mixed Oxide Fuel program. It has about fourteen additional tons in France.

All of Japan's plutonium emanated from its nuclear power plants, since the country has no nuclear weapons program. However, it has not escaped observation that given Japan's extraordinary inventory of plutonium, it could quickly transition to nuclear weapons manufacture.

Japan also has 1.2 tons of enriched uranium. All told, Japan has the capacity to build around 5,000 atomic bombs. Officially, the country continues to swear off nuclear weapons development. But with global volatility and instability on the increase, precipitated as much by climate change pressures as by saber rattling from hostile neighbors, that situation could quickly change.

While nuclear weapons and nuclear power programs may largely diverge at the enrichment and electricity generation stage, they meet again at the waste phase. In the United States, prior to the 1970s, some irradiated fuel from commercial nuclear power plants – also known misleadingly as "spent" fuel – was sent to a reprocessing plant in South Carolina. There, the plutonium, which is a product of the fission process even in a civilian reactor, was extracted to be used in the production of nuclear weapons. Reprocessing was subsequently banned, first by President Gerald Ford and then by President Jimmy Carter, out of proliferation concerns.

Two countries that have focused heavily on reprocessing are France and the United Kingdom. In both countries, reprocessing has produced enormous radioactive waste streams – into the English Channel and Irish Sea, respectively – and in the case of France, 10 million tons annually.

Gaseous releases from reprocessing plants are the most radiologically toxic along the entire uranium fuel chain, and leukemia clusters have been found around both the UK and French sites. Contamination from radioactive reprocessing effluent has been found as far north as the Arctic. The Irish Sea has been designated the most radioactively contaminated sea in the world as a result of the UK's Sellafield reprocessing site, which has now closed.

In addition to the highly contaminative nature of reprocessing, it has not solved the nuclear waste problem. The UK and French reprocessing sites each house an enormous inventory of surplus plutonium – an estimated 140 tons at Sellafield and at least 80 tons at the La Hague site in France, where it is stored in Coca-Cola-sized containers, a clear security risk.

Reprocessing has sometimes erroneously been referred to as "recycling." Nuclear proponents have even made specious claims that France "recycles" all of its nuclear waste. In reality, almost all the irradiated reactor fuel reprocessed at La Hague has remained as waste. In fact, while reprocessing may reduce the radiological intensity of irradiated reactor fuel, it actually *increases* its volume. And since France, like every other country in the world, has no open, functioning radioactive waste repository, there is no disposition solution for any of this radioactive waste, before or after reprocessing.

During reprocessing, so-called low-level and intermediate-level radioactive wastes are released into the water – in the case of La Hague, into the English Channel, and from Sellafield into the Irish Sea. In addition, waste gases are released into the air, including krypton, xenon, and carbon-14. The bulk of the remaining high-level waste – mainly uranium too contaminated with other isotopes to be usable for anything – is transported to another nuclear storage facility in the south of France. Only about 4 percent of the waste – too radiologically hot to move – is stored at La Hague. And then there is the separated plutonium, about 1 percent of all the reprocessed waste, a tiny fraction of which is manufactured into a reactor fuel known as mixed-oxide, or MOX, a blend of uranium and plutonium.

However, the proportion of plutonium in MOX fuel used in French reactors is between just 5 and 8 percent, and the proportion of MOX fuel within the traditional fuel that is then fed into reactors able to use MOX fuel is only 30 percent. Worse yet, since irradiation of uranium creates plutonium, and reactors are unable to fission all the plutonium in the MOX fuel, even after the MOX fuel has been irradiated in the reactor, there is *still* plutonium in the waste produced by these reactors.

No country reprocesses irradiated MOX fuel because it is too complex and therefore too expensive. Thus, despite all the effort and expense, and the enormous amount of waste and contamination produced by reprocessing itself, there is little to *no net reduction* of plutonium at the end of the day!

In the United States, plans were under way for decades to build a MOX fuel fabrication plant close to the Savannah River Site reprocessing plant in Aiken, South Carolina.

The US MOX program was born originally out of an agreement with Russia signed in 2000 – and amended in 2010 – that committed each nation to dispose of 34 metric tons of surplus weapons-grade plutonium, enough for a total of 17,000 nuclear weapons. MOX was the agreed vehicle to substantiate that agreement, with a condition that the United States supply Russia with the MOX fuel fabrication technology, an endeavor the Russians said they could not afford.

Nonproliferation experts and activists had pushed hard instead for vitrification as a management solution for surplus plutonium. This would have solidified the plutonium in ceramic and encased it in glass logs, categorizing it as waste and making it permanently inaccessible. It is also potentially a cheaper alternative than MOX. The United States for a time pursued both the MOX and vitrification options. However, vitrification was finally dropped under the George W. Bush administration. The Russians withdrew from the MOX agreement with the United States in 2016.

The US MOX plant was canceled in 2019 after squandering more than $5 billion. Ironically, with plans now afoot to convert the abandoned US MOX plant into a facility to manufacture plutonium pits for nuclear weapons, a plan originally designed to reduce the US nuclear weapons arsenal could instead be used to expand it.

The problem of radioactive waste generated by both the nuclear energy and nuclear weapons programs has never been satisfactorily addressed anywhere in the world. In the United States, the Waste Isolation Pilot

Project (WIPP) near Carlsbad, New Mexico, has been receiving what is known as Transuranic waste, principally plutonium-239, plutonium-240, and americium-24, from the US nuclear weapons program.

WIPP, a deep geological repository in salt dome deposits, was licensed to last 10,000 years, but 15 years in it suffered a serious accident that shut the facility down. In February 2014, a radioactive leak followed an earlier underground truck fire, contaminating at least seventeen workers who were working on the surface at the time with americium-24. Plutonium was detected by air sensors half a mile away.

The WIPP accident raised serious questions about the repository's suitability to accept commercial high-level radioactive waste, as some nuclear proponents are advocating. Although there was an official "reopening ceremony" in January 2017, part of the site remained closed and there are problems with tunnel collapse within the repository.

The problem of what to do with high-level radioactive waste, ever since the first cupful was generated back in 1942 with Fermi's first chain reaction, has never been solved. Not only is there no disposal solution, there is no safe, long-term management or storage plan.

In the United States, a political decision to try to dump all the country's high-level radioactive waste – mainly commercial but some weapons wastes – at the Yucca Mountain site in Nevada, was eventually defunded and canceled by the Obama administration. The volcanic site had few scientific merits and studies showed it would have leaked long before its lethal cargo had decayed to harmless levels.

Instead, while the search for a permanent repository site continues, a new plan has been established called Consolidated Interim Storage (CIS), which seeks sites that "voluntarily" agree to accept high-level radioactive reactor waste "temporarily." While Yucca Mountain would have been on sacred lands of the Western Shoshone tribe, CIS candidate sites so far are located in low-income majority Hispanic communities in West Texas and New Mexico.

So what has become of the high-level radioactive waste generated by nuclear power plants? It remains at the nuclear power plants sites, either in the fuel pools or in outdoor casks, poorly protected from sabotage or accident. The Nuclear Age heralded not only the terror unleashed by the invention of nuclear weapons but also the danger posed by the radioactive waste indefinitely – and maybe permanently – left behind at civilian reactors.

As we have seen, the genesis of nuclear energy and nuclear power are bound together, leading to what is known today as the Nuclear Club. The are nine nations known to possess nuclear weapons – the United States, Russia, China, France, the United Kingdom, India, Pakistan, North Korea and Israel. All possess either commercial or research reactors, which enabled the development of nuclear weapons or the production of the necessary materials for the atomic bomb. In the case of the United States, nuclear weapons came first but led to the creation of the civilian nuclear program dubbed Atoms for Peace.

For example, India's first "civilian" reactor technology was provided by Canada – with the heavy water supplied by the United States. The reactor went critical in July 1960, and it provided the plutonium used to manufacture India's first nuclear bomb, which it exploded in May 1974. North Korea insisted it was conducting nuclear energy research for peaceful purposes before quitting the NPT in 2003 to continue its pursuit of the bomb.

Today India and Pakistan each have around 140 nuclear weapons. Studies have shown that even a so-called limited nuclear exchange between these two hostile countries – using fifty nuclear weapons on each side – could result in global agricultural failure similar to the effects of a nuclear winter.

Israel is what is known as an "undeclared" nuclear weapons state, a disingenuous moniker, since there is absolutely no doubt whatsoever that Israel has nuclear weapons – probably close to a hundred. Its nuclear energy program was kick-started by the French, after which ensued an extraordinary cloak-and-dagger tail of subterfuge, theft, and secret deals that led to Israel's atomic weapons program.

However, not all of the official nuclear weapons states are willing to play by United Nations (UN) rules established to, in theory, endeavor to reduce, if not get rid of, all nuclear weapons. Article VI of the nuclear Non-Proliferation Treaty, which entered into force in 1970, reads: "Each of the Parties to the Treaty undertakes to pursue negotiations in good faith on effective measures relating to cessation of the nuclear arms race at an early date and to nuclear disarmament, and on a treaty on general and complete disarmament under strict and effective international control." Even though the nuclear weapons states have reduced the sizes of their atomic arsenals, they are clearly not disarming.

Furthermore, India, Pakistan, Israel, and North Korea are not even signatories to the treaty. There is a clause within it that allows for three months' notice to withdraw from the NPT, which is precisely what North Korea did once it decided to transition from nuclear power to nuclear weapons. The other three countries never signed it in the first place.

There is an equally problematic additional requirement in Article IV of the treaty that further complicates disarmament. It reads: "Nothing in this Treaty shall be interpreted as affecting the inalienable right of all the Parties to the Treaty to develop research, production and use of nuclear energy for peaceful purposes without discrimination and in conformity with Articles I and II of this Treaty."

Article IV is viewed among the UN arms control hierarchy as the cornerstone of the treaty and is considered one of its "three pillars," along with nonproliferation and disarmament.

Clearly, though, allowing countries to develop the technology that embarks them on the same pathway as the one to nuclear weapons is utterly counterproductive. Why, one must ask, is developing nuclear power considered a consolation prize, or even a reward, for forgoing nuclear weapons? If electricity production is the need, then why not reward those countries with not only the right – but with the financial support and infrastructure – to develop safe and sustainable renewable energy?

The answer, of course, is that the "inalienable right" to develop nuclear power has absolutely nothing to do with electricity generation, or even energy. It is all about the nuclear cache. Until we are rid of that, we will not be rid of nuclear weapons.

It is also the reason we do not yet have – and may never have – a nuclear-free Middle East, despite attempts to establish this. And, even were this measure to be successful, suspicion will always hang in the air so long as those same countries are allowed, under Article IV of the NPT, to develop nuclear power programs.

Indeed, there are at least fourteen Middle Eastern countries that have expressed an interest in developing nuclear power. As we have seen with the case of Saudi Arabia, they do not need it, given their highly sunny and often windblown climates are tailor-made for solar and wind power.

As North Korea demonstrated, and Iran may well have been attempting to do, a country with a nuclear energy program can both threaten and actually transition to a nuclear weapons program if and when it so chooses. This remains an important power play in a conflict zone like the Middle East.

On July 7, 2017, however, there was a breakthrough at the UN when 122 nations voted in favor of a treaty outlawing nuclear weapons, a concept first launched in 2016. This is viewed as a major breakthrough on the path to global abolition. The UN Treaty on the Prohibition of Nuclear Weapons (TPNW) opened for signatures in September 2017 and, at time of this writing, seventy countries had signed and twenty-three had ratified the treaty. Once fifty countries ratify it, the treaty will come into force. The terms of the TPNW include an agreement not to "develop, test, produce, manufacture, otherwise acquire, possess or stockpile nuclear weapons or other nuclear explosive devices." One of the organizations that took the lead in seeing the TPNW become a reality was the International Campaign to Abolish Nuclear Weapons, which went on to receive the 2017 Nobel Peace Prize.

The success of the TPNW may be aided and abetted by the fact that commercial nuclear power is waning globally. The pathway back to nuclear weapons may, too, eventually disappear.

For that to happen, we must begin to rid ourselves of the illusory belief that the end of the Cold War ushered out the nuclear weapons danger and that a Chernobyl – or even a Fukushima – nuclear power plant disaster could not happen on US soil. As we have seen, thousands of nuclear weapons remain poised on hair-trigger alert. Another nuclear power plant meltdown is only a question of "when," not "if." The pressures of climate change, water shortages, unstable governments, ever-increasing conflict zones around the world, and the increasing inventory of military and civilian nuclear materials add to these risks.

The challenge is on to separate the twin demonic powers of nuclear weapons and nuclear energy. That is likely only possible by abolishing them both.

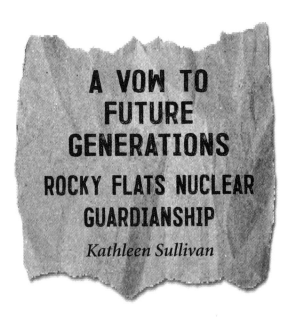

A VOW TO FUTURE GENERATIONS

ROCKY FLATS NUCLEAR GUARDIANSHIP

Kathleen Sullivan

On a warm September day in 1985, I drove down Highway 119 heading south from Boulder, Colorado, with my maternal great aunt Anice Carlise Swift. I was just beginning my freshman year at the University of Colorado, and Aunt Anice said she had something very important to share. In her bumper sticker–clad car ("Be Alert We Need More Lerts") she pulled up to a nondescript industrial gateway. The sign read, "The Rocky Flats Plant." To the west rose the foothills of the Front Range. Just beyond the West Gate, indented into the land and unseen from the roadway, was situated the sole plutonium-pit production plant for the US nuclear arsenal. From 1952 to 1989 some 70,000 plutonium triggers, essentially a Nagasaki bomb at the core of all US nuclear weapons, were manufactured at Rocky Flats.

Growing up during the Reagan administration, I thought about nuclear weapons a lot and had already considered myself an activist for disarmament. But on that warm autumn day, I learned for the first time about plutonium. And from that moment my life took a different course, thanks to an invisible poison that has a half-life of 24,000 years, can increase cancer risks manifold, and can mutate the genome of living organisms.

The history of the once-secret nuclear weapons site has been well documented.[1] Activists, academics, and concerned citizens can readily access information on the catastrophic account of Rocky Flats' radioactive legacy.[2] These comprise but are not limited to multiple fires, including two major accidents involving plutonium in 1957 and 1969; on-site storage and burial of transuranic materials[3] in leaking drums and unlined trenches contaminating the land and groundwater; radioactive contamination of nearby creeks and reservoirs; plutonium trapped in building ductwork; missing plutonium and so-called infinity rooms deemed too highly radioactive and dangerous to enter; the incineration of plutonium-contaminated waste that eventually brought the attention of the FBI, who shut down operations in 1989; and the much maligned "cleanup" operation that permitted the burial of plutonium and contaminated buildings in-situ.

After decades of activism and research, letter campaigns and lawsuits, Rocky Flats shuttered its operation, the buildings were taken down, and much radioactivity was borne away from the site, but much remains. The first six feet of level earth were partially "cleaned" of contamination, but for six feet below the surface, any amount of plutonium and other radioactive and toxic materials were left on-site. And the surface of land that comprises the former nuclear bomb production site shifts often due to bioturbation, the handiwork of burrowing animals. Ecologist Shawn Smallwood has documented the presence of some eighteen species at Rocky Flats whose bailiwick is to move earth from below to above. Smallwood's research has shown that burrowing animals play a significant role in the redistribution and further dispersal of radioactive contaminants that remain in the ground at Rocky Flats.

> They take surface material down and bring buried material up. Major diggers, like pocket gophers, harvester ants, and prairie dogs, burrow to depths of 10 to 16 feet and disturb very large areas on the surface, while coyotes, badgers, rabbits, and other animals move additional soil. Plants loosen soil and create passages animals can use. Smallwood estimated that burrowing animals disturb 11 to 12% of surface soil at Rocky Flats in any given year. Undisturbed soils do not exist at this site. The plutonium, which at Rocky Flats

is only partially remediated down to a depth of six feet and is not remediated at all below that level, is being constantly re-circulated in the environment. What is now buried is likely someday to be brought to the surface for wider dispersal by wind, water, fires or other means. (Moore 2013)

Far from "guarding" or watching over the nuclear legacy of Rocky Flats, the US Department of Energy transferred ownership and management of most of the site to the US Fish and Wildlife Service. In September 2018, the Rocky Flats National Wildlife Refuge opened to the public —with plans for a visitors center, picnic areas, and 20 miles of hiking, biking, and bridle trails. Given the matrix of invisibility, near timelessness, and contaminant migration due to construction, weather, and burrowing animals, how can people approach the responsible care of Rocky Flats' radioactive heritage? And how can visitors be assured safety from exposure to plutonium and other radionuclides?

Nuclear Guardianship is one philosophy and action idea that entails mindful responsibility for nuclear materials produced in the manufacture of nuclear weapons and nuclear power technology. Since 2010, the Rocky Flats Nuclear Guardianship Project (RFNGP) has been established as a community-based concept that works at the nexus of art, science, and spirituality to protect people and the environment from further radioactive poisoning and to educate present and future generations about their nuclear inheritance.

This chapter will explore the genesis and meaning of Nuclear Guardianship and how it has been and can be applied to Rocky Flats, where radioactivity has already contaminated the once-active nuclear weapons plant and continues to migrate on- and off-site in unpredictable ways that require awareness and community response. The ideas, art, and action that continue to imbue the Rocky Flats story will be addressed by those Nuclear Guardians engaged in passing the legacy of responsible care on to future generations.

From Greenham Common to Nuclear Guardianship

Huddling under the stars in the dark, on the edge of a devastatingly bleak military base, guarded constantly by US Army personnel, might have been a daunting experience, but the women were sustained by their convictions, and unified by a fervent desire to forward the cause of peace by resisting the installation of Cruise missiles on our soil. (Lowry 1983, 73)

The women's peace camp at Greenham Common, a UK military base jointly operated by the US and British armies, was established in 1981 with a walk from Cardiff, Wales, to Greenham, England, where women opposed the presence of US nuclear weapons on what once was common land. For nearly two decades, women lived at Greenham in order to draw attention to both the site and the increasing threat of nuclear annihilation that the site symbolized. The thousands of women who took their turn living there made the presence of nuclear weaponry visible for an international community. Greenham became a worldwide inspiration, and in a fundamental way, changed the nature of antinuclear protest – by making the site visible as a symbol for US nuclear weapons in Europe and most importantly by sustaining that gaze through physically residing outside the fenced border of the military base. Women lived under tarps in all weather, cooked over open fires, and dealt with, if not daily, weekly evictions, with spells in the local jail whereupon release they reinhabited the base time and again. In the end it was the Greenham women and their sustained presence that forced the hand of the US and British military establishments. After nineteen years of women living on-site, the cruise missiles were returned to the United States and the base was closed.

Ecophilosopher and activist Joanna Macy visited the women's peace camp in 1983, and had a feeling that she'd seen these same gatherings, not in the past, but in the future.

> Sitting in the rain at Greenham Common I suddenly realized that [my] feeling of déjà vu was not about the past so much as the future. Of course! For life to go on, this is what would have to happen around the nuclear power and weapons stations.... Even after nuclear disarmament, even after the closing of the last reactor, something like these citizen encampments would be necessary to ensure that the radioactivity was contained. (Macy 2000, 246)

Out of Macy's future vision came the Nuclear Guardianship Project. A citizen initiative established in Berkeley, California, in 1988, the project emphasizes that present proposed "solutions" to the problem of radioactive waste further displace the practice of its responsible care. Early work is archived on-line at the Nuclear Guardianship Library (Nuclear Guardianship Project, n.d.). Tabloid-sized publications called *The Nuclear Guardianship Forum* were produced in the early to mid-1990s, and filled with scholarly research, poetry, art, and process ideas. Fertile imagination and collaboration across disciplines typified the early Nuclear Guardians in their quest to understand the "poison fire" – a fire that destroys our DNA, that must be contained and capped, protected from the biosphere. There were nuclear scientists, cosmologists, authors, artists, educators, anthropologists, and spiritual teachers in the "Fire Group" that met monthly for six years.[4]

The Guardianship Ethic, a guiding document that has evolved with the latest research and sociopolitical assessments for current nuclear realities, outlines how best to look after radioactive waste and create a culture of awareness and care. And here the understanding of what radioactive waste is extends beyond the categorization given by government and industry. Nuclear Guardians recognize that every process involved in the production of nuclear weapons and nuclear electricity creates radioactive "waste." The products of nuclear technology and the instruments used to produce them will eventually require isolation from the environment. That is, every nuclear bomb, nuclear reactor, glove box, radiation suit, and production facilities themselves will require containment. And in the case of plutonium, this containment needs to be achieved for nearly half of 1 million years (Capra 1982, 246).

And yet, deep geologic disposal remains the current and only resolution on offer after seventy-five years since the brightest minds of science worked tirelessly to split the atom and weaponize it. Deep geologic disposal is a euphemism for dumping or burying radioactive contaminants, which only serves to hide this poison fire from a future gaze. Through this act of hiding, deep geologic disposal robs our capacity to contain human-made radioactivity, and denies our responsibility to future generations.

Monitored, Retrievable, and Where Possible, On-Site

The practice of Nuclear Guardianship is purposefully low-tech, requiring the storage of radioactive material in a monitored, retrievable configuration. When radioactive material is stored where present and future generations understand it to be, and are made aware of its presence, the maintenance needed for its continual isolation from the environment is more readily facilitated. Nuclear Guardianship acknowledges that this form of responsible care will entail ongoing monitoring and maintenance. These materials will need to be routinely repackaged because of their uniquely vast temporal nature. To wit, no human-made vessel can "outlive" the radioactive materials they attempt to contain. This storage is likewise envisioned as decentralized, occurring where possible at the site of generation. Storing radioactive materials where they have been produced avoids the risk of further contamination that, given the sheer volume of waste, would no doubt occur in the transportation of these materials.

Nuclear Guardians understand that there is no technological solution to the so-called disposal of radioactive materials. For materials that remain life-threatening beyond any conventional notion of time, disposal can never actually be achieved. Wherever the material is placed, it will continue to be both mutagenic and carcinogenic. Therefore, it is paramount that the materials are not hidden from the public but rather remain in mind in order that their safe containment be achieved. Guarding the radioactive materials, monitoring and correcting any found problems, is how the poison fire can be continually isolated from the environment. Moreover, keeping the existence of the material in mind through public education and community involvement further serves to develop people's commitment to its responsible care, which could be recognized as humanity's most enduring artifact for future generations.

> No technology by itself can banish [radioactive materials] and when we attempt to hide it (or hide from it), the radioactivity spreads beyond our control.... We can contain the radioactivity if we pay attention to it. The act of paying attention may be the last thing we want to do, but it is the one act that is required. And increasing numbers of citizens and scientists are recognizing today that the only realistic, viable response to nuclear waste is on-going, on-site, monitored storage – keeping waste containment... accessible for monitoring and repair by present and future generations. (Macy 1992, 3)

Nuclear Guardianship works to restore and recall "nuclear memories." On behalf of the future, people living today must not forget what happened at the Trinity test site in New Mexico in July of 1945, or what occurred one month later in Hiroshima and Nagasaki. According to Macy, these events "must be enshrined in our collective memory so that we can learn [from them] and be vigilant" (Macy 1991b, 4).

Nuclear Guardianship at Rocky Flats

LeRoy Moore, cofounder of the Rocky Mountain Peace and Justice Center (RMPJC), has kept a finger on the pulse of Rocky Flats' issues for more than three decades, working tirelessly to stop plutonium processing, and since the plant shut down, he has relentlessly pursued proper "cleanup" and remediation through monitoring plutonium migration and education of the public. Moore, together with Christopher Hormel, Judith Mohling, and others, established the Rocky Flats Nuclear Guardianship Project in 2010 through the RMPJC. They were inspired by a six-month series of presentations focused on an ethic of care "providing education and leadership regarding the source, nature, danger and care of nuclear materials, particularly materials associated with Rocky Flats" (Moore personal interview, Sept. 4, 2016). There are a growing number of citizen groups, research actions, public campaigns, and art and education initiatives that continue to raise awareness about the history of Rocky Flats, what has been left behind and what remains, and how to move forward in recognition of our nuclear inheritance.

Much of Moore's dedicated activism and scholarly research is owed to Dr. Carl Johnson, former head of the Colorado Department of Health for Jefferson County in the jurisdiction of Rocky Flats. His early monitoring of dust samples downwind of the plant site found levels of plutonium forty-four times higher than previously reported; he later documented a spike in cancers and leukemia in the residential and farming communities near the site. According to Moore, Johnson's collection method was novel and had not happened before or since.

> [Carl Johnson] found levels of plutonium on average 40 times greater than what the Colorado Department of Health

had found at the same locations with their whole-soil sampling method. Johnson tried to get the state to adopt his dust sampling method for all of the state's off-site sampling; they rejected his proposal. No dust sampling has ever happened on the Rocky Flats' site and very little off-site, other than that done by Johnson and his colleagues. (Moore, personal interview, Sept. 4, 2016).

Given the paucity of attention and research involving Johnson's innovative method, RMPJC conducted a dust sampling of their own in 2010.

[We] hired Todd Margulies of Golden [Colorado] to collect a small number of samples in areas east of the Rocky Flats site. He and I went together. It was very dry, the ground was barren and hard, the wind having blown loose soil away. The only plutonium we found in this windblown area was in a pocket at the base of a yucca plant, where loose soil could not be picked up by wind. The most striking result was a sample collected in the crawl-space of a house about one mile east of the Rocky Flats boundary. In that crawl-space, pipes and conduits were heavily covered with dust. If there was any plutonium in the dust, as we suspected, it was not deposited by the plume from the 1957 fire – the biggest airborne release from the plant – because the house was built in 1960. Samples were sent for analysis to Marco Kaltofen of the Boston Chemical Corp. The crawl-space dust contained hot particles with heavy concentrations of plutonium and lesser amounts of thorium and lead. The plutonium in this dust had accumulated under the house for 50 years. Kaltofen said anyone who spent time in this crawl-space could readily inhale plutonium particles, endangering one's health. We concluded that what we found at this house could appear in other structures. (Moore, personal interview, Sept. 4, 2016).

Christopher Hormel, a founding member of the Rocky Flats Nuclear Guardians, was part of a later sampling expedition in 2012. Hormel found that sampling not only produces the empirical evidence of the presence and migration of plutonium off-site, but can also point to faults with existing sampling methods conducted by the Department of Energy.

> When any sampling is conducted as part of the process we may be able to point out the flaws in their methods, and bring more awareness to the public about the lack of certainty regarding where and how many contaminants actually remain on the site and how they move over time. My experience with sampling has given me a deep appreciation of how little we know about how radioactive contaminants move in the environment, and makes DOE statements about how their science proves that the site is safe, a sick joke. (Hormel, personal interview, Sept. 8, 2016)

Plutonium is an alpha emitter and can enter the body through an open wound or can be ingested or inhaled. Many experts agree that it is most damaging in its respirable form, which means downwind of Rocky Flats death can cling on invisible particles in the very air we breathe. But to the public mind, especially those living nearby or recreating at the former plutonium bomb site, the dangers of radiation exposure are not so urgently imagined.

Dr. Karl Z. Morgan, the reputed "father" of health physics, offers a compelling point of view. He worked on the Manhattan Project and also at Oak Ridge National Laboratory, a nuclear weapons plant in Tennessee. Yet he later became an opponent of nuclear weapons and nuclear power when he realized that the US nuclear industry was suppressing the dangers regarding radiation exposure. Dr. Morgan pioneered research that suggests there is no safe level of radiation. In 2006, the National Academy of Sciences report on *Health Risks from Exposure to Low Levels of Ionizing Radiation* (BEIR VII) affirmed that there is no "safe dose threshold" and that any dose of radiation may be harmful.

Fears of further release of plutonium from the land, and the migration of respirable particles, prompted the cancellation of a proposed controlled burn at Rocky Flats scheduled for the spring of 2015. While the US Fish and Wildlife Service considers this a deferment, the Colorado Air Quality Control Commission has no future permit to offer. According to Moore, "The Commission terminated the burn permit for the Rocky Flats Refuge. It said Fish & Wildlife could not do a burn at Rocky Flats without applying for a new permit, and that the public will be invited to attend the hearing and to comment on any proposal" (Moore, personal interview, Sept. 4, 2016).

Another project that denies the dangers at Rocky Flats is the proposed Jefferson Parkway, a highway slated to be built on the eastern edge of the site, known to be contaminated with plutonium and other radionuclides. Thanks to activists, scientists, and academics who have been watching developments at Rocky Flats, the project now seems to be somewhat stalled due to the risk of redistributing radioactive contaminants, particularly plutonium, through road construction.

> The Denver Regional Council of Local Governments added the road to its master transportation plan for the Denver area on the condition that no state or federal taxpayer funds can be used to build it. If it is ever built it will be a privately financed toll highway. Ongoing opposition of RMPJC and others and waning support for toll roads has resulted in the failure of parties with funds to invest in the road. Things are relatively quiet for now, though this wrong-footed, dangerous proposal may be revived (Moore, personal interview, Sept. 4, 2016).

The 100-Year Flood

The very serious issue of migrating plutonium due to construction of roadways, hiking trails, and housing projects has the common theme of human engagement. These are ventures, imagined or real, that construction workers, project managers, investors, and communities are driving or postponing. Unfortunately, the land has already been disturbed by trail development at the site and housing construction in the buffer zone. Who knows how this has caused the further dispersion of radioactivity. And what happens when the weather intervenes?

In September 2013, Boulder and Jefferson Counties experienced an uncommon, astonishing flood. Within eight days, 17 inches of rain had fallen, 150 miles of roads were damaged, some 345 homes were destroyed, and four people died. Out at Rocky Flats, plutonium migrated off-site, but how much we will never know. The monitors were disabled due to the downpour (Brennan and Aguilar 2013). LeRoy Moore explains:

> The traditional belief regarding migration at Rocky Flats is that the plutonium in the environment will remain in place. The basis for the "cleanup" was the conclusion of the Actinide Migration Evaluation Pathway Analysis Report (2002) that plutonium in soil and groundwater was "relatively immobile." This was refuted in the Spring of 1995 by Rocky Flats engineer Iggy Litaor, who with instruments set up in the environment near the 903 Pad[5] detected rapid subsurface movement of plutonium in the unusually wet conditions of that Spring. He had previously accepted the industry orthodoxy that plutonium in soil will remain in place, but, in his words, "Mother Nature taught me a lesson." We befriended Litaor and sponsored public presentations by him in Boulder, Denver and Fort Collins. Despite the fact that his work was well-known, the cleanup was done, as noted, on the assumption that plutonium in the environment will stay in place. One little known fact is that both Litaor and I asked DOE to provide him with data he knew they had so he could publish a peer-reviewed report of his findings; they promised to provide what we requested but never did.... And in the 2013 flood, plutonium in the environment moved exactly as Litaor said it would. The quantity that left the site in the streambeds of Walnut and Woman Creeks, however, was not measured because the monitors in both creeks were so flooded with water that they were immobilized and did not function. In addition, any plutonium in the large amount of water leaving the site via sheet flooding was also not monitored, because there is no equipment to measure this kind of flow. No one really knows how much plutonium escaped the site and flowed onto land to the East (Moore, personal interview, Sept. 4, 2016).

Education and Public Awareness Campaigns

South of Rocky Flats, and directly adjacent to the site, is a vast housing development called Candelas. On the company website is a promotional video entitled *Candelas Is Family*, where the narrator, a mother and community enthusiast, espouses the health and well-being of the vast open space "where kids can simply be kids." "Home, where there is every opportunity to be a healthier you."[6] Studies have found that women and children are more susceptible to radiation exposure.[7] The life test of how "to be the best mother you can be" would likely not include raising a family next to what the US Department of Energy once called the most dangerous nuclear site in the United States.

Candelas is one of Colorado's largest housing developments, although the online brochure says nothing about plutonium. However, a small group of concerned citizens is taking the education of prospective buyers into their own hands. Michelle Gabrieloff-Parish is leading the charge through a project she founded called Candelas Glows/Rocky Flats Glows, which seeks to educate new or would-be homeowners about the true nature of Rocky Flats.

We believe Rocky Flats needs to be remembered for what it was, with plant workers recognized as the atomic veterans that they are. The wildlife refuge designation needs to be immediately stripped and the area must not be opened to the public. We believe the site should be memorialized, calling on artists to help us build permanent structures that speak to the site's past. Optimally, an institution should be created to oversee Rocky Flats and monitor the site – focusing on remediation and monitoring – especially in the case of extreme weather such as the 2013 floods, which caused the migration of plutonium off-site. Our primary focus is to stop the development of the area around Rocky Flats.[8]

Just east of the former Rocky Flats Plant site, and directly downwind and downstream from the radioactive contamination that remains there, is the Westminster Hills Dog Park and Open Space. This beautiful area is very popular among residents and dog owners, although it is unfortunately the likely cause of a spike in cancers in the local dog population. Veterinarians in the Arvada and Westminster area report alarmingly high incidences of cancers in dogs. Bill Johnson, a retired veterinarian who owned animal hospitals in California and Colorado, was quoted in the

Denver Post: "My biggest concern when I came back to Arvada to practice was seeing all these dogs with cancer. I saw more in one week than I would in a few months in California" (Briggs 2014).

Dogs that frequent the park are known to get bone cancers primarily in their front legs as well as cancerous growths between the pads of their paws. Sadly, there are no signs warning visitors of the potential hazards, so family pets continue to recreate there, bringing any number of known carcinogens back with them into their homes. Activist Alesya Casse has been outspoken in her attempts to warn residents after dogs she knew contracted rare cancers.

The campaign to Keep Kids Off Rocky Flats, facilitated by nuclear guardians Chris Allred and Brittany Gutermuth, at first authored a petition directed to school districts throughout the region, educating about the risk of visiting the wildlife refuge, particularly to children. Ann Parker, a retired public school teacher, appealed to the Boulder County Board of Education to stop students from visiting the refuge. At present, seven school districts including Denver and Boulder have vowed to protect children from radiation exposure.

Others have committed to use the law, including LeRoy Moore:

> We are taking legal action to require the DOE and US Fish and Wildlife to conform with the language in the Rocky Flats National Wildlife Refuge Act requiring that the whole site be cleaned up prior to transfer of land from DOE to Fish and Wildlife to establish the refuge. As things stand, the refuge encircles DOE land, the former industrial area, which remains on the Superfund list of the most contaminated sites in the country. Conceivably, the present refuge could disappear and the DOE land could be cleaned sufficiently to be removed from the Superfund list. (Moore, personal interview, Sept. 4, 2016)

Rocky Flats Nuclear Guardians (RFNG) members work closely with other concerned citizens throughout the region. According to Hormel, these include,

> Rocky Flats Downwinders, a group of people seeking to support those downwind of Rocky Flats who have health

problems due to exposure to radioactivity and other toxins released from the site; the Alliance of Nuclear Worker Advocacy Groups (ANWAG), an organization that helps former Rocky Flats workers get the compensation due to them because of workplace exposures; and Rocky Flats Right to Know, locals from Arvada who are committed to educating the public about the reality out on the site. All these are assisted by an informal group of scientists called The Rocky Flats Technical Group, which helps the general public understand the risk Rocky Flats continues to pose to this day (Hormel, personal interview, Sept. 8, 2016).

Education is essential for raising awareness and taking action. To assist, RFNGP members have created a content-rich website that provides carefully researched material on the history of Rocky Flats, the dangers of the radioactivity released into the environment from the site, and what can be done to effect change.[9] On the horizon there will be courses offered through Naropa University on the science and spiritual practice of Nuclear Guardianship. The RFNGP is a partner with the Joanna Macy Center at Naropa, which will develop curriculum for Nuclear Guardianship and training opportunities for undergraduate and graduate students.[10]

Conclusion

If there is a single positive element of our nuclear legacy it can be found through a profound and urgent connection with future generations. By burying radioactive materials, future people are excluded from a discussion that they are necessarily a part of. While it is not possible to "speak" to the future generations, it is still possible to take their well-being into consideration in relation to the nuclear materials that they will, buried or not, inherit. There is no other product of human societies that will so fervently stand the test of time. No work of art, no system of language will outlast the near timeless radioactive materials of the present/past. For this reason alone (although there are others), the containment of radioactive waste must remain part of our history and collective duty. We must maintain the knowledge of human-made radiation – where it is stored, how it got there to begin with, and how to guard against the poison fire going forward, forever.

Although no signage or information about the site's previous use exists currently at the Rocky Flats Wildlife Refuge, there is a guardian in Jeff Gipe's *Cold War Horse* – rearing slightly as if to take off running, a formidable stallion in a red hazmat suit looking out across the plain toward Rocky Flats.[11] The life-size sculpture is the only monument to what truly happened, and continues to happen. "The site has been buried," Gipe says. "It's a physical and mental cover-up, in that the most contaminated buildings in America are still buried out there."[12]

Awareness presupposes taking responsibility. When Macy joined the women at Greenham Common she was a part of the enactment of conscientious care in the nuclear age. The women there protested the presence of nuclear bombs, and because they maintained their gaze through a physical witness at the base for nearly two decades, Greenham Common became a subject of the world's gaze. Their presence questioned the validity of nuclear weapons. After nineteen years, the US nuclear bombs were removed. What will happen in the same number of years at Rocky Flats Wildlife Refuge remains to be seen, which is the essential point: that radioactive materials cannot be seen. A fundamental goal of Rocky Flats Nuclear Guardianship is to maintain the gaze through keeping the history of the site alive from one generation to the next and infusing the narrative with action and responsible care, to study, understand, and further contain what has been left behind. And to make a vow to future generations, that we respect and revere them enough to inform them of the nuclear inheritance they are about to receive.

Endnotes

1. Well documented yes, but hidden too. After the FBI raided Rocky Flats in 1989, there was a grand jury that heard evidence about the day-to-day operations, routinely flouting safety regulations and resulting in radioactive contamination both on- and off-site. All evidence at the trial has been sealed, and the jurors have been gagged with the threat of prison sentences if they go public with what they know. In an effort to fully inform the public jury foreman Wes McKinley and lead FBI

agent on the case Jon Lipsky have gone public with what they know in an astonishing book, *The Ambushed Grand Jury: How the Government Covered Up Nuclear Crimes and How We Caught Them Red Handed.* The book and vast reference materials are available online at http://rockyflatsambushedgrandjury.com/rocky-flats/.

2. Also see Kristen Iversen (2012) and the writings and research of Le-Roy Moore, which can be found on his blog site, https://leroymoore.wordpress.com.

3. Transuranic is defined by the US Nuclear Regulatory Commission as "an artificially made, radioactive element that has an atomic number higher than uranium in the periodic table of elements such as neptunium, plutonium, americium, and others." That is, human-made radioactive materials that in the case of plutonium remains carcinogenic and mutagenic for 240,000 years.

4. For an excellent interview with Joanna Macy on the early days of the Nuclear Guardianship Project, see "Guardians of the Future: An Interview with Joanna Macy by Alan AtKisson" (1991b).

5. Waste oil and solvents that were known to be contaminated with plutonium and uranium were stored outside in barrels for decades in the 903 Area. Unprotected from the elements, of course these barrels became corroded and leaked their contents into the ground, which would have been taken up by the wind migrating wherever/whenever, depositing deadly radionuclides along their pathway, https://docs.wixstatic.com/ugd/cff93e_2f63f79212f8431e8b04cc88195f95db.pdf.

6. The video is archived online at http://www.candelaslife.com.

7. https://www.nirs.org/wp-content/uploads/radiation/radhealth/radiationwomen.pdf.

8. https://candelasglows.com/about/.

9. https://www.rockyflatsnuclearguardianship.org.

10. http://naropa.edu/academics/jmc/index.php.

11. http://coldwarhorse.com.

12. https://observer.com/2019/07/rocky-flats-plant-american-chernobyl-history-documentary.

Works Cited

Ackland, Len. *Making a Real Killing: Rocky Flats and the Nuclear West.* Albuquerque: University of New Mexico Press, 1999.

Beck, Ulrich. *Risk Society: Towards a New Modernity.* London: Sage, 1992.

Bertell, Rosalie. *No Immediate Danger: Prognosis for a Radioactive Earth.* London: The Women's Press, 1985.

Brennan, Charlie, and John Aguilar. "Eight Days, 1,000-Year Rain, 100-Year Flood: The Story of Boulder County's Flood of 2013," *Boulder Daily Camera*, Sept. 21, 2013. http://www.dailycamera.com/news/boulder-flood/ci_24148258/boulder-county-colorado-flood-2013-survival-100-rain-100-year-flood.

Briggs, Austin. "Activist at Westminster Dog Park Warns of Proximity to Rocky Flats," Denver Post, Apr. 8, 2014. http://www.denverpost.com/2014/04/08/activist-at-westminster-dog-park-warns-of-proximity-to-rocky-flats-2/.

Candelas Glows. www.candelasglows.com, accessed March 6, 2019.

Capra, Fritjof. *The Turning Point: Science, Society and the Rising Culture.* London: Flamingo, 1982.

Chaloupka, William. *Knowing Nukes: The Politics and Culture of the Atom.* Minneapolis: University of Minnesota Press, 1992.

Cold War Horse. http://coldwarhorse.com, accessed Aug. 9, 2019.

Iversen, Kristen. *Full Body Burden: Growing Up in the Nuclear Shadow of Rocky Flats.* New York: Crown Publishers, 2012.

Keppler, Marliese. "Adopt-A-Reactor: A Practical Proposal to Bring Nuclear Reality into Everyday Awareness." *Nuclear Guardianship Forum,* Spring Issue (1992).

Lowry, Maggie. "A Voice from the Peace Camps: Greenham Common and Upper Heyford." In *Over Our Dead Bodies: Women Against the Bomb.* London: Virago, 1983.

Macy, Joanna. *World as Lover, World as Self.* Berkeley, CA: Parallax Press, 1991a.

———. "Guarding the Earth: An Interview with Joanna Macy by Alan AtKisson." *Inquiring Mind*, Spring Issue (1991b.)

———. "Technology and Mindfulness: A Call to Attention to the Radioactive Results of Nuclear Technology." *Nuclear Guardianship Forum*, Spring Issue (1992).

———. *Widening Circles: A Memoir.* Gabriola Island, Canada: New Society Publishers, 2000.

McKinley, Wes. *The Ambushed Grand Jury: How the Justice Department Covered Up Government Nuclear Crime and How We Caught Them Red Handed.* New York: Apex Press, 2004.

Moore, LeRoy. "Science Compromised in the Cleanup of Rocky Flats." Boulder, CO: Rocky Mountain Peace and Justice Center, 2013.

Moore, LeRoy et al. *A Citizen's Guide to Rocky Flats: Colorado's Nuclear Bomb Factory.* Boulder, CO: Rocky Mountain Peace and Justice Center, 1992.

Nuclear Guardianship Forum. www.ratical.org/radiation/NGP/, accessed March 6, 2019.

Nuclear Guardianship Project. "Nuclear Guardianship Library." www.univ-great-turning.org/nuclear-guardianship/, accessed March 6, 2019.

Roberts, Chris. "Half-Life of Memory: Unforgetting the 'American Chernobyl,'"

Observer, July 27, 2019. https://observer.com/2019/07/rocky-flats-plant-american-chernobyl-history-documentary.

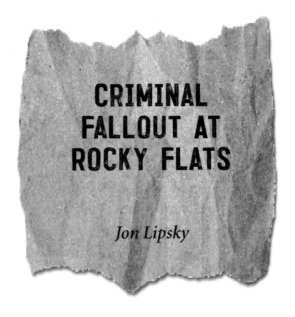

CRIMINAL FALLOUT AT ROCKY FLATS

Jon Lipsky

Despite the denial of the US government, criminal fallout of the Rocky Flats Nuclear Weapons Plant has been devastating, occurring at the expense of our citizens, nuclear workers, and environment. Rocky Flats activities and operations resulted in uncontrolled fusion chain reactions (criticalities), spills, and fires from which the secret veil of US national security failed – and is failing – to protect public health. This volume and its contributing authors articulate a nuclear history that should never be repeated. I have the deepest respect and admiration for the authors of this book, whose voices and conscience reveal important truths about Rocky Flats. I care about the harm done by the plant, a "state-created danger." As the Honorable Wes McKinley, who served as the foreman on the Rocky Flats grand jury, has noted, "Democracy is NOT a spectator form of government." (Eco Ed, 3:30).

My official involvement with the Rocky Flats Nuclear Weapons Plant began in May 1987.[1] In 1984, I felt fortunate to be assigned as a new agent with the FBI in Denver, Colorado, despite the tree-hugging jabs from colleagues that accompanied federal environmental crime investigations at that time. The advent of federal environmental investigations was trailblazing, and I was considered to be qualified to join these investigations because – rather amusingly – I had previously written littering tickets as a police officer at Las Vegas, Nevada. After several successful environmental crime cases, by 1987 I was involved in the first US criminal prosecution and convictions related to the Resource Conservation Recovery Act (RCRA) Knowing Endangerment violations with the Protex Industries, Inc. case (Associated Press, 1). RCRA is a federal waste minimization and cradle-to-grave law intended to also apply to US nuclear weapons facilities, including Rocky Flats. However, the US Department of Energy (DOE) has resisted applying the law to their nuclear weapons facilities. The legal requirements of RCRA Knowing Endangerment were so steep – requiring "substantially certain" proof – that US Department of Justice (DOJ) attorneys ordered prosecution to be postponed in April 1987. (Title 42, US Code, Section 6228[f][1][C]). During the December 1987 Protex Industries, Inc. criminal trial, the presiding US district court judge James R. Carrigan intimated several comments that a larger polluter (Rocky Flats) existed in Colorado. The judge's comments elicited our confident agreement. Protex Industries, Inc. bore the cost of its RCRA remediation, as it should have, but my resolve was about to be tested.

Also in 1987, a DOE internal memorandum concerning Rocky Flats, leaked by a congressional oversight and investigation committee, fell into our laps. The internal DOE memorandum was a smoking-gun document, written by a DOE attorney for DOE management to principally assuage or mitigate regulatory action and maintain a cooperative public image, but it highlighted for criminal investigative purposes that some Rocky Flats RCRA operations were "patently illegal" (Barton 1986, 4). The internal memorandum was an undeniable admission of criminal guilt that exceeded a "reasonable factual predicate" and to open a "Toxic Waste Matter"; however, politics has its own half-life of persistence (DOJ 2017, 1; Lipsky 1987, 1).

1987 was the Reagan era, and environmental protection was remiss due to scandal, the Cold War, and the raging nuclear weapons buildup in both the United States and the Soviet Union. In other words, nuclear production minimized environmental laws and health and safety in and around Rocky Flats. A full field investigation would be delayed for more than a year as Colorado US attorney Robert N. Miller at the time was not approachable about investigating Rocky Flats' environmental crimes. Then a different Denver US attorney, Michael J. Norton, would be appointed in 1988, who initially remarked that prosecution of environmental violations at Rocky Flats would be a "win-win" for his [political career].

As a result of this political change, we were able to begin a full-field criminal investigation into Rocky Flats. The collection of evidence and witness interviews began in earnest in August 1988.

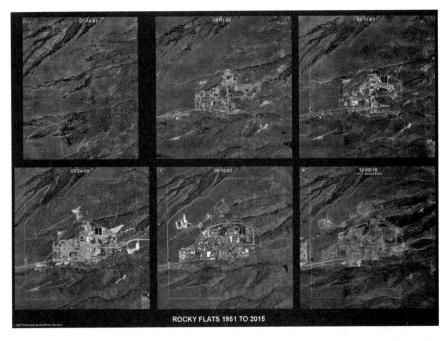

Aerial photographic collage of the Rocky Flats Site
in 1951, 1955, 1962, 1969, 2002 and 2015.
Reprinted by permission: Colorado Aerial Photo Services
and Google Earth.

We took a number of investigative steps to gather physical evidence about what was peripherally happening at the plant. Influent and effluent "monitors" around Rocky Flats surface waterways were situated to collect evidence of potential environmental contamination. (Eco Ed 1988, 1). I learned that Rocky Flats security had surface-to-air missiles to protect from aerial overflight intrusions. Despite this deadly capability, we flew over the site on four separate occasions (December 9, 10, and 15, 1988, and February 24, 1989) to collect aerial thermal-imaging video.[2] (Eco Ed 1988, 1) These videos provided valuable information regarding potential on- and off-site contamination. The October 1988 orientation overflight of Rocky Flats with one of the federal prosecutors, Ken Fimberg, was not recorded.

Further, a review of the 1987 Rocky Flats thirty-nine-volume *Waste Stream Identification and Characterization* report gleaned strong and convincing facts of potentially significant levels of contamination, and we were able to pursue an affidavit for a criminal search warrant.

The beginning of 1989 showed promise for a Rocky Flats investigation under a newly elected US president, George H. W. Bush. The Land and Natural Resources Division of the DOJ supported our allegations and our intention to plan a search warrant for Rocky Flats. The alternative was to serve federal grand jury subpoenas without the benefit of surprise. The incoming secretary of energy, James D. Watkins, also supported our proposed criminal investigation. Back in 1984, the US Environmental Protection Agency (EPA) had evaluated Rocky Flats and determined that it was eligible to be and should have been designated a Superfund site. The official government position of hands-off management at Rocky Flats was evaporating.

However, in January 1989, the US attorney general Dick Thornburgh was closely monitoring the Rocky Flats case, and DOJ Criminal Division assistant attorney general Martin Carlson asserted several "practical considerations," meaning that justice would be slow at Rocky Flats (Carlson 1989, 1).

One consideration raised was DOE's position that RCRA did not apply to government-operated nuclear weapons facilities, including Rocky Flats, and the issue was not legally clear. This uninformed legal opinion had actually been cleared up by a federal judge who had ruled five years earlier that RCRA did apply to DOE nuclear weapons operations, including Rocky Flats (*L.E.A.F. v. Hodel*, 586 F. Supp. 1163; E.D. Tenn. 1984). Another Criminal Division concern was that if DOE had tacitly approved and ratified improper environmental practices by Rockwell International Corporation at Rocky Flats, then a criminal prosecution of Rockwell employees would be more difficult and could undermine prosecutive appeal of this matter. DOE enjoys sovereign immunity as an agency; however, its employees may be held culpable for crimes.

Finally, Carlson was concerned that legitimate questions might arise regarding whether criminal prosecution was warranted at Rocky Flats; DOE and Rockwell already had plans to close the site and correct environmental damage with a seven-year, $323-million cleanup proposal. Rockwell and its employees were not immune from criminal prosecution, but civilly the company was indemnified by DOE at taxpayer expense. Closing Rocky Flats would have satisfied one of the Lamm-Wirth Task Force goals – to close Rocky Flats completely – from a decade earlier. Later, in January 1989, DOJ assistant attorney general Edward S. G. Dennis formulated a more constructive and supportive memo. (Dennis 1989, 1).

In March 1989, the secretary of energy facilitated personnel to meet with me and discuss logistics to raid Rocky Flats. I was personally assured by Under Secretary of Energy W. Henson Moore that no DOE personnel would be transferred from Rocky Flats. Specifically, I was assured that Albert E. Whiteman, the DOE manager at Rocky Flats, would not be transferred prior to the raid. The DOE Rocky Flats manager was integral to Rocky Flats decision-making and personally responsible for regulatory RCRA compliance at the site. The unusual circumstance in obtaining peaceful access to Rocky Flats through DOE headquarters should not have allowed the manager to be provided sanctuary – particularly after the promises to not transfer him were made. Of course the manager had the right to not self-incriminate himself and could have refused to submit to an interview; however, his office papers would be subject to a lawful search and seizure. After being transferred the DOE Rocky Flats manager would have had the opportunity to sanitize important Rocky Flats documents. Obstruction of justice and tampering with evidence came to my mind.

Events began to move quickly. I was attending a wedding[3] in Delaware in early June 1989 when I was abruptly advised to return to Denver to begin the execution of the federal search warrant at Rocky Flats. Unbeknownst to me, the Denver assistant US Attorney, Ken Fimberg, had provided my search warrant affidavit to a Denver US magistrate to expedite the review process.

On June 5, 1989, I was present with the cadre of FBI and EPA Office of Criminal Enforcement agents and professional support personnel to attend mandatory radiation training. At this training, we learned about radiation dangers and safety, personnel radiation monitoring, and that

EPA radiation personnel would be available for decontamination. Later, when my clothes indicated signs of radiation, I did not have to rely on DOE or Rocky Flats personnel for decontamination, an abhorrent thought to me.

On the morning of June 6, 1989, I met with US magistrate Hilbert Schauer concerning my Application and Affidavit for Search Warrant at Rocky Flats (Lipsky 1989, 1–116). I was amazed that Magistrate Schauer had no questions of me; usually the magistrate has something to say or a question to ask, particularly with regard to a 116-page document to search at such an explosive site. We were able to move forward with the raid. I filed the paperwork, including a separate Motion to Seal the Search Warrant and Affidavit, with the clerk of the court, and off I went. Selected officials were waiting for my arrival with the search warrant at the Rocky Flats conference room, and the majority of the team was staging at the Denver Federal Center. Service of a federal search warrant required handing a paper copy of the propounded search warrant, not the affidavit, to the person in charge of the place to be searched with the affiant noting the time of service.

My route included the Boulder Turnpike, and I caught a glimpse of the Boulder Flatirons one more time from outside of Rocky Flats before facing the challenge that lay before me.

June 1989 photo of Jon Lipsky at Rocky Flats.
Reprinted by permission: Eco Ed, Inc.

The Rocky Flats raid began with a ruse. DOE scheduled a conference at the plant that morning with FBI and EPA agents and DOJ attorneys under the pretense that we were to discuss a potential plot by Earth First!, a radical environmental advocacy group, to sabotage nuclear power plants in Arizona, California, and Colorado. I entered through the Colorado Highway 93 entrance at Rocky Flats. I was running a bit late, but not as late as the Rockwell manager. The under secretary of energy was occupied with DOE personnel actions, and one high-level DOE Albuquerque official displayed quite a look of anxiety and embarrassment as I entered the conference room area.

The DOE resident manager, who had been replaced by the DOE manager from Hanford, Washington, in late May 1989, was nowhere to be seen. Important personal papers that the transferred DOE Rocky Flats manager possessed was the only real cleanup at Rocky Flats. The manager's documentary evidence was not available. I then learned that a DOE "Tiger Team" was already in place, conducting an audit at Rocky Flats (DOE 1989, 1).

Our criminal investigative teams comprising seventy-five people were issued DOE access badges to Rocky Flats along with separate individual dosimeters. Each member of the FBI and EPA teams were required to wear a dosimeter, which was meant to collect information regarding potential exposure to radiation during our time at the Rocky Flats site. The housing for the dosimeter included a slot on the bottom-front to hold the access badge in place with a common lanyard clip on the top and the in-place access badge covering the dosimeter-sensor probably blocked at least alpha radiation. We were encouraged by DOE personnel to wear the access badge over the front of the dosimeter. Weapons-grade plutonium-239 is an alpha emitter and the principal element for the fabrication of the trigger for the atomic bomb. I got it – Rocky Flats was not safe!

The subsequent Tiger Team reports would prove to be counterproductive to our criminal investigation and later for nuclear worker unique compensation claims, Energy Employees Occupational Illness Compensation Program Act of 2000 (EEOICPA). The Tiger Team name was rooted in US Navy parlance, a designation implemented by retired admiral James

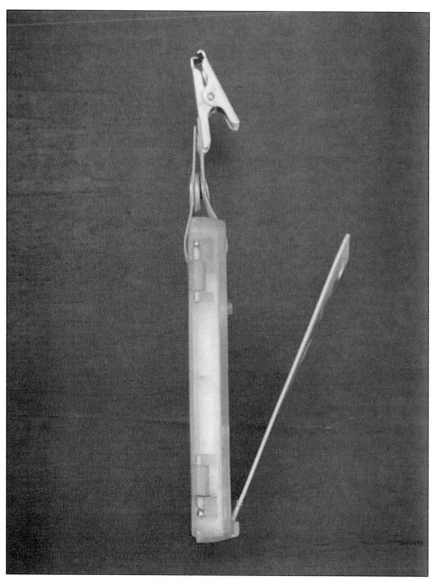

Side view of Rocky Flats' dosimeter and badge.
Reprinted by permission: Eco Ed, Inc.

D. Watkins and the new secretary of energy. The Tiger Team comprised experts from around the United States familiar with Rocky Flats operations, DOE orders, and the Atomic Energy Act.

Further, local Denver news media organizations filed federal court motions to have our search warrant affidavit unsealed (Denver Publishing Company 1989, 1). Unfortunately, the US attorney general callously disregarded the safety of FBI and EPA agents at Rocky Flats and ordered the unsealing of the affidavit during the raid. (Norton and Fimberg 1989, 1). (The book *The Ambushed Grand Jury* expounds on these frustrations – a big case equals big problems.)

On June 7, 1989, the day after Colorado governor Roy Romer aired a "TV tirade" concerning the Rocky Flats raid, the Colorado Department of Health (CDH) personally served its RCRA compliance order at Rocky Flats. (KMGH 1989, 3:15). The CDH enforcement position at Rocky Flats was via administrative or civil sanctions, rather than with criminal sanctions, as allowed by the law. CDH was provided delegated authority to enforce RCRA by the EPA in 1984. It was a hand-delivered compliance order, with allegations of some RCRA misdeeds that had been known and were a year old. (Dowsett 1989, 1). It soon became apparent that CDH prioritized obtaining DOE oversight funds over human health and the environment. The DOE Hanford, Washington, site was the subject of the first tri-party agreement in May 1989, and the state of Colorado wanted a similar agreement to augment their budget. (DOE 1989, 1). By June 16, 1989, Governor Romer exuberantly announced the multimillion-dollar agreement in principle with DOE. (CDH 1989, 1). A second regulatory attempt to close and remediate certain Rocky Flats RCRA waste disposal units was to fail; however, CDH had received their "bribe" money (unnamed DOE Rocky Flats employee). For example, the Solar Evaporation Ponds were closed for use at Rocky Flats by CDH in 1985, and in 1986, the Solar Evaporation Ponds underwent RCRA-closure planning procedures to be completed by 1991. Instead, Rockwell International utilized one of the ponds, among other criminal violations, for routine Rocky Flats activities and operations in 1988 and pleaded guilty to the criminal conduct in 1992. The solar evaporation pond cleanup was specifically cited in the 1989 agreement in principle because the first cleanup attempt in 1986, at taxpayer expense, had failed. As of 2020 the solar evaporation pond footprints remain at the Rocky Flats Superfund Site utilizing a Solar Evaporation Pond Treatment System (SEPTS) with the goal of mitigating Rocky Flats contaminants from the Rocky Flats National Wildlife Refuge and off-site lands.

Federal search warrants have a shelf life of ten days, meaning that a supplemental search warrant was required to complete the search for physical evidence at Rocky Flats. Ultimately, the search took a total of eighteen days and two search warrants. Our efforts involved the seizure of about a million documents, hundreds of interview reports, and 403 bottles of environmental samples that – unfortunately – would not be analyzed, nor would they be considered in the subsequent Rocky Flats Superfund Comprehensive Risk Analysis twenty-seven years later. The Rocky Flats Superfund action was to also include process knowledge that was obviated.

The raid was complete and our work had just begun, but the DOJ moved too quickly to a special grand jury investigation. I thought it was premature for DOJ to impanel the Rocky Flats Special Federal Grand Jury 89-2 (SFGJ) on August 1, 1989, and I believe DOJ knew it. The timing was unusual because the SFGJ "may submit a report to the court" before the evidence could be processed. The political pressure to resolve the criminal investigation sooner rather than later, and perhaps assure the public that the plant was relatively safe, was the DOJ's task at hand, in the shortest amount of time, without consideration of the complexity of the criminal investigation. (Finesilver 1989, 1). However, I am legally constrained from discussing matters presented to the SFGJ, along with classified materials and other matters related to the Privacy Act.

On September 22, 1989, DOE fired Rockwell as the Rocky Flats contract operator. The day before, Rockwell had filed a federal lawsuit in Washington, DC, that, in part, stated it was impossible to legally operate Rocky Flats; that is, the company claimed it was not possible to produce plutonium triggers for nuclear weapons and comply with environmental regulations. Later that month, the EPA designated Rocky Flats on the National Priority List as among the worst of Superfund sites necessitating prioritized remediation.

In May 2007, EPA delisted from Superfund status the Rocky Flats Buffer Zone portion and off-site – residential – acres, without remediation. (EPA 2006, 1). Today, and decades into the future, the approximately 1,400 acres in the middle of the refuge remains an active Superfund site. The Rocky Flats Buffer Zone was designated as the Rocky Flats National Wildlife Refuge (RFNWR) as legislated in the RFNWR Act of 2001. (P. Law 107–107). The RFNWR Act allocated a 300-foot right-of-way along the eastern edge of the property, west of Indiana Street, in Golden, Colorado, and the right-of-way was eventually deeded to the Jefferson Parkway Public Highway Authority (JPPHA) in 2012. The off-site area has since been the subject of much residential construction.

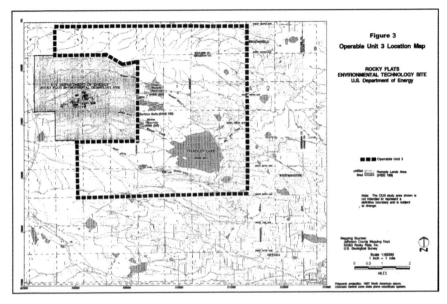

Figure 3. Operable Unit 3 (off-site acres) location map diagram
Rocky Flats, Environmental Technology Site, Jefferson County
Mapping Department, EG&G Rocky Flats, U.S. Geological Survey.

During the SFGJ investigative process, Rockwell's defense attorneys shadowed witnesses who said they testified before the SFGJ and documented their debriefing following their testimony. Rockwell spared no expense to monitor the Rocky Flats criminal investigation. Overtly, criminal target letters were issued during the investigation, after the prosecutive decision was made that no individuals would be charged. I refused to personally deliver any of the "target letters" because of the perceived misconduct by DOJ. The issuance of target letters was publicly known; however, Michael J. Norton testified before the congressional subcommittee in 1992 that the matter was grand jury material, which limited his responses. (Fimberg 1991, 1).

In late 1991, the established DOJ corporate-only plea agreement became the final prosecutive decision of the grand jury investigation. No individuals, including DOE employees, were to be charged with crimes. There were no criminal ramifications for the DOE Rocky Flats manager having been transferred from Rocky Flats in May 1989. Denver assistant US attorney Ken Fimberg, with whom I had worked for several years, called me into a private meeting to inform me that the plea agreement was not to include any allegations by former Rocky Flats nuclear worker and whistleblower James Stone, who had filed a federal False Claims Act lawsuit, or any allegations from a draft SFGJ report. However, the governing statute for the SFGJ and the chief federal judge who had sworn in the panel had authorized a Rocky Flats report to be written. This report was repressed by DOJ, but it was eventually leaked to *Westword*, an independent Denver weekly paper.

My intentions were clearly stated during this meeting – that evidence existed to charge individuals involved in Rocky Flats operations. The assistant US attorney shared this opinion, but he told me he had been outvoted. One unnamed Rocky Flats prosecutor, now a Colorado US congressman, voted to pay Rockwell for the inconvenience of the criminal investigation and issue an official apology. Prosecutors drafted the Government's Sentencing Memorandum, which included concessions to Rockwell that were not investigated (Norton et al. 1992, 1) For example, the US Government stated, "The conduct to which Rockwell has pled guilty did not result in substantial physiological harm, or the imminent threat of substantial physiological harm, to members of the public residing and working outside Rocky Flats' boundaries" (Norton et al. 1992, 124).

I was stunned and physically ill over the plea agreement and some unsubstantiated concessions between the *United States of America v. Rockwell International, Inc.*, case number 92-CR-107.

During one of the last proceedings, an unnamed SFGJ juror asked my opinion on whether evidence existed to charge individuals involved in Rocky Flats operations. Prosecutors interrupted the question and advised that I would not be providing a response. I was pleasantly surprised to learn that the SFGJ did not agree with the plea agreement. In March 1992, the incomplete and misleading plea agreement and factual basis was tendered to the court and it was accepted by the federal judge in early June 1992. (Norton 1992 et al., 1). US government officials were under the impression that the Rocky Flats prosecution information and documents would remain under executive branch lock and key and US District Court seal, but that notion soon changed.

With his looming reelection bid, President George H. W. Bush touted the Rocky Flats plea agreement as one of the successes of his administration. However, others did not agree. Congressman Howard Wolpe, (D-Michigan), who was the chairman of the Subcommittee on Investigations and Oversight of the House Committee on Science, Space and Technology, initiated an investigation into "The Prosecution of Environmental Crimes At the Department of Energy's Rocky Flats Facility" (Wolpe 1993, 1). Initially, the subcommittee's staff would provide questions for me to FBI headquarters, which would be forwarded to Denver for me to answer, and then my written answers would be routed back to FBI headquarters before they were provided to committee staff. I experienced a few rounds of this back and forth before the U.S. marshal's office subpoenaed me to personally testify before the subcommittee.

However, I was informed that DOJ had no intention for me to testify; they attempted to exclude my personal testimony under the guise of executive privilege. Executive privilege is a US presidential power of withholding information in the public's interest. Eventually, DOJ's efforts earned me a contempt of Congress warning letter from the subcommittee chairman. DOJ attorney David Margolis advised me not to worry; Congress relies on DOJ to prosecute contempt citations, and DOJ would not prosecute me regarding this matter. Finally, when cooler heads prevailed, I was authorized to testify before Congress, but only if a DOJ attorney sat with me and if I heeded an admonishment concerning the lack of evidence to charge individuals. (This stick-in-the-mud strategy should be familiar, as William P. Barr was the US attorney general in 1992.)

Of course, the question of whether there was evidence to charge individuals was on the minds of many of the congressional representatives. Subcommittee chairman Wolpe referred to it by saying, "Second, it should be that the most important thing that Federal prosecutors bargained away in negotiations with Rockwell was the truth" (Wolpe 1993, 2). Despite being admonished by DOJ that individual charges lacked sufficient evidence, I continued to testify, based on the evidence, that individuals should have been charged. My DOJ handler, Roger Cubbage, gave me verbal solace in my convictions. DOJ was serious about their warning to me. In between congressional testimony sessions, Denver assistant US attorney Ken Fimberg presented me with an unsolicited two-page jurat (affidavit under oath) to sign that contained seven numbered paragraphs stating that I had made "statements freely and voluntarily, and have not been pressured or coerced to do so" (Fimberg 1992, 2). There was nothing voluntary about signing the document. Congressional rules restricted contact between witnesses, and Kenneth Fimberg demanded that I should recant my congressional testimony. I did not sign and bitterly resented the document and its intentions.

By early January 1993, the subcommittee issued its report, and three weeks later, I was transferred to the Los Angeles office of the FBI. The FBI had fulfilled a special request to transfer me.[4] In 1994, I was interviewed for the "Dubester Report," a DOJ investigation to rebut the 1993 congressional report concerning Rocky Flats initiated by Webster (Web) Hubbell. (Dubester 1994, 1). DOJ garnered as much media attention as it could that the Wolpe report conclusions were influenced by politics. DOJ attorney Mark Dubester chided me several times during my daytime interview concerning restricted information that I was legally not allowed to answer. Then I was summoned to his office that evening. Dubester pressed me again to answer legally restrictive information, and then I walked out the door.

I fondly and reverently recall being contacted in September 2000 by attorney Caron Balkany about her Rocky Flats Citizens' Investigation. The site was contaminated and the public did not know the full story of Rocky Flats. Rocky Flats had been shuttered; however, the government intended to transform it into a plutonium playground. After Caron Balkany explained that the Colorado congressional delegation intended to convert Rocky Flats into a national wildlife refuge to promote, among other things, primary school field trips, I wanted to assist Caron and her project any way I could to inform the public of the truth. Caron Balkany asked me if I recalled what Congressman Wolpe said to me – that if any additional information concerning Rocky Flats was known, I should contact Congress about what I knew. Because of the congressional subcommittee oversight investigation into Rocky Flats, literally thousands of Rocky Flats documents were released to the public. Caron obtained some copies of those congressional documents, many of which had not seen the light of day. These were the types of documents that DOJ had unsuccessfully attempted to conceal from the public with the SFGJ. But the public has a right to know about Rocky Flats and its lingering radiation contamination, a risk analysis of more than 250,000 years.

In March 2004, Caron Balkany and Wes McKinley published their book, *The Ambushed Grand Jury*. Jacque Brever, former Rocky Flats nuclear worker, and I contributed to the book, and I notified Congress about the contents of the nonfiction, nonprofit book. The previous month I had sent a lengthy memo to FBI director Robert S. Mueller III, reminding him of his duty to protect whistleblowers like me (Lipsky 2004, 1–3). In advance of an August 18, 2004, press conference to announce the book and discuss the fact that Rocky Flats was not safe, which I was planning to attend on my own personal time, the FBI issued a gag order to include administrative action against me regarding the Rocky Flats criminal investigation. (*Rocky Mountain News* 2004, 1).

The *Merilyn Cook v. Dow Chemical, Rockwell International* federal civil suit, case number 90-cv-00181(JLK) (Cook), a class action lawsuit on behalf of more than 13,000 residents living near Rocky Flats, was scheduled to begin trial in 2005. The threat I received from my FBI superiors on August 17, 2004, demonstrated that I would not be officially authorized to testify in the Cook case. Cook was the namesake for the federal civil Rocky Flats nuisance and trespass of weapons-grade plutonium-239 litigation that allegedly devalued property values. It was important for the plaintiffs and largely the public that I be able to testify in this case. I had met the requisite criteria for retirement, and, as we call it in FBI-speak, "KMA (Kiss my ass)" day. I was able to retire from the FBI – out the door in '04.

In 2005, I was in contact with Peter Nordberg from the Berger & Montague law firm in Philadelphia, about testifying in the Cook case. That summer I received a "DOJ letter" and follow-up telephone call from a Denver FBI legal adviser. (Goffi 2005, 1). DOJ learned that I was on the witness list for the Cook case, and I was essentially informed that if I testified, I could be arrested, charged with a crime, and sentenced to prison – a sobering thought.

My wife, Patricia, and I discussed the DOJ threat, as we previously had considered other DOJ threats, but she always remained supportive; she said again, "Follow your heart." My research gleaned a DOJ glitch in their rule concerning the relevancy of my proposed testimony as a retired FBI agent. I called Peter Nordberg, and we agreed I would not be subpoenaed to the trial. I then participated in the court-ordered pretrial deposition session and testified before the Cook jury for about forty hours. The trial judge had ruled that my Rocky Flats subject-matter expert witness testimony would be heard. The Kirkland & Ellis lead defense attorney cautioned the judge that he was concerned I might testify in a fashion to expose me for arrest. Judge John Kane said he was concerned for my safety as well. It turned out that more than a handful of attorneys in attendance had told Peter Nordberg they would defend me if necessary, pro bono. On Valentine's Day 2006 the jury's verdict was for the plaintiffs: that Dow Chemical and Rockwell International trespassed with plutonium from Rocky Flats, plutonium is present on the class properties, and that plutonium will continue to be present on the class properties indefinitely. In May 2016, the Cook plaintiffs settled with Dow Chemical and Rockwell for $375 million. Dow Chemical and Rockwell were indemnified by DOE; however, the US president at the time ne-

Jon Lipsky walks to court at Denver, Colorado. Reprinted by permission: Denver Public Library.

gotiated special appropriations from Congress to pay the bills, including Kirkland & Ellis' invoice at taxpayers' expense. No funds were paid from the existing DOE budget.

In 2014, Patricia and I moved back to Colorado after the special symposium at the Arvada Events Center to celebrate the twenty-fifth anniversary of the FBI raid at Rocky Flats. The previous year the Rocky Mountain Peace and Justice Center in Boulder had honored me, whistleblower Jacque Brever, and grand jury foreman Wes McKinley with an award. In 2015, I received an award from the Alliance for Nuclear Accountability.

My work with Rocky Flats continues. I've collaborated with Professor John Whiteley, University of California at Irvine; Ashlyn Velte and Philip Gaddis, University of Colorado, Boulder archives regarding the Rocky Flats collections of the Atomic West Project; and with principal nuclear worker advocates Terrie Barrie and Deb Jerison to promote nuclear worker unique compensation claims under EEOICPA. I work with the Rocky Flats Technology Group, initiated by Professor Harvey Nichols, Randy Stafford, Michelle Gabrieloff-Parish and others, to thwart the opening of the RFNWR and construction of the Jefferson Parkway, and the efforts of the Rocky Mountain Peace and Justice Center, Judith Mohling and LeRoy Moore regarding Rocky Flats Nuclear Guardianship, as espoused by environmental activist and scholar JoAnna Macy. I support the efforts of seven local nongovernmental organizations (NGOs) created to promote the truth about Rocky Flats and work to seek independent verification of Rocky Flats risks, as proclaimed by Anne Fenerty and Dr. Mark Johnson, MD, MPH. Anne Fenerty was a professor of chemistry knowledgeable about Rocky Flats and Dr. Johnson is the executive director of the Jefferson County Colorado Health Department where much of Rocky Flats is situated. As environmental watchdog Snake River Alliance notes, "Nuclear waste is not your friend."

The success of our efforts, on the part of individuals and organizations, has been substantial. With the involvement of Mary McDevitt Harlow, our work prevented a vacuous attempt by the US Fish and Wildlife Service (USFWS) to conduct a 701-acre controlled burn at the RFNWR in 2015. In 2016, our efforts, including those of Sandy Pennington, persuaded the Town of Superior to abandon Rocky Mountain Greenway (RMG) public trails through the refuge. Six other municipalities voted for the RMG trails; however, they decided to require an environmental sampling contingency prior to proceeding. Also in 2016, we launched a community campaign, conceived by Art Burmeister, to inform local school district board members regarding the truths, ignored by the government, about Rocky Flats. To date, seven school districts have banned school field trips to Rocky Flats. The eighth school district is considering a similar ban.

In 2017, our advocacy efforts launched a federal National Environmental Policy Act (NEPA) lawsuit against USFWS to not open the refuge public trails as reconfigured from what was believed to be legally permissible. The case was dismissed, but refiling is still an option. In 2018, our work launched a second federal NEPA lawsuit against USFWS and the US Department of Transportation to not open the refuge public trails as reconfigured; a judicial decision is pending. The Town of Superior also filed its own similar lawsuit. Then-US congressman Jared Polis intervened on our group's behalf on the planned September 2018 opening of the Rocky Flats Refuge, but after about an hour of agency reconsideration, USFWS opened it.

In January 2019, attorney Pat Mellen filed a federal petition on behalf of seven community organizations to obtain a judicial decision to release certain SFGJ records to the public, based on five inherent dangers posed by Rocky Flats activities, operations, and risks. (Mellen 2019, 1).

With Randy Stafford leading the charge, the Jefferson Parkway Public Highway Authority reversed its decision to not sample the Jefferson Parkway soil. In August 2019, JPPHA disclosed that one particular sample resulted in a 264 pCi/g, 8.8 micron high-activity hot particle of plutonium-239 (1,250 times higher than the Rocky Flats Superfund standard and 6,600 times higher than worldwide fallout levels). With the expertise of Professor Michael Ketterer (see Chapter 7), we all should be concerned about fugitive hot particles of weapons-grade plutonium-239. The hot particle discovery has caused a construction delay of the Jefferson Parkway, scheduled to be built by 2020.

The challenges continue. We have grave concerns for the public about DOE plans to breach three Rocky Flats site earthen surface water dams by 2020. The radioactive and hazardous waste–laden soil disturbance will no doubt be entrained by air currents, causing yet another nuisance and trespass against public health and the environment.

It is Rocky Flats all over again – Rocky Flats II – with the National Nuclear Security Administration (NNSA) plans for plutonium pit production at Los Alamos National Laboratory in New Mexico, and the Savannah River site plant to produce new plutonium pits by 2030. (NNSA 2019, 1). Rocky Flats produced plutonium pits until June 1989 when confirmed crimes ceased operations. NNSA has convinced US government actors that Plutonium Aging is somehow an issue in the short-term. However Plutonium Aging is a fallacy meant to mislead the public away from the prevailing pretermitted nuclear waste problems. "Plutonium and people don't mix" and the Precautionary Principle should rule our public policies around the world, not the military-industrial complex (Moore 2019, 1).

Nuclear weapons beget nuclear waste, and the United States is not able to safely store even the existing amount of nuclear waste. It is inconceivable and unthinkable to promote the fabrication of additional nuclear weapons. ICAN, the "international campaign to stigmatize, prohibit and eliminate nuclear weapons," reports that while thirty-four countries have ratified the nuclear-weapons ban treaty, none of the nine nuclear-armed states have signed (ICAN n.d., 1). US officials ignore the ICAN treaty, but the Norwegian Nobel Committee awarded ICAN its Nobel Peace Prize in 2017 for its work on the Treaty on the Prohibition of Nuclear Weapons. On January 28, 2020, I testified before the New York City Council, along with more than sixty others, in favor of their legislation regarding the ICAN Cities Appeal efforts for a nuclear-free zone and to divest public pension funds with companies involved in nuclear weapons production (Lipsky 2020, 1). I invite all readers to learn more about nuclear weapon truths and become involved in a sustainable public policy effort regarding all things nuclear.

Endnotes

1. In July 1984, my wife, Patricia, during our temporary quarters at Denver, read about Rocky Flats and its contamination, and we decided to reside in Aurora, Colorado, east of Denver, to avoid the Rocky Flats' radioactive pollution.

2. Prior to flying over Rocky Flats and exposing photos/video, I secured a letter of immunity from the Denver US attorney to not be prosecuted for such crimes enumerated in the Atomic Energy Act, just in case.

3. Patricia, my wife, was matron of honor, our second daughter, Rachel, was a flower girl and our two other daughters, Trisha and Kristin, attended along with my beloved mother in law, Ruth Bernice Collins.

4. The month prior I learned that the FBI had no remaining transfer funds and was specifically informed that I would not be transferred. Special FBI Denver requests to not transfer me began in about 1986.

Works Cited

The array of Rocky Flats source documents for this essay is the direct result of Congressman Howard Wolpe (D-MI), his staff, and his US Congressional Oversight and Investigations Subcommittee efforts.

Under the leadership, vision, and expertise of Ms. Caron Balkany, Esquire, many of the subcommittee documents, Freedom of Information Act responsive–documents, and donated documents are publicly available for inspection, education, and scholarly works at the Eco Ed, Inc., website, ***https://rockyflatsambushedgrandjury.com/reference-materials/.*** Kristin Lipsky assisted with organizing and scanning of the documents. Eco Ed, Inc. is a New Mexico nonprofit corporation dedicated to environmental justice, education, and sponsorship.

In addition, Ms. Terrie Barrie, Alliance for Nuclear Worker Advocacy Groups, secured the donation of thousands of United Steel Workers, Local 8031, Rocky Flats–related documents at ***https://rockyflatsambushedgrandjury.com/category/safety-concerns/.***

Associated Press. "Protex Industries Convicted in Waste Case," Dec. 22, 1987. *https://apnews.com/cc3a22d2b29483c59540c9e3e13d2473*, accessed Dec.12, 2019.

Barton, John. "Briefing for Mary L. Walker for Meetings with Admiral Foley, General Counsel Farrell and with the Under Secretary on Rocky Flats. July 14, 1986. https://rockyflatsambushedgrandjury.com/3425-2/, accessed Dec. 12, 2019.

Carlson, Martin. "Draft Search Warrant, Rocky Flats Nuclear Weapons Facility. Jan. 10, 1989." https:// rockyflatsambushedgrandjury.com/ draft-search-warrant-rocky-flats-nuclear-weapons-facility-debriefing-memo/, accessed Jan. 31, 2020.

Colorado Department of Health (CDH) and US Department of Energy (DOE). "Agreement in Principle," by Governor Roy Romer, CDH, and DOE Secretary James T. Watkins. https://rockyflatsambushedgrandjury.com/us-dept-energy-colorado-rocky-flats-agreement/, accessed Dec. 12, 2019.

Dennis, Edward S. G., Jr. "Briefing on Operation Desert Glow. Jan. 31, 1989." https://rockyflatsambushedgrandjury.com/us-department-of-justice-briefing-on-operation-desert-glow-at-rocky-flats-january-31-1989/, accessed on Dec. 17, 2019.

The Denver Publishing Company, d/b/a the *Rocky Mountain News.* "Motion to Unseal Materials Regarding Search Warrant," case number 89-730M. June 7, 1989. https://rockyflatsambushedgrandjury.com/wp-content/uploads/19890607-Motion-to-Unseal-SW-DN-Publishing-Co.pdf, accessed Dec. 12, 2019.

Dowsett, Frederick, and David Shelton. "Compliance Order No. 89-06-07-01 cover letter." June 7, 1989. https://rockyflatsambushedgrandjury.com/wp-content/uploads/19890607-CDHOrder-RockyFlats.pdf, accessed Dec. 12, 2019.

Dubester, Mark. "Summary." April 8, 1994. http://sites.uci.edu/e127/files/2018/08/DOJ1.pdf, accessed Dec. 14, 2019.

Eco Ed. "Effluent Monitor Placement on Walnut Creek, East of Rocky Flats." 1988. https://rockyflatsambushedgrandjury.com/1988-effluent-monitor-placement-at-walnut-creek-and-indiana-street-arvada-colorado-at-rocky-flats-perimeter-in-preparation-for-the-june-6-1989-federal-search-warrant-at-rocky-flats/, accessed Dec. 17, 2019.

———. "Overflight FLIR video Rocky Flats Nuclear Weapons Plant. Dec.15, 1988." https://rockyflatsambushedgrandjury.com/overflight-flir-video-rocky-flats-nuclear-weapons-plant-december-15-1988/, accessed Dec. 12, 2019.

Eco Ed, Inc. "Rocky Flats: The Ambushed Grand Jury." RockyFlatsAmbushedGrandJury.com, statement by Wes McKinley, 2002, https://rockyflatsambushedgrandjury.com/rocky-flats/, time mark 3:30, accessed Dec. 12, 2019.

Fimberg, Ken. "Individual Targets' Attorneys." May 2, 1991. https://rockyflatsambushedgrandjury.com/rocky-flats-individual-targets-attorneys-letter-of-may-2-1991/, accessed Dec. 14, 2019.

Fimberg, Kenneth. "Affidavit of Jon S. Lipsky." Oct.1992. https://rockyflatsambushedgrandjury.com/rocky-flats-bullshit-affidavit/, accessed Dec. 14, 2019.

Finesilver, Sherman. "United States District Court, District of Colorado, Information to Special Grand Jury 89-2, Aug. 1, 1989." https://rocky-flatsambushedgrandjury.com/information-to-special-grand-jury-89-2-august-1-1989/, accessed Dec. 20, 2019.

Goffi, Robert. "Re: Cook, et al v. Rockwell International Corp., et al., 90-K-181 (D. Colo.)." Oct. 13, 2005. https://rockyflatsambushedgrand-jury.com/DOJ-letter-to-jon-lipsky-to-not-testify-in-the-merilyn-cook-et-al-v-dow-chemical-and-rockwell-litigation/, accessed Jan. 5, 2020.

ICAN. "International Campaign to Stigmatize, Prohibit and Eliminate Nuclear Weapons." N.d. https://www.icanw.org, accessed Jan. 5, 2020.

KMGH Denver 7. "Live Interview with Colorado Governor Roy Romer." June 6, 1989. https://rockyflatsambushedgrandjury.com/rocky-flats-june-1989-local-denver-news/, time mark 3:15, accessed Dec. 12, 2019.

Lipsky, Jon. "Jon Lipsky no FBI retaliation letter to FBI Director." Feb. 24, 2004. https://rockyflatsambushedgrandjury.com/3436-2/, accessed Dec. 14, 2019.

———. "The Rocky Flats Plant, Application and Affidavit for Search Warrant, case number 89-730M." June 6, 1989. https://rockyflatsam-bushedgrandjury.com/wp-content/uploads/19890606-Rocky-Flats-Applicaton-and-Aff-for-SW-89-730M.pdf, accessed on Dec. 12, 2019.

———. "The Rocky Flats Plant, Application and Affidavit for Search Warrant, case number 89-753M, June 14, 1989." https://rocky-flatsambushedgrandjury.com/second-rocky-flats-fbi-search-warrant-june-14-1989/, accessed Dec. 20, 2019.

———. "The Rocky Flats Plant, Search Warrant Return, case number 89-730M." June 14, 1989. https://rockyflatsambushedgrandjury.com/wp-content/uploads/19890614-Search-Warrant-89-730M-Return.pdf, accessed on Dec. 12, 2019.

———. "The Rocky Flats Plant, Search Warrant Return, case number 89-753M." June 23, 1989. https://rockyflatsambushedgrandjury.com/wp-content/uploads/19890614-Search-Warrant-89-753M-Return.pdf, accessed Dec. 12, 2019.

————. Testimony before the New York City Council, Committees on Governmental Operations & Civil Service and Labor, Jan. 28, 2020. https://youtu.be/JaGfcaYg4ec, accessed on Feb. 2, 2020.

————. "Unknown Subjects; Doing Business as Rockwell International Corporation, Rocky Flats Plant, Golden, Colorado; Toxic Waste Matter; Public Corruption Matter." July 8, 1987. https://rockyflatsambushedgrandjury.com/federal-bureau-of-investigation-letterhead-memo-lhm-rocky-flats/, accessed Dec. 16, 2019.

McConnell, Linda. "Rocky Flats Is Not Safe," *Rocky Mountain News*, Aug. 18, 2004. https://digital.denverlibrary.org/digital/collection/p16079coll32/id/25877/, accessed Jan. 3, 2020.

Mellen, Pat. "Petition for Disclosure of Certain Documents Provided to Special Federal Grand Jury 89-2 opposed by DOJ." Jan. 10, 2019. https://rockyflatsambushedgrandjury.com/petition-for-disclosure-of-certain-documents-provided-to-special-federal-grand-jury-89-2-opposed-by-us-doj/, accessed Jan. 5, 2020.

Moore, LeRoy. *Plutonium and People Don't Mix.* 2019. https://www.boulderbookstore.net/event/leroy-moore-plutonium-people-dont-mix, accessed Jan. 5, 2020.

National Nuclear Security Administration (NNSA). "Plutonium Pit Production." Apr. 2019. https://www.energy.gov/sites/prod/files/2019/05/f62/2019-05-13-FACTSHEET-plutonium-pits.pdf, accessed Dec. 14, 2019.

Norton, Michael, and Kenneth Fimberg. "Motion to Extend Date and Supplement June 6, 1989 Search Warrant Inventory." June 23, 1989. https://rockyflatsambushedgrandjury.com/wp-content/uploads/19890623-Motion-Order-89-730M-Search-Warrant-Return.pdf, accessed on Dec. 12, 2019.

————. "Motion to Unseal Search Warrant and Search Warrant Affidavit," case number 89-730M. June 9, 1989. https://rockyflatsambushedgrandjury.com/wp-content/uploads/19890609-Motion-Order-to-Unseal-SW-USG.pdf, accessed Dec. 12, 2019.

Norton, Michael, Barry Hartman, Kenneth Fimberg, and Peter Murtha. "Information 42 U.S.C. S 6928 (d) (2), 33 U.S.C. SS 1311 (a) and

1319 (c)." March 26, 1992. https://rockyflatsambushedgrand-jury.com/rockwell-international-charged-federal-environmental-crimes-rocky-flats/ [20], https://www.latimes.com/archives/la-xpm-1993-08-15-tm-24105-story.html, accessed Dec. 14, 2019.

―――――. "Plaintiffs Sentencing Memorandum." 1992. https://rocky-flatsambushedgrandjury.com/plaintiffs-sentencing-memoran-dum-rocky-flats-march-26-1992/, accessed Jan. 5, 2020.

Norton, Michael et al. "Plaintiff's Sentencing Memorandum." March 26, 1992. https://rockyflatsambushedgrandjury.com/wp-content/up-loads/1989-09-21-Rockwell-Sues-Government-in-Rocky-Flats-Dis-pute.pdf , accessed Jan. 23, 2020.

―――――. "Waste Stream Identification and Characterization, Overview, U.S.D.O.E. – Rocky Flats Plant. Apr. 6, 1987." https://rockyflatsam-bushedgrandjury.com/wp-content/uploads/19870406-Berger-Mon-tague-P-1258-WSIC-Overview.pdf, accessed Jan. 3, 2020.

Scanlon, Bill. "DOE Cuts Ties with Rockwell. *Boulder Daily Camera*, Sept. 23, 1989. https://rockyflatsambushedgrandjury.com/rockwell-sues-government-in-rocky-flats-dispute/, accessed Jan. 23, 2019.

Title 42 US Code 6228(f)(1)(C).

US Department of Energy (DOE). "Assessment of Environmental Con-ditions at the Rocky Flats Plant, Golden, Colorado, Aug. 1989," with DOE Freedom of Information Act cover letter. https://rockyflatsam-bushedgrandjury.com/u-s-department-of-energy-tiger-team-re-port-at-rocky-flats-august-1989/, accessed Dec. 20, 2019.

―――――. "Tri-Party Agreement." May 15, 1989. https://www.hanford.gov/page.cfm/TriParty, accessed Jan. 2, 2020.

US Department of Justice (DOJ). Attorney General's Guidelines on General Crimes, Racketeering Enterprise and Domestic Security/Terrorism Investigations. Updated March 2, 2017. See "Preliminary Inquiries" and "Investigations." https://www.justice.gov/archives/ag/attorney-generals-guidelines-general-crimes-racketeering-enter-prise-and-domestic, accessed Dec.12, 2019.

US Environmental Protection Agency (EPA). "Preliminary Closeout Report: Rocky Flats Plant (DOE) Central and Peripheral Operable

Units," 2006. https://semspub.epa.gov/work/08/1020362.pdf, accessed Dec. 12, 2019.

Westword. "True Lies." Aug. 19, 2004. https://www.westword.com/news/true-lies-5080629, accessed Dec. 14, 2019.

Wolpe, Howard. "The Prosecution of Environmental Crimes at the Department of Energy's Rocky Flats Facility." https://rockyflatsambushedgrandjury.com/wp-content/uploads/19930114-Congressman-Wolpe-Report-re-Rocky-Flats-Prosecution.pdf, accessed Dec. 14, 2019.

CONTRIBUTOR BIOGRAPHIES

Becky Alexis-Martin, PhD, is a lecturer in political and cultural geographies at Manchester Metropolitan University. She is also a senior research fellow in human geography at the University of Southampton. Her research interests include the health and well-being of nuclear communities and nuclear culture. She also researches the consequences of nuclear warfare, irregular warfare, and terrorism, with a focus on the long-term socio-environmental consequences of each scenario.

Jeff Gipe grew up near Rocky Flats Nuclear Weapons Plant, where his father worked for many years. He has been exploring a variety of avenues for portraying Rocky Flats' secret and highly politicized legacy through the arts. Gipe created a public memorial for Rocky Flats, he has curated several art exhibits, and he is currently directing the film, *Half-Life of Memory*. Gipe earned his bachelor of fine arts degree from Rocky Mountain College of Art and Design in Denver, and his master of fine arts degree from the New York Academy of Art in New York City.

Linda Pentz Gunter founded Beyond Nuclear in 2007 and serves as its international specialist as well as its media and development director. Prior to her work in antinuclear advocacy, she was a journalist for twenty years in print and broadcast, working for USA Network, Reuters, *The Times* (UK), and other US and international outlets. In 2018, Linda launched a new web platform, BeyondNuclearInternational.org.

Heidi Hutner, PhD, director of sustainability studies and associate professor at Stony Brook University, writes about the environment for magazines, books, and academic journals. She is the author of *Colonial Women* (Oxford University Press). Hutner is working on two books, *Earth Room: Notes from a Professor and Mother*, and *Nowhere: An Atomic Memoir*. She holds a PhD from the University of Washington.

Kristen Iversen, PhD, is author of *Full Body Burden: Growing Up in the Nuclear Shadow of Rocky Flats* (selected by numerous universities for their First Year Experience/Common Read programs and now a forthcoming documentary), *Molly Brown: Unraveling the Myth*, and *Shadow Boxing: Art and Craft in Creative Nonfiction*, and a forthcoming biography of Nikola Tesla. Her work has appeared in the *New York Times, The Nation, The American Scholar, Fourth Genre*, and many other publications. Originally from Colorado, Iversen has taught at universities around the country and is professor of creative writing at the University of Cincinnati, where she also serves as Literary Nonfiction editor of *The Cincinnati Review*. She holds a PhD from the University of Denver, and in spring of 2021, she will be a Fulbright Scholar at the University of Bergen, Norway.

Carol Jensen, RN, MEd, is a retired professor emeritus in integrative health care at Metropolitan State University in Denver, Colorado. Carol created the integrative health care program at Metro State, which was the first of its kind in the United States. Carol began as a clinical nurse and administrator but found her true avocation in working with and teaching Metro State students. Her background includes expertise and practice related to alternative medicine, aging and gerontology issues, and integrative health and wellness. Carol initiated the Rocky Flats Community Health Study when members of the public and community groups became concerned about environmental health impacts related to Rocky Flats.

Dr. Mark B. Johnson has been the executive director of Jefferson County Public Health since April 1990. He graduated from medical school at Loma Linda University and received his medical specialty training and master of public health degree from Johns Hopkins University. He is board certified in preventive medicine and public health and is a past president of the American College of Preventive Medicine.

Michael E. Ketterer studied chemistry at the University of Notre Dame and University of Colorado-Boulder, receiving a PhD in analytical chemistry. Michael has conducted studies of plutonium in the environment, using inductively coupled plasma mass spectrometry; current research interests include studying plutonium dioxide particles in soils near the former Rocky Flats facility. Michael is Professor Emeritus of Chemistry and Biochemistry at Northern Arizona University, and is Adjunct Professor in the Chemistry and Biochemistry Department at University of Denver.

Jon Lipsky, MAS and Retired FBI, was the lead FBI criminal investigator of federal environmental crimes at the Rocky Flats Nuclear Weapons Plant, in Golden, Colorado from 1987 to 1992. He was also a Las Vegas, Nevada Metropolitan Police Officer. He contributed to *The Ambushed Grand Jury* nonfiction and nonprofit book to enlighten the public concerning U.S. government misdeeds and about the fact that Rocky Flats will never be safe. He testified as a subject-matter expert witness for plaintiffs in the *Cook v. Rockwell* federal lawsuit.

Heidi Maibom, PhD, is professor of philosophy at the University of Cincinnati. She holds a PhD from University College London, and has held fellowships at Cambridge University and Princeton University. Her work concerns emotion, empathy, psychopathology, responsibility, and interpersonal understanding. Her books include *Empathy and Morality* (Oxford University Press 2014), *Routledge Handbook of Philosophy of Empathy* (Routledge 2017), and *Empathy* (Routledge forthcoming). She is currently writing a book about perspective taking.

Stephanie A. Malin, PhD, is an environmental sociologist specializing in natural resource sociology, governance, and rural development, with a focus on the community impacts of resource extraction and energy production. Her main interests include environmental justice, environmental health, social mobilization, and the socio-environmental effects of market-based economies. Stephanie serves as an associate professor in the Department of Sociology at Colorado State University and she is an adjunct associate professor with the Colorado School of Public Health. She completed a Mellon Foundation Postdoctoral Fellowship at Brown University after earning her PhD in sociology from Utah State University.

Writer and former academic **LeRoy Moore**, PhD, has been devoted to Rocky Flats issues since he learned about the plant in 1978. He worked successfully with others to end nuclear weapons production at the plant, then sought the best possible cleanup of a site badly contaminated with radioactive plutonium. Because of the inadequacy of the cleanup, he now seeks to make people aware that Rocky Flats poses a public health danger forever. He is the author of *Plutonium and People Don't Mix: Rocky Flats: Colorado's Defunct Nuclear Bomb Factory* (2019).

Dr. Harvey Nichols, emeritus professor of biology at University of Colorado–Boulder, was born and educated in England and then recruited to a postdoctoral position at Yale. Following an appointment in the Department of Meteorology at University of Wisconsin–Madison, he spent forty years as a professor in biology at CU–Boulder. His primary field is arctic paleo-ecology and ancient and modern climate history of the Arctic (northern Canada and Arctic Siberia), resulting from his expeditions into those regions. His esoteric studies of windblown pollen in the Arctic led the Department of Energy to ask him to do similar research on windblown plutonium particles at the nuclear weapons establishment at Rocky Flats, which led to his forty-five years of scientific criticism of their air-sampling equipment, operations, and hazardous residues. Nichols won the Boulder Faculty Assembly prize at CU–Boulder for Excellence in (Public) Service in recognition of his Rocky Flats work.

Shannon Perry currently manages exhibitions and loans for the Brooks Museum of Art in Memphis, Tennessee. She holds degrees in art from James Madison University (BS) and in art history from the University of Maryland–College Park (MA). She has more than twenty-five years of experience working with art museum collections and exhibitions, including spending a decade at the Smithsonian Institution, first at the Smithsonian Institution Traveling Exhibition Service (SITES) and later the Smithsonian American Art Museum.

E. Warren Perry, Jr. (1963–2019) was a writer, lecturer, and curator for seven museums and five universities from 1981 to 2019. He held degrees in literature and drama from the University of Memphis (MA) and the Catholic University of America (MFA). Among his many publications are *Echoes of Elvis* (2012) and *Swift to My Wounded: Walt Whitman and the Civil War* (2010). He was the former Curator of Collections for the American Museum of Science and Energy, (Oak Ridge, TN), and was the programs administrator for the Pink Palace Family of Museums (Memphis, TN).

Louise M. Roselle is a civil litigator who is of counsel to Biller & Kimble, LLC, in Cincinnati, Ohio. She has practiced law for more than forty-seven years and was co-trial counsel for the plaintiffs in the *Cook v, Rockwell* lawsuit, the class action for the residents around Rocky Flats. Her civil trial practice has focused on plaintiffs' complex environmental class action and personal injury litigation in both state and federal courts. She has successfully litigated and resolved cases that include environmental lawsuits for both workers and neighbors, automobile accidents, and chemical plant explosions.

Randy Stafford is a senior manager at Oracle, with a thirty-two-year career in software architecture. He holds a bachelor of science degree in applied mathematics, with graduate coursework in computer science, from Colorado State University. Mr. Stafford has contributed to four books on software architecture and speaks frequently at software conferences. His mother grew up in Arvada, and her siblings worked at Rocky Flats. Mr. Stafford served on the Jefferson Parkway Advisory Committee.

Kathleen Sullivan, PhD, has been engaged in the nuclear issue for more than thirty years. Director of Hibakusha Stories, an arts-based initiative that has brought atomic bomb survivors to some 45,000 students, she produces nuclear-themed films, including two documentaries (*The Last Atomic Bomb* and *The Ultimate Wish: Ending the Nuclear Age*) and projects that focus on art for disarmament – utilizing visual arts, music, and dance (*The Nuclear Age in 6 Movements, The Hiroshima Panels Project,* and *If You Love This Planet*). Kathleen is a Nagasaki peace correspondent and Hiroshima peace ambassador. www.hibakushastories.org.

INDEX